LOCATIONAL ANALYSIS
FOR MANUFACTURING

A Selection of Readings

Gerald J. Karaska

David F. Bramhall

THE M.I.T. PRESS
Massachusetts Institute of Technology
Cambridge, Massachusetts, and London, England

Library of Congress catalog card number: 68-27424
Printed in the United States of America

To W. I.

THE REGIONAL SCIENCE STUDIES SERIES

edited by Walter Isard

1 *Location and Space-Economy*
  Walter Isard

2 *The Location of the Synthetic-Fiber Industry*
  Joseph Airov

3 *Industrial Complex Analysis and Regional Development*
  Walter Isard, Eugene W. Schooler, and Thomas Vietorisz

4 *Methods of Regional Analysis*
  Walter Isard

5 *Domestic Airline Efficiency*
  Ronald E. Miller

6 *The Spatial Dynamics of U.S. Urban-Industrial Growth: 1800–1914*
  Allan R. Pred

7 *Locational Analysis for Manufacturing: A Selection of Readings*
  Gerald J. Karaska and David F. Bramhall

8 *General Theory: Social, Political, Economic, and Regional*
  Walter Isard

FOREWORD

This volume on *Locational Analysis for Manufacturing* by Drs. Karaska and Bramhall is the seventh in the Regional Science Studies Series. It is not a volume intended for the scholarly location theorist. It does not purport to refine existing abstract studies, or creatively to forge new doctrine. Rather it aims to fill a major gap in the literature — a gap that exists between abstract location theory on the one hand, and highly specific investigations of single industries and industrial complexes on the other hand. It is designed to cast light upon general location factors, as they may affect all kinds of manufacturing industries in the world of reality, as observed by many sharp, specialized analysts. First, it gives proper emphasis to the role of theory and proceeds to sift out of the theory the more valid and relevant elements. Then it focuses upon each of the key factors — transportation costs, labor costs, power, fuel and energy costs, scale and agglomeration economies, demand and revenue potentials, competition, and decision-making procedures — and looks at each of these topics at some depth.

Within the Regional Science Studies Series itself, this book by Drs. Karaska and Bramhall very effectively complements the existing volumes. It bridges the broad theoretical, historical, and methodological works (those on *Location and Space-Economy, The Spatial Dynamics of U.S. Urban-Industrial Growth, 1800–1914,* and *Methods of Regional Analysis*) and the highly specific, single-sector studies (*The Location of the Synthetic-Fiber Industry, Industrial Complex Analysis and Regional Development,* and *Domestic Airline Efficiency*). It thereby adds considerable balance and value to the series.

Without question, *Locational Analysis for Manufacturing* will prove to be a valuable work for many generally interested in the problems of industrial location. It should provide basic background materials for those concerned with industrial development and the identification of types of industries which might be developed in their own regions. It should be extremely useful to urban and regional planners attempting to foresee the kinds and size of industries which might locate in their local areas. It should be of key interest to industrial geographers, management scientists, and business analysts concerned with possible markets in their own and other regions. And finally it should be of real value to many scholars — geographers, economists, planners, engineers, regional scientists — generally interested in understanding the spatial distribution of economic activity.

The book should provide excellent reading materials for courses in industrial geography, geography of manufacturing, location theory, economic geography, planning techniques, methods of regional analysis, and related areas. It can serve alone as a basic text in undergraduate courses. It can also serve as supplementary reading for graduate courses where *Location and Space-Economy, Methods of Regional Analysis,* or other similar books are used as texts.

I welcome this book to our series.

WALTER ISARD

CONTRIBUTORS

John W. Alexander	General Director, Inter-Varsity Christian Fellowship, Chicago, Illinois (former Professor of Geography, University of Wisconsin)
William Alonso	Professor of Regional Planning, University of California, Berkeley
Joseph S. Bain	Professor of Economics, University of California, Berkeley
Mark Barchas	Staff Economist, Experimental City Project, University of Minnesota
Marvin J. Barloon	Professor of Economics, Case Western Reserve University
Edward H. Bowman	Comptroller, Yale University
David F. Bramhall	Professor of Economics and Director, Center for Regional Economic Studies, University of Pittsburgh
Benjamin Bridges, Jr.	Office of Research and Statistics, Social Security Administration, Washington, D.C.
S. Earl Brown	Professor of Geography, The Ohio State University
Benjamin Chinitz	Chairman, Department of Economics, Brown University
Michael Chisholm	Reader in Economic Geography, University of Bristol, Bristol, England
Thomas C. Cochran	Professor of History, The University of Pennsylvania
Kalmon J. Cohen	Professor of Economics and Industrial Administration, Carnegie-Mellon University
Marshall R. Colberg	Professor of Economics, Florida State University
Richard M. Cyert	Dean of the Graduate School of Industrial Administration and Professor of Economics and Industrial Administration, Carnegie-Mellon University
Richard E. Dahlberg	Associate Professor of Geography, Syracuse University

Frank T. de Vyver	Professor of Economics and Vice Provost, Duke University
John F. Due	Professor of Economics, University of Illinois
Edgar S. Dunn, Jr.	Research Associate, Resources for the Future, Inc.
Richard W. Epps	Federal Reserve Bank of Philadelphia
Victor R. Fuchs	Associate Director of Research, National Bureau of Economic Research, Inc., New York
Abraham L. Gitlow	Dean, School of Commerce, New York University
Melvin L. Greenhut	Professor of Economics, Texas A. & M. University
Margaret Hall	Somerville College, Oxford
Peter Isard	Stanford University
Walter Isard	Professor of Economics and Regional Science The University of Pennsylvania
Gerald J. Karaska	Associate Professor of Geography, Syracuse University
Robert E. Kuenne	General Economic Systems Project, Princeton, New Jersey
James N. Morgan	Program Director — Survey Research Center and Professor of Economics, The University of Michigan
Eva L. Mueller	Program Director — Survey Research Center and Professor of Economics, The University of Michigan
Thomas A. Reiner	Associate Professor of Regional Science, The University of Pennsylvania
William M. Shenkel	Professor, College of Business Administration, The University of Georgia
Benjamin H. Stevens	Professor of Regional Science, The University of Pennsylvania, and President, Regional Science Research Institute, Philadelphia
Raymond Vernon	Professor of International Trade and Investment, Harvard University
Vincent Whitney	Professor of Sociology, The University of Pennsylvania
Robert A. Will	Manager, Plant Location Surveys, The Austin Company, Cleveland
Christopher Winsten	Fellow of Nuffield College, Oxford

CONTENTS

Foreword   vii

PART I
The Book in Perspective   1

PART II
Partial Equilibrium Approach

Introductory Note   15

THEORETICAL BACKGROUND

1. The Partial Equilibrium Approach to Location Theory:
   Graphic Solutions   22
   Gerald J. Karaska

2. A Reformation of Classical Location Theory and Its Relation to
   Rent Theory   42
   William Alonso

COSTS AS THEY VARY OVER SPACE

Transportation Costs

3. Freight Rates: Selected Aspects of Uniform and Nodal Regions   65
   John W. Alexander, S. Earl Brown, and Richard E. Dahlberg

4. The Effect of Transportation Forms on Regional Economic Growth   83
   Benjamin Chinitz

5. The Interrelationship of the Changing Structure of American
   Transportation and Changes in Industrial Location   97
   Marvin J. Barloon

Labor Costs

6. Labor Factors in the Industrial Development of the South   108
   Frank T. de Vyver

7. Hourly Earnings Differentials by Region and Size of City   125
   Victor R. Fuchs

Contents

8. Wages and the Allocation of Employment   130
   A. L. Gitlow

Energy Costs

9. Atomic Power and the Location of Industry   152
   Walter Isard and Vincent Whitney

Taxes and Subsidies as Cost Factors

10. Studies of State-Local Tax Influences on Location of Industry   167
    John F. Due

11. State and Local Inducements for Industry   178
    Benjamin Bridges, Jr.

12. Federal Influences on Industrial Location: How Extensive   210
    Robert A. Will

Land Costs

13. Agricultural Rent Functions and Bid Price Curves of the Urban Firm   221
    William Alonso

14. The Economic Consequences of Industrial Zoning   244
    William M. Shenkel

Costs Associated with Internal Scale Economies

15. The Measurement of Economies of Scale   255
    Christopher Winsten and Margaret Hall

16. Economies of Scale, Concentration, and the Conditions of Entry in Twenty Manufacturing Industries   265
    Joe S. Bain

17. Scale of Operations — An Empirical Study   290
    Edward H. Bowman

Costs Associated with External Scale Economies

18. Production and Distribution in the Large Metropolis   299
    Raymond Vernon

19. Contrasts in Agglomeration: New York and Pittsburgh   314
    Benjamin Chinitz

VARIATIONS IN DEMAND OVER SPACE

20. Size of Markets Versus Transport Costs in Industrial Location Surveys and Theory   326
    Melvin L. Greenhut

21. When is the Demand Factor of Location Important?   339
    Melvin L. Greenhut

22. The Market Potential Concept and the Analysis of Location   349
    Edgar S. Dunn

23. Tendencies in Agricultural Specialization and Regional Concentration of Industry   361
    Michael Chisholm

PART III

Alternative Views and Analyses of Decision-Making

Introductory Note   369

MARKET COMPETITION AND STRATEGIES IN LOCATIONAL EQUILIBRIUM

24. An Application of Game Theory to a Problem of Location Strategy   372
    Benjamin H. Stevens

25. Aspects of Decision-Making Theory and Regional Science   387
    Walter Isard and Thomas A. Reiner

THE DECISION PROCESS OF THE FIRM

26. New Considerations in the Theory of the Firm   396
    Kalman J. Cohen and Richard M. Cyert

27. The Entrepreneur in Economic Change   419
    Thomas C. Cochran

EMPIRICAL EVIDENCE OF THE SUBJECTIVE BASES OF LOCATION DECISIONS

28. Location Decisions of Manufacturers   429
    Eva Mueller and James N. Morgan

29. Factors in the Location of Florida Industry: Summary of General
    Findings of Florida Survey   443
    Melvin L. Greenhut and Marshall R. Colberg

PART IV

Manufacturing Locations in a General Equilibrium

30. An Introduction to Spatial General Equilibrium   467
    David F. Bramhall

31. The Impact of Steel Upon the Greater New York-Philadelphia
    Industrial Region   477
    Walter Isard and Robert E. Kuenne

32. On a General Political-Social-Economic Equilibrium Theory Oriented
    to Cooperative Solutions and Conflict Resolution   497
    Walter Isard, Peter Isard, Mark Barchas and Richard Epps

Author Index   508

Subject Index   512

PART I
The Book in Perspective

THE BOOK IN PERSPECTIVE

It is the intent of this book to present a sounder and more comprehensive framework in which to pursue an analysis of the location of manufacturing. This is done partly by reviewing the literature in location theory and in spatial general equilibrium theory. From this review, we first identify certain key factors and second show how these factors are interrelated and may be integrated. The selections from the literature represent the current status of research illuminating the role and significance of each of the key factors. The combination and integration of these works form the basis for a more complete analysis of manufacturing location.

After examining the literature of manufacturing location theory, we have recognized two critical approaches. One is a partial equilibrium approach with primary emphasis on minimizing cost factors, largely initiated and developed by A. Weber; the other follows a general equilibrium framework along the lines of Walras, Pareto, and Cassel. Each approach has a long history and tradition. However, the partial equilibrium method presents a reality too naive to represent the complex industrial world; and the general equilibrium method grapples with a task presently too difficult for the state of the economic sciences. It is our conviction that the research relating to these two approaches has reached a stage of maturity in which a set of relationships more adequate then that currently employed may be deduced. We present this volume as a survey of progress made in the development of a more satisfactory analysis for the location of manufacturing. We consider it extremely important that the analysis be firmly grounded in reality, and heavily dependent upon empirical information. Also, we feel that the analysis must reflect the complex, spatial interrelationships of the "region"; hence the logic of abstract models is a requisite ingredient.

We are concerned with the manufacturing establishment as an element or basic unit in the spatial pattern of all manufacturing. This pattern, however, is only one of a large number of spatial distributions in the region. The overriding problem is concerned with the geometry of the manufacturing pattern as it influences and is influenced by the total regional structure. It is recognized that any change in the character and linkages of any one site reverberates throughout the entire system; the

3

goal of the spatial analysis (the regional science) is to comprehend the action space of all possible configurations of the manufacturing pattern.

While there are an infinite number of possible geometric patterns of manufacturing distribution, the intent of regional science is not only to explain or account for any one site or pattern, but to predict the impact upon the regional system of another pattern, or change, in the existing geometry. Simply put, the goal of a theory for the location of manufacturing is to understand the spatial interactions of the manufacturing process. If this goal is to be reached, it is imperative that the manufacturing process be better understood in the context of a complete regional system. To this end we present the most important contributions appearing in the literature which shed light upon the role of the numerous forces influencing the spatial pattern of manufacturing.

At the outset it is perhaps instructive to raise a concern with the validity of an equilibrium approach to location theory. Isard in his Preface to *Location and Space-Economy* notes that "A presentation of conditions of equilibrium in a theoretical system may seem to imply a tendency toward the attainment of a state of equilibrium in the real world. But in a full historic sense, actual economic life never does realize a state of equilibrium. There are always changes impinging upon the economy. The process of adjustment is constantly in operation."[1]

While there are numerous disturbances in the socioeconomic world whose long-run adjustments raise serious limitations to the notion of a state of equilibrium, there is still some heuristic value in viewing the location problem as a system tending toward some optimal steady state, or in analyzing locational situations with reference to the extent of disequilibrium of the system. In Isard's words, the equilibrium approach "necessarily casts light upon the long-run interaction of diverse forces and can yield valuable insights for historical trend projection in any concrete situation.[2]

The first book in the Regional Science Studies Series was Walter Isard's *Location and Space-Economy*, subtitled *A General Theory Relating to Industrial Location, Market Areas, Land Use, Trade, and Urban Structure*. The Preface to that book expressed concern that theoretical deliberations have the habit of turning in upon themselves, tending to grow more and more remote from reality. Isard states, "Admittedly the general theory of location and space-economy evolved in this volume is of little direct utility for handling specific problems of reality." However, this statement is followed by another that general principles and constructs do have the facility of guiding the choice of those structural relations subject to empirical estimations which are "the more significant

---

[1] Walter Isard, *Location and Space-Economy* (New York: M.I.T. Press and Wiley, 1956), p. ix.
[2] *Ibid.*, p. x.

ones for analytic purposes."[3] The origin of this present book and its subsequent outline were guided by these thoughts. We envision this book as a "filling-in" of the thoughts and abstractions of *Location and Space-Economy* with empirical research[4] and more recent theoretical thought.

Location Theory Reviewed

Industrial location theory has a long history in the economic literature, essentially beginning as a part of the more encompassing general theory of location and space-economy and the general equilibrium theory of economics.[5] While the spatial dimension was neglected in most early formulations of economic theory, Isard notes that these were stated "in a manner pregnant with spatial implications."[6] The explicit consideration of the spatial dimension in theory is attributed as beginning with von Thünen, Launhardt, Weber and Lösch and culminating in the present work of Hoover and Isard and the discipline of regional science.[7]

Both von Thünen and Weber attempted formulations of abstract theories in the direction of general equilibrium solutions. Von Thünen sought laws which determined the production best carried on at a given place, but restricted his analysis to agricultural production and land rent as influenced by distance from the market place (explanation of rent is further expanded to consider differences in wage levels).[8] Weber's pursuit of general location theory was directed to the study of forces introduced as people occupy an undeveloped country and establish economic systems.[9] The formulation of this general theory is abortive and most of Weber's contribution concerns a partial equilibrium solution to industrial location problems, with emphasis upon variation of costs over space. Weberian location theory is usually conceived as evolving under

---

[3] *Ibid.,* p. viii.

[4] For an excellent review of the industrial location literature, see Benjamin H. Stevens and Carolyn A. Brackett, *Industrial Location: A Review and Annotated Bibliography of Theoretical, Empirical, and Case Studies* (Philadelphia: Regional Science Research Institute, 1967), 240 pp.

[5] For an excellent and detailed review of the development of this literature, see Walter Isard, *Location and Space-Economy,* Chapter 2, pp. 24–54.

[6] *Ibid.,* p. 25.

[7] Johann Heinrich von Thünen, *Der isolierte Staat in Beziehung auf Landwirtschaft und Nationalökonomie* (Hamburg, 1826). Wilhelm Launhardt, "Die Bestimmung des zweckmässigsten Standortes einer gewerblichen Anlage," *Zeitschrift des Vereins deutscher Ingenieure, XXVI,* No. 3 (Berlin, 1882). Alfred Weber, *Über den Standort der Industrien* (Tubingen, 1910); English translation with introduction and notes by Carl J. Friedrich, *Theory of the Location of Industries* (Chicago: The University of Chicago Press, 1929). August Lösch, *The Economics of Location,* translated by William H. Woglom with the assistance of Wolfgang F. Stolper (New Haven: Yale University Press, 1954), 520 pp. Edgar M. Hoover, *The Location of Economic Activity* (New York: McGraw-Hill, 1948), 310 pp. Walter Isard, *Location and Space-Economy.*

[8] Friedrich, *Alfred Weber's Theory,* p. xxi.

[9] Isard, *Location and Space-Economy,* p. 29, and Friedrich, *Alfred Weber's Theory,* pp. 219–220.

these special conditions: (1) location and size of place of consumption are fixed; (2) the locations of the material deposit are given; and (3) the geographic cost pattern of labor is given, and at any one site labor is unlimited in supply at constant cost.[10] It is worthy of note that this formulation by Weber does not assume an even distribution or "equal fertility" throughout the region as does the model of von Thünen.

Contemporary research in industrial location theory has been concerned only implicitly with the formulation of general theory. It has been even less concerned with the formulation of a general theory of location and space economy which encompasses the entire milieu of a region. With only a few exceptions, the bulk of the research has followed a partial equilibrium approach holding constant most extraneous locational forces; it has by and large considered the locations and cost of all resources as fixed, and neglected the mutual relations and interdependence of all economic elements as well as the temporal and spatial character of the interrelated economic processes.

A common procedure utilized to relax certain forces or assumptions and fixed relationships is the substitution principle. For example, starting with differences in transportation costs as a function of distance, an equilibrium point or site for a manufacturing plant may be determined which minimizes the total transportation costs on deliveries of raw materials and the finished product. This initial site can then be reevaluated by introducing the geographic variation of another factor, for example, labor. Cost savings on labor at a second site may more than balance the additional transportation costs involved by location at the second site. In effect, it pays to substitute transport outlays for labor outlays. Isard suggests that the substitution principle offers the most fruitful tool for development of the general theory of location and space-economy.[11] He advocates strengthening the theory by distinguishing between two types of substitution: (1) that among transport inputs; and (2) that among outlays, among revenues, and among outlays and revenues. Isard contends that if there is any sense at all to location economics, it is because of regularities in the variations of costs and prices over space stemming from the fact that transport cost is some function of distance. "The problem of production becomes a problem of choosing the right combination of the various types of capital, labor, land, and transport inputs."[12] Isard's work is essentially rooted in the transport input as a simple, common concept to express the complex spatial relations of an economy. He defines a transport input as the movement of a unit of weight over a distance, for example, pound-miles, ton-miles, etc. "In an indirect sense, transport inputs correspond to the exertions of effort and other factor

[10] Isard, *Location and Space-Economy*, p. 28n.
[11] *Ibid.*, pp. 35 ff.
[12] *Ibid.*, p. 36.

6

services required to overcome resistance encountered in movement through space where friction is present."[13]

While the emphasis on transport inputs places location at the center of the analysis, and while the substitution principle nicely illuminates the way in which tradeoffs varying over space enter economic theory, serious problems develop when this avenue of analysis is matched with empirical observations. For one, the interdependence and mutual interrelations of all factors significantly influence the location of economic activity. For another, even in this partial sense, transportation costs *per se* have come in many production location decisions to be recognized empirically as a relatively unimportant factor. In only a few industries — heavy manufacturing and bulk processing like iron and steel and petroleum refining — is the transport input likely to be a determining factor. This is not to conclude that the "transport input" or "friction of distance" is negligible or unimportant, but rather that it needs to be reexamined and redefined in terms of the observed communication patterns and face-to-face contacts. Also, certain factors, less quantifiable, such as flexibility, speed, and availability of supply, must be explicitly confronted.

Another analytical approach of relevance to location theory is general equilibrium. The general equilibrium approach has a long history in the economic literature. For example, Adam Smith alluded to an "invisible hand" guiding economic decisions. This allusion is a recognition of the pervasiveness of interdependence in an economic system, an implication that a complete understanding of the economy is more than the sum of separate elements. Because of the elusiveness and complexity of this notion, general equilibrium formulations have been treated in abstract and mathematical terms, and have found only restricted articulation in empirical research.

The general equilibrium model usually consists of a set of statements about an entire economic system. More ambitious models have attempted to control, or at least recognize, the behavior of such elements as space, time, decision-making behavior, uncertainty, political goals, and even psychological differences among individuals. It is the articulation of the first of these elements which we deem critical to the problem of the location of manufacturing.

Isard defines spatial general equilibrium analysis as an attempt to comprehend the regional economy in its totality, wherein the mutual relations and interdependence of all economic elements — both collectively and atomistically — are of fundamental importance.[14] Emphasis is placed upon the interdependence or linkages of all sectors, all regions, and all sectors in all regions. Spatial models and formulations of inter-

[13] *Ibid.*, p. 79.
[14] *Ibid.*, p. 26.

dependence might be put in three categories: (1) abstract formulations defining the complexity of the sectoral and interregional linkages, the decision rules of transactors, and the conditions for equilibrium; (2) highly aggregated formulations such as multisectoral multiplier and regional growth models; and (3) models which are more restrictive in their assumptions and less general in their interest, but which lend themselves to empirical application, such as input-output and linear programming techniques. In all of these models and formulations rarely is the manufacturing activity not of central importance.

Manufacturing Defined

Before elaborating upon the location problem in manufacturing, we must first define manufacturing operationally, keeping in mind both the economic perspective and the spatial dimension. Our definition outlines and focuses upon four aspects of the manufacturing phenomenon: (1) the engineering process and its technology; (2) the site and physical facility containing the process; (3) the "inputs" or amount and value of purchased goods and services; and (4) the "outputs" or amount and value of goods produced.

The manufacturing *process* generally involves a mechanical or chemical transformation of inorganic or organic substances into some new product. This transformation also includes the assemblage of component parts into a "new" product and sometimes is considered as a service performed upon some *in situ* materials. Important considerations of this process are the level of technology with its related mechanization and energy component, and the size or scale of operation. Technology can be expressed as a function relating inputs to outputs at various scales and in different combinations.

Aspects of the manufacturing process relevant to locational analysis may deal with exogenous natural conditions such as climate, topography, steam-flow, etc., which act to influence the efficiency of the process at different locations. Another exogenous factor, economic in character, is the presence or absence of other technically linked processes and the general level of technology.[15] Still another locationally relevant factor is the shape and dimensions of the physical plant as it may influence optimization of the process-flow.

The manufacturing *site* assumes numerous and sometimes confusing labels. Common or popular usage such as factory, mill, or plant is here accepted to mean the physical structure housing the manufacturing

---

[15] See the industrial complex analysis of Walter Isard *et al., Methods of Regional Analysis: An Introduction to Regional Science* (New York: M.I.T. Press and Wiley, 1960), Chapter 9, pp. 375–412.

process. The legal connotations of company, corporation, or firm refer to the financial control and decision-making mechanism; while the economic term, establishment, denotes the single facility or site. The term *establishment* is taken to refer to either a single-plant firm or the branch plant of the multiplant firm. In considering the site aspect of manufacturing, the analyst must clearly distinguish between location decisions regarding a single-plant establishment or a branch plant, and with respect to a new establishment or a relocated establishment. The context of the location problem may be different for each of these situations.

Definition of the *input* aspect of manufacturing recognizes a multiplicity of concepts. The input is a good or service which is treated as an expenditure or purchase by the establishment and is here classified as either material or value-added. Material inputs are materials consumed in the manufacturing process; supplies and containers for packaging of the manufactured product; fuel consumed in the manufacturing process; fuel consumed in energy transformation or purchased energy which subsequently become components of the manufacturing process; and subcontracting work to either competitive or complementary firms. In their spatial dimension the material inputs find critical importance since they refer to geographic linkages or ties with the numerous suppliers or "vendors." These sources of supply can be classed as natural — mine, farm, forest, or water; other manufacturing establishments; or retail and wholesale trade establishments. The value-added inputs or expenditures are commonly recognized as labor; management costs, including sales and administration; taxes; land costs and rents; current operating expenses, including charges for maintenance and repair; water and related utilities; research and development; advertising; engineering and management consulting; telephone and telegraph; insurance; and fees on royalties and patents. In order to complete the financial accounts for a firm, additional items should be considered in the value-added statement: changes in the value of current inventories or of items purchased for resale (without processing), capital investment on fixed assets (including depreciation and interest charges), bad debts, and dividends and profits (additions to surplus). The spatial dimension of the value-added components of manufacturing focuses upon the geographic variation in costs and availability of these items.

The *output* aspect of the manufacturing definition describes the product or shipments of the establishment and represents its sales or receipts. In addition to physical products which are created, it commonly includes services rendered, sale of scrap or refuse, installation work, repair work, and resale items. It is especially characteristic of American manufacturing that this output also defines *secondary* products and services. That is, the outputs are frequently not "singly classed" products, but several related products. Further complicating a valid designation of the firm's output is the multifaceted character of the products, i.e., the output is of varying sizes, shapes, etc. The spatial significance of output relates to variation of both demand and delivered price over space, depending upon the locations of consuming centers and the producing establishment. The market is envisioned as a spatial surface, embodying both direct and indirect demand for the product at each geographic point.

The Location Problem

The location problem of manufacturing has been posed in the literature in several ways. It has been formulated as a decision by management to select the best site at which to locate or relocate an establishment. While it has also been presented as explanation or rationale for a plant currently located at a site, or for an existing pattern of plants, we choose to emphasize the search for an optimal location. As Lösch put it, "The real duty of the economist is not to explain our sorry reality, but to improve it. The question of the best location is far more dignified than determination of the actual one."[16]

In most discussions of the location problem the overriding economic bias has regarded the goal of maximizing profits for the firm as dominating the locational choice, where profits are taken as the difference between revenues and costs. This book is organized primarily around that principle. The theory of location of manufacturing is essentially an exposition of the complex interdependence of forces and reactions implicit in the maximum profits objective. We describe the major elements of an equation expressing this objective as cost items defined as the inputs of each firm, industry, and region; and revenue items covering output and demand factors. These elements are qualified through the influence of time and inertia; exogenous forces such as national goals, technology, and nature; and spatial limits to competition.

We begin by considering the production function of a single establishment and by observing geographic variation in costs of the establishment's major inputs and the spatial variation in the demand for its output. For each material input, specified by quality, there is a cost associated with each point in the region. Thus for each material input a contoured surface appears, the slope of which represents the initial cost of the input plus its transportation charge to any point qualifying as a location for manufacturing. Accordingly, the establishment may in its location decision initially focus upon the selection of a production site which minimizes the total costs of collecting all of its important material

[16] Lösch, *The Economics of Location,* p. 4.

inputs. At a later stage modifications may be introduced since value-added inputs can be ensured only if the firm locates at specific sites. Thus alternative plant sites which provide cost advantages in value-added inputs may turn out to be the locations with overall minimum total costs. This locational analysis can be neatly (if abstractly) portrayed diagrammatically and mathematically so as to yield the optimum or equilibrium point where all costs are minimized.

For this same single-plant establishment, the demand factor is considered in a similar way. The region is portrayed as a surface of consumers with products flowing from the plant to a set of distribution or consumption points. An equilibrium solution which minimizes total delivery costs again becomes feasible.

To this point our approach is *partial* in that we consider only those elements which directly influence production at the plant site. We assume all costs to be fixed or stable, and analyze the influence of total costs of each input as its cost and/or availability varied over the surface of the region. We introduce multiple cost elements, still pursuing the partial analysis, by substituting the costs of one input for another. Further, we initially assume the demand factor to be constant, and other forces such as time and exogenous variables to be fixed, as the cost items are played off against one another. The locational decisions of other firms are also not allowed to constrain the analysis.

The assumptions of the partial model are then relaxed as the region is considered a spatial system wherein locational interdependence and general equilibrium factors influence costs and revenues. We recognize the following: (1) the prices of the inputs (material and value-added) are a function of the total quantity supplied and demanded, and are influenced by the bidding of competitive and complementary firms; (2) the prices of inputs are influenced by certain noneconomic factors whose importance to entrepreneurs is not easily measured in monetary terms; (3) decision-making at all levels is something less than completely rational or optimum; (4) the performance or efficiency of any one firm, through agglomeration effects, influences the behavior of all firms and values in the local subsystem, and hence the costs of all value-added inputs; (5) the demand for the product of the firm is not fixed but rather is influenced by changing demands of the total system which may result from changes in technology or other exogenous economic forces; and so forth.

In summary, our book begins by introducing abstract formulations of the partial equilibrium model. The selections from the literature next describe those cost and demand factors which assume critical spatial importance. Subsequently, locational decision-making is presented as a multidimensional process, followed by its interpretation with respect to space. Empirical studies are included so as to compare theoretical and rational behavior with actual decisions. Finally, the general equilibrium approach is posed, and a relevant empirical study using restrictive assumptions is presented. The last selection represents the most recent work and exploratory thought in the formulation of spatial general equilibrium models.

PART II
The Partial Equilibrium Approach

INTRODUCTORY NOTE

The first section of this part of the book treats in detail abstract and theoretical formulations of the partial equilibrium approach to industrial location problems. The paper by Karaska develops the partial equilibrium logic using graphic solutions. Beginning with only differences in transportation costs on one supply item and a one-point market, the author derives solution points which minimize total transportation costs. Similar minimum total transportation cost solutions are obtained for situations involving several inputs and a single-point market. These solutions to two-dimensional spatial problems use isotims, lines of equal transportation cost, and isodapanes, lines of equal total transportation costs. The substitution principle is employed to expand the partial equilibrium model so as to include additional cost variables. The final graphic solutions are directed to market factors and their areal patterns.

The theoretical article by Alonso treats similar problems but provides solutions utilizing vector analysis. This more elegant portrayal of the Weberian location problem provides another look at the minimum transportation cost site as an optimal location for a plant. Alonso notes that if one relaxes the strict assumption of the spatial approach — that everything but transport costs remains constant — it does not follow that the firm will locate so as to minimize transportation costs. He demonstrates how the optimal location will vary with factor mix, with economies of scale, with the structure of demand, with pricing policy, and with the objectives of the firm. His model becomes even more general as he is able to demonstrate its complementarity with rent theory.

Following this review and elaboration of abstract formulations of industrial location theory we present empirical studies which serve to establish the relative importance of those variables or forces which may influence the equilibrium solutions. Studies of the influence of cost factors are presented first, followed by materials on the demand or revenue factors.

The order in which the cost factors are presented follows the logic of the preceding theoretical models. The influence of transportation costs is first examined. Then the significance of labor costs, energy costs, taxes and subsidies, land costs, and indirect costs associated with internal economies of scale and external economies of scale are each investigated in turn.

The first selection on transportation by Alexander, Brown, and Dahlberg presents a detailed portrayal of the spatial variation (and irregularities) of actual transportation rates. This set of real-world observations, together with the temporal developments in rate structures discussed by Chinitz, expand upon the relevance of the transport input in the Weberian model. The research by Chinitz and by Barloon further refines the analysis by elaborating upon the changing role of transportation costs in industrial location and development. While the costs associated with shipping commodities may have been critical in earlier periods of American history, and while the locations of certain industries have always been determined by transportation consideration, many industries have today become freed from the restrictions imposed by the transportation structure.

For evaluating the influence of labor costs we present three studies focusing upon the notion of "wage differentials," which may be interpreted as reflecting the geographic variation in labor cost. The literature on wage differentials in the United States has frequently emphasized disparities between the South and the North. Since the South has lagged behind the rest of the United States in industrial development, and since American history has witnessed a migration of certain industries to the South, the lower wage levels of the South have received considerable attention as an important force in industrial location. As de Vyver reveals, however, this southern lag in wage differentials has been growing smaller. Further, unionism and restrictive and cost-producing wage legislation have only temporarily favored location in the South. Fuchs presents another quantitative study of wage differentials which underscores more critical reasons for wage differentials. One of his most important findings is the substantial difference in hourly earnings across city size. This city-size differential is also shown to have significant spatial relationships with other variables such as skill levels and education, sex, and race. The third article, by Gitlow, serves to elaborate upon the dimensionality of wage differentials. One must consider wages not only in monetary terms but in terms of such opportunity costs as security, hazards, job prestige, etc. The spatial relevance of these dimensions is directly related to job mobility; Gitlow finds wages only one element of job attractiveness, and finds job attractiveness to be closely related to job availability.

Since power or energy is characteristically a very small cost item in practically all American industries, it appears as a relatively unimportant locational force or attraction. Isard and Whitney emphasize that only a few industries have traditionally been oriented to fuel and power sites. They focus their analysis on the question of relocation of the power-oriented industries (cement, glass, aluminum, and iron and steel) consequent upon the development and availability of cheaper atomic power. They conclude that even if atomic power were developed so as to substantially reduce the power costs to these industries, it is highly unlikely that a major relocation of American industry would ensue. The locational attraction of power does not appear as a major discriminating force in location decisions.

The next section of readings deals with still another set of variables often considered in the location equation — taxes and local subsidies to industry. With respect to taxes as a force attracting or repelling industrial location, Due presents a review of numerous studies and surveys on this topic. His conclusions provide a certain consensus of opinion — that taxes are not a major factor or influence, but are rather a secondary consideration. They also point up a major difficulty inherent in the partial approach — the attempt to evaluate the importance of just one factor in the location problem. For example, if low taxes arise because of actual economies (efficiency) in the provision of public services, then the tax factor does reflect an economic advantage; if not, then the lower taxes in an environment of relatively inadequate public services may well reflect an economic disadvantage. Coupled with this point is the notion that the tax "burden" may actually represent a somewhat irrational reaction by business groups, in part reflecting a personal, political bias. Due presents the tax factor as a complex notion reflecting the "image" or business climate of the state or region, and in which actual taxes paid are only one element. Bridges expands upon the subject of taxes as an influence upon location decisions. Concentrating upon financial inducements to industry — tax concessions and low-interest loans — he examines the major types of inducement programs, then proceeds to evaluate the economic effects of each. While he concludes that the evidence suggests that inducement programs are only of secondary importance, their significance in terms of the "image" or business climate cannot be underestimated. Will underscores the presence of the federal government in all location decisions, as well as its relevance to locational theory.

The treatment of *land* as a cost in the production function of a manufacturing firm must deal not only with the direct monetary outlay in the form of a payment for use of a unit of space, but also with the somewhat abstract notion of land *rent*. To this point, in our selection of readings, we have considered the manufacturing establishment or site to be represented as a dimensionless point appearing on a map. Viewed as a point, without competition for space (other firms are essentially "piled up" at the same site), we are essentially in the realm of classical location theory. Once we consider competition for the use of space we are in another realm of economics — rent theory. In this context, land is not simply an input which is purchased. Rather, the firm occupies a location in space which significantly affects its expenditures on other inputs (in our problem, principally transport cost). The logical basis for analyzing the value of each parcel of land, and therefore its price or rent, stems from the classical work of von Thünen. Alonso presents the von Thünen model first for agricultural rent and land use, and subsequently extends it to account for location with respect to urban firms. The earlier paper by Alonso (in the first section of this part of the book) elaborates upon the complementarity of rent and location theories. The Shenkel article adds another dimension to our consideration of land as an input by its discussion of the influence of zoning as a negative and positive force in industrial location.

The next section is concerned with the optimal size or scale of operation of a manufacturing firm as a location factor. Economies of scale — the agglomeration economies — reflect a certain level of output whose spatial relevance may be seen with respect to the size and number of branch plants operated by a single firm. Too many branch plants may preclude the full attainment of these economies. The article by Winsten and Hall discusses in a conceptual way the nuances inherent in the notion of internal economies of scale. While they address themselves to the retail and distribution sectors of a regional economy, their logic is appropriate to the industrial firm as well. The article by Bain presents results of a detailed survey of twenty industry types in which data were gathered from managerial and engineering estimates to document the effect of the size of the plant or firm on the cost of production and distribution, and on entry and concentration. The next article, by Bowman, provides another empirical study of agglomeration, in this case the problem of the optimal size of an ice cream branch plant and its territory. Bowman's study reveals that the company's ten plants were too small and that a system with fewer and larger plants would be a less costly one. Interestingly enough, independently of the Bowman study, the same company reduced the number of plants following its own accounting rationale and decision-making framework.

External economies of scale is another factor which only indirectly affects the cost structure of a manufacturing location. While it has received some attention in the literature, it remains as an elusive, complex, but extremely critical locational force. The external agglomeration economies have been recognized to include the *localization* and the *urbanization* types. Hoover defined these as localization economies — economies gained for all firms in a single industry at a single location, consequent upon the enlargement of the total output of that industry at that location; and urbanization economies — the economies gained for all firms in all industries at a single location, consequent upon the enlargement of the total economic size (population, income, output, or wealth) of that location, for all industries taken together.[1]

[1] See Isard, *Location and Space-Economy* (New York: M.I.T. Press and Wiley, 1956), p. 172.

Vernon discusses the scale economies in the context of the large markets of the metropolitan areas. He notes the increasing "pull" of the market in the location problem, and extends this logic to consider the reduced costs for certain types of industry which substitute external economies of scale for the efficiency which may be gained elsewhere from internal agglomeration. This depiction of the industrial structure of a large metropolitan area as an intricate and highly articulated set of linkages among establishments is further elaborated upon by Chinitz. By comparing results from detailed studies of New York and Pittsburgh he offers some hypotheses about interindustry influences on factor costs.

The last set of selections on the partial equilibrium approach to a theory for the location of manufacturing discusses the demand or revenue side of the profit maximation equation. Up to now we have been concerned with that part of the entrepreneur's locational strategy which seeks to reduce production and other costs; the other side of the profit-maximizing equation is his objective of raising as high as possible the firm's total sales or receipts. Greenhut in two articles attempts to develop more fully the importance and meaning of the demand factor. His first paper stresses a distinction between the goal of increasing the size of markets and that of reducing transportation costs on delivery of the manufactured product. The second paper elaborates upon the meaning of the revenue factor by considering demand as a prime location factor, being on the one hand an *area-determining* factor of location, and on the other hand a *site-determining* factor. Still considering the demand force in industrial location, Dunn presents an operational procedure which suggests a broader treatment of spatial market analysis. Following the concept of population potential (regarding the gravity model), he uses contours of market potential more accurately to portray the areal shape and size of a firm's market. In its analytical form he derives an index of location which combines a measure of market potential with a measure of transport cost analogous to the isodapane solutions presented earlier; and in this way he suggests a more comprehensive solution to the problem of the optimal location for the establishment.

The final selection is a brief paper by Michael Chisholm dealing with a futuristic viewpoint of the market. Chisholm's major thesis is the increasing mobility of the market and its relation to certain natural amenities. He couples the notion that the entrepreneur caters to the desires of workers to live in a more pleasant environment with the identity of workers as consumers, and with the multiplier relationship of workers and consumers. The market has always been mobile in the sense that workers are mobile, but he notes the new mobility of markets because consumers *as consumers* have a greater freedom of choice of where to live, which in turn is reinforced by the fact that workers can also be more selective about where they work.

Theoretical Background

THE PARTIAL EQUILIBRIUM APPROACH TO LOCATION THEORY: GRAPHIC SOLUTIONS

Gerald J. Karaska

Introduction

As discussed previously, the objective of the partial approach is to simplify the location problem by considering the operation of only a few relevant factors.[1] While the first simplified model is quite unlike reality, when more variables are introduced into the analytical framework the resulting models begin to portray better the behavior of forces in a real locational situation. Regardless of the complexity of a model — that is, the number and variety of forces or factors which are considered for a particular industry — the approach remains *partial* in that interdependence and feedback are not allowed to influence the values of the relevant factors.

Our intent in this section is to present the basic elements traditionally considered in the partial equilibrium approach. We wish to examine their behavior and especially illustrate their importance in a fictitious solution to the question of a best location for the establishment of a manufacturing plant. We present here graphic solutions which are sub-

[1] The material presented here is part of a large literature in which the subject matter is well articulated. We present a simplified and introductory interpretation of this literature so as to illustrate certain principles and ideas which are the subject matter of the readings in this volume. While this material is available in the original works, the absence of any discussion on solutions to the partial equilibrium, location problem presents a serious gap in the readings. The following are the important works in the field of location theory: Alfred Weber, *Theory of the Location of Industries,* translated with an Introduction and Notes by Carl J. Friedrich (Chicago: University of Chicago Press, 1929), 256 pp. Edgar M. Hoover, *Location Theory and the Shoe and Leather Industries,* Harvard Economic Studies, vol. LV (Cambridge: Harvard University Press, 1937). Edgar M. Hoover, *The Location of Economic Activity* (New York: McGraw-Hill, 1948), 310 pp. August Lösch, *The Economics of Location,* translated by William H. Woglom with the assistance of Wolfgang F. Stolper (New Haven: Yale University Press, 1954), 520 pp. Walter Isard, *Location and Space-Economy* (New York: M.I.T. Press and Wiley, 1956), 350 pp.

The specific contents and outline of this section draw heavily from the works listed above, but are especially dependent upon the author's interpretations of lectures by Walter Isard of the Department of Regional Science, University of Pennsylvania. A similar treatment of this topic can be found in William Alonso, "Location Theory" in John Friedmann and William Alonso, *Regional Development and Planning: A Reader* (Cambridge: M.I.T. Press), pp. 75–106.

The assistance of Michael S. Ontko is gratefully acknowledged.

ject to limitations in dimension and complexity. A more elegant mathematical solution to the same problem has been developed, but it is not given here.[2]

It perhaps needs to be noted that the models presented herein are not intended to be "useful" in the sense of furnishing "know-how" or control of the environment in determining the best location for a manufacturing plant. The purpose of these models is to generate ideas and insights as to how space influences decisions of businesses. The models attempt with some rigor to develop a logical approach.

The basic part of the analysis attempts to unravel the influence of space — distance and direction from each point to all other points in a region. Further, it is assumed that the decision-makers are rational entrepreneurs who choose locations for sites of their plants which maximize the excess of revenues over cost, i.e., profits. The traditional Weberian analysis concentrates upon the minimization of costs holding demand fixed or constant; we initially follow this Weberian scheme, and later consider markets and market areas as equally important variables.

Transportation Costs and Rates

We begin by examining transportation costs as consisting of two elements. One is a "terminal or handling" charge c, and the other is a "line" or delivery charge which is some function of distance. Figure 1

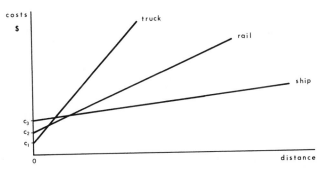

Figure 1.   Linear Transportation Costs by Mode of Transportation.

portrays this relationship as a linear function for three different modes of transportation — truck, rail, and ship. The costs of shipping commodities are seen to increase with an increase of distance from the terminal at O. A somewhat more realistic portrayal of the influence of distance upon

2 See Walter Isard, *Location and Space-Economy*, and William Alonso, "A Reformulation of Classical Location Theory and Its Relation to Rent Theory," *Papers of the Regional Science Association, 1967, XIX* (1967), pp. 23–44.

transportation costs is seen in Figure 2. This diagram shows the functional relationship to be nonlinear, indicating that transportation costs increase but at a decreasing rate with distance. The realism sought is the lower line costs per ton-mile associated with shipments moving greater distances — the economic advantages associated with "long hauls." Fur-

Figure 2. Nonlinear Transportation Costs.

ther realism is introduced in Figure 3, which portrays the transport cost to be a step function, that is, to be constant over a specified distance or zone. The costs per zone increase with distance from the terminal, and conform to earlier notions by increasing at a decreasing rate.

Numerous peculiarities of the transportation system can be introduced. Carriers may establish "rates" in accordance with their policies regarding competitive situations. For example, transportation companies may

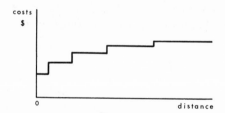

Figure 3. Zonal Nonlinear Transportation Costs.

gain economic advantages in certain regions through "back haul" rates wherein a lower rate is charged for shipment on vehicles which normally would return empty; "fabrication-in-transit" rates wherein the rate absorbs unloading and loading charges so that the commodities can be fabricated or manufactured at some point enroute; "shadow pricing" wherein those routes in direct competition with the route of another transportation company receive a lower rate; special rates for carload lots, or bulk commodities, or any special commodity; etc.

The Location Problem: Competition In One-Dimensional Space

Our first concern in the location problem is finding the point or site of manufacturing where total transportation costs are minimized. For the moment we assume that all other costs (labor, power, etc.) are fixed and everywhere equal.

An initial model considers the problem of the location of a manufacturing plant so as to minimize total transportation costs on the procurement of one item of input or supply situated at S and distribution of the output, or product to a single market point, M. Figure 4 illustrates this problem when both the supply item and the product are charged the same transport rates, that is, the transportation costs on delivery from S and delivery to M are identical functions of distance. If the plant were

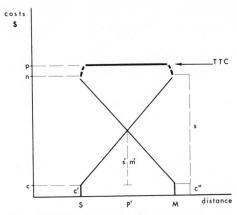

Figure 4.   Total Transportation Costs in One-Dimensional Space with Equal Delivery Costs.

established at M, the total transportation costs (TTC) on supply and distribution would be n; this total cost n is the sum of the loading charge of the supply item, namely, c', and the line costs of the supply item to M, namely, s. A plant location at M would incur no delivery costs on final product.

As Figure 4 shows, the minimum total transportation cost is n, and occurs at either the supply site or the market site. Any other location for the plant would incur a higher total transportation cost in Figure 4.[3] At mid-point P', for example, the total transportation cost, namely, p, would include delivery of the supply item from S — which includes a loading charge of c' plus the line cost of delivery, s'; and delivery of the product to M — which involves a delivery cost of m' plus an unloading charge of c''.

The model portrayed in Figure 4 points up an important location principle, namely, that the equilibrium point or site of the manufacturing plant, where transport costs are minimized, will be found at either the

[3] The dashed vertical stretches of the total transportation cost line (TTC) indicate that this line is discontinuous at S and M.

material (input) site or the market site, and not at any other point. Other factors being equal, when the transport cost on the supply item is higher than on the product, there results a supply-oriented location for the plant — this is illustrated in Figure 5 by the steeper slope of the

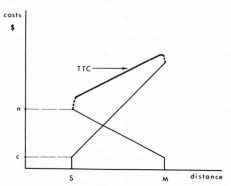

Figure 5. Total Transportation Costs in One-Dimensional Space with Unequal Delivery Costs.

delivery line from S, and the minimum TTC of n at S. When the transport cost on the final product is higher than on the supply item, the opposite configuration obtains.

Close inspection of these diagrams and those to follow plus some thinking quickly reveals that two factors essentially determine the solu-

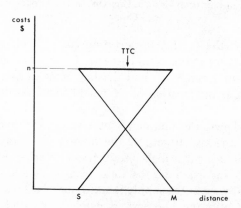

Figure 6. Total Transportation Costs in One-Dimensional Space with Linear Delivery Costs and without Loading Charges.

tions — the definition of the loading charge, c, and the shape of the TTC curve (linear vs. curvilinear). If the problem were presented without a loading charge, and if the curves were linear and of the same slope, then the exercise would indicate a solution wherein all points had the same TTC (see Figure 6). If the problem were presented without a loading charge, and if the curves were *nonlinear*, like those of Figure 7, then the exercise would reveal a solution wherein a terminal point is an optimal (minimal) solution and intermediate points represent continuously increasing costs with increasing distance from the minimum

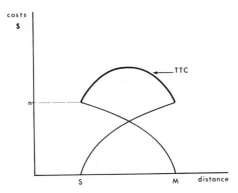

Figure 7. Total Transportation Costs in One-Dimensional Space with Nonlinear Delivery Costs and without Loading Charges.

cost terminals (see Figure 7). Perhaps the most realistic portrayal of this problem is that of Figure 8, which shows the requisite handling charges and the steplike, zonal rate structure, with costs per ton-mile decreasing with increasing distance from each terminal. As shown in Figure 8, a terminal point is again an optimal solution.

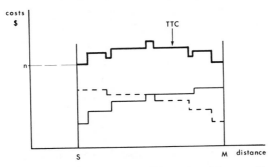

Figure 8. Total Transportation Costs in One-Dimensional Space with Zonal Delivery Costs.

One variation of the preceding model does result in an equilibrium position at a site between the source and the market. Figure 9 portrays this situation as a "fabrication-in-transit," transportation-cost advantage wherein the commodity being shipped is transferred from one mode, for example rail, to another mode, say ship. Figure 9 shows the total transportation cost (TTC) at the market, M, to include the following:

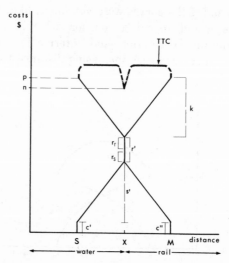

Figure 9.   Total Transportation Costs for a "Fabrication-in-Transit" Situation.

the cost of loading the supply item onto a ship, namely, c'; the cost of delivery by ship to the railhead at X, namely, s'; the cost of unloading the item from the ship and reloading upon the rails, namely, r'; and the cost of delivery by rail to the market, namely, k. Since there are no delivery costs on the final product, the total transportation cost (TTC) at M is p. In the situation illustrated by Figure 9, the TTC at M is equal to the TTC at S, for the transportation rates on both supply and distribution are taken as equal.[4] But note that Figure 9 reveals the lowest total transportation cost to be n, when location is at X, the transshipment point. This situation obtains because at X the plant is faced with only two handling charges — loading of the input at S, and unloading of product at M — since a "fabrication-in-transit" arrangement does not include in the transport rate the loading and unloading charge normally involved in transshipment.

The Location Problem: Competition in Two-Dimensional Space

Before pursuing an equilibrium solution to the lowest total-transportation-cost site for a manufacturing plant considering competition among numerous locations, it is instructive to introduce the concepts of *ideal weight* and Weber's *material index.*[5] The graphic solutions we are following become simplified by standardizing the commodities being shipped,

---

[4] In this example the rates for water and rail transportation are made equal so as to simplify the problem; as Figure 1 revealed, however, these rates are normally different.

[5] Weber, *Theory of the Location of Industries*, pp. xxiv and 59 ff.

for it is obvious that inputs of varying weight and value will be charged different transport rates, and that the manufactured products will also vary in weight, value, and transport rate. For example, consider the location problem in which one ton of final product, shipped at $2.00 per ton per mile, requires three tons of material input which is delivered at the rate of $1.50 per ton-mile. If the product is taken as the standard, one ton of product is considered to have one ton of *ideal weight*. The ideal weight of one ton of raw material is therefore $1.50/$2.00 × one ton = 0.75 ton. In other words, one ton of raw material costs as much to move as 0.75 ton of finished product. So the one ton of raw material is said to have an ideal weight of 0.75 ton. Hence, the three tons of material input has an ideal weight of only 2.25 tons.

Weber's material index is a ratio of the ideal weight of the localized material to the ideal weight of the final product. If the material index is greater than one, the plant would locate at the input site so as to minimize total transport costs; if it is less than one, the plant becomes market-oriented. For the preceding example the material index is 2.25 ÷ 1.00, or 2.25; hence the plant is supply-oriented. When more than one localized input is being considered, the material index is the ratio of the combined ideal weights of all localized materials to the ideal weight of the product. Unfortunately, in this last instance a material index greater than one does not distinguish the single optimum site for a plant. However, a material index less than one still indicates location at the market as the most desirable.

When more than two sites are considered, the solution space of the location problem becomes two dimensional and is mapped as a polygon. In this more complex space, the equilibrium point may occur within the locational polygon as well as at its vertices. The following discussion illustrates a graphic solution for the point of minimum total transportation cost considering more than two competing sites.

We begin by postulating a location situation in which the manufacturing process requires two different inputs which are located at different sites, and in which the product is delivered to one market. We further postulate the solution space to form an equilateral triangle with the

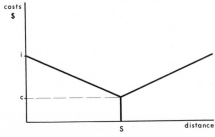

Figure 10. Transportation Costs in Two Directions from a Supply Point.

input sites and the market site being the vertices, and all three sites commanding equal transport costs per unit-weight, i.e., being associated with equal ideal weights. Figure 10 shows the influence of distance upon costs for one of the sites in the location triangle and notes the cost of each delivery to include the loading or unloading charge, c; and the line transport cost, i. The straight-line distance of the graph, Figure 10, is now transformed to the two dimensions of a map (see Figure 11). The lines on this map are isorithms of equal delivery cost for each pertinent item — whether a material input or the finished product — and are called *isotims*. For example, the first isotim coursing around S_1 indicates the locus of points each of which incurs $8.00 in obtaining one ton of raw material from S_1. Since the ideal weights of supply and product are equal, the isotims in Figure 11 appear as equally spaced, concentric circles.

Pursuing a solution, we compute aggregate, total transportation costs for all points in the solution space by summing the values of the intersecting isotims. For example, at point R, three isotims intersect and the sum of the costs associated with these isotims is $20.00 (on material from S_1) + $40.00 (on material from S_2) + $24.00 (on finished product to M), namely, $84.00. Lines connecting points of equal, total transportation costs are called *isodapanes*. Such isodapanes are indicated by the bold lines in Figure 11. They portray a surface with the minimum point of total transport costs at P — $66.00. By thus depicting the variation in total delivery costs at different locations, the isodapane surface describes the influence of space upon the location of a manufacturing plant.

The isodapane surface has been described in the literature as similar to a balance or scale. In the one-dimensional case where equal ideal weights were postulated for two competing sites (Figure 4), the scale was balanced with the fulcrum at the exact center and the optimum location was at either end; with unequal weights, the scales were tipped to either the supply terminal or the market terminal (Figure 5). As a two-dimensional case where a locational polygon is considered, the balance can be represented by an apparatus invented by Varignon[6] whereby each material and market site becomes a small weight attached to a string which moves along a frictionless roller. Each string, in turn, is coupled with the strings and weights of the other sites at a single common point. All of the rollers with their weights and strings are appropriately affixed to a horizontal, circular disc upon which the connecting point, where the strings are coupled, moves to an equilibrium position in response to the "weights" or pulls of each site.

Our graphic solution of the location problem is comparable to the Varignon mechanism. To illustrate we present Figure 12, which postulates a different ideal weight for supply point S_1. As seen in this sequence,

[6] Weber, *Theory of the Location of Industries*, p. 229.

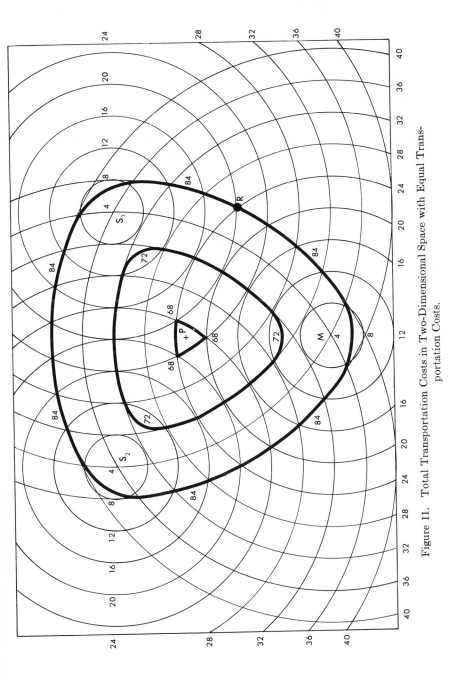

Figure 11. Total Transportation Costs in Two-Dimensional Space with Equal Transportation Costs.

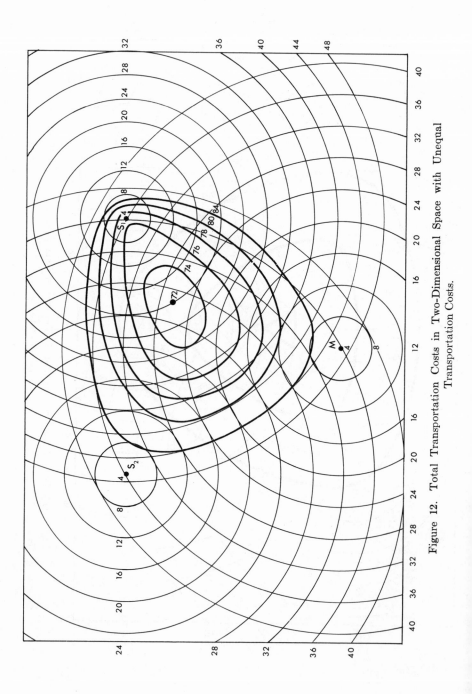

Figure 12. Total Transportation Costs in Two-Dimensional Space with Unequal Transportation Costs.

Figures 11 and 12, the isodapanes and the point of minimum transport cost "move" in response to the greater pull or heavier weight of the S_1 site.

The significant principle invoked here is that the equilibrium point is located at that site where the pulls of all relevant transport costs are balanced. Figures 11 and 12 illustrate the case where no dominant weight exists. If a dominant weight does exist, that is, if the ideal weight of the commodity at one site (supply or market) is equal to or greater than the sum of the ideal weights of all other points, then the equilibrium point will be at the point having the dominant weight (preponderant pull).

The Location Problem: Additional Forces

We have evaluated the relevance of distance as portrayed by transportation costs upon the solution of the optimal site for the location of a manufacturing plant. Our approach has been partial in that we have considered only transport-cost minimization and have held all other costs as constant or nonvarying in the solution space. Nor have we permitted interdependence, since we have not allowed the location solution or decision to influence or change the costs at any point in the space. Following the isodapane exercise we may introduce other costs for consideration in the solution by the principle of substitution. Consider the location polygon of Figure 13, which shows a solution space bounded by three requisite inputs, S_1, S_2, S_3, and a single market point, M. The isodapanes are drawn at $1.00 intervals and reveal an equilibrium point at P. We now evaluate another prospective site for the plant — L — where labor inputs of equal productivity may be acquired at a cheaper cost than at other sites in the bounded solution space. If the labor costs at L are 25 percent cheaper than at all other sites, and if this represents a difference of $5.00 in total costs, we may translate the relevance of L to the location problem by delimiting a *critical isodapane*. A critical isodapane corresponds to the locus of all points which incur transport costs greater than the minimum transport cost point by an amount equal to the potential savings in labor cost at the cheaper labor location. If at L the "gain" from labor is greater than the loss in transportation costs — that is, if point L lies within the critical isodapane — we may substitute L for P as the equilibrium point. In Figure 13, L lies outside the critical isodapane (that is, it incurs more than $5.00 additional transport cost when compared with P). Thus L does not represent a desirable alternative site for the location of the manufacturing plant.

At this stage in the analysis we may reject the cheap labor site as a location for the plant, or we may continue the analysis by seeking a replacement deposit for one of the requisite inputs (S_1, S_2, or S_3) which

33

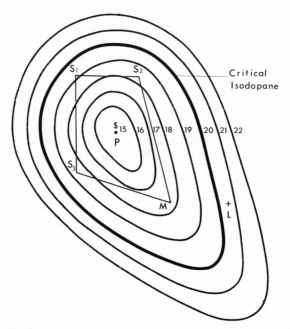

Figure 13. Isodapane Surface with Critical Isodapane.

would reorient the locational polygon so that point L would lie within the critical isodapane.

This substitution procedure can be extended by introducing other, previously constant, cost factors and by reevaluating replacement deposits. The number of additional location factors which can be considered depends only upon the "capacity" of the analyst.

Consider another example of the substitution principle, in this case where efficiencies are associated with internal economies of scale. Figure 14 naively portrays the scale of operation for a manufacturing process

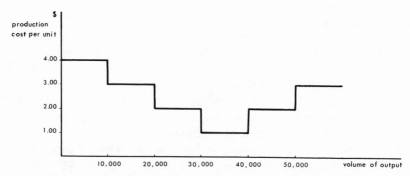

Figure 14. Production Costs as a Function of Volume of Output.

as a stepwise increase of output volume (capacity). In Figure 14 the lowest level of production is established at 10,000 units and at a cost of $4.00 per unit. The next level or scale of output is 20,000 units at a cost of $3.00 per unit, etc.

A question of agglomeration is now introduced to achieve a higher level of production. Agglomeration is here presented as the possibility of consolidation by two or more branch plants of a company producing identical products. The location question is concerned with a new location wherein one large plant would undertake the production instead of two smaller plants so as to gain some cost advantage. Figure 15a shows

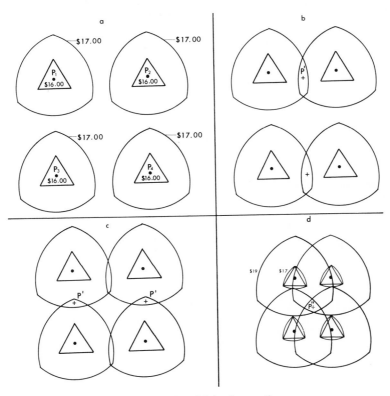

Figure 15. Spatial Agglomeration.

a study region containing four identical branch plants, each producing 10,000 units of output and each requiring two supply inputs and one market. Each plant is portrayed as a locational triangle with the plant site at P each having a minimal, total transportation cost of $16.00 per unit of output. Savings from agglomeration are estimated at $1.00 per unit output. Thus the critical isodapanes connecting all points which would incur $17.00 transport cost per unit product, that is, *$1.00 additional transport cost when compared to P,* are constructed. The question of two plants consolidating resolves to the critical isodapane test wherein the $1.00 cost saving per unit from agglomeration into a 20,000 unit-level is balanced against the additional transportation costs of a new plant location (producing 20,000 units) intermediate between the two existing branch plants. In Figure 15a no critical isodapanes intersect. Agglomeration is not feasible.

Figure 15b shows the same situation for plants less distant from each other. The $17.00 isodapanes, the critical isodapane (with $1.00 tradeoff), do intersect. A new plant P' in the zone of intersection producing 20,000 units would operate at a lower total cost (including delivery from four supply points and delivery to two market points) than two branch plants at P_1, and P_2. Figure 15c illustrates an alternative arrangement, and Figure 15d illustrates a feasible solution of consolidation by the four plants into a new single plant, P'', producing 40,000 units.

The Location Problem: Market Area Analysis

Following the Weberian scheme, our partial equilibrium analysis has concentrated upon reducing *costs* in the profit maximization equation of the firm. We now focus on the *demand* variable in this equation by evaluating conditions which produce an equilibrium solution in the process of enlarging the market for the manufactured product.

Our previous models had relegated the market to a single point. We now relax this constraint by viewing the market as occupying two-dimensional space or area. First consider the market area in cross-section, with two manufacturing plants at fixed locations and delivering identical products. The problem deals with minimization of transport costs on delivery of the product and the determination of the market area over which each plant is able to gain control or economic dominance. For each point within a given plant's market area, the delivered price of that product from that plant is cheaper than the delivered price of the same product from any other point. In Figure 16, for example, at point M_j, the total cost of the product delivered from P_1 is m, which is appreciably lower than the delivered total cost of p of the product from P_2. At M_j, the total cost of the product includes its manufactured value, a, plus the transportation cost, d', of delivery from P_1. The total cost of the same product at M_j, delivered from P_2 includes the same manufacturing cost, a, plus the larger transportation cost, d'', associated with greater distance from P_2.

Point M_k in Figure 16 is equally distant from P_1 and P_2 and represents a boundary (indifference) point where the transportation cost on

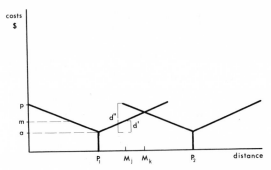

Figure 16. Market Areas as a Function of Equal Transportation Costs for Two Competing Plants.

the delivered product, d, is equal whether delivered from P_1 or P_2. The area to the left of M_k including that to the left of P_1 is served more cheaply from P_1, while the area to the right of M_k (including that to the right of P_2) is dominated by the cheaper delivered price from P_2.

In competition among plants for market areas, dominance is thus attributed to lower manufacturing costs, lower transport costs, or both. An example of the influence of differential costs is illustrated by Figure 17, which shows that the plant at P_1 is able to ship the product at a lower transport rate than P_2 and hence "controls" the larger area P_1M_k. An interesting configuration is shown in Figure 17, which illustrates the market "enclave," M_kM_m of plant P_2. In this model the market area beyond (to the right of) M_m is served more cheaply by the plant at P_1 even though P_1 is more distant than P_2.

In two-dimensional space, competition for market space extends in all directions and a new type of diagram is required. Figure 18 shows three manufacturing plants, at P_1, P_2, and P_3, which manufacture identical products of equal value, and which deliver this product at equal transportation rates. The market areas of these plants are seen to be of

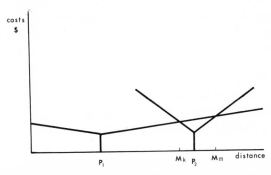

Figure 17. Market Areas as a Function of Unequal Transportation Costs for Two Competing Plants.

37

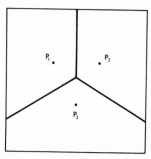

Figure 18. Market Areas as a Function of Equal Transportation Costs for Three Competing Plants.

equal size. Figure 19, on the other hand, illustrates the same plants but with the plant at P_2 incurring a higher transport cost (or a higher cost of manufacturing). The market area of P_2 in Figure 19 is smaller than the market areas of P_1 and P_3.

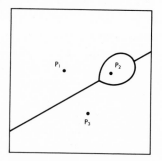

Figure 19. Market Areas as a Function of Unequal Transportation Costs for Three Competing Plants.

A logical extension of the analysis at this stage is the distribution of plants completely servicing a region. Figure 20 illustrates possible arrangements of plants as a continuum from a uniform pattern, to a random pattern, to a clustered pattern.[7] Figure 20a represents a uniform pattern whereby the market area of each plant is of equal size. Figure 20b shows the plants arranged as a random pattern in which the market areas are of unequal size, but in which each plant maintains a required minimum (threshold) area. Figure 20c illustrates a clustered pattern in which the same number of plants are situated next to each other. The clustered pattern appears to represent an inefficient distribution system in terms of the customer or market, but it may be an efficient and feasible solution in terms of advantages gained from external economies of scale.

[7] Michael F. Dacey, "Analysis of Central Place and Point Patterns by a Nearest Neighbour Method," *Lund Studies in Geography, Series B, Human Geography 24* (1962), 55–75.

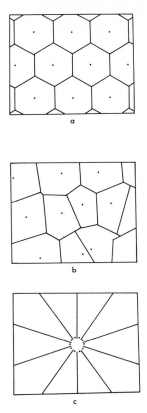

Figure 20. Market Areas for Uniform, Random, and Clustered Distributions of Plants.

The graphic exercises we have been pursuing can be extended to arrive at an equilibrium solution involving an overall areal market pattern. We closely follow Isard by considering location triangle $M_1S_1S_2$ in Figure 21, which is composed of two supply points and a one-point market.[8] From this location triangle a "weight triangle" OS_1S_2 is constructed on one of the sides of the location triangle. It is constructed by laying out three straight-line segments whose relative lengths correspond to the weights of forces at the three apexes of the location triangle. These three lengths are then drawn together and closed to form the weight triangle. Figure 21 shows the weight triangle OS_1S_2 and its relation to the original location triangle $M_1S_1S_2$, where the side S_1S_2 is the common side.

[8] The following discussion follows closely the work of Isard, *Location and Space-Economy*, 256–257, and George Pick, "Mathematical Analysis," in Weber, *Theory of the Location of Industries*, pp. 227–236, and is derived from the work of Launhardt, "Die Bestimmung des weckmassigsten Standortes einer gewerblichen Anlage," *Zeitschrift des Vereins deutscher Ingenieure, XXVL,* No. 3 (Berlin, 1882), and Tord Palander, *Beiträge zur Standortstheorie,* Uppsala: Almquist E. Wiksells Boktryckeri-A.-B., 1935.

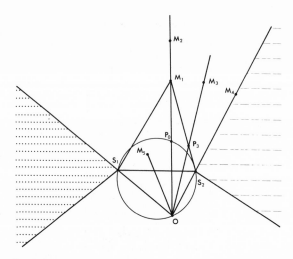

Figure 21.   Equilibrium Solutions Utilizing a Weight Triangle and Pole Lines.

Having determined the weight triangle, a circle is circumscribed around it and the two opposite apexes M_1 (of the original location triangle) and O (of the weight triangle) are connected by a straight line, OM_1. The intersection P_0 of this straight line and the circumscribed circle can be shown to be the equilibrium point which a vectoral solution would yield (the angles of the weight triangle bear a definite relationship to the angles formed at the equilibrium point, as precisely shown in Figure 22).

In Figure 21 we first consider the location for the plant so as to minimize transport costs on the supply inputs and delivery to the one-point market M_1. The line connecting O and M_1 intersects the circumscribed circle at P_0 and therefore, as already indicated, is the equilibrium point for the location triangle $M_1S_1S_2$. We next consider a market site at M_2, which is located on the same line which connected O and M_1. P_0 would also be the equilibrium point for the location triangle $M_2S_1S_2$, since the corresponding weight triangle is again OS_1S_2. It can be similarly shown that P_0 is the optimal plant site for all market-sites on the stretch of the line OM_1 extending from P_0 to M_1 and beyond.

Consider another market-site at M_3, with a corresponding location triangle $M_3S_1S_2$. The respective weight triangle constructed on the side S_1S_2 remains as OS_1S_2, since the relevant weights or forces of the apexes have not changed, and since the circle circumscribing the triangle OS_1S_2 remains the same. The plant site which can serve M_3 optimally is located at the intersection of line OM_3 and the circumscribed circle. It is point P_3.

For a market point at M_4 the line connecting O with M_4 intersects the circle at S_2, a supply point; hence S_2 is the logical production point. Actually, all market points in the dashed zone are best served from S_2; and, it can be demonstrated that all market points in the dotted zone are

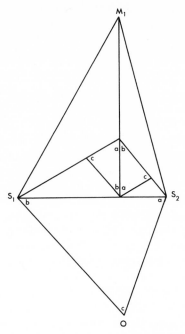

Figure 22.   Geometric Congruencies Between Location Triangle and Weight Triangle.

best served from S_1, the other supply point. For a market point at M_5 we note a situation where the pole line OM_5 does not intersect the circumscribed circle within the location triangle $M_5S_1S_2$. In this case M_5 is the logical site of production.

It can be further demonstrated that for markets located below line S_1S_2, the pertinent solutions are an exact mirror reflection of the situation above the line.

We may thus generalize. A weight triangle will exist when there is no dominant weight, or preponderant pull of the market, as when Weber's material index is greater than one. When a weight triangle does exist, for all market sites along any pole line outside the circumscribed circle, the optimal production site is located at the intersection of that pole line and the circumscribed circle; for market sites within the circumscribed circle, location should be at the market.

We conclude our graphic solutions at this point as their extensions become quite complicated, and as these are well described by Isard.[9] Isard demonstrates how additional location factors such as agglomeration economies, labor, and raw material supply areas may become incorporated into the preceding model.

[9] See Isard, *Location and Space-Economy*, Chapter 11, pp. 254–287.

A REFORMULATION OF CLASSICAL LOCATION THEORY AND ITS RELATION TO RENT THEORY

WILLIAM ALONSO

This paper has three purposes. The first is to illustrate a method of conceiving and solving the problems of classical location theory by the use of vector analysis. The second is to extend this theory into the consideration of such factors as economies of scale, factor substitution, and elastic demands. The principal conclusion is that the minimizing of transport costs is a doubtful criterion of location. The third purpose is to define the common ground between the theories of rent and location, showing that they are equivalent.

It must be understood that the intent here is not to provide techniques of solution for actual problems of location. The approach, in common with most of classical location theory, considers only those factors that are continuous differentiable functions over geographic territory. It neglects discontinuities, such as steps in transport costs functions, actual transport networks, terminal costs, cheap labor, power, or other factors that exist at particular locations, etc. The interest of the partial model presented here is to show how certain factors affect the logic of location; actual decisions would consider other factors as well. Such partial models are an aid to the understanding and insight which must underlie the solution of actual problems. For instance, learned books on economic development often dismiss the location issue by stating that industry will locate where it minimizes its transport costs. It will be seen below that this is true only under certain restrictive assumptions, even for industries that are particularly sensitive to transport costs. Needless to say, a great many industries are far more oriented to production costs, which may be affected by externalities or other localized advantages, or to other factors such as ease of marketing, safety from civil disturbance, and that great imponderable, happenstance.

A RESTATEMENT OF WEBER'S THEORY

In the back pages of C. J. Friedrich's *Alfred Weber's Theory of the Location of Industries*, in Georg Pick's "Mathematical Appendix," there is an etching of a handsome device called a Varignon frame, on which an ingenious arrangement of weights and pulleys simulates Weber's classic three-point location problem.[1] This is to find the location of least transport costs for a factory that uses two raw materials and sells its product at a city. It is assumed that

---

This work was begun within the Joint Center for Urban Studies of the Massachusetts Institute of Technology and Harvard University. It was concluded and written under the Program in Regional and Urban Economics sponsored by the Economic Development Administration at Harvard.

[1] Chicago: University of Chicago Press, 1929.

Reprinted from *Papers, The Regional Science Association*, 19 (1967), 23–44, by permission of the author and editor.

the producer bears all transport costs, that factor proportions are constant, that there are no economics of scale, and that the amount of product to be sold as well as the price is known.

In this physical analogue, the pulleys are placed corresponding to the locations on a map of the sources of materials and of the market. Through each pulley is passed a string from which hangs a weight, and the other ends of the three strings are tied together into a knot over the table. The weight at each location is proportional to the product of the technical coefficient times the relevant transport rate. Weber called this product the "ideal weight." If this machine is allowed to find its equilibrium, the knot will come to rest at the point of least transport costs. We shall see that this machine is a perfect physical model of the vector solution.[2]

Perhaps the best known method of solution is that of isodapane mapping, developed by Weber and improved upon by Hoover.[3] This method, in effect, computes total transport costs at each point on the map. The resulting surface of transport costs will reach its low point somewhere within the polygon defined by the sources of materials and the markets, or else at one of these points. The solution is found by inspection of the map, on which the transport cost surface is represented by contour lines (isodapanes). It may be noted that this technique has become much more accessible than when first proposed, thanks to the recent coupling of the calculating and graphic potentialities of computers.

The equation for the surface of transport costs is a deceptively simple one:

$$K(x_0, y_0) = \Sigma_i a_i r_i s_{i,0}$$

where $K(x_0, y_0)$ would be total transport costs per unit of product if the firm located at (x_0, y_0); a_i is the weight of material i per unit of product, or the technical coefficient of that input, and is unity in the case of the product itself; if there are several markets, the technical coefficient for each market will be the fraction of production sold at that market; r_i is the transport rate applicable to that good; and $s_{i,0}$ is the distance from the source or market at (x_i, y_i) to (x_0, y_0).

The problem is to find the low point of the surface of transport costs. I-sodapane mapping may be called a pattern of total search, since it plots the value of K for all points. An analytic solution would set the partial derivatives of K with respect to x and y equal to zero and then solve for x and y,

$$\partial K/\partial x = 0 = \Sigma_i a_i r_i (\partial s_i/\partial x) = \Sigma_i a_i r_i (x-x_i)[(x-x_i)^2 + (y-y_i)^2]^{-1/2}$$
$$\partial K/\partial y = 0 = \Sigma_i a_i r_i (\partial s_i/\partial y) = \Sigma_i a_i r_i (y-y_i)[(x-x_i)^2 + (y-y_i)^2]^{-1/2} . \quad (1)$$

Unfortunately, no method is known to solve these equations analytically,

---

[2] Pick realized this, but he did not present the mathematics. He also saw that the Varignon frame is not limited to three-point problems.

[3] E. M. Hoover, *The Location of Economic Activity* (New York: McGraw-Hill, 1948). A brief summary is offered in my "Location Theory," in J. R. P. Friedmann and W. Alonso, *Regional Development and Planning* (Cambridge: Massachusetts Institute of Technology Press, 1964).

and we are forced to solve them numerically. The basic approach is to make a series of successive approximations that get as close to the exact solution as one wants. The most common techniques are based on the Newton-Raphson method or to the closely related secant method. If we have an estimate u_t for the t approximation of the value of u for which $f(u)$ is zero, the next $(t+1)$ approximation is obtained by $u_{t+1} = u_t - f(u_t)/f'(u_t)$. The logic of this is simple. To our earlier estimate we add or subtract the amount from which $f(u)$ still differs from zero divided by the rate of increase or decrease of the function at the point of the earlier estimate. A very effective numerical technique for solving Weber's problem recently presented by Kuhn and Kuenne appears to be based on this principle.[4] The technique of graphic solution next presented is basically equivalent to the Kuhn and Kuenne algorithm but more tiresome and time consuming and less accurate, both because it relies on graphics, and because it uses the secant as an approximation to the derivative. However, it is helpful for visualizing the behavior and the economics behind the mathematics and prepares the groundwork for the more interesting problems discussed later.

Rather than by inspection of the isodapane mapping, if a physical model of the K surface were at hand, one could conceive of letting a small ball roll downhill and come to rest at the bottom. More formally, one could follow a slope line or line of steepest descent from any point on the K surface down to the bottom, where all such lines intersect. The successive approximations of the Kuhn and Kuenne algorithm trace, in effect, an approximation of such a slope line. These lines all run at all points normal to the contour or isodapane lines. At any point, by definition, the isodapane points in the direction of no change in K, and the slope line in the direction of greatest change.[5]

In terms of vector analysis, K is a scalar surface, and, at any point (x, y), its gradient, grad K, consists of (a) the maximum rate of increase of K at that point, and (b) the direction in which this change occurs. Grad K is a vector and may be interpreted as a pull or force, having both magnitude and direction. If, starting at any point, we proceeded by infinitely small steps, always in the direction of the gradient at each successive step, we would trace out a slope line.[6] It must be noted that the gradient is defined as going uphill, and that,

[4] H. W. Kuhn and R. E. Kuenne, "An Efficient Algorithm for the Numerical Solution of the Generalized Weber Problem in Spatial Economics," *Journal of Regional Science*, Winter, 1962.

[5] An interesting exposition of these concepts applied to geographic matters is found in W. Warntz, "The Topology of a Socio-Economic Terrain and Spatial Flows," *Papers of the Regional Science Association*, XVII, 1966. Other treatments of the mathematical tools presented here may be found in standard texts of mathematics, particularly those for engineers, under sections dealing with analytic geometry and vector analysis.

[6] For this reason, slope lines are also sometimes called integral lines, for they are the integral of the direction of the gradient. One could conceive of solving the Weber problem by integrating $(\partial K/\partial y)/(\partial K/\partial x)$ in equations (1) to find the general equations of slope lines and then discovering low point by the intersection of any two slope lines, each defined by any point (x, y). Unfortunately, the same complexity that prevents the analytic solution of those equations places this integration beyond our reach.

as we are looking for a minimum, we would wish to go downhill. In other words, we would follow the negative of the gradient. However, to avoid unnecessary awkwardness of language, we shall generally disregard the sign.

The gradient of a function which consists of the sum of other functions is equal to the vector sum of the gradients of the component functions:

$$\text{grad } K = \Sigma_i \text{ grad } (a_i r_i s_i) \,. \tag{2}$$

The gradient of the component transport cost functions will have the magnitude $d(a_i r_i s_i)/ds_i = a_i r_i$ and will point directly toward the source of the material or toward the market.[7] Thus, we see that the gradient at any point is the vector sum of Weber's ideal weights, which, in the Varignon frame, are literally locational pulls, and the arrangement of pulleys and the central knot are the means of pointing them in the right directions. The path traced by the knot in the Varignon frame is a course line. At equilibrium, these locational pulls will balance off exactly, or grad $K = 0$. These conditions require careful restatement in the case of solutions at the sources of materials or the markets, and the interested reader may find them in Kuhn and Kuenne. However, it is easy to determine in advance whether such a solution will occur by means of Weber's dominant weight.[8] Weber showed that if one of the ideal weights is greater than the arithmetic sum of the rest, location will be at that source or that market. This is equivalent to saying that if one of the pulls is greater than the vector sum of all the others, regardless of their directions, it will pull the location to its source.

Figure 1 is the graphic equivalent of equation (2) at some arbitrary point (x_e, y_e). Figure 2 shows the graphic tehnique for going from one approximation to the next. Grad K_e is obtained as in Figure 1. Grad $K_{e'}$ is similarly obtained at some point $(x_{e'}, y_{e'})$ along the direction of grad K_e. Grad $K_{e'}$ is then projected

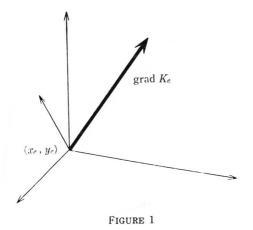

grad K_e

(x_e, y_e)

FIGURE 1

[7] I am reversing the sign. More accurately, they point directly away.

[8] This will be the case for convex location polygons. In concave ones, the solution may be at one of the singular points even in the absence of a dominant weight.

onto the extended grad K_e line, and both grad K_e and the projection of grad $K_{e'}$ are rotated 90° to be vertical to the path of grad K_e.[9] A line is then drawn across the ends of these rotated vectors; this line will intersect the path of grad K at some point (x_{e+1}, y_{e+1}), which becomes our next approximation. The procedure is repeated until the steps become very small, indicating the neighborhood of the low point of the surface K. This procedure is a graphic equivalent of the secant method, and those familiar with the algebra of vectors will recognize the simple operations involved.

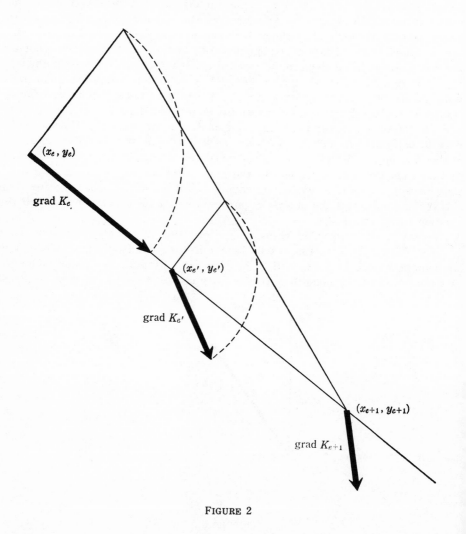

FIGURE 2

---

[9] If the projection of grad $K_{e'}$ on the path of grad K_e is in the opposite direction of grad K_e, it is rotated 270°, and (x_{e+1}, y_{e+1}) will be found between (x, y_e) and $(x_{e'}, y_{e'})$.

EXTENSION OF THE THEORY

One of the most commonly accepted truisms is that industry will locate to minimize transport costs, unless it finds some localized advantage such as cheap labor which compensates for added transport costs. As the problem is stated in Weber, the quantity sold and the price at each market is known, and technical coefficients are constant. Then, "since total revenue and costs on all inputs (except transport inputs) are thus fixed, the firm's customary problem of maximizing profits... is reduced to the problem of minimizing transport costs."[10] It will be shown, however, that if we relax the strict assumptions that everything but transport costs remains constant, it does not follow that the firm will locate to minimize transport costs. It will be seen that the optimal location will vary with factor mix, with economies of scale, with the structure of demand, with pricing policy, and with the objective of the firm. In other words, there is no one optimal location, and most optimal locations do not, except in a special sense which will be discussed, minimize transport costs.

Variable Production Function

In Weber's formulation, the quantity of a factor per unit of product is assumed constant. This assumption of fixed technical coefficients is a frequent one in applied economics as, for instance, in input-output and linear programming. In a pure theory, however, we are interested in the effects of factor substitution and economies of scale. Moses has pointed out that, if factor substitution is considered, since delivered prices of inputs will vary from location to location, the factor mix will vary in such a way that the ratio of the marginal productivity of the factors will equal the ratio of their delivered prices. Thus, "it would be purely by chance if transport costs were at a minimum" at the optimal location.[11]

We shall now examine this proposition in terms of locational pulls. We know for a firm:

P = the price of its product at the market;
Q = the quantity of the product to be sold;
$B(x, y)$ = delivery costs function per unit of product;
$P_i(x, y)$ = delivered price function of input i; and
A_i = the quantity of input i used.

The function $B(x, y)$ is a general form of the delivery costs function. Its simplest explicit form would be rs, where r is the transport rate per mile per unit product, and s the distance from (x, y) to the market. Similarly, $p_i(x, y)$ is a general form of delivered price, of which the simplest explicit form would be $p_i^* + r_i s_i$, where p_i^* is the price per unit of material i at the source, r_i is the transport rate per mile per unit of material i, and s_i is the distance from (x, y)

---

[10] W. Isard, *Location and Space-Economy* (Cambridge: The Technical Press of the Massachusetts Institute of Technology and New York City: John Wiley & Sons, Inc., 1956), p. 223.

[11] L. Moses, "Location and the Theory of Production," *Quarterly Journal of Economics*, May, 1958, p. 265.

to the source of the material. The problem is to find at what point (x, y) profits are maximized.

In the classical formulation $A_i/Q = a_i$, a constant. But here we permit factor substitution, and we permit a_i to vary. We have a technical production function $Q = f(A_1 \ldots A_n)$, and we construct the cost function $C = \Sigma_i p_i A_i$. Minimizing cost for the fixed quantity Q, we obtain the usual statements concerning the ratios of prices and marginal products. However, we wish to regard prices as variables, and we conceive of deriving a set of equations from those above of the form $A_i = A_i(p_1 \ldots p_n)$. That is to say, any set of factor prices $(p_i \ldots p_n)$ will determine a set of factor quantities $(A_1 \ldots A_n)$.

The objective is to maximize profits, G,

$$G = Q(P - B) - \Sigma_i p_i A_i . \tag{3}$$

One may think of a profit surface $G(x, y)$, which will have its maximum where $\dfrac{\partial G}{\partial x} = \dfrac{\partial G}{\partial y} = 0$. Differentiating with respect to x, and keeping in mind that the partial with respect to y will be perfectly symmetrical, we have:

$$\frac{\partial G}{\partial x} = - Q \frac{\partial B}{\partial x} - \Sigma_i A_i \frac{\partial p_i}{\partial x} - \Sigma_i p_i \frac{\partial A_i}{\partial x} . \tag{4}$$

From the function $A_i = A_i(p_i \ldots p_n)$, we have

$$\frac{\partial A_i}{\partial x} = \Sigma_j \frac{\partial A_i}{\partial p_j} \cdot \frac{\partial p_j}{\partial x} .$$

Substituting into equation (4),

$$\frac{\partial G}{\partial x} = - Q \frac{\partial B}{\partial x} - \Sigma_i A_i \frac{\partial p_i}{\partial x} - \Sigma_i \left[p_i (\Sigma_j \frac{\partial A_i}{\partial p_j} \cdot \frac{\partial p_j}{\partial x}) \right] , \tag{5}$$

from which, rearranging the terms,

$$\frac{\partial G}{\partial x} = Q \frac{\partial B}{\partial x} - \Sigma_i \left[\frac{\partial p_i}{\partial x} (A_i + \Sigma_j p_i \frac{\partial A_j}{\partial p_i}) \right] . \tag{6}$$

Although it is easy to set $\dfrac{\partial G}{\partial x}$ and $\dfrac{\partial G}{\partial y}$ equal to zero, the solution for (x, y) is as intractable to analytic methods as was the simpler problem without factor substitution. Thus, one would have to proceed by a technique of successive approximations such as was presented earlier. The gradient of the profit surface is grad $G = \left[\dfrac{\partial G}{\partial x}, \dfrac{\partial G}{\partial y} \right]$ at all points. One could start at any arbitrary point and, by the technique of estimating the rate of change of the gradient, make successive approximations climbing to the point of highest profit.

It is unlikely, however, that many of us will meet with problems of this sort to which we want an actual solution. Actual problems will have other complications. It is useful, however, to examine the components of the gradient for the light they throw on the effects of the factors we are considering. The gradient of the profit surface can be disaggregated into the various pulls of market and sources of materials. The pull toward the market is unchanged

48

from the pure Weber problem, except that here we use total product Q instead of unit product, as we used total quantity of each material instead of the technical coefficient. The pull toward the market will be $Q\left[\dfrac{\partial B}{\partial x}, \dfrac{\partial B}{\partial y}\right]$.[12] That is, a pull toward the market of a magnitude equal to total product times the marginal transport cost per unit or $Q\dfrac{\partial B}{\partial s}$. If we are using a linear transport function, $\dfrac{\partial B}{\partial s} = r$, and the market pull will be Qr.

In this case, however, we are more interested in the pulls of the materials. From equation (6), the pull of the material is

$$\frac{\partial p_i}{\partial s_i}\left(A_i + \Sigma_j p_j \frac{\partial A_j}{\partial p_i}\right). \tag{6a}$$

The first of this term, $(\partial p_i/\partial s_i)A_i$, is the Weberian pull; marginal transport costs times weight and represents the direct change in costs from the change in the delivered price of the material.

The product of the marginal transport costs times the second term within the parentheses may be termed the substitution effect on costs. It is the change in p_i times the resultant change in each of the inputs times its price, or the rate of change of value of each input with changes in delivered price of i. For a decrease in p_i, this term will be negative for substitute factors, positive for the good i and its complements, and zero for those inputs for which no substitution is possible. As might be expected, then, if no substitution is possible, this term will be zero, and the problem reduces to its Weberian form. However, if this term is positive, the pull will be greater than in Weber, and smaller if the term is negative. This term reflects the rate of substitution between transport inputs and other inputs. The classical formulations consider only substitution among transport inputs, not the substitution between space and things.

The expression (6a) can be represented in alternative ways by using the concept of cross-elasticity. The cross-elasticity e_{ji} is the rate of change in the quantity of input j associated with a rate of change in the price of input i, or with the ratio of the prices of j and i. Either definition reduces to

$$e_{ji} = \frac{\partial A_j}{\partial p_i}\frac{p_i}{A_j}.$$

Making use of the fact that $(\partial A_j/\partial p_j) = (\partial A_i/\partial p_j)$,[13] by substitution and manipulation, the pull of material i in expression (6a) may also be written

$$\Sigma_i\left[\frac{\partial p_i}{\partial x}(A_i + \Sigma_i e_{ji}\frac{p_j}{p_i}A_j)\right], \tag{6b}$$

---

[12] The reader is reminded that for verbal simplicity we are disregarding the sign. To simplify the notation, we shall write $\partial B/\partial x$ for $(\partial B/\partial s)(\partial s/\partial x)$. In polar terms, the pull would be $Q\{\partial B/\partial s, \theta\}$. Of course, $\partial B/\partial s = [(\partial B/\partial x)^2 + (\partial B/\partial y^2)]^{1/2}$.

[13] See J. M. Henderson and R. E. Quandt, *Microeconomic Theory* (New York City: McGraw-Hill, 1958), pp. 74–5.

or

$$\Sigma_i \left[\frac{\partial p_i}{\partial x} A_i (1 + \Sigma_j e_{ij}) \right].$$ (6c)

All three ways of expressing the pull of a material are revealing, but (6c) is the most elegant. If i is a substitute for j, e_{ij} will be positive; it will be negative for the factor itself (e_{ii}) and its complements. Thus, $\Sigma_j e_{ij}$ may be positive or negative, and the pull of a material will be equal to its ideal weight only if the cross-elasticities happen to cancel. If factor i is a ready substitute for others, (6c) makes clear that the sum of the cross-elasticities will be positive; on the other hand, if the factor can be readily substituted for, it will be vulnerable to its own price changes, and the negative e_{ii} will be substantial.

We may thus distinguish "gaining factors," for which $\Sigma_j e_{ij}$ is positive and "losing factors," for which it is negative. A gaining factor will be far more dominant than in the Weberian formulation, and more than would at first appear from expression (6c). The pull is larger than the ideal weight at any point in our search procedure. Further, from one step of the search to the next, the quantity A_i will grow larger, and thus the pull will become stronger. If, as is common, marginal transport costs are lower for long hauls, as the location is pulled toward the source of i, $\partial p_i / \partial s_i$ will become larger and the pull stronger. Conversely, the symmetrically opposite effects will weaken the pulls of the other factors. These effects are comparable to a gravitational pull that gets stronger as you get nearer a planet. On the other hand, decreasing returns to factor i and increasing returns to the others might be reducing $\Sigma_j e_{ij}$, perhaps even making it negative at some point and weakening the pull. On the whole, however, it is clear that it is far likelier that one of the materials will have a dominant pull than appears in a formulation using fixed coefficients.[14] The reader may think, for instance, of a steel industry which can substitute ore and scrap.

It can be seen from the preceeding that the most profitable location, where the vector sums of these pulls add to zero, will not coincide with the least transport costs location unless by chance all the substitution effects cancel out. Further, there is no clear and useful meaning to the minimizing of transport costs since factor proportions change with location, and the eventual factor mix is unknown until the location is determined.

Economies of Scale and a Single Market

If there are economies of scale, the optimal location will vary with the scale of production. If greater production is more efficient, the quantities of materials per unit of product will decrease and the pulls of the materials with them. In such a case, a large city might be a served by a market-oriented firm and a small city by a material-oriented one in the same industry. The opposite will be true for industries that suffer diseconomies of scale. Thus, if economic development means larger markets and increased efficiency of production, one of its consequences is increasing market-orientation for industry as a whole.

---

[14] Moses, *op. cit.*, arrives at a similar conclusion for a special case.

These effects of scale and associated changes in the factor-mix indicate that the most profitable location will vary with the scale of production. One may conceive of a geographic expansion path representing the locus of optimal locations with changing scale of production.[15]

We shall consider a small firm which is to supply a market with perfectly elastic demand at price P. The firm has constant factor proportions but diseconomies of scale in the range which will interest us,[16] so that

$$A_i = f_i(Q) \, ; \, f'_i > 0 \, ; \, f''_i > 0 \, . \tag{7}$$

The profit function is given by

$$G = Q(P - B) - \Sigma_i p_i f_i \, . \tag{8}$$

Maximizing G at any location, we have

$$0 = \frac{\partial G}{\partial Q} = P - B - \Sigma_i p_i f'_i \, , \tag{9}$$

which says, as expected, that marginal cost equals marginal revenue. The profit gradient $\left\{ \dfrac{\partial G}{\partial x} , \dfrac{\partial G}{\partial y} \right\}$ is

$$\frac{\partial G}{\partial x} = - Q \frac{\partial B}{\partial x} - \Sigma_i \frac{\partial p_i}{\partial x} f_i = - Q \frac{\partial B}{\partial x} - \Sigma_i \frac{\partial p_i}{\partial x} A_i \tag{10}$$

and the symmetrical $\partial G/\partial y$. The pulls of the market and the materials are quantities times marginal transport costs. It might appear that the Weberian solution applies, but this would be an oversimplification. As we follow grad G, Q will increase, and the diseconomies of scale will make the firm more material oriented. The final Q and the corresponding quantities of materials will only be determined simultaneously with the optimal location. Only if we knew the eventual quantity to be produced could we substitute the criterion of minimizing transport costs for the maximizing of profits.

One can find the solution to this problem by the general technique described earlier; the procedure is unchanged but the inner workings are slightly more complex. When we start the search at an arbitrary location, we determine the quantity to be produced to maximize profits at that location. The gradient of profits (the resultant of the location pulls) will point us to an approximation of the best location for that level of production, which is a point on the geographic expansion path mentioned earlier. But, as we move toward the expansion path, transport costs per unit of product are lowered, thus reducing marginal costs and making profitable a larger production. The next step will aim at the point on the geographic expansion curve corresponding to the new level of production. We are, in short, approximating a moving point along a curve. The final solution is the point of least transport costs for the most profitable (and in

---

[15] Moses, op. cit., makes this same point.

[16] Of course, for a horizontal demand curve, a firm with continuing economies of scale would produce to infinity.

this case, largest) level of production.[17]

Demand Elasticity and the Number of Markets

If there is more than one market, and markets have perfectly elastic demand, each plant will serve a single market, except in some cases in which the optimal location is at a source of material. In the case of constant returns to scale, if a plant can serve a market at all, it will sell an infinite quantity. It was to avoid this illogicality that the Weberian formulation supposed one knew the quantity to be sold at each market as well as the price. In cases of decreasing returns to scale, a firm would still sell at only one market if it sought to maximize profits. This derives from the general condition that, in the case of multiple markets, marginal revenue must equal marginal cost at each market for maximum profits. Thus, a firm would sell at more than one market, if, at all markets served, price minus delivery costs are equal, and this would only happen by chance. Any solution that served more than one market from a single plant would otherwise be less profitable than a multiple plant solution. The Weberian treatment of economies of scale focuses on the problem of increasing returns. If there is perfect elasticity, this would lead to infinite sales, and, to avoid illogicality, recourse is had again to fixed quantities as well as prices.

Fixed prices and quantities seem valid for firms which form part of a cartel or which are built to produce according to the terms of a large single contract. Such are very special cases. The important thing is to realize that the concepts of perfect competition and infinitely elastic demand are poorly suited to the analysis of spatial economics. They assume that the producer is very small and the demand very large. But spatial economics, in effect, disaggregates the economy by location. Demand as seen by any producer is smaller and likely to be sloped. Consequently, it is more often useful when considering spatial problems to think of the relation of supply and demand as in terms of monopoly or competitive monopoly.[18] Space acts as a differentiator of products and producers.

In the next pages, we shall examine three cases of alternative objectives and pricing policies by producers faced with several markets with sloping demand curves. We shall return to constant technical coefficients to simplify the mathematics and to concentrate on the interplay of demand, location, and pricing policy. This will imply an inconsistency, however, for we shall consider the location of a single plant. If there are no economies of scale, the producer would do better by serving each market with its own plant. It is only when there exist economies of scale over at least part of the production function that it will be sensible to serve more than one market from a single

---

[17] One might imagine that one could solve for Q in equation (9) and substitute in equation (8), thus obtaining a grad G that considers the concurrent changes in (9). This would be $dG/dx = \partial G/\partial x + (\partial G/\partial Q)(\partial Q/\partial x)$. But equation (9) has made $\partial G/\partial Q = 0$, and therefore $dG/dx = \partial G/\partial x$. In other words, $\partial G/\partial Q = 0$, by definition, at all points on the scalar surface G.

[18] See E. Chamberlin, *The Theory of Monopolistic Competition* (Cambridge: Harvard University Press, 1950).

ant. We shall deal only with cases in which, for whatever reason, a single ant is to be built. This plant may choose not to serve certain markets, it we exclude the possibility of the firm's building more than one plant. ot only is this problem far simpler to handle, but it is a perfectly realistic ie for many firms for reasons dealing principally with limitations of manage- al and entreprenurial capacity. Under proper circumstances, such a firm can ake more money than if it restricts itself to a single market but less than the multiplant solutions.

The three cases we shall consider are: (1) a firm which sells f. o. b., (2) a rm which discriminates perfectly among markets, and (3) a government-own- l producer which seeks to maximize consumer surplus. It will be seen that ie optimal location will be different in all three cases and that only in the ist two can it be said that transport costs are minimized, but even in these nly after the fact. It is ironical that, in the case of f. o. b. pricing, transport psts are in no sense minimized, for the classical literature in this subject, al- lough assuming this minimizing, has traditionally spoken of f. o. b. pricing.[19]

. O. B. Pricing

Assume a producer contemplates a number of markets with sloping demand urves. He will quote a single price R for his product, and the customer will ay for delivery costs. Thus, the price as perceived by the customer is

$$P_w = R + B_w \tag{11}$$

/here

P_w = cost to customer at market w,
R = f. o. b. price, and
B_w = delivery costs to market w.

We shall assume linear demand functions at each market. The conclusions re unchanged by this restrictive assumption, but the mathematical manipula- ions are easier to follow. The relations between price and quantity demanded re given in various forms by

$$P_w = R + B_w = t_w - u_w q_w$$
$$q_w = \frac{P_w - t_w}{-u_w} = \frac{R + B_w - t_w}{-u_w} \tag{12}$$

where

t_w , u_w = constants for market w and
q_w = demand quantity at market w.

Total sales, Q, are the sum of sales at each market

$$Q = \Sigma_w q_w = \Sigma_w \frac{R + B_w - t_w}{-u_w} . \tag{13}$$

---

[19] For instance, one text says, "As a provisional hypothesis we postulate that all prices are quoted f. o. b. factory by sellers ... this seems to be the customary assumption in economic analysis." S. Weintraub, *Price Theory* (New York: Pitman Publishing Co., 1949).

Profits, G, are given by the equation:

$$G = Q(R - \Sigma_i a_i p_i),$$ (1

where

a_i = the technical coefficient of input i and

p_i = its delivered price.

The entrepreneur operates on two variables to maximize his profit: his f.o. price, R, and his location, (x, y). At any given location, he would maximize profit with respect to R

$$0 = \frac{\partial G}{\partial Q} = R + Q \frac{\partial R}{\partial Q} - \Sigma_i a_i p_i.$$ (1

From equation (13), we have that

$$\frac{\partial R}{\partial Q} = - \frac{1}{\Sigma_w u_w^{-1}}.$$ (1

From the definition of elasticity, total elasticity E as seen by the producer is

$$- E = \frac{\partial Q}{\partial R} \cdot \frac{R}{Q} = - \Sigma_w u_w^{-1} \frac{R}{Q}.$$ (1

By substituting equations (16) and (17) into (15), we have

$$0 = \frac{\partial G}{\partial Q} = R - \frac{Q}{\Sigma_w u_w^{-1}} - \Sigma_i a_i p_i,$$ (1

$$R\left(1 - \frac{1}{E}\right) = \Sigma_i a_i p_i.$$ (1

Equation (19) is the ordinary statement of profit maximization that marginal revenue equals marginal cost.

We now wish to obtain the locational pull vectors. By substitution from equations (18) and (13) into (14), we obtain

$$G = - \frac{Q^2}{\Sigma_w u_w^{-1}}$$

$$Q = - \frac{\Sigma_w u_w^{-1} \Sigma_i a_i p_i + \Sigma_w (B_w - t_w) u_w^{-1}}{2}.$$ (20

Differentiating to obtain $\partial G / \partial x$ and keeping in mind the formal symmetry of $\partial G / \partial y$

$$\frac{\partial G}{\partial x} = - Q \Sigma_i a_i \frac{\partial p_i}{\partial x} - \frac{Q}{\Sigma_w u^{-1}} \Sigma_w \left(\frac{\partial B_w}{\partial x} u_w^{-1} \right).$$ (21

By substitution from equation (17) into equation (21) and from the definition of elasticity for market w as perceived by the producer[20]

---

[20] It is here that the assumption of linear demand simplifies the notation by permitting us to ignore the distinction between the elasticity as perceived by the customer which is based on P_w, and that perceived by the producer, which is based on R.

$$e_w = - \frac{\partial Q}{\partial R} \frac{R}{Q} = - \frac{R}{u_w q_w} ,$$

e obtain

$$\frac{\partial G}{\partial x} = - Q \Sigma_i a_i \frac{\partial p_i}{\partial x} - \Sigma_w \frac{e_w}{E} q_w \frac{\partial B_w}{\partial x} . \qquad (22)$$

The first term on the right-hand side of equation (22) is simply the Web-rian pull of materials: $Q a_i = A_i$ is the quantity of material i, $\frac{\partial p_i}{\partial s_i}$ is the trans-ort rate. It is the second term which is of interest. The Weberian pull $\frac{\partial B_w}{\partial s_w}$ is weighted by the ratio of the elasticity of market w to the total elastic-ty as perceived by the producer. This is a very sensible outcome. A market vith a comparatively elastic demand either because it is a contested market or ecause of local tastes and incomes will pull the firm toward itself out of pro-ortion to the size of the market. The producer's sales and profits increase aster by his moving toward a price-sensitive market than they decrease from noving away from an insensitive one.[21] It should be noted that at the profit-naximizing location, where $\partial G/\partial x = \partial G/\partial y = 0$, transport costs will not be min-mized in any sense of the word unless by chance, since transport costs are weighted by relative elasticities.

A Perfectly Discriminating Monopolist

The f. o. b. monopolist just considered did not differentiate among markets' We shall now consider the location of a producer which will change the price nost advantageous to himself at each of several markets. Again, for simplicity n the proof and to facilitate comparison, we will assume linear demand func-tions identical to those of the previous case. The profit function is now

$$G = \Sigma_w q_w (P_w - B_w - \Sigma_i a_i p_i) . \qquad (23)$$

The producer will maximize his profit at any location by setting P_w at each market according to

$$0 = \frac{\partial G}{\partial q_w} = P_w - B_w - \Sigma_i a_i p_i + q_w \frac{\partial P_w}{\partial q_w} , \qquad (24)$$

which, by manipulation and the definition of elasticity, becomes

$$P_w + q_w \frac{\partial P_w}{\partial q_w} = B_w + \Sigma_i a_i p_i , \qquad (25)$$

---

[21] It is interesting to note that market pulls as a whole are likely to be less than in the Weberian formulation or in the other cases considered here. This derives from the generally greater elasticity of demand curves in space, which will make E greater than most, if not all, e_w's. For a recent discussion of this phenomenon of demand in space, see B. H. Stevens and C. P. Rydell, "Spatial Demand Theory and Monopoly Price Policy," *Papers of the Regional Science Association*, XVII, 1966.

or
$$P_w\left(1 - \frac{1}{e_w}\right) = B_w + \Sigma_i a_i p_i .$$

By substitution from equations (24) and (12) into (23), we obtain

$$G = \Sigma_w q_w^2 \frac{\partial P_w}{\partial q_w} = \Sigma_w - q_w^2 u_w$$

$$q_w = \frac{t_w - B_w - \Sigma_i a_i p_i}{2 u_w} . \tag{2(}$$

It is interesting to compare the new restatement of profits in equation (26) t that of the f.o.b. monopolist in equation (20). In the former case, the sum of th quantities was squared; in this case, the squares are summed. In the forme case, the quantities term was multiplied by the inverse of the sum of the in verses of the $u's$; in this case, each squared quantity is multiplied by its proper u

To obtain the location pull vectors, we differentiate equation (26) with re spect to x and y and, after simplifying, obtain

$$\frac{\partial G}{\partial x} = -\Sigma_w q_w \Sigma_i a_i \frac{\partial p_i}{\partial x} - \Sigma_w q_w \frac{\partial B_w}{\partial x} . \tag{27}$$

The first term on the right side is again a collection of simple Weberian pull of materials. The second term is the pull of each market. It is a simple pu of quantity times transport rate, but the quantity will change after each itera tion in the search procedure. Thus, at equilibrium, transport costs will b minimized for delivery of the equilibrium quantities to each of the markets, but of course, these quantities cannot be known until the equilibrium location i found, and, in this sense, transport costs are minimized only after the fact.

By contrasting the last terms in equations (22) and (27), it is clear that th equilibrium locations will be different under the two pricing systems, as wil be the quantities sold at the various markets.

Maximizing Consumer Surplus

Imagine a theoretically-minded public official in charge of a government owned manufacturing plant who sets himself the goal of finding the location which maximizes consumer surplus, charging only production plus delivery costs at each market

$$P_w^* = \Sigma_i a_i p_i + B_w \tag{28}$$

where

$$P_w^* = \text{price charged at market } w .$$

Demand at market w is given by

$$P_w = f_w(q_w) . \tag{29}$$

Consumer surplus at market w is the area under the local demand curve above P_w^*

$$S_w = \int_0^{q_w^*} (P_w - P_w^*) dq_w = F_w(q_w^*) - F_w(0) - P_w^* q_w^* \tag{30}$$

56

where

$$S_w = \text{consumer surplus at market } w,$$
$$q_w^* = \text{the quantity sold at price } P_w^*, \text{ and}$$
$$F_w = \int f_w dq_w.$$

Total consumer surplus is

$$S = \Sigma_w \left[\int_0^{q_w^*} (P_w - P_w^*) dq_w \right] = \Sigma_w F_w(q_w^*) - \Sigma_w F_w(0) - \Sigma_w P_w^* q_w^*. \tag{31}$$

To obtain the locational pull vectors, we differentiate equation (31) with respect to x and y

$$\frac{\partial S}{\partial x} = \Sigma_w P_w^* \frac{\partial q_w^*}{\partial x} - \Sigma_w P_w^* \frac{\partial q_w^*}{\partial x} - \Sigma_w q_w^* \frac{\partial P_w^*}{\partial x}, \tag{32}$$

or

$$\frac{\partial S}{\partial x} = - \Sigma_w q_w^* \frac{\partial P_w^*}{\partial x}. $$

From equation (28),

$$\frac{\partial P_w^*}{\partial x} = \Sigma_i a_i \frac{\partial p_i}{\partial x} + \frac{\partial B_w}{\partial x}. \tag{33}$$

Substituting into equation (32), we obtain

$$\frac{\partial S}{\partial x} = - \Sigma_w q_w^* \Sigma_i a_i \frac{\partial p_i}{\partial x} - \Sigma_w q_w^* \frac{\partial B_w}{\partial x}. \tag{34}$$

The terms of the right represent locational pulls of weight times transport rates, but once again we are faced with the problem that equilibrium quantities sold at various markets are unknown until they are determined simultaneously with the equilibrium location, so that transport costs are minimized only after the fact.

Equation (34), by comparison to equations (22) and (27), reveals that the objective of maximizing consumer surplus results in yet a third optimal location. The pulls in this case are clearly, except by chance, different from those of the f. o. b. monopolist, since there is no weighting by relative elasticity. They are different from the discriminating monopolist in that the quantities sold at different markets are different. Only if, in both cases, the quantities sold at various markets are exactly proportional will the two locations coincide. The only likelihood of this happening is if all demand curves are strictly linear, in which case the consumer surplus quantities are in all cases exactly twice the discriminating monopolist's quantities. And this will only be true if we do not admit of economies or diseconomies of scale, which would change the values of the pulls of the materials.

It is interesting to consider the way in which the "weights" applied to the marginal transport costs in the market pulls vary with a slight displacement in these three cases.

	weight	$\dfrac{\partial\,(\text{weight})}{\partial x}$
f. o. b.	$\dfrac{e_w}{E}q_w$	$-\dfrac{e_w q_w}{P_w}\left[\dfrac{\Sigma a_i\dfrac{\partial p_i}{\partial x}}{E-1}+\dfrac{\dfrac{\partial B_w}{\partial x}}{E}\right]$
discriminating monopolist	q_w	$-\dfrac{e_w^2}{e_w^{-1}}\dfrac{q_w}{P_w}\left(\Sigma a_i\dfrac{\partial p_i}{\partial x}+\dfrac{\partial B_w}{\partial x}\right)$
consumer surplus	q_w^{*}	$-e_w\dfrac{q_w}{P_w}\left(\Sigma a_i\dfrac{\partial p_i}{\partial x}+\dfrac{\partial B_w}{\partial x}\right)$

This is further proof that, if we started our search procedure for all three cases at a common point, the paths to the optimal locations would diverge.

THE COMPLEMENTARITY OF RENT AND LOCATION THEORIES

It has long been recognized that rent and location theories are twins, but the linkages are elusive. Many linear programming formulations now exist in which the dual of the minimizing of transport costs is the maximizing of rents, and in the early and simplest forms of agricultural and urban rent theories this complementarity was stressed. Thus, Haig, using his vivid phrase "the friction of space," said "while transportation overcomes friction, site rentals and transport costs represent the cost of what friction remains." Rent is "the saving in transport costs."[22] Perhaps the most persuasive demonstration of the symmetry of these two bodies of theory is the fact that many of the same diagrams can be used interchangeably and that many authors slide from one to the other without seemingly realizing it.

But the two theories, for all their commonalities, are still distinct. The key to the difference seems to me to be that rent theory deals with competition for the use of space and location theory does not. The common approach in formal location theory represents the firm as a dimensionless point to be placed on the map. As long as the firm is viewed as a point, there cannot be competition for space, since we could crowd as many industries as we wished on the head of a pin. These industries might compete for markets or for inputs, but they cannot compete for land. It is only when the firm is recognized as having the attribute of spatial extension that the two theories can be joined.

It is difficult to handle rent because land is an unusual good. A firm does not simply buy the input land; in the same transaction it chooses a location in space which significantly affects its requirements of other inputs, principally transport. Although the space it occupies is, at least in the abstract, a homo-

---

[22] R. M. Haig, "Toward an Understanding of the Metropolis," *Quarterly Journal* of *Economics,* May, 1926.

geneous good (an acre here is as roomy as an acre there), location is a highly differentiated good. Insufficient recognition of this complexity has often led to error. In this respect, it is instructive to examine the linear programming solutions, in which a minimum of transport costs in the direct problem is married at a saddle point with the maximum of aggregate rents in the dual. A typical form of these problems is to find the most efficient serving of a number of customers from a given number of warehouses. These problems regard the warehouse as a unit and thus avoid the complexity of distinguishing between where and how much space by associating indissolubly the size of the site with its location. In other words, they have transferred the problem from one of continuous space (and hence usually treated by the use of calculus or diagrammatics) to one of discrete, regionalized, bounded space (and hence suitable to matrix analysis and finite mathematics). This simplification has permitted powerful advances, but it remains a simplification.

There is no conceptual difficulty in introducing consideration of land costs into the analysis of the location of the firm as it has been stated in the preceding pages. In fact, this has already been done implicitly whenever we have written $\Sigma_i A_i p_i$. One of these inputs is land, and it is multiplied by its price or rent. There is no difference from other inputs in that, if we use constant coefficients, the pull vector of a material is the quantity times the delivered price or transport costs gradient. For land, it is the acreage times the rent gradient. It is true, from an operational standpoint, that although transport gradients are always aimed at the source of the material, the rent gradient is likely to vary less systematically in its direction, especially if we are dealing with large territories. Whereas the transport costs functions increase monotonically from their source, the rent surface may well have many peaks and pits. This would lead to practical problems of distinguishing local maxima of profits, and, unless rent is stated as an explicit function, it will require numerical estimation of the gradient. But no conceptual difficulty exists. Further, in expressions (6a, b, c) the conditions of substitution among land and other inputs are given, and they state, as might be expected, that higher land prices lead to less use of land and more of other inputs. These expressions state the process of substitution among the usual inputs, transport costs, and ground rent.

The key point is that in the search for the best location, the vector pull of rent is of the same kind as the pulls of materials and of markets. If we limit ourselves to constant technical coefficients, we might speak of the "ideal weight" of land as the area occupied times the rent gradient. Examine the dimensionality implied. The pulls of markets and materials are in terms of pounds times the marginal transport rate, which is in dollars per pound per mile. Thus these pulls are, as components of the gradient of the profit surface must be, in terms of dollars per mile. The pull of rent is in terms of quantity of land (square miles) times the rent gradient (dollars per square mile per mile), which again reduces to dollars per mile. The same holds true for the cases in which input substitution is possible, or in which demand elasticities weight the pulls, for elasticities and marginal rates of substitution are pure numbers.

But these still deal with the problem of the location of a firm. Rent theory deals with the competition of firms and other land users for the right to occupy the land, since it is this competitive process for a scarce commodity that causes ground rent to exist.[23] Land, as we have mentioned, is a difficult good to deal with because of its dual nature; land as space is a homogeneous good, and land at a location is a continuously differentiated good. Whereas we may speak of *the* price of a homogeneous good, a differentiated good calls for a *pattern* of prices, stating prices at locations. To study the competition for land we will make use of bid-price curves or bid-price surfaces.[24] A bid-price surface is a pattern of land values such that the firm is indifferent among locations. It bears no necessary relation to the actual pattern of land prices. It merely says that if the price of land were such here and thus there, the firm would be equally satisfied at either location. Equal satisfaction for a firm in the normal use means equal profits.

The equation for a bid-price surface is easily obtained. We denote bid-price by r, and substitute r for p_L (the actual price of land) in the profits equations, such as (3), (8), (14), or (23). Rearranging the terms, we put r in terms of all the other variables. If we hold profit constant at some arbitrary value, the various marginality conditions reduce r to a function of (x, y). This function is the bid-price surface for that level of profits. At any point (x, y), it tells us how much that firm could or would pay to maintain that level of profits. Of course, all the other variables are determined simultaneously, so that the price at that location implies not only a certain level of profits but also a certain level of sales and certain quantities of inputs, including land. Different levels of profits lead to similarly shaped but higher or lower surfaces, with higher profits resulting in lower surfaces. Thus, a firm will have a family of bid-price surfaces layered like an onion.

One may think of solving the firm-location problem in terms of bid-price surfaces. Introduce the surface of actual land prices, P_L, into the same three-dimensional diagram with the family of bid-price curves. The surface of actual land prices represents the options available in fact; the layered family of bid-price surfaces represents a mapping of the preferences of the firm, so constructed that the firm is indifferent among points on one surface but prefers lower surfaces. The optimal location of the firm, then, is the point of tangency of the surface of actual prices with the lowest bid-price surface with which it comes in contact. This solution, of course, will be the same as that obtained by other means, and, unless very restrictive assumptions are made about fixed demand and technical coefficients, it is unlikely to minimize either transport costs or transport costs plus rents. It will simply maximize profits.

The concept of bid-prices is most useful for the study of competition for space, rather than for the analysis of the location of a single firm. The locational

---

[23] Location theory, in its more complex forms, has dealt with the competition of firms for markets and resources, as far as I know, rather than for the right to occupy land.

[24] To avoid lengthening this paper, the definition and discussion of bid prices will be brief. A more thorough presentation of the basic concepts can be found in W. Alonso, *Location and Land Use* (Cambridge: Harvard University Press, 1964).

ull of a firm with respect to rent is the quantity of land, perhaps weighted y elasticities, times the gradient of land costs. But these locational pulls cannot be compared directly among firms and, for that matter, among firms and ther users of land such as residences and agriculture, because different quanties of land are involved. The concept of bid rents in effect sorts out location and quantity of land by stating the pulls in terms that are standardized er unit of land. With such a common scale, the pulls become comparable, and becomes easier to study the competition among users. For instance, several heorists of agricultural and urban rent have observed that, in cases of a single enter of orientation, the users with steepest bid-price surfaces will gain the nore central locations. Thus, a firm may have a powerful pull towards a center, but if it is a heavy user of land or it cannot substitute other inputs for and, its pull per acre (gradient of bid-price) will be weak, and its increased ids for land in that direction will be small and unlikely to succeed. Similarly, t provides a possible answer to the paradox of residential location in American metropolitan areas, in which the rich live on cheap suburban land and the oor on expensive central land. The locational pull for residences amounts to he price times the marginal rate of substitution between land and travel time ninus marginal transport costs. However, the bid-price gradient or pull per cre is the total pull divided by the quantity of land. Therefore, in many cases, vhere price and income elasticities for land are high, the slope of the bid-price urfaces of those with higher incomes will be less steep.[25]

The major models of rent theory concern themselves principally with single-enter cases and are, in a sense, abstractions of two-dimensional geographic space nto a one-dimensional locational space defined by distance from that center. The second dimension is incorporated in terms of quantity of land available as a function of distance from the center. This simplification eases the task of lefining and finding the market solution. To illustrate this, consider the rule f steepness of bid-price surfaces mentioned above. In the single-center case, he bid-price surfaces are tent-shaped and peak at the common center; their gradients all point at all times toward that center. Thus the comparison of he gradients is made easy, involving only comparisons of magnitude. But, if ve have more than one orientation, as we do in location theory and, indeed, in nost situations of residential and commercial location, the bid-price gradients f the competing users will point in different directions, so that comparison must involve both magnitude and direction and involve true two-dimensional geographic space. Imagine, for instance, the case of a firm which is outbid by another in the direction of its own gradient, but whose slope in a second direction, although smaller than its own gradient, is steeper than the gradient of a third firm which is oriented in this second direction. Limiting ourselves to these two directions, the firm will move along the second direction, since it can bid more successfully there than along the direction of its own gradient.

The process of finding the market equilibrium is obviously far more complex in two-dimensional geographic space than in the one-dimensional case. I shall present here only an impressionistic description of the process of solution.

[25] For a more detailed exposition of this point, see Alonso, op. cit., pp. 106–16.

Imagine that we have a great number of potential users of land, including in dustries, commerces, households, and farms. For each of these, we generate its family of bid-price surfaces. We have already described the method of generating them for industry. In the residential case, a conceptually simila method is applied, and surfaces are generated such that satisfaction (utility) b constant at all points in one such surface, but lower surfaces yield more sati faction.[26] The bid-price surfaces for different users will rise to peaks at differen locations and fall away at different rates. Some may be fairly flat with a fev sharp peaks; others may rise in gentle swells like a rolling countryside.

Pick a bid-price surface at some arbitrary level for each potential user o land, then assign to each user all of the land over which his bid-price surfac is higher than any of the others. The result will be that a few users have far mor land than they would want at that price and that location, some will have fa less, and many will have no land at all. Shift to lower bid-price surfaces thos who have too much land, and to higher ones those who have too little or none Continue to do this until each user has precisely the appropriate quantity o land implied by the location and level of his successful bids. The envelope o least upper bound of all the individual equilibrium bid-price surfaces is th function which describes actual rents, $p_L(x, y)$. When we studied the locatio of the firm in the earlier sections, we had taken the rent function p_L as given If we were now to take our derived p_L and solve for the location of one of th users, we would arrive within the limits of our accuracy to the same locatio and quantity of land for that user as in the market solution.

The rule of the single-center case that the steeper curves take the mor central locations takes on a new and more complex form. For any user o land, his uphill neighbors must have bid-price surfaces with a slope greate than the gradient of his bid-price surface when the neighbors' slope is measure in the direction of the gradient of the user. Conversely, the slope of the user' bid-price surface, measured in the direction of his downhill neighbors' gradient must be steeper than their gradient. In other words, his uphill neighbors, wh stand in the direction in which he would like to move, must be able to bes his best offer to shift, and he must be able to best the best offers of his downhil neighbors, in whose way he stands.

In summary, the common ground of rent and location theories is their use of locational pulls in the form of vectors, although this is generally done only implicitly. If we are dealing with the location of a single firm or household the pull of rent is identical to the pulls of markets or materials, with the gra dient of the actual rent surface standing in place of a transport rate. In the

---

[26] This is done for the one-center case in Alonso, op. cit., chap. 4. It can be easily extended to cases in which a family has several orientations such as various jobs of dif ferent members, shopping, recreation, in-laws, etc. Instead of the single all-purpose dis tance, the utility function considers the distances to each of these orientations, and the budget function includes travel costs functions to each. By manipulation of the differen tials of the utility and budget functions, one arrives at an expression for the gradient of the bid-price surface as the vector sum of the locational pulls to each of these orientations divided by the quantity of land.

ase of problems of the competition for space, which is to say problems in rent heory, the pulls of the competing users must be standardized to pulls per unit f land in order to be able to compare them. Rent and transport costs will be omplementary in rent theory only if severe assumptions are made about every hing else being constant, including such things as value of sales and con- tant technical coefficients, including that for land. This will be so for much he same reason that the minimizing of transport costs in location theory is an bjective valid only in those tautological cases in which everything else is eld constant.

Costs as They Vary over Space

Transportation Costs

FREIGHT RATES: SELECTED ASPECTS OF UNIFORM AND NODAL REGIONS*

John W. Alexander, S. Earl Brown, and Richard E. Dahlberg

IN a commercial economy having specialized transportation, the movement of goods is influenced by several forces, one of which is the freight rate structure. The spatial differences in transport charges is not only a geographic factor influencing the circulation of goods but also a geographic element in terms of which the character of a region may be expressed. "Mankind is not spread evenly over the face of the earth but tends to cluster in certain areas, which vary from each other. . . . Within such areas relationships arise. . . . It is through the means of transportation and communication that these interrelationships are set up and maintained. . . . But the cost of its use is often as great an element in the importance of a transportation line as its actual presence. Hence freight rates are of greatest value in outlining regions and in affecting their

organization. This is seen in the practice of zoning rates and of offering special inducements for the movement of certain commodities. . . . If transportation facilities serve to consolidate regions, it must also be observed that freight rates are to regions and to cities what tariffs are to nations. They form a part of the cost of connections with other regions and may be manipulated to the advantage or disadvantage of a given region in almost exactly the same way."[1]

Thus, as a geographic element lending character to regions and as a geographic factor influencing the location of economic activities freight rates have significance for the regional analyst.

OVER-SIMPLIFIED GEOGRAPHIC CONCEPTS OF FREIGHT RATES

Unfortunately, some geographic concepts of freight rates have been over-simplified. As a result, there are spatial differences in such costs which either are not known or are not generally

*This study is based in part upon a research grant from the Graduate School of the University of Wisconsin for the 1952–1953 academic year. Mr. Brown and Mr. Dahlberg carried the entire burden of copying and mapping all the statistics pertaining to Wisconsin's freight rate structures presented herein. They also participated in drafting the manuscript.

[1] Harry E. Moore: *What is Regionalism?* Southern Policy Papers, No. 10, University of North Carolina Press, Chapel Hill, 1937, pp. 2–4.

Reprinted from *Economic Geography*, 34 (1958), 1–18, by permission of the authors and editor.

recognized in many geographic studies. This prevents the regional analyst from clearly understanding the relationships between regional economies and the flow of goods both within a region and between regions.[2] In general, there seem to be two misconceptions: (1) From any given point, freight rates (assessed by the same form of transport) increase similarly in all directions; i.e., the rail rate on a carload of coal from Milwaukee to a point 100 miles northwest is the same as the rail rate on a similar carload of coal from Milwaukee to a point 100 miles southwest. (2) The second misconception is that freight rates always increase with distance. The extreme expression of this fallacy is that rates increase *directly* with distance; i.e., it costs twice as much to ship a commodity 1000 miles as 500 miles. Less erroneous is the idea that rates increase with distance but always at a diminishing rate.[3]

It is difficult to document these two criticisms. In most geographical treatises dealing with economic activity, scarcely any but the most cursory mention is made of transport costs. Without so stating (and therefore not quotable) such studies apparently assume the two concepts expressed above. In any case, the very absence of recognition of freight rate analysis in geographic studies supports the conclusion that geographers are rather uninformed on spatial variations in such costs. On the other hand, a few studies do recognize the role of

transport costs but, for want of evidence, assume that freight rate structures are concentric around transport centers. For example, Harris employed this expedient in his analysis of the American market[4] but frankly raised the question "How nearly does the actual freight-rate structure approximate the generalized transport bands used in the calculations of this paper?"[5]

Geographers have made comparatively few investigations of spatial variations in freight rates probably because of rate complexity. "Rate structures are so complex that to generalize them into significant geographic patterns is extraordinarily difficult. . . . In spite of all these difficulties, it would be worth while to attempt some geographic generalization of rate patterns. . . . Rate structures can be studied from a geographic point of view."[6] Nevertheless, in view of the fact that freight rates are fundamentally important in the geography of flow (which in turn is the dynamic aspect of transport geography), because they are spatial variables contributing to regionalism, and because of misconceptions easily drawn regarding freight rates, this article will consider freight rates from two regional viewpoints: uniform regions and nodal regions.

UNIFORM FREIGHT RATE REGIONS

A uniform region, as defined by Whittlesey, is homogeneous because all parts of its area contain the feature or features by which it is defined, in this case,

---

[2] "As an example, under the system of freight rates prevailing before 1925, it cost less to ship fruit from California to New York than from the Ozark fruit region to the same city, while the cost of shipping fruit from California to New York was less than twice that of moving it from Florida and California . . . ." Harry F. Moore, *op. cit.*, p. 3.

[3] For more detailed discussion of these misconceptions, see E. F. Penrose: "The Place of Transport in Economic and Political Geography," United Nations' *Transport and Communications Review*, Volume V, Number 2, April-June, 1952, p. 4.

[4] Chauncy D. Harris: "Market As a Factor in Localization of Industry," *Annals Assn. Amer. Geogrs.*, Vol. 44, 1954, p. 323.

[5] *Ibid.*, p. 348.

[6] Edward L. Ullman and Harold B. Mayer: "Transportation Geography" in *American Geography, Inventory and Prospect*, Preston E. James and Clarence F. Jones, edits., Syracuse, 1954, reference on pp. 326–327.

Fig. 1.   United States Freight Rate Territories, 1937. (Source: United States Government, 75th Congress, 1st Session, House Document No. 264, *The Interterritorial Freight Rate Problem of the United States, 1937*.)

similar freight rates.[7]   An example of uniform freight rate regions is the structure of railroad class freight rates which prevailed for years in the United States. Since 1887 the rates charged by the nation's railroads have been regulated by the federal government's Interstate Commerce Commission (I.C.C.).   It has not been a case of the Commission prescribing rates but rather of either approving or disapproving rates which the railroads proposed.   For years the Commission recognized different regions within which the railroads had decided to charge characteristic prices.   The five major regions, as mapped by a congressional committee in 1937, appeared in an official House Document

[7] Derwent Whittlesey: "The Regional Concept and the Regional Method," Chapter II in *American Geography, Inventory and Prospect*, references on pp. 36 and 39.

and is reproduced as Figure 1 in this article.   Table I shows the *average* rate prevailing in each of the five regions. In such a rate structure, a shipment of any given commodity moving X miles in Official Territory was priced, on the average, at a lower freight rate than a shipment of the identical commodity moving the same distance in any other

TABLE I

LEVELS OF FIRST-CLASS FREIGHT RATES

Index numbers indicate the *average* levels of applicable class rates mile for mile in other territories in relation to Official Territory for shipments of up to 1000 miles.

Territory	Index of rate
Official or Eastern....................	100
Southern.............................	139
Western Trunk Line..................	147
Southwestern........................	175
Mountain-Pacific....................	171

Source: United States 75th Congress, 1st Session, House Document No. 264 *The Interterritorial Freight Rate Problem of the United States*, 1937.

rate region, so long as *class rates*[8] applied in both cases. It must be emphasized that the figures presented in Table I and portrayed graphically in Figure 1 are *averages* for all such movements within the region.

The reasons for this regional variation in class rates are exceedingly complex and comprise a sizable body of literature in transportation economics.[9] In general they reflect (a) the principle that efficiencies in mass movement warrant lower rates where heavy traffic occurs, and (b) the influence of competitive forms of cheaper transportation such as waterways along the Atlantic, the Pacific, and the Gulf coasts. In any case, division of the United States in terms of this geographic element produced clearly defined regions of the uniform type.

As a geographic factor, this regionalism in the nation's freight rate structure had a profound impact upon the nation's economic geography. It gave the Northeast a definite rate advantage making it less expensive, on the average, to ship goods in that region than in any other part of the nation. In recent years the I.C.C. received increasing protest from other portions of the country, especially the South, whose leaders complained that the rate structure was regionally discriminatory in favor of the

economy of the Official (or Eastern) region. Beginning in the 1940's the I.C.C. reviewed these regional discrepancies in the class rate structure[10] and, in a series of decisions spaced several years apart, gradually erased most of the regional differentiations. By 1952 uniformity had been achieved from the Atlantic Coast to the Rocky Mountains. Nevertheless, the effect of the regional differences in class rates which prevailed from 1887–1952 will be observable in the regionalization of the American economy for many years to come.

NODAL FREIGHT RATE REGIONS

"Nodal regions are homogeneous with respect to internal structures or organization. This structure includes a focus, or foci, and a surrounding area tied to the focus by lines of circulation. . . . Hence the nodal region is bounded by the disappearance or differential weakening of the tie to its own focus in favor of some other focus. Its boundary lines tend to run at right angles to the lines that tie it together."[11] Nodal freight rate regions are delimited in terms of rate structures to/from transport foci. The remainder of the present article is essentially a study of nodal regions[12] discernible in a case study area: the State of Wisconsin.

The specific objectives of the research reported in the following pages are (a) to

[8] Where the movement of a commodity is particularly heavy between any two points, the railroad may publish a reduced rate termed a *commodity* rate. By law, railroads are required to file each new rate with the Commission 30 days before its effective date. Unless protested at least 12 days before the effective date, it becomes an official rate. If protested, the new rate is suspended by the Commission pending investigation at the end of which time it may be disallowed or approved.

[9] For example, Roland B. Eutsler: *Transportation in North Carolina, A Study of Rate Structure and Rate Adjustment*, University of Pennsylvania, 1929; William H. Joubert: *Southern Freight Rates in Transition*, University of Florida Press, 1949; D. Philip Locklin, *Economics of Transportation*, 1947; D. A. MacGibbon, *Railway Rates and the Canadian Railway Commission*, 1917.

[10] F. L. Barton: "The Interstate Commerce Commission Considers The Class Rate Structure," *Journ. of Land and Publ. Utility Econs.*, Vol. 17, 1941, pp. 10–16.

[11] Derwent Whittlesey, *op. cit.*, p. 37.

[12] Examples of other studies in which freight rate regional nodality is implicit, although not always identified as such are: John W. Alexander: "Freight Rates As a Geographic Factor in Illinois," *Econ. Geogr.*, Vol. 20, 1944, pp. 25–30; Stuart P. Daggett and John Carter: *The Structure of Transcontinental Railroad Rates*, University of California Press, Berkeley, 1947; Olaf Lindberg: "An Economic-Geographical Study of the Localization of the Swedish Paper Industry," *Geografiska Annaler*, Arg. XXXV, 1953, Hafte I, pp. 28–40.

present facts with some analysis of freight rate structures in a case study area and (b) to consider problems of methodology in the study of freight rates from the geographical viewpoint.

This is a progress report in a study of Wisconsin's freight rate geography which is still in the descriptive stage. As yet little has been done in interpreting these rate structures or correlating them with other phenomena. The report is issued at this stage with the thought that it will be of interest to specialists concerned with the spatial variations of transport costs.

All maps are of Wisconsin's rate structures during the period 1952–1953.

The State of Wisconsin was selected for study because: (a) At least some types of spatial differences in transport costs prevailing over the earth were assumed to be discernible in an area the size of Wisconsin; (b) transport costs frequently are assessed on a "state" basis; a political state is a meaningful area in the consideration of transport charges;[13] (c) data on transport charges applicable to this political unit are on file in a central place (the Wisconsin Public Service Commission) which is easily accessible in Madison.

Procedure

Maps were constructed of several different freight rate structures: (a) *class* rates on *rail* shipments to/from all points in Wisconsin from/to Chicago, Milwaukee, Green Bay, Superior and Duluth (the first being the major out-of-state shipping center on the southeast and the last being a major out-of-state shipping point on the north-west); (b) *class* rates on *truck* shipments to/from all points in Wisconsin from/to

[13] Rates on an *intrastate* flow of goods to a major terminal, or rate-breaking point, are often different than rates on an identical flow of goods destined via that same terminal for another state.

the same five shipping centers listed above; (c) commodity railroad rates on *coal* to all Wisconsin points from the southern Illinois-Indiana coal field, from Milwaukee, from Green Bay, and from Superior.

Data Sources

Data were procured from the State Public Service Commission which has on file in the Capitol all rate tariffs which apply to the movement of freight in Wisconsin.[14]

Mapping Techniques

Rates were plotted on base maps (provided by the Public Service Commission) which show the location of all railroads and shipping points in the State. Plotting of truck rates required interpolating from the State's official highway map for location of points not on railways.

Isarithms, herein termed *isophors*,[15] were constructed as lines connecting the innermost points of equal freight rates. "Innermost" has significance because in the structure of any nodal rate region it is possible for consecutive places on a radiating transport artery to have the same rate to the transport center around which the rate structure is oriented. In such a case the isophor is drawn through the place nearest the transport center

[14] The authors gratefully acknowledge the cooperation of the personnel in the Wisconsin Public Service Commission office, especially Mr. Ivan A. Sherman, Transportation Rate Analyst, and Mr. Harold Hueblein. "Tariffs" are tables of freight charges or transport prices published by the carriers.

[15] The term isophor is derived from the Greek "isos" (equal) and "phora" (charge for carrying freight). Scandinavian scholars have used different terms. Tord Palander employs the term "isotim" defined as a line connecting points of equal delivered price. See E. H. Hoover's discussion of terminology on page 8 of his *Location Theory and the Shoe and Leather Industries*, Harvard University Press, Cambridge, Massachusetts, 1937. Olaf Lindberg uses the term "isovecture" defined as a line joining points of equal transport costs, *op. cit.*, p. 28.

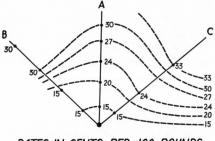

RATES IN CENTS PER 100 POUNDS
TO/FROM A TRANSPORT CENTER

FIG. 2.

which serves as the focus of the nodal region.

Several problems arise in the drawing of such isarithms. How should they be drawn where a sequence of shipping points along one radiating transport artery has a sequence of rates ascending in several small increments while a neighboring radiating line has rates ascending in a few large increments (Fig. 2)? Can the isophors be continuous lines located as per the quoted rates on line A and interpolated on lines B and C? This requires isophors to cross a transport line (thus indicating rates of a given value) where no such rates exist. Figure 3, a portion of a Wisconsin rate structure, illustrates this problem. The rail first class rate per 100 pounds to Chicago is 143 cents from Klevenville and 126 cents from Riley. Rates from all other shipping points (for which rates are published) are plotted on Figure 3. Isophors are drawn for only those rates which are quoted for places which are located in the area mapped. Between Klevenville and Riley there is no shipping point; no quoted rate exists. Yet three isophors (133, 136, and 140) run between the two. Is this realistic? Should isarithms be drawn in locations where there are nonexistent values?

A second problem is a visual one.

Closely spaced isarithms give the impression of steeper gradients than do isarithms farther apart. Figure 4 illustrates this problem by showing the first class rate structure on rail shipments between Chicago and all Wisconsin points. It has been constructed according to the "interpolated isophor" technique: viz., drawing isophors for rates which are quoted for specific stations, and extending them across all rail lines (even where no such rates are quoted) in order to give form to the rate structure. Thus, there are isophors for values 129, 133, and 136 but none for 130, 131, 132, 134, or 135 because there are no stations in Wisconsin for which such rates are quoted. The visual impression is one of a steep gradient extending through Wonewoc and Kiel because isophors are close together. Actually the rate contrast through this belt is only 10–11 cents.

One solution to these mapping problems could be the construction of isophors at selected constant intervals. However, this might hide important

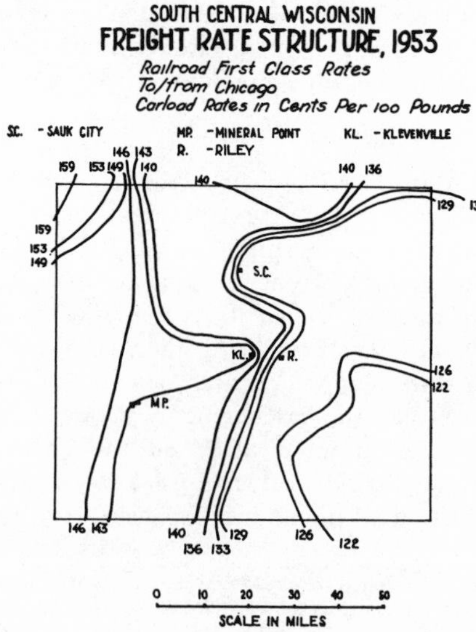

SOUTH CENTRAL WISCONSIN
FREIGHT RATE STRUCTURE, 1953
Railroad First Class Rates
To/from Chicago
Carload Rates in Cents Per 100 Pounds

SC. - SAUK CITY   MP. - MINERAL POINT   KL. - KLEVENVILLE
R. - RILEY

SCALE IN MILES

FIG. 3.

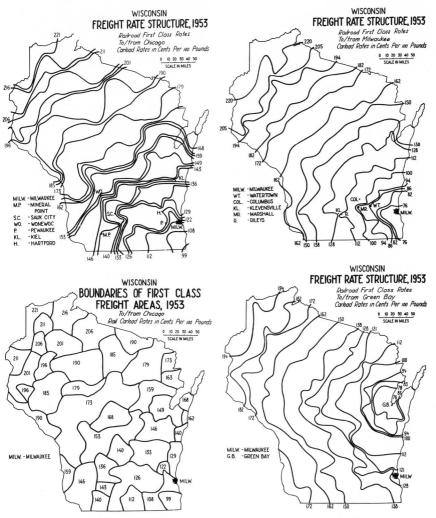

FIGS. 4 (upper left), 5 (lower left), 6 (upper right), and 7 (lower right).

deviations from the general structure. For example, application of 10-unit intervals selected at 126, 136, and 146 on Figure 4 would fail to reveal rather abrupt structure changes in the vicinity of Mineral Point. Another difficulty with this technique is that rates may not be quoted for values fitting into a regular interval; for example, there is no 156 rate and no 116 rate anywhere in Wisconsin to continue the sequence proposed in the foregoing illustration.

An alternative mapping technique abandons the use of isarithms in favor of rate area boundaries. Each line would encompass all contiguous places with the same rate. Figure 5 has been constructed on this basis for rail first class rates to/from Chicago. Cartographically this is more accurate than the isarithmic technique, i.e., no rate is represented in any place if it does not exist there. On the other hand, the selection of adequate symbols is a problem since there are 26 different categories (from the area having a 99 cent rate in the extreme southeast to the area having a 221 cent rate in the extreme northwest). Also, this does not give a clear visual impression of the relationship between rates and distance nor does it give an easily grasped view of a rate structure.

In any case, there is need for improving the technique of mapping freight rate structures.

Railroad First Class Freight Rate Structures

Figures 4, 6, 9, 10, and 11 employ the interpolated isophor technique, showing Wisconsin's structure of rail first class freight rates to/from five major transport centers as of 1952–1953.

Figure 4 shows the rate structure between all Wisconsin rail stations and *Chicago*. Only very broadly is the pattern one of concentric circles, which should prevail if rates increased uniformly in all directions from Chicago. The capricious path of isophors is illustrated by numerous examples. For instance, the rate between Milwaukee and Chicago is 108 cents per 100 pounds. Just north of Milwaukee (on the rail routes along the lake shore) the rate increases abruptly to 129. Between these two values rates of 112, 122, and 126 are quoted elsewhere in Wisconsin. Though closely spaced just north of Milwaukee, these isophors diverge to the west; the 126 and 129 isophors are parallel to a point beyond Hartford where the 129 isophor bends sharply *northwest* while the 126 isophor bends sharply *southeast*. Similar variation involves other pairs of isophors: e.g., 146 and 149, 153 and 159, 185 and 190. Obviously, in this

particular structure, rates increase differentially in different directions from the focal city.

The complexity of a freight rate structure is illustrated by the profusion of isarithms on Figure 4 on which every existing rate quoted for any place in the State is represented. For the sake of simplicity, most maps to follow are not, in this respect, complete replicas of Wisconsin's rate structure. Only selected isophors will appear, in order to present more clearly the essence of the structure. The total visual impression of subsequent maps therefore cannot be compared directly with that of Figure 4; however, the complexities of isophor patterns are comparable.

Figure 6 shows the structure of rail first class rates between all Wisconsin shipping points and *Milwaukee*. There is some tendency toward a concentric pattern, yet sharp irregularities in many isophors indicate that increase with distance apparently is not consistent in all directions. Profiles of freight rate gradients to the north, west, southwest, and south of Milwaukee show marked variations (Fig. 8).

It might be supposed that places on a direct route to the focal city of the structure would have lower rates than neighboring places not on such routes. This is not true. For instance, Figure 9 shows Fort Atkinson to have a lower rate to Milwaukee than does Eagle, which is not only on a direct route but also closer to Milwaukee. Figure 9 also reveals sharp structure contrasts between two places on separate direct routes. For example, Columbus and Marshall are on direct routes to Milwaukee, in fact their routes converge at Watertown. Yet the Marshall rate to Milwaukee is 86 cents while that of Columbus is 100 cents. Note the steep gradient between Riley and Klevenville on Figure 8 as well as Figure 3.

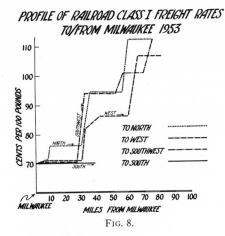

FIG. 8.

The structure of rail first class rates around *Green Bay* (Fig. 7), *Superior* (Fig. 10), and *Duluth* (Fig. 11) reveals the same general arrangement: a tendency toward concentricity but strange deflections in and congestions of isophors. There is an anomaly in the Superior structure north of Milwaukee where nine stations on two different railroads have a 186 rate, in sharp contrast to the 214 rate prevailing around them. This actually represents an error in the published tariffs.[16] In the Duluth rate structure the 159 and 196 isophors are particularly distorted.

Inspection of the foregoing rail rate structures around five focal points reveals the structures of isophors to be very asymmetrical. Rates do not increase consistently with distance in any one direction, or similarly in different directions.

To understand what appears to be capriciousness on the part of rail first class rates one needs to consider three

[16] Since determining the exact rates to Superior for all Wisconsin points required several computations, it was first thought that an error had been made in computations; however, Mr. Ivan A. Sherman checked the computations, found them to be correct, and verified the conclusion that the tariffs quoted rates for this small area out of harmony with the general rate structure.

principles which apply in the philosophy of rate making adhered to by the railroads in this nation: (a) the "grouping" principle, (b) the "short line distance" principle, and (c) the "rate step" principle.

The *grouping principle* enables railroads to simplify the publication of class rates. Theoretically, if all rates were assessed on the mileage basis, a separate rate would have to be published between every pair of shipping points in the nation. As a result, each freight agent in the country would have to refer to volumes of tremendous size to determine rates on shipments to/from his depot. By treating several proximal stations as one, the railroads greatly simplify their rate tariffs. In essence, the grouping principle declares that all the stations in a group take the same rate to any other group of stations. The group's specific rate is computed in terms of the group's "control point" which often is the largest settlement in the group's area. Figure 12 shows the location of the 67 areas of station groups which the railroads proposed

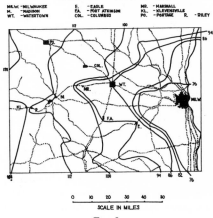

FIG. 9.

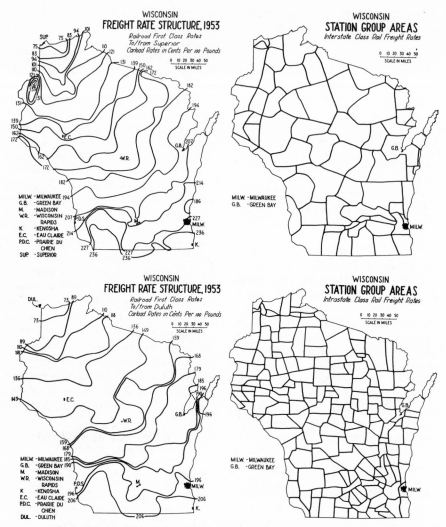

FIGS. 10 (upper left), 11 (lower left), 12 (upper right), and 13 (lower right).

(and the Interstate Commerce Commission approved) for the *interstate* class freight rate structure. The major dimension of each group's area is approximately 40 miles although some are longer and a few are shorter. Figure 13 shows that for *intrastate* rail shipments, Wisconsin's class freight rate structure comprises many more (180 to be exact) group areas.[17] Group areas are smaller

on Figure 13 than on Figure 12 because intrastate shipments tend to be shorter than interstate.

The *"short line principle"* prescribes that rates shall be computed on the basis of the mileage of the shortest route over which carload freight can be

[17] Figures 12 and 13 are copied from manuscript maps prepared in the Tariff Section of the Wisconsin Public Service Commission, courtesy of Mr. Ivan A. Sherman.

transported without transfer of lading. In application this means that a shipment needing to move from one railroad to another would have to move through interchange points which the railroads have established, analogous to "transfer stations" on a city's rapid transit system. For this reason alone, rate structures could not be expected to be concentric around a transport center unless numerous railroad routes extended outward from it radially.

The third principle followed by the railroads is the *quoting of rates "in steps."* For instance, no *interstate* rates are quoted on shipments of less than 40 miles, but from 40 to 100 miles the rate increases in steps of five miles and is computed in terms of the distance between the control points of groups. For distances between 100 and 240 miles the steps are 10 miles in length; they are 20 miles long for distances over 240 miles. *Intrastate* rates in Wisconsin are quoted in terms of five mile steps on shipments of 100 miles or less and of 10 mile steps on shipments exceeding 100 miles.

Such methods of computing rates by railroads have evolved gradually over the years and have been permitted by the government commissions.

The group-area philosophy portrayed by the patterns of Figures 12 and 13, the "short line" principle, and the philosophy of increasing rates in steps are fundamental to the understanding of the isophor maps of class rates presented in this study, and are excellent examples of a cultural geographic factor (philosophy of rate-making) operating to influence the locational pattern of a geographic element, the freight rate structure of Wisconsin.

Truck First Class Freight Rate Structures

Maps of Wisconsin structures of common carrier truck rates are shown in

Figures 14–18. Admittedly, more traffic probably moves by *private* truck and by *contract* truck, but it is impossible to construct rate maps for such flow. The structures of rates to/from *Chicago* (Fig. 14) are represented by selected isophors and reveal more irregularities in the nearer rather than the distant portions of the State. By contrast, the structures of rates to/from *Milwaukee*, *Green Bay*, and *Superior* (Figs. 15, 16, and 17) show surprising concentricity. The Milwaukee structure (Fig. 15) is shown in its entirety; i.e., all isophors are drawn. For the sake of simplicity, alternate isophors have been omitted on Figures 16 and 17.

A different philosophy of rate making has prevailed in determining truck rates. The trucking authorities, in contrast to the railroad men, proposed to the commissions that truck rates be computed generally in terms of *airline* distances rather than the "short-line-involving-no-transfer-of-lading" principle. This is the main explanation for Wisconsin's truck rate structures being more symmetrical than the rail rates. Nevertheless, the fact that truck rates, like rail rates, increase in shorter steps for short hauls and, on interstate shipments, also respond to the location of control points means that the interstate truck class rate structures for Chicago and Duluth, Figure 20, tend to be less symmetrical in their inner areas.

Class Rate Nodal Regions

Synthesis of rail rate structures and truck rate structures just presented enables the delimitation of nodal regions around the five focal centers, Figure 18. The nodal region for each focus was constructed by delimiting all shipping points linked by a lower rate to that center than to any other. For example, the first class rail rate per 100 pounds from Madison is 126 to Chicago, 107

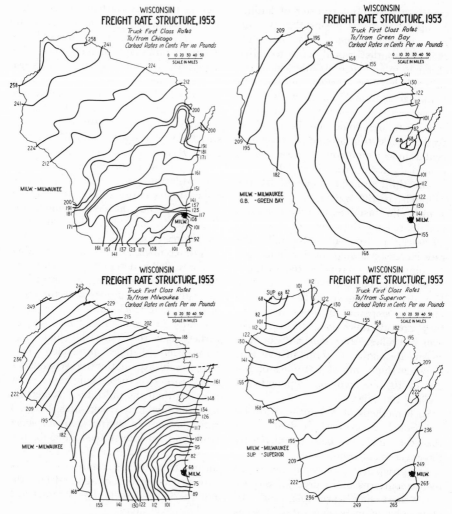

FIGS. 14 (upper left), 15 (lower left), 16 (upper right), and 17 (lower right).

to Milwaukee, 138 to Green Bay, 211 to Superior, and 190 to Duluth. Therefore, Madison is in the Milwaukee nodal region of rail rates. Where truck rates are lower than rail rates a solid black symbol is employed.

Two broad observations can be drawn from the map of nodal regions. First, over most of Wisconsin, first class rail rates are lower than first class truck rates.[18] However, in the immediate hinterlands of each focus the truck rates are lower. Chicago and Duluth have no such "truck advantage regions" in Wisconsin, and Superior's is small. The Milwaukee nodal area in which truck

[18] The reader is reminded that the areas delimited on Figure 18 as having lower truck rates are delimited in terms of common carrier rates, it being impossible to procure data on private truck movements and contract truck movements.

rates are less than rail rates exceeds Green Bay's which, in turn, exceeds Superior's. At least in the structures mapped herein, it appears that the larger the transport center, the more extensive the area in which truck transport has a favorable rate differential over railroads. Whether this principle is true or not for other transport centers in the State and in the nation is yet to be investigated.

The extent of the truck nodal regions within the rail nodal regions noted above relates to the well-known fact that on short hauls the truck is more efficient than the train. Recognition of this division of talent is demonstrated in the "piggy-back" development in which trucks accumulate loads in the hinterlands of major rail centers, assemble at the center, are loaded bodily onto rail flat cars and carried by rail over a long haul to another rail center where the truck disembarks, finishing its movement in short hauls to distributing points in the center's hinterland.

The second observation is that nodal rate regions can have peculiar shapes and locations, the most unusual situations resulting where a nodal region involving intrastate shipments is enmeshed with one involving interstate traffic. That any part of Wisconsin should have lower rates to Chicago than to Milwaukee may seem surprising, yet Chicago's nodal region penetrates the extreme southwestern corner of the State which is served by the Chicago, Burlington and Quincy Railroad's main line between Chicago and the Twin Cities. Milwaukee's nodal region blankets most of southern Wisconsin and actually reaches the Mississippi River at two places: (a) in the vicinity of Prairie du Chien where rates via the Milwaukee Railroad's direct line to Milwaukee are lower than the Burlington's rates to Chicago, thus fragmenting

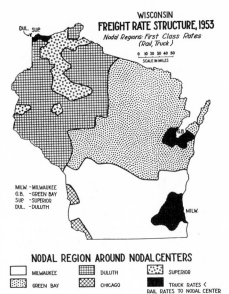

WISCONSIN
FREIGHT RATE STRUCTURE, 1953
*Nodal Regions: First Class Rates
(Rail, Truck)*

0 10 20 30 40 50
SCALE IN MILES

MILW. -MILWAUKEE
G.B. -GREEN BAY
SUP -SUPERIOR
DUL. -DULUTH

NODAL REGION AROUND NODAL CENTERS

☐ MILWAUKEE	▦ DULUTH	⠿ SUPERIOR
▨ GREEN BAY	▧ CHICAGO	■ TRUCK RATES RATES < RAIL RATES TO NODAL CENTER

FIG. 18.

the Chicago nodal region, and (b) in the vicinity of LaCrosse where another direct line to Milwaukee has effected lower rates than to the other four centers.

Even more unusual is the relative location of the Duluth and Superior nodal regions. Duluth's extends much farther south. In spite of the fact that Duluth itself is west of Superior, its nodal region also extends farther east than Superior's. Superior's nodal region actually is an aggregate of several fragmented areas within the Duluth nodal region. Incongruous as it may seem, Figure 18 reveals that shippers and consignees in most of northwestern Wisconsin have lower first class rates on shipments to/from Duluth, Minnesota than to/from Superior, Wisconsin. Comparison of Figures 10 and 11 reveals that, even outside the Duluth nodal region, rates from Wisconsin to Duluth are generally lower than to Superior. For example, comparative rates for selected points are presented

TABLE II

RAILROAD FIRST CLASS RATES

(per 100 pounds)

From	To Duluth, Minnesota	To Superior, Wisconsin
Eau Claire............	$1.36	$1.39
Wisconsin Rapids.......	1.53	1.62
Green Bay.............	1.79	1.99
Prairie du Chien........	1.90	2.07
Madison..............	1.90	2.11
Milwaukee.............	1.96	2.27
Kenosha..............	2.06	2.36

in Table II. A graphic view of this information is presented in Figure 19, a comparative profile of the Duluth and Superior rate structures along the rail routes connecting Superior with Eau Claire, Portage, Milwaukee, and Kenosha. In the northern half of this route the two profiles intersect eight times, indicating that there are four segments where lower rates to Superior prevail alternating with four segments of lower rates to Duluth. The route's southern half sees the Superior structure climbing high above Duluth's. The differential reaches 30 cents in the vicinity of Oconomowoc, shrinks to 26 cents in the Milwaukee area, and expands again to 30 cents between Racine and Kenosha. Similar intertwinings of profiles would result if the Duluth and Superior structures were compared along other routes. At first glance, such a relationship of structures would appear illogical unless one remembers that the dotted graph portrays an interstate structure of rates, whereas the solid line represents intrastate structure which both result from rate computation methods which differ in terms of (a) size of group areas of stations and (b) length of steps by which rates increase.

Commodity Rate Structures: Coal

Figures 21, 22, and 23[19] show Wisconsin's freight rate structures as of 1952–1953 on movement of a selected

commodity, coal, chosen because it moves between more points in larger tonnage than any other commodity.

Figure 21 portrays the structure on coal rates from the southern Illinois bituminous coal field from which most Wisconsin localities receive coal. The original map showed a confusion of isophors in the southern part of the State; for simplicity of reproduction 10 isophors have been deleted between the 344 and 437 rates. North of the 437 isophor only three have been deleted. The map reveals clearly the rate advantage enjoyed by southeastern Wisconsin. Most places have rates of 388 or 420 cents per ton. Northward the

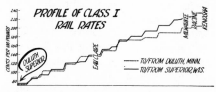

FIG. 19.

rates increase at rather long intervals, but the increases are abrupt. Figure 21 illustrates one of the mapping problems discussed earlier. A steep gradient is implied by the congestion of three isophors between Waukesha and Sussex, separated by a 25 cent differential (between 395 and 420). By contrast, a gentle gradient appears to prevail across the central portion of the state through Blair, Wisconsin Rapids, and Green Bay, where there is no close spacing of isophors. Yet here the rate increases sharply in a single step from 445 to 475, a differential of 30 cents per ton.

The lowest rates on Figure 21 occur, not along the Lake Michigan shore, but 60 miles westward along the Rock River Valley. Beloit's rate of 341 is the lowest

[19] These maps are based on coal rates filed with the Public Service Commission and recorded also by Mr. W. F. Ehmann for the Wisconsin Coal Bureau, Inc., who provided the data for this portion of the study.

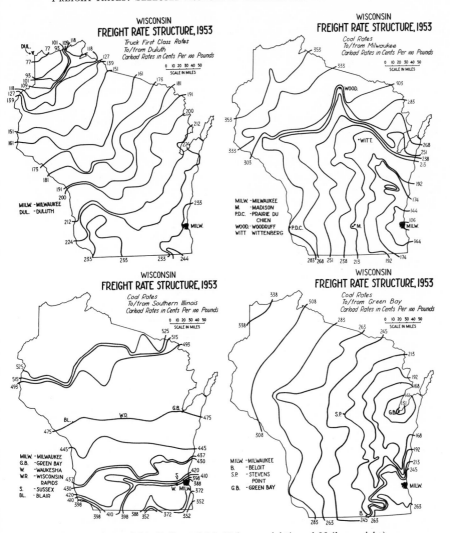

FIGS. 20 (upper left), 21 (lower left), 22 (upper right), and 23 (lower right).

in the State, 47 cents lower than Milwaukee's, 12 cents lower than Racine's. This concession was granted the Beloit area by the I.C.C. in response to vigorous persuasion by manufactural interests in the Rock River Valley, and is of significance in perpetuating this small industrial belt as one of the nation's more intensely developed industrial nodes.[20]

The complexity of the structure on rates from *Milwaukee* almost defies description (Figure 22). The original map was so intricate as to be illegible in reduced form. The map reproduced here omits two-thirds of the isophors in

[20] For further analysis of this adjustment on coal rates see John W. Alexander: *Geography of Manufacturing in the Rock River Valley*, University of Wisconsin School of Commerce, Bureau of Business Research Service, 1949, pp. 163–164.

an effort to portray the major structural characteristics which reveal an asymmetrical arrangement of rates very low to the northwest. For instance, the rate from Milwaukee to Madison, a distance of 90 miles, is 208 cents per ton; but in a northerly direction the 208 rate carries 200 miles to Wittenberg. Two hundred miles west of Milwaukee the rate is 278 at Prairie du Chien. A 278 rate in a northwesterly direction carries as far as Woodruff, almost to the Michigan border. It is difficult to explain all such idiosyncracies in the freight rate structure. However, certain factors can be identified. For example, the northward looping of isophors in the eastern portion of Wisconsin (e.g., the 213 isophor) is due to the competitive position of other coal gateways such as Green Bay. The railroads, with the approval of the Commission, have given Milwaukee a favorable competitive rate in Green Bay's hinterland. The result is that some communities in eastern Wisconsin enjoy lower rates on dock coal from Milwaukee than do communities closer to Milwaukee but located in southwestern Wisconsin. The strange pattern of isophors in north-central Wisconsin, like a prong pointing northward, is the result of what rate analysts term "holddowns" to give manufacturing firms in the Wisconsin River Valley competitive rates as compared to industry in the Fox River Valley to the east.[21] The same principle has been observed already in the case of the Rock River Valley on Figure 21.

Another unusual aspect of a rate structure portrayed by Figure 22 is the "negative anomaly" 50 miles north of Milwaukee. This is one result of the "equalization clause" which, in the words of Ivan A. Sherman of Wiscon-

[21] Mr. Ivan A. Sherman in personal interview.

sin's Public Service Commission, "permits railroads to equalize without undue discrimination the rates to destinations from more distant ports, or to reduce the spread in rates from more distant ports over those from nearer ports; but such equalization or reduction in rates shall be to a level not lower than the rate that would be produced by the scale at 50 per cent of the rate-making distance from the more distant port." This equalization clause has been in effect for decades, ever since Appalachian coal began moving through Wisconsin's ports. This clause states another philosophy of rate making which, as a spatial variable, is both a cultural geographic factor and a geographic element.

The coal rate structures portrayed in Figures 21–23 are unique in the United States, according to the Wisconsin Public Service Commission. In no other state is there the overlapping of so many rate structures on coal movements.

To the absolute rate values on Figure 22 should be added $3.45, the rate on coal from the Appalachian field via rail and water to Milwaukee. Appalachian coal moving via the Great Lakes to Milwaukee, Green Bay, Superior, and other Wisconsin ports is termed "dock coal." The rate on "dock coal" to Madison would be $3.45 plus $2.08 equalling $5.53 which has a differential of $1.58 above Madison's $3.95 rate from southern Illinois. This is a major reason why inland consumers who do not require the higher quality Appalachian coal prefer the Illinois product.

Wisconsin's major nodal regions in terms of "*dock* coal" commodity rates are shown in Figure 24 which is based not only on Figures 22 and 23 but also on individual rate structures constructed around all other important coal ports (Racine, Port Washington, Sheboygan,

Manitowoc, Marinette, Ashland, and Superior). In every case the transport charge from Appalachian coal fields to lake port was added to the charge from lake port to Wisconsin points. Nodal regions then were delimited in terms of over-all rates from coal fields to destination.

The large blank area on Figure 24 indicates that the pattern of dock coal rate nodal regions is more complex than the construction of class rate nodal regions. Figure 18 reveals no areas of overlap; every place in the State can be ascribed to a single nodal region. This is impossible for dock coal rates. Nodal regions involving no overlap are outlined in Figure 24 and, in the aggregate, comprise less than half of Wisconsin. In most of southern Wisconsin a station is likely to enjoy equally low rates on dock coal from at least two, and often more, of the coal receiving ports. This appears to result from at least two causes: (a) Transport charges from the Appalachian coal producing fields are quoted for groups of Wisconsin ports rather than on a distance basis. Table III illustrates this point with data on shipments from Pittsburgh. (b) The equalization clause (mentioned earlier) enables railroads to quote equal rates between a point and two or more ports.

However, when rates on Illinois coal are considered, all of Wisconsin is in the Illinois nodal region excepting the

WISCONSIN
FREIGHT RATE STRUCTURE, 1953
Nodal Regions: Railroad Rates on Coal
0 10 20 30 40 50
SCALE IN MILES

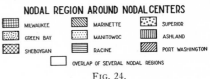

NODAL REGION AROUND NODAL CENTERS

MILWAUKEE   MARINETTE   SUPERIOR
GREEN BAY   MANITOWOC   ASHLAND
SHEBOYGAN   RACINE   PORT WASHINGTON
OVERLAP OF SEVERAL NODAL REGIONS

FIG. 24.

extreme north (i.e., northernmost portions of the nodal regions ascribed to Green Bay, to Marinette, to Ashland, and to Superior) and the seven communities having ports receiving dock coal (Racine, Milwaukee, Port Washington, Sheboygan, Manitowoc, Green Bay, and Marinette).

Summary Comments

1. Maps of selected components of Wisconsin's freight rate structure, on both *interstate* and *intrastate* shipments, reveal that rates vary markedly with distance. Isophors are not spaced at regular intervals.

2. The maps reveal that rates vary greatly with *direction*. Isophors twist and bend; they do not follow circular paths.

3. The explanation for these patterns or locational arrangements of rates is found, in part at least, in the philosophy of rate making which the railroads follow. Five important aspects of this

TABLE III
TRANSPORT CHARGES PER TON ON COAL FROM
PITTSBURGH TO WISCONSIN DOCKS

Superior	$3.31
Ashland	3.31
Marinette	3.38
Green Bay	3.38
Manitowoc	3.38
Sheboygan	3.38
Port Washington	3.38
Milwaukee	3.45
Racine	3.45

Source: Mr. W. F. Ehman, Wisconsin Coal Bureau, Inc.

philosophy have been shown to be: (a) the grouping principle, (b) the short line principle, (c) the rate-step principle, (d) the equalization principle, and (e) the hold-down principle. All five policies help effect spatial differences in transport charges.

4. Freight rate structures can be used to define nodal regions which may be useful in analyzing functional regions of the more important transport centers. Such nodal freight rate regions may be based on class rates or on commodity rates.

5. Many problems posed in mapping isophors remain unsolved. Should an isophor be constructed in only that part of the state where its value is quoted as a rate, thereby "dangling" in other parts of the state or terminating against other isophors? Or should an isophor once plotted in the area of its rate's occurrence be constructed continuously across the state maintaining its position relative to the other isophors? Should isophors be constructed for every value of rate quoted, or should only selected intervals be represented? The latter alternative often leads to the predicament where a consistent interval cannot be maintained, where no rates exist for some values which would appear in a consistent scale of intervals.

6. Logical steps in further research on freight rate structures include (a) an investigation of causes (other than the five cited in No. 3 above) behind the strange structural patterns and deviations of the isophors from concentricity, (b) a study of the actual movement of goods to determine the degree of conformance with the nodal regions as defined in terms of freight rate structures, (c) research into the influence of freight rate structures on the location of economic activities, and vice versa, (d) additional commodity studies to appraise their similarity with the class rate structures and the coal rate structures, and (e) experiments with techniques for mapping freight rate structures.

The Effect of Transportation Forms on Regional Economic Growth

BENJAMIN CHINITZ

FOR at least a hundred years or more, manufacturing has grown at a more rapid pace in the rest of the country than it has in New England and the Middle Atlantic states. Each of these areas has suffered a marked decline in its share of national manufacturing employment. Moreover, all areas of the country—including those whose population growth has been comparatively slow—have gained in manufacturing at the expense of the heavily industrialized Northeast.

In short, manufacturing has pulled away from the Northeast faster than population, and has come to be much more evenly distributed throughout the nation. In the twentieth century, the number of manufacturing workers per 1,000 population has declined in New England, increased but slightly in the Middle Atlantic region, and increased substantially in almost all other areas. (See Table I.)

If we look behind these basic shifts, we can discern two phases, with transportation playing rather a different role in each. The first phase, covering the westward and southward drift of manufacturing during the latter half of the nineteenth century, occurred

Reprinted from *Traffic Quarterly*, 14 (1960), 129–142, by permission of the author and editor.

when the prevailing tendency in many industries was toward greater geographical centralizing of production facilities. That is, while manufacturing as a whole was coming to be more evenly dis-

TABLE I—PERCENTAGE GEOGRAPHIC DISTRIBUTION OF UNITED STATES MANUFACTURING EMPLOYMENT, SELECTED YEARS, 1860-1954

	1860	1899	1929	1954
United States	100%	100%	100%	100%
New England	30	18	12	9
Middle Atlantic	42	34	30	26
North Central	16	29	35	35
South Atlantic)		10	10	11
South Central }	8	6	7	9
Mountain and Pacific	4	4	6	10

Source: 1860 figures from George Rogers Taylor, *The Transportation Revolution 1815–1860* (New York, 1951), p. 247. Other figures from U. S. Department of Commerce, Office of Area Development, *Long-Term Regional Trends in Manufacturing Growth 1899–1955* (Washington, 1958), p. 5.

tributed around the nation, individual industries were being drawn more tightly together. The regions that grew fastest during this period did so by attracting certain industries on a large scale.

In the twentieth century, however, the trend has been toward a more evenly distributed production in relation to the distribution of population *in a large number of individual industries*. The southern and western regions that have increased their share of the nation's manufacturing employment in recent decades have done so primarily by increasing their shares of many industries which were and still are concentrated in the older industrial areas. Let us consider each of these phases in turn.

THE CENTRALIZATION PHASE

The declining cost and increasing speed of freight transport in the nineteenth century paved the way for concentration of many manufacturing industries; especially industries once organized on the basis of small plants supplied from local sources and selling to local markets. Whereas, previously, manufacturers had sought ways to economize on transport costs, they now sought ways to reduce production costs. How could they take advantage of lower transport costs to reduce production costs? There were a variety of ways, depending on the kind of industry.

Technological progress in fabrication made available cost-reducing methods and machines that could be profitably exploited only when production was conducted on a large scale. Reduction in cost of shipping the product to distant markets now made it possible to adopt these techniques. More was saved by using these techniques than was spent on transport costs in distributing the product.

The clearest manifestation of this trend was the substitution of factory for home as the manufacturing unit. "From their predominant position in 1815," writes one historian, "household manufacturers, outside the field of food preparation, had largely disappeared by 1860 in most parts of the country . . . this primitive form of production throve where transportation was most difficult and expensive; it was least able to hold its own wherever canals, steamboats, or railroads were introduced."

But where should the factory be located, now that it was possible to stray from the local market? Often the dominant consideration was availability of superior raw materials. The typical iron works of the early nineteenth century depended upon iron from a nearby bog or mine and upon charcoal fuel provided by trees of the immediate countryside. Once the opportunity for large-scale production appeared, the superior ore and coal resources of western Pennsylvania and Ohio made them attractive as locations for large mills.

Raw-material sources also attracted production facilities away from the local market, independently of the shift to large-scale production. The mere fact that it was now cheaper to ship the product made it possible for the manufacturer to seek out the superior raw material. True, he could also maintain his factory at the market and have the better raw material shipped in from a greater distance. But it was often cheaper to ship the finished product than the raw material because of the reduced weight and bulk resulting from processing.

Whether independently or in combination with economies of scale, the attraction of sources of raw materials proved very strong in many industries. New England and the eastern parts of the Middle Atlantic states did not fare too well in competition for these industries. Of course there were important exceptions. Those processes that relied heavily on imported materials were attracted to port cities, mainly on the East Coast.

Raw materials aside, the favored location of large plants with far-flung markets was also shifting westward in response to the westward shift of population and buying power. Reduced transport costs made it possible to satisfy national demand from fewer locations, but these locations were nevertheless chosen with a view to keeping the freight bill as low as possible.

The advent of rail transport—which was largely responsible for the sustained reduction in transport costs throughout the nineteenth century—reduced the cost and increased the speed of overland transport relative to water transport. To be sure, the full effect of the change in the structure of transport costs as viewed by the carrier, was not allowed to be reflected in charges as viewed by the shipper.

Instead, railroad managements engaged in widespread discrimination, cutting their rates where they faced water competition and maintaining them where no such competition existed. Points served by water were favored, therefore, and those with no water alternative were made to bear high rates. But the enormous reduction in overland freight costs nevertheless was a greater boon to areas in the interior than to coastal areas.

In time, the inherent cost characteristics came to be more and more reflected in the structure of rates. After the Interstate Commerce Commission came into existence in the late nineteenth century, its activities whittled away at the various discriminations practiced in favor of the old cities of the Northeast. One of the Commission's policies conducive to reducing discrimination was to make distance a more important determinant of the price of freight service.

After the initial spurt of rail, the cost of moving freight by land, relative to the cost of water haul, continued to decline. For one thing, the railroad grid was being filled out. More points were being connected to each other and to the main lines. A manufacturer could count on having facilities for rail transportation in a rapidly increasing number of places.

For another, the operating costs of water transport were rising more rapidly than the operating costs of railroads. Both rail and water carriers confronted steeply rising wage rates as the productivity of labor made rapid strides in other sectors of the nation's economy. But labor costs occupied a lesser position in the rail cost structure than in the water cost structure.

The railroads detracted from the advantages of coastal ports for still other reasons. By promoting the development of land-locked areas, they helped to redistribute the nation's markets so that a smaller proportion of the total was found in places accessible to water transport. Furthermore, the services of water carriers could now be exploited by combination rail-water movements from points farther in the interior. In short, the emergence of a satisfactory alternative to water transport tended to reduce the attraction of the East Coast as a location for plants serving national markets.

THE DECENTRALIZATION PHASE

Until 1929, the relative decline of the New England and Middle Atlantic states was largely matched by relative growth in the East North Central states. The other broad areas of the country also grew faster than the Northeast, but their combined gains were not equal to that of the East North Central region.

Since 1929, while the Middle Atlantic and New England have continued to decline, relative to the nation, the East North Central region has about held its own, while relative growth has occurred in all other areas. We shall hereafter refer to these fast growing areas as the South and West for purposes of brevity.

The main thesis of this article is that the shift in regional distribution of manufacturing between 1929 and 1954 was associated with a reversal of the trend toward geographic concentration of particular industries which had characterized the earlier period, and that transport factors had much to do with this reversal of trend. The South and West have grown more rapidly than the Northeast since 1929, in the main by becoming more self-sufficient in a wide range of industries. As a rule, they have not tightened their hold over industries in which they already dominated by 1929.

This characterization of the changing geographic distribution of manufacturing activities is based on a careful study of data provided in the Census of Manufactures on some 120 categories of industry.[1] For each industry in each of four broad regions—Northeast, North Central, South and West—the actual number of employees was compared to what that number would be if each region had a share of the national total, equal to the region's share of the nation's population. This calculation was made for 1939 and 1954, for comparable industrial categories.

[1] The details of this study can be found in the author's contribution to the New York Metropolitan Region Study: Benjamin Chinitz, *Freight and the Metropolis*.

Results of this analysis showed quite clearly that each of the four regions—including the slow-growing Northeast—had reduced its deficiencies in a large number of industries; that is, it had narrowed the gap between actual employment and expected employment on the basis of population. However, since the South and the West had the greatest deficiencies to start with, the trend toward self-sufficiency naturally was a greater boon to these regions than it was to the mature regions.

When we rank industries by the degree to which they have become more evenly distributed around the country in relation to population, we discover that, generally, industries with relatively high freight costs have been more responsive to the decentralization trend. To be sure, all kinds of industries have decentralized; but among those that have resisted the trend there is a much greater preponderance of industries manufacturing high-value, low-weight products. This finding suggests that developments in freight transport may have had something to do with this trend.

Let us see how changes in transport costs and facilities have helped to alter the distribution of manufacturing employment in this manner.

TRANSPORT COSTS AND OTHER COSTS

One reason that the trend toward concentration of industries has been reversed is that the rapid relative decline of transport costs in the nineteenth century did not extend far into the twentieth century. As shown in Figure 1, average rail revenue per ton-mile has been rising in absolute terms during this century; when adjusted for changes in the price level, these ton-mile revenue figures indicate that the downward trend of the nineteenth century was changed into a widely varying trendless movement in the twentieth century. To the extent that movement has occurred, it has been the result of the peculiar cyclical behavior of freight rates, which tend to fall more slowly and rise less rapidly than other prices.

The trend in average revenue per ton-mile is an imperfect measure of the trend in transport costs. Any such average revenue figure reflects not only a change in the price of some given transport service but also a change in the nature of the transport services being performed over the years. There have been two significant changes in the bundle of transport services being performed, each of which would tend to depress average revenue per ton-mile and hence give it a downward bias as a measure of the change in transport costs.

AVERAGE FREIGHT REVENUE PER TON-MILE ON ALL U. S.
RAILROADS, BY FIVE-YEAR PERIODS, 1890-1955

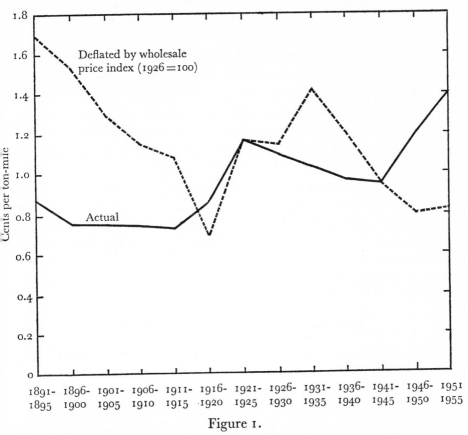

Figure 1.

Sources: Average revenue per ton-mile and wholesale price index from 1890 to 1945, U. S. Bureau of the Census, *Historical Abstract of the United States, 1789–1945* (Washington, 1949), p. 203. Average revenue per ton-mile, 1946–1955, from Association of American Railroads, *Railroad Transportation, A Statistical Record, 1921–1957* (Washington, 1958), p. 24. Wholesale price index, 1946–1955, from U. S. Bureau of the Census, *Statistical Abstract of the United States* (Washington, 1957), p. 324.

One of these is the increasing average haul; the other, the decline in relative importance of less-than-carload traffic. If we could adjust for these biases, therefore, the picture of relatively rising transport costs would be even stranger.

Various attempts have been made to measure more accurately the average increase in freight charges in recent years. Since 1947, the Interstate Commerce Commission has been taking a one per-cent sample of all waybills on carload freight originating and ter-minating in the United States. Each waybill provides information on the commodity being shipped, its origin and destination, the revenue received by the railroad for the shipment, and other characteristics of the shipment.

By comparing the revenues received in successive years for shipments with the same characteristics as to commodity and length of haul, it is possible to derive a more accurate measure of the changing level of transport costs than is provided in Figure 1. The results of such a test for the period 1947 to 1954 show that the level of freight rates rose forty-one percent during that period, while the level of wholesale prices rose fourteen percent.

As transport costs rise, relative to other costs, producers seek ways of avoiding transport costs even at the expense of higher production costs, by locating closer to the market. But suppose that getting close to the market means getting farther away from sources of raw materials? Will this not stop the trend? Here, too, we find that developments in transport cost have favored market orienta-tion.

RAW MATERIALS VS. FINISHED PRODUCTS

Freight rates on raw materials and semifinished goods are generally lower than freight rates on finished products. In part, the reason for this is that those who price freight services assume that the demand for transport by shippers of low-value products is quite sensitive to the cost of transport. But in part, the reason is simply a reflection of lower costs. A ton of coal is easier to handle than a ton of steel, and a ton of steel is easier to handle than a ton of auto-mobile.

As nearly as we can tell, this gap in freight rates for different types of products has actually widened over time. By comparing railroad revenues in 1954 to those in 1947 on the basis of the Inter-state Commerce Commission one percent sample, it was found that since the war the rates on products of mines—representing a major group of raw materials—have risen less rapidly than rates on manufactured products. Less reliable evidence for longer periods suggests a similar tendency in the rate structure. Between 1928 and 1957, the average revenue per ton of mine-products hauled by the railroads increased 63 percent, while the average revenue for manufactured products increased 122 percent.

This tendency apparently resulted from a series of innovations in freight handling, most of which have tended to reduce the relative cost of handling unfinished goods. In addition, the railroads have persisted in their long-cherished practice of discriminating in favor of commodities of low value per ton. Each time they introduced across-the-board percentage increases in freight rates, they made exceptions favoring low-value commodities such as raw materials. As a result, the gap between rates on raw materials and rates on finished products has widened.

The railroads' progressive discrimination in favor of raw materials is manifested in the ratio-trend of revenue to cost, as shown in Table II. While the ratio has fallen for all categories of freight, it has fallen faster for the products-of-mines group than for manufacturers. Paradoxically, the railroads have continued their traditional pricing practices despite the increasing intensity of truck competition for the movement of manufacturers' goods.

TABLE II—RATIO OF REVENUE TO OUT-OF-POCKET COST,
CLASS I RAILROADS, SELECTED YEARS

Commodity Class	1939	1947	1951	1955
Products of agriculture	1.35	1.21	1.34	1.30
Animals and products	1.25	1.06	1.17	1.18
Products of mines	1.78	1.32	1.27	1.22
Products of forests	1.53	1.27	1.29	1.31
Manufactures and miscellaneous	2.03	1.65	1.80	1.76
Total	1.72	1.41	1.50	1.46

Sources: Interstate Commerce Commission, Bureau of Accounts, Cost Finding and Valuation: *Distribution of the Rail Revenue Contribution by Commodity Groups—1955* (Washington, 1957), p. 6, and *Distribution of the Rail Overhead Burden by Commodity Groups—1939 and 1947* (Washington, 1949), p. 9.

So far, two factors have been adduced that worked toward greater market orientation of industry: the rise of transport costs relative to other costs, and the rise of transport costs on manufactured products relative to transport costs on raw materials. But a third and more important factor was the rise of transport costs on long hauls relative to transport costs on short hauls.

LONG HAULS VS. SHORT HAULS

The shipment of freight involves two kinds of costs: terminal and line-haul. Terminal costs are those incurred in the handling of freight at origin and destination. Line-haul costs mean those incurred on the trip between origin and destination, and are roughly proportional to distance. But terminal costs do not vary with distance; they constitute a more or less fixed cost whatever the length of the trip. Consequently, total costs per mile go down with distance because the terminal costs are spread over a longer trip.

Terminal costs depend on many factors, including size of shipment and type of commodity. But on the average, many cost studies have demonstrated that terminal costs are higher for water carriers than for rail carriers, and higher for rail carriers than for motor carriers. When viewed in these terms, it is clear that the sequence of technological development has reduced terminal costs more than it has reduced line-haul costs. As a result, the cost of short hauls has fallen relative to the cost of long hauls. And in this respect the most important event has been development of the truck.

So much for costs. What about rates? Has the change in the structure of costs, as viewed by the carrier, been imparted to the structure of rates, as viewed by the shipper? Our view is that it has—in a variety of ways.

To begin with, if rates did not reflect the change in cost structure, the shipper could exploit the advantages of trucking by operating his private truck fleet. Since almost half of all intercity trucking moves in privately operated vehicles, it is evident that this prerogative has commonly been used. To be sure, resort to private trucking has not always been a real alternative to shippers. For some, the volume and pattern of freight movement have been of a kind to prevent shippers from operating a truck fleet at costs comparable to commercial rates.

Other restraints also have existed. Manufacturers, for instance, have been reluctant to place truckdrivers directly on their payroll because they often consider being involved with the International Teamsters Union a major disadvantage. Despite these restraints on the expansion of private transportation, many firms have resorted to it.

But the shipper who continued to rely on the common carrier felt the impact of the change in structure of freight costs. Let us assume for the moment that the motor carrier's rate structure did not differ very much from that of the railroad, and that motor-rail competition had no effect on rail rate-structure. Still, the shipper was now being offered a service that was superior to rail, particularly for the short haul.

Take the matter of elapsed time. On the average, according to a recent study, the excess of elapsed time by rail over elapsed time by truck can be reckoned by the following formula: 48 hours plus 8.55 hours for each 100 miles. The figure of 48 arises out of the truck's greater efficiency at origin and destination; the figure of 8.55 from the truck's greater efficiency on the trip between origin and destination.

Saving 48 hours irrespective of length of haul means, of course, that the shipper saves relatively more, the shorter the haul. On a 100-mile trip, truck time is only nine percent of rail time. On a 500-mile trip truck time is twenty-four percent of rail time. Thus, the truck represents a greater boon to the short-haul shipper than to the long-haul shipper.

Aside from time-saving, the truck also offered pick-up and delivery service to the shipper, which the railroad performed only when the shipper had a rail siding. After the railroads instituted pick-up and delivery on less-than-carload shipments, they still required the carload shipper without a siding to pick up and deliver his freight at his own expense.

This additional expense constituted a relatively greater burden on the shipper, the shorter the haul. By the same token, once he could tender his freight to a motor carrier with pick-up and delivery service as routine, his freight costs were reduced, especially for the shorter haul. And for the less-than-carload shipper, this was true whether he shipped by rail or truck.

In these ways, the truck would have reduced the relative cost of short-haul transportation from the standpoint of the shipper, as well as the carrier, even though it had not disturbed existing relationships between rate and distance in freight tariffs. However, the railroads have attempted to combat motor-carrier competition by rate adjustments, and this fact has resulted in a change in the rate-distance relationship favoring the short haul. It is difficult to demonstrate this assertion by citing changes in rates as quoted in freight tariffs. But other kinds of evidence are available.

PERCENTAGE INCREASE IN RAIL AVERAGE REVENUE
PER TON BY LENGTH OF HAUL, 1947-1954

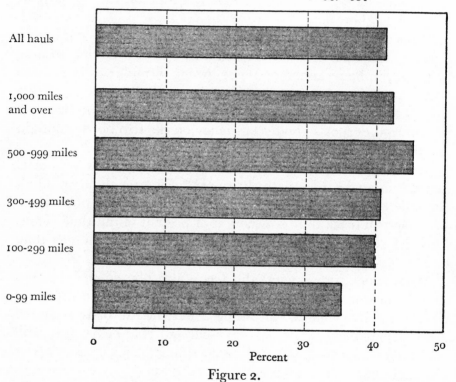

Figure 2.

Source: Benjamin Chinitz, *Freight and the Metropolis*, Harvard University Press, 1960.

For instance, from 1947 to 1954, as Figure 2 indicates, percentage increases in average revenue received by railroads was greater for longer hauls, except for hauls of 1,000 miles or more. These figures, it will be recalled from the earlier discussion, are based on comparison of average revenues in 1947 and 1954 for the same traffic mix. They reflect changes in actual charges rather than in quoted rates.

To be sure, the differences between lengths of haul are not very impressive. But one can justifiably regard the 1947-54 period as a sample from a longer period stretching back to the 1930's, when the railroads began to react to the pressure of truck competition. If comparable figures covering a longer period were available, they would doubtless exhibit a much sharper divergence in the trend of rates between various lengths of haul.

LARGE SHIPMENTS VS. SMALL SHIPMENTS

Trucking promoted the decentralization of industry not alone because of its impact on short-haul transport costs, but also because it brought down the cost of shipping in small lots relative to the cost of shipping in large lots. By doing so, it cut into one of the advantages of the large-scale producer—the advantage of receiving materials in large lots at lower average freight costs.

The disadvantage suffered by the receiver of small lots of merchandise has changed dramatically with each new phase of the transport revolution. The three major modes of transport—water, rail, and truck—have had distinctly different impacts in this respect. As long as the movement of goods depended on vessels with a total capacity running into thousands of tons, the small producer was at a hopeless disadvantage, by comparison with the large producer whose needs more closely approximated the capacity of a vessel.

The advent of rail reduced the discrepancy, offering the delivery of individual cars with an average capacity of thirty tons. Introduction of the truck with its capacity of about ten tons reduced the spread further. It is apparent, therefore, that new modes of transport, with their increasing divisibility, facilitated the problem of small producers. As a result, the establishment of plants on a smaller scale, closer to the market, became feasible.

If the change in structure of carrier costs favoring small shipments had not been reflected in their rates, innovations would have been of little help to the small shipper. But rates have been affected by changes in costs. For one thing, the lower rates that motor carriers charge for truckload shipments—rates usually approximating those charged by railroads for carload shipments—are applicable on shipments of around 20,000 pounds, for which the railroads charge the higher, less-than-carload rates.

And when the shipper substituted truckload shipments for less-than-carload shipments, he not only paid a lower rate but also got much better service—an improvement in service far greater than the improvement that resulted from substituting truckload for carload service. For a small shipment moving at less-than-truckload rates, the shipper paid a rate usually no lower than, and often higher than, the less-than-carload rate, but again the service was far superior. At the same time, motor-carrier competition induced the railroads to favor small shipments by providing free pick-up and delivery service for less-than-carload shipments.

All of the transport trends described so far have had the same effect, with respect to the location of industry. They have encouraged a greater degree of market orientation. Partly as a consequence of these shifts in the structure of transport costs, there has been a marked tendency, as observed earlier, for employment in individual industries to become more evenly distributed around the country in proportion to population. On the whole, this trend has favored the relatively underindustrialized areas of the nation.

However, one major development in recent decades—the spread of air freight—has favored the older manufacturing areas. Without doubt, air freight is a greater boon, the longer the haul. Thus it is a factor tending to favor the concentration of industry.

Even so, air freight is not altogether favorable to established centers. In those industries in which such advantages as lower wages have helped less industrialized areas, the increasing speed of freight transport has worked against high-wage areas. With the aid of air freight, manufacturers have strayed as far as Puerto Rico and even Japan, in search of cheap labor.

The Interrelationship of the Changing Structure of American Transportation and Changes in Industrial Location

By MARVIN J. BARLOON

Introduction

THIS ANALYSIS is concerned with changes in industrial location as between regions and localities in the United States and not, as a central emphasis, as between sites within metropolitian areas. While passenger transportation doubtlessly undergoes a significant interaction with industrial location, the central attention of this paper is on inter-city freight transportation.

A change in industrial location does not ordinarily mean an actual migration of an industry, that is, an expansion in one area concomitant with contraction in another. More usually, during a period of over-all expansion, it means a differentially greater expansion in certain regions and, during a period of contraction, a differentially lesser contraction in these same regions.

Generalizations on the subject of industrial location must, of course, admit of many exceptions. Furthermore, industries are highly diverse and, in the extremely intricate patterns of locational influences, much is not known nor understood. Subject to these limitations, I believe it may be said that transportation requirements are of little, or of limited, influence in the selection of industrial locations with respect to a growing portion of the periodic increment to the nation's industrial establishment. Insofar as transportation needs are concerned, an ever greater segment of the nation's industry is becoming relatively footloose. Changes in the structure of transportation appear to be principally responses to changes in the structure of the national product and in the consequent changes in transport requirements of the shipping and receiving industries. For the most part, changes in industrial output and in location appear to alter the structure of transportation, rather than the converse.

I should like to sketch these relationships: first, with respect to the expanding percentage of the tangible national product consisting of more highly processed products, generating a more rapidly growing demand for a particular type of transportation service. This development relates most generally to fabricated and assembled components and products. In addition, the higher degree of processing in the category of bulk commodities is most conspicuous in its effect on the locational pattern of the iron and steel industry. Finally, with respect to the differentially greater growth in minimum service and lowest cost modes of transportation, such as water carriage and pipelines, there is reason to believe that these are not exercising any substantial influence on locational distribution of the industries they serve but reflect, rather, a growth of cer-

Reprinted from *Land Economics*, 41 (1965), 169–179, by permission of the author and editor.

tain major industries on a locational pattern previously prevailing.

The Declining Role of Transportation as a Factor in Plant Location

With respect to a growing portion of the nation's industrial establishment, transportation is very probably a minor influence in the determination of plant location. As time passes, a growing segment of industry requires higher standards of transportation service, accepting the associated higher cost, and becomes less preoccupied with, or even indifferent to, the availability of those modes which, at the sacrifice of premium service, provide for the movement of goods at minimum cost. In the selection of location, premium transportation service is a less confining influence than minimum cost. A shipping or receiving industry whose executives are preoccupied primarily with transportation service will ordinarily find a wider range of sites where their transport requirements can be fulfilled. Therefore, within this wider range of sites, locational influences other than transportation will more usually be determinant of final site selection.

In speaking of premium transportation service, I refer to the movement of goods in small lots, with short door-to-door delivery time, subject to low levels of loss and damage, and with a high predictability of arrival time. These are features of a large portion of inter-city trucking, of Trailer On Flat Car, piggyback movement, (Trailer on Flat Car, hereinafter referred to as TOFC) and of air cargo. A growing portion of high-speed, long-haul rail service in cars of special design may also be placed in this category. At the other extreme, minimum cost transportation would include much of water transportation and of rail

carriage, either in conventional facilities or in unit trains, representing very large minimum-lot shipments. In referring to levels of cost, I have in mind the cost of the transportation service only, recognizing that much premium service transportation is associated with a minimum cost of the over-all function of physical distribution.

The almost limitless variety of commodities requiring transportation, of course, calls for all gradations of service-cost combinations. Nevertheless, for purposes of discussion, it may be convenient to note two major groups within the tangible national product at the extremes, on the one hand, of minimum cost and, on the other, of premium service requirements. That portion of the tangible national product consisting of relatively homogeneous commodities, amenable to transport in very large units of movement, representing relatively uncomplicated inventory control problems and, characteristically although not universally, of relatively low value per unit of weight, calls for industrial site selection subject to a high preoccupation with low cost transportation for which service values can be sacrificed. But, at the other extreme, products of markedly high value per unit of weight, of heterogeneous and changing design and composition, and calling, therefore, for minimum inventory levels consistent with delivery requirements, generate a demand for premium levels of transportation service, the high cost of which can more readily be absorbed in the delivered price of the product.

The preoccupation with transportation service in a growing segment of industry reflects, in substantial measure, the changing composition of the tangible national product which is moved by the transportation agencies. The segment consisting of commodities and products subject to more exacting standards of inventory control appears to be growing substantially faster than the output of those commodity groups which can tolerate medium and low-level service standards. This change is related in part to the rise in the level of real income and expenditure per household and in the greater intricacy of design of numerous consumer and capital goods. It is associated, as well, with technological innovations in the field of communications.

Looking first at consumer goods, income and expenditure per household are substantially altering the composition of the output of consumer goods requiring transport. The reported expenditures per household for consumers' durable and non-durable goods, stated in 1954 dollars, rose irregularly from $3,241 in 1950 to $3,621 in 1963, a rise of 11.7 percent.[1] If the price deflators could have reflected more adequately improvements in product design, the reported increase would almost surely have been greater. Stated in popular terms, the standard of living has been going up.

Obviously, a household with rising real levels of expenditure for tangible goods does not increase in full proportion with this rise in the physical quantity or tonnage of the goods it consumes. A significant portion of the increase in expenditure represents, rather, the purchase of goods of higher quality and of higher value per unit of weight. Looking at freight volume as a whole, we must, of course, concede a considerable increase in the tonnage of goods transported. This arises, in part, from the increase in number of households and from a limited increase in tonnage of consumption per household. But, in its influence on the level of transportation

service required, it is important to note the rising percentage of the national product of consumer goods in the higher quality brackets.

In part, the upward shift in quality level is a shift from a lower grade to a higher grade of existing goods. But, in addition, it is a shift to newly developed and more highly processed or more intricately fabricated goods than those formerly available. Examples would include certain food products. Flour and other ingredients of home baking have been substantially replaced by special mixes and semi-finished or fully-prepared baked goods. A wide variety of frozen foods and pre-cut meats and poultry have entered the composition of food lines. Turning to domestic appliances, the two-oven kitchen stove with automatic temperature and timing controls exemplifies a trend apparent as well in refrigerators, dishwashers, sewing machines, and various other appliances. The television set, a more complex instrument, has largely displaced the living room radio. The miniaturized radio, itself, represents a higher concentration of value per unit of weight than its predecessor.

Turning to producers' goods, it would be outside the scope of this paper to trace the effects of rising saving and investment levels per household or per worker, an intricate subject in its own right. Suffice it to say that evidence abounds here, too, of a product mix which includes a rising component of highly processed and more intricately fabricated cargo. Let me cite certain examples. Office equipment now includes

---

[1] United States Department of Commerce, *Statistical Abstract of the United States.* (Washington, D. C.: United States Government Printing Office, 1964) pp. 35, 323.

electronic computers, electric type-writers, and a wide variety of sophisticated filing, posting, billing, and other machines not formerly available. In factories, the paraphernalia of automation and numerical controls has accompanied a general incorporation of higher precision and metallurgical refinement in production equipment. Other categories of producers' goods might be cited, as well: more complex equipment for mining, farming, and road building, and the widespread use of prefabricated building components in the construction industry. All of these developments tend in the direction of imparting an average higher value per ton to the nation's physical product moved by the transportation agencies.

It would appear axiomatic that a rising component in the nation's tangible product of more highly fabricated goods would induce a growing preoccupation on the part of shipping executives with transportation service rather than with transportation cost. Quite clearly this development involves a more intense effort towards minimizing inventories while maintaining delivery standards. But the prevalence of more precise inventory control is induced, not only by rising values of product per unit of weight, but, in addition, by a more varied assortment in many lines of final product assemblies.

Producers of finished goods have been making available to the buyer a much wider choice of colors, models, styles, horsepower, and the like. An automobile called a "Buick" in 1963 was available in 25 models; that called a "Ford" in 46 style, color, and power combinations, not counting the Thunderbird.[2] The same type of development has occurred in domestic appliances and in office equipment. In manufacturing

equipment, special tooling and fixtures, individualized to the requirements of the particular customer, have become more prevalent. In a recent instance which has come to my attention, a basic machine tool costing $40,000 was sold in association with special tooling to the buyer's specification, costing an additional $15,000. This is fairly typical.

The individualization of assembled products in both consumers' and producer's goods has enormously complicated the structure of inventories, generating a control problem which would be almost insoluble under medium or low standards of transportation service. We cannot overlook, of course, the role of improved communications in meeting this problem. These include substantial service improvements in the long distance telephone, often utilizing private wire systems and microwave transmission, short-wave radio systems, integrated and computerized reporting and processing of inventory and sales data from geographically dispersed production and distribution centers, and the growth of executive air travel, both public and private. The consequence has been an immediacy and completeness of information with respect to widely dispersed operations, calling for a corresponding promptness of response in the transportation service.

Products and operations of the type I have been discussing require small lot shipment with short door-to-door delivery time, even over long distances, and a high predictability of arrival time. These are characteristics of inter-city trucking, of TOFC service, and of air cargo. All of these are forms of trans-

---

[2] *Automotive News, 1963 Almanac Edition* (Detroit, Michigan: Slocum Publishing Company, 1963), p. 10.

portation which, over a long period of years, have been undergoing a differentially more rapid growth than, for example, conventional railroad freight haulage.

The differentially greater growth of inter-city trucking over the past generation is commonly regarded as an instance of a technologically newer mode of transportation taking over traffic formerly carried by a less advanced competitor. This is a view of dubious validity. Since the end of World War II, trucking has admittedly been undergoing substantial technological improvements, including the construction of improved highways. But, so has railroading, and, when we consider the enormous transformations wrought by the complete dieselization of motive power, the electronic classification yard, centralized traffic control, and telephonic radio communication, there is reason to suspect that, over the past 20 years, the railroads have undergone more technological advancement than the trucking industry. But, until recently, railroad advancement was too largely cost-related and too little service-related to attract a growing volume of freight requiring premium service.

The loss of position by the railroads has apparently been arrested during the past two years. There is a strong presumption that this change reflects, in part, improvements in railroad service, particularly such innovations as TOFC, the new automobile cars, expedited interchange of freight cars in blocks, specialized freight car designs, and great improvements in long-haul freight schedules. As long as the railroads continue to develop service improvements, particularly for small-lot movements, with short door-to-door delivery time, and a high predictability of arrival time,

I should think it quite likely that they will at least hold, and possibly improve, their position with respect to the more remunerative categories of freight traffic. In sum, it is my thesis that a continuing growth in that segment of the national product of tangible goods consisting of higher valued, more highly processed, and more intricately designed goods has generated a differentially greater growth in demand for higher service standards of transportation and enabled a growing percentage of the cargo moved to absorb the associated higher costs. The consequence has been the liberation of a growing portion of industry from the locational confinements of medium and low cost transportation.

The locationally liberating influence of high transportation service standards is derived from the particular character of those modes emphasizing premium service rather than low cost of movement. These modes include air cargo, TOFC service, some aspects of high-speed, long-haul rail carriage, and, most emphatically of all, highway transportation. Most of these modes represent the superior service standards of small-lot movement, short door-to-door delivery time, and a high predictability of arrival time, all peculiarly suited to the type of cargo I have been describing. Their rapid development is associated with a greater latitude of industrial site selection both as between regions of the country and, within any particular region, as between particular localities and sites.

The broader latitude as between regions relates to service in long-haul movements. Expeditious long-haul service obviously means that the distance of a site from materials sources and markets is a declining restraint on plant location. The service appeal of air cargo is obviously directed primarily at long-haul movements. The same is true of TOFC. TOFC terminal costs and delays virtually rule it out for most movements of less than 250 miles, so that the advantages of this growing mode are bestowed principally on long-haul carriage. High speed schedules of trains of conventional freight cars are likewise reducing the distance restraint. An increasing number of rail deliveries are now being made in only three days between Chicago and the Pacific Coast. With regard to highway transportation, the continuing development of the interstate highway system bestows its principal benefits on movements of greater distance. Thus, all of these developing features of the transportation system reduce substantially the handicap of great distance from materials sources and from markets with respect to plant sites attractive in other respects. These modes are thus closely associated with a growing freedom from confinement to particular regions. The differentially more rapid growth of light industries in such regions as Florida, Arizona, and Southern California appears to be a feature of this interregional liberation of a growing sector of American industry.

In addition to greater latitude of choice as between regions, latitude is increasing as between individual localities and sites within any given region. In substantial measure, this appears to reflect the ubiquitous character of the highway system. While virtually all overland modes of transportation serve every major region of the United States, the density of service availability varies considerably.

The differentially greater density of the highway system is reflected in the mileage figures. In 1962 there was a total of 621,684 miles of surfaced rural road in the United States under state control.[3] Total surfaced mileage of rural roads under all jurisdictions amounted to 2,228,570.[4] An unknown but large portion of even locally-controlled rural mileage is capable of carrying heavy inter-city trucks, at least under light or moderate traffic densities. The railroads, by contrast, operated only 228,484 miles of road.[5] The commercially navigable inland and intracoastal waterways have an extent of 20,153 miles.[6]

The highway system is a locationally liberating influence within a region or locality because the number of properties abutting roads and highways and suitable, therefore, for the initiation and termination of direct inter-city movement of loaded vehicles, is much greater than that of properties abutting railway lines or waterways.

The rapid growth of railway TOFC service and of air cargo, in their linkage with highway transportation, share in this influence. All of the TOFC plans, with the exception of Plan II, are amenable to expeditious interchange as between rail and highway. A growing portion of air cargo, likewise, is assembled at major airports by means of short inter-city truck movements, subject, of course, to rehandling of cargo at the air-

---

[3] United States Department of Commerce, Bureau of Public Roads, *Highway Statistics, 1962* (Washington, D. C.; United States Government Printing Office, 1964), p. 123.

[4] Ibid., p. 137.

[5] Interstate Commerce Commission, *Transport Statistics in the United States, 1962*, Part I (Washington, D. C.: United States Government Printing Office, 1963), Table 156, p. 109.

[6] United States Senate, Committee on Interstate and Foreign Commerce, *National Transportation Policy*, Preliminary Draft of a Report by the Special Study Group on Transportation Policies in the United States, 87th Congress, 1st Session, (Washington, D. C.: United States Government Printing Office, 1961), Table VI, p. 178.

ort. The growth of these two premium-service modes of transportation, to the xtent that they interchange expediously with inter-city truck transportaon, reflects, as well, a liberating influnce in the choice of particular sites 'ithin a region.

The more rapidly growing portion of 1e tangible national product, therefore, quiring the type of service provided y highway trucking, by TOFC, and by ir cargo enjoys a wider range of sites litable as to transportation requirelents, both interregionally and within egions, than is true of the product roups seeking lower cost at medium or 1inimal service standards and reliant, herefore, on such modes as convenional rail or waterway haulage.

Thus far I have been considering the hange in locational influence for that ortion of the tangible national product menable to transport by premium-servce modes. I have sought to indicate hat this change is associated with the lifferentially more rapid growth of 1ighly processed and intricately fabriated goods representing transportation lemand. But, the higher degree of procssing has been under way as well with espect to some commodities not suit-ble to these modes and continuing to nove, therefore, primarily by water and :onventional rail transport. The influnce of this change is most notable in ts locational influence on the iron and teel industry. I am not prepared to say 1ow far it extends in other industries, ut its substantial impact on iron and teel merits special attention.

Throughout the history of the modern ron and steel industry, the location of integrated plants has most commonly represented a resolution of three counteracting geographical attractions. These three are the accessibility of coking coal, of iron ore, and of markets for products. The lowest aggregate transportation cost of all three combined (subject, further, to the desirability of premium service in moving certain products to markets) has been one of the principal influences on the geographical distribution of the integrated portion of the industry. This is not to rule out other factors, but rather to focus attention on those of greatest importance.

Probably the greatest single influence on changes in optimum iron and steel location since the early 1950's has been a restructuring of the ore supply. For one thing, the very large development of ore sources in the Quebec-Labrador region and in Venezuela accessible to U. S. Atlantic Coast furnaces and, with respect to Venezuela ores, accessible to Southern furnaces, has bestowed a substantial advantage on these two regions. In 1952, 7.5 percent of all ores received at U. S. iron and steel plants were imported via the Atlantic and Gulf Coasts. In 1962, this percentage had increased to 24.3.[7]

But, an even more pervasive influence has been a substantial upgrading in the quality of ores as shipped, associated both with these new origins and with long-established internal sources. The principal quality improvements have been a very large growth in the portion of the ore supply of high iron content and of optimum sizing. The higher concentration of iron content has been achieved, and is still going on, both in the Quebec-Labrador region and in the Great Lakes district. As an indication of the magnitude of this change, U. S. ores as shipped in 1952 had an average iron

---

[7] American Iron Ore Association, *Iron Ore, 1959* (Cleveland, Ohio, 1960) pp. 52, 72; and *Iron Ore, 1963*, pp. 32, 51.

content of 50.3 percent. Imports from Canada that year were too small to have altered this significantly. But, in 1962, all domestic ores plus those imported from Canada had an average iron content of 56.5 percent.[8]

The increase in iron content of ores has been accomplished by the construction of a virtually new industry incorporating elaborate processes for concentrating low-grade iron-bearing minerals, such as taconites and jaspers. Since 1952, such plants have been constructed at or near mine sites in the United States and Canada, accessible to the American iron and steel industry, with a total annual capacity of 50,000,000 gross tons of concentrate having an iron content averaging 64.4 percent.[9] This is the equivalent of over 64,000,000 gross tons of ore at the iron content of eleven years previously, 1952, that is, of over 62 percent of total U. S. and Canadian ore production in the earlier year. This segment of the American iron ore supply is still growing rapidly.

The consequence of improvement in ore quality is a substantial reduction in the tonnage of ore, coking coal, and limestone which has to be shipped for each ton of iron and steel to be produced. Obviously, in using an ore of higher iron content, less ore has to be shipped for any given tonnage of pig iron. With respect to coking coal and limestone, the consumption of these materials per ton of pig iron varies inversely with the iron content of the ore. Improved sizing of the ore further reduces the required tonnages. In consequence, the total of ore, coal, and limestone transported to blast furnaces per net ton of pig iron produced throughout the United States declined from 6,885 pounds in 1952 to 5,634 in 1962, a reduction of 1,251 pounds, or 18 per cent.[10]

Mineral Requirements per Ton of Steel. It should be noted that this development has not had as great an influence on optimum location for steel production as these figures indicate. While the quantity of raw materials to be assembled per ton of pig iron has declined, the quantity of pig iron utilized per ton of steel has gone up. In 1952, steelmaking furnaces of all type consumed 1,145 pounds of pig iron per ton of steel ingots. In 1962, this had risen to 1,236 pounds.[11] This change is associated, in part, with the growing use of the basic oxygen furnace, requiring a higher charge of hot metal and a smaller charge of ferrous scrap than is true of other principal types of steelmaking furnaces.

The net effect of these two offsetting influences has, nevertheless, remained one of a significantly smaller tonnage of mineral materials to be transported to the iron and steel plant per ton of steel produced. For all American steelmaking furnaces, the amount of ore, coal, and limestone required for pig iron production declined from 3,942 pounds per ingot ton in 1952 to 3,481 pounds in 1962,

---

[8] These percentages are derived from tonnages as reported by The University of Minnesota, *Bulletin, Mining Directory Issue* (Minneapolis, Minnesota 1964), pp. 275, 278; and iron content as reported by United States Bureau of Mines, *Minerals Yearbook*, 1952, Vol. I; Jachin M. Forbes, *Iron Ore* (Washington, D. C.: United States Government Printing Office, 1955), p. 509; and by the American Iron Ore Association, *Iron Ore, 1963* (Cleveland, Ohio, 1964) pp. 104, 111.

[9] James B. McComb, *Iron Mining and Taxes in Minnesota* (Saint Paul, Minnesota: Macalester College, 1963), p. 16.

[10] Calculated from American Iron Ore Association, *op. cit.*, 1959, p. 89; also 1963, p. 60. Required coal derived from United States average coke rate reported by American Iron and Steel Institute, *Annual Statistical Report, 1952*, (New York, New York: 1953), p. 46; and 1962, 1963, p. 17.

[11] American Iron and Steel Institute, *Annual Statistical Report, 1952* (New York, New York: 1953), p. 46; and 1962, 1963, p. 17.

a reduction just short of 12 percent. With the continued construction of taconite processing plants, this decline is still going on. The average tonnage of these materials per ton of ingot steel declined from 1962 to 1963 by still an additional 114 pounds, for a total decline since 1952 of 14.6 percent.

The reduced quantity of materials to be assembled, per ton of steel produced, clearly means a reduction in the attraction of low-cost materials assembly as a locational influence for integrated works. The geographical center of equilibrium between the offsetting attractions of low-cost materials assembly, on the one hand, and access to markets, on the other, moves closer to the market. This influence is accentuated in recent years by the increased importance of premium service transportation for finished steels. The reduced steel inventories held by consumers appears to be a long-continued condition, requiring the movement of a larger portion of finished steels than previously in small-lot deliveries with short door-to-door transit time and precise scheduling of arrival.

Still other developments are, to a moderate degree, releasing the steel industry, both integrated and non-integrated, from the requirements of minerals accessibility. The increasing transport of coke over long distances tends to liberate blast furnace location, in some measure, from the attraction of low cost access to coal and from coke by-product markets. The increasing use of pig iron in steel production has reduced the demand for ferrous scrap, and the accompanying decline in scrap prices encourages the growth of nonintegrated steel works using scrap as their sole metalliferous material in such regions as Hawaii, the Pacific Northwest, Arizona, Florida, and Puerto Rico. But, the growing portion of the iron ore supply consisting of highly processed concentrates, associated, in part, with new fields in the Quebec-Labrador region and, to a lesser extent, in Venezuela, remain the principal influences altering the geographical distribution of the iron and steel industry.

In the past, a large body of analytical literature on iron and steel location was produced, with principal attention on the transportation cost of assembling mineral raw materials at respective centers of production. This literature is now primarily of historical interest. Changes of great magnitude are still underway, so that any current analysis based on present conditions is subject to rapid obsolescence. Probably the principal element of fluidity in the changing geography of this industry is the continued up-grading of its raw materials and the consequent decline in the influence of their transportation cost on iron and steel location.

Thus far, I have sought to indicate that the major changes in the interrelationship between transportation developments and industrial location relate to a differentially greater growth in that portion of the tangible national product incorporating a high degree of processing and intricate fabrication. I have dwelt on this theme with respect to products seeking the highest transportation service standards and, also, with respect to major materials utilized by the iron and steel industry.

Meanwhile, what shall we say about the rapid growth of certain low-cost technologies for moving bulk commodities in large units? We may note, especially, pipelines, water transportation, and such rail technologies as the unit train. The interaction of these developments with industrial location is, of course, very complex. But, I must generalize and shall do so by saying that these appear to be related in substantial measure to growth industries whose locational economics are not basically changing.

I have been emphasizing the differentially greater growth in the higher quality component of the tangible national product. But, the residual component has been growing, as well, and, within its overall content, certain industries, such as petroleum, chemicals, and electric utilities, generating movement of large-volume, bulk materials by low-cost, minimum service modes have been an important element in the changing structure of transportation. It appears, however, that, for the most part, this growth reflects expansion on an existing pattern of locational distribution.

Much of the growth of the mass movement modes is associated with the growth of the petroleum industry. This is obviously true in the case of oil pipelines. It is also true with respect to a very large portion of waterway carriage. By far the greater part of domestic coastal transportation on the high seas represents the movement of petroleum and products, and this is also the largest sector of inland waterway movements, representing, in 1962, 34.6 percent of all internal waterborne tonnage.[12] Without doubt, there are significant changes under way in the locational distribution of the various segments of the oil industry. However, they are not nearly as thoroughgoing as those in the broad area of light manufactures or in the iron and steel industry. By and large, I believe it is a reasonable generalization to say that the growth in oil pipeline transportation and in waterborne petroleum and products reflects the growth of the oil industry, without altering very drastically its basic locational distribution.

A second product group contributing to the growth of waterborne commerce, potentially to pipeline development, and to carriage by railroad unit trains is bituminous coal. In 1962, bituminous coal represented 18.3 percent of all rail carloadings and 24.7 percent of all tonnage moved internally on the waterways.[13] To some extent these coal movements are competitive with each other, but, probably to a comparably great degree, they are competitive either with long distance transmission of electric power or with oil and gas. In their effect on the location of bituminous coal mining, it may be said that, to the extent these movements are competitive at destination with oil and gas, they tend to sustain the volume of coal production at existing locations, particularly in the basin of the Ohio River and in southern Illinois, while restraining the growth of fuel production in the oil and gas fields. In this respect, they tend to retard change in the locational status quo.

A large portion of the mass movement of coal by water and rail is consigned to electric utilities. One segment of this movement tends to encourage the growth of electric generating capacity at existing energy consuming locations. This is conspicuously true of the waterborne coal movements from the Ohio Valley and southern Illinois to the Twin Cities, to the Chicago area, to Pittsburgh and Cincinnati, and to Gulf Coast generating stations. It is true, as well, of

---

[12] Corps of Engineers United States Army, *Waterborne Commerce of the United States, 1962,* Part 5 (Washington, D. C.: United States Government Printing Office, 1963) pp. 12, 14.
[13] Association of American Railroads, *Statistics of Railroads of Class I in the United States* (Washington, D. C.: United States Government Printing Office, 1964) p. 5; and Corps of Engineers, United States Army, *op. cit.,* pp. 12, 14.

unit train movements to northern Illinois, to the Great Lakes, and to the Delaware River. Existing and projected coal pipeline installations are, likewise, calculated to serve generating stations at energy consuming centers, such as the Lake Erie Shore and the Delaware River.

With respect to waterborne utility coal, much of the movement competes with long distance, high voltage transmission of electric energy. In recent years, a growing portion of the incremental generating capacity of the country has been located at the mouth of the coal mine rather than in proximity to energy markets, a reflection of the growing feasibility of transmitting energy long distance over high voltage lines. An additional large portion, however, has located at intermediate points on navigable waterways, receiving coal by barge or deep-draft ship. This development would seem to represent a modification of the location of new generating sites closer to the mine mouth, attendant upon rising voltages of transmission.

Another large industry undergoing rapid growth and generating a rising volume of bulk traffic, notably by waterway, is the chemical industry. For a large portion of this industry, the growth in waterborne traffic would seem to represent rapid industrial expansion, for the most part, on the existing locational pattern. As with the electric utility, the chemical plant is a voracious user of water. In addition, it consumes large tonnages of crude bulk materials and originates correspondingly large quantities of bulk products amenable to waterborne carriage. For these reasons, a large part of the industry has historically been located on navigable water, and, as it grows, this orientation continues. It is probably true, therefore, that, speaking generally, most of the growth in the waterborne movement of chemical materials and products reflects the rapid growth of this industry without major alteration in the transport orientation of plant sites.

In sum, it appears probable that the technological innovations and volume expansion at the lowest-cost levels of mass transportation, particularly by pipeline, water carriage, and rail innovations of the multiple-car variety, are not associated with substantial changes in the pattern of industrial location. Their rapid growth would seem to be related primarily to the corresponding rapid expansion of certain industries which they serve. With respect to these industries, and with respect, as well, to the coal mining industry, they may tend, for the most part, to preserve the existing geographical dispersion of the shipping and receiving industries.

Subject, of course, to numerous exceptions and qualifications, it would appear that the major changes in industrial locational patterns in the United States relate to that growing percentage of the industrial structure receiving and shipping materials, components, and assembled products incorporating a higher degree of processing and greater intricacy of fabrication and that, in this segment of industry, the structure of transportation is reacting to shipping and locational needs, rather than the converse. In consequence, a growing portion of the nation's industry is being progressively liberated from earlier locational confinements.

Labor Costs

LABOR FACTORS IN THE INDUSTRIAL DEVELOPMENT OF THE SOUTH[1]

FRANK T. DE VYVER

Any analysis of accelerating and decelerating factors in the economic development of the South must include discussion of labor factors. It may be assumed that enterprisers seeking to establish new industries in a given site will not only investigate freight rates, raw material, and powers costs, but also will seek information concerning the labor supply, wage rates, the labor climate, and various aspects of labor legislation. To be sure the weight to be attached to each of these several factors will depend upon the type of industry involved. If the new plant is material oriented, labor factors may be relatively unimportant; if the plant is market oriented, labor factors may not be taken into account; if the plant is labor oriented, the labor factors will be deemed of great significance.[2] Actually, in respect of all but market oriented plants, the labor factor must be considered. Furthermore, other things being equal, costs tend to be relatively low when there is an adequate labor supply of efficient workers to be had at reasonable pay rates, and when there is a minimum of restrictive and cost-producing legislation.

In this paper the adequacy of the labor supply will not be discussed. The analysis will be limited to wage differentials, the extent of trade unionism, and the extent of restrictive and cost-producing labor legislation in the southern states as compared with certain northern industrial centers. These are factors which may influence the economic development of the South, and, according to a recently published legislative report from Massachusetts, these same factors have affected the development of that state's textile industry.[3]

Within the past ten years considerable study has been made of wage differentials. It is well, therefore, to examine the facts which these studies have revealed and to consider those facts in the light of the problem before us, viz., are wage differentials an accelerating or decelerating factor in the economic development of this area.

Professor Richard Lester did considerable study and analysis of North-South wage differentials. In a series of articles published in the *Southern Economic Journal* and other scientific or literary periodicals, he sought to find the facts

---

[1] In this discussion the South includes the following states: Virginia, North Carolina, South Carolina, Georgia, Florida, Alabama, Mississippi, Tennessee, Louisiana, Arkansas, and Kentucky.

[2] For a discussion of specific plants falling in each of these three categories see G. E. McLaughlin and Stefan Robock, *Why Industry Moves South* (National Planning Association, Committee of the South, 1949).

[3] Commonwealth of Massachusetts, *Report of the Special Commission Relative to the Textile Industry and to Prevent the Removal Thereof from the Commonwealth* (Boston, May 12, 1950). (Hereafter cited as Massachusetts Report.)

Reprinted from *Southern Economic Journal*, 18 (1951), 189–205, by permission of the author and editor.

and apply to those facts principles of economic theory.[4] Professor Lester also tried to discover some facts about productivity of the workers. Professor Sufrin and two assistants, Swinyard and Stephenson, have also examined the facts using a different approach, that of comparing differentials in average annual wages according to the size of the community.[5] The Bureau of Labor Statistics has published two articles on Regional Wage Differentials giving the facts as shown by the Bureau's figures as far back as 1907.[6]

A survey of these articles would indicate that these several writers reached the following conclusions: (1) Although measuring differentials is difficult statistically, different rates of pay for the same jobs have been paid in southern industries and northern industries. (2) These differentials are not uniform as between industries. (3) In most southern industries the differentials have been decreasing during the past twenty years. (4) Differentials within the southern states and even within the same labor market area are as great as those existing between southern and northern states. (5) There is very little evidence to indicate any great degree of difference between labor efficiency north and south. (6) Wage rates vary according to the size of the community, being highest in great metropolitan areas; the South has few metropolitan areas. Therefore, wage rates are naturally lower in the South than in a section like New England.

Recently the state of Massachusetts has become interested in why its textile industry is losing ground to the South. The report of a special commission issued May 12, 1950, considers wage differentials as one of the important factors involved in the removal of the industry from that state.[7] Furthermore, that commission found that in the textile industry at least, productivity was higher in the South than in New England. They said, "Evidence was presented to the Commission to the effect that although the skill and efficiency of the textile worker in the Commonwealth and the rest of New England was greater than in the newer textile areas, productivity of workers in the latter area was higher, due to differences in work assignments."[8] In other words, rather than the lower paid southern workers being lower paid because of lower efficiency, this commission seems to think that even if wages and fringe benefits were the same in

---

[4] Richard A. Lester, "Trends in Southern Wage Differentials since 1890," *Southern Economic Journal*, XI (Apr. 1945). Lester, "Diversity in North-South Wage Differentials and in Wage Rates within the South," *ibid.*, XII (Jan. 1946). Lester, "Southern Wage Differentials: Developments, Analysis, and Implications," *ibid.*, XIII (Apr. 1947). Lester, "Must Wages Differ North-South," *Virginia Quarterly Review*, XXII (Winter 1946). Lester, "Wage Diversity and Its Theoretical Implications," *Review of Economic Statistics*, XXVIII (Aug. 1946).

[5] S. C. Sufrin, A. W. Swinyard, and Francis M. Stephenson, "The North-South Differential—A Different View," *Southern Economic Journal*, XV (Oct. 1948). Swinyard and Stephenson, "North-South Differentials—A Different View," *Management Review*, XXXVII (Apr. 1948).

[6] U. S. Department of Labor, Bureau of Labor Statistics, "Regional Wage Differentials," *Monthly Labor Review*, LXIII (Oct. 1946). *Ibid.*, LXVI (Apr. 1948), "Trends in Regional Wage Differentials in Manufacturing, 1907–46."

[7] Massachusetts Report, *op. cit.*, p. 19.

[8] *Ibid.*, p. 28.

both areas, the labor factor in the cost of cloth would be higher in the Commonwealth.

With an array of facts such as those brought out in these studies, analysis of wage differentials as an accelerating force is made extremely difficult. As mentioned above, however, it can be assumed that, other things being equal, the business man will seek lowest labor costs which may or may not mean lower wages. If, therefore, the findings of the Syracuse economists are true and wage rates are lower in smaller communities, and if (as certainly may be assumed) labor efficiency is just as high as in a small community, then the South has a distinct advantage as a manufacturing area because its population is not concentrated. Its advantage, to be sure, may be over areas where the population is concentrated and not over the thousands of small communities in the United States which likewise have the wage differential that comes from smallness. Yet the probable surplus population in this area, which has been called the hidden unemployment in agriculture, will affect the labor supply in these rural areas and tend to keep the wage rates down.

Although wage differentials in the South arising from the size of the southern communities may be an accelerating factor, this will be true only if the lower wages are accompanied by lower costs. The new enterprise must, of course, consider the psychic advantages arising from location in a smaller community as well as the obvious disadvantages. Particularly, however, if the plant is labor oriented and in a highly competitive industry, the differential because of the size of the community in which the plant is located may well become an important factor.

Despite the findings of the Commonwealth Commission, let us next assume that the regional wage differentials arise because of the differences in labor productivity. When current productivity studies of the U. S. Department of Labor have been completed, there may be more light on the facts of regional productivity. Obviously, if regional wage variations are equal to regional differences in productivity, there is no gain to the employer, and the wage differential cannot act as an accelerating factor. It has even been argued that an artificial increase in the wages by law or trade union action would cause employers already operating to increase their own efficiency by seeking greater efficiency from their working forces. But the repeated establishment of higher wage levels will have progressively less effect upon the efficiency of management, and other factors of production will eventually be substituted for high priced labor. The theory that high wage levels will "shock" management into greater efficiency, while it may be valid in the case of a single wage increase, cannot be applied to a series of increases.

With similar methods and organization, however, neither the average nor the imputed physical product per worker as between regions should differ greatly within given industries. It is not the average output per worker that is significant, given any set of wage rates, but the marginal revenue value of his imputed product per time period compared to the price of his labor for this time period. Differences must originate in differences in the money price of labor.

This money price of labor should probably be lower in the South than in other sections of the country because there is much concealed unemployment in agriculture, and because there still predominate here industries in which for reasons not here relevant the marginal revenue value productivity of labor is low.

In general, then, labor must be lower priced in the South than in much of the Northeast, and, for this reason, it should be cheaper to produce divers goods in the South.

It has long been recognized, of course, that wage rates paid do not necessarily reflect a competitive wage and that rates may, therefore, be raised by law or union activity We would expect to find southern wage rates lower for reasons given above. If they are not, then wages have been raised higher than a true market rate.

How, then, can the effect of wage differentials upon southern economic development be analyzed? The differential should be an accelerating factor because the enterpriser should be able to hire as efficient labor at lower cost because of supply conditions in the labor market. If a wage differential reflects only inferior methods of production, there is no accelerating factor.

Although lower wage rates may be expected in the South, there is apparently some question as to whether these differentials actually accelerate the development of southern industry. Professor Lester found, for example, that many northern industries have brought northern wage rates to the South despite the labor market conditions found where they located.[9] To these plants, wage differentials were certainly not factors leading to a move South. In fact, Lester concludes, along with McLaughlin and Robock,[10] that wage differentials are not now bringing industry South. Nevertheless, a rational employer must realize that the market value of labor in the South is lower than it is in the Northeast.

TRADE UNIONISM

McLaughlin and Robock after asking new industries why they located in the South found that, ". . .where labor has been the primary factor in locating new plants, more emphasis has been placed on availability and on labor attitudes than on wage rates."[11] The phrase "labor attitudes" may be translated as "labor climate," thus including not only the attitude of labor itself but also the attitude of other citizens toward labor relations. The Massachusetts Commission likewise gave considerable importance to labor relations and labor legislation as factors making for a competitive disadvantage to Massachusetts textile mills.[12]

Under this broadened definition of labor attitude, there will first be discussed the problem of unionism as an accelerating or decelerating factor and then the

[9] Richard A. Lester, "Southern Wage Differentials: Developments, Analysis, and Implications," *Southern Economic Journal*, XIII (Apr. 1947), p. 387.

[10] McLaughlin and Robock, *op. cit.*

[11] *Ibid.*, p. 67.

[12] Massachusetts Report, *op. cit.*, p. 33.

various types of labor legislation which may throw light upon the community feeling toward labor relations and the effect that feeling may have on economic growth.

Once again assumptions must be made before any analysis can be attempted concerning the role of unions as accelerating or decelerating factors in economic development. We can assume that if the choice were entirely his own an employer would prefer to operate without a union.

Any other assumption would belie the effort made by employers to keep unions out of their plants even, in times past at least, to the extent of spying upon their workers so that the union members could be discharged. This assumption does not mean that management has not learned to accept the inevitable and even work with the greatest cooperation with the union of its employees. It does not mean that new enterprises try to escape unions—that is probably impossible. It does mean, however, that again, other things being equal, new enterprises will start in unorganized areas rather than in organized areas, to take advantage of a time lag between the time the new business starts and the time it is organized.

Before discussing the facts about union strength, another assumption must be made. Within limits a union may, through economic strength, raise the wages and improve the working conditions of the workers in a particular industry in a given area. Higher wages may mean increased purchasing power for the low income groups. Again this assumption does not mean that workers may not get all the market requires even without unions or the threat of unions. It merely recognized that within the extremes of wage rates, strong bargaining may help move the worker toward the maximum.

The extent of unionism in the South as compared with the rest of the United States can only be estimated. Table 1 shows these estimates for several major southern industries and indicates that union membership in relation to employment is lower in the South than in the country as a whole in all industries except tobacco manufactures.

The statistics upon which this statement is based are not entirely comparable. Total employment figures are taken from the 1947 United States Census of Manufactures except for employment in the construction and mining industries for which the figures are found in the Sixteenth Census of the United States. Total union membership figures, uncorrected for Canadian membership, are from the Department of Labor's Directory of Labor Unions in the United States 1950 (B.L.S. Bulletin No. 980) which gave membership figures for 1949. Southern membership figures are from a study of union membership as of 1948.[13] There may also be discrepancies because union jurisdiction and census divisions do not coincide. Despite the limitations of the presented statistics, there is little doubt that the widely held view concerning the weakness of southern labor organization is based upon fact.

Nor has there been any great change in this situation within the last few years.

[13] F. T. de Vyver, "The Present Status of Labor Unions in the South—1948," *Southern Economic Journal*, XVI (July 1949).

The CIO contends that its southern drive is continuing, but claims no great success. Whatever the reason, southern workers are staying out of unions in large numbers. A check upon elections in textile and knitting mills in the South from Virginia through to Mississippi between January 1, 1950, and July 1, 1951, shows 40 elections. Of this number the unions have won 13 and lost 27, but most of the elections have been in small places.[14] A report of the Advisory Council on the Virginia Economy indicates that in the state of Virginia the extent

TABLE 1

Comparison by Industry of Percentage of Total National Employment and Percentage of Total Union Membership in Selected Southern States[1]

INDUSTRY	TOTAL EMPLOYMENT	EMPLOYMENT IN SOUTH	PERCENTAGE OF TOTAL EMPLOYMENT IN SOUTH	PERCENTAGE OF TOTAL UNION MEMBERSHIP IN SOUTH	ESTIMATED TOTAL UNION MEMBERSHIP FOR INDUSTRY [c]	ESTIMATED UNION MEMBERSHIP IN SOUTH [d]
Tobacco manufactures	103,289[a]	66,057[2][a]	64	75	45,571	34,180
Textile mill products	1,147,194[a]	544,521[3][a]	47	20	460,770	103,967
Apparel and related products	972,897[a]	120,833[a]	12	3	798,010	25,968
Lumber and timber basic products	388,665[a]	208,515[a]	54	13	90,000	11,800
Furniture and fixtures	282,780[a]	68,304[a]	24	10	95,000	9,635
Construction industry	1,073,655[b]	178,216[b]	17	9	1,428,000	135,363
Coal industry	370,636[b]	90,764[b]	24	15	600,000	87,500

[1] Alabama, Arkansas, Florida, Georgia, Kentucky, Louisiana, Mississippi, North Carolina, South Carolina, Tennessee, Virginia.

[2] Excludes Alabama, Arkansas and Georgia for which employment figures are not available.

[3] Excludes Arkansas.

Sources:

[a] U. S. Department of Commerce, Bureau of the Census, *Census of Manufactures 1947.*

[b] U. S. Department of Commerce, Bureau of the Census, *Sixteenth Census of the United States.*

[c] U. S. Department of Labor, Bureau of Labor Statistics, Bulletin No. 980.

[d] F. T. de Vyver, "The Present Status of Labor Unions in the South—1948," *Southern Economic Journal*, XVI (July 1949).

of unionization of workers in such important industries as lumber and wood products and furniture and fixtures was extremely low in 1949.[15]

Since organization in the South is comparatively small and since the South as yet is apparently not ready for organization, the effect of these factors upon the economic development of the area must be considered.

[14] Compiled from a running check of figures published in *Weekly Summary of N.L.R.B. Cases*, a news release of the National Labor Relations Board.

[15] State of Virginia, Advisory Council on the Virginia Economy, *Skills, Wages and Unionization of Workers in Virginia Manufacturing* (Oct. 1950).

To the extent that new industries are seeking at least to get started without the bother and cost of dealing with unions, the weakness of organization in this area is an accelerating factor in industrial development. We have assumed that, other things being equal, a manufacturer would prefer to get along without having to negotiate with a union. The new enterpriser, therefore, will undoubtedly take his plant South to keep away from organization provided he has an adequate labor supply and other factors in the location are relatively equal. Let it be repeated that this does not mean that industry will move South in an attempt to flee organization. Generally speaking, business men are hard headed and know, therefore, that their plants may be organized at any time. They know further, nevertheless, that the union, acting under present laws, cannot possibly organize them immediately and that fellow employers in the area have continued to remain unorganized through various devices. In other words, they can always hope; although even hope may be denied to them in some of the highly organized industrial areas of the country. It is interesting to note that the Massachusetts study recommends repeal of the Taft-Hartley law so that the southern industry may more easily be organized and competition between the areas thereby made more even.[16]

Nevertheless, granted the other assumption that unions will tend to raise wages at least in the short run toward the marginal productivity of the worker, the absence of unionism in the South may possibly act as a decelerating factor in economic development. To the extent that higher wages bring greater business activity because of the wider spread of purchasing power among a lower income group, to that extent the South may have been held back by the payment of wages lower than the true market rate. Some students, too, for example, Sufrin, have found that trade unions tend toward making management more efficient. The short-run wage bargains, says Professor Sufrin ". . .cause management to undertake technological changes or more efficient managerial practices in order to meet the wage demands made upon it." "Thus," he concludes, "union activity helps to develop a progressive economy."[17] Other factors, of course, bring more efficient management, but to the extent that unions may bring more efficiency; to that extent the absence of labor organization in the South has been detrimental. When a Mississippi cotton mill in 1948 paid a minimum wage of $.41 and an average wage of $.53 (while North Carolina mills paid $.94 as a minimum wage and $1.21 as an average), efficiency of operation was of small importance.

LEGISLATIVE FACTORS

Examining the labor laws of the several states as presented by Commerce Clearing House,[18] one finds seven pages for Mississippi and nearly two hundred pages covering the labor laws of Massachusetts. This may mean, of course, that an industrial state needs more labor legislation than a non-industrial area or that

[16] Massachusetts Report, *op. cit.*, p. 50.
[17] Sidney C. Sufrin, *Union Wages and Labor's Earnings* (Syracuse University Press, 1950), p. 51.
[18] Commerce Clearing House, *Labor Law Reporter* (4th ed.), IV, 1950. See also for subsequent analysis of state labor laws.

Mississippi is simply backward in the field of labor legislation. The very quantity of legislation in Massachusetts does give pause to anyone who remembers operations under war-time regulations. Furthermore, some of these regulations may be costly and some can be classified as pro-union or anti-union. A third group of laws are more annoying than costly but may make operations more difficult.

1) *Cost Increasing Legislation*

Labor legislation which increases costs of operation will surely decelerate economic development. This does not mean that a new industry will seek out the area with the lowest cost workmen's compensation insurance or with unemployment insurance most favorable to the employer's pocketbook. It does mean, however, that the manufacturer seeking a new location must consider those factors along with other matters before making his decision.

The employer considering the workmen's compensation laws would have little to choose as between the northern and southern states, although his insurance costs would probably be slightly lower in the South. The length of the waiting period, the percentage of wages used as the basis for benefits, the maximum weekly benefit, the maximum time period, and the minimum benefits are all requirements of workmen's compensation laws which will affect the cost of insurance to the employer. Table 2 gives in summary form this information for the two groups of states. Unfortunately, statistics are not available concerning the actual cost per accident in the selected states. The analysis summarized in the table does, however, help to determine cost differences.

This table shows that the waiting period in the southern states is slightly less than in the selected northern states. The usual time in both sections is seven days, but in both sections there are states requiring only three days' waiting. More significant as a cost item than the actual waiting period is the length of time disability has to continue before the benefits are retroactive to the first day. Three of the southern states and two of the northern states have no provisions for retroactive payments. The northern laws having such provisions, however, are more generous toward the injured worker than are the southern laws, and the insurance costs would, therefore, be greater.

Workmen's compensation benefits are calculated as a percentage of average weekly earnings. The percentage of earnings required in any state, therefore, will affect the cost of insurance. On this point there are only slight differences between the two areas, with the southern laws, nevertheless, having in general lower standards than any of the northern states except Connecticut and Rhode Island. Mississippi, requiring a payment of $66\frac{2}{3}$ per cent of wages, is higher than any southern state and as high as any of the selected northern states.

Having an even greater influence upon costs are the maximum benefits and the maximum length of time those benefits run. Here again, of course, the amounts differ in individual states from a high of $32 a week in New York and Connecticut to a low of $20 a week in Virginia. The southern average, however, is about $23 a week, and the average for the selected northern states approaches $29 a week. Both the time limit for these benefits and the maximum total payments are also lower in the South. Massachusetts, New York, and Ohio provide payments for life under certain circumstances. The remaining states have a definite limitation of weeks amounting to 300 in New Hampshire to 1,000 weeks in Rhode Island. The southern states average 456 weeks, and the northern states 585 weeks. Total monetary payments are also higher in the North ($12,600)

TABLE 2

Comparison of Workmen's Compensation Laws in Selected Southern and Northern States

	BENEFITS FOR PERMANENT TOTAL DISABILITY					WAITING PERIOD	DURATION OF DISABILITY REQUIRED FOR RETROACTIVE PAYMENT
	Maximum Percentage of Wages	Maximum Weekly Payment	Minimum Weekly Payment	Time Limit	Amount Limit		
	%			Weeks		Days	Weeks
Alabama	65	$21.00	$5.00	550	$8,400	7	—
Arkansas	65	25.00	7.00	450	8,000	7	4
Florida	60	22.00	8.00	350		4	—
Georgia	50	24.00	7.00	350	8,400	7	—
Kentucky	65	21.00	7.00	520	9,500	7	3
Louisiana	65	30.00	3.00	400	12,000	7	6
Mississippi	66.6	25.00	7.00	450	8,600	5	2
North Carolina	60	24.00	8.00	400	6,000	7	4
South Carolina	60	25.00	5.00	500	6,000	3	2
Tennessee	60	25.00	10.00	550	7,500	7	4
Virginia	55	20.00	6.00	500	7,800	7	6
Average, southern states	61	23.82	6.64	456	8,220	6.2	
Connecticut	50	32.00	9.00	624	20,000	7	2
Maine	66.6	24.00	12.00	500	9,000	7	4
Massachusetts	66.6	30.00	18.00	Life		7	1.14
New Hampshire	66.6	30.00	15.00	300	7,500	7	1
New York	66.6	32.00	15.00	Life		7	5
Ohio	66.6	30.00	10.00	Life		7	—
Pennsylvania	66.6	25.00	12.50	500	12,500	7	—
Rhode Island	60	28.00	15.00	1,000	14,000	3	2
Average, northern states	63.8	28.88	13.31	585	12,600	6.5	

Source: Analysis of Provisions of Workmen's Compensation Laws, Chamber of Commerce of the United States, 1950.

than in the South ($8,220). It can be argued, of course, that since wages are lower in the South, maximum benefits should be lower if malingering is to be checked. Nevertheless, insurance costs will be considerably lower, of course, if the amounts of benefits are lower.

The minimum benefit required by compensation laws is not an important cost item unless wage rates themselves are low and expense is involved in bringing the percentage of benefits to the minimum. Sixty per cent of average weekly benefits may well be high enough so that a minimum of five or ten dollars a week will

pply only in exceptional cases. The extra cost will only arise when the minimum
ayment is high in a state where the average wages are low. The average mini-
num benefit in the South is $6.64 and ranges from $3.00 a week in Louisiana to
10 a week in Tennessee. The northern average is $13.31 with ranges from $9.00
week in Connecticut to $18 in Massachusetts.

In their study of decelerating factors for the textile industry of Massachusetts,
he commission in that state collected some figures showing costs per $100 of
ay roll for the northern and southern states.[19] Table 3 gives the information
or the states found in both studies and shows clearly that the costs for $100 of
ay roll are considerably lower in most of the southern states than in the northern
states. Part of these differences in cost, of course, may arise because of better

TABLE 3

*Insurance Rates for Workmen's Compensation Insurance per $100 Payroll
for Selected States, 1950*

Alabama	$0.41	Connecticut	.68
Arkansas	.85	Massachusetts	1.18
Georgia	.48	New Hampshire	.90
Kentucky	.69	New York	1.61
Louisiana	.96	Pennsylvania	.30
North Carolina	.50	Rhode Island	1.46
South Carolina	.93		
Tennessee	.67		
Virginia	.57		
Average for southern states	.67	Average for northern states	1.02

Source: Massachusetts Report, *op. cit.*, p. 15.

accident records and better equipment, but there is no doubt that the more
generous laws of the northern states, particularly of Rhode Island, Massachusetts, and New York account for some of the greater cost of insurance.

Workmen's compensation laws are certainly less costly in the South. Probably,
therefore, these laws will be accelerating factors in economic growth. Whether an
employer who would come South for a cheaper workmen's compensation law is
the type of employer who would do the area any good is another question, but the
fact remains that it costs an employer less for compensation insurance in Georgia
than it does in New York or Massachusetts. In a highly competitive industry
such cost differentials may be important.

Because all state unemployment compensation laws have experience rating
provisions, the tax rates and hence the costs of this type of insurance vary among
states. Again it must be said that low unemployment compensation costs will not
necessarily be the factor which draws a new industry to an area, but it will be a
cost that will be watched in a competitive industry in which labor is an important
cost item.

The costs of unemployment compensation are based upon numerous provisions

[19] Massachusetts Report, *op. cit.*, p. 15.

in the several state laws. Although the Social Security Law was probably designed to get states to pass unemployment compensation laws thus eliminating inter state competition, during the years the states have experimented with their laws and by administration and otherwise have sought ways of reducing costs to the employers. Thus, inter-state competition is again apparent. No attempt will be made in this paper to give a full analysis of the several unemployment compensation laws. Several cost producing factors, however, will be discussed.

TABLE 4

Average per cent Insured Unemployment (Average Insured Unemployment as a per cent of Average Covered Employment), Selected States, 1948, 1949, and the First Nine Months of 1950

	1948	1949	1950 (1ST 9 MONTHS)
United States..............	3.0	6.0	5.4
New England States			
Connecticut..............	2.8	7.4	4.6
Maine....................	4.9	9.5	9.2
Massachusetts............	3.8	7.9	6.6
New Hampshire...........	4.4	10.6	9.9
Rhode Island.............	6.0	13.0	8.6
Vermont.................	2.8	7.3	6.4
Average, New England States..	4.1	9.3	7.6
Southern States			
Alabama.................	2.8	6.4	5.7
Florida..................	3.5	5.6	4.4
Georgia.................	2.0	4.4	4.0
Kentucky................	2.5	6.4	6.1
Louisiana................	2.5	4.9	5.7
Mississippi..............	2.9	6.2	7.2
North Carolina...........	2.4	5.3	4.9
South Carolina...........	2.1	5.3	4.7
Tennessee...............	4.4	8.4	7.2
Virginia.................	1.7	4.0	3.8
Average, southern states.......	2.7	5.7	5.4

Source: U. S. Department of Labor, Bureau of Employment Security.

In the first place, there is in general a lower percentage of insured unemployment in the southern states than in the New England states. This percentage of insured employment as calculated by the Bureau of Employment Security is the average insured unemployment as a per cent of average covered employment. It is a good index of unemployment and perhaps is an indication of the relative stability of the economy of a state. Table 4 indicates that the employment experience of most of the southern states was better than the national average except during the months May to September, 1950. The table likewise shows

hat the experience of the southern states as a group was uniformly more favor-
ble than that of the New England states. With less unemployment to pay for,
he costs will, of course, be lower, provided experience rating is part of the law.

Duration of benefits and the size of the benefits compared to the average
weekly wage are two other factors affecting the costs of unemployment compensation to the employer. In general the laws of the southern states provide for
shorter duration of benefits than the New England laws, and the average weekly

TABLE 5

Average Employer Unemployment Compensation Tax Rates, Selected States,
1948, 1949, and 1950[a]

STATE	1948	1949 (PRELIMINARY)	1950 (PRELIMINARY)
United States...............	1.24	1.3	1.5
New England States			
Connecticut...............	.33	.75	1.2
Maine.....................	1.64	1.67	1.7
Massachusetts.............	1.31	1.41	1.9
New Hampshire.............	1.36	1.60	1.9
Rhode Island.............	1.44	1.78	2.7
Vermont...................	1.56	1.27	1.5
Average, New England States..	1.27	1.41	1.8
Southern States			
Alabama...................	1.01	1.08	1.2
Florida...................	.97	.92	.9
Georgia...................	1.04	1.24	1.3
Kentucky..................	1.55	1.68	1.3
Louisiana.................	1.84	1.61	1.6
Mississippi...............	2.04	1.33	1.3
North Carolina...........	1.65	1.36	1.6
South Carolina...........	1.26	1.12	1.4
Tennessee.................	1.39	1.32	1.5
Virginia..................	.68	.74	.9
Average, southern states.......	1.34	1.24	1.3

[a] U. S. Department of Labor, Bureau of Employment Security.

benefits are generally a smaller proportion of the average weekly wages in the
South than in New England.

Less unemployment, lower benefits, and shorter duration of benefits should
provide lower tax rates to the employer. Table 5 shows the average tax rates for
selected states and for the United States for 1948, 1949, and 1950. Variations, to
be sure, are great within the areas. Despite this, in neither 1949 nor 1950 did any
New England state have a tax rate as low as the lowest of the southern states, nor
did any of the latter have a rate as high as the highest among the New England
states.

Employer tax rates for unemployment compensation can be important cost items. Individual employers, to be sure, can change their own rates by careful planning and administration, but the benefit provisions of the laws themselves can greatly affect the individual employer's rate, no matter what he does in his own plant. Unemployment insurance costs, therefore, may be decelerating or accelerating in economic development, depending how far the particular state law departs from the norm of the country or the area.

Workmen's Compensation Laws and Unemployment Compensation Laws may provide decelerating and accelerating factors in economic development because of costs involved. Another group of laws may bring equally important economic results because those laws are favorable or unfavorable to union development.

2) *Union-Restricting Legislation*

The assumption has been made earlier that, given the choice, employers would rather operate without a union than with a union. This assumption as has been said would be particularly true during the early days of a business when the new employer is trying to establish work assignments and work out the problems involved in getting the best workers on the jobs they can do best. Laws, therefore, which do not encourage unions will have an accelerating effect upon economic development even though most businessmen have no idea that by moving to another state they can permanently operate their plants without carrying on collective bargaining.

In this general field of labor legislation southern states have been most conservative. In the South only Kentucky has legislation dealing with collective bargaining which can be called protective for unions.[20] Anti-closed shop laws on the other hand are found in at least six of the southern states,[21] and in the other southern states no protective legislation has been passed.

In the selected northern states, on the other hand, are found five of the eleven laws called "little Wagner Acts." Connecticut, Massachusetts, New York, Pennsylvania, and Rhode Island all have state labor relations acts which must be classified as protective for the unions. The Massachusetts law does contain some restrictions upon union activities by requiring, as does the Taft-Hartley Law, a written request for a check-off. There are also some restrictions upon the administration of the closed shop both in Massachusetts and New Hampshire, but those restrictions are less severe than those found in the federal law. In fact, even the most restrictive features of the northern laws are much less restrictive than the definite right to work laws passed within the past few years as a result of the Barden amendment to the Taft-Hartley law.

Undoubtedly, to the plant which seeks a new location free from union restrictions for a short time at least, the southern states with their right-to-work laws offer many attractions. Certainly the states which follow the federal law in

[20] Kentucky, see *Labor Law Reporter, op. cit.*

[21] Such laws are found in Arkansas, Florida, Georgia, North Carolina, Tennessee, and Virginia.

encouraging collective bargaining offer fewer advantages to the new industry seeking to avoid for a time at least the organization of the new plant.

Likewise important as indicating the economic climate of the two areas are the laws regulating the uses of injunctions in labor disputes. This is not the place to discuss the use of the labor injunction in industrial disputes, but the fact is, of course, that the Norris-LaGuardia act in limiting the use of the injunction in federal courts has sought to correct alleged abuses of the injunction procedures. This law has made the granting of injunctions in labor disputes extremely difficult in the federal courts and has probably forced a greater use of the state courts for this purpose. It becomes important, then, to consider state laws on the injunction procedures.

Only one southern state, Louisiana, limits the application of the injunction in labor disputes, while six of the eight northern states being considered here regulate its use in industrial conflicts. The history of the use of the injunction in labor disputes shows that the procedure can be a very potent weapon in the labor conflict. The purpose of the anti-injunction legislation according to the law of one state is to "protect labor from the unrestrained issuance of injunctions in industrial disputes."[22] The legislation usually defines lawful and unlawful union acts, provides that injunctions can be granted only after open hearing and sets up conditions under which temporary restraining orders may be issued.

New industry which seeks to continue unorganized would no doubt find fighting unions easier if there were no anti-injunction laws to keep the employer from appealing to the courts during periods of labor disputes. Industry of this type will surely think of the South as more favorable for location than in states which regulate injunctions. To this extent the absence of anti-injunction laws may be an accelerating factor in southern development.

There are few differences between northern and southern labor laws regulating strikes, picketing, and boycotts. To be sure, the northern anti-injunction laws do make carrying out these activities easier, but only in a few southern states and in no northern states have there been definite restrictions, except those concerning public utility strikes. Florida, Alabama, and Georgia have, however, provided severe restrictions upon the right to strike. Alabama passed a law requiring that all strikes must be authorized by a majority of the regular employees voting by secret ballot. Florida enacted a similar law, and Georgia requires thirty days' written notice of intent to strike. The Alabama law has been declared unconstitutional by the state courts, and the Georgia law has also been interpreted by the courts as being unconstitutional. Nevertheless, these statutes express the intent of the state legislatures, and they are definitely restrictive as compared with the regulations found in the northern states.

Such laws do indicate that some southern states are quite willing to restrict the activities of labor unions. Again it may be concluded that the industry seeking to remain unorganized will find it easier to do so under the more restrictive laws of the South.

[22] Connecticut, see *Labor Law Reporter, op. cit.*

3) *Legislation Interfering with Management's Freedom of Operation*

A third type of labor law which may have some bearing upon the new employer's decision to locate in a given area or state may be called bothersome rather than costly or anti-union. No employer today, of course, can escape regulatory legislation, but he can hope for varying degrees of interference in the employment function and working conditions.

It is doubtful that any employer would come to one of the southern states because of the absence of minimum wages. He would probably find that he had to meet the standards of the Fair Labor Standards Act with its seventy-five cents minimum wage and time and one-half for overtime. Only three of the eleven southern states have minimum wage laws on their books, and in one of these three states (Louisiana) no minimum wages were in effect at the beginning of 1949. Kentucky and Arkansas are the other southern states having minimum wage legislation. All of the northern states considered in this study have such legislation. Furthermore, seven of the northern states provide that equal pay must be provided for equal work regardless of the sex of the worker.

Laws regulating the hours of labor for adults are found in all of the northern states and in all but two of the southern states (Alabama and Florida). These laws vary a great deal but in general none of them may be called particularly oppressive in so far as the outside limits of the regulations. It is the special restrictions for special groups that makes operation of plants difficult and thus may have an effect upon the growth of industry in a particular state.

No southern state, for example, restricts night work by women, but five of the northern states have regulations to this effect. In the operation of an industry like textiles where competition usually necessitates three shift operations in order to reduce costs, restrictions upon night work for women can be particularly burdensome. Connecticut provides that the Commissioner of Labor *may* permit employment of women between 1 A.M. and 6 A.M. if adequate transportation is available, and if the health and welfare of the women workers is protected. Massachusetts prohibits night work by women between 11 P.M. and 6 A.M. although in this state too the Commissioner of Labor is authorized to suspend the application of the legislation until July 1, 1952. New Hampshire has established a maximum day of 10 hours work for women, but if the women are employed at night, the maximum becomes 8 hours. Such a law, under the present federal regulations, would not be a hindrance. In Pennsylvania women may be employed at night only if adequate transportation is provided, special safety precautions taken, adequate lighting provided, etc.

It is little wonder that the Massachusetts Commission drew particular attention to such restrictions as a factor hindering the state's textile industry. They pointed out that although the Commissioner did have the right to suspend the hours regulation, the producer would none the less find such a situation difficult for long-term planning. In addition, permission is granted only in emergency and the law itself which provides discretionary power is in itself a temporary law extended from year to year. But since there had been no complaint against the Commissioner of Labor the Commission did not recommend the repeal of the restriction upon night work for women when a plant operates beyond two shifts.[23]

Massachusetts further provides for meal periods for any woman or minor working seven and one half hours. This law too has been found restrictive and the Commission has recommended its repeal.[24] No such laws are found in the southern states.

There are many other restrictive laws found particularly in the northern states. No doubt there has been need for these laws or they would not have been passed. Nevertheless, to an employer seeking a place to locate, the Massachusetts regulation that records must be kept of the temperature in textile mills, and a given ratio of humidity to temperatures must not be exceeded, must seem a nuisance at least. Some of the northern states have provided many other restrictions dealing with the payment of workers. In Maine in all textile companies where workers are paid on a piece rate basis, pick clocks must be placed on each loom and weavers must be paid according to the clocks. That's the way it's done in the South too, but no labor inspector enforces the rule. In Massachusetts pick clocks must be used, specifications for piece work must be posted, tickets must be placed on each machine stating the number of roving or yarn, and the maximum length of a piece may not exceed its intended length by more than 3 per cent. In Rhode Island pick clocks must be employed, and rates for piece work must be posted.

Such regulations may be necessary to insure proper payment of piece rate workers. Nevertheless, any employer would find such restrictions onerous indeed and the absence of such restrictions must no doubt be considered as an accelerating factor in the development of southern industry.

Other restrictive laws not found in the southern states are the so-called fair employment practice acts. These laws have as their purpose the elimination of racial, religious, or national-origin discrimination in employment. Massachusetts, Connecticut, Rhode Island, and New York all have such laws and the Massachusetts law has been amended to provide for protecting workers between the ages of 45 and 65 from discrimination in employment.[25] However laudable such laws may be, the fact is they restrict the employer a great deal in selecting the workers he wishes. An employer will, therefore, if the choice can be made, go to states where such restrictions are not found. No such laws have been enacted in the South and the absence of them may be called an accelerating factor in the economic development of the area.

The effect of restrictive legislation upon industry is well expressed in the Massachusetts report which says, "Management representatives testified that in general the attitude of governmental agencies in other jurisdictions was more favorable to industry than in the Commonwealth. This was evidenced in many ways, it was stated, but particular emphasis was placed on the number of legis-

23 Massachusetts Report, *op. cit.*, p. 46.

24 *Ibid.*

25 *Labor Law Reporter, op. cit.*

lative proposals and enactments in the Commonwealth which were detrimental to the competitive position of the industry, and it was felt that little attention or weight was given to the objections raised by management representatives to such proposals."[26]

The Commission found, in other words, that the labor climate was an important factor in the decline of the Massachusetts textile industry. There is no doubt that a more favorable labor climate is an accelerating factor in this area.

CONCLUSIONS

This paper has attempted to show the labor factors which affect the economic development of the South. Due consideration must, of course, be given to the different types of industries involved. If an industry comes to a market, the labor factors may be of no importance. If the industry comes to an area because of labor supply or because of raw material supply, labor factors which affect costs will be of great importance. The degree of importance will depend upon the part of the total costs of production which are labor costs and upon the competitive condition of the industry of which the new plant is a part. Nevertheless labor factors must be considered and are considered by rational enterprises seeking to minimize costs.

Although the Massachusetts legislation committee seems to disagree, other students have found that wage differentials are no longer a strong factor in pulling industry to this area. Differentials have been growing smaller, and many industries putting branches in the South bring their northern wage scale with them rather than paying the going rate for the area. The weakness of the trade unions in the area, however, certainly is an accelerating factor in the South's development. Once again let it be said that this does not mean that industrialists have an idea that their plants will remain permanently unorganized nor are these industrialists fleeing the unions. The lag in the organizational program after the start of the new industry may give the new employer a chance to develop his plant without the restrictions of union regulations having to do with the operation of the plant. Those early years are most important for a new industry.

Finally, the lack of labor legislation and the nature of the legislation which does exist in this area undoubtedly are accelerating factors. It costs less to insure workers against accident and unemployment in the South than in the North. The legislation in the South regarding trade unions is restrictive rather than protective as it is in the North. And protective legislation, excellent though it may be, may become very burdensome to a manufacturer. The laws in the southern states will burden very few employers.

[26] Massachusetts Report, *op. cit.*, pp. 41–42.

Hourly Earnings Differentials by Region and Size of City

VICTOR R. FUCHS

THE EXISTENCE of lower wages in the South than in the rest of the United States has been a subject of continuing practical and scientific interest. For businessmen, union leaders, and public officials, the regional wage differential has significant implications for policy purposes. Some economists have concentrated their research on explaining the differential. Others have found it to be of considerable value in testing economic theories and in deriving quantitative estimates of important economic relationships.

Thus, the fact that the price of labor relative to the price of capital differs between regions permits the estimation of production functions for individual industries and the calculation of elasticities of substitution between labor and capital.

Similarly, if it is true that the regional wage differential is significantly greater for unskilled than for skilled labor, it should be possible to use this information to gain insights concerning the elasticity of substitution of human capital for raw labor. Such insights would contribute to an understanding of interindustry differences in rates of change of output per man over time. In addition to its role in the estimation of production

* This paper is an excerpt of a larger paper published by the National Bureau of Economic Research as part of its study of productivity in the service industries undertaken with the assistance of a grant from the Ford Foundation, *Differentials in Hourly Earnings by Region and City Size*, 1959, National Bureau of Economic Research Occasional Paper, 101, Columbia University Press, 1967.

Reprinted from *Monthly Labor Review*, 90 (1967), 22–26, by permission of the author and editor.

functions, the wage differential is important in the analysis of income distribution, population migration, and changes in the location of manufacturing.

Geographical Standardization

Standardization for geographical differences in industry or occupation mix is a useful way of getting at the question of geographical differences in labor quality, but it is deficient to the extent that there are labor quality differences within the same industry or occupation. An alternative approach to the problem would be to look at such labor quality proxies as color, age, sex, and education, since it is well known that there are significant wage differentials at the national level associated with each of these variables.

The purpose of this paper is to present new estimates of geographical wage differentials based on average hourly earnings of all nonagricultural persons as calculated from the *1960 Census of Population*. The availability of a 1/1,000 sample of the census on punched cards makes it possible to standardize simultaneously for color, age, sex, and education [1] and to investigate the relation between city size and wages along with the analysis of regional differentials.

The population studied included all persons who were employed in nonagricultural industries during the Census "reference" week (varying weeks in April) in 1960, and who had some earnings in 1959. The total number of persons covered in the sample was 56,247. Estimates of annual hours worked were obtained for each worker by multiplying the number of weeks worked in 1959 by the number of hours worked in the Census reference week in April 1960. Though the use of hours for a single week in a different year and inaccuracy in reporting of hours may produce considerable error for any single worker, no large or systematic error is present in comparisons of groups. Annual hours and annual earnings were each aggregated across

[1] The computer program was written by Charlotte Boschan of the National Bureau of Economic Research with the assistance of a grant of computer time from International Business Machine Corp. Details concerning the program are available upon request to the author.

Certain data used were derived from punch cards furnished under a joint project sponsored by the U.S. Bureau of Census and the Population Council. Neither the Census Bureau nor the Population Council assumes any responsibility of the validity of any of the figures or interpretations of them, published herein, based on this material.

workers in each group. Average hourly earnings for each group in 1959 were estimated by dividing aggregate earnings by man-hours. These estimates are referred to as "actual" hourly earnings to distinguish them from "expected" earnings.

"Expected" earnings for each region or city size were obtained by multiplying, for each worker, the estimated number of hours worked in 1959 by the national hourly earnings rate for his particular color, age, sex, and education cell. (There are 168 such cells.) These earnings were then aggregated and divided by the aggregate man-hours to get "expected" hourly earnings. To the extent that labor quality is associated with color, age, sex, and education, differences in average "expected" earnings across regions and city size groups measure differences in labor quality; differences in the ratio of estimated actual earnings to "expected" earnings measure differences in wages, holding labor quality constant.[2]

It should be noted that the differentials studied in this paper are *relative* differentials; they are obtained by dividing "actual" by "expected" earnings. It is also possible to study *absolute* differentials by subtracting expected from actual earnings. Because our primary interest is how demand for labor responds to changing wage rates, the relative differentials appear to be more relevant. If one were primarily interested in questions concerning the supply of labor, absolute differentials would be used.

Regional Differentials

The regional differentials in average hourly earnings in dollars and in index-number form with the South equal to 100, are shown in table 1. The figures contain few surprises. Earnings are significantly lower in the South than in other regions; earnings in the West are slightly higher than in the Northeast or North Central divisions. The difference between the South and the rest of the country is much greater for nonwhites than for whites; within each color group, the differentials for males and for females appear to be about the same.

---

[2] Systematic differences in national hourly earnings rates by color, age, sex, and education suggest that these variables do, to some extent at least, measure labor quality. The white-nonwhite differences are probably due in part to market discrimination, but color is relevant to quality because of the likelihood that, at given levels of education, nonwhites have received poorer quality schooling and less on-the-job training than have whites.

The following tabulation shows the extent t which regional earnings differences can be ex plained by differences in color, age, sex, an education.

"Expected" Average Hourly Earnings, by Region, 1959 (dollars per hour)

	South	Non-South	North-east	North central	W
Total	2.38	2.54	2.53	2.52	2.
White males	2.82	2.89	2.90	2.85	2.
White females	1.77	1.76	1.72	1.75	1.
Nonwhite males	1.74	1.91	1.90	1.88	2.
Nonwhite females	1.16	1.24	1.19	1.21	1.

Where the comparison is for a given color-se group, the effect of differences in age and educa tion is reflected in the "expected" earnings. Labo quality, as measured by these variables, appear to be somewhat lower in the South than in the res of the country, and highest in the West. Th regional difference is slightly greater for male than for females. In fact, white females in th South have slightly higher "expected" earning than in the Northeast and North Central.

A significant regional wage differential remain after standardizing for color, age, sex, and educa tion. (See table 2.) For all nonagricultural em ployed persons, the differential between the Sout and the rest of the country is approximately 1 percent. It is much greater for nonwhites tha for whites and is smallest for white males wher the differential is of the order of 14 percent.

It is worth noting that the standardization pro cedure used here is not the only one available fo studying this problem. It would be equally appro priate to standardize by using the actual earnings rates for each color, age, sex, and education cel in each region, weighted by the national distribu tion of man-hours. When the two standardization

TABLE 1. AVERAGE HOURLY EARNINGS, NONAGRICUL-TURAL EMPLOYED PERSONS, BY REGION, 1959

Item	South	Non-South	North-east	North Central	West
	Dollars per hour				
Total	$2.12	$2.65	$2.62	$2.60	$2.76
White males	$2.54	$2.99	$2.97	$2.94	$3.09
White females	1.56	1.83	1.84	1.75	1.97
Nonwhite males	1.40	2.22	2.07	2.25	2.43
Nonwhite females	.92	1.50	1.55	1.40	1.56
	Index, South=100				
Total	100	125	124	123	130
White males	100	118	117	116	122
White females	100	117	118	113	126
Nonwhite males	100	159	149	161	174
Nonwhite females	100	163	168	152	170

SOURCE: *U.S. Censuses of Population and Housing: 1960 1/1,000 Sample.*

procedures yield markedly different results, interpretation is difficult. Fortunately, in this instance the two standardization procedures give similar results. For white males the difference in results is of the order of 1 percent. For nonwhite females it goes as high as 2 percent.

This section has shown that only a portion of the gross non-South/South wage differential is attributable to demographic differences in the labor force. It is sometimes argued that the remainder is largely attributable to differences in city size, rather than to a regional differential at given city sizes. The next section deals with the question of wage differentials associated with city size.

City-Size Differentials

A strong and consistent positive relation exists between earnings and city size. Average hourly earnings tend to rise with city size in every region and for every color-sex group. The rate of increase is sharpest in the South, and least pronounced in the Northeast and West. It is also sharper for nonwhites than for whites. Because the South has a relatively large proportion of nonwhites, a question arises whether the sharper city-size gradient is predominantly a regional or color phenomenon. The last four rows of table 3 show that only the regional difference is significant. Holding color constant, the city-size gradient is steeper in the South than in the non-South for both whites and nonwhites. Holding region constant, there is no evidence of a steeper gradient for nonwhites than for whites.

TABLE 2. RATIO OF ACTUAL TO "EXPECTED" HOURLY EARNINGS, BY REGION, 1959

Item	South	Non-South	North-east	North Central	West
	Ratio				
Total	0.89	1.04	1.04	1.03	1.06
White males	.90	1.03	1.02	1.03	1.05
White females	.89	1.04	1.07	1.00	1.07
Nonwhite males	.80	1.16	1.09	1.20	1.21
Nonwhite females	.79	1.21	1.30	1.16	1.19
	Index of ratio, South=100				
Total	100	117	117	116	119
White males	100	114	113	114	117
White females	100	117	120	112	120
Nonwhite males	100	145	136	150	151
Nonwhite females	100	153	165	147	151

Little of the city-size wage differential can be explained by differences in color, age, sex, or education (table 4). There is a slight tendency for "expected" earnings in rural areas to be below average, but on the whole the labor force "mix" is similar in all city-size categories.[3] Strictly speaking, similarity of expected earnings only proves that the "mix" is similar on average; there could be significant offsetting differences in the distributions by years of schooling or other variables. In fact, the distributions are quite similar, but there is a tendency for the larger cities in the non-South to have a greater than average share of workers in the lowest and the highest educational classes.

The sharp variation in actual earnings, combined with great similarity in "expected" earnings, means that the ratio of actual to "expected" varies greatly with city size. These ratios indicate that within each region there is a very considerable range of earnings, after standardizing for color, age, sex, and education. They also show that within each color-sex group, wages vary considerably by city size after standardizing for age and education.[4]

Regional Differential Adjusted

The South has a much larger share of its nonagricultural work force outside of Standard Metropolitan Statistical Areas and a much smaller share in SMSA's of 1 million and over than does the non-South. This fact, plus the existence of a significant wage differential across city sizes within regions, suggests the possibility that a substantial portion of the regional wage differential observed in table 2 is a reflection of the city-size effect. One method of adjustment consists of taking the ratio of actual to expected in each city size in each region and weighting it by the share of that city size in national total man-hours.[5]

[3] When the differences in "mix" are very small, the problem of choosing between alternative standardization procedure is unimportant.
[4] The city-size differential may be biased upward to the extent that some nonagricultural employed persons may have been employed in agriculture in 1959, and a disproportionate share of such persons may be in the areas outside SMSA's. The chances of this being an important source of bias seem very slight.
[5] The possibility of an alternative standardization procedure arises again and again, fortunately, the other procedure gives very similar results, except for nonwhites in the individual regions of the non-South.

TABLE 3. AVERAGE HOURLY EARNINGS, NONAGRICULTURAL EMPLOYED PERSONS, BY CITY SIZE, 1959

Item	Rural	Urban places		Standard Metropolitan Statistical Areas			
		Under 10,000	10,000-99,999	Under 250,000	250,000-499,999	500,000-999,999	1,000,000 and more
		Dollars per hour					
Total	$2.00	$2.12	$2.23	$2.39	$2.43	$2.56	$2.84
South	$1.71	$1.82	$1.94	$2.15	$2.31	$2.34	$2.62
Non-South	2.22	2.30	2.39	2.54	2.50	2.67	2.87
Northeast	2.33	2.37	2.41	2.41	2.36	2.51	2.79
North Central	2.11	2.22	2.33	2.61	2.61	2.79	2.90
West	2.36	2.43	2.50	2.65	2.62	2.71	2.98
White males	2.24	2.43	2.61	2.78	2.77	2.96	3.29
White females	1.45	1.49	1.57	1.65	1.69	1.82	2.00
Nonwhite males	1.28	1.26	1.33	1.53	1.89	2.00	2.08
Nonwhite females	.83	.69	.91	.85	1.05	1.24	1.47
South:							
Whites	1.80	1.98	2.14	2.34	2.46	2.54	2.86
Nonwhites	1.06	.99	.99	1.13	1.28	1.37	1.54
Non-South:							
Whites	2.22	2.31	2.40	2.56	2.52	2.71	2.96
Nonwhites	[1]1.80	1.62	1.84	1.90	2.13	2.18	1.96

[1] Based on fewer than 50 observations.

Whereas, after adjusting for color, age, sex, and education, the differential between the non-South and the South was of the order of 17 percent; it is about 9 percent after city size is also taken into account. City size does make some difference, but does not explain all of the regional differential. It makes the greatest difference in the Northeast, and the least in the North Central. The regional differential continues to be much greater for nonwhites than for whites.

It is also possible to recalculate the city-size differentials holding region constant. The effect of this adjustment proves to be relatively small. In general, hourly earnings in the largest urban areas are approximately 30 percent higher than in the rural areas and small towns, and approximately 15 percent higher than in the small Standard Metropolitan Statistical Areas.

Conclusions

The observed average hourly earnings in the non-South are about 25 percent higher than in the South. About one-third of this differential is attributable to regional differences in the labor force as measured by color, age, sex, and education; about one-third is related to regional differences in city size; and about one-third of the differential remains, after adjusting for labor force composition and city size.

These estimates cannot be precise, partly because of the limitations of the data, and partly because the standardization techniques are necessarily imperfect. Some experimentation with alternative standardizations produced similar results; these estimates therefore are probably reasonably good guides to the order of magnitude of the various factors that contribute to the regional wage differential.

For white males alone, the gross non-South/South differential is approximately 18 percent. Differences in education and age explain less than one-fourth of the differential; city-size differences explain more than one-third; and the regional differential, after adjusting for all these factors, is slightly more than one-third the gross differential. In the case of white females, education and age do not explain any of the 17 percent regional differential, but city size explains about one-half of it. For nonwhites, the gross differential is of the order of 60 percent. Differences in education and age explain about one-fourth of the differential for males, but only one-tenth for females. The reverse is true for city size, so that both nonwhite groups show the same net differential, approximately 35 percent.

An attempt to explain interindustry differentials in average hourly earnings through multiple regression analysis offers some confirmation of these findings. The percentage of employment in

TABLE 4. "EXPECTED" AVERAGE HOURLY EARNINGS, BY CITY SIZE, 1959

Item	Rural	Urban places		Standard Metropolitan Statistical Areas			
		Under 10,000	10,000-99,999	Under 250,000	250,000-499,999	500,000-999,999	1,000,000 and more
		Dollars per hour					
Total	$2.41	$2.53	$2.48	$2.49	$2.50	$2.50	$2.53
South	$2.26	$2.39	$2.35	$2.41	$2.46	$2.43	$2.47
Non-South	2.53	2.62	2.55	2.54	2.52	2.54	2.54
Northeast	2.56	2.59	2.55	2.51	2.46	2.53	2.54
North Central	2.49	2.60	2.51	2.54	2.54	2.52	2.51
West	2.59	2.72	2.64	2.63	2.62	2.57	2.61
White males	2.70	2.89	2.86	2.86	2.85	2.91	2.95
White females	1.74	1.77	1.78	1.76	1.76	1.78	1.76
Nonwhite males	1.63	1.68	1.76	1.86	1.82	1.87	1.89
Nonwhite females	1.10	1.09	1.18	1.17	1.18	1.23	1.23
South:							
Whites	2.37	2.56	2.53	2.57	2.59	2.60	2.66
Nonwhites	1.44	1.45	1.49	1.55	1.55	1.56	1.61
Non-South:							
Whites	2.54	2.63	2.57	2.57	2.55	2.61	2.63
Nonwhites	[1]1.67	1.55	1.63	1.74	1.63	1.77	1.69

[1] Based on fewer than 50 observations.

the South, the percentage of employment in large cities, "expected" hourly earnings, extent of unionization, and size of employer were used as explanatory variables. Taken alone, the regional variable is significantly related (inversely) to hourly earnings. The significance of the relationship is sharply reduced when account is taken of "expected" earnings and is further reduced when account is also taken of the percentage of employment in large cities. The remaining relation between earnings and percentage in the South is entirely explained by industry differences in extent of unionization.

One of the important conclusions of the paper is the findings of a substantial difference in hourly earnings across city size. Furthermore, these differences are relatively unaffected by standardization for labor force composition and regional mix. Standardized hourly earnings in the SMSA's of 1 million and over are typically 25 to 35 percent higher than in the areas outside SMSA's within the same region, and about 15 percent higher than in SMSA's of less than 1 million. The city-size gradient is steeper in the South than in the rest of the country. Multiple regression analysis across industries again tends to confirm these findings. Furthermore, the regression analysis rejects the hypotheses that the higher earnings in the large cities can be attributed to unionization or size of employer.

The non-South/South differential is found to be inversely related to skill level as measured by education, sex, and color. The fact that the regional differential varies with education within each color may help to shed new light on an old problem—the reason for the large regional wage variation for nonwhites compared with whites. This has usually been explained in terms of greater market discrimination against nonwhites in the South than in the non-South. But there is an alternative explanation. It may reflect, at least in part, the fact that nonwhites are disproportionately of low skill, both in the South and the non-South, and that the regional differential is greater, the lower the skill level, regardless of color. This hypothesis appears worthy of further study. An alternative way of interpreting the data would be to say that there is more economic segregation in the South than in the non-South. This depresses the price of nonwhite unskilled labor but raises the

relative price of nonwhite skilled labor because of its relative scarcity.

The city-size differential in hourly earnings appears to be about the same at all levels of education. One possible explanation of this differential is differences in cost of living. Adequate data are not available for a thorough check of this hypothesis. Fragmentary information provided by the Bureau of Labor Statistics on the cost of living in different cities suggests some slight correlation between hourly earnings and prices,[6] but intercity differences in cost of living appear to be small relative to differences in hourly earnings. However, it should be noted that conventional measures of cost of living do not include items like length of time needed to get to work which may vary systematically with city size.

One of the most promising hypotheses to explain the city-size differential is that it reflects differences in labor quality not captured by standardization for color, age, sex, and education. This might take the form of better quality schooling, more on-the-job training, selective in-migration to the big cities of more ambitious and hard working persons, or other forms. Another possible explanation is the existence of a disequilibrium in the supply of labor and capital. Surplus labor from agriculture may tend to move first to the small towns, and then later to the larger cities. Capital may be more readily available in the large cities. If there is disequilibrium, we should observe a tendency for labor to migrate from small to large cities, and for industry to move in the reverse direction.

Possible explanations of the city-size differential such as unmeasured labor quality, cost of living, and disequilibrium are not mutually exclusive. Since the differential to be explained is quite large, it is possible that all of them are valid and significant, with each explaining a part. Just as the regional differential has been put to good use in the testing of economic theories, it would appear that the large city-size differentials in hourly earnings revealed in this paper could provide a fruitful basis for considerable new economic analysis.

[6] See "City Workers Family Budget for October 1951," *Monthly Labor Review*, May 1952, pp. 520–522, and "The Interim City Workers Family Budget," *Monthly Labor Review*, August 1960, pp. 785–808.

WAGES AND THE ALLOCATION OF EMPLOYMENT

A. L. GITLOW

THE THEORETICAL VIEW

Fundamentally, wages have two functions: (1) to allocate productive resources; and (2) to provide the incentive to work which is necessary in a free society. Wages, as one price within a price system, share these functions with other factor-prices. Labor reacts to wage differentials by moving to the jobs offering the most favorable terms and conditions. Workers compare alternative jobs and choose the ones which are superior. We assume implicitly that workers are rational and concerned basically with improving their material position.

The *specific* employment of the nation's labor force involves its allocation on two levels: (1) among labor markets; and (2) within given labor market areas. The former involves the geographical location of the nation's employment. The latter involves the location of the nation's employment as among industries, firms, and skills or occupations.

This distinction is necessary because a truly national labor market is lacking in the United States. This is true despite the relatively high degree of labor mobility characterizing our country. Though significant, this mobility is insufficient to avoid the existence of a number of local labor markets. Considerable segments of the labor force resist changes in location for various reasons, viz., (1) the cost of relocating, (2) inertia and fear of the unknown, (3) lack of knowledge of the alternative opportunities in other labor market areas, and (4) attachment to the area of one's birth and social and family contacts.

Geographical Location

Geographic wage differentials exist in the United States. The economic reasons underlying them are: (1) different ratios of labor to capital in various labor market areas; (2) varying population growth rates; and (3) different capital formation capacities. As a consequence of these differences, there will be unemployment (idleness) and underemployment (inefficient employment) of labor in certain market areas, simultaneously with shortages in others.

A reallocation of labor and capital is, therefore, desirable. The wage-price is our economic instrument for the allocation of labor. Since wages is the basic cost of production, geographic wage differentials involve geographic cost-price differentials, thereby influencing the attractiveness of investment. Geographic wage differentials tend to attract labor to capital, and capital to labor. Such differentials appear necessary as a consequence of continuing variations, among the different areas, in population growth and capital formation capacity. They are necessary to overcome the economic, psychological, and social costs of relocation. We have noted above the costs which cause labor to resist moving. Geographic wage differentials act to overcome these reasons against movement.

Reprinted from *Southern Economic Journal*, 21 (1954), 62–83, by permission of the author and editor.

In a 1951 supplement to the *Survey of Current Business*, entitled *Regional Trends in the United States Economy*, the United States Department of Commerce supported the above observations. The department noted[1] that, in the past two decades, economic differences among the several regions of the United States have become relatively less pronounced, due to the freedom with which population and capital can move from region to region. Consider, for example, the growth of per capita incomes in the Middle East and the Southeast. In order for the rate of increase between 1929 and 1949 to have been in both regions the same as the national average—or 96 per cent—the amount added over this period to 1929 per capita income would have had to be $889 in the Middle East and in the Southeast $330. However, *as long as workers were free to leave the Southeast in order to look for higher incomes, elsewhere—and as long as capital was free to flow in greater volume to the Southeast in search of lower costs of production—the discrepancy between $889 and $330 was too large to be maintained in a free and expanding economy.* Because of these factors, the actual increase in per capita incomes in the Middle East was $639 compared to $538 in the Southeast. But the $538 increase in the Southeast was a much larger percentage advance than the $639 increase in the Middle East. Consequently, regional incomes tended to be leveled.

Another example, more specific, of the relationship between wages and the geographical location of employment, is provided by George P. Shultz's study of the Brockton shoe industry.[2] Shultz explained[3] that his evidence *indicated that unemployment, the quantity axis of wage decisions, had been an effective pressure within the union.* Particularly in preparation for bidding on Army orders in 1940, *the union adjusted wage rates in an effort to increase the volume of employment in Brockton.*

Industrial Location

Our economy is dynamic, reflecting changes in tastes, as well as innovations. Industries grow and die. Consequently, the demand for labor in a given industry may be expanding or contracting. If the former is the case, labor must be attracted from those industries which are declining. Wage differentials are the basic instrument of our economic system for effecting this reallocation of labor. Such differentials reflect, in part, an expanding or declining demand. They are, consequently, performing a vital function. In this connection, it must be recognized that the magnitudes of the differentials may have to be substantial to affect a reallocation of labor. Further, it is necessary to consider the differentials labor *expects* as well as the *actual* differentials. Expectation may vary significantly from actuality.

We have been using the term wage differential with the implication that it

[1] *Regional Trends in the United States Economy*, 1951 supplement to the *Survey of Current Business*, U. S. Department of Commerce, pp. 1, 2, 4, 7.

[2] George P. Shultz, *Pressures on Wage Decisions*, Technology Press of M.I.T. and John Wiley and Sons, New York, 1951.

[3] *Ibid.*, pp. 73, 74.

covered only variations in money wages. This is inaccurate. The opportunity costs (alternative opportunities) of labor are assessed on a more extensive basis than mere comparisons of money wages. Security, hazard, prestige, pleasantness of surroundings (attitudes of one's fellows and superiors as well as the physical workplace), discipline, vacations, sick leave, rest periods, pension and welfare benefits—all these enter the scales and influence the costs of labor. They will, therefore, exercise an influence on the level and slope (elasticity) of the labor supply curve.

Location by Firm

Firms expand or decline. The former must attract labor from the latter. Generally, the expanding firms will be those which are more efficient. Efficiency includes intelligent financing as well as technical competence in production arrangements. Greater efficiency involves lower unit costs, with consequent stimulation of the individual firm's demand for labor. Efficient firms will outbid the inefficient ones for labor. Competitive bidding involves wage differentials, although theoretically these differentials would disappear with the achievement of an equilibrium between the demand for and supply of labor in the market. Of course, in a dynamic market, demand and supply conditions do not remain static long enough for a long-run equilibrium to be achieved. Usually, equilibrium is something towards which there is a tendency, rather than something which is achieved. Therefore, wage differentials are to be expected as a normal market phenomenon.

Location by Skill or Occupation

The more skilled an occupation is, the greater the *time* and *effort* required for its mastery. The expenditure of *effort* necessary to become technically competent involves disutility (human cost). The learning effort involves also the passage of time. There is a more subtle disutility (human cost) involved in this connection. When a worker spends a portion of his life in training for a skill or occupation, he foregoes immediate pleasures for those more remote in time. These disutilities (human costs) must be offset by more attractive compensation, in order to induce free men to expend time and effort. Any generalization concerning the disutilities involved in training should consider also individual differences in (1) preference to undergo training, (2) estimation of *expected* yield as a result of the training, (3) financial ability or willingness to undergo training, (4) preferences among occupations for which training is necessary, and (5) the differential force exerted by changes in the partial and total economic environment.[4]

As an example, the *New York Times* reported in November 1952 a shortage of apprentice tool makers.[5] The newspaper stated: "Semi-skilled workers on a production line do better in terms of take-home pay than apprentices looking

[4] Louis R. Salkever, "Toward a Theory of Wage Structure," *Industrial and Labor Relations Review*, vol. 6, no. 3, April 1953, p. 308.

[5] *New York Times*, November 23, 1952.

head to becoming master machinist or tool designers. That is why there is a shortage of apprentices. It is why there are few young men willing to start the long road to becoming a skilled tool worker."

It is interesting that the Soviet Union has long recognized the importance of wage differentials as an inducement for workers to attain higher levels of skill. In an important speech at a meeting of factory managers in June 1931, Stalin said:[6]

. . . in a number of establishments the wage rates are established in such a manner that the difference almost disappears between qualified labor and unqualified labor, between heavy labor and light labor. Equalitarianism leads to this, that the unqualified (unskilled) laborer is not interested in becoming a qualified laborer. . . . We cannot tolerate a situation where a railway locomotive driver earns only as much as a copy clerk. . . . We must give the unskilled worker a stimulus and prospect of advancement, of rising to a higher position. . . It is necessary to organize such a system of wage scales as will take into account the difference between qualified labor and unqualified labor, between heavy labor and light labor. . . . Marx and Lenin say that the difference between qualified and unqualified work will exist even under socialism, even after the destruction of classes. . . . Who is right—Marx and Lenin or the equalitarians?

MOBILITY STUDIES

Here and there, in the above discussion, we have presented evidence concerning the wage-employment allocation relationship. In this section, we bring together some available evidence of the relationship on a more ambitious scale. Since allocation involves movement, we are concerned with mobility. More specifically, we are concerned with these types of mobility: region to region, industry to industry, firm to firm, and skill level to skill level. It must be understood, in this connection, that there is a difference between the *inclination* (*propensity*) *to move* and *actual movement*. Opportunity must be coupled with willingness before any actual movement will occur.

Mobility of the American Labor Force

We have noted already the geographical mobility of the American labor force, by commenting on the significant movement from the Southeastern portion of the United States since 1929.

In a report entitled "Job Tenure of American Workers," the Bureau of Labor Statistics made a more sweeping observation when it said:[7] "Mobility always has been a major characteristic of the American labor force. Changes from one occupation or industry to another have been accompanied by extensive geographical shifts and appear to form a common pattern in the working lives of substantial numbers of people."

In this same report, which was based on a survey by the Bureau of the Census of the United States Department of Commerce, the Bureau of Labor Statistics

---

[6] Abram Bergson, *Structure of Soviet Wages*, Harvard University Press, Cambridge, 1944, p. 178.
[7] *Monthly Labor Review*, vol. 75, no. 3, September 1952, p. 257.

A. L. GITLOW

TABLE 1[8]

Experience of Workers at their Current Jobs, by Major Occupation Group and
Sex, January 1951

OCCUPATION	PER CENT WITH JOBS ACQUIRED BEFORE WORLD WAR II			MEDIAN YEARS ON CURRENT JOB		
	Total	Men	Women	Total	Men	Women
All Employed Persons...............	22.0	25.4	13.9	3.4	3.9	2.2
Farmers and Farm Managers..........	50.0	50.4	42.4	9.4	9.6	7.1
Managers, Officials, Proprietors, except farm...............................	33.0	34.9	22.7	5.1	5.3	4.2
Craftsmen, foremen, and kindred workers............................	27.9	28.2	20.2	4.3	4.3	4.2
Professional, technical, and kindred workers............................	24.9	27.8	20.3	3.7	4.3	2.5
Clerical and kindred workers..........	17.4	25.7	12.7	2.9	3.9	2.5
Operatives and kindred workers.......	16.9	18.7	12.4	2.9	3.1	2.3
Farm laborers and foremen............	18.2	9.7	33.9	2.7	2.4	4.8
Sales Workers........................	14.0	16.2	10.3	2.2	2.6	1.6
Service workers, except household.....	14.1	19.2	7.9	2.0	2.9	1.2
Laborers, except farm.................	11.6	11.6	—	1.6	1.6	—
Private household workers.............	10.2	—	10.2	1.2	—	1.2

analyzed the job stability of the American labor force. It did so in the belief
that job shifting (mobility) can be gauged effectively by the extent to which
workers remain on the same job for long periods of time. The Census survey
found that 13 million of the 59 million civilian workers employed in January
1951 had been with the same employer continuously since November 1941 or
earlier. In other words, more than a fifth of the workers employed at the time
of the survey were still working in the same jobs they had prior to Pearl Harbor
and the beginning of World War II. Thus, a significantly large proportion of
workers remained with the same employer or business despite the war and
postwar (including Korea) dislocations, notwithstanding the mass movement
of men into and out of the Armed Forces and of women into and out of the
labor force, and in the face of the extensive variations in industrial demand
of the past decade. *The corollary must also be noted: the labor force was extremely
mobile. In the total, job tenure was less marked than job shifting.*

The January 1951 total includes many persons who could not possibly have
had a continuous job for 9 or more years simply because of their age. It also
includes many men who involuntarily interrupted their job holding, by entry
into the Armed Forces. The proportion with long-term job tenure, calculated
on a base consisting of those with continuous labor-force participation throughout
this period, would therefore be considerably higher.

This study concluded that the most mobile segments of the American labor
force are to be found in these groups: (1) the young (under 45 years of age);

[8] *Monthly Labor Review*, vol. 75, no. 3., *op. cit.*, p. 261.

2) the unskilled; (3) the industries in which seniority is not so important, or in which employment conditions are less stable; and (4) the non-whites. Conversely, the most stable segments of the American labor force are to be found in these groups: (1) the older workers (over 45 years of age); (2) the semi-skilled, managerial, and self-employed persons; (3) the industries in which seniority is important or in which employment conditions are stable; and (4) the whites. The major reason for the disparity between whites and non-whites is the greater concentration of non-white jobs in casual or part-time work and in occupations with characteristically lower job stability.

Mobility of Tool and Die Makers

We noted: (1) that skilled workers are less mobile than semiskilled or unskilled; and (2) that a shortage of skilled tool makers characterized the Korean "police" period. Therefore, a study of the mobility of tool and die makers, *with special attention to the importance of economic considerations in choice of occupation and job changes*, should be of special interest. Such a study, covering the period 1940–1951, was made by the Bureau of Labor Statistics for the Department of the Air Force.[9] The study is based primarily on the analysis of 11-year work histories (1940–1951), obtained by personal interviews in the spring of 1951 with 1,712 tool and die makers.

The precision which tool and die making demands requires a high degree of skill, which is obtained by four or more years of training or experience. Qualified tool and die makers are at the top of the occupational ladder. They are among the highest paid workers in the metalworking field.

The survey analyzed four types of movement by tool and die makers: (I) movement in and out of the occupation; (II) movement between employers; (III) movement between industries; and (IV) movement from one geographic area to another.

I. Movement in and out of the Occupation

During the 11-year period, there was very little movement in and out of the occupation. *After becoming qualified journeymen*, more than 90 per cent of the group surveyed worked only as tool and die makers.[10]

II. Movement between Employers

All of the industry and geographic shifts made by the workers included in the study, as well as most of the moves in and out of the occupation, involved changes of employer. Measurement of movement between employers was, therefore, a comprehensive measurement of all movement.

[9] *The Mobility of Tool and Die Makers*, 1940–1951, U.S. Department of Labor, Bureau of Labor Statistics, Bulletin No. 1120, November 14, 1952.

[10] *Ibid.*, p. 32. The work histories of these men began only after they became qualified journeymen. The occupational movement involving a skill progression up to tool and die maker was considered in this study as part of the training experience for the trade, but it *was excluded from the measurement of mobility of fully qualified members of this craft.*

Nearly three-fifths (979 of the 1,712 workers in the survey) had worked for only one employer. The 733 tool and die makers who had changed employers one or more times made 2,127 moves, or an average of 2.9 per person. More than half of those who had shifted made only one or two moves. *Three-fifths of the movement between employers was made by 229 workers (about one-seventh of the total number of workers in the survey) who made four or more shifts each. Thus, tool and die makers, as a group, were relatively immobile. However, within the group, there was a rather mobile minority.*[11]

Of the 733 tool and die makers who had made employer shifts, 605 (82.5 per cent) had made at least one voluntary move. About two-thirds (1,258) of the 2,127 moves between employers were voluntary. If the frequency of voluntary movement between employers of the estimated 100,000 tool and die makers employed in early 1952 was the same as was found for the 1,712 craftsmen in the survey sample, it is estimated that about 9,000 voluntary employer shifts would be made annually by the tool and die makers in the country. Most of the job changes would involve a change of industry, but less than 12 per cent of the shifts would involve a change of employment from one labor market to another. Of course, 9,000 job changes does not mean that 9,000 different craftsmen would change employers. A small number of men would change jobs more than once during a given year.[12]

Workers with fewer months in the labor force *after qualifying as tool and die makers* made proportionately more job changes in relation to the length of their work experience. While age differences were an important factor, there were differences even for workers in the same age group. *The relationship between months in the labor force and degree of mobility tends to substantiate the belief that when workers enter the labor market, either as new workers, or as in this case, as new journeymen, they look for "good" jobs. In this search they move from job to job until they find one that satisfies their requirements, and once they obtain such a position, they are likely to remain there.*[13]

III. *Movement between Industries*

There appeared to be a significant degree of interindustry movement. Slightly more than a quarter of the workers employed in the machinery and motor vehicles industry had changed employers. Also, more than half the workers employed in the aircraft industry and about two-thirds of those working in the machine tool accessories industry had changed jobs during the period. Although the average age of the workers differed by industry and was to some extent a factor, the interindustry differences in mobility still appeared when age was held constant. These differences may be partially explained by the nature of the industries, particularly their recent growth and the degree to which employment has fluctuated. For example, only about half the tool and die makers employed in the machine tool accessories industry had qualified as tool and die makers in that industry. Thus, the other 50 per cent would necessarily

---

[11] *Ibid.*, p. 33.
[12] *Ibid.*, pp. 33, 34.
[13] *Ibid.*, p. 36.

ave made at least one job (and industry) move in order to be employed in a machine tool accessories plant.[14]

IV. *Movement from one Geographic area to another*

There was relatively little movement from one geographic area to another.)nly 143 (8.4 per cent) of the 1,712 men reported changing their cities of em->loyment during the 11 years. These men made only 250 such shifts in job ocation or an average of 1.7 moves each. Nearly half of those who had changed heir cities of employment moved only once, and five-sixths had made only one)r two locational moves.[15]

The tool and die makers interviewed were asked to give their reasons for changing 'obs. The information called for the entire explanation for changing employers, ncluding both the reason for leaving a particular job and for taking the next)ne. The reasons given were divided into two broad groups: voluntary job :hanges and involuntary job changes. The results are contained in Table 2.

Of the 2,127 job changes 1,258 were voluntary and 675 were involuntary. [n 194 cases the workers gave no reason or the reason was so vague as to be unclassifiable. Of the changes made voluntarily, the reason given most fre-quently was the desire for higher pay (27.5 per cent), including a higher wage rate or higher take-home pay because of a longer workweek. The next largest category (24.9 per cent) of all voluntary job changes covered a variety of re-sponses which could be summed up as a desire to get a "better job." This in-cluded such reasons as "to gain experience," "to get a promotion," or "to take

TABLE 2[16]

Job Changes of Tool and Die Makers, by Nature of Change and Reason for Voluntary Changes, 1940–1951

JOB CHANGES	PERIOD OF CHANGE (1940–1951)	
	Number	Per cent
All Job Changes...............................	2,127	100.0
Voluntary.......................................	1,258	59.1
Involuntary....................................	675	31.7
Reason not reported...........................	194	9.2
Voluntary changes.............................	1,258	100.0
Better Pay.................................	—	27.5
Better Job.................................	—	24.9
Working Conditions.........................	—	11.6
Location...................................	—	5.1
Return to Former Employer..................	—	5.0
Differences with Foreman...................	—	3.3
Other......................................	—	22.6

[14] *Ibid.*, p. 37.
[15] *Ibid.*, p. 39.
[16] *Ibid.*, p. 41.

a job which would lead to promotion." The desire to improve working conditions accounted for 11.6 per cent of the voluntary job changes made. Included in this group were changes made to secure different work shifts, more desirable hours of work, or better physical conditions in the tool room or shop. 5.1 per cent of the voluntary job changes were made because of plant location or transportation difficulties. Five per cent of the workers left jobs to return to plants from which, in most cases, they had been laid off. 3.3 per cent of the voluntary job changes were made because of "differences" with supervisors. In 22.6 per cent of the voluntary job changes, vague reasons or reasons not related to a particular job were given.[17]

Commenting upon these results, the Bureau of Labor Statistics observed:[18] "The above enumeration of reasons for changing jobs suggest the important conclusion that *most of the voluntary movement of tool and die makers was for specific and rational reasons calculated to improve the worker's job situation.*" (Italics added.)

Each worker was asked to identify the influences leading him to this occupation. 1,287, or 75.2 per cent of the 1,712 workers surveyed,[19] cited these three major reasons: (I) 621 said they became tool and die makers because they were mechanically inclined and *had looked for an occupation in which they could use their aptitudes*; (II) 384 reported entering the occupation because of the *advice or example of their families or friends*; (III) 282 reported entering the trade because *they expected it to provide them a good income at once or in the immediate future.*

The first and third reasons appear to be rational decisions associated with economic betterment. They account for 903 (70.2 per cent) of the 1,287 tool and die makers able to provide definite reasons for entering the occupation. Further, there is a strong likelihood that the influence of family and friends was exerted in connection with the argument that entry into the occupation was economically advantageous. The basic *conclusion* is: *Rational economic factors have been most potent in influencing tool and die makers: (1) to enter the occupation; and (2) to change jobs.*

Patterns of Mobility, Skilled Workers, Six Cities[20]

This study is based primarily on an analysis of 10-year work histories obtained in interviews with a sample of 2,578 male skilled workers who were employed during 1950 in six large cities. The sample includes not only workers who were on skilled jobs in 1950, but also those who held a skilled job sometime during 1940–50.

As a part of the 10-year work history collected for this study, a direct question was asked the worker about each job he left, "Why did you leave that job?"

[17] *Ibid.*, p. 42.
[18] *Ibid.*, p. 42.
[19] *Ibid.*, p. 24.
[20] *Patterns of Mobility of Skilled Workers and Factors Affecting Their Occupational Choice Six Cities, 1940–51*, Survey of Occupational Mobility Conducted by Cooperating University Research Centers and the Social Science Research Council for the U.S. Department of the Air Force and U. S. Bureau of the Census, Industrial Relations Section, Massachusetts Institute of Technology, Cambridge, Mass., February 1, 1952, mimeographed.

TABLE 3[21]

Specific Reason for Shifts, 1940–50

SPECIFIC REASON FOR SHIFT	WEIGHTED PER CENT (ROUNDED)
a. *Voluntary Reasons*	*48*
1. Wages	7
2. Chance for Improvement	9
3. Going into own Business	3
4. Physical characteristics	4
5. Fairness of Treatment	4
6. Independence and control	0
7. Steadiness of Employment	2
8. Wanted a Change	1
9. Emigration to U.S.A.	0
10. General dissatisfaction with job or occupation	3
11. Nearness to home	1
12. Other voluntary reasons	7
13. Went into defense work	3
14. Wanted a geographical shift, just "moved" to a city	4
b. *Involuntary Reasons*	*51*
1. Economic reasons (layoffs)	33
2. Personal reasons	2
3. Health reasons	4
4. Discharge	1
5. Other involuntary reasons	1
6. Military Service	8
7. Unclassified reasons	2

For the purpose of analyzing the positive motivations of workers in leaving jobs, it is the voluntary shifts that are of interest to us. We must proceed with caution in interpreting these data, for the problem of motivation is a deep one and the data are based on only brief interviews. Further, previous studies have shown that no fixed scale of "job satisfactions" can be drawn. The worker's response may thus be expected to change as his personal or community environment changes.

With these qualifications in mind, the reasons for voluntary job shifts, as given by the skilled workers in the sample, revealed *two main points:* (1) the *"economic" factors, "wages" and "chance for improvement," represented the most important grouping of reasons, accounting for one-third of the voluntary shifts;* and (2) *the so-called "human relations" factors, "fairness of treatment" and "independence and control," were relatively unimportant (4 per cent of the voluntary reasons).* (Table 3.[22])

This statement about the importance of "economic" motives may be challenged on the grounds that the shifts for these reasons may have resulted in no greater wage gain during this period of full employment than the shifts

---

[21] *Ibid.*, p. 50.

[22] It must be kept in mind that 51 per cent of the reasons for shifting jobs were *involuntary.*

TABLE 4[23]

*Per Cent Wage Change on Job Shifts for Reasons of "Wage" or "Chance for Advancement"
as Compared with "Layoffs"*

PER CENT WAGE CHANGE	WAGES AND CHANCE FOR ADVANCEMENT, PER CENT	LAYOFFS, PER CENT
No Wage Change.........................	8	19
1–10% Increase.........................	11	9
10–30% Increase........................	21	10
Over 30% Increase......................	33	9
1–10% Decrease........................	4	7
Over 10% Decrease.....................	14	25
No Information.........................	9	22
Total...............................	100	100

that followed layoffs. Thus, other studies have found that workers' knowledge of alternative jobs was slight and that there was no particular tendency for movement toward the higher wage firms. In order to check on this point, this study compared the percentage wage changes resulting from voluntary shifts for "wage" and "chance for advancement" reasons with involuntary shifts resulting from layoffs. (Table 4.)

A marked difference between these two groups is apparent: 65 per cent of the former group increased their wages whereas only 28 per cent of the latter group secured an increase in wages. These data must, of course, be accepted with caution, for they are based on unverified statements by the individual workers. Nevertheless, this particular result seems pronounced enough to warrant confidence in its validity. Combining it with the apparent importance of "economic" motivations cited above, *we may advance this evidence as confirming, at least, the finding of other studies that skilled workers are relatively purposeful and rational, in an economic sense, as they behave in the labor market.*

Another direct question was put to the skilled worker by the interviewer. After collecting a 10-year work history, the interviewer selected the job held longest during the period from 1945–1950. The worker was then asked, "You spent the most time as ——— during the last five years. Why did you go into this kind of work?" Some of the answers will be related to an occupation that is not skilled, since the length of time in the skilled trade and the date of entry vary within the group analyzed. Such cases are not considered in the following discussion.

These craftsmen apparently felt a natural aptitude and liking for what they considered to be interesting work. They were often encouraged in this feeling by a father, an uncle, or some other relative. (Table 5.)

The fact that such direct economic factors as wages and chance for advancement were not emphasized by a large proportion of these skilled workers raises

[23] *Ibid.*, p. 53.

TABLE 5[24]

Reason for Choosing Skilled Occupation held Longest since January 1, 1945
(Percentage totals do not equal 100 because of rounding)

REASON	PER CENT
a. Job-Oriented Reasons	*22*
1. Wages	2
2. Proximity to home	0
3. Physical characteristics of job	1
4. "Like the work"	1
5. Security	1
6. Anticipation of Advancement	0
7. Independence and Control	0
8. Influence of relatives	1
9. Assistance of relatives and friends	3
10. Job scarcity	3
11. Chance	5
12. Promotion	3
13. Special training	0
14. Other, unclassified	2
b. Occupation-Oriented Reasons	*53*
1. Wages	5
2. Job Interest and feeling of aptitude	13
3. Physical Characteristics of occupation	2
4. "Like the trade"	8
5. Security	1
6. Anticipation of advancement	2
7. Independence and control	0
8. Influence of relatives	6
9. Job scarcity	1
10. Chance	3
11. Special training	6
12. Informal training	3
13. Other, unclassified	3
c. No information or not applicable	*23*
Total	98

a further question of interpretation. Does this mean that the economic motive was not an important consideration in the choice of a skilled trade? Such a conclusion seems unwarranted. Material presented earlier on reasons for job shifts showed that many voluntary shifts were made for "wage" or "chance for improvement" reasons. Thus, the emphasis placed on direct economic factors as explanations for job to job movement indicates their basic importance. Since skilled jobs are generally thought of among wage earners as at the top of the economic ladder, it would seem likely that this fact and its general im-

[24] *Ibid.*, p. 57.

portance was assumed by those explaining their occupational choice. At th
very least, one should not conclude from these data that the economic attraction
of skilled jobs were unimportant factors in the choice of skilled occupations.

The Movement of Factory Workers

In a study bearing the above title, Charles A. Myers and W. Rupert Maclaurin
reported their observations of the operation of a local labor market in a medium
sized Massachusetts manufacturing community. Their investigation concerned
the employment experience of 1,500 workers who moved between 37 principal
manufacturing and public utility firms in the community during 1937, 1938
and 1939. All the firms still in business in the summer of 1942 were interviewed
again to provide comparative data and information on the 1942 labor market.

Attention was focused on the extent to which workers moved *voluntarily*
or *were forced to move* from one firm to another or in and out of employment
during this period, and the effect of this movement. Myers and Maclaurin
sought to answer these questions: (1) How much inter-factory movement took
place within the community? (2) What was the nature of that movement; who
were the people that moved? (3) What were the principal barriers to movement
between local firms? (4) Did the movement of workers fulfill its functions of (a)
equalizing wages and other conditions of work for comparable jobs, (b) distributing labor where the need was greatest, and (c) enabling workers to better
themselves and to learn new occupations?[25]

The study covered the period 1937–1942, involving substantial unemployment (1937–1939) and growing labor shortages (1942). The fact that there
was a labor surplus during most of this period is important. It establishes an
important distinction between this study and those discussed earlier.[26]

Myers and Maclaurin summarized their principal findings as follows:

I. Only a small proportion of the total movement of workers during 1937–39
took place among the principal factories of the community.

II. Less than 30 per cent of the moves among the 37 firms in 1937–39 were
voluntary, and 70 per cent were forced by layoffs and discharges. Thus only a
small group of workers were willing or able to quit their jobs because they
were dissatisfied or because they hoped to "better themselves." Forced movements were still predominant in the wartime labor market of 1942.

III. There was a strong tendency for workers to move between industries
and firms located in the same neighborhood. Some movement occurred in the
direction of higher-wage firms, although it was not very great.

IV. The workers who moved *voluntarily* were mostly young, short-service

[25] Charles A. Myers and W. Rupert Maclaurin, *The Movement of Factory Workers*, John
Wiley and Sons, New York, 1943, pp. 70–76.

[26] The authors note that an important limitation of the study is the fact that the data
provided very little information on the experience of three groups of workers: (1) those
factory workers who took non-factory jobs or were unemployed after leaving a factory,
(2) those who remained with one employer after entering the manufacturing labor market
late in 1937, 1938, or 1939, and (3) those who were not employed at any time during the
period in the principal manufacturing firms. If complete information had been available
on these workers, the conclusions on movement might have been modified.

orkers, frequently women, whose earnings were relatively low in the job they uit. These workers had less to lose by moving than did the older, longer-ervice workers who held the better-paying jobs. Forced movements were also oncentrated on the young, short-service workers, since even the non-union rms gave considerable weight to length of service in making layoffs.

V. Despite labor surpluses and differences in skill requirements between ndustries, many more workers could have moved than actually did, if it had ot been for certain other barriers to free movement of workers within the abor market. On the demand side, there was a gentleman's agreement among mployers not to hire labor away from each other. Employers also had certain ther restrictive hiring practices which limited movement to particular groups f workers.

VI. On the supply side of the labor market, there were non-competitive ractices which likewise constituted barriers to movement. Workers tended to eek and accept jobs within their immediate neighborhoods, largely because hey learned of openings or secured jobs through the influence of employed riends and relatives. Long service and attachment to the job or firm was another actor limiting movement in response to immediate financial incentives. Unionism nd unemployment compensation had little direct influence on movement in he period studied.

VII. Movement from lower-wage to higher-wage firms was largely ineffective n reducing differentials in rates for comparable jobs. Increases by the lower-vage firms between 1937 and 1942 were brought about more by minimum-wage orders and the pressure of unions than by voluntary movement away from these firms. Higher-wage firms also made increases, thus leaving the ranking of firms in the community's wage structure unchanged, for the most part.

VIII. The low-wage firms generally did not compensate for their poorer wage rates by providing better working conditions, welfare plans, or good "informal relations."

IX. Because of the various barriers to movement, the high-wage, expanding firms probably did not succeed in getting the best working force that could be obtained. On the other hand, there was probably sufficient movement among the workers in the sample to prevent the development of a "hard core" of unemployment during 1937–39.

X. Movement between the principal factories was not successful in giving workers an opportunity to utilize their capacities and abilities as effectively as possible. The fact that more than a third of the voluntary moves during 1937–39 resulted in lower earnings, and frequently some unemployment, indicates that voluntary movement was not too intelligent and often disappointing to the workers.

The above conclusions appear to undermine our earlier evidence relative to differentials and the rational allocation of employment. Before we discard that evidence, however, we must recall that these conclusions related to a period of labor surplus. Thus, Myers and Maclaurin observed:[27] "The pressure

[27] *Ibid.*, p. 74.

on some firms to get and hold workers late in 1942, however, had forced certain changes which were in contrast with the 1937–39 period." They noted these significant changes:

I. There was a stronger tendency for workers to move from the lower-wage to higher-wage firms. All the low-wage firms were losing workers in 1942; whereas only four-fifths were losing workers in 1937.

II. The attraction of war jobs with better wages was overcoming somewhat the attachment of workers to neighborhood firms and industries.

III. The willingness of workers to move voluntarily, and hence the potential amount of voluntary movement, was great. For example, nearly a fourth of the community's labor force, most of whom were already employed, applied for jobs with a large firm which acquired a plant in the community early in 1942. This firm was known for its good wages and personnel policies.

IV. Employers with war contracts observed the "gentleman's agreement" with other war plants, but not with non-war employers. Some firms modified it further to accept any applicant who said he had quit his job in another war plant.

On balance, therefore, our earlier evidence and reasoning retain vitality. The Myers and Maclaurin study, however, introduces a warning note relative to periods of severe unemployment. At such times, level of employment problems may overwhelm the effective functioning of wages as a basic instrument for securing the rational and effective allocation of employment.

A New England Textile City

In *The Dynamics of a Labor Market*, Charles A. Myers and George P. Shultz reported the results of their study of a medium-sized (35,000) New England community, which had suffered a partial mill shutdown that resulted in considerable unemployment. The textile mill had been the dominant employer in the community for over a century. Occurring in 1948, the partial mill shutdown was accompanied in 1949 by layoffs in other local industries. Amidst a general atmosphere of business recession, the local labor force suffered its peak unemployment of about 12 per cent in April 1949.[28]

In making the study, Myers and Shultz sought answers to these questions: (1) How do displaced workers look for and find new jobs? (2) What part is played by unemployment benefits and by the State Employment Service? (3) What satisfactions do these workers seek in their jobs? (4) How, if at all, do they change their viewpoint as the level of unemployment rises and falls? (5) How are employers, employed workers, and unions affected by the changed conditions?

Though the study's results indicated the importance of *chance* in worker mobility and the existence of wide variations in hiring rates within a small geographic area, the authors appeared convinced that the evidence indicated that the labor market concept of wage theory was helpful in explaining events in the community. Myers and Shultz presented their evidence in four points.

[28] Charles A. Myers and George P. Shultz, *The Dynamics of a Labor Market*, Prentice-Hall, New York, 1951, pp. 3–4, 198–204.

I. The vast majority of workers interviewed were not willing to make any immediate change in their place of residence. This was more true of those with dependents than of those without. Also, many workers were willing to take jobs outside the city if these jobs were within commuting distance.

II. Unemployment in the community did have an effect on worker, union, and employer behavior. Displaced workers tended to emphasize employment security and wages as more important job satisfactions. The attitudes of employed workers also changed. With increased unemployment, employers found: a) Where they could not staff plants adequately before the shutdown, they were able to adopt a selective hiring policy afterwards, (b) Where they were previously lax in discipline, they now replaced unsatisfactory employees with qualified and more conscientious workers, and (c) Where pressure on low hiring rates was pushing the minimum slowly upward, this pressure was relieved. In a few cases, these rates were actually lowered.

Weak unions discovered that hostile employers could undermine their bargaining position by using the pool of unemployed as a way to increase worker dependence on the employer. Even where unions were strong and union-management relationships were friendly, unemployment and short-time work in the particular plant moderated the collective bargaining demands of many unions and resulted in settlements far below those of immediately previous years.

III. The wide range in minimum rates and average rates of pay that evidently existed in the community must be modified by two considerations: (a) Employers generally felt that the available labor supply was heterogeneous; the quality varied widely and relatively high wages, they believed, attracted relatively good employees; and (b) Many employers believed that they hired from a restricted labor market. Machinists and woodworkers, for example, were virtually noncompeting groups, and variations in rates between them could be explained on those grounds.

IV. The displaced workers appeared to have considerably more knowledge about wages and working conditions in various local plants than previous studies of local labor markets had indicated. Only a small percentage knew nothing about jobs they took after the shutdown. *A majority of the workers interviewed, both employed and unemployed, named "good" and "poor" places to work in the community, with "wages" being the most important differentiating factor. While chance and the scarcity of other employment opportunities explained many job choices, workers would move toward the high-wage firms, given that opportunity.*

Another New England City

The crux of this discussion is the relationship between labor mobility and wages. Precisely this question constituted the central purpose of Lloyd G. Reynolds' book *The Structure of Labor Markets*.[29] In that work he did two things: (1) reported the results of a case study of wages and labor mobility

[29] Lloyd G. Reynolds, *The Structure of Labor Markets*, Harper and Bros., New York, 1951.

145

in a medium-sized New England city; and (2) engaged in an extensive discussion of labor market theory and policy. Our interest centers in the case study.

The city's population was 352,036 in 1947. This size enabled its leaders to meet frequently and be well known to each other, but prevented labor from moving freely throughout the metropolitan area in search of employment.[30] The study was restricted to manual labor, with the basic field work being conducted during the years 1946–48.[31] This was a period of extremely low unemployment both in the city and nationally, although the labor market became less tight by the end of 1948.

The study's data were drawn from three main sources: (1) worker interviews; (2) management interviews; and (3) other sources of statistical and interview information (the manufacturers' division of the Chamber of Commerce, the state headquarters of the National Metal Trades Association, the State Employment Service, the unemployment compensation system, the State Department of Labor, and the local school system).[32]

The worker interviews involved three samples (separate groups of workers). Sample 1 included some 450 workers, constituting a cross-section of the city's manual working population as of October 1945. This group included few war veterans. It was relatively old, skilled, and immobile. Sample 2 included some 350 workers employed in manufacturing industries. This group was relatively young, contained many war veterans, and was more mobile than sample 1. Sample 3 was a small group of 50 unemployed workers. They were questioned intensively on their methods of job hunting and their minimum standards of an acceptable job. These samples are, of course, not so extensive as the first two studies discussed in this section, which covered 1,712 and 2,578 workers respectively.

Reynolds' conclusions relative to mobility were stated briefly under four headings: (I) factors affecting a worker's mobility rate; (II) the relative frequency of different types of movement—industrial, occupational, and geographical; (III) the characteristics of interindustry movement; and (IV) the significant lines of cleavage within the labor market.[33]

I. *Factors Influencing Mobility Rates*

A. Most labor turnover occurs within a small segment of the labor force.

B. Unskilled workers change jobs more frequently than the semiskilled, and these in turn move more frequently than skilled workers.

C. Labor's inclination to change employers decreases with increasing length of service. It appears that the acquisition of seniority is the result of an employee's earlier decision that the particular firm is a good place to work.

D. Older workers are less mobile. Age, of course, is related to length of service. This seems to indicate that labor, after a certain amount of "shopping around"

[30] *Ibid.*, pp. 56.
[31] *Ibid.*, pp. 9, 11.
[32] *Ibid.*, pp. 15, 16.
[33] *Ibid.*, pp. 38–41.

n youth, makes an occupational adjustment and settles down to acquiring seniority, pension rights, and other forms of security.

Skill, length of service, age, and other factors are related to labor's inclination (propensity) to change jobs. The extent of *actual movement* is, however, somewhat different. It may depend equally, or more, on the rate of expansion in the total demand for labor.

II. *Relative Frequency of Various Types of Movement*

Interplant movement is most frequent because (except for intraplant promotions) it is a prerequisite for any other sort of movement. Next most common is interindustry movement.

III. *Characteristics of Interindustry Movement*

The walls around specific industries are like sieves. Not many workers remain in the same industry throughout their working lives. Some workers show an amazing variety of movement. Reynolds found that within a single year about half the workers hired by firms in the city studied came from other types of industry. Although a worker leaving a company is somewhat more likely to go to another company in the same industry, or to certain "neighboring" industries, this tendency is not very strong and appears capable of being overridden by war emergencies or other drastic shifts in the demand for labor.

IV. *Labor Market Lines of Cleavage*

Reynolds draws from his study the impression that the most important boundaries among labor markets run along geographical lines. Thus, a labor market can be identified with a locality small enough so that people can readily travel from homes in any part of the area to jobs in any other part.

Having noted the above characteristics of mobility, Reynolds analyzed the factors influencing workers to take a job.[34]

The relative frequency with which different job elements were mentioned in the answers to various questions is indicated in Table 6. An entry of "1" in a particular column of the table means that that job element was mentioned more frequently than any other in response to a particular question. An entry of "2" indicates that that element was mentioned next most frequently. Similarly with entries of "3", "4", or more. The rank order shown in the table is a rough measure of relative significance.

Some of the terms used in Table 6 require explanation. *Wages* includes two elements: (1) living costs; and (2) wage comparisons. The cost-of-living element was mentioned about twice as frequently as the comparative wage element. This may be due to the fact that the study was made during a period of rapidly increasing living costs. *Physical Characteristics of the job* includes: (1) the nature of the job itself (degree of cleanliness, arduousness, and hazard); (2) physical plant conditions (cleanliness, ventilation, etc.); and (3) the type of machinery (modern or obsolete, and in good or bad condition). The first (nature of the

---

[34] *Ibid.*, pp. 91–181.

A. L. GITLOW

TABLE 6[35]
Factors in Job Satisfaction

FACTOR	AVERAGE RANK	LEFT LAST JOB BECAUSE		DISSATISFIED WITH PRESENT JOB BECAUSE		SATISFIED WITH PRESENT JOB BECAUSE		LAST 3 JOBS RATED "GOOD" OR "BAD" BECAUSE (S2)		INT. IN TRANSFER TO OTHER JOB IN PLANT BECAUSE (S2)		WOULD OR WOULD NOT WORK IN OTHER SPECIFIED PLANTS BECAUSE (S1)		WHAT MAKES A JOB A "GOOD"
		S1	S2	S1	S2	S1	S2	Good	Bad	Int.[a]	Not Int.[b]	Would work	Would not work	
	(1)	(2)	(3)	(4)	(5)	(6)	(7)	(8)	(9)	(10)	(11)	(12)	(13)	(14)
Wages	1	1	1	2	2	2	1	1	2	1	2	2	1	1
Physical characteristics of the Job	2	2	2	3	3	4	3	2	1	3	3	3	2	2
Independence and control	3	3	3	1	1	1	2	4	3	6	4	5	4	3
Job interest	4	4	4	5	5	7	4	3	5	2	1	1	6	4
Fairness of treatment	5	5	5	4	4	6	5	6	4	5	5	6	3	5
Relations with fellow workers	6	6	6	6	6	3	7	5	7	4	6	4	5	6
Steadiness of work	7	7	7	7	7	5	6	7	6	7	7	7	7	7

[a] Interested.
[b] Not interested.
The symbols S1 and S2 refer to Samples 1 and 2 respectively.
The overall ranking of a factor (column 1) was obtained by taking an arithmetic mean of its rank in the other 13 columns of the table.

job itself) was mentioned most frequently. *Independence and control* means: (1) freedom from too close supervision; and (2) a chance to voice one's opinion on how the job should be done. Generally, this factor involves the worker's relation with his supervisor. *Relations with fellow workers* refers to: (1) the type of person with whom the worker is associated on the job; (2) the degree of cooperative spirit in the group; and (3) the degree to which others in the group look to the worker for leadership. The other terms used in the table seem self-explanatory.

The ranking of the various job factors by the workers covered by samples 1 and 2 is markedly consistent. *Wages* appears in first or second place in each instance. *Physical characteristics of the job* stands almost invariably in second or third place. On the other side, *steadiness of work* stands at the bottom in ten of the 13 columns. This seems to indicate *consistency* in the worker's responses to different questions. It *may* also indicate a basic *reliability* in the responses, i.e., a correspondence between the worker's statements to the interviewer and his actual feelings and behavior.

Some interesting variations appear, however, in connection with the other

[35] *Ibid.*, p. 93.

b factors. *Independence and control* ranks third in overall standing, but it ses to first place when the worker is appraising his present job (columns 4–7). his may indicate that workers forget how good or bad their supervisors were on evious jobs, and have no way of judging how good they will be on prospective bs. *Job interest* stands fourth on average, but it rises to the top when the orker is considering a transfer to another job (columns 10 and 12). Workers ho said they would not leave their present jobs most commonly cited the teresting *nature of their present work* (column 11). Workers who wanted to ave their present jobs most commonly cited *wages* as the reason, with *job terest* ranking second (column 10). Workers expressing a preference for work some other plant also gave the *interesting nature of the work* as their most ommon reason (column 12).[36]

Recognizing limitations in coverage and technique, Reynolds nevertheless oncluded that the main criteria in worker job evaluation are: (1) money income; ?) the physical nature of the work; (3) the degree of independence on the job nd the agreeableness of supervision, (4) the degree of interest in the work; and 5) the fairness with which the worker feels he has been treated by management. eynolds suggests also that a relation of substitution between money income nd other job elements may be reasonably assumed. Thus, higher wage rates an serve as an offset to poor working conditions, irregular employment, disgreeable supervision, and so on. The relationship, however, does not seem o be a continuous one, for workers did not seem very sensitive to small variaions in income. Thus, it would have required sizeable increases in wage rates o compensate for a worsening of jobs in other respects.

Reynolds made a special effort to determine how workers decide whether particular wage rate is good enough to warrant taking (or staying on) the ob. The reasons which workers gave for regarding their wage as fair or unfair re shown in Table 7.

Cost-of-living stands out prominently. This may be due to the fact that all he interviewing was done during 1947, a period of rapidly rising prices. Simulaneously, peak wartime earnings had diminished somewhat due to reductions n weekly hours of work. A study made during a period of falling prices and ising real incomes might have revealed less concern with the cost-of-living actor.

Comparisons were important. Three major factors in Table 7 involved comarisons: (1) rates for similar work in other plants; (2) nature of the work; and 3) rates for other jobs in the same plant. In connection with *nature of the work*, vorkers seemed to express an absolute judgment that a certain kind of work is vorth just about so much. Actually, these judgments rested on an implicit

---

36 The sampling technique used involved two limitations, in particular: (1) there was o careful attempt to measure the *intensity* of the worker's feelings about each of the ob characteristics he mentioned; and (2) there was no systematic exploration of how far he worker's job attitudes were conditioned, not by job characteristics, but by he worker's own personality, intelligence level, family life, and other non-job factors. *bid.*, p. 96.

A. L. GITLOW

TABLE 7[37]

Workers' Standards of Fair Wages

FACTOR	REASONS FOR REGARDING WAGE AS UNFAIR (%)		REASONS FOR REGARDI WAGE AS FAIR (%)	
	Sample 1	Sample 2	Sample 1	Sample
Cost of Maintaining an adequate living standard.	35	30	15	30
Rates for Similar Work in Other Plants.	10	27	27	27
Nature of the Work.	35	21	23	21
Rates for Other Jobs in the same plant.	6	6	8	6
Union scale.	2	2	5	2
Length of service.	1	2	4	2
Company's ability to Pay.	6	1	2	0
Others, and no reason given.	5	11	16	12
Total.	100	100	100	100

comparison with previous jobs held by the worker or with other jobs which saw around him in the plant. The basis of these comparisons, however, were n made explicit. Workers stressed these job elements most heavily in explainin why a certain kind of work deserves a certain rate of pay: (1) the degree physical effort required, tempo of work, or quantity of work accomplishe during the day; (2) safety hazards and other working conditions; and (3) degre of responsibility. On the other hand, management, in setting relative wag rates, usually emphasizes skill, education, experience, and training requirement Although Reynolds believes the importance of comparisons to be overstate with workers often using them as a peg on which to hang discontent originatin in some other factor, the factor still seems important.

On the basis of the above evidence, Reynolds' study appears to indicate significant degree of rationality in worker behavior with regard to the relation ship between wages and job choice. Reynolds, however, expresses profoun doubt as to this relationship. He notes: (1) that workers' comparisons wer imprecise or inaccurate;[38] and (2) that wage differentials do not, in importan degree, redistribute labor among firms and occupations.[39]

In this connection, we must recall our previously reported and somewha more extensive studies. Myers and Schultz noted that workers appeared to hav more knowledge about wages and working conditions in various local plants tha indicated in other studies. The six city survey of occupational mobility indicate that workers making voluntary job shifts generally increased their wages a against the group making involuntary job changes. The Bureau of Labo Statistics' study of tool and die makers, as well as the others reported, indicate that workers, particularly skilled ones, are relatively purposeful and rational i their labor market behavior.

[37] *Ibid.*, p. 99.
[38] *Ibid.*, p. 100.
[39] *Ibid.*, p. 224.

SUMMARY

The labor market is not perfectly competitive. In terms of "workable" though imperfect" competition, however, we may say the following about wage determination and its relation to labor mobility.[40]

I. Workers have some knowledge of jobs other than those on which they e currently employed, have some freedom of choice among employers, and ake some calculation of the relative attractiveness of alternative jobs. This lculation is not based *solely* on wage considerations. Labor takes into consideration any aspect of a job which it considers relevant. It is not necessary at workers have full knowledge of job opportunities or that all workers have ll knowledge of job opportunities or that all workers make careful comparisons. ompetition may be effective despite the ignorance or inertia of the majority.

Within the limits set by knowledge and market structure, workers will choose tter jobs in preference to poorer ones. Voluntary movement of labor will show drift toward more desirable jobs. Employers offering especially desirable bs will have a surplus of applicants for work. Employers offering less desirable bs will experience labor shortages.

II. An employer who wishes to keep a constant share of the area labor force ust keep the over-all attractiveness of his jobs in line with the attractiveness ' jobs offered by other employers. The employer may have some latitude in lecting ingredients for the "package" of employment conditions which he fers. He is bound, however, by the requirement that the "package" as a whole ust be as attractive as that offered by other employers.

III. In consequence of this behavior of workers and employers, there may be tendency toward equalization of the net attractiveness of all jobs in the area. he tendency toward equalization of job attractiveness requires time. Actually, could be effective only if each employer in an area desired to retain the same roportion of the area's labor force forever. But the demand for labor is dynamic. n expanding firm may need to offer more attractive terms than others. A eclining firm may offer poorer terms, and lose labor. The quality of labor is also factor. Employers willing to hire low-quality labor may be able to offer relatively poor employment terms.

IV. Movement arises also from changes in the availability of jobs in particular rms, trades, and areas. People move away from situations where jobs have been estroyed. They move to places where new jobs are opening up and rivalry for hese jobs is not so severe.

The view that workers can be redistributed *only* by changes in wage differentials is incomplete. They are reallocated also by differentials in the availibity of obs. When workers are no longer needed, they are discharged. To get them where hey are needed, in such instances, it is necessary only to indicate job availability. n sum, the allocation of labor seems to be a function of *job attractiveness* (with vages of special importance) and *job availability*.

[40] *Ibid.*, pp. 208–210, 244.

Energy Costs

ATOMIC POWER
AND THE LOCATION OF INDUSTRY

Walter Isard and Vincent Whitney

The well-defined physical consequences of nuclear fission contrast sharply with the speculative social and economic consequences. Diverse opinions, ranging from undocumented wishful thinking to shrewd analysis based on necessarily inadequate data, have attempted to cover the gamut of possible effects. One of the areas in which speculation has been particularly widespread is that of the probable effects that the commercial application of nuclear energy will have on industrial location. It is this aspect which we want to examine here. How may atomic power affect the world-wide pattern of industrialization? How may it influence the location of particular industries in this country?

Costs of Atomic Power

Basic to any analysis of the location of industry is a consideration of the costs of operation at various sites. One of these costs is, of course, that of power to industrial consumers. Existing costs for fuel and power, taken as a whole, represent a spatial pattern which may be modified in any one of several ways by the introduction of nuclear energy as a new power source.

When we ask how, specifically, atomic power will affect this pattern of fuel and power costs and ultimately the distribution of industry, two principal questions occur: (1) If atomic power is made generally available to industry in a particular area, how much will it cost for varying sizes of plant and varying scales of operation? (2) How will differences among areas in conditions of demand and in availability of capital, labor, and other factors affect the cost of constructing and operating nuclear plants in these areas?

The Invalidity of Cost Estimates

Unfortunately, no realistic basis exists for making estimates of the cost of atomic power. This may seem a bald statement in view of the

Reprinted from *Harvard Business Review*, *28* (1950), 45–54, by permission of the authors and editor.

several optimistic estimates which have appeared in print. But it has a substance which none of the estimates so far made can claim.

Of the earlier estimates, the most hopeful is that of Menke, who suggests that a cost of 3 mills per kilowatt hour "might be achieved in, perhaps, ten to twenty years of further active development."[1] Menke's estimate, like most of those made prior to the last two years, appears unduly optimistic in light of the continuation of experimental work with nuclear reactors, which has clearly shown a more complex and costly situation than engineers were earlier aware of. Specifically, the engineers failed to comprehend the extent to which materials used in the construction of reactors deteriorate in operation. They were in general far too optimistic about the ease with which the technical engineering problems involved in the construction of high-power nuclear piles could be solved.

A growing awareness of the real extent to which such problems had been underestimated has apparently put an end among engineers to the popular pastime of making estimates of the cost of atomic power. At least no figures have been published by engineers, so far as the authors are aware, since 1947. And it appears to be the consensus among engineers, physicists, and other natural scientists today that the uncertainties involved in the construction and operation of atomic power plants preclude any meaningful cost estimates.

The Thomas Report

Although cost estimates lack significance at this stage of the game, the questions we have raised about atomic power and industrial location can nevertheless be tackled. Fortunately, we can set down certain significant items of information about cost *relations*, which in turn have important implications for the location of industry, without having to depend on specific cost *estimates.*[2]

The significance of these relations can best be understood by reference to some set of hypothetical cost figures. The figures we shall use are the most reliable and, at the same time, the most conservative of the early optimistic cost estimates, namely, those presented in a report made under the direction of Dr. Charles A. Thomas of the Monsanto Chemical Company and presented by the State Department to the United Nations Atomic Energy Commission.[3] We want to emphasize

[1] John R. Menke, "Nuclear Fission as a Source of Power," *Econometrica*, Vol. 15, No. 4 (October 1947), p. 329.

[2] Our position is thus at variance with that of analysts on the staff of the Cowles Commission for Research in Economics. For an example of their view, applying specific cost estimates, see Sam H. Schurr, "Atomic Power in Selected Industries," *Harvard Business Review*, Vol. XXVII, No. 4 (July 1949), pp. 459–479.

[3] U. S. Department of State, *The International Control of Atomic Energy: Scientific Information Transmitted to the United Nations Atomic Energy Commisison, June 14, 1946–October 14, 1946* (Washington, Government Printing Office, 1947), Vol. 4, "Nuclear Power."

that, as we use the figures, they are purely hypothetical. Their use, however, lets us summarize a well-known set of estimates, which for our purposes are as meaningful as any imaginary figures we might adopt.

The Thomas Report suggests that an atomic power plant generating 75,000 kilowatts would cost in the neighborhood of $25,000,000 when built in a typical area of the eastern United States. With such a plant operating at 100% of capacity and with interest charges on investment set at 3%, the operating costs estimated by the Thomas group are about 8 mills for each kilowatt hour.

Conventional (i.e., nonatomic) power stations operate at some point below 100% of capacity. With the customary irregularity of loads, and with time out for necessary maintenance and repair, this is inevitable. For this reason, we have adjusted the Thomas-group figures to operation at 80% of capacity, the highest level of operation for existing steam stations; and at 50% of capacity, an operating level which is typical of existing system loads. This gives revised cost estimates of 9.4 mills and of 14.5 mills per kilowatt hour for atomic power plants.

By contrast, when operating figures are adjusted to a 50% plant factor, most actual steam stations of 50,000 kilowatts or greater capacity in the United States in 1945 operated at costs of not over 8 mills per kilowatt hour and a good many with costs of under 6 mills.[4] Thus, in the light of our revisions for less than capacity operation, it would seem that the Thomas-group estimates actually offer more ground for pessimism than optimism.

In Foreign Countries

Now let us examine some implications of certain cost relations for the world-wide pattern of industrialization.

Capital Costs

It is a significant point, and one accepted generally by engineers, that the capital cost of an atomic power plant will, under comparable conditions, considerably exceed that of a conventional steam station. Thomas, for example, suggests that the capital cost for his hypothetical atomic power plant will be two-and-one-half times that of his comparable modern steam station.

This important fact is apparently disregarded by those who argue enthusiastically that the many regions of the world which are under-developed and which lack adequate fuel and energy sources will experi-

[4] Walter Isard and John B. Lansing, "Comparisons of Power Cost for Atomic and Conventional Steam Stations," *Review of Economics and Statistics,* Vol. XXXI, No. 3 (August 1949), pp. 217–228, contains a technical discussion of this and related cost analysis.

ence an industrial awakening if atomic power becomes available at reasonable cost. Argentina is frequently referred to as the classic example of a nation now handicapped by a poor endowment of fuel and energy sources, which has the aggressive leadership necessary to take advantage of atomic power at competitive cost levels, and which would not be held back by any tradition, taboo, or other cultural hindrance. In consequence, it is implied, many plants located elsewhere would be relocated in Argentina, especially those having important markets in South America.

Suppose for a moment that atomic power does become generally available to industry at competitive cost levels. In that case, we would agree, existing transport disadvantages on fuel for nations such as Argentina might be expected to disappear. Even if all fissionable material were imported, transport costs would have no significance since one ton of nuclear fuel generates potentially as many kilowatt hours of electricity as two to three million tons of coal.

But this is not the whole story. We may anticipate, for instance, that atomic energy might increase the significance of other differentials between nations. One such vital differential is that of capital availability and interest costs, since the generation of atomic power will probably require considerably greater amounts of capital than are needed for the generation of power in conventional stations.

For purposes of illustration, we can use the figures of the Thomas Report, including the assumption that interest cost in the United States will be 3%. If future interest costs in Argentina should be 6%, an assumption which is in no way unreasonable, then the cost of atomic power in that country would be roughly 2.5 mills greater for every kilowatt hour on the basis of higher interest costs alone. Even though no interest appears in the bookkeeping, as might be the case if the government supplied capital, an imputed interest charge belongs in the comparison of costs, either because it represents actual outlays somewhere else along the line or because it measures the return on the same money put to alternative uses.

We know that there are sharp differences in the price at which capital is available in various parts of the world. But, beyond this, there is also marked variation in the availability and hence in the cost of skilled labor, of technical competence, of construction materials, of repair facilities, and so on. Fissionable material must be processed if its potential energy is to be released. The costs of such processing will hardly be uniform throughout the world.

Considerations of this sort make it very unlikely that, as commonly assumed, atomic power costs for similar plants will be about the same everywhere. Countries like Argentina, which now are clearly disadvantaged in terms of coal, oil, and water power sources, are not likely to

155

better their positions relative to the more highly industrialized nations if, as seems fairly certain, their costs for atomic power will also be relatively high in comparison with other areas. Such a conclusion hardly suggests industrial relocation.

What is more, the experience of many countries in which industrialization has lagged in the past indicates that there may be just as powerful obstacles to the development of atomic power in the nature of their social institutions. There are a number of areas which are not lacking in natural wealth but where efforts to utilize resources have been shackled by tremendous resistances — political instability, unbalanced economies, social institutions which are not oriented toward industrialization, illiterate and poverty-stricken populations. In Rhodesia, for example, where there are excellent coal deposits and where excellent hydro sources are within easy reach, economic backwardness certainly is not due to a lack of power resources.

In the case of such countries, it seems foolish to think that the introduction of a new power source will bring about any transformation. On the contrary, those nations which have already accepted industrialization and which have the advantage in terms of capital availability and costs, of technical know-how, of a large pool of skilled labor, and so on, are the very nations which will be likely to reap the benefits from any commercially available atomic power in the foreseeable future.

Economies of Scale

This conclusion is reinforced by still another set of factors. Although there has been relatively little discussion of the topic on the part of engineers and although there might be less general agreement on it than on capital costs, indications are that atomic power plant operations will involve significant economies of scale — in other words, that unit costs of product will decline with increases in the scale of operation. Moreover, these economies will probably extend to larger size plants than is true in the case of conventional steam stations.

The best cost study we have for steam stations in this country,[5] while emphasizing the wide range of conditions under which such stations operate, suggests that on the average economies of scale are likely to go along with increases in size of plant up to a capacity of about 75,000 kilowatts. Beyond this capacity further economies of scale may occur; for a variety of reasons, however, these larger plants tend to become more elaborate so that investment per kilowatt fails to show further decline.

At this stage of our knowledge, it looks as though atomic plants will show significant economies of scale beyond the figure of 75,000 kilo-

[5] John B. Lansing, "An Investigation Into the Long Run Cost Curves for Steam Central Stations"; doctoral dissertation, Harvard University, 1949.

watt capacity. We emphasize that this is our impression rather than established fact. There are indications, however, that a substantial part of the investment in pile and in necessary chemical and metallurgical facilities will not increase in proportion to the scale of operation. For example, the complicated and costly control mechanisms will be necessities regardless of size of plant. To state this as cautiously as possible, it seems a better assumption that significant economies of scale will exist than that they will not.

If our assumption proves correct, then presumably countries which are already in a position to utilize substantial amounts of new power will build larger plants and as a result have lower atomic power costs. Which countries are these? Again, they are not the underdeveloped nations, for the latter can be expected to have only a minimum unfolding demand for new power. Rather, they are the already heavily industrialized nations like the United States, England, and the Soviet Union. So on this score, too, there seems to be little reason to expect the kind of change in the world-wide pattern of industrialization which would favor the economically backward countries.

Developmental Subsidies

Another factor which leads to the same conclusion is the heavy hidden investment in nuclear development in the form of governmental subsidy. The major development programs in this country, in Great Britain, in France, and inevitably in Russia involve a great number of aids and services in effect donated by government. Just as the various government subsidies to aviation, which are intended to encourage its development, do not enter into airline costs, so subsidization of atomic research and engineering would, in all likelihood, be omitted in any cost calculations for atomic power. This too would serve to favor the more industrialized nations which could and presumably would offer the greatest amounts of subsidization.

To summarize in terms of location, the advent of atomic power should mean that American businessmen who sell in foreign markets, or who may consider foreign locations for securing United States markets, will have less rather than more impetus to relocate abroad. The advantage of location in the fuel-abundant and capital-rich countries would appear to be heightened and that of location in less favored countries diminished by the introduction of atomic power on a commerical scale.

In the United States

It has frequently been asserted that atomic power will erase the differences in fuel and power costs which now exist for different parts of the United States, thereby encouraging the dispersion of industry.

We may ignore regional differences in capital availability, interest cost, and the presence of skilled labor and technical competence. In terms of atomic operations they are not likely to produce important cost differentials within the United States. One factor which we cannot ignore, however, is that of probable economies as scale of operation is increased. We may anticipate that in those particular regions where new power can be installed in large blocks, power costs will be more moderate than in other regions.

Effect on Regional Cost Differentials

The picture is more complex, of course. For example, what information we have suggests that fixed costs will be responsible for a greater part of the whole cost of generating electricity in atomic stations than they are in steam stations. But while increases in the power output of an atomic plant will entail greater total outlay, it is unlikely that any direct cost item will cause this outlay to rise as sharply as would the expenditure for greater quantities of oil, coal, or gas in a steam station. In other words, atomic plants may enjoy the advantage of having lower marginal costs than conventional plants in the short run. If we are correct, the advantage will be striking for those areas which can utilize an atomic plant most fully because of widespread and regular demand for power.

Writers with a contrary point of view have suggested that if atomic power were eventually to become cheap enough to supplant all other sources of power and to be used as a substitute for all direct fuels, fuel and power cost differentials among regions of the United States would be drastically reduced or even eliminated entirely. But a major joker here is that atomic power seems unlikely to become sufficiently cheap to take the place of all power now based on conventional sources.

Let us examine the facts a little more closely. John B. Lansing, in an unpublished analysis of 1945 fuel costs for 197 randomly selected central steam stations of 5,000 kilowatts capacity or above, found distinct regional cost differentials. Cost comparisons in terms of cents per million B.t.u. showed that New England (except Maine, for which no stations were included) and Florida had the highest median fuel costs — 26 cents to 41 cents per million B.t.u. States with the lowest costs — 6 cents to 12 cents — are all part of or immediately adjacent to areas of oil and gas production and constitute the block of states from Missouri through Texas. Next lowest — 12 cents to 18 cents — are oil-producing California and the coal-producing states of Kentucky, West Virginia, Illinois, Wyoming, Colorado, Pennsylvania, and Alabama. The remaining states, which fall in the center of the distribution, with median costs of from 17 cents to 25 cents, are not important fuel producers but at the same time are not distant from fuel deposits.

Such data may serve as one very rough indication of those regions in which atomic power has maximum and minimum chances of becoming a competitive power source. Definitive analysis would demand consideration of many other relevant factors — for example, marginal costs, new capacity, and the size of the market area involved. On this basis, however, it certainly is not unreasonable to suppose that atomic power, if it becomes commercially feasible, will probably (1) replace the poorer alternate sources of fuel and power, and (2) be used simultaneously with, rather than supplant, the better sources. Through such use, differentials in regional costs might well be reduced somewhat, but it seems doubtful that they will come near being eliminated, particularly in view of the economies of large-scale operation in areas with higher power utilization.

Relocation of Industry

If power cost differences do decline, will American industry relocate? To answer such a question fully demands a more complete analysis than can be undertaken here of the complex of location forces which are constantly operating, but an approach can be indicated.

Two major sets of differentials among sites are those in transport costs and in processing costs. Further, there are certain forces which tend, up to a certain point, to lower transport and processing costs whenever the scale of a plant's operations rises or whenever the geographic concentration of similar, or sometimes even dissimilar, plants increases. Likewise, still another set of forces tends toward the dispersion of industry. Within the involved series of forces the differential in power costs is only a subdivision of the differentials in processing costs. Clearly, any narrowing of the gap between power costs in different areas will have little meaning except to industries whose power needs are large and whose power costs constitute a fair proportion of all costs.

But even those industries which have been oriented to fuel and power sites may not find it expedient to relocate production if (as is not necessarily the case) the differential advantage of the historic site is largely lost with the development of atomic power. General dispersion may be no more probable for such industries than it is for industries which were originally oriented to the use of coal in production processes but are no longer. A number of these latter, located in areas like the Pittsburgh district, have not migrated for good reason: relocation may be an expensive process.

The established pattern of transport facilities, financial institutions, and skilled labor; the established relationships with markets, sources of raw materials, and allied industries; and the developed agglomeration of economies — all these, built up over a long period, may in many cases be more important than lowered power-cost differentials. Such considerations, while not denying the possibility of a dispersion of power-oriented industries, nevertheless suggest that such a possibility is easily exaggerated.

Another consideration is that cheap atomic power, by encouraging the use of more power-consuming operations in the fabrication of specific products, would tend to increase rates of production. Because of this, cost differentials for atomic power, though smaller, may become more important than present differentials for conventional power in determining the concentration of power-oriented industries at favorable sites. By comparison, current differentials may be associated with lower rates of production and a lesser use of power machinery.

An example from the past makes this clearer. The early development of hydro power tended to even out energy resources. But because aluminum and certain other electro-process industries, which grew with hydro development, make use of such large quantities of power, they are now concentrated at and largely bound to hydroelectric sites. Hydro development encouraged the growth of those industries, both old and new, which were most sensitive to differences in energy costs. In consequence, the narrowing of such cost differentials, growing out of hydro development, injected new concentrations of industry into the economy. Atomic power may conceivably act in the same way — that is, to encourage the concentration rather than the dispersion of industry.

Finally, political factors cannot be overlooked. These extraeconomic considerations may ultimately determine a relatively intensive development of nuclear facilities in a few locations which may be selected for reasons of military security rather than economic logicality. It is conceivable that by-product power may be available at such locations at low cost based on government subsidy. Such sites might serve as foci of attraction for power-consuming industries and thus lead to relatively intense concentrations. Defense considerations would probably require that these be spread over an area of concentration rather than pressed into any compact physical proximity, but the overall effect would be in the direction of concentration.

The Location of Specific Industries

We can now turn to the possible effects of atomic power on the location of some sample industries which are large consumers of power. In examining these, no attempt will be made to predict actual levels to which atomic power costs *may* fall, since such accuracy is not yet possible. Instead, we shall recognize that there are various strategic areas in which an industry, given a new spatial pattern of fuel and power costs, might relocate; and, where necessary to use cost terms, we shall ask to what levels the cost of atomic power *must* fall to make an actual shift of plant feasible. Such considerations have the incidental value of pointing up certain applications of locational principles which are basic to any decisions on plant location.

Which industries are most likely to be locationally affected by atomic power? For guidance we have those tables which list the various industries according to the ratio of their fuel and power costs to product value.[6] However, it should be emphasized that a high ranking alone is not an indication of the relative locational pull of fuel and power sites. The cement industry, for example, attests clearly to that fact.

The Cement Industry

Among all industries cement ranks high in the number of kilowatt hours of power consumed for every dollar of value of product. Moreover, its ranking is high for tons of bituminous coal, for barrels of fuel oil, and for cubic feet of natural gas consumed, all per dollar of value of product. In 1937, for instance, the cost of fuel and purchased energy for the industry was 18.73% of value of product, a very high figure comparatively.

Despite all this, access to fuel and power sources is only a secondary location factor for the cement industry in the United States. Access to market and raw materials is more important — at least in a country where the discrepancy among various regions in the availability of fuel and power is not pronounced.

Without question, savings would result from the concentration of cement plants at the best fuel and power sites. But both raw materials and final products are bulky and low in value and accordingly subject to relatively high transport charges. In consequence, savings in fuel and power would be less than the additional costs incurred in transporting raw materials and finished product to and from the superior but relatively distant fuel and power sites. Technical developments since the turn of the century have permitted the use of lower grade raw materials, which are fairly widespread in this country. Accordingly, the distribution of cement production has come to correspond in general with that of its chief market, the construction industry, which in turn is closely patterned to the distribution of population.

Consequently, there is little point in attempting to find to what levels the cost of atomic power must fall to make relocation of plant feasible in the cement industry. The reason is evident: even if atomic power reduces the cost differentials based on access to fuel and power, it will hardly affect the differentials in transport cost, which are likely to continue to be the chief single determinants of plant location.

A minor and somewhat speculative consequence is that if nuclear energy does reduce differentials in the costs of fuel and power, it may

[6] See, for example, National Resources Planning Board, *Industrial Location and National Resources* (Washington, Government Printing Office, 1943), Table 4, p. 161.

well serve to strengthen the tendency of the industry to orient its location according to transport factors such as the nearness and accessibility of markets. Take, for example, the implications of lower power costs through atomic energy for regions like New England where fuel and power costs are relatively high and the need for fuel economy has tended to bring about larger scale operation. It is conceivable that relatively lower power costs may tend to lessen the necessity for this larger scale operation and thus to bring forth a larger number of small plants, which will follow still more closely some of the present and anticipated trends of population distribution and thus accentuate the transport-orientation of the industry.

The manufacture of bricks and of ice are other industries whose locational pattern resembles that of cement. High transport costs, related especially to perishability in transit in the case of ice, tie these industries to their markets in even greater degree than cement. Location of such large power-consuming industries, therefore, is unlikely to be changed by whatever reduced cost differentials for fuel and power are brought about by any utilization of nuclear energy.

The Glass Industry

The glass industry differs sharply from the cases discussed above. For in the glass industry costs of fuel and purchased energy take up a considerably smaller percentage of product value than they do in the manufacture of cement. Such costs in 1937, according to National Resources Planning Board data, were only 6.9% of value of product.

Yet, historically, the glass industry has always shown a pronounced tendency to be oriented to fuel. Before the discovery of natural gas, glass plants were concentrated near sources of fuel around Pittsburgh and in other coal mining areas. Later these plants were drawn to sites where newly opened oil wells provided natural gas, a fuel of especial excellence for glassmaking. Moreover, as old wells were exhausted and new ones discovered, a sizable part of the industry moved from one gas site to another.

Thus today natural gas is largely used to supply the heat for melting the batch, and the glass industry is, to a great extent, oriented to cheap natural gas sites. Though sizable quantities of fuel are employed, utilization of cheap fuel near its point of origin keeps fuel costs moderate relative to total value of product. Clearly, this is a case in which the importance of fuel and purchased-energy costs in determining location cannot be understood from a table of percentage cost figures.

There is one further major consideration here. Because of breakage and costly packaging, transport expenses are high for the glass industry. In consequence, it is possible that, were it not for the very strong attraction of cheap fuel sites, plant location would be closer to markets. In fact, the present construction of natural-gas pipelines for long-distance transmission of the fuel seems likely to bring about a relocation of the industry near the markets. If this occurs soon, then, as the Cowles Commission study has pointed out,[7] atomic power may come on the scene too late to have any major locational impact upon an industry which in the main will have already moved to the market. This would be true even if rates for atomic power were low enough to justify the use of electric glass furnaces.

The Aluminum Industry

Aluminum is another major industry which even more than glass has been oriented to fuel and power. Again, because of the extremely cheap power it utilizes, power costs are not an adequate measure of the extent to which superior hydro-power sites have exerted a dominating pull on the industry.

The locational structure of the aluminum industry in the United States today is a product of conflicting forces. On the one hand, the considerable weight loss which occurs when alumina is extracted from bauxite ores has been a primary influence in locating alumina plants either at the source of domestic ores in Arkansas or at such ports as Mobile and Baton Rouge, which in terms of transport cost are close to foreign ore sources and which are supplied with cheap natural gas by pipeline. On the other hand, the tremendous quantities of electricity which are necessary to reduce alumina to aluminum ingots — from 18,000 to 22,000 kilowatts per ton of ingots — have drawn reduction plants to superior hydro-power sites.

Further to complicate the picture, a third pull is exerted by the market. The freight charges on one pound of aluminum ingot are considerably less than those on one pound of semifabricated aluminum. Moreover, because of the subsequent addition of alloys one pound of ingot yields more than one pound of fabricated product. In consequence, semifabrication and final fabrication plants are located at the market.

This split structure adds large transportation costs to the final cost of aluminum products. If atomic power were sufficiently cheap, its availability at the market or at strategic gateway points would theoretically make possible sizable savings in transportation and, perhaps, some economies resulting from integrated operation.

The possibility of such relocation based on atomic power has been carefully explored by Orah Cooper.[8] Her study is concerned with the possibility of an all-electric integrated operation near major markets rather than at present ore sources or points of ore importation. Since the latter

[7] Sam H. Schurr, *op. cit.*, pp. 471–472.
[8] "Aluminum As a Power-Conscious Industry," unpublished report to the Teaching Institute of Economics, the American University, Washington, 1949.

points are themselves distant from major markets, they would, as sites, entail unnecessary transport expense.

One possibility would be to import bauxite to a point near New York City. At this site the alumina could be extracted, reduced, and the aluminum fabricated for the important market in this general area. Using the best data available, Cooper concluded that to make such an operation feasible the maximum permissible cost for atomic power would be 4 mills per kilowatt hour. Similarly, an all-electric integrated works at Chicago would be economically sound only if the cost of atomic power did not exceed 3.5 mills per kilowatt hour. In contrast, the present costs of hydro power to reduction plants are only about 2 mills per kilowatt hour.

Atomic power costs not exceeding the ceilings indicated by Cooper, though doubtful even with subsidization, are conceivable. If such low costs should in fact be attained, a considerable relocation of aluminum operations in market areas might be expected. It seems more likely, however, that cheap atomic power would orient *new* aluminum capacity to market locations since the better alternative hydro-power sites will probably have been pre-empted by existing plants.

The Iron and Steel Industries

The basic iron and steel industry cannot be overlooked in our analysis.

Historically, the iron and steel industry has been subject to three major locational pulls: coal sites, ore sites, and markets. Before the middle of the last century, coal sites unquestionably exercised the dominant locational pull for iron and steel. That this is no longer true is largely a result of advances in technology which, among other things, have greatly diminished the amount of coal needed to produce a ton of pig iron or a ton of steel. The pull of ore sites likewise has weakened. Ordinarily, each ton of pig iron requires two to three tons of ore, a ratio which has shown no significant decline over the years. However, the increasing use of scrap as a substitute for pig iron has led directly to sharply reduced requirements of ore, as well as of coal, in steel production.

Today the market pull seems the strongest. This is true especially when the market is one which has been long established and which, consequently, generates sizable amounts of scrap. This factor is not so much greater, however, that it dominates the combined pulls of ore and coal sites. What is more, a given market can exert no decisive pull until it becomes large enough in size to absorb fairly completely the output of a fully integrated works. The failure to establish integrated operations on the Pacific Coast before the recent war was partly a function of the limited market. Not only does present increased capacity in this area reflect the fact of an expanding market; along with the relative decline of capacity in the Pittsburgh area, increased capacity in the Detroit area and along the Eastern Seaboard, and the talk of constructing a plant in

New England, it also emphasizes the expanding significance of markets as a locational factor in the iron and steel industry.

What effects might be expected from the introduction of low-cost atomic power? Probably it would encourage a continuing, and perhaps faster, growth of electric furnace operations based on the use of large amounts of local scrap. This should be true particularly in those areas which are distant in terms of transportation from major production points and which have sufficiently large amounts of scrap to suggest low-to-moderate scrap prices. Any such development would contribute to a more even geographical distribution of iron and steel production in the United States.

The possibility of using an electric smelting furnace, based on atomic power, as a substitute for the coal-burning blast furnace has been suggested. Any remarks that might be made about the locational implications of electric smelting, however, would be pure speculation at this time. The feasibility of the operation, at least for this country, has not been established. The most reliable figures available are from the efficient Tysland-Hole furnace in Norway, and careful analysis of such foreign operating data suggests that the use here of electric smelting furnaces based on atomic power would be feasible only if such power fell to the low figure of 4 mills per kilowatt hour while at the same time the price of coal rose to $22 a ton.

Similarly, the locational implications of the sponge iron process (iron reduced by hydrogen, which is produced by the electrolysis of water using atomic electricity)[9] depend upon too many suppositions to permit meaningful analysis at present.

It is possible, also, that cheap atomic electricity would lead to greater beneficiation of iron ores at the mine. This would reduce the quantity of ore transported for each ton of pig iron and would lower somewhat the amount of coal required for smelting operations. In this way the locational influence of ore and coal sites, as against the pull of markets, would be still further reduced.

But, by and large, aside from the possible consequences of greater development of electric furnaces utilizing scrap, no major locational changes in the iron and steel industry seem likely to result from the introduction of atomic power. Neither a geographic shift nor a splitting up of the present highly integrated structure of the industry is to be expected.

Conclusion

The industries we have briefly examined are representative of the group which have sizable fuel and power requirements. It is to be expected that

---

[9] Sam H. Schurr, *op. cit.*, pp. 473–474.

the advent of a new source of cheap power would be more likely to influence the location of industries in this group than those, such as the tobacco industry, whose use of power in terms of dollar value of product is relatively slight.

Careful examination of the cement, glass, aluminum, and iron and steel industries, for all of which power requirements are important, turns up little evidence that atomic power, even at prices competing with the better conventional sources, is likely to induce very much plant relocation. Nor does atomic power seem destined to induce industrial development in economically backward areas outside the United States. Rather, it appears more likely that present power differentials, which favor the heavily industrialized nations, will be strengthened. Obviously, therefore, we should not expect American plants to relocate in such countries as Brazil or India because of the introduction of cheap atomic power.

Further, it must be emphasized that such cheap atomic power is at present only conjecture. As the authors have stated elsewhere, with fuller documentation, "In the short run at least, all available evidence supports the belief that atomic power will cost more — and perhaps considerably more — than will power from existent energy sources."[10]

At any rate, the fact that utilizable power from nuclear fission is nowhere commercially available in the United States means that so far no records of operating experience are available for examination. This, when coupled with other uncertainties, such as developments which hinge on new processes and other technological advances, some of which are not now even conceived, makes it impossible to estimate the future cost of atomic power.

But we do know that unit costs for conventional types of fuel and power in this country are low, especially at or adjacent to the better sources. Furthermore, there is nothing to indicate that the historic cheapening of conventional power costs has reached an end. The costs of atomic energy, in other words, must fall to really low levels before this new power source can effect any changes of consequence in the distribution of industry, whether in this country or abroad. And unless government subsidization is extremely heavy in a given country, the chances are that cost levels will never become low enough to achieve that effect.

In short, not only is a general relocation of industry unlikely to follow the introduction of commercial atomic power at competitive prices, but the likelihood of the introduction of such power at costs which are as low as those of the better conventional fuel and power sources is itself a moot question.

[10] Walter Isard and Vincent Whitney, "Atomic Power and Economic Development," *Bulletin of the Atomic Scientists*, Vol. 5, No. 3 (March 1949), p. 78.

axes and Subsidies as Cost Factors

STUDIES OF STATE-LOCAL TAX INFLUENCES ON LOCATION OF INDUSTRY

JOHN F. DUE

FOR decades, one of the most contro- versial issues in the field of state-local inance has been that of the effects of ax differentials on location of economic ictivity, particularly of industry. No rgument has been so consistently and iniversally used against new state taxes r increases in rates, especially those af- ecting business, than the " drive indus- ry out " thesis. On the reverse side, tates frequently have used claims of ow taxes as a lure to business, and in the south many local governments have sought to lure industry by property tax concessions. Supporters of various tax measures argue that the taxes have no effects upon location whatsoever. Some studies were made many years ago to ascertain actual effects, but most of these early ones were not sufficiently so- phisticated in their techniques for the results to be of great significance. In the last decade, with growing state-local tax burdens and increased attention to economic development, there has been a great increase in attention to the prob- lem, with a number of studies under- taken, and published in a wide variety of sources, some not readily available. It is the primary purpose of this article to review the major studies and the vari- ous approaches taken, and to draw some conclusions from them.

Statistical Studies of Relative Tax Burdens and Growth Rates

One approach to the problem has been that of a statistical comparison of the relative rates of growth in various states and the relative tax burdens. There have been two studies of this type of major importance in recent years. An Iowa study by C. C. Bloom ascer- tained, by simple correlation, the rela- tions between growth in manufacturing employment and capital outlays of manufacturers with per capita state- local tax collections, and growth in such tax collections in the period 1939-1953 and 1947-53.[1] No significant correla- tions are found: there was a slight posi- tive one between growth in taxes and growth in manufacturing employment; that is, the higher-tax states enjoyed more rapid expansion of manufacturing. There was no isolation of other factors influencing manufacturing growth, and the taxes considered were not limited to those on manufacturers. Accordingly the significant conclusion of the study is a negative one: there was no demon- strable evidence that high tax levels had retarded the growth of the states in- volved.

A much more elaborate and signifi- cant study was that of W. R. Thompson

[1] C. C. Bloom, *State and Local Tax Differentials* (Iowa City: Bureau of Business Research, State Uni- versity of Iowa, 1955).

Reprinted from *National Tax Journal*, 14 (1961), 163–173, by permission of the author and editor.

and John M. Mattila.[2] Confining their study to taxes paid by business firms (which were compared on the basis of amount paid per employee) and employing modern econometric techniques, they concluded that for the period 1947-1954, there was no significant correlation of interstate tax differentials and employment growth in the 29 manufacturing industries concerned. However, even this study suffers from limitations, since it does not concentrate attention on the marginal zone—on the group of firms which have any significant choice in location. Differences in type of tax are ignored, and the tax burden used as a measure includes that on all business, not merely manufacturers. Finally, this study, as all of this type, can never provide answers to the question: would the rapidly growing states have grown still more rapidly had it not been for their higher tax burdens? Nevertheless, they do indicate that higher business tax burdens are not having any measurable effects in slowing down the rate of growth. Clearly the taxes are not producing the economic stagnation which the opponents of higher state taxes claim.

The Interview Approach

In an effort to pinpoint more precisely the effects of taxation on industrial location, interview and questionnaire enquiries have been made of the factors affecting location decisions. There have been two types: those enquiring about the general factors affecting location, and those specifically asking about tax influences. Naturally the results are quite different.

Representative of the former, and a survey obviously not conducted for the purpose of proving a preconceived conclusion, was that of *Business Week* in 1958. Enquiry of a number of business firms about factors influencing location brought some 747 references to location decisions, of which only 5 per cent referred to taxation, and some of these related only to property tax influence on selection of a site within a particular area.[3] An extensive field interview study by the Survey Research Center of the University of Michigan in 1950 of Michigan firms concluded that taxes were not significant in location decisions. Only 9 per cent of the firms interviewed (in terms of employment represented) mentioned taxes as an unfavorable location factor, although Michigan has received great notoriety as a high tax state.[4]

Of the interview studies which specifically mentioned taxes, one of the most recent was that undertaken in Massachusetts for the Federal Reserve Bank of Boston. This is another notoriously high tax state.[5] Of 196 manufacturing firms from which replies were obtained, 16 per cent indicated that local taxes had influenced location decisions, and 19 per cent indicated that state taxes had done so. And 25 per cent indicated that state taxes would influence future location decisions. A survey of firms moving out of New

[2] *An Econometric Model of Postwar State Industrial Development* (Detroit: Wayne State University Press, 1959).
A study by W. D. Ross showed that Louisiana tax concessions to industry had very meager results so far as location is concerned. See " Tax Concessions and Their Effect," *Proceedings of the National Tax Association* for 1957, pp. 216-24.

[3] " Plant Site Preferences of Industry and Factors of Selection," *Business Week Research Report*, 1958.

[4] See *Industrial Mobility in Michigan* (Ann Arbor: University of Michigan Press, 1950).

[5] See J. D. Strasma, *State and Local Taxation of Industry* (Boston: Federal Reserve Bank of Boston, 1959), p. 14.

York City was made for the years 1947-55 by the Regional Plan Association; some 14 per cent indicated taxation as the major reason.[6] Comparable results were found in Minnesota and Wisconsin studies. While these results are not to be disregarded, it must be kept in mind that they do not indicate the magnitude of the tax influence in location decision making. Likewise the anti-tax attitude of many business men conditions them to stress the tax factor, as does the belief that their answers may influence the conclusions of the survey and thus ultimately bring lower taxes.

Somewhat related to the interview results are public announcements from business firms about the effects of taxation, particularly when legislative bodies are considering higher levies affecting business. Firms will frequently announce the suspension of building plans pending legislative action. Such announcements must be recognized for what they almost always are: purely strategical moves designed to influence the outcome of the legislative action.

Analysis of the Role of State-Local Taxes in Costs

One of the most common approaches in recent years has been that of an analysis of the significance of tax costs in various areas, to ascertain the extent of tax difference among taxing jurisdictions and thus the potential role of taxes in location decisions. Most of these studies have been made as a part of general analyses of state tax systems. There are two approaches: the use of data of actual firms operating in more than one state, and data built up for typical hypothetical firms.

Of the multi-plant studies, one made in Pennsylvania showed a ratio of state and local taxes to net investment for interstate multi-plant firms ranging from 4.34 per cent in Wisconsin to .57 per cent in Delaware.[7] One of the most exhaustive studies of this character was that by D. B. Yntema[8] for 1956-57, showing relative tax costs of actual operations in Michigan and neighboring states. The study showed a range in ratio of state-local taxes in other states to Michigan taxes ranging from 33 in Illinois to 78 in Wisconsin.

Of the hypothetical studies, one of the most thorough was that by J. S. Floyd, who ascertained tax costs for firms in three industries in a variety of locations, as a part of a general study of the influences of location.[9] Fairly substantial differences were found; for hosiery mills, for example, the difference in state-local tax cost between highest and lowest cost locations was equal to 2 per cent of sales; for furniture factories, 3.40.

A more extensive study was that of the Pennsylvania Economy League, covering 237 localities in ten states, and a variety of firms with diverse ratios of inventories, fixed investment, and sales. The Federal Reserve Bank of Boston study by Strasma was similar, with two types of typical firms and seven industrial states. For the typical manufacturing firm, state taxes ranged from $4,105 in Illinois to $28,468 in Massachusetts. In contrast, local taxes were

6 See A. K. Campbell, " Taxes and Industrial Location in the New York Mertopolitan Region," *National Tax Journal*, Vol. XI (Sept. 1958), p. 198.

7 Commonwealth of Pennsylvania, Tax Study Committee: *The Tax Problem* (Philadelphia, 1953), p. 145.

8 *Michigan's Taxes on Business* (Holland, Mich.: Hope College, 1959), p. 2.

9 *Effects of Taxation on Industrial Location* (Chapel Hill: University of North Carolina Press, 1952), p. 68.

lowest in Burlington, Massachusetts, and highest in Chicago ($16,788 vs. $65,-862).[10]

A study by the Fantus Factory Locating Service of state-local tax burdens for a typical corporation in 11 midwestern cities showed a high state tax cost in Kentucky ($46,576) and a low in Illinois ($193); a local tax high in a Michigan city of $107,254 vs a low of $19,590 in a Kentucky city, and a combined high of $143,358 for a Michigan city and a low of $54,056 for an Ohio city.[11] The Campbell study of the New York metropolitan areas was of the same character as was a 1960 study by D. Soule at the University of Kentucky.[12]

These studies, in themselves, are of greater significance for particular states and particular business firms than they are for throwing light on the question of the effects of taxation on location. For the latter they are mainly of consequence for giving some idea of the extent of interstate and intrastate differences. The precise figures are of course open to serious question, a fact well recognized by those who have made the studies. The multi-plant studies, while using actual tax data, suffer from the problems of noncomparability of operations in various states, and inadequate samples, and yield results significant only for the particular industries. High tax firms are particularly willing to cooperate, and thus bias the sample. The hypothetical-firm studies permit the selection of more adequate and representative data, and can be adjusted more easily to reflect the situations of particular industries or to adapt to changing tax laws. There are, however, limitations. The typical figure may not be at all representative for many industries; and, particularly because of local property tax differences, tax burden may vary tremendously between locations within a state. Thus care must be employed in interpreting results. The most difficult problem, however, is that of estimating local property tax burdens, because of variations in assessment ratios, and the frequent bargaining element involved, particularly with new large firms.

Analysis of Tax Effects in Terms of Cost

Various studies of the role of taxation in location decisions, including those just referred to involving interstate comparisons, have analyzed the importance of state-local taxes in total business expenses. The results of several studies can be summarized briefly. A Michigan study showed state taxes to constitute about ½ of 1 per cent and local taxes about 1½ per cent of value added by manufacturers.[13] The Pennsylvania Economy League study noted above showed a state-local tax differential between the highest tax state and the lowest tax state equal to .3 per cent of sales.[14] The Campbell study of the New York metropolitan area showed an average ratio of state and local taxes to sales of 1.5 per cent (1954).[15] An extensive Minnesota study for 1953 showed a ratio of state and local tax cost to sales of .82 per cent for all manufacturing in

[10] Strasma, *Taxation of Industry, op. cit.*, Chap. VIII.

[11] W. Haber, *et al.*, *The Michigan Economy* (Kalamazoo: The W. E. Upjohn Institute for Employment Research, 1959), pp. 341-54.

[12] A. K. Campbell, "Taxation and Industrial Location," *op. cit.* D. Soule, *Comparative Total Tax Loads of Selected Manufacturers*, University of Kentucky (Lexington: 1960).

[13] *Michigan Tax Study: Staff Papers* (Lansing: 1958), pp. 86-87.

[14] See Haber, *Michigan Economy, op. cit.*, p. 314.

[15] Campbell, "Taxes and Industrial Location," *op. cit.*, p. 209.

Minnesota.[16]

The fact that state-local, and particularly state, taxes represent such a small percentage of total costs does not in itself prove that taxes have no significant effect on location. As many writers have pointed out, a small percentage difference in cost can have substantial dollars-and-cents effect upon profit if the taxes cannot be shifted. However, two points must be noted. First, some shifting is frequently possible; secondly, the major cost items such as wages are so much greater in total magnitude that very small differentials will have tremendously greater influence on relative costs in different locations than great percentage differences in taxation.

The significance of the tax cost element is reduced still further by the deductibility of all state business taxes in calculating federal income tax liability. The net result, for the typical large corporation most likely to be influenced by taxation for location, is to reduce the net cost of state-local taxes roughly in half, since the marginal federal rate is 52 per cent.

Finally, business firms making a careful enquiry into location will consider governmental services as well as taxes. When low taxes mean poor services, as they often do, the firm will find it necessary to supply the services—such as sewage disposal, police and fire protection, streets—itself. And low-tax poor-service areas may be very unattractive to employees. The importance of considering the services rendered has been noted in various guides to location;[17] and is a factor considered by the factory

locating services. It is, however, somewhat difficult to measure in any completely objective way.

Conclusions of Various Studies

Numerous students of the problem of taxation and location have for the most part reached much the same conclusion. A few quotations are typical:

Greenhut—" From these studies, it would seem that tax incentives are at best a relatively unimportant secondary factor of location." [18]

Campbell: " In most studies based on the interview technique, industrialists tend to agree that taxes are a secondary consideration in location choice, and the actual cost of taxes as revealed here would tend to indicate the correctness of this view." [19]

University of Wisconsin State Tax Study Committee: " The contention that economic growth in Wisconsin or elsewhere has been considerably affected by tax differentials has not been established by credible evidence. Neither has it been disproved, though the general failure to establish correlation between economic development and tax differentials is indicative that at present levels of differentiation effects on economic growth cannot be very serious." [20]

Floyd's conclusions are somewhat less categorical: " As has been pointed out, the investigations analyzed, whether based on interviews, questionnaires or correlation analysis, have failed to demonstrate conclusively that tax cost differentials do or do not affect the selec-

16 *Report of the Governor's Minnesota Tax Study Committee* (St. Paul: 1956), p. 121.

17 See Dun's Review, Special Report to Management, *Industry's Plant*, March 1960.

18 M. L. Greenhut, *Plant Location in Theory and Practise* (Chapel Hill: Univ. of North Carolina Press, 1955), p. 139.

19 " Taxes and Industrial Location," *op. cit.*, p. 209.

20 *Wisconsin's State and Local Tax Burden* (Madison: 1959), p. 35.

tion of all types of plant sites. The theoretical analysis undertaken in the present study, however, leads to the conclusion that under certain conditions tax considerations may influence the selection of location for some, but by no means all, types of industrial plants." [21] It should be pointed out that the two most significant correlation analyses have been made since Floyd's book was written.

Perhaps the most significant statements of experts are to be found in the paper by Maurice Fulton in the volume, *Taxes and Economic Growth in Michigan*.[22] Fulton, an official of the Fantus Factory Locating Service, has had perhaps as much contact with actual location decision making as anyone in the United States. While he recognizes that taxes may have some influence, particularly along the " image " lines noted in the next section, he concludes: " The writer is keenly aware of the fact that state taxes are not as important in the location process as many other measures. Very few, if any location decisions are based solely on tax reasons.—p. 71. . . . a universal principle seems to apply, viz., tax costs, primarily state tax costs, are rarely, if ever, the principal factor in plant location. . . . p. 72.

Taxation and the General Business Climate of a State

In the last few years increased recognition has been given to the role which state taxation may have on the general business climate or reputation of a state, or, in other words, the state image in the eyes of the national business community. Without question certain states have

21 *Effects of Taxation, op. cit.,* p. 109.

22 P. W. McCracken, ed. (Kalamazoo: The Upjohn Institute for Employment Research, 1960), pp. 69-84.

built up an unfavorable image; Massachusetts, Pennsylvania, Michigan, Wisconsin, and to some extent Minnesota are prime examples, among the major industrial states, although Pennsylvania has worked hard in recent years to improve its position. These reputations are the product of a variety of forces: extent of unionization and state policy toward unions and management; unemployment and workmen's compensation legislation; financial responsibility of the state; magnitude of state debt; and tax levels and structures. Normally taxation alone is not responsible; at best it is only one factor. But clearly it does play a part, and some students of location decision-making argue that it has come to be regarded as a major index of general business climate.

There are several elements in the tax influence. One is the magnitude of taxation, particularly as affecting business; this depends in part upon the overall level of state-local expenditures, in part upon the division of tax burdens between business and individuals. Another is the type of tax; many business men have developed a particular dislike of the corporation franchise tax based on income; proposals for this type of tax have, in some states, such as Michigan and Illinois, become a prime center of legislative battles between " conservative " and " liberal " groups. In other states which have had such taxes for many years, they are accepted without question—so long as the rates are not out of line. By contrast business groups with, exceptions—mainly the retail organizations—are inclined to favor sales taxes and to regard reliance on them as reflecting a pro-business attitude. Another is the precise structure of the tax; there is reasonable resentment against interstate allocation formulas which result in multiple taxation.

The significance of this business climate factor for location is hard to assess. But clearly it plays some role. As stated by Fulton, " Many firms categorically reject Michigan from preliminary consideration because of an unsatisfactory image, one strengthened by the realization that taxes on business are higher than those across the state line." [23] Factory locating services report that some of their clients instruct them not even to consider certain states in looking for sites. As a result in some instances the firms undoubtedly rule out lowest cost locations because of this. In large measure this attitude reflects prejudice based on very little factual evidence, and in part upon the fear of uncomplimentary remarks from officials of other business firms, to the effect that " Are you out of your mind, man, to locate in that state? ". The notion that other firms are studiously avoiding a state—even if in fact they are not—encourages particular business men to reject consideration of it.

Along these lines Strasma, in the Federal Reserve Bank of Boston study, concludes that the tax climate factor plays a primary role in the second of the three stages of the location selection process, that of selecting the particular state in a general region, rather than at the first (selection of the region) or the third (selection of the precise site).[24] A bad reputation of a state or a certain metropolitan area will simply cause business men to disregard possible sites in the area without any review of relative costs.

[23] *Taxes and Economic Growth in Michigan, op. cit.*, p. 72.

[24] *State and Local Taxation, op. cit.*, Chap. II.

The role which taxation plays in the general business climate is in part obviously a function not of actual tax differences, as noted, but a somewhat irrational reaction on the part of business groups. Largely because of high Federal taxes, the average business man is inclined to have a strong anti-tax emotional bias, and to be quick to emphasize tax elements relative to others. Secondly, when legislatures are considering tax changes, business associations typically bring forth wildly exaggerated propaganda about the effects of taxation on location, which many business men come to believe. When a bitter fight develops in a legislature over tax changes, and the " liberals " win, this is inevitably taken as anti-business action and a factor lessening the business climate. When tax changes are pending, strategy moves become significant, as noted in an earlier section. Or, if a business firm finds it desirable to relocate, it may announce that the action is taken for tax reasons, in the hope of discouraging further tax increases. All of these actions tend to stir up the anti-tax attitude.

The significance of the tax climate image in actual location decisions is difficult to assess. Factory location experts regard it as one of considerable importance, and point to specific examples such as the selection by a number of firms of sites on the Illinois rather than the Wisconsin side of the border for tax-climate reasons alone. As Fulton concludes in the paper cited above with respect to Michigan, " Certainly a shift in Michigan's tax impact away from business cannot prove anything but salutary; it should do much to improve the state's " business climate ", the morale of its businessmen, and should increase the possibilities for industrial and economic development and growth ".[25]   And yet it is obviously easy to exaggerate the influence of this force.   Some evidence that the tax reputation of a state and the use of corporate income taxes can not have dire results was given by the empirical studies noted above, and is shown by the following table, which in-

the ones with bad tax reputations, had the most rapid growth, and Illinois and Ohio, the two lowest tax states, had the lowest rates. All of the southern states except Florida have corporate income taxes, and yet all showed higher than typical rates of industrial growth in this period.   High-corporate-tax Colorado

TABLE I

INDEX OF CHANGE IN VALUE ADDED BY MANUFACTURE, BY STATE, 1954–58

(U. S. Average 100)

Percentages Indicate 1958 State Corporate Income Tax Rates

High Business Tax States	Index	Low Tax States (No Corporate Income Taxes)	Index
Industrial-Belt States			
Pennsylvania (6%)	97		
Michigan *	83	Ohio	92
Wisconsin (2–7%)	99	Illinois	93
Iowa (2%)	107	Indiana	96
Minnesota (7.3%)	104		
Kentucky (5%)	119		
Southern States			
Maryland (5%)	108		
Virginia (5%)	108		
North Carolina (6%)	116		
South Carolina (5%)	111		
Georgia (4%)	110		
Alabama (3%)	110		
Mississippi (2–6%)	113		
Tennessee (3.75%)	108		
Louisiana (4%)	100		
Arkansas (1–5%)	106		

* Value added and capital stock franchise taxes.
Source: U. S. Department of Commerce, *Area Development Bulletin*, Feb.–March 1960.

dicates, for various states, the index of changes in value-added in manufacturing for the period 1954-58, expressed in terms of a U. S. average of 100.   In the central industrial belt extending westward from Pennsylvania to Minnesota and Iowa, with the exception of Michigan (suffering in this period from decline in defense spending for wheeled vehicles and decentralization of the automobile industry) the high tax states,

25 *Taxes and Economic Growth in Michigan*, op. cit., p. 75.

(index 135), New Mexico (144), Arizona (185), California (118) and Idaho (113), also showed high figures, whereas noncorporate income tax and generally low tax Nevada (90) and Wyoming (93) were among the lowest in the country.   Obviously many other influences were at work, and comparison between regions or even between the widely diverse states of the far west are not very significant.   But clearly the figures indicate that relatively low tax rates in themselves cannot protect a state rom declining relative growth when ther factors are unfavorable, whereas high tax rates and bad reputations tax-wise appear not to have very significant ffects in the opposite direction.

Some Conclusions

Out of this review come three general conclusions:

1. On the basis of all available studies, it is obvious that relatively high business tax levels do not have the disastrous effects often claimed for them. While the statistical analysis and study of location factors are by no means conclusive, they suggest very strongly that the tax effects cannot be of major importance.

2. However, without doubt, in some instances the tax element plays the deciding role in determining the optimum location, since other factors balance. This is most likely to be the case in the selection of the precise site in a metropolitan area (property taxes being the ones of chief concern), or when a suitable area for site location straddles a state border. But state and local taxes represent such a small percentage of total costs that the cases in which they are controlling cannot be very significant.

3. The tax climate factor, as one element in the general business reputation or climate of the state, without doubt influences some location decision making, by causing firms to exclude certain states or urban areas from consideration. Again, these cases are probably not a significant portion of the total.

Gresham's Law of Location

To the extent that firms are influenced by tax factors, a species of Gresham's Law operates: these firms will tend to gravitate to the low tax cost areas. If these low taxes arise from actual econo-

mies in the provision of public services, the tax factor reflects a real economic factor and its influence does not distort location from the sites which are most economic. But if this is not the case, tax influences do exercise an undesirable influence, by leading firms to locate in places other than those which involve maximum efficiency in the use of resources. If, for example, the taxes reflect a high level of community services, which the business firm does not take into consideration, or regards as unimportant, or from a community decision that equity requires placing a higher portion of the over-all tax burden on business, the location influence of the taxes does distort the location pattern from the optimum.

More serious is the effect on the development of tax structures of the belief of state legislative bodies about the influence of taxation on location. The endless propaganda on the subject and the strategy-inspired announcements of business firms when tax changes are being considered lead many legislators to exaggerate the influence of the taxes beyond any effect which they may have. The result is a potential danger of state cutthroat competition, and more seriously in fact, a major obstacle to reform of tax structures. In terror of " driving business out," legislatures become unwilling to adjust taxes to levels necessary to meet the desires of the community for services, and to bring the tax structures in line with popularly accepted ideas of equity in taxation. States which have made the adjustments seldom retreat from the changes, and find that losses in business activity are not great enough to be noticeable. But efforts of other states to improve their tax structures are seriously impeded. Not infrequently two adjacent states are both in urgent need of tax reform but in each the main obstacle is the fear that industries will be lost to the other. Illinois and Indiana provide a good illustration.[26]

Locational Influences, Tax Reform, and Business Associations

There is no simple solution to the problem of this obstacle to tax reform, as with most questions of public finance. Obviously increased centralization of tax collection at the federal level, with greater use of grants, shared revenues, etc., would lessen the problem, but is regarded as objectionable by many persons in the interests of preserving state autonomy and other factors. Outright state agreements on tax structures and levels, as outlined by Floyd,[27] are very difficult to attain in a governmental system characterized by separation of powers and constitutional restrictions on taxation. For each state to adjust its taxes downward on any industry where locational decisions are being influenced would tend to reduce all taxes on business to the least common denominator, contrary to popular views about equity in taxation.

One important step toward a solution is a detailed exploration of the locational effects of taxation by state tax agencies and study commissions and various unbiased research organizations, such as university Bureaus of Business Research, in an effort to ascertain the actual effect of taxation on location decisions. This work will not only suggest some modifications where a particular tax system provides unusually severe burden on a certain industry, but is almost certain to explode the widely used arguments about the disastrous effects of taxes on location. Brazer has suggested, very appropriately, that further work in this field must stress motivational research, studying actual decision making influences in various types of industries.[28]

A further very helpful influence would be that of a careful reconsideration by major business associations, such as state chambers of commerce, manufacturers associations, and the like, of the whole question of state-local taxation. These organizations have tended to take rigid unyielding positions against use of any state corporation income tax in many states, or any increases in taxes affecting business, regardless of the circumstances. In Illinois, for example, most business groups fight any change in the corporate franchise tax, even though at present it is merely nominal, and the general Illinois tax picture is such that a very substantial increase in business taxation would be possible without elimination of the state's relatively advantageous tax situation and favorable business climate.

Such positions have several undesirable effects in terms of the groups directly involved. By blocking any increases, they may bring about recurrent financial crises, such as those of Michigan, which can do more to harm the business reputation of a state than higher tax levels. There is always the danger of an impasse, "liberal" groups resisting fur-

---

[26] The 1952 Indiana Tax Study Commission was so obsessed with this fear of Ohio and Illinois that it concluded its recommendations with emphasis on the following statement: "It is of the utmost importance to maintain Indiana's tax position as compared to competing industrial states, and any adjustments in rate or structure must give this position first consideration." (*Report*, p. 9.) The 1959 Indiana commission on state tax and finance policy took the same position.

[27] *Effects of Taxation, op. cit.*, Chap. VII.

[28] H. E. Brazer, "Taxation and Industrial Location in Michigan," in Haber, *Michigan Economy, op. cit.*, pp. 305-27.

ther sales tax increases until there is an adjustment in other levies. Also, resistance to the adjustments in state tax structures often leads to increased demand for aid for various functions from the federal government, even though the function can be most efficiently operated and financed primarily at the state level. Experience in the highway field gives strong evidence of the consequences when states, blocked by various lobbies from increasing taxes, fail to provide a level of services which a large portion of the community seeks. And, of course, the longer that the organizations fight reasonable reform legislation instead of cooperating in a sensible program the greater become the pressures for a revolution in the tax system, with possible strong punitive anti-business tax legislation, with harm to all concerned.

The question of the appropriate position of business associations on taxation is one not easily answered. Clearly, they have an obligation to their members to fight detrimental legislation; this is one of their primary functions. But presumably, as representatives of the business community of a state, they also have an obligation to assume some responsibility to the community as a whole, in working toward improved governmental operations, provision of levels of services which reflect community wishes, and a generally acceptable tax system. Rigid opposition to any tax reform which might increase the tax load of business, vigorous use of misleading and often deliberately fact-distorting propaganda and strong lobbying pressure can in the end not only interfere with the development of the state or community, but also build up substantial ill will which destroys the good business climate. Such organizations may ultimately lose all influence on legislation, as has happened with various associations of this type at the federal level. These organizations appear at times to suffer from a malady which also afflicts labor unions, farm groups and others, one which may be called organizationitis: determined to appear as vigorous fighters for the interests of their members, they end up with positions far more extreme than the consensus of thinking on the part of their members as a whole, and hold rigidly to these positions so as to avoid appearing to " appease their enemies "—despite the fact that failure to be realistic and reasonable may in the end prove disastrous to all concerned.

STATE AND LOCAL INDUCEMENTS
FOR INDUSTRY *

PART I

BENJAMIN BRIDGES, JR.

I N THE postwar years there has been rapid expansion in state and local efforts to promote economic growth by giving financial inducements to industry. These inducements usually take the form of low-interest loans or tax concessions. Some of the inducement programs are publicly financed, while others are privately financed.

In view of this rapid expansion, it is becoming increasingly important for researchers to examine these inducement programs. This paper examines the five

* This paper is based upon a study done by the author for the Wisconsin Department of Resource Development (B. Bridges, Jr., *State and Local Industrial Development Incentives: Wisconsin, Its Neighbor States, and the Nation,* Wisconsin Department of Resource Development, Madison, Wisconsin, 1965). The author would like to thank Professor Harold Groves and Mr. Gerald Sazama of the University of Wisconsin who served as consultant and research assistant respectively for this study; he would also like to thank Professor Robert Lampman of the University of Wisconsin for his comments on an earlier draft of this paper.

major types of inducement programs. Three of these, state industrial finance authorities, local industrial bond financing, and tax concessions, are publicly financed. The other two, statewide development credit corporations and local development corporations, are privately financed. In an effort to shed new light concerning these programs, considerable use is made of unpublished data and of relatively inaccessible publications. Part I of the paper provides a description of the programs and discusses their use and scope in the various states and regions of the nation. In Part II an attempt is made to determine and evaluate the economic effects of such programs.

I. NATURE AND USE OF INDUCE-
MENT PROGRAMS

A. STATE INDUSTRIAL FINANCE
AUTHORITIES [1]

[1] In this section heavy reliance is placed on (1) unpublished data from Edwin C. Gooding of the Federal Reserve Bank of Boston, and (2) published and unpublished reports of various state industrial finance authorities.

Reprinted from *National Tax Journal,* 18 (1965), 1–14, 175–192, by permission of the author and editor.

The state industrial finance authority is a creation of the postwar years. Since New Hampshire authorized the first such authority in 1955, the use of this inducement technique has expanded rapidly. By the end of 1959 five states had authorized such programs and four of these were active. By September, 1963, the number of authorized programs and of active programs had increased to nineteen and fifteen, respectively (Table I).

There are two distinct types of state authorities. One guarantees industrial loans made by private lenders, while the other makes direct loans of state funds to industry.

1. State Loan Guarantee Programs

In 1955 New Hampshire authorized the first state loan guarantee program. By the end of 1959 four states had authorized such programs, and two of these (Maine and Rhode Island) were active. By September, 1963, the numbers of authorized programs and of active programs had increased to seven and six, respectively. Maine and Rhode Island account for about 90 per cent of the dollar volume of loans guaranteed under such programs (Table II).

State loan guarantee authorities typically guarantee the repayment of first mortgage industrial loans made by private lenders.[2] To back these loans, states pledge their full faith and credit and usually provide reserve funds for claims in the case of defaults. Rhode Island pledged up to $30 million and provided an initial reserve fund of $100,000, Maine pledged up to $20 million and provided a reserve of $500,000.

[2] In a similar way the Federal Housing Authority guarantees the repayment of first mortgage housing loans made by private lenders.

Most guaranteed loans go to manufacturing firms. Ninety-three per cent of the number of loans and 60 per cent of the dollar volume of loans go to plants with under 500 employees; five-sixths of the number of loans and one-half of the dollar volume go to plants with under 200 employees. Three-fourths of the number of loans go to firms already established in the state; most of the rest go to firms relocating from outside the state.

Guaranteed loans have maturities of up to 20 to 25 years, and go mostly to finance construction of plants and purchases of land. The authorities insure loans ranging up to 90 per cent of the land and building costs; privately-financed local development corporations often provide loans to finance the remaining 10 per cent of project cost.[3] In several states such local participation is required. In Rhode Island the privately financed state development credit corporation often provides loans for the remaining 10 per cent of project cost.[4] The average state loan guarantee is $500,000; the loan guarantees of Rhode Island and Maine average $770,000 and $300,000, respectively. Loan guarantees are not restricted to areas of substantial unemployment or underemployment.

Loan guarantee authorities charge an insurance fee of ¾ to 1 per cent on outstanding balances, and private lenders charge interest rates of 5 to 6 per cent. When the insurance fee is added to the basic interest rate, the total cost to the borrower for these high-risk loans is 6 to 6¾ per cent. For the small and medium-sized firms which receive

[3] See below, section E, for a discussion of local development corporations.

[4] See below, section D, for a discussion of statewide development credit corporations.

TABLE I

STATE AND LOCAL INDUSTRIAL DEVELOPMENT INCENTIVES
AS OF SEPTEMBER 30, 1963 [a]

State	(1) State Industrial Finance Authority	(2) Local Industrial Bond Financing [b]	(3) Tax Concessions [c]	(4) Statewide Development Credit Corporation	(5) Local Development Corporations [c] (number)
New England					
Maine	yes (A)	yes (N)	no	yes (A)	67
New Hampshire	yes (A) [d]	no	no	yes (A)	45
Vermont	yes (A)	yes (N)	yes	yes (A)	33
Massachusetts	no	no	no	yes (A)	30
Rhode Island	yes (A)	no	yes	yes (A)	10
Connecticut	yes (A)	no	no	yes (A)	32
Middle Atlantic					
New York	yes (A)	no	no	yes (A)	82
New Jersey	yes (N)	no	no	yes (A)	36
Pennsylvania	yes (A) [d]	no	no	no	205
East North Central					
Ohio	no	yes (N)	no	yes (N)	125
Indiana	no	no	no	yes (N)	59
Illinois	no	yes (N)	no	no	52
Michigan	no	yes (N)	no	yes (N)	149
Wisconsin	no	yes (N)	no	yes (A)	196
West North Central					
Minnesota	yes (A)	yes (N)	no	yes (N)	219
Iowa ....,	no	yes (N)	no	yes (N)	131
Missouri	no	yes (N)	no	yes (A)	168
North Dakota	yes (N)	yes (A)	no	no	28
South Dakota	no	no	no	yes (A)	15
Nebraska	no	yes (A)	yes	no	47
Kansas	no	yes (A)	no	yes (N)	96
South Atlantic					
Delaware	yes (A)	no	no	no	2
Maryland	yes (A)	yes (N)	yes	yes (A)	22
Virginia	no	no	no	yes (A)	84
West Virginia	yes (A)	yes (N)	no	yes (N)	65
North Carolina	no	no	no	yes (A)	152
South Carolina	no	no	yes	yes (A)	13
Georgia	yes (N)	yes (A)	no	no	139
Florida	no	no	no	yes (A)	46
East South Central					
Kentucky	yes (A)	yes (A)	yes	yes (A)	68
Tennessee	no	yes (A)	yes	yes (N)	111
Alabama	no	yes (A)	yes	no	19
Mississippi	no	yes (A)	yes	yes (A)	18
West South Central					
Arkansas	no	yes (A)	yes	yes (A)	141
Louisiana	no	yes (A)	yes	no	49
Oklahoma	yes (A)	yes (A)	yes	no	74
Texas	no	no	no	no	107
Mountain					
Montana	no	no	yes	no	10
Idaho	no	no	no	yes (N)	14
Wyoming	yes (N)	no	no	no	3
Colorado	no	yes (N)	no	no	28
New Mexico	no	yes (A)	no	no	12
Arizona	no	no	no	no	15
Utah	no	no	no	no	14
Nevada	no	no	no	no	4

TABLE I (*Continued*)

STATE AND LOCAL INDUSTRIAL DEVELOPMENT INCENTIVES
AS OF SEPTEMBER 30, 1963 [a]

State	(1) State Industrial Finance Authority	(2) Local Industrial Bond Financing [b]	(3) Tax Con- cessions [c]	(4) Statewide Development Credit Corporation	(5) Local Development Corporations [c] (number)
Pacific					
Alaska	yes (A)	no	yes	no	0
Washington	no	yes (A)	no	yes (N)	14
Oregon	no	no	no	yes (N)	55
California	no	no	no	no	38
Hawaii	yes (A) [d]	no	yes	yes (N)	7
TOTAL .... {	15 yes (A) 4 yes (N) 31 no	14 yes (A) 11 yes (N) 25 no	15 yes [c] 35 no	18 yes (A) 13 yes (N) 19 no	3,149 [c]

A : active.
N: not active.
[a] Column (5) is as of November 1, 1963.
[b] "Yes" is listed no matter how limited or extensive the statutory authority is; "yes" means that bonds may be issued to finance one, several, or all of the following: sites, buildings, machinery, and equipment, other business costs.
[c] Some are active and some are not active.
[d] Have 2 different programs (see below, Tables II and III).
Sources: Columns (1), (2), (3), and (4): Edwin C. Gooding, "New War Between the States: Part I," *New England Business Review*, October 1963, Federal Reserve Bank of Boston; and unpublished data from Edwin C. Gooding, Federal Reserve Bank of Boston. The findings of Gooding's survey of state and local industrial development incentive programs differ slightly from those of several other recent surveys. Column (5): Unpublished data from Joseph L. McAuliff, Area Redevelopment Administration, U. S. Department of Commerce, Washington, D. C.

these loans, comparable loans are either not available from commercial lenders, or if available, only at higher rates. The well-established authorities of Maine and Rhode Island are now operating profitably. Both of these authorities experienced net losses (operating expenses in excess of gross income) in the first three years of operation and net profits in all subsequent years. No losses on loans have been sustained so far by the six active corporations.

TABLE II

STATE LOAN GUARANTEE PROGRAMS

State	(1) Date Activated	(2) Loans Guaranteed Through Sept., 30, 1963 Number	(3) Amount (million $)
Connecticut	Aug., 1963	5	$ 2.5
Delaware	Feb., 1962	2	2.7
Maine	Jan., 1958	29	8.7
New Hampshire	July, 1962	1	0.2
Vermont	Aug., 1961	1	0.1
Rhode Island	Jan., 1959	22	17.0
Pennsylvania	N	..	...
Total		60	$31.2

N: not active.
Source: Delaware: Letter from Delaware Industrial Building Commission. Other states: Unpublished data from Edwin C. Gooding, Federal Reserve Bank of Boston.

By the end of September, 1963, these authorities had guaranteed $31 million of loans. Current legislation authorizes a maximum of $110 million of outstanding loan guarantees.

2. State Direct Loan Programs

In 1955 New Hampshire authorized the first state direct loan program. By the end of 1959 three states had authorized such programs and two of these (New Hampshire and Pennsylvania) were active. By September, 1963, the numbers of authorized programs and of active programs had increased to fourteen and ten, respectively (Table I).

There are two distinct types of state direct loan authorities. One is restricted to lending jointly with the federal government's Area Redevelopment Administration, while the other is not so restricted.

a. *State Loans Limited to ARA Projects.* Four state authorities are restricted to lending jointly with the federal ARA for projects located in depressed areas, and two of these (Maryland and Minnesota) are active (Table III). Funds come from state appropriations or borrowing from the state treasury. As of September 30, 1963, Maryland had made one loan for $51,000 and Minnesota had made nine loans for $132,000. All 10 loans have gone to plants with under 500 employees; and nine have gone to plants with under 200 employees. These loans go to finance construction of plants, purchases of machinery and equipment, and purchase of land. State funds typically finance 5 to 20 per cent of the cost of an industrial project; the federal ARA provides a maximum of 65 per cent and local development corporations 5 to 10

TABLE III
STATE DIRECT LOAN PROGRAMS

State	(1) Date Activated	(2) Loans Made Through Sept. 30, 1963 Number	(3) Amount (million $)
	Loans limited to ARA Projects		
Maryland	June, 1962	1	$ 0.1
Minnesota	July, 1961	9	0.1
New Jersey	N	...	...
Wyoming	N	...	...
	Loans not limited to ARA Projects		
Alaska	June, 1963	2	0.1
Georgia	N	...	...
Hawaii [a]	N	...	...
Hawaii [b,c]	July, 1961	2	0.1
Kentucky	July, 1960	12	1.8
New Hampshire	Nov., 1955	8	3.8
New York [c]	Jan., 1962	40	4.6
Oklahoma	July, 1960	9	1.2
Pennsylvania [c]	May, 1956	322	43.4
West Virginia [c]	Feb., 1962	9	0.8
Total		416	$56.0

N: not active.
[a] Hawaii Capital Loan Program.
[b] Hawaii Economic Redevelopment for Depressed Areas.
[c] Restricted to labor surplus areas as defined by the state.
Source: Unpublished data from Edwin C. Gooding, Federal Reserve Bank of Boston.

er cent. Minnesota and Maryland charge only 3 and 4 per cent, respectively, for these state loans. No losses n loans have been sustained so far.

b. *State Loans Not Limited to ARA Projects.* Ten state authorities are not estricted to lending jointly with the ederal ARA, and eight of these are ctive (Table III). Pennsylvania, New Hampshire, Oklahoma, and Kentucky ccount for most of the years of experience to date. Pennsylvania alone accounts for about four-fifths of the dollar volume of loans made under such programs.

Six of these authorities are permitted o make direct industrial loans in all reas of the state. The loans of the other four authorities are restricted to abor surplus areas as defined by the tate.

The funds of state authorities come from state appropriations and/or sales of *tax-exempt* bonds by the authority. The state appropriation may, in effect, also be financed by the sale of tax-exempt bonds. The Pennsylvania authority is financed by state appropriations, while the authority of New York is financed by bond sales.

Most direct loans go to manufacturing firms. Ninety-seven per cent of the number of loans and 90 per cent of the dollar volume of loans go to plants with under 500 employees; four-fifths of the number of loans and three-fifths of the dollar volume go to plants with under 200 employees. Half of the loans goes to firms already established in the state; another third goes to entirely new firms; and the remaining fifth goes to firms relocating from outside the state.

Most direct loans have maturities of 10 to 20 years. These loans go mostly to finance construction of plants and purchases of land, but some funds finance purchases of machinery and equipment. State funds typically finance 25 to 50 per cent of the cost of an industrial project; typically local development corporations provide 5 to 25 per cent and conventional lenders 50 to 60 per cent. The average state loan is $140,000. The average Pennsylvania loan is $130,000; the loans of New Hampshire, Oklahoma, and Kentucky average $470,000, $140,000, and $150,000, respectively.

The Pennsylvania and New York authorities charge about 2½ and 3 per cent, respectively, for these loans, while most other authorities charge 4 to 5 per cent. At present most corporate bonds which are traded nationally bear interest rates of 4¼ to 4¾ per cent. Thus when state authority and local development corporation loans bear interest rates of only 2 to 3 per cent, even very large firms which have easy access to the national security market would find it cheaper to borrow from these development agencies. However, most state direct loans go to small and medium-sized firms. For state direct loans the ratio of losses sustained on loans to loans made is only .05 per cent.

By the end of September, 1963, these authorities had made loans of $56 million.

B. LOCAL INDUSTRIAL BOND FINANCING

In 1936 Mississippi became the first state to authorize local industrial bonds, but no other state authorized such bonds until 1948. Since 1948 the use of this inducement technique has also expanded rapidly. By the end of 1959 thirteen states had authorized such bonds, and bonds were issued in ten states. By September, 1963, the number of states authorizing bonds had increased to twenty-five, and the number of states in which localities issued bonds increased to fourteen (Table I). Five southern states (Alabama, Arkansas, Kentucky, Mississippi, and Tennessee) account for most of the experience to date.

Local governments are authorized to issue bonds to finance the construction of industrial facilities for lease to private firms. State government approval of individual local bond issues is not required in most states. The aided firms pay rentals just sufficient to cover the principal and interest of the bonds and the maintenance of the facilities. The interest income from these local bonds is exempt from federal income taxation. *In addition these industrial facilities are generally exempt from state and local property taxation as long as these facilities continue to be publicly owned.*

There are two types of local industrial bonds, general obligation bonds and revenue bonds. General obligation bonds are secured by the taxing power of the issuing government; revenue bonds are secured only by the property acquired with the proceeds of the bond sale and the income the property produces under the terms of the lease contract. One state authorizes only general obligation bonds; fifteen states authorize only revenue bonds; and nine states authorize both general obligation and revenue bonds. In most states industrial bond financing is not restricted to labor surplus areas.

General obligation bonds are primarily used to finance small manufacturing firms locating in rural areas with surplus farm labor. These bonds have maturities up to 25 to 40 years and finance up to 100 per cent of plant cost. During the period 1960-1963 the mean general obligation bond issue reported by the Investment Bankers Association (IBA) was $450,000; the median issue

was $300,000. The interest rate depends mainly upon the credit rating of the issuing local government. Exemption of interest on these bonds lowers the interest rate by perhaps 1 to 1½ per cent. At present the rates of Aaa and Baa general obligation bonds are approximately 3.2 per cent and 3.6 per cent respectively. Thus even without the usual property tax exemptions very large firms would find these to be a very cheap source of credit. However, most general obligation bonds have financed small or medium sized firms. Cases of long-term default on these bonds have been rare.

Before 1961 tax-exempt revenue bonds were also primarily used to finance small manufacturing firms locating in rural areas. Recently, however, revenue bonds have financed a number of large industrial projects for very large firms; recently financed plants include those of Harvey Aluminum ($50 million), Armour ($25 million), U. S. Rubber ($21 million), and Olin Mathieson ($17 million). During the period 1960-1963 the mean revenue bond issue reported by the IBA was $3,000,000; the median issue was only $750,000. In addition revenue bonds recently have financed firms locating in the immediate vicinity of large cities. Revenue bonds have maturities up to 25 to 40 years and finance up to 100 per cent of plant cost. The interest rate depends upon the credit rating of the firm financed by the bonds. Even in the absence of the usual property tax exemptions very large firms find these bonds to be a very cheap source of credit. Cases of long-term default have been rare.

No good estimates of the volume of local industrial bond issues are available. The IBA estimates that issues through 1962 and 1963 totaled $300 million and

$420 million, respectively; [5] and the Advisory Commission on Intergovernmental Relations (ACIR) estimates that issues through 1962 totaled $460 million.[6] Professors Roland I. Robinson and Joe S. Floyd, Jr. think that the IBA and ACIR estimates are much too low because they do not include issues sold locally and neither reported to the IBA or to state agencies nor nationally advertised. In a 1963 article Robinson guessed that total local issues were in the vicinity of $1 billion; [7] and in a 1962 article Floyd guessed that total state and local issues were in the vicinity of $2 billion.[8] In addition to omitting many locally sold bonds the IBA and ACIR estimates also omit (1) bonds issued to finance state industrial finance authorities and (2) industrial bonds issued by port authorities. Bonds issued to finance state industrial finance authorities amount to less than $50 million, and industrial bonds issued by port authorities probably amount to a relatively small sum. Thus the difference between the IBA and ACIR estimates on the one hand and the Robinson and Floyd estimates on the other hand is

largely due to different treatment of locally-sold bonds. This writer has seen mention of only one instance of a large private placement by a locality; the Philadelphia Industrial Development Corporation has made private placements of some $40 million. This writer believes that the Robinson guess of $1 billion is more accurate than the Floyd guess of $2 billion.

The use of local industrial bonds has expanded rapidly. According to the ACIR less than $10 million of bonds were issued in each of the years from 1951 through 1956; for each year from 1960 through 1962, $80 million to $100 million of bonds were issued; and according to the IBA, in 1963 bond issues amounted to $120 million. Revenue bonds, according to the IBA, accounted for 28 per cent of the dollar volume of industrial bonds issued during 1960; the comparable figures for 1961, 1962, and 1963 are 80 per cent, 80 per cent, and 88 per cent, respectively.

C. TAX CONCESSIONS

In a number of states *legally* authorized tax concessions to new industries have been granted by state and local governments for many years. During the past seventeen years the number of states authorizing such tax concessions increased slightly from 12 to 15 (Table I). In seven of these states such tax concession programs are quite active.

Typically new businesses (usually manufacturing firms) are granted exemptions from certain local property taxes for five to ten years. A few states also provide such property tax exemptions for expanding firms. Exemptions may be for all local property taxes, all local property taxes except school taxes, only municipal property taxes, only taxes on plant and equipment, only taxes on

---

[5] Investment Bankers Association of America, *Report of the Subcommittee on Municipal Industrial Financing*, Municipal Securities Committee, Investment Bankers Association of America, 52nd Annual Convention, Hollywood, Florida, December 1-6, 1963, mimeographed, Washington, D. C., 1963; and Investment Bankers Association of America, annual lists of municipal industrial bond issues, mimeographed, Washington, D. C.

[6] Advisory Commission on Intergovernmental Relations, *Industrial Development Bond Financing*, A Commission Report, Washington, D. C., 1963.

[7] Roland I. Robinson, "Subsidizing Industry at Everyone's Expense: Tax-exempt Industrial Bonds," *Challenge: The Magazine of Economic Affairs*, October 1963, pp. 24-27.

[8] Joe S. Floyd, Jr., "Federal, State and Local Government Programs for Financing Industrial Development," *Proceedings of Fifty-fifth Annual Conference on Taxation, National Tax Association*, 1962, pp. 444-454.

plant, etc. In addition, some states provide exemptions from certain state taxes. In two states (Rhode Island and Vermont) a local government may guarantee a new firm that its property tax will not increase for a specified number of years.

Legally authorized property tax concessions are widely used in only seven states—Alabama, Kentucky, Louisiana, Mississippi, Rhode Island, South Carolina, and Vermont.[9] According to the very rough estimates of William Edward Morgan, during 1958-1961 *new* industrial investments in these states valued at $1.6 billion received tax exemptions.[10] *However, many of these property tax exemptions probably were granted in connection with local industrial bond financing.* Tax-exempt *new* investment averaged $0.4 billion per year; by comparison publicly-financed low-interest loans granted last year amounted to between $0.15 billion and $0.30 billion. The average duration of these property tax exemptions was about nine years. Hence, the value of currently exempted property is probably about $3.6 billion (9/4 of $1.6 billion);[11] by comparison currently *outstanding* publicly-financed low-interest loans probably amount to less than $1 billion. In the absence of exemptions property taxes on exempted property would have averaged about 1.1 per cent of the market value of this property. Thus the annual tax cost reduction resulting from these exemptions

is probably about $40 million (1.1 per cent of $3.6 billion), or substantially larger than the annual interest cost reduction resulting from publicly-financed low-interest loans.

D. STATEWIDE DEVELOPMENT
CREDIT CORPORATIONS

The statewide development credit corporation (often called business development corporation) is another creation of the postwar years. Since Maine authorized the first such corporation in 1949, the use of this technique has expanded rapidly. By the end of 1959 twenty-one states had authorized corporations, and thirteen of these were active. By the end of 1963 the number of authorized corporations had increased to thirty-one, and the number of active corporations had increased to eighteen (Table I). New York, Massachusetts, and North Carolina account for about 60 per cent of the dollar volume of development credit corporation loans to date.

Sources of Funds. Development credit corporations are state chartered, but privately financed. Their funds come from (1) stock sales (external source), (2) borrowing (external source), and (3) retained earnings (internal source).

(1) *Stock* is sold primarily to businesses, individuals, and local development organizations interested in the state's economic development.[12] Stockholders, typically, neither expect nor receive more than token dividends. Most corporations have sold less stock than they have been authorized to issue. Stock sold averages $400,000 per cor-

---

[9] The use of illegal tax concessions is said to be widespread. In addition to low-interest loans (provided via issues of tax-exempt bonds) and tax concessions (legal or illegal), local governments often give various other legal or illegal inducements to industry.

[10] William Edward Morgan, *The Effects of State and Local Tax and Financial Inducements on Industrial Location,* unpublished doctoral dissertation, University of Colorado, Boulder, Colorado, 1964.

[11] Most exemptions granted more than 9 years ago have now expired.

[12] In this section heavy reliance is placed on (1) unpublished data from Edwin C. Gooding of the Federal Reserve Bank of Boston, and (2) published and unpublished reports of the various statewide development credit corporations.

poration and ranges from $1,000,000 for North Carolina to $35,000 for Wisconsin; number of stockholders averages about 300 per corporation and ranges from 1,815 for North Carolina to 22 for New Jersey; stock per stockholder averages about $1,200 and ranges from $10,000 for Virginia to $200 for Wisconsin.

(2) *Borrowing* is primarily from member commercial lending institutions.[13] These member institutions are permitted to extend lines of credit up to a small percentage (typically 1 to 2½ per cent) of ther capital and surplus or its equivalent.[14] Commercial banks comprise three-fourths of the member lenders; the rest are chiefly savings and loan associations, savings banks, and insurance companies. Development credit corporations usually borrow at rates equal to, or one-fourth to one-half per cent above, the prime rate on short-term bank loans to business. At present the prime rate is 4½ per cent.

Most corporations are permitted to borrow up to some multiple (typically 10) of their capital and surplus. For several corporations the ratio of credit pledges to capital and surplus is above the maximum permissible ratio. Thus these corporations could not borrow the full amount pledged by members.

Credit pledged averages about $5 million per corporation and ranges from $18 million for New York to $0.4 million for Wisconsin; number of members averages about 80 per corporation and

[13] Several corporations have sold subordinated debentures. These debentures are senior to stock, but junior to loans from members. In addition several corporations have borrowed from the federal government's Small Business Administration. These loans are authorized by the Small Business Investment Act of 1958 (Public Law 85-699, August 21, 1958).

[14] When a member extends such a line of credit to a development corporation, the member agrees to lend on call to the corporation any amount up to the specified maximum on previously specified terms.

ranges from 190 for New York and Kentucky to 13 for Rhode Island; and credit pledged per member averages about $60,000 and ranges from $300,000 for Rhode Island to $6,000 for Wisconsin. Total indebtedness to members averages about $2.5 million per corporation and ranges from $15.0 million for New York to $0.3 million for Kentucky. Pledges available for call average about $1.5 million per corporation and range from $3.6 million for Virginia to less than $0.1 million for Wisconsin.

Development credit corporations differ significantly in their relative reliance on stock sales and on borrowing from members. The ratio of credit pledged to stock sold averages about 11 to 1 and ranges from 42 to 1 for New York to 2 to 1 for Mississippi. The ratio of indebtedness to members to stock sold average about 5.5 to 1 and ranges from 35 to 1 for New York to 0.4 to 1 for Kentucky.

(3) *Retained earnings* of development credit corporations equal or are slightly less than their after-tax earnings. For the older corporations retained earnings range from 50 to 150 per cent of stock sold; the newer corporations have only small amounts of retained earnings.

Uses of Funds. Development credit corporations make loans (most of them secured) primarily to small manufacturing firms. About 70 per cent of the loans go to manufacturing firms; and most of the rest go to firms in commercial real estate, distribution (wholesale and retail), recreation, and service. Three-fourths of the loans go to firms already established in the state; and the rest are evenly divided between entirely new firms and firms relocating from outside the state.

Most development credit corporation loans have maturities of five to ten years. Most loans go for plant and equipment purposes, but a sizeable number of loans go for working capital purposes. The average development credit corporation loan is about $90,000 and ranges from $340,000 for Virginia to $20,000 for Vermont. Other lenders have participated in about 45 per cent of all development credit corporation loans. For such joint loans the proportion of funds supplied by these other lenders has averaged about one-fifth. In addition because of the development credit corporation loans, other lenders have extended senior credit to about one-sixth of the borrowers from development credit corporations. Corporation loans are not restricted to areas of substantial unemployment or underemployment.

Development credit corporations typically charge 6 to 8 per cent for these high-risk loans. According to Edwin C. Gooding of the Federal Reserve Bank of Boston such loans are either not available from commercial lenders or, if available, only at rates at least twice as high.

Experience. All development credit corporations have made profits. Average annual rates of profit on equity (sum of stock sold, surplus, and reserve for bad debts) range from 15 to 20 per cent down to 1 or 2 per cent. The major factor in explaining the difference in profit rates is the ratio of loans outstanding to equity which ranges from 15.3 to 1 down to 1.1 to 1. Profit rates for a number of the development credit corporations are similar to those for commercial credit agencies. For recent years the rate of profit for all commercial credit agencies averaged 11 per cent. Profit rates for the two types of

commercial credit agencies, commercial banks and commercial credit agencies other than commercial banks, averaged 13 and 8 per cent, respectively. However, member lenders and stockholders provide considerable free help in the investigation of development credit corporation loan applicants.

The ratio of losses sustained on loans disbursed averages about 0.45 per cent. The ratios for Maine, New Hampshire, and Connecticut, are 3.54, 1.17, and 1.05 per cent, respectively; all other corporations have ratios of 0.61 per cent or less. Nine corporations have not yet sustained any losses on loans. The ratio of losses sustained on loans to loans disbursed for development credit corporations is considerably higher than that for commercial bank loans to businesses. All applicants for corporation loans must previously have been rejected by commercial lenders. Of these applicants, development credit corporations reject about 45 per cent.

At the end of 1963 loans made (disbursed or awaiting disbursement) totaled $107 million. Loans made averaged about $6 million per corporation and ranged from $30 million for New York to $0.6 million for Vermont. Loans disbursed totaled $95 million (Table IV). The balance on loans outstanding totaled $52 million. Loans disbursed in 1963 totaled $17 million. For most of the older corporations the annual volume of new loans has increased only slightly in the past few years because the increase in the demand for such loans has been rather small, partly due to increased competition from noncommercial lenders such as the federal government's Small Business Administration.

TABLE IV

STATEWIDE DEVELOPMENT CREDIT CORPORATIONS

State	(1) Loans Disbursed During 1963 (million $)	(2) Loans Disbursed Through 1963 (million $)
Arkansas	$ 0.4	$ 3.5
Connecticut	0.6	4.2
Florida	1.7	1.9
Hawaii	N	N
Idaho	N	N
Indiana	N	N
Iowa	N	N
Kansas	N	N
Kentucky	0.6	1.3
Maine	0.3	3.2
Maryland	0.2	1.9
Massachusetts ...	1.6	18.2
Michigan	N	N
Minnesota	N	N
Mississippi	0.6	1.1
Missouri	N	N
New Hampshire ..	0.2	2.2
New Jersey	0.3	1.3
New York	5.1	26.9
North Carolina ..	3.2	16.6
Ohio	N	N
Oregon	N	N
Rhode Island	0.7	6.7
South Carolina ...	0.1	1.9
South Dakota	ª	ª
Tennessee	N	N
Vermont	0.1	0.6
Virginia	1.1	1.9
Washington	N	N
West Virginia	N	N
Wisconsin	0.3	1.7
Total	$17.1	$95.1

N: not active.
ª The South Dakota corporation has been active, but is now liquidating. No information is available on its activity.
Source: Arkansas and Wisconsin: 1963 annual reports for these two corporations. Other states: Unpublished data from Edwin C. Gooding, Federal Reserve Bank of Boston.

E. LOCAL DEVELOPMENT CORPORATIONS

Local development corporations are not new. They have been used in considerable number for many years. In recent years the use of this technique has expanded rapidly. In 1958 there were more than 1,800 of these corporations. Most of these were established since 1952. By 1963 the number of corporations had increased to more than 3,100 (Table I). However, many of these corporations are not active, and many of the active ones are not very active.

Local development corporations are concentrated in nonindustrialized areas and in industrialized areas with persistent unemployment. In 1958 over 70 per cent of these corporations were in towns of less than 10,000 population; somewhat over 20 per cent in towns of between 10,000 and 50,000 population; and only around 5 per cent in population centers of over 50,000.

In 1963 local development corporations existed in all states except Alaska. Number of corporations averaged 60 per state and ranged from 219 and 205 for Minnesota and Pennsylvania, respectively, to 2 and 0 for Delaware and Alaska, respectively.

Localities use a wide variety of names for these *formally* organized local industrial financing organizations, such as industrial development corporation, industrial foundation, community development corporation, industrial building company, development company, and industrial fund.[15] This paper will always refer to these organizations as local development corporations.

Many local development corporations were promoted and established by local chambers of commerce and many operate under direct chamber auspices. These corporations are organized in various ways. Many are organized as nonprofit corporations; others are organized as profit corporations; and a few are established as charitable trusts.

[15] In addition to the formally organized local development corporations there are a large number of informally organized private local groups which give various inducements to industry. Many railroad and public utility firms also offer inducements.

Local development corporations are privately financed. Most corporations raise initial capital by sale of stock. Stockholders typically neither expect nor receive more than token dividends. Other corporations borrow this capital from individuals and local business firms; and a few corporations raise it by means of donations. Some corporations have only one source of initial capital, while others have several sources. It is estimated that the corporations in existence in early 1958 had raised at least $125 million of initial capital through early 1958.[16] Amount raised per corporation averaged at least $65,000. There is great variation in corporation size. For example, a study of 75 New England corporations found an average of $60,000 with the range from $10,000 to $500,000.

Corporations typically supplement their initial capital by borrowing from conventional commercial lenders. Some corporations have borrowed from the federal government's Small Business Administration. As of June 30, 1964, the Small Business Administration had made $56 million of loans to state and local development corporations. Most of these loans went to local development corporations. These loans were authorized by the Small Business Investment Act of 1958 (Public Law 85-699, August 21, 1958).

Most of the funds raised by local development corporations have been used to finance construction of industrial plants to the specification of particular firms. These plants are then leased by the local development corporations to these firms, frequently with an option to purchase. Rentals have usually been set at levels that would enable the local development corporation to get back its money plus a moderate amount of interest in 10 to 25 years.

Local development corporations engage in a number of other activities. Some corporations make nonbankable loans for plant construction, purchases of equipment, purchases of land, and working capital purposes; some purchase existing vacant plants, modernize them, and then sell or lease them to private firms; and some construct shell or complete plants on an anticipatory basis, i.e., without having plant leases signed before construction begins. Many purchase or take option on desirable industrial sites and sell these sites to manufacturers usually at cost or close to cost. A few make gifts of industrial sites; and a few have purchased stock of business concerns.

In addition, local development corporations often finance projects jointly with statewide development credit corporations, state industrial finance authorities, and with the federal government's Area Redevelopment Administration.

For the year 1957 estimated expenditures of local development corporations totaled $19 million.[17] Expenditures per corporation averaged only $10,000, but again variation around the average was quite large.

Although new investments amounting to less than 5 per cent of current investment in manufacturing plant and equipment now receive the above-discussed financial inducements, the use of such inducements is expanding. In view of this growth, it is becoming increasingly important for researchers (1) to determine the effects of these inducements upon resource allocation, and (2)

[16] Donald R. Gilmore, *Developing the "Little" Economies: A Survey of Area Development Programs in the United States,* Supplementary Paper No. 10, Committee for Economic Development, New York, 1960.

[17] Gilmore, *op. cit.,* pp. 126-133.

190

o evaluate these effects. Such effects re examined in Part II of this paper.

ADDITIONAL REFERENCES

Committee on Banking and Currency, U. S. Senate, *Development Corporations and Authorities: Reports, Statutes and Other Materials on State and Local Development Corporations and Authorities,* Washington, D. C., December 2, 1959.

Floyd, Joe S., Jr. and Luther H. Hodges, Jr., Financing Industrial Growth: *Private and Public Sources of Long Term Capital for Industry,* Research Paper No. 10, School of Business Administration, University of North Carolina, Chapel Hill, North Carolina, 1962.

Floyd, Joe S., Jr., "State and Local Financing for Industrial Development," *Proceedings of the 56th Annual Conference on Taxation* (1963), National Tax Association, pp. 187-203.

Floyd, Joe S., Jr., two papers on state and local financing plans for industry, prepared for the Committee of State Fiscal Officers, mimeographed, School of Business Administration, University of North Carolina, Chapel Hill, North Carolina, 1963.

Gooding, Edwin C., "New War Between the States," Parts I-IV, *New England Business Review,* Federal Reserve Bank of Boston, October 1963, December 1963, July 1964, and October 1964.

New York State Department of Commerce, *The Use of Public Funds or Credit in Industrial Location,* Research Bulletin No. 6, Albany, New York, 1963.

North Carolina Committee to Study Financing for Industrial Development, *Report to the Governor of North Carolina from the Committee to Study Financing for Industrial Development,* mimeographed, Raleigh, North Carolina, November 1, 1962.

Prentice-Hall, Inc., *The Prentice-Hall Guide to State Industrial Development Incentives,* Special Report, Englewood Cliffs, New Jersey, 1963.

U. S. Department of Commerce, Office of Area Development, *Communities with Locally Financed Industrial Development Organizations,* Washington, D. C., 1958.

STATE AND LOCAL INDUCEMENTS
FOR INDUSTRY*

PART II

BENJAMIN BRIDGES, JR.

IN THE postwar years there has been rapid expansion in state and local efforts to promote economic growth by giving financial inducements to industry. These inducements usually take the form of low-interest loans or tax concessions. Some of these inducement programs are publicly financed, while others are privately financed.

This paper examines the five major types of inducement programs. Three of these, state industrial finance authorities, local industrial bond financing, and tax concessions, are publicly financed. The other two, statewide development credit corporations and local development corporations, are privately

* This paper is based upon a study done by the author for the Wisconsin Department of Resource Development (B. Bridges, Jr., *State and Local Industrial Development Incentives: Wisconsin, Its Neighbor States, and the Nation*, Wisconsin Department of Resource Development, Madison, Wisconsin, 1965). The author would like to thank Professor Harold Groves and Mr. Gerald Sazama of the University of Wisconsin who served as consultant and research assistant respectively for this study; he would also like to thank Professor Robert Lampman of the University of Wisconsin for his comments on an earlier draft of this paper.

financed. Part I of the paper provided a description of these programs and discussed their use and scope in the various states and regions of the nation. In this part of the paper (Part II) an attempt is made (1) to determine the effects of such programs upon resource allocation and (2) to evaluate these effects.

II. EFFECTS OF INDUCEMENT PROGRAMS

A. ATTEMPTS TO DETERMINE EFFECTS

Business investment decisions (how much to invest and where to invest) are very complex and involve a large number of pecuniary and nonpecuniary factors. Thus it is very difficult to determine the effect of a single factor, financial inducements, upon the volume and location of investment. Inducements affect investment decisions by reducing firm costs, by making funds available to firms which could not otherwise secure funds, by bringing potential locations to the attention of business officials, and by improving area images in the eyes of business officials.

This section begins with an examination of what business officials have said about the effects of such inducements. Next, the impact of inducements upon firm costs is considered.

1. *Questionnaire Studies*

Numerous researchers have questioned manufacturers (by means of mail questionnaires or personal interviews) in attempting to determine the effects of financial inducements upon plant location.[18] However, most of these studies failed to ask firms about the effect of inducements upon the volume of their investment.

One might expect manufacturers to somewhat overstate the importance of financial inducements as a location factor in the hope that such overstatements will encourage states and localities to make more use of such inducements; on the other hand manufacturers might understate their importance because of the well-publicized opposition to their use. In the great majority of these questionnaire studies inducements rank quite low on lists of location factors. The low rank of inducements is *partly* explained by two typical weaknesses of such studies. (1) In the majority of studies each firm typically was asked about factors in the choice of its *present* location. Many of these firms did not receive offers of inducement. Thus some firms to whom inducements would have been an important location factor did not receive offers of inducements. (2) These studies typically fail to make a distinction between factors affecting choice of region and factors affecting choice of location within a region. Inducements are a more important factor in choice of location within a region than in choice of region. Thus the

questionnaire studies somewhat understate the importance of inducements in the choice of location within a region.

In a small minority of these questionnaire studies inducements appear to be more important. One reason why inducements appear more important in these studies is that firms typically were asked specifically whether inducements were an important location factor, while in the majority studies firms typically were asked to name the most important location factors. Similarly, tax differentials appear as more important in studies which specifically ask about the tax factor than in those which ask about location factors in general.[19] A second reason why inducements appear more important in the minority studies than in the majority studies is that firms not receiving aid to whom aid would have been an important location factor typically appear in the majority studies, but not in the minority studies. In the minority studies firms typically were asked whether or not inducements would be an important factor in their future location decisions if such inducements were offered to them.

For several reasons this writer believes that the second of the two reasons given in the preceding paragraph is probably much less important than the first of these reasons. (1) A number of the majority studies were for states in which financial inducements are widely used, and thus few firms not receiving aid to whom aid would have been important appear in these studies. (2) Despite the fact that interarea tax cost differentials which are similar in magnitude to the cost reductions produced by financial inducements are encountered by *all* firms, tax cost differentials also typi-

---

[18] For two surveys of such questionnaire studies, see Benjamin Bridges, Jr., *Industrial Development Incentives: Wisconsin, Its Neighbor States, and the Nation*, Wisconsin Department of Resource Development, Madison, Wisconsin, 1965, and William Edward Morgan, *The Effects of State and Local Tax and Financial Inducements on Industrial Location*, unpublished doctoral dissertation, University of Colorado, Boulder, Colorado, 1964.

[19] See John F. Due, "Studies of State-Local Tax Influences on the Location of Industry," *National Tax Journal*, 14, June 1961, pp. 163-173.

cally rank quite low on lists of location factors.[20]

In summary it can be said that the findings of these questionnaire studies tend to support the hypothesis that inducements of the type now in common use are and will continue to be a secondary rather than a primary location factor. Inducements are certainly a secondary factor in the choice of region and are probably also a secondary factor in the choice of location within a region.[21]

2. Impact of Inducements upon Business Cost

A second method of attempting to determine the effects of inducements upon business investment is to estimate the impact of financial inducements upon firm costs. Other researchers have made little use of this approach. Here some crude estimates of cost reductions caused by such inducements are presented. First, the impact of property tax exemptions upon business costs is considered. Then the impact of the various low-interest loan programs is examined. Although this section's estimates are for Wisconsin, the general findings of the section should also apply for the other states.

a. *Impact of Property Tax Exemptions upon Business Costs.* First, an attempt is made to estimate the sizes of the cost reductions which would result from exempting new or expanding *Wisconsin* firms from local property taxes. Then these cost reduction estimates are compared in size with estimated interstate labor cost and tax cost differentials.

The size of the cost reductions which would result from exempting Wisconsin firms from property taxes would depend

upon the particular characteristics of the exemptions granted—their recipients, coverage, duration, etc. Property tax exemptions as used in other states usually have the following characteristics: (1) exemption recipients: mostly manufacturing firms, (2) coverage of exemptions: may be for all local property taxes, all local property taxes except school taxes, only municipal property taxes, only taxes on plant and equipment, only taxes on plant, etc., and (3) duration of exemptions: five to ten years.[22]

Wisconsin local property tax on manufacturing property as a percentage of value of shipments is shown in column 1 of Table V for each of 15 Wisconsin 2-digit manufacturing industries. The data are from the *1958 Census of Manufactures.*[23] Since total cost figures are not available in the *Census of Manufactures,* value of shipments figures were used as indicators of total cost.

Wisconsin local property taxes amounted to 0.68 per cent of value of shipments for all manufacturing industries combined, and ranged from 0.37 per cent for the food products industry to 1.10 per cent for the primary metals industry (Table V). In other words, it is estimated that exempting the average new food products (primary metals) plant from *all* Wisconsin local property taxes would reduce its state-local tax costs by 0.37 per cent (1.10 per cent) of its value of shipments from that plant. However, since state-local tax payments are deducted in calculating federal taxable income, this reduction in state-local tax liability would be partly

[20] *Ibid.*

[21] Similar conclusions were reached in Morgan, *op. cit.*

[22] For a more detailed discussion of property tax exemptions, see section C of Part I of this paper.

[23] Actually, value of shipments figures were estimated from the *1958 Census of Manufactures* by Professor Ronald J. Wonnacott of the University of Western Ontario.

offset by the accompanying increase in federal income tax liability.

For a number of reasons these esti-mates need to be interpreted with care. First, they are for rather broadly defined industries. Second, as shown in column 1 of Table VI, for all manufac-

shows the effect on cost of exempting firms from all local property taxes. In some states exemptions are not granted for inventory. In other states exemptions are not granted for either inventory or equipment.

The importance of a tax exemption as

TABLE V

WISCONSIN LOCAL PROPERTY TAX AND VARIOUS PERCENTAGES OF GROSS AND NET DEPRECIABLE
AND DEPLETABLE ASSETS AS PERCENTAGES OF VALUE OF SHIPMENTS,
BY MANUFACTURING INDUSTRIES: 1958

	(1)	(2)	(3)	(4)	(5)	(6)	(7)	(8)	(9)
	Local Property Tax [a]	Gross Depreciable and Depletable Assets				Net Depreciable and Depletable Assets			
Industry		1% of	2% of	3% of	4% of	1% of	2% of	3% of	4% of
20 Food products	0.37	.20	.39	.59	.78	.12	.23	.35	.47
23 Apparel and related products ...	.42	.09	.18	.27	.36	.04	.07	.11	.14
24 Lumber and wood products	.74	.36	.72	1.07	1.43	.18	.35	.53	.70
26 Paper and pulp products	.55	.39	.78	1.18	1.57	.23	.47	.70	.93
28 Chemicals and products	.52	.26	.52	.79	1.05	.13	.27	.40	.53
30 Rubber products	.56	.26	.52	.78	1.04	.08	.15	.23	.31
31 Leather and leather goods	.64	.16	.32	.49	.65	.08	.15	.23	.29
32 Stone, clay, and glass	.42	.29	.59	.88	1.17	.12	.25	.37	.50
33 Primary metals industries	1.40	.48	.96	1.44	1.92	.22	.44	.63	.87
34 Fabricated metal products	.77	.31	.63	.94	1.26	.18	.35	.53	.70
35 Non-electrical machinery	.97	.33	.65	.98	1.30	.15	.31	.46	.62
36 Electrical machinery	.90	.27	.53	.80	1.07	.14	.28	.41	.55
37 Transportation equipment	.68	.30	.59	.89	1.19	.14	.28	.42	.56
38 Instruments and related products	.39	.10	.19	.29	.39	.06	.13	.19	.25
All manufacturing	.68	.30	.60	.90	1.20	.16	.32	.47	.63

[a] In 1961 Wisconsin reduced taxes on manufacturing property.
Sources: Local property tax, gross and net depreciable and depletable assets, U. S. Department of Commerce, Bureau of the Census, *1958 Census of Manufactures*. Value of shipments, Professor Ronald J. Wonnacott, University of Western Ontario.

turing industries combined the ratio of tangible property (at book value) to value of shipments increases steadily as firm size increases. Hence, for most industries the ratio of property tax to value of shipments would also increase as firm size increases. Third, property tax exemptions are granted mainly for new or expanded plants. Such plants may have higher ratios of property tax to value of shipments than do other plants in the industry of comparable size. Fourth, effective property tax rates vary greatly from locality to locality within the state. Fifth, Table V

a location factor depends to a large extent upon how it compares in size with interarea differentials in total costs. Here the estimated cost reductions resulting from property tax exemptions are compared in size with some estimates of interstate cost differentials. Since tax exemptions would be a more important factor in the choice of location within a region than in the choice of location of region, it was decided to limit these cost comparisons to a 7-state region (Wisconsin and six neighboring states—Indiana, Illinois, Iowa, Michigan, Minnesota, and Ohio). Estimates of interstate dif-

TABLE VI

CAPITAL ASSETS LESS RESERVES AND INVENTORY
AS PERCENTAGES OF BUSINESS RECEIPTS FOR
ALL MANUFACTURING INDUSTRIES,
BY ASSET CLASSES

Total Assets ($1,000)		(1) Capital Assets Less Reserves	(2) Inventory	(3) Capital Assets Less Reserves Plus Inventory
$ 1–	25	9	4	13
25–	50	12	7	19
50–	100	12	8	20
100–	250	12	9	21
250–	500	12	10	22
500–	1,000	12	12	24
1,000–	2,500	13	13	26
2,500–	5,000	15	15	30
5,000–	10,000	18	17	35
10,000–	25,000	22	19	41
25,000–	50,000	25	19	44
50,000–	100,000	27	17	44
100,000–	250,000	27	18	45
250,000 or more		37	16	53
All asset classes		25	15	40

Source: U. S. Treasury Department, Internal Revenue Service, *Statistics of Income: 1959–60, Corporation Income Tax Returns.*

ferentials in labor costs and in tax costs were derived from a study by Professor Ronald J. Wonnacott.[24] Interstate differentials in transportation costs and in other costs are not available in the Wonnacott study.

Estimated labor cost differentials between Wisconsin and the other six states of the region are available for 18 of the 2-digit manufacturing industries. These differentials for each industry were calculated using average per hour earnings of production workers and Minnesota labor intensities (labor hours per dollar of shipments) from the *1958 Census of Manufactures.* State and local tax cost differentials are available for 12 of the 2-digit manufacturing industries. Taxes

[24] Ronald J. Wonnacott, *Manufacturing Costs and the Comparative Advantage of United States Regions,* Study Paper No. 9, Upper Midwest Economic Study, University of Minnesota, Minneapolis, Minnesota, 1963.

included in calculating these differentials were local property taxes and state income, franchise, license, and gross receipts taxes. Local property tax figures are from the *1958 Census of Manufactures.* For each state tax, total yield, as reported in the *Compendium of State Government Finances in 1958,* was allocated crudely by industries. These labor cost and tax cost differentials are for rather broadly defined industries, and may vary with size of plant, age of plant, location of plant within a state, etc.

Comparison of tax exemptions with labor cost differentials is possible for 13 of the 2-digit manufacturing industries. Wisconsin labor costs are higher than those in neighbor states in 30 cases and lower than those in neighbor states in 47 cases. As shown in Table VII tax exemptions (for all real and personal property) would be large enough to overcome Wisconsin's labor cost disadvantage in 6 of 30 cases. Comparison of tax exemptions with state and local tax cost differentials is possible for 9 of the 2-digit manufacturing industries. Wisconsin state and local tax costs are higher in $31\frac{1}{2}$ cases and lower in $15\frac{1}{2}$ cases.[25] The one tie was counted as $\frac{1}{2}$ higher and $\frac{1}{2}$ lower. As shown in Table VII tax exemptions would be large enough to overcome Wisconsin's state and local tax cost disadvantage in $25\frac{1}{2}$ out of $31\frac{1}{2}$ cases. Since both state-local tax costs and labor costs are deducted in calculating federal taxable income, federal deductibility would not change the significance of property tax exemptions *relative* to labor cost or tax cost differentials.

b. *Impact of Low-Interest Loan Inducements upon Business Costs.* State industrial finance authorities, local gov-

[25] In 1961 Wisconsin reduced taxes on manufacturing.

:nments (via industrial bonds), state-
'ide development credit corporations,
nd local development corporations all
rovide firms with funds at interest
ites lower than those charged by con-
entional lenders. Here an attempt is
iade to estimate the sizes of the cost
:ductions or savings which would re-
ilt from such low-interest loan in-
ucements. Then these cost reduction
stimates are compared in size with esti-
iated interstate labor cost and tax cost
ifferentials.

firms receiving these loans. Accordingly, estimates of various different interest cost reductions as percentages of
value of shipments are shown in Table
V for each of 14 Wisconsin 2-digit
manufacturing industries. For each interest rate reduction there are two estimates of the cost reduction. The first
estimate was obtained by multiplying
the interest-rate reduction times the
ratio of gross depreciable and depletable
assets to value of shipments; and the
second estimate was obtained by mul-

TABLE VII

NUMBERS OF CASES IN WHICH VARIOUS COST REDUCTIONS WERE LARGE ENOUGH TO OVERCOME
WISCONSIN'S LABOR COST AND TAX COST DISADVANTAGES: 1958

	Labor Cost Differential [a]	State and Local Tax Cost Differential [b, c]
,ocal property tax [c]	6	25½
% of gross depreciable and depletable assets	3	7
% of " " " " "	8½	20
% of " " " " "	11	30½
% of " " " " "	14	31½
% of net depreciable and depletable assets	2	3½
% of " " " " "	3	6½
% of " " " " "	4	13½
% of " " " " "	7	18½

[a] Wisconsin disadvantage in 30 cases and advantage in 47 cases.
[b] Wisconsin disadvantage in 31½ cases and advantage in 15½ cases.
[c] In 1961 Wisconsin taxes on manufacturing property.

The size of the cost reductions which
would result from extending the various
ow-interest loan inducements to Wis-
:onsin firms would depend upon the
:ype of inducement extended and upon
:he particular characteristics of that inducement—its recipients, size, purpose,
maturity, interest rate, etc. As the discussion of Part I of the paper indicated,
no unique interest-rate reduction or saving can be attributed to each type of
low-interest loan inducement. For example, the size of the interest-rate reduction resulting from statewide development credit corporation loans
depends heavily upon the size of the

tiplying the interest-rate reduction
times the ratio of net depreciable and
depletable assets to value of shipments.
Gross and net asset figures are from the
1958 Census of Manufactures. It is
not clear whether the gross asset ratios
or the net asset ratios produce the better
estimates of the ratios of market value
of depreciable and depletable assets to
value of shipments for firms receiving
these low-interest loans. These asset
figures are book value figures. Net asset figures are designed to be better indicators of market value than are gross
asset figures. In most cases, however,
the book value of net assets is probably

lower than the market value of these assets. In addition, these loans are made primarily for plant construction or expansion. These new or expanded plants may have higher ratios of depreciable and depletable assets to value of shipments than do other plants in the industry of comparable size.

An illustration of the meaning of the cost-reduction estimates presented in columns 2 to 9 of Table V should prove useful. Suppose that a food products firm receives a state direct loan (noninstallment type) to finance 100 per cent of the cost of its depreciable and depletable assets at an interest *rate 2* percentage points below that charged by conventional lenders. There are two estimates of the resulting interest *cost* reduction —0.39 per cent and 0.23 per cent of the value of shipments from this new plant. Since interest payments are deducted in calculating federal taxable income, this reduction in interest cost would be partly offset by the accompanying increase in federal income tax liability.

One per cent (four per cent) of gross depreciable and depletable assets amounted to 0.30 (1.20) per cent of the value of shipments for all manufacturing industries combined and ranged from 0.09 (0.36) per cent for the apparel and related products industry to 0.48 (1.92) per cent for the primary metals industry (Table V). One per cent (four per cent) of net depreciable and depletable assets amounted to 0.16 (0.63) per cent of the value of shipments for all manufacturing industries combined and ranged from 0.04 (0.14) per cent for the apparel and related products industry to 0.23 (0.93) per cent for the pulp and paper products industry. For all manufacturing industries combined net assets account for about one-half of gross assets.

For several reasons these estimate need to be interpreted with great car First, they are for rather broadly de fined industries. Second, as shown i column 1 of Table VI, for all manu facturing industries combined the rati of net capital assets (depreciable an depletable assets plus land) at bool value to value of shipments increases a firm size, as measured by total assets, in creases. However, the ratio is virtuall constant over the range from $25,00 to $2,500,000 of total assets. Accord ing to one writer the minimum size firn having access to the national securit market has total assets of $1,000,000 t $3,000,000.[26] The ratio also generall increases for all 2-digit manufacturin industries except tobacco, apparel an related products, and rubber products For most of these industries the ratio at first show no upward trend as firn size increases, but as firm size continue to increase the ratios begin to trend upward. Third, these loans are usually installment loans. The principal of an installment loan is repaid in installment during the life of the loan, while the principal of a noninstallment loan is not repaid until the end of the life of the loan. For a given loan size and maturity the present value of the interest-rate reduction on the installment loan is equal to the present value of an interest-rate reduction on the noninstallment loan which is approximately 60 to 70 per cent of the interest-rate reduction on the installment loan. For example, for a given loan size and maturity, a 3 percentage point interest-rate reduction on the installment loan is approximately equivalent to a 2 percentage point in-

[26] George W. Mitchell, "A Review of Survey Findings," *Financing Small Business,* Report to the Committees on Banking and Currency and the Select Committees on Small Business of the U. S. Congress by the Federal Reserve System, Parts 1 and 2, April 11, 1958, Washington, D. C.

rest-rate reduction on the noninstallment loan. Fourth, some low-interest
loans finance both plant and equipment.
Others finance only plant. Both plant
and equipment are included in depreciable and depletable assets. For all
manufacturing industries, equipment
amounts to perhaps one-fourth of depreciable and depletable assets.

Comparison of interest cost reductions
with labor costs differentials is possible
for 13 of the 2-digit manufacturing industries. Wisconsin labor costs are
higher than those in neighbor states in
0 cases and lower than those in neighbor states in 47 cases. As shown in
Table V, interest cost reductions of 1,
2, 3 and 4 per cent of gross depreciable
and depletable assets would be large
enough to overcome Wisconsin's labor
cost disadvantage in 3, 8½, 11, and
14 cases, respectively. Interest-cost reductions of 1, 2, 3, and 4 per cent of net
depreciable and depletable assets would
be large enough to overcome Wisconsin's
labor cost disadvantage in 2, 3, 4, and
7 cases, respectively. Comparison of interest cost reductions with state and
local tax cost differentials is possible for
9 of the 2-digit manufacturing industries. Wisconsin state and local tax costs
are higher in 31½ cases and lower in
15½ cases. As shown in Table V,
interest cost reductions of 1, 2, 3, and
4 per cent of gross depreciable and depletable assets would be large enough to
overcome Wisconsin's state and local
tax cost differential in 7, 20, 30½,
and 31½ cases, respectively. Interest
cost reductions of 1, 2, 3, and 4 per
cent of net depreciable and depletable
assets would be large enough to overcome Wisconsin's state and local tax
cost disadvantage in 3½, 6½, 13½,
and 18½ cases, respectively.[27] Since

interest costs, state-local tax costs, and
labor costs are all deducted in calculating federal taxable income, federal deductibility would not change the significance of interest cost reductions
relative to labor cost or tax cost differentials.

c. *Impact of Inducements upon Business Costs: A Summary.* In size of cost
reduction per annum, the property tax
exemption is roughly equivalent to 2
per cent of gross depreciable and depletable assets and to 4 per cent of net depreciable and depletable assets.

The ratio of cost reduction due to a
property tax exemption to value of
shipments increases as firm size increases.
On the contrary, the ratio of *cost* reduction due to low-interest loans to
value of shipments decreases as firm size
increases from small to medium, and is
larger for small firms than for large
firms. For a given inducement program, the interest-*rate* reduction decreases as firm size increases. This is
true because the interest rate charged on
these low-interest loans typically does
not decrease markedly as firm size increases, while the interest rate charged
by conventional lenders for similar loans
does decrease markedly as firm size increases. For most manufacturing industries the ratios of depreciable and depletable assets to value of shipments at
first show no upward trend as firm size
increases, but as firm size continues to
increase the ratios begin to trend upward. For all manufacturing industries
combined this ratio is virtually constant
over the range from $25,000 to
$2,500,000 of total assets.

The importance of an industrial development inducement as a location factor depends to a large extent upon how
the cost reduction produced by the inducement compares in size with interarea differentials in *total* cost; however,

27 Remember that most local industrial bond financing involves both low-interest loans and property tax
exemptions.

location decisions depend to some extent upon factors other than considerations of money cost. Cost reductions which are large enough to overcome tax cost and/or labor cost differentials may not be large enough to overcome differentials in total cost. For example, they may not overcome transportation cost differentials. A cost reduction which overcomes a tax cost differential may not overcome a labor cost differential and vice versa. On the other hand cost reductions which are not large enough to overcome tax cost and/or labor cost differentials may be large enough to overcome differentials in total cost.

Industrial development inducements affect the volume as well as the location of investment. In some cases both volume and location are affected. In other cases only volume or only location is affected. In still other cases neither is affected. The importance of inducements in affecting volume of investment depends to a large extent upon how much such inducements reduce costs and hence increase profits. One study found pre-tax profit income averaged about 5 per cent of value of shipments.[28] Thus a cost reduction equal to 1 per cent of value of shipments would produce a 20 per cent increase in pre-tax profit income.

3. *Attempts to Determine Effects: Some Conclusions*

Despite the difficulty of determining the effect of a single factor, industrial development inducements, upon the volume and location of investment, the following conclusions can be drawn.

Industrial development inducements are a more important factor in the

choice of location within the region tha? in the choice of location of region. On? reason for the above is that differentia? in total costs within regions are generall? smaller than such differentials betwee? regions. In addition intraregional di?ferences in capital availability and i? image are often smaller than such inter? regional differences.

Even in the choice of location withi? a region inducements of the commonly? used types are probably a secondar? factor. In most cases cost reductior? due to inducements are probably sma? relative to differentials in total cos? Primary factors include such things ?? labor cost differentials, transportatio? cost differentials, etc. On the basis o? available evidence it is impossible to es? tablish just how important a secondar? location factor industrial developmen? inducements are.

In some cases, however, offers of in? ducements *might* significantly affect th? decision of a number of firms as t? whether to locate in a particular state o? in the adjoining state. For example? offers of industrial development induce? ments by Wisconsin groups *might* sig? nificantly affect the decision of a num? ber of firms as to whether to locate i? Wisconsin or Illinois. The bulk of Wis? consin's industry is located in south? eastern Wisconsin not far from the Il? linois state line. In a number of case? total cost differentials between south? eastern Wisconsin and northern Illinoi? may be relatively small. In addition t? reducing costs, offers of inducements by? Wisconsin groups *might* noticeably im? prove Wisconsin's image in the eyes of? business officials. State images depend? only partly on costs and partly on less? tangible (and often less rational) fac? tors.[29]

[28] Governor's Minnesota Tax Study Committee, *Report of the Governor's Minnesota Tax Study Committee: 1956*, St. Paul, Minnesota, 1956.

[29] See Due, *loc. cit.* and Wonnacatt, *op. cit.*

According to studies by Wallace and Ruttan and by Ross a majority of the firms receiving inducements did not consider them to be a crucial location factor.[30]

Property tax exemptions increase in importance as a location factor as firm size increases for the following two reasons. First, as firm size increases the number of alternative locations under consideration generally increases. Second, the ratio of cost reduction due to a property tax exemption to value of shipments increases as firm size increases. The Ross study found that property tax exemptions were more important as a location factor for large investments than for small investments.

Low-interest loans probably are a more important location factor for small firms than for medium-sized or large firms. The ratio of cost reduction due to low-interest loans to value of shipments decreases as firm size increases from small to medium. This ratio is also larger for small firms than for large firms. In addition, the unavailability of capital is a more important problem for small firms than for medium-sized or large firms. These two factors are probably more than enough to offset the fact that small firms consider a smaller number of alternative locations than do medium-sized or large firms.

Inducements affect the volume as well as the location of investment. On the basis of available evidence it is impossible to establish just how important a factor inducements are in determining the volume of investment. Most studies of business investment show that the volume of investment is rather insensitive to changes in the cost and availability of capital.[31] The arguments presented one paragraph earlier suggest that low-interest loans are more important as a factor in determining the volume (and location) of investment for small firms than for medium-sized or large firms. Some studies of business investment find that the investment of small firms is considerably less insensitive than the investment of large firms to changes in the cost and availability of capital.[32] On the contrary, the argument presented two paragraphs ealier suggests that as firm size increases property tax exemptions increase in importance as a factor in determining the volume (and location) of investment. Ross (op. cit.), however, did not find any consistent relationship between size of investment and the importance of tax exemptions.

The financing of these inducement programs is of some importance. If the programs are financed by borrowing, funds are diverted mainly from other investment. If the programs are financed by taxation, funds are mainly diverted from consumption. Furthermore, funds are more likely to be diverted from other in-state investment if borrowing is from state individuals and/or institutions than if borrowing is from out-of-state individuals and/or institutions.

[30] L. T. Wallace and V. W. Ruttan, "The Role of the Community as a Factor in Industrial Location," *Papers and Proceedings of the Regional Science Association*, Vol. 7, pp. 133-142; William D. Ross, *Louisiana's Industrial Tax Exemption Program, Louisiana Business Bulletin*, Vol. 15, December 1953, College of Commerce, Louisiana State University, Baton Rouge, Louisiana; and Ross, "Tax Concessions and Their Effect," *Proceedings of the 50th Annual Conference on Taxation, National Tax Association*, 1957, pp. 216-224.

[31] For a summary of such studies see U. S. Congress, Joint Economic Committee, *Staff Report on Employment, Growth, and Price Levels*, Washington, D. C., 1959.

[32] For a summary of such studies see *ibid*.

B. AN ATTEMPT TO EVALUATE THE EFFECTS

In this section an attempt is made to evaluate the economic effects of financial inducements to industry. These effects are evaluated both from the point of view of a state and from the point of view of the nation. Some inducement programs are operated at the state level and others at the local level. However, many of the local programs require state authorization. These state-local programs may have significant effects upon national resource allocation. If the resource allocation effects of some of these programs are considered to be harmful, the national government may want to discourage the use of such programs by states and localities.

1. Evaluation from a State Viewpoint

Each of the various inducement methods of attempting to increase a state's economic growth involves both benefits and costs to the state. For each method one would like to compare benefits with costs. In addition, one would like to compare the outcomes of the various inducement methods with each other and with the outcomes of various non-inducement methods.[33] On the basis of the preceding discussion the general magnitude of benefits and costs can be estimated. Unfortunately, however, only very imprecise benefit-cost comparisons are possible.

[33] For attempts to compute benefits and costs to localities of financial inducements see (1) John E. Moes, *Local Subsidies for Industry*; (2) James R. Rinehart, "Rates of Return on Municipal Subsidies to Industry," *Southern Economic Journal*, 29, April 1963, pp. 297-306; and (3) Rinehart, "Rates of Return on Municipal Subsidies to Industry: A Reply," *Southern Economic Journal*, 30, April 1964, pp. 359-361. For a criticism of Rinehart's work see Lewis E. Hill, "Rates of Return on Municipal Subsidies to Industry: Comment," *Southern Economic Journal*, 30, April 1964, pp. 358-359.

Inducement programs (via attracting plants to the state) increase state population by discouraging out-migration and encouraging in-migration. In addition migration which is unaffected by inducement programs causes state population to change over time in size and composition. In estimating benefits and costs to the state of inducements it seems most sensible to include only those benefits and costs which accrue to persons who were residents of the state at the time the decision to give the inducements was made ("original" residents). For example, in estimating the time streams of benefits and costs to the state of inducements which were granted in a particular year (year t), we might include only those benefits and costs which accrue to persons who were residents of the state at the beginning of that year (year t).

The benefit to the state consists of the present value of the increase in the income of the "original" residents which was caused by the inducement program. The income increase results from the net increase in investment undertaken in the state because of this inducement program. The *net* increase in investment is the excess of the investment undertaken because of the inducement program over the investment *not* undertaken because of this program. A sizeable part of the income increase consists of the income increases of the new employees of the firms which undertook investment because of the inducement program. Some of these employees were previously unemployed, and others previously earned substantially lower incomes.[34] Another sizeable part

[34] If the inducements prevented the out-migration of some "original" residents, the increase in the total income of "original" residents which would have occurred as a result of such out-migration should be subtracted out in estimating benefits.

of the income increase results from the state income multiplier effect. On the other hand, there are some decreases in state income resulting from the investment *not* undertaken because of the inducement program. In the absence of the program some of the funds used to finance the program would have been used to finance other investment projects within the state. For example, a local bank which supplied a loan under a state loan guarantee program might in the absence of the guarantee program have lent at least part of these funds to some local firm. The failure of the bank to make this loan might have caused this local firm to cancel its plans to build a new plant.

The cost to the state consists of the present value of the decrease in "original" resident income resulting because some of the "original" residents financing the inducement program would as a result have lower (actual or potential) incomes. For example, taxpayers would have lower incomes because of the higher taxes they had to pay in order to (1) recover the tax revenue lost because of a tax exemption program or (2) cover the deficit of a bond-financed state direct loan program.

Local Industrial Bond Financing. For a revenue bond program which does not involve state-local tax exemptions it seems likely that benefits to the state substantially exceed costs to the state, especially if these bonds are sold to out-of-state individuals or institutions. Funds are less likely to be diverted from in-state investment if the bond sales are to out-of-state individuals and/or institutions than if borrowing is from in-state individuals and/or institutions. Costs are quite small. For a low-interest loan inducement the cost to the state equals the sum of (a) the difference

over the life of the loan between the cost of the funds to the state and the interest paid by the aided firm for these funds, and (b) in the case of default the lost loan principle. For bond-financed loans in most cases the cost of funds to the state is the interest paid on these bonds. This is so because the appropriate assumption in most cases is that in the absence of the low-interest loan these bonds would not have been issued. For the following reasons the costs of a revenue bond program are quite small. (a) Local governments lend at approximately the same interest rates at which they borrow. (b) The risk of default is borne by the bondholders. (c) For these bonds the interest-rate reduction is primarily due to the exemption of the interest income from these bonds from federal income taxation. Thus the cost of this interest-rate reduction is borne by the federal government, and residents of the state pay only a small portion of federal taxes. However, if the bond program also involves property tax exemptions, costs are much larger and benefits to the state may or may not exceed costs to the state.

The benefits to a state of a revenue bond program are often exaggerated. Even in the choice of location within a region financial inducements such as revenue bonds (especially in the absence of property tax exemptions) are probably a secondary location factor.

For a *general obligation* bond program which does not involve state-local tax exemptions benefits to the state may or may not exceed costs to the state. For loans to large firms it seems likely that benefits substantially exceed costs, but for loans to small firms benefits may or may not exceed costs. The following factors affect costs. (a) Local governments lend at approximately the

203

same interest rates at which they borrow. (b) The risk of default is borne by local governments. This risk is small for loans to large firms, but may not be small for loans to small firms. (c) The interest income from these bonds is exempt from federal income taxation. (d) As a result of their industrial bond programs, local governments may have to pay higher interest rates on their nonindustrial bonds. If the bond program also involves property tax exemptions, costs to the state are much larger.

Tax Concessions. According to the rough estimates of William D. Ross, the present value of the investments (not the increase in income resulting from these investments) undertaken in Louisiana during 1946-1950 because of its property tax exemption program was less than the present value of the property tax revenue lost because of the program.[35] In other words, if Louisiana governments instead of granting tax exemptions had collected this tax revenue and invested it themselves in new plant and equipment they would have created more jobs than were created by the exemption program. On the other hand, the present value of the increase in state income resulting because of the exemption program *may* have been greater than the present value of the tax revenue lost because of this program.

State Loan Guarantee Authorities. For a well-established state loan guarantee program it seems likely that benefits to the state exceed costs to the state. These loan guarantee authorities have relatively small reserve funds and operate profitably, and thus costs are small. The well-established authorities of Rhode Island and Maine have reserve funds of $100,000 and $500,000 respectively and are now operating profitably.

35 Ross, *op. cit.*; and Ross, *loc. cit.*

State Direct Loan Authorities. Bond-financed state direct loan authorities often lend at interest rates equal to or lower than those at which they borrow. For the revenue bond authority which lends and borrows at approximately the same interest rate it seems likely that benefits to the state substantially exceed costs to the state. The reasoning is the same as that presented above in the section dealing with the benefits and costs of local revenue bond programs. For the authority which lends at interest rates considerably lower than those at which it borrows the additional benefits to the state of this additional interest-rate reduction (the difference between its borrowing and lending rates) may or may not exceed the additional costs to the state. The deficit of the authority is an additional cost which is borne entirely by the state government rather than by the federal government.

For the *general obligation* bond authority which lends and borrows at approximately the same interest rate benefits to the state may or may not exceed costs to the state. The reasoning is the same as that presented above in the section dealing with the benefits and costs of local general obligation bond programs. For the authority which lends at interest rates considerably lower than those at which it borrows the additional benefits to the state of this additional interest-rate reduction may or may not exceed the additional costs to the state.

For the *tax-financed* state direct loan authority the benefits to the state may or may not exceed costs to the state. For tax-financed loans the cost of funds to the state is the return on these funds in their alternative use. The state's taxpayers suffer losses (costs) if the interest rate charged by the state authority is lower than the interest rate at which hese funds could be invested if they were not used to finance the authority's loan program. In addition the authority bears the risk of default.

Statewide Development Credit Corporations. For a well-established statewide development credit corporation it seems likely that benefits to the state exceed costs to the state. The profit rates of many of these corporations are comparable or almost comparable to those of commercial credit agencies, and thus costs to the state are probably small.

Local Development Corporations. Local development corporations offer various types of financial inducements. For some types of inducements benefits to the state may exceed costs to the state; and for other types of iducements costs to the state may exceed benefits to the state.

Concluding Comments. A new plant increases state income more if located in an area with a labor surplus than if located in an area without a labor surplus. However, in many cases larger inducements are needed to attract new plants to the former type of area than to the latter type of area.

The preceding discussion of the benefits and costs of inducements was based upon the assumption that the increased use of inducements in the given state does not provoke retaliatory increases in the use of inducements in neighboring states. Such retaliatory action substantially reduces the benefits to the state and/or increases the costs to the state of its inducement programs. In the event that the given state increases the use of inducements some such retaliatory action is likely. However, even in the absence of increases in the use of inducements in the given state, the use of inducements in neighboring states is likely

to increase, thus somewhat weakening the given state's competitive position.

In addition to inducement programs various other measures for attempting to increase a state's economic growth, such as increased expenditures for vocational education and job retraining, have been suggested. Some of these measures might well be more effective with regard to benefits and costs to the state, than some of the financial inducement programs.

2. Evaluation from the National Viewpoint

The discussion of earlier sections indicated the general magnitude of the effect of inducement programs upon national resource allocation, but did not attempt to determine whether these effects were desirable or undesirable from the national viewpoint. Various economic arguments have been used to justify inducements from the national viewpoint, i.e., to show the desirability of the resource allocation effects of inducements. One commonly used argument asserts that inducements are needed to fill a gap in the credit market. Another argument asserts that inducements are needed to compensate for wage rate inflexibility in the labor market. The following is an attempt to evaluate these arguments.

a. *Credit Gap Argument.* It has been argued that inducements improve national resource allocation by helping to fill a gap in the credit market. What is meant by the credit gap? A credit gap is not simply the existence of some borrowers who cannot get funds at terms acceptable to them. Meeting the demands of such borrowers would not necessarily produce better resource allocation. For example, firm A would be willing to pay up to 8 per cent per an-

205

num for a loan, but cannot secure such a loan. Supplying firm A with a loan enables it to divert resources away from other firms that may have been able to make more productive use of them. A credit gap means that there are some borrowers who cannot get funds at terms acceptable to them, but it means much more. It means that supplying some of these firms with loans enables them to divert resources away from other firms that would have made less productive use of them.

Economists agree that the credit gap, if it exists, applies mainly to the long-term financing of small firms (especially young ones). Long-term loans have maturities of at least five years. However, economists do not agree as to whether or not small firms actually encounter a significant long-term credit gap. Moreover, those who agree that such a gap exists do not agree as to its magnitude.[36]

In a recent article Professor Alfred J. Gobar argues that the experience of Small Business Investment Companies shows that small firms do not encounter a significant long-term credit gap, but rapidly growing medium-sized firms may encounter such a gap.[37]

On the other hand the experience of privately-financed statewide development credit corporations provides *some* support for the proposition that such a gap exists for small firms, but that it is not a large one. These corporations make loans primarily to small manufacturing firms. These loans average about $90,000, have maturities of 5 to 10 years, and bear interest rates of 6 to 8

per cent. According to Edwin Good ing of the Federal Reserve Bank o Boston, comparable loans are usuall either not available from commercia lenders or, if available, only at rates a least twice as high.[38, 39]

The *existence* of a credit gap fo small firms is *suggested* by the profi and loss experience of developmen credit corporations. Despite the fac that they charge interest rates well be low those charged by commercial lend ers for comparable loans, all develop ment credit corporations have mad profits. Several of the well-establishe corporations whose annual reports wer available to this writer had average an nual rates of profit on equity (sum o stock sold, surplus, and reserve for ba debts) ranging from 7 to 8 per cent t 15 to 20 per cent. These profit rates ar similar to those for commercial credi agencies. The rate of profit for all com mercial credit agencies was 11 per cent profit rates for the two types of com mercial credit agencies, commercia banks and commercial credit agencie other than banks, were 13 and 8 pe cent, respectively.[40] However, membe lenders and stockholders provide consid erable free help in investigation of devel opment credit corporation loan appli cants. A rough guess would be that th value of this donated labor average about 1 or 2 per cent of the value o outstanding loans. Thus if develop ment credit corporations had to cover al of their costs (including the value o these donated services), they would hav

[36] See (1) U. S. Congress, *Financing Small Business;* and (2) "Small Business Financing: Corporate Manufacturers," *Federal Reserve Bulletin,* 47, January 1961, pp. 8-22.

[37] Albert J. Gobar, "Continuing Problems of Small Business Investment Companies in Closing the Equity Gap," *Quarterly Review of Economics and Business,* 4, Autumn 1964, pp. 33-40.

[38] Edwin C. Gooding, "New War Between th States: Part I," *New England Business Review,* Fed eral Reserve Bank of Boston, October 1963, pp. 1-5

[39] For a detailed discussion of statewide develop ment credit corporations, see section C of Part I o this paper.

[40] Calculated from U. S. Treasury Department, In ternal Revenue Service, *Statistics of Income: Corpo ration Income Tax Returns* for seven recent years.

charge interest rates of 7 to 10 per cent instead of 6 to 8 per cent in order to maintain their current profit rates.[41] On the other hand the experience of development credit corporations *suggests* that the credit gap is probably a small one. In 1963 loans disbursed by development credit corporations totaled only $17 million or only $1 million per corporation. For many corporations the annual volume of new loans has increased only slightly mainly because the increase in the demand for such loans has been rather small. However, this slow growth in demand is in part due to increased competition from other nonprofit lending agencies (Small Business Administration, Area Redevelopment Administration, state industrial finance authorities, local industrial bond programs, and privately-financed local development corporations).

A small credit gap may be of more importance than its dollar size suggests. It may be that the firms unable to secure funds because of this gap would contribute more than their share of economic and technological innovations.

Small firms in rural areas probably have more difficulty in securing adequate long-term financing than do small firms in urban areas.[42]

At its strongest, the credit gap argument calls for the granting of loans to small firms at interest rates of perhaps 7 to 10 per cent, and thus provides some support for statewide development credit corporations and state loan guarantee authorities. Development credit corporations lend primarily to small firms and usually charge rates of 6 to 8 per cent. Most loans guaranteed by state industrial finance authorities cost 6 to 6¾ per cent. Most direct loans by state industrial finance authorities go to small firms, but bear interest rates of only 2 to 5 per cent. Most general obligation bonds finance small firms, but bear interest rates of 3 to 4½ per cent. Most of the dollar volume of revenue bonds finances large firms at interest rates of 4 to 5 per cent. From the point of view of national resource allocation, charging too low an interest rate may be as bad or worse than charging too high an interest rate.

b. *Wage-Rate Inflexibility Argument.* It has also been argued that financial inducements improve national resource allocation by helping to compensate for wage-rate inflexibility in the labor markets of labor surplus areas.[43] John E. Moes is the leading proponent of this argument. He suggests that the unemployment and underemployment of labor surplus areas are directly attributable to the inflexibility of wage rates. According to Moes, if wage rates were flexible, they would fall until full employment was reached. He attributes much of the inflexibility of wage rates to minimum wage laws and to union activity, and argues that financial inducements should be employed to compensate for wage-rate inflexibility. Inducements will attract firms to labor surplus areas as lower wage rates would have if wage rates had been flexible.

---

[41] This is true if the demand for development credit corporation loans is relatively inelastic with respect to the interest rate.

[42] See Advisory Commission on Intergovernmental Relations, *Industrial Development Bond Financing*, A Commission Report, Washington, D. C., 1963; and Edwin C. Gooding, "New War Between the States: Part 3," *New England Business Review*, Federal Reserve Bank of Boston, July 1964, pp. 2-7.

[43] See: (1) Moes, *op. cit.*; (2) Moes, "The Subsidization of Industry by Local Communities in the South," *Southern Economic Journal*, 28, October 1961, pp. 187-193; (3) Moes, "Local Subsidies for Industry: Reply," *Southern Economic Journal*, 29, July 1962, pp. 119-126; and (4) James M. Buchanan and Moes, "A Regional Countermeasure to National Wage Standardization," *American Economic Review*, 50, June 1960, pp. 434-438.

It is this writer's judgment that Moes overstates the importance of wage-rate inflexibility as a basic cause of unemployment and underemployment in labor surplus areas.[44] (1) At present a sizeable portion of this unemployment and underemployment is due to the weakness of overall demand in the economy. This weakness of overall demand calls for stimulative fiscal and monetary measures by the federal government rather than for financial inducements to industry. (2) A portion of this unemployment and underemployment is due to lack of knowledge on the part of workers and businessmen. Many unemployed or underemployed workers are not aware of job opportunities in other areas, and a number of businessmen may not be aware of investment opportunities in labor surplus areas. This problem calls for measures to increase such knowledge rather than for financial inducements.

An unknown portion of the unemployment and underemployment of labor surplus areas is basically due to wage-rate inflexibility. However, a sizeable amount of wage-rate inflexibility must be attributed to factors other than minimum wage laws and union activity, such as notions concerning "fair" wage rates, etc.

At most the Moes argument provides *some* support for the use of financial

inducements in labor surplus areas. definitely does not support the use of such inducements in areas not havin labor surpluses. In addition, from th point of view of national resource allo cation the use of inducements in labo surplus areas could become too inten sive, by overcompensating for wage-rat inflexibility.

The activities of statewide develop ment credit corporations and local de velopment corporations are not limite to labor surplus areas. Most state loa guarantee programs, local industria bond programs, and tax concessions pro grams are not limited to labor surplu areas. However, a number of state di rect loan authorities, including those o Pennsylvania and New York, can oper ate only in labor surplus areas. A num ber of other state direct loan authoritie can operate in all areas of the state.

Although the use of financial induce ments in labor surplus areas may im prove national resource allocation, alter native methods of aiding the people o these areas such as job retraining, mor effective employment services, etc., ma be even more desirable with regard t their resource allocation effects. O course such methods could be used a supplements to as well as substitutes fo financial inducements.

C. EFFECTS OF INDUCEMENT PROGRAMS
A SUMMARY

Financial inducements of the type now in common use are certainly a secondary location factor in the choice of region and are probably also a secondary factor in the choice of location within a region. On the basis of available evidence it is impossible to establish precisely how important a secondary location inducements are. In some cases offers of inducements *might* signifi-

[44] For other appraisals of Moes' argument see (1) Ralph Gray, "Industrial Development Subsidies and Efficiency in Resource Allocation," *National Tax Journal*, 17, June 1964, pp. 164-172; (2) Irving J. Goffman, "Local Subsidies for Industry: Comment," *Southern Economic Journal*, 29, July 1962, pp. 111-114; (3) James H. Thompson, "Local Subsidies for Industry: Comment," *Southern Economic Journal*, 29, July 1962, pp. 114-119; and (4) Joe S. Floyd, Jr. and Luther H. Hodges, Jr., *Financing Industrial Growth: Private and Public Sources of Long Term Capital for Industry*, Research Paper No. 10, School of Business Administration, University of North Carolina, Chapel Hill, North Carolina, 1962.

antly affect the decision of a number of firms as to whether to locate in a particular state or in the adjoining state. In addition to reducing costs, offers of inducements by groups in a particular state *might* noticeably improve that state's image in the eyes of business officials.

Inducements affect the volume as well as the location of investment. On the basis of available evidence it is impossible to establish just how important a factor inducements are in determining the volume of investment. Most studies of business investment show that the volume of investment is rather insensitive to changes in the cost and availability of capital.

For local revenue bond programs and for one type of state direct loan program it seems likely that benefits to the state substantially exceed costs to the state; for well-established state loan guarantee authorities and for statewide development credit corporations it also seems likely that benefits to the state exceed costs to the state; for the other types of financial inducement programs benefits to the state may or may not exceed costs to the state. Some of the various noninducement programs which have been suggested for attempting to increase a state's economic growth might well be more effective with regard to benefits and costs to the state than some of the financial inducement programs.

Various arguments have been put forth to justify from the national viewpoint the use of industrial development inducements. Two of these are the credit gap argument and the wage-rate inflexibility argument. The credit gap, if it exists, may be small. At most the credit gap argument provides support for state loan guarantee authorities and statewide development credit corporations. The proponents of the wage-rate inflexibility argument usually overstate the importance of this inflexibility as a cause of unemployment and underemployment in labor surplus areas. At most this argument provides support for the use of financial inducements in labor surplus areas. Neither argument supports the use of state direct loans, local industrial bonds, or tax concessions in areas not having labor surpluses.[45] With regard to national resource allocation effects, other methods of aiding the people of labor surplus areas may be preferable to financial inducements.

[45] In addition the exempting of the interest income from state and local industrial bonds from federal income taxation produces serious inequity in the federal income tax structure.

FEDERAL INFLUENCES ON INDUSTRIAL LOCATION: HOW EXTENSIVE?

Robert A. Will

Whether the influences are overt or oblique, every plant location decision — including the initial step of when to consider a new location — is affected by the federal government. At one extreme is the establishment and direct ownership of a manufacturing plant by the government itself. At the other extreme is the small, privately-held manufacturer who selects a location near a ninety percent-government-financed interstate highway to take advantage of speedy truck service (after first taking into consideration the effect of government regulated freight rates at this location). In the broad spectrum between these two extremes are the regional development programs, tax inducements, subsidies, legislation and other governmental instruments affecting industrial site selection.

There are four fundamental ways in which the federal government influences industrial plant location. In most location decisions, certain of these effects are overlapping; however, they may be categorized as: (1) Establishment and ownership of plants by governmental agencies (such plants are usually operated by private contractors). Corollary to this is the location of privately owned plants near government facilities that utilize their products, as evidenced in the space and missile program. (2) Provision for direct governmental economic aid, tax benefits or subsidies to industries locating in specific areas. (3) Development and improvement projects affecting the attractiveness to industry of regions, areas or sites. (4) Legislative and legal action which affects the essential elements of plant location.

Direct Government Ownership

Traditionally the federal government has kept its ownership of manufacturing facilities to the minimum held necessary for national defense, preferring to contract with privately-owned suppliers to meet its needs.

Reprinted from *Land Economics, 40* (1964), 49–57, by permission of the author and editor.

In recent decades this policy has been modified by several circumstances, and government ownership has been broadened.

Federal government ownership of manufacturing facilities dates back to the establishment of the Springfield Arsenal in 1794. For more than a century after this, ownership was largely confined to the armaments industry, notably arsenals.[1] However, beginning in World War I, and continuing through the depression and World War II, the government entered a number of fields under emergency circumstances, and has not yet seen fit to extricate itself from certain of these. The role of the federal government in business was included within the scope of the widely publicized study made by the Hoover Commission. Findings of this Commission have been summarized as follows:

"After two years of study the Commission on Organization of the Executive Branch of the Government was unable to discover the full extent of business enterprises owned and operated by the Government. No one knows how much goods and services are produced by them or how much profit or loss they make in any year. Nevertheless, it is obvious that the Government is in business in a big way and that it competes unfairly with privately owned business . . . The Government has found three major pretexts for creating its own businesses that invade the field of private enterprise: (1) the existence of economic emergencies; (2) emergencies caused by war; and (3) the need for development of projects which are not adaptable to private industry because of their nature or magnitudes."[2]

The Hoover Commission found that there were no fewer than 2500 separate industrial or commercial facilities owned by the armed services alone, with an investment in excess of $15 billion. Manufacturing operations included paint, clothing, lumber, chemicals, chains, photographic equipment, watches, and others.[3] A major non-military government manufacturing operation noted by the Commission was the production of phosphate and nitrate fertilizer since 1933 by the Tennessee Valley Authority. Annual production of this fertilizer has amounted to $20 million, or four percent of the nation's total.[4]

It was during World War II that the federal government played a direct and truly major role in the location of American manufacturing facilities. Ordinance requirements alone resulted in the establishment of 73 government-owned, contractor-operated plants in all parts of the country, employing 400,000 persons.[5] Even more significant from a long range viewpoint was the establishment of two completely new major in-

---

[1] Levin H. Campbell, Jr., *The Industry-Ordnance Team* (New York, New York: McGraw-Hill, 1946), pp. 37–40.
[2] Neil MacNeil and Harold W. Metz, *The Hoover Report 1953–1955* (New York, New York: The MacMillan Company, 1956), pp. 154–155.
[3] *Ibid.*, p. 157.
[4] *Ibid.*, pp. 172–173.
[5] Campbell, *op. cit.*, p. 102.

dustries, synthetic rubber and nuclear products, and the development of the aluminum industry.

In early 1941, the Rubber Reserve Company was established by the government to provide a synthetic rubber program. This program eventually resulted, by the end of World War II, in the construction of 51 plants capable of producing 1 million tons of usable rubber yearly. All of the rubber plants were government-built and owned but were operated by private contractors.[6] Following World War II, the government began a program for sale of the plants at a rate calculated not to jeopardize national defense interests. By 1955 this disposal was completed.[7]

A second major wartime program which still retains considerable locational significance for a sizable segment of the economy is the atomic energy program. The Atomic Energy Commission, which now directs this effort as the successor to the wartime Manhattan project, owns an estimated $7.2 billion (before depreciation) in plant and equipment, and requires more than $2 billion annually for its programs.[8] Total employment in the atomic energy field is estimated at 193,000, of which 138,000 are employed in 318 privately-owned and government-owned contractor-operated industrial plants.[9] Plants are scattered in all sections of the country with available low cost power a major locational criterion in some instances.

A third direct government plant location effort whose consequences are still important today occurred in the aluminum industry. In this case, existing privately-owned production facilities in 1941 were inadequate to meet the sudden heavy demand for aluminum precipitated by World War II. Additional facilities were constructed and owned by the government but were mostly operated by the Aluminum Company of America. In 1946 these facilities were leased by, and later purchased by, Reynolds Metals Company and Kaiser Aluminum and Chemical Corporation; the pattern of Alcoa's competition in the aluminum industry had been established by the government.[10]

By and large then, we see that direct government ownership of industrial plants has diminished greatly since the World War II surge, although the disposal process still continues (e.g., General Services Administration was selling a considerable amount of industrial property

[6] The Assistant to the President, *Synthetic Rubber-Recommendations of the President* (Washington, D.C.: United States Government Printing Office, 1950), pp. 21–28 and 94–105.

[7] J. G. Glover and R. L. Lagai, *The Development of American Industries* (New York, New York: Simmons-Boardman Publishing Corporation, 1959), pp. 402–408.

[8] Atomic Energy Commission, *Annual Report to Congress* (Washington, D.C.: United States Government Printing Office, 1962), pp. 530–540.

[9] *Ibid.*, 295–299.

[10] Glover and Lagai, *op. cit.*, pp. 233–234.

even as recently as 1962: 47 such properties with an original cost of $406 million in that year alone).[11]

A significant revival of governmental influence, parallel in certain respects to that in wartime, has occurred in the past several years. Although this influence stops short of wartime measures, an examination of recent space and missile industry plant locations reveals a strong trend — even a stampede — to be near government-established facilities which utilize space age products, (e.g., witness the agglomerating effect of Cape Canaveral, around which facilities of such companies as Martin-Marietta, Pratt Whitney, Thiokol and Aerojet-General are or will be located).

Nor are all of the new space age facilities necessarily company-owned. The summer and autumn of 1961 saw a scramble by 36 firms to bid on the Saturn rocket contract, to be fulfilled in a plant selected by the government. The plant ultimately chosen was the government's large Michoud Arsenal at New Orleans. While the prospective contractors prepared their bids for operating in the Michoud plant, a number of them were simultaneously searching the Gulf and Southeast Atlantic Coasts for large uninhabited areas suitable for testing the rockets, should they obtain the contract.[12] This concern proved to be needless when the National Aeronautics and Space Administration entered the picture and acquired ownership or easement rights to 140,000 acres of land conveniently located to New Orleans. This acquisition involves moving 650 families from the site, an accomplishment which would be extremely difficult for a private organization.[13]

With the increasing complexity of technology and the large expenditures required in many industrial product development programs, it is difficult to see how the trend toward higher plateaus of direct government involvement in industry and industrial location will be reversed.

Direct Government Influences

The existence of economic hardship areas in the country in the midst of a generally high level or prosperity since World War II has been a

[11] Administrator of General Services, *Annual Report of the Administrator of General Services 1962* (Washington, D.C.: United States Government Printing Office, 1962), p. 11.

[12] The author's firm was engaged by one of the interested space hardware companies to investigate New Orleans and also to search for a test site. From this vantage point the author was able to observe first-hand many of the events preceding establishment of the Saturn manufacturing and test program.

[13] Most of the land area is in three large timber holdings and the communities involved are small and unincorporated. The publication, *Industrial Development and Manufacturer's Record*, March 1963, p. 30, reports that NASA will "actually only deal with a handful of private owners." Nevertheless, the potential problems of acquiring a multiownership site without the right of condemnation made other areas more attractive to site seekers for private organizations.

matter of concern to the federal government. This concern has led to attempts to ameliorate the hardships in designated areas by encouraging the location, establishment and expansion of manufacturing plants in such areas. To further these aims, the Office of Area Development of the United States Department of Commerce was established in 1947. This office was charged with helping communities get better organized to work on their own problems, including industrialization, and to give them the technical guidance and tools necessary to do the job. Conversely, the Office of Area Development also maintained community files for assistance to industries seeking new locations but did not render field assistance in these projects. To further encourage manufacturing growth in areas of chronic unemployment, rapid tax amortization on a portion of qualified new plants was permitted. This feature has since expired but there has been talk in the government of its revival.

The year 1961 saw increased impetus given to improving the lot of so-called "distressed areas," or "Redevelopment Areas" as they have been designated by the government. The instrument created by the Area Redevelopment Act of 1961 to carry out this program is the Area Redevelopment Administration. The ARA is empowered to assist both chronic areas of unemployment and low wage rural areas by providing up to $100 million in loans and $75 million in grants over a four-year period, to communities for facilities that provide jobs. A $200 million revolving fund was also created for loans up to sixty five percent of total cost of commercial and industrial projects in the Redevelopment Areas.[14] The program is being implemented by a field staff which works with the areas and with prospective industries. For obvious reasons, no aid is given to relocation of industries from one area to another; only expansions and new industries are qualified for assistance.

It is still too early to assess the over-all success of the ARA program in view of the program's cost versus its benefits, and the difficulty of separating ARA's influence from what may have happened anyway. Recent ARA news releases speak of that agency's successes in such glowing terms as "1045 permanent new jobs to result from ARA project in Providence, R.I."[15] "More than 1,500 new direct and indirect jobs result from this week's project approvals by ARA,"[16] and "$250,000 public facility grant to save 48 jobs, add 260 new jobs in Claiborne County, Tennessee approved by ARA."[17] Certainly one cannot deny that there

[14] "Aid to Depressed Areas Picks Up Momentum," *Engineering News-Record,* September 21, 1961, pp. 260–261.

[15] Area Redevelopment Administration, *News Release 62–172* (Washington, D.C.: United States Department of Commerce, 1962).

[16] Area Redevelopment Administration, *News Release 62–146* (Washington, D.C.: United States Department of Commerce, 1962).

[17] Area Redevelopment Administration, *News Release 62–203* (Washington, D.C.: United States Department of Commerce, 1962).

has been considerable interest in the ARA program within the areas affected.

The problem of safeguarding American industrial capacity from enemy attack led to another government effort to influence the location of industry. This was the National Industrial Dispersion Program, announced by the President in 1951.[18] Purpose of the program was to encourage the construction of new industrial facilities in areas which were considered non-target. As an added inducement, capital expenditures for protective construction in a defense plant were allowed a 5-year tax amortization, a feature which expired at the end of 1959. The industrial dispersion program has proven to be largely ineffectual in influencing plant locations.

Side Effects of Government Programs

The federal government, in its role of upgrading the economy of the nation by instigating, promoting, coordinating and financing all manner of projects from harbor improvement to census taking, has figured vitally in the plant location plans of private industry. Many of these efforts have been extremely controversial. Some are regional or area wide; others are ubiquitous. Regardless, the industrialist must consider this form of government action as an increasingly important factor in plant location plans.

Regional development projects culminate in importance in the very extensive Tennessee Valley Authority project. This project was begun in 1933 to develop the Tennessee River basin by flood control, navigation improvement, power generation and reforestation. Of these improvements, power generation subsequently has received the lion's share of the approximately $2 billion investment, accounting for four-fifths of the total. Water power resources have long since proven to be inadequate, and three-fourths of the power generation is presently done by steam. Ironically enough, TVA now advertises itself as the world's largest consumer of coal.

TVA has been bitterly assailed in certain quarters as "a sullen and indigestible lump in the free economy."[19] It has been defended devoutly in other quarters — including many persons who fall under its suzerainty — as a self-supporting proposition beneficial to the area and the nation.[20] (It is interesting to note that, since 1960, TVA must sell power bonds

[18] Office of Area Development, *The National Dispersion Program* (Washington, D.C.: United States Department of Commerce, 1957).

[19] "Promising Switch — TVA May Become the Yardstick for Public Power," *Barron's* November 21, 1960, p. 1.

[20] The author has discussed TVA benefits with industrial development officials in the TVA area and has yet to find anyone locally who is not happy with the economic effects of that project on the area.

on the open market. Such bonds are free of state and local taxes, however, and the agency continues to pay no federal taxes).

Irrespective of the arguments advanced by the opponents and proponents of TVA, much of the industrial plant location in the area can be attributed directly to the low power costs, navigation, water supply and other economic inducements which TVA has provided. Prime examples of such industry are the chemical complexes around Florence, Alabama, and Calvert City, Kentucky. The Atomic Energy Commission has found TVA attractive also, and purchases more than half of the power produced by that supplier.

The Bonneville Power Administration of the northwestern United States represents another government power project which has drawn new industrial plants to its service area to take advantage of low power rates. (It is interesting to note that the Hoover Commission Task Force estimated that on seven large power projects, the federal government lost $75 million in 1953 because of failure to recover the true cost of power. Power was estimated to have been disposed of at forty percent below true value.) [21] As to the future, the President hopes for a long-range comprehensive development plan for every major river basin by 1970.

No plant location determinant has been directly affected by the government to a greater degree than interstate commerce, whose instrument is transportation. The federal government began earnest efforts to establish a measure of control over the national transportation system by passing the Interstate Commerce Act of 1887. It has since taken an increasingly direct hand in transportation by financing improvements of navigation, new roads and air facilities.

The federal government has been responsible for the development and maintenance of the inland and coastal waterway system and in effect has subsidized this form of transportation. The Hoover Report estimated that just the maintenance of facilities developed for intracoastal and river navigation was costing the government 74¢ per 1000 ton miles of traffic carried.[22] From the standpoint of plant location, however, what is important is the freight cost to the company concerned.

One has only to search for an attractive, flood-free site along a major waterway to see to what extent good-waterserved sites have been preempted by industry. Certainly the chemical and basic metal complexes of the upper Ohio Valley and its tributaries and the petrochemical concentration of the Gulf Coast and lower Mississippi River offer ample proof of the attractiveness to private industry of the government's waterways projects. The well-known Houston ship channel is an excellent illustration of the magnetic powers of water-served sites on many types of industry. This project was begun in 1910 when the city of Houston and the federal

---

[21] MacNeil and Metz, *op. cit.*, pp. 126–128.
[22] *Ibid.*, p. 124.

government split the cost of a 25-foot channel to the city. The most recent development was Congress' appropriation of $19 million in 1961 for further deepening of the channel.

The federal government in 1956 increased its longtime influence on the nation's roads by instituting the $41 billion interstate highway program. This program calls for construction of a 41,000 mile system of limited access, high speed roads, ninety percent supported by federal funds; it is now more than half completed, constructed, or engineered. The popularity of these roads is attested to by industry's predilection to location near interchanges and the appreciated price of industrial land near these same interchanges.

Nor can air transportation be overlooked. Government subsidy of the feeder airlines has had a secondary effect on plant location by making areas remote from the main plant more accessible for branch plants and more palatable to busy executives. The government also regulates airline operations through air traffic controls. Presently, the Administration is supporting a $500 million, five-year program for modernizing air traffic control which is intended to increase air safety and improve service.

The role which the government has played in harnessing atomic power for peaceful uses should become increasingly important within the next decade. The Atomic Energy Commission has already spent about $1.3 billion to develop atomic power plants (vs., $432 million contributed by private industry), and after initial disappointments it now appears that sizable nuclear plants can be competitive with conventional power plants by 1966 in certain areas of the United States.[23] Further improvements in the efficiencies of nuclear power plants could result in diminishing some of the inter-regional differences in power cost, which in turn could affect locational plans of large power consuming industries.

The examples cited above represent some of the more salient illustrations of the indirect influence of government programs on industrial plant location. Many more programs in effect subtly influence the company considering a new location, and must be reckoned with.

Legislative and Legal Effects

The fourth major influence that the federal government exerts on the plant location decision is that which has been enacted by its legislative branch, interpreted by its judicial branch and enforced by its executive branch. It is, in brief, the myriad of legislative and legal factors affecting all phases of our economy.

The zenith of laissez-faire in America occurred in the period from approximately 1850 to 1870. Since 1870 there has been a trend, accelerated

---

[23] Norman G. Miller, Jr., "Atomic Power Push," *The Wall Street Journal,* May 24, 1962, p. 1.

by wars, toward greater governmental legal controls on all segments of business. In 1887 the Interstate Commerce Act was passed, prohibiting freight rate discrimination between persons, commodities or localities. Three years later, in 1890, the Sherman Anti-Trust Act further restricted American business by prohibiting mergers or agreements which produced restraint or monopoly in interstate trade.[24] Both of these restrictive acts were portents of similar legislation. Beginning in 1933, with the Roosevelt administration, business was forced to consider federal government regulations as a major factor in its operations — including plant location.[25]

No major plant location criterion has escaped the influence of government regulations. Transportation, labor, utilities, and of course taxes, must accept some degree of control from Washington. Witness the power of the Interstate Commerce Commission in the field of transportation. This agency controls rates on all interstate rail freight traffic and about one-third of the truck traffic. With its considerable power, the Interstate Commerce Commission is in a position to influence when many plant location decisions will be made and where the plants will be located, both regionally and locally.

The Interstate Commerce Commission has been under increasing criticism in recent years as the result of the economic problems plaguing the nation's railroads. The Transportation Act of 1958 directed the ICC to develop keener competition among different modes of transportation which, if implemented successfully, can be of considerable significance to site selection. It is noteworthy also that the President has proposed that the ICC be deprived of its power to set minimum rail rates. (On the other side of the coin, the American Waterway Operators believe that the unrestrained competition which would result from this move could be the end of the waterway system.[26] Certainly the readjustment which would follow would play an important part in plant location plans.)

A post-World-War-II transportation readjustment of unusual significance to industrial location occurred in 1948 when the Supreme Court outlawed the basing-point freight rate system. In this instance it was private industry, not the government, which had built-up an artificial framework of controls over freight. (More than 20 types of industry, including steel and cement, set the freight rates from certain "base point" locations to all customers from all plants.) Opinions were varied on the effect the basing-points system had had on plant location prior to its overthrow in 1948. The American Iron & Steel Institute admitted, however, that "many plants have been located in places . . . which would not be desirable places from which to distribute steel products if the basing-

[24] Thomas G. Cochran, *Basic History of American Business* (Princeton, New Jersey: Van Nostrand Company, Inc. 1959) pp. 166–170.

[25] *Ibid.*, pp. 97–98.

[26] "'Splitting Headache' on the River," *Dun's Review,* June 1962, p. 111.

point method of quoting prices were not continued."[27] The upset of this system by the Supreme Court provided a stimulus to the decentralization of certain consumers of the commodities affected but did not result in a sudden major overall relocation of industry.

Federal tariffs and import quotas have figured prominently in the development and location of American industry. An extreme example of these controls and their effects occurs in the sugar industry. About one-fourth of the domestic sugar used is subsidized beet sugar, produced in more than 70 factories located mostly in California, Colorado and Idaho. Imported quota and price-controlled cane sugar accounting for the balance of the production is refined in 24 plants, all but three of which are located in or near major coastal cities. A free market in this case would undoubtedly have resulted in no beet sugar production and consequently no beet refining factories in the interior of the country — but additional refineries for cane sugar on the coast.

Government controls over labor began much more recently than regulation of trade or transportation. In fact, it was not until the 1930's that effective regulations were instituted, regulations which solidly entrenched the federal government as a factor to be considered in this facet of plant location.

Labor controls which have particularly affected the locational aspect of industry are: (1) minimum wage laws, (2) laws governing collective bargaining, and (3) recent court rulings regarding employee job rights.

1) *Minimum wage laws* can exert an influence in certain low paying industries by reducing regional labor cost differentials and in some cases even handicapping an industry facing low cost foreign competition. On government contracts the minimum wage level may be still higher than that established for all interstate commerce industries, paring regional differences even further.

2) *Laws governing collective bargaining,* such as the National Labor Relations Act in force from 1935 to 1947, encouraged the growth of labor unions until they are now a major consideration in American industry.[28] From the locational standpoint it is significant that certain regions of the country have five times as high a percentage of organized labor as do others.

3) *Recent court ruling regarding employee job rights* have a direct impact on plant location and are being watched with considerable interest by industries contemplating a move. Two 1961 court rulings involving the Glidden Company and the Gemmer Manufacturing Company relocations were handed down as a result of suits by employees and the union, respectively, to require the companies to offer jobs to old employees in their new locations. Courts upheld the plaintiffs, citing that seniority is a vested right earned by long-time employees in a firm. In July, 1962, a Federal Appeals Court overturned the Gemmer ruling due to wording in the union contract limiting the union's

[27] Fritz Machlup, *The Basing Points System* (Philadelphia, Pennsylvania: Blakiston Company, 1949), p. 236.
[28] Cochran, *op. cit.,* pp. 170–172.

representation right to a local area.[29] The final outcome of these legal battles could significantly affect many future plant location decisions.

Another interesting governmental legislative measure which has had an indirect but noticeable effect on industrial location is the exemption of municipal bond interest from federal income taxes. In certain states, particularly in lesser industrially developed areas, communities have constructed industrial buildings to attract manufacturer occupants. Such buildings offer industry financing at a low interest rate and, because the buildings are municipally owned, they also offer exemption from local real estate taxes. There has been agitation from certain sources to prohibit municipal bonding power from this application.[30]

The above examples of regulatory influence represent several of the more prominent cases of the federal government's role in plant location. Many more examples can be cited both in the fields which are mentioned above and in other areas such as utility regulation, pollution control and even building height restrictions on sites near airports. We have seen enough, however, to realize that consideration of federal regulations, both direct and indirect, cannot be avoided in the plant location decision.

Conclusions

Four fundamental facets of government activity affect plant location, namely: (1) direct ownership or sponsorship of industrial facilities; (2) subsidization programs to directly encourage industrial development; (3) economic development and improvement projects; and (4) legislative and legal actions.

Since 1930 all of these areas of activity have experienced a governmental influence which has been gaining in both absolute and relative importance. In our complex and technological society this influence appears to be here to stay and even to continue to gain. This is not necessarily an indictment of government policy for, as we have seen, in some cases it is industry itself which has built up the restrictions and the government which has cleared away the red tape. And certainly the government must play the role of coordinator and contractor of our defense effort as it must also be the entrepreneur for worthwhile regional development projects — both functions which are beyond the capabilities of private enterprise.

Government influence on industrial location patterns and plant location criteria has been on the increase. Much is directly apparent; much is indirect and must be looked for if it is to be recognized. In either form, it is a major force in every plant location decision.

[29] "Court Bars Seniority Right of 5 Rehired by Unit of Ross Gear," *The Wall Street Journal,* July 18, 1962, p. 6.
[30] "Industrial-Aid Bonds Draw Fire," *Engineering News-Record,* January 18, 1962, p. 70.

Land Costs

Agricultural Rent Functions and Bid Price Curves of the Urban Firm

William Alonso

A. INTRODUCTION

In chapter 2 we have seen how the equilibrium solution of the individual resident may be found. We now wish to arrive at a formulation of market equilibrium. However, the classical form of solution for the individual cannot be used in this case to derive the structure of demand in the market. In the usual case, from the individual solution, one may derive a miniature demand curve for that person by varying the price of the commodity. If the demand curves of all persons are aggregated, one obtains a demand curve for the market. But in this case, land and distance are so intertwined that we cannot derive such a curve.

To illustrate this point, let us examine the variations in the quantity of land bought by an individual at a given location, t_0, as the price of land, $P(t_0)$, varies. The individual must maintain his budget balanced, so that equation (2:1) must hold:

$$(2:1) \qquad y = p_z z + P(t_0)q + k(t_0).$$

The individual decides how he will spend his money between land, q, and the composite good, z, by comparing the ratio of their prices to their marginal rate of substitution in equation

$$(2:14) \qquad u_q/u_z = P(t_0)/p_z.$$

By allowing the price P at location t_0 to vary, and solving for q and z, we can obtain the demand curve, which relates q to $P(t_0)$. But this demand curve will obtain only for that individual at *that* location. Variations in distance will affect the amount of money at his disposal by affecting the commuting costs term in equation (2:1). Equally as important, since both the marginal utilities u_q and u_z in

Reprinted from William Alonso, *Location and Land Use: Toward a General Theory of Land Rent* (Cambridge, Massachusetts: Harvard University Press, 1964), pp. 36–58, by permission of the author and publisher.

equation (2:14) are functions of z, q, and t, the marginal rate of substitution will vary as t varies. Consequently, the demand curves for the same individual will vary with his location. Since part of the problem of finding the market solution consists of finding individual locations, not knowing the locations of individuals we would not know which of their demand curves to use to build up our market demand curve.

There are difficult problems on the supply side as well. The principal one is that of defining the supply of land. While there is a fixed supply of land at any given distance from the center of the city, the total supply of land may be regarded as infinite for any practical purpose. The total supply of land, therefore, cannot be regarded as a fixed, finite quantity; rather, it must be viewed as a collection of stocks of land differentiated by their location.

These problems are similar to those encountered in the theory of agricultural rent and land use. In this chapter we shall examine a greatly simplified agricultural model to learn the method by which it handles the land market. The problem of the location of urban firms will be investigated as one that shares characteristics with the problems of both the agricultural and the residential land uses. In the light of this analysis, individual equilibrium will be restated in chapter 4 in a form that can be used to arrive at a market solution.

B. A SIMPLE MODEL OF AGRICULTURAL RENT AND LAND USE

The theory of spatial structure of agricultural production originated in 1826 in J. H. von Thünen's theory of the isolated city. Two recent and more complete statements are those by W. Isard and E. S. Dunn.[1] While this analysis can reach a very high level of complexity, the version presented here will be greatly simplified.[2]

In this type of model there is a single market at which agricultural produce can be sold, and all produce is shipped to this market. All land is on a featureless plain. Various crops may be considered, but for simplicity we shall deal with only one at first.

Let that crop be, for instance, corn. One acre of land will produce

---

1. Von Thünen, *Der isolierte Staat* (Hamburg, 1826); Isard, *Location and Space-Economy*; Dunn, *The Location of Agricultural Production.*
2. The principal omissions from the analysis are: (1) variations in the intensity of use, (2) variations in the costs of production with distance, (3) crop mixtures, and (4) the effects of varying fertility of land.

30 bushels of corn at a cost of \$10 in labor and machinery. The price of a bushel of corn is \$1 at the market, and consequently one acre's production sells for \$30. If corn were produced right at the market, value would exceed costs at the rate of \$20 per acre. However, corn produced at any distance from the market must pay shipping costs. If these costs are \$0.05 per bushel per mile, an acre of land at 10 miles from the market would have \$15 in shipping costs in addition to \$10 in production costs. Since revenue remains at \$30, the gap between revenue and costs is only \$5. At distances greater than $13\frac{1}{3}$ miles, costs will exceed revenues, and no corn will be produced.

The gap between revenues and costs is economic rent in the technical sense and becomes rent paid to the landlord in the ordinary sense. Suppose no rent is paid. A farmer notices that the gap between costs and revenues one mile nearer the market is \$1.50 per acre greater than at his location, and 2 miles nearer the market the gap is \$3 per acre greater. He will bid rents for these locations up to these amounts. The competition among farmers for the more favored locations converts this gap into rent and "wipes away any surplus profit which might befall the operator at any site."[3] The farmer retains only "normal profits," which may be regarded as a form of labor costs.

The rent at any location may be calculated from the expression

$$p_c(t) = N[P_c - C - k_c(t)],$$

where $p_c(t_0)$: the rent per unit of land at a distance t_0 from the market;

N: number of units of the crop produced per unit of land;

P_c: price per unit of the crop at the market;

C: cost of producing one unit of the crop;

$k_c(t_0)$: cost of transporting one unit of the product a distance t_0 to the market.

This rent function[4] is shown as $p_c(t)$ in Figure 11. The location t_e is that location at which rent is zero. At distances greater than t_e corn could be produced only at a loss.

3. Isard, *Location and Space-Economy*, p. 196.

4. This is the term used by Isard and Dunn. E. M. Hoover (*Location Theory and the Shoe and Leather Industries* [Cambridge, Mass.: Harvard University Press, 1937]), prefers "rent surface," emphasizing its three-dimensional nature.

We can now compute the total production of corn. It will be

$$\text{total production} = N \cdot S(t_e).$$

The function $S(t)$ denotes how much land is bounded by a circle of radius t around the market; t_e is the most distant location at which the crop is grown. In a featureless plain, $S(t)$ would be πt^2. $S(t_e)$ represents, then, the area over which the crop is grown, and N the number of units of the crop produced per unit of area. Should the total amount of corn produced at price P_c exceed the demand at

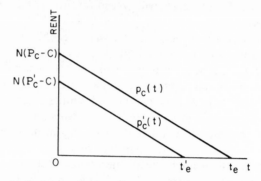

FIGURE 11. Agricultural bid rents for the same crop at two different market prices

that price, the price will drop to some lower value P'_c. There results a generally lower rent function (curve $p'_c(t)$ in Figure 11); the farthest distance at which corn would be produced would be t'_e (smaller than t_e), and the total production of corn would be reduced. Thus, through changes in the market price of the produce, the total production of the crop is brought into line with the demand for it. Rents, which are a residual, are downgraded as the price of the good drops.

This analysis has been at the level of the industry: in this case, corn-growing industry. How does it relate to the individual farmer at the level of the firm? The competition among farmers insures that all surplus profits go to the landlord in the form of rent, but at the same time it insures normal returns to the farmer whatever his location to motivate him to work his land.[5] "Thus, theoretically,

5. These normal profits are now considered as part of the costs of production, C.

the farm operator is indifferent to the position at which he is located, provided, of course, he is within the rent-yielding hinterland. Hence, observing the adjustments of the individual agricultural entre- preneur at each possible distance from the market yields, for the given crop, a theoretically valid rent function."[6] In other words, the industry's rent function for a given market price may be viewed also as the rent a farmer would be willing to pay the landlords at each of these locations.

Let us introduce another crop, wheat, with a rent function $p_w(t)$ as shown in Figure 12. Assume that the over-all supply and demand

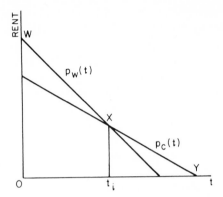

FIGURE 12. Bid rent functions for two crops

quantities are in balance.   Wheat farmers can pay a higher rent for land than corn farmers in the area between the market ($t=0$) and distance t_i, and landlords will rent their land to wheat farmers in this range. On the other hand, corn producers can pay a rent higher than wheat producers at distances greater than t_i, and that land will be put into the production of corn. The function denoting the rents actually paid will be *WXY*. The meaning of the $p_c(t)$ curve to the left of t_i and of $p_w(t)$ to the right of that point, then, is that these are unsuccessful bids for the land rather than the rents actually paid. A distinction must be drawn between rent functions which are rents actually paid and those which represent rents someone is willing to pay. The latter type may be unsuccessful in securing the land; if

6. Isard, *Location and Space-Economy*, p. 196.

they are successful they represent actual rents. For example, the equation $p_c(t) = N[P_c - C - k_c(t)]$ represents a *bid rent function* for corn; that part of the curve to the right of t_i represents successful bids; that part to the left of t_i represents unsuccessful bids.

More crops might be added to this analysis without changing its main features. Finally, when "... it is desirable to consider each firm by itself ... each firm can be considered as an industry. More boundary variables are introduced but so are more equations to determine the variables ... Thus firm and industry are mutually consistent in the spatial framework, and in the extreme case may be considered as one and the same thing."[7]

This very brief review suffices to point to the principal means of aggregating demand for the agricultural production factor land. First, for each of the competing users (firm or industry) a family of bid rent curves is derived, each curve corresponding to a given market price for the product and to a given level of profits for the farm operator (in the agricultural model these profits are "normal" in every case). Then, taking from the family of curves for each bidder the bid rent curve that corresponds to the appropriate market price for the produce, the curves of all the potential users of land are compared at all locations, and the land at each location is assigned to the highest bidder. These highest bids, taken together, constitute the actual rent structure. However, the "appropriate market price for the produce" must be found simultaneously. This is done by establishing the price at which sufficient land and no more is secured to produce the correct amount of the produce according to the demand schedule.[8] This price identifies which curve of the family of bid rent curves should be used. This curve states the rent for land the producers of that commodity are willing to pay at various locations, given that market price for their produce.

Abstracting from the particulars of agriculture, the method reduces to: (1) for each potential user of land, a family of bid rent functions is derived, such that the user is indifferent as to his location along any *one* of these functions; (2) equilibrium price at any

7. *Ibid.*, p. 248. The problem is stated in the form of a system of simultaneous equations, and a general statement is found in the section "Agricultural Location Theory Embraced and Generalized," pp. 243–251. The problem of finite vs. infinite price elasticities of demand faced by the industry and the firm cannot be discussed here. However, if market price is regarded as fixed, the statement is accurate.

8. This involves either an iterative series or a simultaneous solution.

location is found by comparing the bids of the potential users and choosing the highest; and (3) equilibrium quantities of land are found by selection of the proper bid rent function for each user. In the solution, the second and third steps are interdependent and must be brought into agreement either through a simultaneous or an iterative solution.

C. EQUILIBRIUM OF THE FIRM

Before trying to apply the general method of agriculture to residential land use, we shall examine commercial firms in the city as an intermediate problem, sharing characteristics of both. Moreover, whereas no formal theory of residential land use has been put forward in the literature, there has been some discussion of the possibility of extending the method of agricultural theory to urban commercial land uses.

Two authors who consider this possibility are E. Chamberlin and W. Isard. The latter is optimistic: "Yet it suffices to disclose the rather obvious interconnections of agricultural location theory and urban land use theory. In each, rent functions (surfaces) guide the allocating hand of the market. For both, relations to transportation facilities and systems are critical in the definition of effective economic distance."[9] Chamberlin, on the other hand, is pessimistic: "Urban rent for retailing purposes is a different sort of income from agricultural rent—in fact, although the two types are ordinarily thought of as analogous, the only resemblance between them appears to be that they are both paid for land."[10] But he goes on to say: "The rent of urban land is explained wholly, that of agricultural land partly, by the factor of location." He seems to be referring here to the differences in the fertility of land in agriculture. However, the theory of agricultural location is based almost exclusively on location: fertility differences are introduced later, as a complicating factor.[11] Both Isard and Chamberlin, then, are saying much the same thing, though they differ in their attitude.

9. Isard, *Location and Space-Economy*, p. 205.
10. E. Chamberlin, *The Theory of Monopolistic Competition* (6th ed.; Cambridge, Mass.: Harvard University Press, 1950), p. 266.
11. This is true only of modern post-von Thünen theorists. The earlier theorists, from Ricardo on, concentrated principally on fertility differentials, to the neglect of the location factor.

Chamberlin mentions some further differences between agriculture and urban retailing. He points out that the farmer pays for the productive ability, the retailer for the selling ability of land; that the farmer's site is at a given distance from the market, while the retailer's carries its market with it, sites differing from each other in the size and quality of this market. Moreover, the individual farmer is in the position of a seller in a perfectly competitive market, faced by a demand curve which is, from his point of view, perfectly elastic. The urban retailer is in the position of a monopolist, faced with a sloping demand curve.[12] The several farmers sell in the same market, the urban store has—to some extent— its own market.[13] Chamberlin's conclusion is that the rent paid by retailing activities is monopoly rent, in contrast to that arising in the perfect competition of the agricultural market. This is a thought-provoking distinction, but not fatal to the extension of rent theory from agricultural to urban land uses.

Isard, who has translated agricultural theory into terms of substitution analysis,[14] suggests that "... the urban land use problem can be presented in terms of substitution analysis and as an integral part of general location theory, much as agricultural location theory has been. In essence the businessman substitutes among various outlays ... he incurs additional rent outlays to acquire additional revenue potentials ... Thus, although the typical businessman may not attack his problem in such a comprehensive fashion, tracing out in a substitution framework what his reactions would be allows us to arrive at optimal patterns of land use."[15]

The analysis below will employ an orthodox or classical substitution analysis to find the equilibrium location of the urban firm.

12. This point is not very clear, for agricultural theory finds its equilibrium at the industry level, and it is the demand for the product as a whole that determines rents. This demand is sloped for the industry, if not for the individual farmer.

13. See Chamberlin, *The Theory of Monopolistic Competition*, appendix D, "Urban Rent as Monopoly Income," for these arguments.

14. Essentially of land rent for transport costs. The bid rent function $p_c(t) = N[P_c - C - k_c(t)]$ traces a path where the substitution between increasing transport costs and reduced land costs is such that the entrepreneur is indifferent among locations. "As the enterprise moves away from the market, it substitutes transport outlays for rent outlays, *ceteris paribus*," Isard, *Location and Space-Economy*, p. 196.

15. *Ibid.*, p. 205. It is not clear, however, what is meant by "optimal." Presumably this refers to Haig's "highest and best use," or else to the best location from the point of view of profits for the firm.

However, this analysis of the equilibrium of the firm will suffer from the same shortcomings as the analysis of individual residential equilibrium in the previous chapter. Therefore, in the last pages of this chapter we shall reformulate the equilibrium of the firm in accordance to the principles derived from our analysis of agricultural theory.

A word of explanation is needed, however, before going on with the analysis. What follows is intended to apply to urban firms in general. But, because the language sometimes becomes quite awkward when one tries to describe the behavior of firms in general, the firm will occasionally be viewed as a retail or wholesale concern. The analysis, however, will refer to urban firms in general, including retail and wholesale, office, financial, and manufacturing firms.

General Considerations

In considering the rent of an urban site, Isard cites the following determining factors: "(1) effective distance from the core; (2) accessibility of the site to potential customers; (3) number of competitors, their locations, and the intensity with which they vie for sales; and (4) proximity of land devoted to an individual use or set of uses which are complementary in terms of both attracting potential customers and cutting costs, whether they be production, service, advertising, or other."[16] Chamberlin adds "the prices that can be charged and the type of business which can best be conducted on the location." We shall consider the first of Isard's factors, the distance from the core. In our completely centralized city this implies the second factor; accessibility of the site to potential customers will decrease with distance from the center. The other factors, which relate to the interdependence of business locations, are too complex for analysis here.[17] The tendency of certain businesses to spread or gather may best be understood by Lösch's theory[18] in the former case and by the less clearly formulated theory of linkages in the latter.

16. Isard, *Location and Space-Economy*, p. 200.

17. The consideration of mark-up, to which Isard devotes considerable attention, can probably be explicitly incorporated into the analysis presented here. However, this has not been done at this writing. It is assumed that the firm will have optimized mark-ups, or else that they remain constant.

18. August Lösch, *The Economics of Location* (New Haven: Yale University Press, 1954).

The businessman in this case is very like the resident we considered in chapter 2. He is faced with a given structure of prices[19] for land, according to distance, which is described by the function $P(t)$. He will decide on his location and on the amount of land he wishes to occupy[20] in such a way that he will make the greatest possible profits. These profits may be defined as the remainder after operating costs and land costs have been deducted from the volume of business. This relation may be expressed in the following equation:

$$(3:1) \qquad\qquad G = V - C - R,$$

where G: profits, in dollars;
$\quad\quad V$: volume of business, in dollars;
$\quad\quad C$: operating costs, in dollars;
$\quad\quad R$: land costs, in dollars.

Let us examine the elements of the right-hand side of equation $(3:1)$. The volume of business, V, will depend on the location of the firm, t, and on the size of the site, q, used for selling, display, parking, and inventory. This may be expressed as

$$(3:2) \qquad\qquad V = V(t, q).$$

The operating costs, C, will depend on the location, t, in such matters as distance from warehousing and transportation terminals, and on the size of the site, q, in such matters as maintenance and ease of handling merchandise within the store. Of course, operating costs will also depend on the volume of business, V. Thus operating costs, C, will be a function

$$(3:3) \qquad\qquad C = C(V, t, q).$$

Site rent has been purposely abstracted from these costs to receive

19. We return now to using the word "price" rather than "rent" for the reasons given in the first chapter.

20. The size of the site is seldom if ever considered in the literature, most references being to rent for the site without mention of size. However, it should be clear that market equilibrium cannot be found without consideration of quantities. A notable exception to this neglect is found in Marshall, *Principles of Economics*, book V, chap. XI: "... industries are willing to pay a high value for additional land in order to avoid the inconveniences and expense of crowding their work onto a narrow site" (p. 450), and "If land is cheap he will take much of it; if it is dear he will take less and build high" (p. 448).

separate treatment. The businessman's site rent, R, will be the number of units of land he occupies, q, times the price of land at his location, $P(t)$:

$$(3:4) \qquad\qquad R = P(t)q.$$

The businessman will seek to maximize his profits by adjusting his location and ground space.[21] The marginal analysis of profit maximization could be shown diagrammatically in three dimensions, but it would be extremely difficult to read such a diagram. Consequently, only two-dimensional partial solutions will be shown diagrammatically, and the complete solution will be derived mathematically.

Diagrammatic Solution

First, let us assume that the businessman's location has already been fixed at $t = t_0$. The only variable he can manipulate to maximize profits will be the quantity of land, q. Marginal revenue (changes in V) will eventually decrease as q increases, and will eventually become negative when the store reaches excessive size. (See Figure 13.) Marginal costs consist of changes in operating costs, C, which are shown as decreasing with economies of scale (though, of course, they may increase after the premises reach a certain size) and the marginal cost of land, which remains constant at the price of land at that location, $P(t_0)$. Total marginal costs are the sum of marginal operating costs and the marginal cost of land. The most profitable amount of land will be q_e in Figure 13, where marginal costs equal marginal revenues. The dashed line, indicating marginal profits, is derived by subtracting total marginal costs from marginal revenues. It is positive up to q_e, and negative thereafter. If the businessman had a site smaller than q_e it would pay him to acquire additional land since the marginal costs would be smaller than the marginal revenue. However, he would not expand beyond q_e because mar-

21. Implicit in this is the problem of floor-area ratio. For completeness, we should include the firm's consideration of the number of stories in the structure and of the marginal costs of vertical versus horizontal expansion. However, in order to keep the analysis simple this has not been done. It should be noted that Marshall has something to say on this point. He writes of a "margin of building," such that an additional floor will be added "instead of spreading the building over more ground, [when] a saving in the cost of land is effected, which just compensates for the extra expense and inconvenience of the plan" (*ibid.*, p. 448).

ginal costs would be greater than marginal revenues. Thus, the marginal analysis with respect to the size of the site is of the type usually encountered in classical economics.

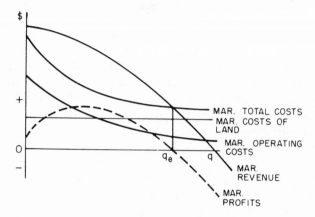

FIGURE 13. Marginal costs and revenue of the firm according to size of site, at a given location

Let us now consider the size of the site as fixed at $q = q_0$, and allow distance t to vary. As the distance from the core of the city increases, sales (revenue) would decrease. This is shown in Figure 14. This means that marginal revenue is negative as in Figure 15. Marginal costs are more complex. There are two components: operating

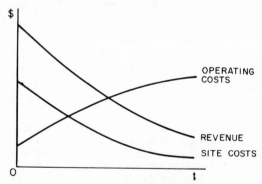

FIGURE 14. Costs and revenue of the firm according to location, holding the size of the site constant

costs and rent. Operating costs will increase with distance from the center (Figure 14), and consequently marginal operating costs will be positive (Figure 15).[22] The other component, rent, will diminish with distance from the center as land becomes cheaper (Figure 14). Therefore, the marginal site costs are in reality savings, and are represented by a negative curve in Figure 15. Total marginal costs, then, are the algebraic sum of a negative and a positive quantity, and may themselves be either positive or negative, depending on whether increases in operating costs exceed savings in rent or not.

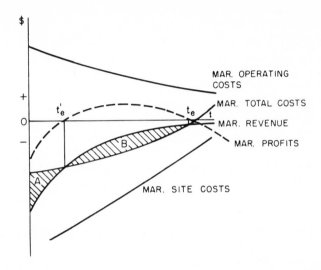

FIGURE 15. Marginal costs and revenue of the firm according to location, holding the size of the site constant

The dashed line representing marginal profits is the result of the algebraic sum of marginal revenues and marginal costs.

The equilibrium location will be at t_e in Figure 15, where marginal revenue equals marginal cost. This is not affected by the meeting of the curves in the negative quadrant. In the situation depicted in the diagram marginal costs are savings and marginal

22. In Figure 15 marginal operating costs have been shown as decreasing with distance because they are probably associated principally with transport costs, which in general increase at a decreasing rate.

revenue is gross income lost with movement away from the center of the city. Maximum profits, and equilibrium, will be achieved at that location (t_e) as long as marginal revenue intersects marginal costs from above. At the earlier intersection, t'_e, marginal revenue intersects marginal costs from below, and consequently further increases in distance would be profitable.

The fact that the marginal revenue curve cuts the marginal costs curve from above at some point is no guarantee, however, that that is an equilibrium point. In Figure 15 there are two shaded areas, A and B. Area A is the total loss involved in moving from the center to t'_e, whereas B is the gain in moving from t'_e to t_e. Obviously, then, area B must be larger than area A for t_e to be the equilibrium location. If area A is larger, profits will be maximized at the center where $t = 0$.[23]

Mathematical Solution

While the optimization of location and size of site have just been presented separately, the equilibrium of the firm requires their simultaneous solution. This can best be done through differential equations. A particular advantage of the mathematical approach is its generality. In the diagrammatic solution, above, we considered a case in which the volume of business decreased with increasing distance from the center of the city. However, in the case of a manufacturing concern, location may not affect the volume of business. In the mathematical solution, the first case would have a negative partial derivative of V with respect to distance, while in the second case the value of the partial derivative would be zero. Thus, a single solution will be general and embrace all possible cases. The equations representing revenue, costs, and profits for the firm, it will be

---

23. The other diagrammatic possibilities are covered by this criterion. (1) If the marginal revenue curve is at all points below the marginal costs curve, area A is infinite and area B is zero. Profits will be maximized at the center. (2) If the marginal revenue curve is over the marginal costs curve at all points before the intersection at t_e, and below beyond that point, area A will be zero, area B will be finite but greater than zero, and profits will be maximized at t_e. (3) For logical completeness, we should consider the possibility of the marginal revenue curve being above the marginal costs curve at all points to infinity. Then area A would be zero, area B would be of undefined size, possibly infinite, and a location at an infinite distance from the city would be optimal. A moment's thought will show this to be absurd.

remembered, are:

(3:1)   profits $G = V - C - R$

(3:2)   volume of business $V = V(t, q)$

(3:3)   operating costs $C = C(V, t, q)$

(3:4)   land costs $R = P(t)q.$

Our problem is, given the function $P(t)$, to maximize profits, G. Differentiating equation (3:1), we obtain

$$dG = dV - dC - dR.$$

Since G is being maximized, $dG = 0$, and

(3:5) $0 = dG = dV - dC - dR.$

Differentiating equations (3:2, 3, 4) yields

$$dV = V_t \, dt + V_q \, dq$$

$$dC = C_V \, dV + C_t \, dt + C_q \, dq^{24}$$

$$dR = P(t)dq + q(dP/dt)dt.$$

Substituting these into equation (3:5):

$$0 = dG = V_t \, dt + V_q \, dq - C_V \, dV - C_q \, dq - C_t \, dt - P \, dq - q(dP/dt)dt.$$

Substituting again for dV in the third term of the right-hand side of the equation,

$$0 = dG = V_t \, dt + V_q \, dq - C_V(V_t \, dt + V_q \, dq)$$
$$- C_q \, dq - C_t \, dt - P \, dq - q(dP/dt)dt.$$

This may be rewritten as

(3:6) $0 = dt(V_t - C_V V_t - C_t - q \, dP/dt) + dq(V_q - C_V V_q - C_q - P).$

Holding q constant in equation (3:6), so that $dq = 0$, we have

$$0 = dt(V_t - C_V V_t - C_t - q \, dP/dt),$$

from which, since $dt \neq 0$, dividing through by dt,

(3:7) $0 = V_t - C_V V_t - C_t - q \, dP/dt.$

24. Here C_t and C_q are partials of $C(V, t, q)$, considering V as a third independent variable. The dependence of V on t and q is introduced below.

Conversely, holding t constant so that $dt=0$, equation (3:6) becomes

$$0 = dq(V_q - C_V V_q - C_q - P),$$

and, since $dq \neq 0$, dividing through by dq, we obtain

(3:8) $$0 = V_q - C_V V_q - C_q - P.$$

The two equations (3:7, 8) enable us to solve for the two unknowns, t and q, since all the variables are expressed parametrically in terms of these two. The values of G, V, C, and R can be calculated from equations (3:1, 2, 3, 4) by putting in the appropriate values of t and q. Of course, the necessary steps must be taken, where there are multiple solutions, to find the *maximum maximorum*. The absolute value of G at the center ($t=0$) should be tested, with equation (3:8) holding, for dP/dt is discontinuous there.

Interpretation of the Mathematical Solution

Equations (3:7, 8) are of the usual form, stating that at equilibrium, profits having been maximized, marginal cost must equal marginal revenue. In this sense, they are restatements of Figures 13 and 15. Verbally, we may interpret the terms of these equations as follows:

Location equation: (3:7) $0 = V_t - C_V V_t - C_t - q\, dP/dt$.

V_t: marginal revenue lost from moving an additional distance dt away from the center;

$C_V V_t$: marginal operating cost (presumably negative) arising from the change in volume of business V_t (indirect effect of movement on operating costs);

C_t: marginal increases in operating costs arising directly from movement dt;

$q\, dP/dt$: decrease in rent payments arising from the change in the price of land with movement dt;

Size of site equation: (3:8) $0 = V_q - C_V V_q - C_q - P$.

V_q: marginal change in the volume of sales arising from the increase in area dq;

$C_V V_q$: change in operating costs arising from the change in the volume of sales arising from the increase in area (indirect effect of the change in area on operating costs);

C_q: marginal change in operating costs arising directly from the increase in area, dq;

P: cost of the marginal unit of area.

D. Derivation of the Bid Price Curves of the Urban Firm

In section B of this chapter it was noted that in the agricultural models a set of bid rent functions was derived for each farmer, such that he was indifferent as to his location along any one of these functions. We shall now establish a family of such curves for the urban firm. They will be called, however, bid price rather than bid rent functions for the reasons adduced in the first chapter. Though the analysis must be pursued much further before arriving at the market equilibrium solution, this chapter will conclude with a demonstration of how these curves may be used to find the equilibrium location of the firm.

We wish to derive a bid price function for the urban firm, such that the firm would be indifferent among locations at these prices. This would occur if all locations yielded the firm the same profits. It is clear that such a bid price function bears no necessary relation to actual prices. It is a hypothetical price-of-land-with-distance function, and might be termed an iso-profit curve. In short, it merely says: if price of land varied thus with location, the firm would make the same profits at any location, and consequently it would be indifferent among locations. (In chapter 4 we shall explore the similarities and differences between indifference curves and bid rent functions.)

We shall denote this function as

$$p_f(t)[\![G_0$$

which may be read as the price (p) bid by a firm (f) at each location t, such that, when the quantity of land is optimized, the firm can achieve a constant level of profits G_0, and no more. Since the level of profits is constant, the firm will be indifferent as to its location. Where the referees (f, G_0) are clear, we shall abbreviate this notation to

$$p(t).$$

In the future, the capital letter P will refer to an actual price, the lower case p to a bid price. We shall now show how such a bid price curve may be derived.

The bid price function describes prices that the firm would be willing to pay in order to make exactly G_0 profits. The quantity of land at each location will be optimized to make the maximum profits. Therefore, the equation for the optimization of land (3:8) will hold at every location. In our new notation this now reads

$$0 = V_q - C_V V_q - C_q - p_f(t) [\![G_0,$$

or, in the abbreviated notation,

(3:9) $$0 = V_q - C_V V_q - C_q - p(t).$$

The original set of equations (3:1, 2, 3, 4), must, of course, continue to hold. They will now be written:

(3:10) $$G_0 = V - C - R$$

(3:11) $$V = V(t, q)$$

(3:12) $$C = C(V, t, q)$$

(3:13) $$R = p(t)q.$$

We have, then, five equations (3:9, 10, 11, 12, 13), and six variables: $p_f(t) [\![G_0, q, t, V, C, R$. We may therefore designate one of these variables as a parameter, in terms of which to express the others. Therefore, the expression $p(t)$, which thus far has been a notational device to designate p, now becomes a function in which bid price, p, is uniquely defined by the single variable, t. This is the bid price function.

There are a number of corollaries to be proved concerning the properties of this function:

(1) *The bid price function is single-valued.* This means that, for any given level of profits, G_0, there is one and only one value of p possible at any given t. (See appendix G, note 1 for the formal proof.)

(2) *Two bid price curves, corresponding to different levels of profits for the same firm, will not cross.* (See appendix G, note 2 for the formal proof.) These two corollaries enable us to use an alternative notation for bid price curves. Since they are

single-valued and do not cross, any such curve can be identified by any point on it. It is possible to use the notation

$$p_f(t) [\![t_0, p_0,$$

where t_0, p_0 is any point on the curve (that is, $p_0 = p_f(t_0)[\![t_0, p_0)$, rather than using the level of profits as the referee, as in the notation $p_f(t)[\![G_0.$ This new notation will be preferred since it will permit direct comparison of bid prices among urban firms, residences, and agriculture.

(3) *The lower bid price curves represent higher levels of profits, and consequently are preferable from the point of view of the firm.* This is obvious since profits are a residual after operating costs and land costs are paid, so that the lower the price of land, the higher the residual profits. This implies that curves above the curve for zero profits ($G = 0$), correspond to operation at a loss, and may be disregarded. The firm would not choose to enter the market at a loss, and would not make such bids.

(4) *Bid price functions in general will slope downward.* This may be expected from common sense: since, as a rule, revenue decreases and operating costs increase with distance, bid prices must decrease for the level of profits to remain constant. This slope (whether or not negative) may be stated precisely. (See appendix G, note 3 for the derivation).

(3:14) $dp/dt = (V_t - C_V V_t - C_t)/q.$

The change in bid price is equal to the change in the volume of business minus the change in operating costs, divided through by the quantity of land so as to obtain a per-unit-of-land figure. Since, as a rule, (1) the volume of business will decrease with increasing distance, so that V_t is negative, (2) operating costs will rise, so that change will be positive, but preceded by a minus sign,[25] and (3) the quantity of land must be positive, the slope of the bid price curve must be negative.

25. The term $C_V V_t$, representing the indirect decrease in operating costs arising from the decrease in the volume of sales, will be negative. As it is preceded by a minus sign, its effect will be positive. However, the marginal costs per marginal change in volume of business must be less than unity at any equilibrium position, so that $(V_t - C_V V_t) < 0$.

*The slope will be such that the savings in land costs are just
equal to the business lost plus the increase in operating costs.*

In short, then, a family of bid price curves for a firm is very like
an indifference map: the curves are single-valued, do not cross, and
slope downward to the right. However, though both indicate a
preference mapping, in the case of bid price curves, preference is
downward rather than upward.[26] Equally important is the comparison with the agricultural bid rent curve. Both families of curves
are such that the user is indifferent as to his location along any one
of these functions. Both, as will be shown in chapter 5, can be used
in the same way to find the highest bidder, urban firm, or farmer,
for a location. They differ in that each bid rent function in the
agricultural family corresponds to a different market price for the
agricultural produce, while profits to the farmer are held constant
throughout at "normal profits." On the other hand, in the bid
price mapping of the urban firm, each curve corresponds to a
different level of profits, while prices (p_z) are assumed either held
constant or adjusted by the firm as in the usual monopoly problem.

Another difference between the bid price curves of the urban
firm and the bid rent curves of the agricultural sector is that, in the
latter, the individual farmer has no preference as to higher and lower
curves, since his profits are everywhere "normal." The level of the
curves is determined by a combination of derived demand for the
product and the entry and exit into the market of producers. As
will be seen below, in the urban case the level of the curve is determined by comparing the preferences of the firm with the opportunities available to it.

Yet another significant difference is that there is no highest
agricultural bid rent curve or indifference curve. The price of a
commodity and the level of satisfaction of an individual have no
logically necessary upper limit. The highest bid price function of an
urban firm, on the other hand, will be that for which its profits are
zero. Higher curves are conceptually possible, but they would mean
that the firm would operate at a loss. Accordingly, the firm would
not make these bids for land.

26. The more complex question of what is measured on the axes in either type of
analysis is examined in chapter 4, where a bid price curve mapping for a resident will
be derived from his indifference map.

E. Equilibrium of the Urban Firm through Bid Price Curves

In Figure 16 a map of bid price curves for a firm is shown. According to our notation, curves BPC_1, BPC_2, and BPC_3 are, respectively, $p_f(t)[\![t_i, p_i, p_f(t)[\![t_i, p_i']\!]$, and $p_f(t)[\![t_i, p_i'']\!]$. From the point of view of the firm, BPC_1 is preferable to BPC_2, which in turn is preferable to BPC_3. The firm is faced with an existing structure of land prices $P(t)$ such as that in Figure 17. Figure 16 represents a mapping of

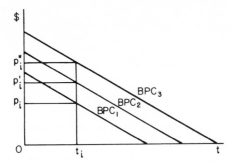

Figure 16. Diagrammatic mapping of bid price curves

the firm's preferences, while Figure 17 is a mapping of the opportunities available to it; preferences and opportunities are shown in the same diagram in Figure 18. The firm will locate at the point at which the price structure touches the lowest of the bid price curves with which it comes in contact.[27] At this point, t_e in Figure 18, the profits of the firm are maximized.[28]

The diagram does not tell us what the optimal quantity of land at this point will be, but this is not important. The bid price curve was defined in such a way that it took into account the optimization of the quantity of land for that price and location. Once the location and the price are known, finding the quantity of land is a simple problem corresponding to Figure 13. The quantity may be computed from equations (3:1, 2, 3, 4). Alternatively, just as we found

27. If the highest bid price curve, for which profits are zero, is at all points below the price structure, the firm can nowhere operate except at a loss and will not enter the market.

28. A price structure more concave from the origin than the bid price curves would yield end point locations.

the parametric form $p_f(t)\llbracket G_0$ in section D, we can at the same time find the parametric form for optimal land quantities as a function of distance for that level of profits.

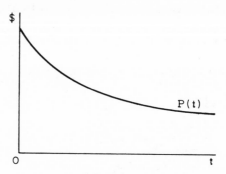

FIGURE 17. Diagrammatic price structure

At the point where $P(t)$ comes in contact with BPC_2 in Figure 18, the two curves are tangent. If they were not, they would intersect, and there would exist some bid price curve below BPC_2 which would be in contact with $P(t)$ and yield a higher level of profits. In other words, at that point the slopes of the two curves are equal:

$$\frac{d}{dt} pf(t_c)\llbracket t_c, p_c = \frac{dP(t_c)}{dt}.$$

To the left of t_c, $P(t)$ is steeper than the bid price curve. Since the

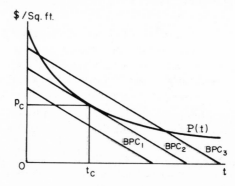

FIGURE 18. Diagrammatic bid prices and price structure: equilibrium of the firm

slope of the bid price curve is the change in the price of land necessary to offset the loss in sales and the increased operating costs, where $P(t)$ is steeper the savings in land costs exceed the loss of revenue and the increased operating costs of outward movement, and the firm would increase its profits by moving farther out. To the right of t_c, on the other hand, the bid price curve is steeper than the actual price structure, meaning that the savings on land are not sufficient to offset lost sales and increased operating costs. The firm would move to the left and come to equilibrium at t_c.[29]

Nothing new has been added to the equilibrium of the firm in this analysis. The equilibrium position was found, without using bid price curves, in section B of this chapter. In the last two sections the same assumptions have been marshaled in another way to arrive at the same conclusions. The point of this exercise has been to gain a view of the equilibrium of the firm such that it may be used as a starting point for arriving at the market equilibrium. In the next chapter residential consumer bid price curves will be derived and used to find individual equilibrium. After that, in chapter 5, we shall arrive at a market solution.

29. Where the lowest bid price curve and the price structure come in contact at the center of the city, the curves need not be tangent. In fact, since there is no left-hand derivative at that point, they cannot be tangent in the full sense. However, to the right the bid price curve must be steeper than the price structure. The reader can visualize this condition by viewing Figure 18 as having the origin at t_c.

The Economic Consequences of Industrial Zoning

WILLIAM M. SHENKEL

TODAY SPACE for industry is one of our principal urban problems. Colin Clark believes the most serious question facing America in the next twenty years will be "that of *location*, the distribution of industry and population between regions in the United States, and the apportionment of land for industry, housing, shopping centers and open space in the metropolitan area."[1] Indeed the shortage of suitable land zoned for industry is partly responsible for the migration of industry from urban centers.[2] The importance of providing space for industry and the central role of industry to local communities is demonstrated further by the various development commissions established in all states. Clearly providing suitable space for industry plays an important part in increasing the rate of industrial growth.

Yet despite the general importance of new industry—and its location—industrial zoning that affects locational decisions is often based on outmoded concepts—in most instances concepts that are founded on colonial nuisance controls. The needs of industry and the interests of the community are therefore in conflict with industrial zoning practices. This paper deals with several aspects of this conflict. First, to show the economic effects of industrial zoning practices, which are usually quite archaic, the economic justification for zoning is reviewed. Secondly, objectives of zoning and their application to industrial land are given. Thirdly, preferred objectives of industrial zoning are then compared to current, mostly obsolete, industrial zoning

practices. Finally, the economic consequences of misdirected zoning ordinances are suggested. The conclusion includes a discussion of industrial zoning measures that might better serve the community and claimed zoning objectives.

Urban land may be viewed as an economic resource that is relatively fixed, durable and, more significantly, relatively scarce. And because land also has utility, it has an economic value. The utility of urban land arises from its capacity to earn a return over costs. In the larger sense the concept includes public land since opportunity costs of publicly-owned land are evidence of economic value though the land is not devoted to private production.

To gain the maximum return (or satisfaction), land resources must be allocated rationally among the more urgent uses. To the economist, zoning is a device encouraging the distribution of land among those uses public, residential, commercial and industrial that result in maximum satisfaction, given the goals of the community.

Such a view goes beyond the popular view of planning. For instance, F. Stuart Chapin, Jr., states ". . . for land use planning purposes it would appear that the economics of use location can be giv-

[1] *Problems of United States Economic Development*, Vol. I (New York, New York: Committee for Economic Development, 1958), p. 289.
[2] Paul A. Wilhelm, "Industrial Development Planning," *Journal of American Institute of Planners*, August 1960, p. 218.

Reprinted from *Land Economics*, 40 (1964), 255–265, by permission of the author and editor.

en *crude recognition* by reference to the broad pattern of land values and trends of change in this pattern."[3] But if zoning is to serve the community, more than a cavalier treatment of urban land economics is needed. For many of the land use problems associated with industry, traffic congestion, depressed industrial areas, poorly maintained buildings, neighborhood obsolescence and the like have resulted from the "crude recognition" of the economics of industrial land use.

A controversy arises, however, over the conflict between zoning and the master plan. It is generally accepted that zoning is one of the devices by which city plans may be carried out.[4] The failure to co-ordinate the zoning ordinance with the master plan has produced three effects. It is contended that unplanned zoning (1) freezes development, (2) produces undesirable zoning, and (3) changes arbitrarily through ordinance amendments so that no comprehensive land use plan can be recognized.[5] The record shows that the absence of community planning may soon be remedied. The latest study published by the International City Managers' Association showed that 645 cities of 1,227 cities recently surveyed used comprehensive plans. Another 406 cities were preparing master plans at the end of 1961[6]

Consequently the more universal adoption of planning may be expected to correct industrial zoning practices developed from nuisance laws. But as zoning is made subordinate to planning, as suggested, the economic effects of zoning would seem to deserve additional emphasis.[7] In sum, planning is more than a means to create a satisfactory social life, it is a means to advance the economic and social goals of the community.[8] Zoning can be used to serve economic objec-

tives so that the limited supply of urban land is rationed among the most urgent uses. This concept also requires that each land use be given the optimum location leading to the maximum production of goods and services at the least cost.

If zoning is considered one means to implement the master plan, then we are vitally concerned with the efficiency with which zoning allocates scarce land resources among competing needs. And further, if zoning follows objectives of the master plan, zoning would appear adequate to accomplish the allocation function.[9] Hence the effectiveness of zoning regulations may be measured by their contribution to the orderly development of the community as guided by the master plan.

The Demand for Industrial Land

The effect of zoning policies are understood more clearly by reviewing the characteristics of the demand for industrial space. It is then possible to identify requirements that industrial zoning regulations must meet if industrial land uses are served. In the first place, indus-

[3] F. Stuart Chapin, Jr., *Urban Land Use Planning* (New York, New York: Harper & Brothers, 1957), p. 18. Emphasis supplied.
[4] Mary McLean, ed., *Local Planning Administration*, Third ed. (Chicago, Illinois: The International City Managers' Association, 1959), p. 307.
[5] *Ibid.*
[6] *The Municipal Year Book 1961* (Chicago, Illinois: International City Managers' Association, 1962), p. 305.
[7] *E.g.*, Carl Feiss, "Planning Absorbs Zoning," *Journal of American Institute of Planners*, May 1961, p. 126.
[8] M. P. Fogarty, *Town and County Planning* (London, England: Hutchinson's University Library, 1948), pp. 72-73.
[9] Zoning is technically described as the division of land into districts that regulate (1) building height and bulk, (2) structural coverage, (3) population density and (4) land use. See Mary McLean, *op. cit.*, p. 306 and Edward M. Bassett, *Zoning* (New York, New York: Russell Sage Foundation, 1940), p. 9.

trial land is subject to a relatively low rate of utilization. Table I shows the projected demand for industrial land compared to the demand for other urban land uses in the San Francisco Bay area, 1960 to 2020.

TABLE I — The Estimated Demand for Urban Land in the San Francisco Bay Area: 1960-2020
(*In square miles*)

Property Type	1960	2020	Increase 1960-2020	Average Annual Increase
Total Urban	616	2,389	1,773	29.6
Residential and Commercial	518	2,079	1,561	26.0
Industrial	98	310	212	3.6

Source: Adapted from Office of Area Development, Business and Defense Services Administration, United States Department of Commerce, *Future Development of the San Francisco Bay Area, 1960-2020* (Washington, D. C.: Government Printing Office, 1959), pp. 63-71.

These data show an average increase in the demand for urban land of 29.6 square miles per year. The major part of urban land is required for residential and commercial purposes—26.0 square miles per year according to data of Table I. But industrial uses account for only *3.6 square miles* annually. While it may be inappropriate to relate industrial land requirements with all other urban land requirements, these data seem consistent with other evidence.[10] Even for industrial land uses that would be expected to show the highest rates of land absorption, observers have noted that investors in industrial land must be willing to hold vacant land over comparatively long periods. According to some investigators full utilization of an industrial park may take ten years or more.[11]

The relatively low rate of utilization for industrial land places industry in an unfavorable bargaining position. The more intensive uses, residential and commercial, may absorb land that may have a higher comparative advantage for industrial purposes. Non-industrial land uses that utilize a greater share of urban land will tend to use sites more appropriately reserved for industrial purposes. Later, it will be shown that industrial zoning weakens the bargaining power of industry compared to other businesses.

Yet another characteristic of industrial land use is worth mentioning: Purchasers of industrial land must acquire land for immediate and future needs. As industry expands, it is more economical (within limits) to enlarge an existing plant than to vacate an existing site. An expanding firm has the alternative of purchasing land beyond current needs or of buying the minimum space for immediate use and planning for later relocation. But under the typical zoning ordinance, industry, once sited, must compete for available land with commercial and sometimes residential uses. The result leads to a mixed, uneconomic allocation of land for either commercial or industrial purposes. Also price reservations among industrial landowners may in-

[10] See, for example, Harland Bartholomew, *Land Uses in American Cities* (Cambridge, Massachusetts: Harvard University Press, 1955), pp. 159-188; and Marion Clawson, R. Burnell Held, Charles H. Stoddard, *Land For the Future* (Baltimore, Maryland: John Hopkins Press, 1960), pp. 51-123. It may be noted that the number of acres of occupied area per one-hundred persons is .39 for commercial use and .84 for industrial use. See *ibid.*, p. 78. See also, Raleigh Barlowe, "Our Future Needs For Non-Farm Lands," *Land, the 1958 Yearbook of Agriculture* (Washington, D. C.: United States Department of Agriculture, Government Printing Office, 1958), pp. 274-79.
[11] See Robert E. Boley, *Industrial Districts Restudied* (Washington, D. C.: Urban Land Institute Technical Bulletin 41, 1961), p. 40; and Theodore K. Pasma, *Organized Industrial Districts* (Washington, D. C.: Government Printing Office, 1954), p. 7.

crease to the point where relocation is the preferred alternative.[12]

One other fact stands out in the case of industrial land users: they require a high level of municipal services. The relatively small firm is handicapped by the inability to invest in land improvements, *i.e.*, a water supply, a sewage disposal system, land grading, drainage and other utilities. For residential subdivisions, the necessary utilities may be readily supplied because the higher rate of land utilization decreases the cost of holding and risks associated with land development. Industrial zoning, therefore, that allows industrial land to be used for other uses contributes to the shortage of improved industrial sites. In addition, the utility services required by industry would seem to justify the allocation of sites that may be improved at the least expense. But in fact the zoning ordinance frequently relegates the land area with the lowest utility and the highest cost of development for industrial use.

And finally, industrial prospects require relatively low cost land.[13] One reason accounting for the migration of plants to suburban areas is the cost of sites in areas of high population density. Because of the zoning treatment of industrial land only the most intensive industries may compete successfully for centrally located space—in itself supporting the generalization that industry uses relatively low-cost land, *i.e.*, land that does not have a higher economic use.[14]

If these characteristics of industrial land use prevail generally, it would seem that the zoning code would include regulations adapted to the unique demands of industrial land use. In the absence of other meaningful guides, the zoning code ideally would serve the following objectives: (1) to allocate industrial land according to anticipated industrial land needs; (2) to reserve industrial land for the exclusive use of industry and related businesses; (3) to reserve space for industries that use land extensively and for industries that generally lower the utility of surrounding land; (4) to provide areas for the development of prestige industrial districts (organized industrial districts) ; and (5) to conserve industrial real estate districts by regulating building bulk and height, building setbacks, parking and truck loading.

The first point constitutes recognition of the fact that industrial land is a limited resource. Under this assumption the problem facing the community is to reserve sufficient space of quality that seems most suitable for industrial purposes. In making the allocation, communities may be guided by the master plan, an expression of community goals. Then once the selection of land for industrial purposes is accomplished, it is most essential to reserve industrial land for only industrial and associated purposes. Flexibility may be provided by rezoning techniques presently used to change residential uses to commercial uses or other

---

[12] The extent of intra-regional relocation is suggested by *Industrial Movements and Expansion, 1947-1957* Economic Base Study Series 3 (Chicago, Illinois: Department of City Planning, 1961); *Industrial Study* (Detroit, Michigan: Department of City Planning, 1956), Master Plan Technical Report Second Series. Also see Institute for Urban Studies, *Industrial Land and Facilities for Philadelphia* (Philadelphia, Pennsylvania: University of Pennsylvania, 1956).

[13] See James H. Thompson, *Methods of Plant Site Selection Available to Small Manufacturing Firms* (Morgantown, West Virginia: Bureau of Business Research, West Virginia University, 1961), West Virginia University Bulletin, Series 62, No. 3-3, p. 81.

[14] For a discussion of land prices viewed as processing costs, see Melvin L. Greenhut, *Plant Location in Theory and in Practise* (Chapel Hill, North Carolina: The University of North Carolina Press, 1956), pp. 124-27.

zoning revisions as provided by ordinance. But once land is zoned for industry, the community must be willing to enforce the exclusive use for industrial purposes.[15] Otherwise land zoned for industry may revert to commercial and other non-industrial purposes if the second point is not observed in the zoning process.

The next two points are concerned with the sub-classification of industrial property. By segregating industrial uses on the basis of the intensity of use, many of the objections to industry may be removed. That is, by segregating the more extensive uses, *i.e.*, steel mills and the processing of bulk products to more isolated areas, the remaining industries may have a minor effect on the utility of surrounding areas. In this manner the utility of industrial space may be conserved even further. Furthermore, the final point suggests that reserving space for prestige industries is another way to classify industrial space demands. The industrial parks (or other special industrial districts in which landscaping controls, architectural controls, and structural coverage ratios meet the demands of the more discriminating industries) are a means to enhance the utility of industrial space and surrounding non-industrial space. The establishment of districts zoned for planned or organized industrial districts is further recognition of the need for quality industrial space.[16] Performance standards that control the operation of industry are additional measures that conserve the utility of industrial space. The urgent need to revise industrial zones to meet actual industrial needs has been recognized in several leading sources.[17]

If the goals of industrial zoning are accepted at least tentatively, it is then relevant to compare desired objective with actual practice. For it is submitted that industrial zoning has developed, not from the analysis of the need for industrial space but from a desire to protect property owners from the assumed nuisances or dangers of industrial property. A re-examination of industrial zoning and its development shows how these early practices affect current zoning regulations.

The Development of Districts Zoned for Industry

Probably the first attempt to form industrial districts began with regulations banning gun powder mills and powder houses in residential districts. Such measures were common in colonial times.[18] The early safety regulations against powder storage were broadened to control the location of wooden buildings, justified because of the fire hazard of wooden buildings. A Wisconsin Act of 1889 authorized cities to designate zones for buildings and structures according to the fire risks involved.[19]

---

[15] Under this philosophy zoning is viewed as an instrument to promote a rational land use plan. See Norman Williams, Jr., "The Evaluation of Zoning," *The American Journal of Economics and Sociology*, April 1956, pp. 262-63.
[16] See *Planned Industrial District Zoning* (Chicago, Illinois: American Society of Planning Officials, 1959), Information Report No. 120.
[17] For example, see *Steps to Secure Sound Zoning* (Columbus, Ohio: National Industrial Zoning Committee, 1958); *Principles of Industrial Zoning* (Columbus, Ohio: National Industrial Zoning Committee, 1962); and *Industrial Zoning Standards* (Chicago, Illinois: American Society of Planning Officials, 1955), Information Report No. 78.
[18] James Metzenbaum, *The Law of Zoning* (New York, New York: Baker, Voorhis & Company, 1930), p. 9.
[19] Erling D. Solberg, *Rural Zoning in the United States* (Washington, D. C.: Bureau of Agriculture Economics, United States Department of Agriculture, 1952), Agriculture Information Bulletin No. 59, p. 2.

Later, certain property uses were segregated from residential areas because of their nuisance classification. The laundry cases of San Francisco developed as a means of restricting the location of Chinese laundries in residential and in certain business districts. Such districting measures were defended because of fire hazards, poor drainage and the presumed moral hazards associated with Chinese laundries.[20] Ordinances were subsequently enacted that restricted the location of dance halls, livery stables, slaughter houses, saloons, pool halls and other uses generally regarded as nuisances.[21]

In 1916 Los Angeles enacted an ordinance that protected residential areas from commercial and industrial encroachment by establishing exclusive residential districts. Zoning at this time was merely a matter of protecting single family dwellings from the presumed nuisances of other urban land uses. Though districting tended to maximize the utility of residential space, it was not recognized that land must also be set aside for other urban, and equally necessary functions.

Comprehensive zoning, introduced by New York City in 1916 resulted in what has since been termed Euclidian Zoning —zoning based on the establishment of use districts, building height and bulk controls and density regulations.[22] The term comprehensive was used to describe the inclusion of other controls besides the establishment of districting. The comprehensive zoning of New York followed partly from the undesirable land use pattern documented by an investigation beginning in 1910. At the time it was claimed that the mixed commercial, residential and industrial uses developed because of inadequate land use (zoning) controls.[23]

Thus zoning for industry started with the segregation of dangerous uses from residential areas. The principle was extended to include those uses not only dangerous but regarded as a nuisance to residential occupants. Until 1916 zoning was considered largely a means to protect residential property. The reforms introduced by the comprehensive zoning of 1916, though introducing intra-district regulations, did not change the philosophy of districting in favor of residential use. More recent zoning techniques have departed from the Euclidian concept by permitting districting flexibility.[24]

Yet on analysis, zoning is still largely administered as a means of providing maximum protection to residential areas. It would seem that current industrial practices based on antiquated zoning regulations dating from colonial times violate objectives of the master plan. Some of the industrial zoning practices that appear inconsistent with (or directly opposed to) the master plan are covered next.

Industrial Zoning Practices

Of all zoning practices affecting industrial property, two practices stand out: selecting suitable industries on the basis of "prohibited" lists and making industrial districts progressively inclusive. The

[20] W. L. Pollard, "Outline of the Law of Zoning in the United States, Zoning in the United States (The Annals of the American Academy of Political and Social Science, Vol. CLV, Part II, May 1931), pp. 16-19.
[21] Ibid.
[22] Village of Euclid v. Ambler Realty Co., 272 U. S. 365 (1926). See also Stephen Sussna, "Zoning Boards: In Theory and In Practice," Land Economics, February 1961, p. 83; and Charles M. Haar, Land-Use Planning (Boston, Massachusetts: Little, Brown and Company, 1959), pp. 192-252.
[23] Gordon Whitnall, "History of Zoning," Zoning in the United States, op. cit., p. 11.
[24] Charles M. Haar, op. cit., p. 246.

latter practice is illustrated by the typical ordinance that begins with single family dwellings—that district receiving preferred protection. Each district of the ordinance following usually permits all land uses of the preceding district. Under this system typically, virtually all property uses permitted under the zoning ordinance are allowed in the final district—the industrial district. So then, residential districts are given *maximum* protection; industrial districts receive the *least* protection. The undesirable effects of the two issues warrant further discussion.

Prohibited Industries. The zoning ordinance will usually state that land and buildings in the industrial districts may be used for any purpose *except* listed industries, the prohibited industries. Frequently the list of prohibited industries will end with the qualification that "any further industry or use which creates corrosive, toxic or noisome fumes, gas, smoke, or odors, obnoxius dust or vapor, or offensive noise or vibration" is prohibited.[25]

Prohibited lists are subject to three criticisms: They are obsolete; they are incomplete and they are misdirected. The obsolescence follows from the list of industries that are presumed to lower the utility of surrounding land. Technical advances in manufacturing, the preference for one-story construction, modern industrial architecture and a tendency to increase the ratio of land to total floor area make prohibited lists, often copied from 1920 or 1930 ordinances, markedly out of date.

Prohibited lists are incomplete in the sense that the 77 pages of manufacturing industries listed in the *Standard Industrial Classification Manual,* any of which might conceivably lower site utility of

surrounding land, cannot be incorporated into local zoning ordinances.[26] In addition, many of the manufacturing industries not included in lists of prohibited industries may also be operated so as to lower the utility of surrounding land. An industry that uses public streets for loading and employee parking or permits outside storage of rubbish would fit in this category. It is virtually impossible to "protect" surrounding properties by limited lists of industries presumed offensive.

But the misdirection of prohibited lists constitutes their greatest weakness. For the acceptability of industry in reality is answered *not by the type* of industry in question but *by the operation* of that industry. Performance standards are based on the concept that if industries are operated in a manner that would not lower the economic usefulness of land, the industry should not only be accepted but encouraged.[27] In fact, because of variations in the method of operation, industries that are omitted in most prohibited lists could seriously lower the utility of industrial land.

In sum, prohibited lists stem from the earlier practice of isolating industries from residential improvements. But if industries are desired as part of the program to implement the master plan—an expression of community goals—then prohibited lists are inconsistent with zoning objectives. The important issue here is that industry acceptability is judged by the effect an industry has on

---

[25] Section 10, *Zoning Atlas,* City of Jacksonville, Florida, Corrected to June 1, 1955.
[26] (Washington, D. C.: Government Printing Office, 1957), pp. 45-121.
[27] See *Performance Standards in Industrial Zoning* (Columbus, Ohio: National Industrial Zoning Committee, 1960); and Robert B. Garrabrant, "Performance Standards for Industrial Zoning: An Appraisal," *Urban Land,* June 1956, pp. 3-6.

he surrounding environment. The list of *permitted* industries together with performance standards represents a preferred means to select industries in contrast to prohibited lists that follow from the "nuisance" theory of zoning.[28]

Progressively Inclusive Districts. Progressively inclusive districts started from the early practice of granting exclusive protection to residential districts.[29] Zoning districts typically begin with the single family dwelling district in which uses other than residential are prohibited. With the addition of multiple family districts, commercial districts and industrial districts in the zoning ordinance, permitted uses are made cumulative so that the final district—usually industrial—permits virtually all uses.

Zoning ordinances based on this principle (and this includes the large majority) give virtually no protection to industrial uses. The one exception concerns residential uses which are now customarily excluded from industrial districts.[30] To the extent that industry must compete for the available space with non-industrial users, three results may be anticipated: First, the competition for industrial space, increased because of non-industrial demands, may raise industrial land prices to a point above price reservations held by industry. Secondly, the industrial district is more comparable to a district with no zoning restrictions. The result is to create a mixed district— a district improved with businesses that have a low priority for land use. The effect produces land with the least possible utility for industrial purposes. Uncontrolled, non-industrial use in the industrial zone leads to traffic congestion, on-street truck loading, inadequate parking and, clearly, a supply of low quality industrial land. To the extent that commercial and recreational uses, *i.e.,* skat-

ing rinks, dance halls and the like, absorb industrial land, the master plan is not only ignored, but hindered.

A third consequence of progressively inclusive districts, and quite serious for cities with a shortage of industrial space, is the absorption of industrial sites by non-industrial uses. If the supply of industrial space is critical and the industrial area represents the most appropriate use of given land area zoned for industry, then it would seem that maximum productive efficiency would be gained by giving industry the same exclusive protection afforded residential use.

Surely the importance of industry and its contribution to the local economy furnish even stronger arguments for exclusive protection relative to the specious reasons offered in support of exclusive zoning for residential property. If the goals of the master plan are to be realized, industrial districts and their regulation must conform more closely to *economic* reality. Industrial zoning characterized by obsolete, incomplete, misdirected prohibited lists and progressively inclusive districts gives little support to the master plan.

The Relative Elasticity of Demand for Industrial Space

The effects of industrial zoning practices are amplified by the relative elasticities of demand for industrial and commercial space. Industry is placed at a distinct disadvantage because of the high-

---

[28] For example see *Cook County Zoning Ordinance,* adopted March, 1960 as amended to January 15, 1962, pp. 119A-155A.
[29] See Richard B. Andrews, *Urban Growth and Development* (New York, New York: Simmons-Boardman Publishing Corporation, 1962), p. 340.
[30] Seward H. Mott and Max S. Wehrly, *The Prohibition of Residential Developments in Industrial Districts* (Washington, D. C.: Urban Land Institute Technical Bulletin No. 10, 1948).

ly *elastic* demand for industrial space in comparison to the relatively *inelastic* demand for commercial space. The highly elastic demand for industrial land follows because most manufacturers may choose among a wide range of sites. For industries that are market or raw material oriented, this selection is considerably narrowed but even here transportation advances are increasing industrial mobility. The availability of sites for the expansion of existing industries, the establishment of new industries, and plant relocation among competing communities lead to a highly elastic demand.[81] In addition, the detailed study that many industries undertake before selecting a community and site also suggests a high demand elasticity for industrial sites.[82]

In contrast to the demand for industrial space, the demand for commercial space is a derived demand dependent on potential sales. In a given community, commercial enterprises would seem more restricted in the choice of sites than industry in general.[83] Moreover the limits imposed by population and personal disposable income restrict the amount of land that can be used for commercial space. So for these reasons the demand for commercial space would appear relatively inelastic.

But the supply curve of industrial land is probably elastic only to the point where the available vacant land is absorbed.[84] Beyond this point the marginal cost rises abruptly as the supply of industrial space is increased by conversion of existing non-conforming uses, the rearrangement of public improvements, the succession of commercial-residential land to industrial use and the like.[85]

Given these facts the land use pattern may be distorted from the ideal allocation as follows: The demand for commercial space in industrially zoned areas will cause land prices to rise above offer submitted by industrial users. The resulting price will tend to discourage industrial use for only the most intensive industries with price reservations corresponding to commercial land value will site in the industrial district. Because of the higher prices bid by non industrial businesses the best sites will be devoted to commercial use; the least usable areas will remain vacant or will be gradually purchased by industry at commercial land prices. For industry to compete successfully with commercial businesses, an additional condition is necessary: the demand for industrial land must increase substantially. But it is quite unlikely that the demand for industrial land in an area encroached by business would increase to the point where all land would be absorbed by industry. Yet another more serious result follows from the discriminatory effects of progressively inclusive districts: That is in the long run further expansion of industry is possible only at points where the demand for industry intersects the rising portion of the supply curve since the commercial demand for low-cost space will probably absorb the available supply. In other words, as the demand

[81] Richard U. Ratcliff, *Urban Land Economics* (New York, New York: McGraw-Hill Book Company, Inc., 1949), p. 139.
[82] See James H. Thompson, *op. cit.*, pp. 42-92.
[83] For a discussion of the demand for commercial space, see Richard U. Ratcliff, *op. cit.*, pp. 126-33; Ralph Turvey, *The Economics of Real Property* (London, England: George Allen & Unwin Ltd. 1957), pp. 28-33; Ernest M. Fisher and Robert M. Fisher, *Urban Real Estate* (New York, New York: Henry Holt and Company, 1954), pp. 315-17.
[84] For a fuller discussion of factors affecting the elasticity of secular land supply curves, see Raleigh Barlowe, *Land Resource Economics* (Englewood Cliffs, New Jersey: Prentice-Hall, Inc., 1958), pp. 21-22.
[85] This point corresponds to the point referred to by Turvey as the intersection of the supply curve with the rate of interest. See *op. cit.*, p. 11.

for urban land increases, the industrial space tends to be used for non-industrial uses until vacant land is utilized. Communities that subscribe to progressively inclusive districts then have little opportunity to attract additional industry. With industrial land prices distorted upward by the demand for non-industrial space, it then becomes necessary to subsidize industry so that land costs are equal to alternative costs in other locations.[36] Such subsidies are typical of urban renewal projects that redevelop mixed, industrial districts to exclusive industrial districts.

The latter effect has even more serious consequences when prohibited lists of industries are enforced by the local community. Then the result is to prevent entry of industry, further lowering the effective demand for industrial space under conditions in which commercial space demand distorts industrial land prices upward. Therefore, communities enforcing progressively inclusive districts and prohibited lists are relatively handicapped in attracting new industry. The remedy lies in constructing zoning ordinances more in accordance with economic objectives. But if zoning ordinances continue to be based on nuisance controls or Euclidian zoning, prospects for industrial expansion are considerably lowered.

Conclusion

Industrial zoning represents a paradox in community development. On the one hand, chambers of commerce, state development commissions, trade associations and the community in general, apparently favor new industry or the expansion of existing industry. The economic benefits of industrial expansion are widely accepted.[37]

On the other hand, negative industrial zoning is without doubt inconsistent with community objectives. To the extent that the master plan is evidence of community intent and, if the enthusiasm shown for new industry is indicative of community desires (or even need), then industrial zoning not only fails to conform to public desires but may even retard community growth. The seeming conflict between industrial zoning practices and community desires follows from the continued observance of nuisance controls developed in colonial times. Yet nuisance controls violate claimed objectives of zoning controls and the master plan, even in view of the special land use requirements of industry.

The list of prohibited industries, a negative type of control, and progressively inclusive districts distort the land use pattern. Industry is unable to compete for scarce land more appropriately used for industrial purposes by reason of non-exclusive zoning. Prohibited lists bar industry that otherwise might use lower cost sites. In addition, progressively inclusive districts detract from the utility of sites supposedly reserved for industry and further result in increased industrial land prices.

If industrial zoning is to serve as a positive land use control, two zoning

---

[36] For arguments in support of local subsidies see John E. Moes, *Local Subsidies for Industry* (Chapel Hill, North Carolina: University of North Carolina Press, 1962), pp. 3-46.

[37] For example see Wesley C. Calef and Charles Daoust, *What Will New Industry Mean to my Town?* (Washington, D. C.: Government Printing Office, 1955); *The Effect of an Industry on a Small Rural Community* (Little Rock, Arkansas: Department of Labor, 1958); *The Effect of Industrialization on Six Small Wisconsin Cities* (Madison, Wisconsin: Bureau of Business Research and Service, University of Wisconsin, 1959); and *What New Industrial Jobs Mean to a Community* (Washington, D. C.: Chamber of Commerce of the United States, 1954).

reforms would appear necessary: (1) the introduction of permissive lists of acceptable industries with performance standards as a substitute for prohibited lists, and (2) the extension of exclusive zoning privileges (usually granted only to residential uses) to industrial uses. The first point requires performance standards instead of prohibited lists of presumed nuisances. Performance standards have been criticized on grounds of administrative difficulties.[38] However, the importance attached to industry surely justifies administrative expenses that would overcome the economic loss associated with inadequate zoning procedures.

The second point calls for a departure from existing zoning practices. But such steps have already been taken in part. The exclusive use of urban renewal sites for industrial purposes and the trend to exclusive zoning with limited court approval are steps in this direction.[39] Special zoning districts, e.g., planned industrial district zoning and governmental ownership of land reserved for industry are other developments supporting the need for the exclusive reservation of land for industrial purposes.[40] Many of these land use practices, though necessary to overcome industrial zoning deficiencies, are a poor substitute for zoning that is consistently applied to all land uses, especially for industrial uses.

---

[38] John Delafons, *Land-Use Controls in the United States* (Cambridge, Massachusetts: Joint Center for Urban Studies of the Massachusetts Institute of Technology and Harvard University, 1962), pp. 43-44; Robert E. Boley, "Performance Standards-Practical Considerations," *Urban Land*, June 1960, pp. 2-8; James Alan Null, *Selected Administrative Problems Caused by Performance Standards in County and Industrial Zoning* (Washington, D. C.: National Association of County Officials, 1960), Information and Educational Service Report No. 11, n.p. and Marvin A. Salzenstein, "Industrial Performance Standards: Do They Work?" *Zoning Digest*, March 1962, pp. 73-76.

[39] Donald R. Bentz, "Industrial Zoning to Exclude Higher Uses," *New York University Law Review*, November 1957, pp. 1261-76.

[40] *Planned Industrial District Zoning* (Chicago, Illinois: American Society of Planning Officials, 1959), Information Report No. 120.

Costs Associated with Internal Scale Economies

THE MEASUREMENT OF ECONOMIES OF SCALE[1]

CHRISTOPHER WINSTEN and MARGARET HALL

1. In this paper we discuss a number of problems which arise in the attempt to assess the extent of economies of scale in an industry. The work was provoked by, and indeed partly comes from, a statistical study of the data collected in the various Censuses of distribution taken both in Great Britain and in the United States in recent years.[2] Our quantitative findings are being published separately, here we restrict ourselves to some theoretical problems of interpretation. But because of the nature of our source of inspiration, our examples will be taken from the field of shops and distribution, they have the advantage of being familiar and also present interesting special problems. We found that the immense volume of data collected from many different trades, and covering a wide area, provided a fascinating challenge.

2. We have already published a discussion of the notion of efficiency in economics,[3] and it may be useful to take first an idea considered there.

Efficiency analysis is essentially a comparison of a range of entities which either exist or *could* exist. One does not always take one's standards from something that exists: sometimes one takes them from something that one merely judges as possible. Thus it is important to define in any particular investigation the group of real or possible entities which are allowed in the analysis; or, in other words, enter into the population. In defining this population one may also be defining the field of choice which is being considered as open to the units under study. Different investigators may have different ideas of the possible: i.e. of the opportunities open to the firms or units in mind. Such differences of judgment on the part of the analyst may have important effects on the statistical analysis, which thus may contain an element of the subjective, blended with its apparently objective form. It is thus important for the investigator to state his range of comparison as precisely as possible.

A second point, which arises in efficiency analysis, but is important here also, concerns the way we define the economic units which we are considering. In comparing different units, one must be quite

---

[1] This paper was read at the European meeting of the Econometric Society, held at Naples in September 1960.

[2] Hall, Knapp and Winsten: *Distribution in Great Britain and North America: A study in structure and productivity*. Oxford: Clarendon Press (to be published shortly).

[3] 'The Ambiguous Notion of Efficiency': Margaret Hall and Christopher Winsten, *Economic Journal*, March 1959.

Reprinted from *Journal of Industrial Economics*, 9 (1960–1961), 255–264, by permission of the authors and editor.

sure what is being taken as the defining characteristic of the unit. We will take our example from distribution again; in fact it is in the econometric analysis of shops that the problem arises in its most obvious form.

At any one time a shop is a conjunction of a variety of elements and these may not stay together. There are: the firm — the legal entity, the managers, the technique used in running the shop, the site of the shop, its building, etc. (which may conceivably be included in the category of technique). These are different aspects, and as time goes on they may be separated from each other. An aggressive firm may move to a better site, yet still leave another firm to operate a shop on the old one. Or it may switch its technique at the old site — switching from counter-service to self-service for example. The management may or may not stay with the firm, or the shop. These and other examples emphasize that it is necessary to identify which aspect of the unit interests us. Of course it is possible to think of these different aspects as factors of production, but in the examples we have mentioned this does not seem a particularly constructive way of seeing the problem. We are not thinking of these factors being added at will to some productive unit apart from themselves, but rather of them as individual entities with some permanence through time, some particular one of which is taken, in fact, to define the unit. In a time series analysis the importance of identifying these different aspects, as soon as mentioned, seems obvious. Cross-section studies, of the kind made on the basis of Census data, of a number of shops at the same time, do not call attention to this difficulty; but it is present, all the same. The problem is important because one has to interpret cross-section data in terms of response functions, as we shall see, and these will be different with the different definitions of unit. For example, the response of output to change of input with the site unchanged may be very different from that which is obtained when expansion takes place by moving to a more appropriate site. An analogous problem arises in the study of household budgets through time. Should a household be considered as associated with the 'head of the household', remaining the same unit as long as he is the same, or be associated with the same place of residence, or should it only continue to exist as long as the same people are together? The problem is often a difficult one. Here as in other places, economic problems have something in common with those of biology, where also the unit can be difficult to define. Since the nature of the response function affects the statistical interpretation of the data, so also must the definition of unit used.

3. We come now to the question of the different dimensions of

scale. For the sake of definiteness we will, in what follows, think of the firm as being defined as a legal entity. Roughly these different dimensions can be classified as input dimensions and as output dimensions. Input dimensions are such things as value of assets or size of labour force. But we are primarily interested in the different dimensions of output, since our study concerned the effects on its structure and productivity of the environment in which distribution is carried out. Dimensions of scale have often been enumerated, but usually without this distinction being made between input and output dimensions. We were, in our study, especially interested in the way enterprises adapt to the different calls on them occasioned by the different economic environments in which they find themselves. They partly adapt by adjusting their inputs to the job they want to do, i.e. their desired outputs. Thus measures of size by output would seem logically to have priority over measures of size by inputs.

The dimensions of scale of output along which a distributive unit can expand can be listed as follows:

(*a*) Turnover can increase, so that the unit or organization is performing more of its services per week (we might call this a greater intensity of output).

(*b*) The operations of the organization may be carried out at more outlets (as when an independent shop expands to become a chain of shops).

(*c*) The range of operations may be widened, in the sense that the shop (or each shop of the chain) sells a wider range of goods. This is an aspect of scale that is quite prominent at the moment, as supermarkets, for example, carry ranges of goods not previously associated with grocery and in many specialists' trades the process of 'poaching', the selling of merchandize traditionally sold by another trade, is going on.

(*d*) The operations may be 'deepened' in the sense that the organization performs more of the services needed before the goods are consumed. A retail organization, for example, may do its own packaging, wholesaling or even manufacturing.

(*e*) A particular type of operation may be repeated more times. In manufacturing, production runs may be longer; in distribution, the same lines may be carried longer, with the consequent decrease in buying costs.

An aspect of scale which does not altogether fit in with those given above, but is nevertheless important is

(*f*) The quantities actually bought at each transaction may be larger. This may occur either when consumers buy larger quantities of the same goods (bigger packets, for example) or more types of goods at the same time. Though it is arguable sometimes whether such a tendency increases or reduces the task performed by the retailer, this case can well be discussed under the heading of economies of scale, and can have an important effect. It is analogous to the making of a larger article in manufacturing.

These are six of the dimensions of scale which can roughly be classified as scales of output. They can be combined amongst themselves in many different ways (in fact in 2^6-1, i.e. 63 ways), and expansion will often occur along particular combinations of dimensions; for example, as a chain acquires more shops so it will tend to take over more of its own wholesaling. There are, however, other environmental factors which influence the task to be performed by the shop, but which perhaps just escape the classification as scale factors. One such is the time pattern of demand. Demand may be evenly spread or come in sharp peaks and troughs (at and between rush hours, for example). In the latter case, it may sometimes be possible to take advantage of 'economies of scale' at the peaks, without incurring corresponding losses in the troughs. Or, if, for example, the peaks and troughs are not predictable, uneven demand may lead to losses. Thus unevenness of demand is a subject close to that of economies of scale, but cannot be classified under the same head.

4. Now that we have roughly delimited what we mean (or rather, the many things we can mean) by scale of output, we must try to assess how important scale will be in determining the costs of operation. There are two ways of answering this question. The first is to study the theoretical advantages (and disadvantages) of large-scale operations. By this means we will be led to an idea of how, for example, an increase in the demand for goods from a shop might lead to a decrease in unit costs, if the management grasped the opportunities available to them. The second method is to examine the data concerning shops available from the censuses. Such data can help to answer a rather different sort of question: to what extent do economies of scale occur in practice?

Theoretical reasons for the existence of economies of scale in various types of economic organization have been thoroughly discussed in economic literature, from Adam Smith, through Babbage, to the more recent literature, of which J. M. Clark's *Economics of Overhead Costs* is a notable example. We will not list them here, but will interpolate two considerations which must be borne in mind in studying economies of scale by any means.

Firstly, the range of available techniques changes in the course of time, as do the range and price of equipment. Thus, there may be great potential economies of scale at one time and then, following the invention of new small-scale techniques, or the cheapening of previously expensive equipment, the potential productivity of the small unit may in part catch up on the larger. (This kind of thing happened in the transport industry in this country as road transport overtook rail, for example). Some such thing may happen in retailing in the future, for example as cheap automatic vending devices, suitable for use inside or outside shops, become available. In this field, as in all others, the potential economies of scale can change over time. The invention of the supermarket has certainly much increased the economies of large-scale operation in the grocery sector.

Secondly, the difficulty of the job done by an organization and the resources which have to be used to perform it must depend on the relationship of the organization to those whose work is similar or complementary. And it may well be that a series of organizations may co-operate so well that they achieve the efficiency of a large-scale operation; indeed, together they may hardly be distinguishable from a single coherent unit except in name and law. On the other hand, a large organization may easily be in the state where none of the departments knows much of what the others do, and there is little interchange between them of staff or ideas. In that case, it has very nearly broken down into its component organizations.

We come now to the problems of measuring economies of scale from census data. Such data only give a cross-section study at a particular time. Yet the relationships in which one is interested in economics are always those which are useful in describing and explaining the changes which take place from one time to another. Part of the problem will therefore be how far we can switch from cross-section studies to time-series relations. And part will be the question of indicators of input and output.

5. *The question of indicators.* The indicator to be used depends partly on the range of comparison of the study, including both the actual and potential units entering into the comparison, and also partly on the valuation to be used. In retail distribution there are a host of different services which are provided by a shop, and all of them could be considered as output. These services may be valued differently by different people. Thus if the relative proportions vary over the range of comparison, different people would have different ideas of relative output. Partly with this in mind, we restricted our range of comparison to fairly narrow limits: in fact to particular trade groups. Within such groups, the value of sales of a shop is roughly proportional to the volume of throughput, and we can take services

as proportional to throughput. At the worst this imposes a valuation on services, but we think it is a valuation that gives a useful basis for discussion.[4] Of course there are other possible indicators of output: value added and gross margins are often used. If the range of comparison is sufficiently restricted, then these should be highly correlated with value of sales. If not, then all three have potential weaknesses: for example, value added may be affected by monopoly elements in pricing, sales are not affected by an increase of depth of task. Value added, although at first sight an attractive measure of output, involves, especially in retail distribution, the addition of the values of many different services. Yet different people may value these services in different ways. Even if we could get a measure of each of these services directly we should still face the problem of bringing them to a common scale, an idea which involves valuing each of them. The value-added notion gives only one possible way of relating the valuations, that reached by the bargainings and frictions of the market, and it may in fact satisfy no individual member and thus may be irrelevant for any particular analysis.

As an indicator of input, we used persons employed. Here again there is an imposed valuation: each person is valued as equal to all others. The alternative might be to take wages as a valuation, though this can be just as arbitrary in many ways. Again we think that our valuation can form the basis of a useful discussion, though we would agree that others would too.

Once indicators (with their associated valuations) have been selected, it is still possible for units to differ in efficiency because of differences of inputs and of outputs not shown up by the indicators. They may, for example, be able to provide those services which are valued in a particular analysis as the same as others but are cheaper to provide, or use workers valued in the analysis as the same as others but cheaper to hire. These adaptations may sometimes explain the economies or diseconomies of scale we find, but the effects still exist, and should be measured. They are *not* explained away.

6. The data supplied by the census effectively give only the regressions of sales on labour, and labour on sales for particular trades. If we are willing to grant that labour is useful as the sole measure of input in distribution, and it is certainly the dominant one there, then we must question how much these regressions may tell us about economies of scale. Our primary interest is in how much an autonomous change in demand for the services of the industry will

---

[4] However, the restriction of the range of comparison introduces an interesting statistical point, which will be noted in section 8 later.

produce a change in productivity. It would thus appear at first sight that we are interested in the regression of labour on sales, the latter being the independent variable for changes through time.

But in looking at census data we are not looking at a time series, we are looking at a variety of units at the same time. And to interpret the results, we will have to have a theory of how these firms reached their relative positions on the scatter diagram of output against input. To do this we must take into account the possibility that each has in part adapted to its own peculiarities, as well as to the economic climate in which it finds itself, a climate which may be influenced by the numbers and behaviour of its competitors.

The first point has been discussed by one of us (C. W.)[5] It is essentially related to the statistical theory associated with 'simultaneous equation' systems. If one thinks of each firm as having a characteristic production function, and supposes that those firms which are more efficient have higher production functions, they may adapt to these higher production functions by expanding more. This will give a tilt to the scatter diagram, exaggerating in the direction of greater economies, or less diseconomies, of scale. Simultaneous equation theory usually assumes the firms have reached an equilibrium state. Even if they have not done so, however, we can often see what sort of qualitative effect a tendency for firms to adapt themselves in this way will have on the scatter diagram. The point is illustrated in diagram 1.

Something of the sort we have just described must surely go on, though the effect may not be too great in most trades. The market for most shops is limited and they cannot expand without incurring increasing costs, as they have to attempt to take custom from others fairly near them. These costs will, as we said above, depend on the number and actions of the competitors.

7. If we are interested in the responses in productivity of the whole trade (industry) to autonomous increases in demand, then the cross-section studies may underestimate possible economies for another reason. Since some of the costs of each firm are costs of competition, an autonomous increase in demand may give each unit access to new demand without incurring such costs. Thus it may raise the 'cross-section' production functions of many of the firms.

8. Not only this, however, but an autonomous increase in demand may bring new firms into the industry, and a decrease may remove old ones. A cross-section study only takes into account those firms that exist at the time: it cannot in the nature of the case predict the

[5] 'The Present Position in Econometrics', *Journal of the Royal Statistical Society, Series A,* 1960.

new entrants, or those firms that may give up. Any inference from cross-section studies to time series results will have to make allowance for this possibility. It will also have to guess whether the new entrants are more or less efficient on the average than the old. Moreover, the new entrants, being competitors with those already there, may depress their production functions again by causing them to incur extra costs of competition.

A similar point is one which is especially likely to arise when the range of competition is kept narrow. It may be that an efficient firm may find it best to expand in a way that takes it out of the scope

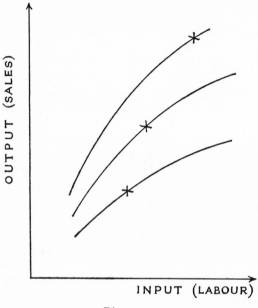

Diagram 1.

of the comparison, a grocer may take on more lines and become a department store, for example. We do not think that this happens to a statistically important extent at any rate over the fairly short run. But the point illustrates the disadvantages of too narrow comparisons. The best economies of scale may be those which involve a quite distinct change of nature of the unit.

9. We decided to examine the scatter diagrams for some trades in more detail, and obtained from the British Census authorities some special tabulations giving the complete scatter of sales and labour employed for some relatively homogeneous trades.[6] When we

[6] These detailed figures will be published in the book cited above.

examined these, some surprising features emerged. If one examined the regression of output on input (the result was not very different if one took the regression of input on output) one usually obtained a line which showed large economies of scale at first, but then flattened off. This would at first sight accord with the *a priori* expectation that at small sizes, an increase can greatly help specialization of labour: after a certain size has been reached there does not seem to be any great change in the way a shop is operated.

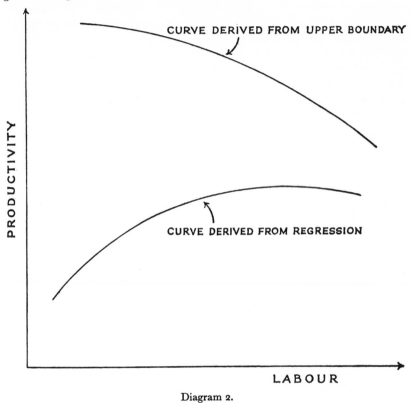

Diagram 2.

But if we look at the upper boundary of the scatter diagram, the result looks quite different (see diagram 2). In the cases we examined this showed a fairly steady *decline* in productivity as the size grew larger. Yet if we hoped to measure a 'best practice' line from actual data, it is to this upper boundary that we would look. And the usual theoretical discussion of 'best practice' hardly suggests such a result.

Two explanations suggest themselves. The most productive small shops usually have one immensely hard working proprietor or manager. The smaller the shop, the more influence his work will have on its productivity. Also there are many more small shops than large ones. Thus from the small ones there is more chance that some will happen to find themselves in extreme conditions (of good site, and continuous demand, for example) that will give high productivity. This latter explanation becomes less convincing when one remembers that the larger shop can bid itself into the good positions.

As for the regression line, it is strongly influenced by the number of shops of very low productivity that occur (perhaps those shops which are just starting, or are alternatively on the point of bankruptcy). As labour size increases, there are proportionately less of these. The point in section 8 above is underlined: one has to have some theory of entry to and exit from the industry, as well as one concerning the production relations within it. Both in the case of the regression lines (lines of averages) and in the case of the upper boundary line (the line of 'best performance') it is a striking fact that the usual theoretical discussions of economies of scale, since they have not acknowledged the variations in environment and efficiency of different firms, have not provided an explanation of the shapes we find.

ECONOMIES OF SCALE, CONCENTRATION, AND THE CONDITION OF ENTRY IN TWENTY MANUFACTURING INDUSTRIES

JOE S. BAIN

Ever since the merger movement of the late nineteenth century, American economists have been recurrently interested in the extent to which large size is necessary for business efficiency. Was the merger movement necessary; was the rule of reason economically justifiable; can this or that concentrated industry be atomized without loss of efficiency? These continue to be important questions to students of recent industrial history and contemporary antitrust policy. In the last three decades, with the notion that plant or firm size is related to efficiency formalized in long-run average-cost or scale curves, there has been much speculation and some inquiry concerning the shapes and positions of those scale curves in various industries and the placement of existing plants and firms on them.

To the economist qua economist, a knowledge for its own sake of the scale curves in particular industries is obviously unimportant. Only idle curiosity could justify his learning without further purpose how many barrels of cement a plant should produce to attain the lowest unit production cost, or how many passenger cars an automobile firm should make to minimize its production costs. But inferences which can be drawn from such knowledge may be important in several ways.

First, the proportion of the total output of its industry which a plant or a firm must supply in order to be reasonably efficient will determine the extent to which concentration in that industry is favored by the pursuit of minimized production costs. In any industry, the minimal scales of plant and of firm which are required for lowest production costs—*when these scales are expressed as percentages of the total scale or capacity of the industry* and are taken together with the shapes of the scale curves at smaller capacities—determine the degree of concentration by plants and firms needed for reasonable efficiency in the industry.

Second, the same relation of productive efficiency to the proportion of the market supplied by a plant or firm in any industry will have a

Reprinted from *American Economic Review*, 44 (1954), 15–39, by permission of the author and editor.

profound effect on *potential competition,* or on the disposition of new firms to enter the industry. If a plant or firm needs to supply only a negligible fraction of industry output to be reasonably efficient, economies of scale provide no deterrent to entry other than those of absolute capital requirements. If, however, a plant or firm must add significantly to industry output in order to be efficient, and will be relatively inefficient if it adds little, entry at efficient scale would lower industry selling prices or induce unfavorable reactions by established firms, whereas entry at much smaller scales would give the entrant a significant cost disadvantage. In this situation established firms can probably raise prices some amount above the competitive level without attracting entry. In general, the "condition of entry"—measured by the extent to which established firms can raise price above a competitive level without inducing further entry—becomes "more difficult" as the ratio of the output of the optimal firm to industry output increases.[1]

Third, the amount of money required for investment in an efficient plant or firm—as determined by size—will affect the availability of the capital necessary for new entry. When the supplies of both equity and loan capital in the range needed for a unit investment are either absolutely limited or positively related to the interest rate, the number of dollars required to establish an efficient plant or firm will clearly affect the condition of entry to an industry.[2]

Finally, a comparison of the scales of existing plants and firms in any industry with the most efficient scales will indicate whether plants and firms are of efficient size, or whether or not the existing pattern of concentration is consistent with reasonable efficiency. Have plant and firm concentration proceeded too far, farther than necessary, just far enough, or not far enough—from the standpoint of productive efficiency? A knowledge of scale curves is prerequisite to an answer.

Although information on the relation of efficiency to scale thus has some importance, relatively little has been done to develop this knowledge through empirical research; economists have relied mainly upon *a priori* speculations and qualitative generalizations of the broadest sort. A popular American view is that economies of large-scale plant do exist—and that the efficiency of plants as large as are built may be conceded—but that further economies of large multiplant firms do not exist, or if they do, are strictly pecuniary in character and hence not to

---

[1] See J. S. Bain, "Conditions of Entry and the Emergence of Monopoly," *Monopoly and Competition and Their Regulation,* E. H. Chamberlin, ed. (London, 1954), for a development of this theory.

[2] But the absolute capital requirement for efficiency need not, as we move from one industry to another, be systematically related to the proportion of industry output needed for efficiency.

be sought or justified as a matter of social policy.[3] At the extreme it is argued that increasing the size of the firm beyond that of an efficient plant does not normally lower costs at all, so that the scale curve is approximately horizontal for some distance beyond this point. The dominant British view, expressed by such writers as Steindl, Florence, and E. A. G. Robinson, gives more credence to the alleged economies of large-scale firms. Both schools rely upon qualitative and substantially untested generalizations about productive and commercial techniques which supposedly determine the response of production costs to variations in the scale of plant or firm. Yet in spite of the extremely sketchy nature of this sort of knowledge, it is common to presume, for instance, that there are numerous examples of each of two sorts of oligopolistic industries—those where scale economies encourage a high concentration, and those where such economies do not but something else does.[4]

Direct empirical investigation has not added much to our knowledge of scale curves. The principal studies employing accounting cost data are found in TNEC Monograph No. 13, and in later work by J. M. Blair,[5] of the Federal Trade Commission. Unfortunately the industries studied have been so few, the periods of time reviewed so remote and brief, and the use and interpretation of the statistical data in most instances so open to question that no reliable generalization regarding scale curves can be drawn from this body of material. There is more available in the way of profit-rate data for firms of various sizes, but here the unsupported assumptions which are normally necessary to argue from higher profits to lower costs are so numerous as to vitiate any attempt to infer scale curves from profit rates. Somewhat more satisfactory information has been developed, for a very few industries only, through "engineering" estimates of the scale curve for plant or firm. But in general our information is such that we are ill-prepared to say much about actual scale curves and their implications.

I. *Scope of the Present Study*

In the course of a recent general study of condition of entry to American manufacturing industries,[6] it has been possible to develop

[3] See, *e.g.*, TNEC Monograph No. 13, *Relative Efficiency of Large, Medium-sized, and Small Business*, pp. 95-139.
It may be noted that the income-distribution effects of strictly pecuniary economies may not be inconsequential in many settings.
[4] See, *e.g.*, Fellner's "Case 1-a," "Case 1-b," and "Case 2" oligopolies, in his *Competition Among the Few* (New York, 1949) pp. 44ff.
[5] See *e.g.* "Technology and Size," *Am. Econ. Rev. Proceedings*, May 1948, XXXVIII, 121-52 and "Relation between Size and Efficiency in Business," *Rev. Econ. Stat.*, Aug. 1942, XXIV, 125-35.
[6] I wish to acknowledge the generous assistance provided for this study since 1951 by

some further data on economies of scale therein. The portion of this information presented here concerns, for each of twenty selected manufacturing industries: (1) the relationship of the output capacity of a plant of lowest-cost size to the output capacity of the industry, together with the shape of the plant scale curve at smaller sizes; (2) the relationship of the capacity of a firm of lowest-cost size to industry capacity, and the firm scale curve at smaller capacities; and (3) the absolute amount of money capital required to establish an optimal plant and an optimal firm as of the current decade.

These data have been developed almost entirely from managerial or "engineering" estimates supplied by certain firms in the industries involved; precisely, they reflect estimates of scale economies and capital requirements which were prepared, in response to detailed prearranged questioning, either by or at the direction of high-level executives in these firms. The general procedure for securing such data included: (1) a lengthy preliminary survey of each of the twenty industries, based on available monographs, documents, and other published and unpublished secondary materials; (2) the subsequent preparation for each industry of a separate, special, and rather lengthy series of questions designed to elicit certain information having bearing on the condition of entry; (3) securing, after explaining the project involved and assuring confidentiality of replies, an advance offer of cooperation in answering these questions from executives in a large number of firms; (4) actual submission of the questions, followed (except in those cases where cooperation was subsequently withdrawn) by obtaining answers, in writing or orally or both. The method used thus involved neither shot-gun dissemination of an all-purpose questionnaire nor postprandial armchair quizzes, but rather a more or less hand-tooled questionnaire procedure in the case of each of twenty industries.

The questions submitted relative to scale economies in each industry were designed in general to elicit information concerning the minimal plant size requisite for lowest unit costs and the shape of the plant scale curve at smaller sizes, the same information for the firm, and the capital required to establish a plant and a firm of most efficient size. Direct and (with exceptions to be noted below) explicit answers to these questions were normally secured. In many cases, there was abundant evidence in the length and documentation of replies of a careful estimating procedure; in some, figures submitted were frankly characterized

the Merrill Foundation for the Advancement of Financial Knowledge, through a grant made to the Research Group on the Monopoly Problem at Harvard University, directed by Dean E. S. Mason. Acknowledgment is also due for the assistance in preceding years of the Bureau of Business and Economic Research, University of California, Berkeley, where essential initial background studies were undertaken.

as unsubstantiated armchair guesses, though in most of these the respondents were very well qualified to guess. By and large, the writer is inclined to feel, on the basis of checks against other sources and of comparisons of different and independent replies to the same questions, that this is generally a fairly reliable body of data, in which the bulk of individual industry estimates are likely to be fairly accurate. The data have the advantage, so far as they are reliable, of reflecting "engineering" estimates in the sense that they represent expert *ex ante* predictions of the net relations of cost to scale, rather than an *ex post* comparison of gross cost results at different achieved outputs. Thus they refer in general directly to scale curves as understood in economic theory.[7]

The twenty manufacturing industries studied may be designated as those producing cigarettes, soap, distilled liquor, shoes, canned fruits and vegetables, meat products, passenger automobiles, fountain pens, typewriters, flour, rubber tires and tubes, refined petroleum products, farm machinery, tractors,[8] steel, copper, cement, gypsum products, rayon, and metal containers. The sample was obviously not drawn at random. It was selected to obtain a maximum possible diversity of industry types consistent with the availability of data, but the fact that data have been more frequently developed for large and for highly concentrated industries than for others has resulted in some systematic differences between the sample and the whole population of manufacturing industries.

The following characteristics of the sample deserve brief note: First, it features large industries, with fifteen of the twenty having value products above a half billion in 1947. Whereas it includes only a little over 4 per cent of the total number (452) of manufacturing industries in 1947, it accounts for about 20 per cent of the value product of all manufacture in 1947.[9] Second, it contains a substantially larger proportion of moderately and highly concentrated manufacturing industries

[7] The general time reference of all estimates is the period 1950 to 1952. From two to five such estimates were received in each of the twenty industries in question. Other sources of data which were available for some industries—such as comparisons of accounting costs or the personal estimates of authors of industry studies—have been deliberately neglected here in order to give a more uniform consistency to the data presented. The only other data presented here, and these largely for expository purposes, are plant and firm concentration data prepared from the 1947 Census of Manufactures. Since the engineering estimates which supply the bulk of our data were generally secured under guarantees of secrecy as to source, no acknowledgments or references to source can be supplied.

[8] For present purposes only we follow the Census in the dubious experiment of segregating tractors from other farm machinery.

[9] The total population of industries described, as well as all data on value products and on concentration by firms, is derived (except as otherwise noted) from the 1947 Census of Manufactures, and in particular from a special analysis of concentration prepared from this Census and published as an appendix in *Hearings, Subcommittee on Study of Monopoly Power, Committee on Judiciary, H. R., 81st Cong., Serial 14, Part 2-B*.

than the total population. Nine industries of the sample had 75 per cent or more of value product controlled by four firms, three had 50 to 75 per cent so controlled, eight had from 25 to 50 per cent, and none less than 25 per cent controlled by four firms.[10] In the total population of manufacturing industries, the corresponding numbers in the four concentration classes were 47, 103, 164, and 138. This bias must be recognized in interpreting findings.

Otherwise, the sample is fairly representative. Eight industries are classed as making consumer goods, eight producer goods, and four goods bought by both producer and consumers. The outputs of eight are nondurable in use, whereas twelve are durable or semidurable. As to type of technique or process, five industries may be classified as engaged in processing farm products and four minerals, three as chemical industries, five as manufacturing or assembling mechanical devices, and three as in miscellaneous fabrication.[11]

II. *Optimal Plant Size and Plant Concentration*

Our first question concerns the shape and position of the plant scale curve (relating unit costs of production to the size of the individual factory or plant) in each of the twenty industries, and the apparent consequences of economies of large plants for entry and for seller concentration. We are interested initially in the scale curve reflecting the relation of production cost to the output or capacity of the plant *when the latter are expressed as percentages of the total output or rated capacity supplying the market to be supplied by the plant.* When output or capacity is expressed in these percentage terms, what is the lowest-cost or "optimal" size of plant and what is the shape of the plant scale curve at smaller sizes?

An initial clue to the potential importance of economies of large plants is supplied by certain data on plant size assembled in the 1947 Census of Manufactures. This Census shows for each of many industries the number of plants in each of several size-classes (size being measured by number of employees), and also the proportion of Census industry employment and of total industry "value added" accounted

---

[10] In three of the twenty cases, value added rather than value product figures were used by the Census in calculating concentration. For automobiles, registration rather than Census figures are followed in describing concentration, in both the sample and the total population, because of deficiencies in Census data.

[11] One further characteristic of the sample may be noted—Census industries have been selected which correspond fairly well to "theoretical" industries, or for which industry concentration as computed tends to reflect closely the relevant theoretical concentration of corresponding or component theoretical industries. This matter is discussed at length in J. S. Bain, "Relation of Profit Rate to Industry Concentration," *Quart. Jour. Econ.*, Aug. 1951, LXV, 297-304.

for by each size-class of plants. From these data[12] certain inferences can be drawn about the sizes of existing plants. For exploratory purposes here I have tried to develop from them some upper-limit estimates of the plant sizes requisite for greatest efficiency in the sample industries, by computing first the average size of plants in the largest size-class in each industry (expressed here as the percentage supplied per plant of the total value added of the Census industry), and second the maximum possible average size (similarly expressed) of the largest four plants in the industry.[13] If we neglect such obvious limitations as those of using value-added data, these estimates may be considered maximum percentages of the national industry outputs requisite for efficiency, on the grounds that in nearly every case we refer to the average size of a few of the largest plants actually built, and that the firms operating them were not restricted from building them to optimal scale. That is, they are generally multiplant firms which could bring a single plant to optimal scale before adding another, if indeed they did not in some cases duplicate optimal technical units on a single location.

The results of these estimating procedures are as follows: Eighteen industries were examined (automobiles and copper being eliminated because of gross deficiencies in Census data); for the eighteen the number of plants in the largest size-class lay between 3 and 15 in all but three cases; in those three it was large enough to make our estimates quite hazardous. The average share of Census industry value added supplied by plants in the largest size-class ranged from 20.1 per cent (typewriters) to 0.7 per cent (shoes), with a median at 3.8 per cent. The maximum possible average share of the largest four plants ranged from 19.1 per cent (cigarettes) to 1.7 per cent (shoes), with a median at 7.9 per cent.

The character of the data is more fully revealed in the frequency distributions in Table I. The first frequency column therein (f_1) classifies industries according to the market-share interval within which the average size of plants in the largest size-class of plants falls, market share being measured by the percentage of the Census industry value-added supplied by a plant. The second frequency column (f_2) shows the same information when the plant size referred to in each industry is the maximum possible average market share of the largest four plants.

[12] The data were previously used by the Federal Trade Commission for its study *The Divergence between Plant and Company Concentration, 1947*. The staff of the Commission has kindly made available its tabulated calculations on plant concentration as based on the Census data.

[13] The latter figure is derived in general by attributing to all but the first four plants in the largest size class the minimum possible market share (*i.e.*, for each the mean share of plants in the second size class) and by dividing the remainder of the total market share in the largest size class among the first four plants.

TABLE I.—CLASSIFICATION OF EIGHTEEN CENSUS INDUSTRIES ACCORDING TO
PERCENTAGES OF INDUSTRY VALUES-ADDED SUPPLIED BY
THE LARGEST PLANTS, 1947[a]

Percentage of Census Industry Value Added Supplied by the Average of the Largest Plants	Number of Industries with the Largest Plant Size in the Specified Percentage Interval	
	When "largest plant size" refers to average size of plants in largest size class of plants (f_1)	When "largest plant size" refers to the maximum possible average size of the largest 4 plants in indsutry (f_2)
0 – 2.4	6	2
2.5– 4.9	5	4
5.0– 7.4	2	3
7.5– 9.9	3	2
10.0–14.9	1	3
15.0–24.9[b]	1	4
Total	18	18

[a] From 1947 Census of Manufactures. The composition of sample is described in the text above.
[b] The highest value in this class was 20.1 per cent.

These findings, showing that in from seven to twelve of the 18 Census industries (depending on the method of estimate) the value added of the largest plants amounted to over 5 per cent apiece of total industry value added and that in from two to seven cases the figure was over 10 per cent apiece, suggest an importance for economies of large-scale plant which is substantial in some of these industries and small in others. But a detailed interpretation of the findings is not justified for several reasons. First, value added in a single year is a rather unsatisfactory measure of "scale" as that term is ordinarily understood. Second, the largest plants as identified by the Census may have resulted from building multiples of optimal technical units on single locations, and if so, the figures presented may overestimate optimal scales. Third, the data in question express the output of the plant as a percentage of the total national value added within the Census industry, whereas in fact the theoretical industry or separate market which a plant supplies may be somewhat smaller.[14] In these cases—where a Census industry is in fact made up of several theoretical industries corresponding to distinct regional markets or product lines—the "percentage-of-industry-output" derived from Census data for large plants is very likely to be below the theoretically relevant figure,[15] and revisions are in order. We

[14] It may also conceivably be larger, as in the case where imports are omitted from Census data or where the Census industry is too narrowly defined, but these contingencies are not realized in any important degree in this sample.
[15] It will be if the plant specializes as to area or product line.

TABLE II.—PROPORTIONS OF NATIONAL INDUSTRY CAPACITY CONTAINED IN SINGLE
PLANTS OF MOST EFFICIENT SCALE, FOR 20 INDUSTRIES, PER
ENGINEERING ESTIMATES CIRCA 1951

Industry	Percentage of National Industry Capacity Contained in One Plant of Minimal Efficient Scale	Industry	Percentage of National Industry Capacity Contained in One Plant of Minimal Efficient Scale
Flour milling	$\frac{1}{10}$ to $\frac{1}{2}$	Rubber tires and tubes[g]	3
Shoes[a]	$\frac{1}{7}$ to $\frac{1}{2}$	Rayon[h]	4 to 6
Canned fruits and vegetables	$\frac{1}{4}$ to $\frac{1}{2}$	Soap[i]	4 to 6
Cement	$\frac{4}{5}$ to 1	Farm machines, ex tractors[j]	4 to 6
Distilled liquors[b]	$1\frac{1}{4}$ to $1\frac{3}{4}$	Cigarettes	5 to 6
Petroleum refining[c]	$1\frac{3}{4}$	Automobiles[k]	5 to 10
Steel[d]	1 to $2\frac{1}{2}$	Fountain pens[l]	5 to 10
Metal containers	$\frac{1}{2}$ to 3	Copper[m]	10
Meat packing:[e]		Tractors	10 to 15
fresh	$\frac{1}{100}$ to $\frac{1}{5}$		
diversified	2 to $2\frac{1}{2}$		
Gypsum products[f]	$2\frac{1}{2}$ to 3	Typewriters	10 to 30

[a] Refers to shoes other than rubber.

[b] Capacity refers to total excluding brandy. Costs refer explicitly to 4-year whiskey, packaged but ex tax.

[c] Optimal balanced integration of successive processes assumed. Outshipment largely by water assumed; optimal scale may be smaller with scattered market and land shipment.

[d] Refers to fully integrated operation producing flat rolled products.

[e] Percentages are of total nonfarm slaughter; diversified operation includes curing, processing, etc.

[f] Combined plasterboard and plaster production assumed.

[g] Purchase of materials at a constant price assumed; production of a wide variety of sizes assumed.

[h] Refers to plant producing both yarn and fibre.

[i] Includes household detergents.

[j] Refers primarily to complex farm machines.

[k] Plant includes integrated facilities for production of components as economical. Final assembly alone—1 to 3 per cent.

[l] Includes conventional pens and ballpoints.

[m] Assumes electrolytic refining.

thus turn at once to direct engineering estimates of optimal plant sizes.

Table II reviews the engineering estimates of the optimal scales of plants for twenty industry groups. In each case, the plant size referred to is the minimal physical production capacity of plant required for lowest production costs, this capacity being expressed as a percentage of total national capacity within the Census industry. In each case also the costs referred to are total production costs, including costs of outshipment where the latter are strategic to the determination of optimal plant scale.

Table III summarizes the data of Table II by classifying industries according to the market-share interval in which the mean estimated size of an optimal plant falls, when size is measured as a percentage of the national industry capacity. These "engineering" data seem generally more satisfactory than those previously developed from Census figures. They reflect rational calculations rather than historical happenstance, and designed plant capacities rather than transient additions to value of output, although they still reflect percentages of the national capacities of Census industries.

TABLE III.—CLASSIFICATION OF TWENTY INDUSTRIES ACCORDING TO PERCENTAGES
OF NATIONAL INDUSTRY CAPACITIES CONTAINED IN SINGLE
PLANTS OF MOST EFFICIENT SCALE

(from Table II)

Percentage of National Industry Capacity Contained in a Plant of Optimal Scale	Number of Industries with Optimal Scale Plant (per mean estimate) in the Specified Percentage Interval (f_3)
0– 2.4	9
2.5– 4.9	2
5.0– 7.4	4
7.5– 9.9	2
10.0–14.9	2
15.0–24.9	1
Total	20

It appears from them that in nine of the twenty industries an optimal plant would account for a quite small fraction of national capacity (under 2½ per cent), whereas in five others the fraction would run above 7½ per cent. In general, the industries with slight economies of scale of plant are engaged in processing of agricultural or mineral materials, whereas greater plant economies are frequently encountered in industries making mechanical devices. The engineering estimates of the importance of economies of large plant present an over-all picture for these industries not greatly different from that derived by calculating average plant sizes in the largest plant-size intervals (column f_1 of Table I), but they clearly ascribe less importance to such economies than the estimates of the maximum possible average sizes of the largest four plants in each of these industries (column f_2 of Table I).

Before we interpret these findings, however, two further matters must be discussed: the shapes of the plant scale curves at capacities short of the estimated optima, and the revisions in the estimates of optima which are needed if the division of Census industries into separate regions or product lines is recognized.

As to the shapes of plant cost curves at capacities short of the estimated optima, relatively fragmentary information has been received. In four industries the plant scale curve appears to be horizontal back to the smallest size considered, or $\frac{1}{4}$ per cent of national industry output; these are flour, shoes, canned fruits and vegetables, and "fresh" meat packing. In ten cases—steel, metal containers, diversified meat packing, gypsum products, farm machinery, automobiles, fountain pens, copper, tractors, and typewriters—quantitative estimates of the shapes of the plant cost curves are not available, although in some cases (*e.g.*, diversified meat packing and metal containers) it is suggested that substantially smaller than optimal plants would entail only slightly higher costs, whereas in some others (*e.g.*, typewriters, automobiles, and tractors) a distinct rise in costs is suggested at half the optimal plant scale. For the seven remaining industries, the estimated relation of production cost to plant scale is shown in Table IV, where costs of 100 represent the lowest attainable costs.

TABLE IV.—RELATION OF PRODUCTION COST TO PLANT
SCALE IN SEVEN INDUSTRIES

	Percentages of National Industry Capacity in One Plant					
	5%	$2\frac{1}{2}$%	1%	$\frac{1}{2}$%	$\frac{1}{4}$%	
Cement	100	100	100	115	130	Relative costs of production
Distilled liquor	100	100	100.5	101	102	
Petroleum refining	100	100	102	104	107	
Tires and tubes	100	100.3	103	104	105.5	
Rayon	100	107	125	Very high		
Soap	100	103	105	Above 105		
Cigarettes	100	101	102	Above 102		

A mixed picture again emerges. In some cases (liquor and cigarettes, for example) the rise of production costs at suboptimal scales is evidently quite small; in others (soap, petroleum refining, tires and tubes) it is moderate but by no means negligible; in some—*e.g.*, rayon and cement—the rise is great.[16] One might hazard the guess that in from a half to two-thirds of all the industries sampled the upturn of the plant scale curve at suboptimal scales is such as to discourage very much smaller operations unless there are forces counterbalancing production cost disadvantages. In the other one-third to a half of cases, a

[16] It will be noted that the industries with the highest degrees of plant concentration are generally those on which it has been most difficult to secure quantitative estimates of the shape of the scale curve. In general, our information on plant scales seems sketchier and perhaps less reliable at this end of the sample.

wide variety of plant sizes might prosper indefinitely in only slightly imperfect markets.

The findings of Tables II and III however—reflecting as they do the percentages of national Census industry capacities supplied by single plants—can hardly be taken at face value so long as the suspicion remains that many Census industries may be broken into several separate and largely noncompeting regional or product submarkets and that a plant may specialize in only one such submarket. In these cases the relevant measure of plant size must be the proportion of the capacity supplying a submarket which is provided by an optimal plant, and this proportion will be larger than the proportion of national capacity provided by the same plant.

In eleven of the twenty cases listed in Table II, a revision of plant-size figures is in order because of the apparent division of the national market into distinct submarkets, coupled with plant specialization among them. In seven of these cases—flour, cement, petroleum refining, steel, metal containers, meat packing, and gypsum products—the important segmentation of markets is geographical in character; national markets are broken into regions, and a single plant will mainly supply only one region. In the other four cases—shoes, canned fruits and vegetables, automobiles, and fountain pens—markets are divided to a significant extent among distinct product lines. In all cases, the relevant measure of plant size is the percentage it may account for of the total capacity supplying any submarket it may supply.

The industries in which market segmentation is important are predominantly those for which the percentages of national industry capacities represented by single plants are quite small. The data for nine of the first ten industries in Table II require revision because of market segmentation, and only two for which revision is required lie in the range of high plant concentration nationally. Where technology does not give some importance to plant economies in industries of our sample, geography and product specialization (by plants) apparently do. Correspondingly, revised plant-size data showing percentages of individual submarket capacities will differ markedly from those in Tables II and III.

To make the revision mentioned, the optimal plant capacity for each of the eleven industries involved has been restated first as a percentage of the capacity supplying the largest submarket identified, and second as a percentage of capacity supplying the smallest of the major submarkets identified. For example, four major regional markets were identified in the petroleum refining industry. The proportion of national capacity supplied by a single optimal refinery had been estimated at 1¾ per cent (Table II); the corresponding percentages for the largest and smallest of the four major regional markets were $3\frac{1}{3}$ per cent and $11\frac{1}{2}$ per cent. In the fountain pen industry the proportion of aggregate national capacity supplied by an optimal plant was estimated at from 5 to 10 per cent. Dividing the market into high-price or gift pens and low-price pens including ballpoints (and recognizing differences in techniques for producing the two lines) the corresponding percentages become 25 to $33\frac{1}{3}$ per cent and 10 to $12\frac{1}{2}$ per cent.

When these revisions have been made for the eleven industries, and the results combined with the unrevised data for the remaining nine, we are prepared to present two frequency distributions parallel to that in Table III above. They classify industries according to the percentage of market capacity provided by an optimal plant, in the first case (column f_4 of Table V) when the capacities of optimal plants in the eleven revised industries are expressed as percentages of the total capacities supplying the largest submarkets in their industries, and in the second (column f_5) when optimal capacities in the eleven industries are expressed as percentages of the total capacities supplying the smallest major submarkets identified. The last column in Table V repeats column f_3 from Table III for purposes of comparison.

Subjective judgments have inescapably influenced the content of

TABLE V.—CLASSIFICATION OF TWENTY INDUSTRIES[a] BY PERCENTAGES OF INDIVIDUAL MARKET CAPACITIES CONTAINED IN A SINGLE-PLANT OF MOST EFFICIENT SCALE

Percentage of Individual Market Capacity Contained in a Plant of Optimal Scale	Number of Industries with Optimal Plant Scale in the Specified Percentage Interval		
	Where percentage is that of the total capacity supplying the largest recognized submarket (f_4)	Where percentage is that of the total capacity supplying the smallest recognized submarket (f_5)	Where percentage is that of the total capacity supplying the national market (f_3 from Table III)
0– 2.4	4	2	9
2.5– 4.9	5	2	2
5.0– 7.4	5	4	4
7.5– 9.9	0	1	2
10.0–14.9	5	3	2
15.0–19.9	0	2	0
20.0–24.9	1	2	1
25.0–29.9	0	2	0
30.0–34.9	0	1	0
35.0–40.0	0	1	0
Total	20	20	20

[a] The meat packing industry is considered for purposes of this table as only involving so-called *fresh* meat packing.

columns f$_4$ and f$_5$, particularly in the identification of regions, the decision as to what is a "major" region or product line, and the decision as to whether market segmentation is significant, but we have tried to follow available information and industry practice systematically. If there is a bias, it is in the direction of defining areas and product lines quite broadly, of considering only a few dominant areas for analysis, and of recognizing segmentation only if there is strong evidence supporting the recognition.

Interpreting Table V with appropriate reference to the earlier discussion of the shapes of plant scale curves, we may emphasize the following conclusions about the importance of economies of large-scale plants within the industries of our sample. First, if the reference is to the largest submarkets of industries with segmented markets (plus the national markets of those with unsegmented markets), then in nine of the twenty cases an optimal plant would supply less than 5 per cent of its market, and in five additional cases less than 7½ per cent. If this is true and if, further, the plant-scale curve is usually fairly flat for a moderate range of suboptimal scales, then in many of these fourteen cases the scale requirements for an optimal plant should not provide a serious deterrent to entry. A firm constructing one reasonably efficient plant should not ordinarily induce serious repercussions from established firms in its market.

On the other hand in six cases—gypsum products, automobiles, typewriters, fountain pens, tractors, and copper—the proportion of the total capacity supplying either the national market or the largest submarket which is provided by a single optimal plant runs from 10 to 25 per cent. Precise data are largely lacking on the shapes of scale curves in these industries, but if they are much inclined upward at suboptimal scales (as is suggested qualitatively in several cases) then the economies of large plant should provide a very significant deterrent to entry to the markets in question. Further, a substantial degree of oligopolistic concentration by firms might easily be justified by the pursuit of plant economies alone. The substantial diversity of situations among industries of moderate to high concentration deserves considerable emphasis.

The picture changes markedly if our attention shifts in the case of the eleven segmented industries from the largest to the smallest major submarkets. Now we find that in eleven of the twenty cases (rather than six) the proportion of the relevant market capacity supplied by an optimal plant exceeds 10 per cent, and in six cases it exceeds 20 per cent. Plant economies sufficient to impede entry very seriously are potentially present in half or more of the cases, and high plant and firm concentration is encouraged by technology. The importance of plant economies thus potentially bulks large indeed in the smaller regional submarkets and the smaller product lines, whereas it is evidently less in the major submarkets and frequently so in the industries with relatively unsegmented national markets.

III. *Optimal Firm Size and Firm Concentration*

The extent to which further economies of large scale are realized if firms grow beyond the size of a single optimal plant has been a subject of controversy among economists. If a distinction is drawn between "production cost" and other advantages of scale—so that sales promotion, price-raising, and similar advantages of big firms are properly distinguished from cost-savings in production and distribution—there is no general agreement among economists as to whether or to what extent the multiplant firm is more economical.[17] It thus may come as no surprise that business executives questioned on the same matter with regard to our sample of industries evidenced a similar diversity of mind. Very distinct differences of opinion relative to the existence or importance of economies of multiplant firms were frequently encountered in the same industry, and in a pattern not satisfactorily explicable in general by the hypothesis that the individual would claim maximum economies for his own size of firm. Any findings presented here on estimates of economies of large-scale firm should thus be viewed as extremely tentative.

Whatever the ostensible importance of economies of the multiplant firm, exploitation of them will not *necessarily* require the multiplant firm to control a larger proportion of any submarket than is needed for one optimal plant. In those instances where national markets are segmented regionally or by product lines, the multiplant firm *may* realize its economies while operating only one plant in each submarket. Then concentration by firms in individual submarkets is not further encouraged and entry is not further impeded[18] by economies of the multiplant firm. An optimal cement plant may supply about 1 per cent of national capacity, or percentages of regional capacity ranging very roughly from 5 to 30 per cent in eleven regional submarkets. The fact that a multiplant cement firm could secure lower costs than a single-plant firm by operating one optimal plant in each of the eleven regions —thus accounting for 11 per cent of national capacity—would not imply that it need have a higher proportion of capacity in any one region than a single-plant firm of optimal size. Except for an increase in absolute capital requirements, the assumed economies of the multi-

---

[17] This disagreement is, as noted above, complicated further by difference of opinion as to whether the disputed economies are real or strictly pecuniary in character.

[18] Except for the increase of absolute capital requirements.

TABLE VI.—THE EXTENT OF ESTIMATED ECONOMIES OF MULTIPLANT
FIRMS IN 20 MANUFACTURING INDUSTRIES

Industry	Percentage of National Industry Capacity Contained in One Optimal Plant	Estimated Extent of Multiplant Economies (as a percentage of total cost)	Percentage of National Industry Capacity Contained in One Optimal Firm	Average Percentage Share of the National Market of First 4 Firms in 1947[a]
Group 1:				
Canned fruits and vegetables	$\frac{1}{4}$ to $\frac{1}{2}$	None	—	6.6
Petroleum refining	$1\frac{3}{4}$	None	—	9.3
Meat packing:[b]				
Fresh	$\frac{1}{10}$ to $\frac{1}{8}$	None	—	—
Diversified	2 to $2\frac{1}{2}$	None	—	10.3[c]
Fountain pens	5 to 10	None	—	14.4
Copper	10	None	—	23.1[d]
Typewriters	10 to 30	None	—	19.9
Group 2:				
Flour	$\frac{1}{10}$ to $\frac{1}{2}$	No estiamte	—	7.3
Distilled liquor	$1\frac{1}{4}$ to $1\frac{3}{4}$	No estimate	—	18.7
Metal containers	$\frac{1}{2}$ to 3	No estimate	—	19.5
Tires and tubes	3	No estimate	—	19.2
Rayon	4 to 6	No estimate	—	19.6
Farm machines, ex tractors	4 to 6	No estimate	—	9.0
Automobiles	5 to 10	No estimate	—	22.5[e]
Tractors	10 to 15	No estimate	—	16.8
Group 3:				
Shoes	$\frac{1}{7}$ to $\frac{1}{2}$	Small, or 2 to 4	$\frac{1}{2}$ to $2\frac{1}{2}$	7.0
Cement	$\frac{4}{5}$ to 1	Small, or 2 to 3	2 to 10	7.4
Steel	1 to $2\frac{1}{2}$	2 to 5	2 to 20	11.2[c]
Gypsum products	$2\frac{1}{2}$ to 3	Small	27 to 33	21.2
Soap	4 to 6	$\frac{1}{2}$ to 1	8 to 15	19.8
Cigarettes	5 to 6	Slight	15 to 20	22.6

[a] Market shares are average percentages of 1947 national values of shipments unless otherwise indicated.

[b] Plant percentages refer to total of nonfarm slaughter, firm percentages to wholesale fresh meat packing only.

[c] Expresses average percentage of total value added rather than value of shipments.

[d] Expresses average percentage of electrolytic plus other national copper refining capacity, 1947.

[e] Expresses approximate average percentage of total 1951 passenger car registrations.

plant firm would not encourage regional market concentration or impede entry.

Suppose on the other hand that there are economies of multiplant firms which are to be realized through operating two or more optimal-size plants either in a single submarket or in a single unsegmented national market. This will evidently encourage a concentration by firms in the relevant submarket or national market greater than that encouraged by plant economies alone, and will further impede entry. If a single plant of most efficient size would supply 5 per cent of the relatively unsegmented national cigarette market, whereas a single firm operating three such plants could lower costs of production and distribution perceptibly, economies of the multiplant firm would favor greater effective concentration and provide further deterrents to entry to the cigarette industry.

Findings relative to the economies of multiplant firms, together with certain related data, are presented in Table VI. The second column therein repeats the estimates of percentages of national Census industry capacities required for optimal plants, from Table II. The third column indicates the estimated extent of economies of multiplant firms (*i.e.,* firms of sizes beyond those of single optimal plants), costs of distribution but not of sales promotion being included. The fourth column indicates the percentages of national industry capacities required for firms with lowest production plus distribution costs, while the final column shows the average percentage per firm of the national market supplied by the first four firms in 1947. The last provides a measure of actual concentration by firms. The estimates in question are entirely those of executives queried in connection with the investigation underlying this study.

The data presented in Table VI shed light on two questions: (1) to what extent do the economies of the multiplant firm tend to enhance concentration and impede entry, and (2) to what extent is the existing concentration by firms greater than required for exploitation of economies of large plants and of large firms?

Concerning the first question a varied picture appears. In eight industries (Group 2 in Table VI) no definite estimate could be obtained of the extent, if any, of economies of the multiplant firm. This is in spite of the fact that in most of these industries the degree of concentration by firms substantially exceeds that requisite for exploitation of estimated economies of the large plant. In six industries (Group 1 in Table VI) it was the consensus that economies of the scale of firm beyond the size of a single optimal plant were either negligible or totally absent. In these cases estimated cost savings of the multiplant firm cannot justify concentration beyond that required by plant economies alone (either in submarkets or in unsegmented national markets) nor can they make entry any more difficult than it is already made by plant economies. With respect to the first four industries in the group, a multiplant firm with plants in several regions or product lines would, according to the estimates received, realize no net cost savings by virtue of this aspect of its organization. In the second three industries in this group, however, economies of the large plant alone are sufficient to support a high degree of concentration by firms and to impede entry.

In the remaining six industries (Group 3 in Table VI) perceptible economies were attributed to the multiplant firm. The extent of these economies is in no case huge, being characterized as slight or small in three cases and as in the two to five per cent range in the remaining three. Nevertheless, two or three percentage points on total cost can be significant in any industry if the ratio of operating profits to sales is not beyond five or ten per cent and if product differentiation and other market imperfections are not dominant. What further tendency toward concentration and what further impediment to entry would the existence of these economies imply?

The optimal multiplant firm as estimated in Group 3 of Table VI includes two or three optimal plants in the soap industry, three or four in the cigarette industry, four or five in the shoe industry, and about ten in the gypsum products industry. Estimates for the steel and cement industries run all the way from one or two to ten plants per optimal firm, and the range of disagreement among authorities is wide. Applying these estimates, the proportion of national industry capacity needed for best efficiency in a multiplant firm is raised; but is the proportion of the capacity supplying any particular regional or product submarket also raised? It will not be if the efficient multiplant firm includes only one optimal plant per submarket, and it will be if it includes two or more per submarket or if the national market is unsegmented.

In Group 3 in Table VI no more than one optimal plant per region is attributed to the optimal firm in cement or in steel, and the proportion of any regional market which need be supplied for efficiency is thus not increased by the incidence of economies of the multiplant firms. In the remaining four cases the conclusion is different. Soap and cigarettes have relatively unsegmented national markets, and the proportion of the market required for best efficiency is doubled, trebled, or quadrupled by the emergence of economies of the multiplant firm. In shoes the assumed specialization to a single product line of the four or five plants needed for efficiency raises the requisite firm concentration by product lines by corresponding multiples. In the gypsum industry it was evidently assumed that an optimal firm would operate several plants in each of one or more major regions. In all of the last four cases, therefore, economies of the multiplant firm encourage greater effective concentration by firms and impede entry. But in these cases (possibly excepting shoes) the economies of the large firm were characterized as slight, so that the effects just listed may be weak.

With respect to the effect of the economies of multiplant firms on concentration and on entry, these conclusions appear. In eight of twenty industries in our sample, no estimate was obtained of the extent of these economies. In two-thirds of the remaining cases, economies of the multiplant firm were held either to be absent, or to take such a form that exploitation of them would not require higher proportions of market control by the firm in any submarket. In one-third of the remaining cases, some encouragement to higher concentration by firms in submarkets was provided, but it was a small encouragement in view of the generally slight economies attributed to the large firm. Economies of the large-scale firm apparently do not represent a major force encouraging concentration or deterring entry in this sample of industries. The data on which this guess rests, however, are far from adequate.

Our second question concerns the extent to which the existing degree of concentration by firms within industries is justified by the estimated economies of large plants and firms. This is a rather complicated question, and may be broken down into three subquestions: (1) Is the existing concentration by firms for national Census industries justified by the economies of single large-scale plants? (2) If not, is the existing concentration by firms nevertheless consistent with no higher concentration within individual submarkets than is required by a single efficient plant—i.e., need there be more than one optimal plant per large firm in any one submarket? (3) In any case, to what extent is the multiplant character of large firms apparently justified by the economies of such firms?

A first approximation to answers to these questions may be made by taking the concentration figure in Column 5 of Table VI as a simple and crude measure of national industry concentration by firms.[19] On the basis of this measure, the answer to the first subquestion is simple and unsurprising—concentration by firms is in every case but one greater than required by single-plant economies, and in more than half of the cases very substantially greater. Generally it is only within some of the industries with very important economies of large plant—e.g., fountain pens, copper, typewriters, autos, tractors, farms machines— that concentration by firms has not been much greater than required by single-plant economies. Even in these cases it may be two or three times as great as thus required. In the other cases concentration by firms tends to be a substantial or large multiple of that required by single-plant economies. Remembering that we are dealing in general in this sample with the more concentrated industries, it might be said in summary that nearly all of the industries tended to become moderately or

---

[19] The average share of national industry output per firm for the first four firms obviously is smaller than the market share for the first firm, larger than that for the fourth firm, etc.

highly concentrated (by firms) whether economies of the single plant were important or not.

The second subquestion is whether the existing degree of concentration by firms is consistent or inconsistent with the existence of a single optimal plant per firm in each recognized submarket. In seven of the nine cases where the national market has been considered substantially unsegmented—copper, typewriters, liquor, tires and tubes, rayon, farm machines, tractors, soap, and cigarettes—the degree of concentration by firms within a single market is greater than required by such plant economies, although in all but two of the seven cases (liquor and tires and tubes) it is greater by at most a multiple of three or four. This last is found probably in part because economies of the large plant seem very important in most of these industries.

In eight of the remaining eleven cases—canned goods, petroleum refining, meat packing, fountain pens, metal containers, cement, steel, and gypsum products—the degree of national concentration by firms is not grossly inconsistent with the larger firms on the average having but a single optimal plant per submarket in each of several submarkets. *(This is certainly not to deny that the largest single firms may have more than this and probably do; we refer only to the average of the largest four firms.)*

In the last three cases—flour, automobiles, and shoes—the degree of concentration by firms exceeds by a multiple of two or three that required for each of the four largest firms on the average to have an optimal plant in each submarket. In general, our showing is that in ten of twenty industries the existing degree of concentration by firms, as measured by the average size of the largest four firms, is significantly greater than required for these firms to have only one optimal plant per submarket; in the other ten cases concentration is at least roughly consistent with such a condition.

The third subquestion concerns the extent to which the existing degree of concentration by firms is justified by the exploitation of economies of multiplant firms. We will go no further with this question here than a comparison of the fourth and fifth columns of Table VI will take us. In Group 1 in that table, the alleged absence of any economies of multiplant firm implies that there is no justification in terms of costs for the excess of concentration by firms over that required for single efficient plants, although in one case (typewriters) the existence of an excess is uncertain, and in four others (all but copper) it is not necessarily accompanied by accentuated concentration in individual submarkets. Here, therefore, the lack of an evident cost justification for multiplant firms raises not so much the issue of concentration in separate markets as the issue of the other advantages and disadvantages of a diversified firm operating in each of several related submarkets.

In Group 2 no estimates of multiplant economies are available; we need say no more than that in five of eight cases (excluding metal containers, farm machines, and tractors) there is a concentration by firms much greater than that required for efficient plants in each submarket, and that this requires evaluation from a cost standpoint. In only one of the industries in Group 3 (shoes) does the degree of concentration by firms seem to have clearly exceeded that required for economies of production and distribution by the large firm.

In the sample as a whole the existing degree of concentration by multiplant firms lacks a clear cost justification in perhaps thirteen of twenty cases, although in seven of these we have a simple lack of any definite estimates. In two more cases the multiplant phenomenon is not very important. Further information is needed on this matter, particularly with reference to cases in which multiplant firm organization has increased effective concentration in individual submarkets or in unsegmented national markets.

IV. *Absolute Capital Requirements and Entry*

The effect of scale economies on the condition of entry so far emphasized is transmitted through their influence on the share of market output which an efficient plant or firm will supply. This impact is important, but it is not proportional to the importance of scale economies measured in such terms as the absolute number of employees or the absolute size of investment required for an optimal plant or firm. This is because the proportion of a market supplied by an optimal plant or firm (which determines the degree of oligopolistic interdependence between the potential entrant and established firms) depends not only on the absolute size of the plant or firm but also on the size of the market. Thus an investment of over $200 million dollars might add only one per cent to national steel capacity, whereas an investment of $6 million might add five or ten per cent to the capacity for producing fountain pens. In addition to the effect of scale economies on entry via the proportion of the market an efficient entrant will supply, there is a distinct and not closely correlated effect via the absolute size of the efficient plant or firm, or, to choose a popular measure, via the total money investment needed to establish such a plant or firm.

To determine the importance of scale economies in establishing sufficient capital requirements to impede entry seriously, we have queried the same sources on the investment requisite for the most efficient plant or firm in the twenty industries sampled. The findings relative to capital requirements for the large plant are fairly compre-

TABLE VII.—Estimated Absolute Capital Requirements for Plants of Estimated Most Efficient Scale, circa 1951, for 20 Industries

Industry	Percentage of National Industry Capacity Provided by One Efficient Plant (from Table II)	Total Capital Required for One Efficient Plant[a]
Category 1:		
Flour milling	$\frac{1}{10}$ to $\frac{1}{2}$	$700,000 to $3,500,000
Shoes	$\frac{1}{4}$ to $\frac{1}{2}$	$500,000 to $2,000,000
Canned fruits and vegetables	$\frac{1}{4}$ to $\frac{1}{2}$	$2,500,000 to $3,000,000
Cement	$\frac{4}{5}$ to 1	$20,000,000 to $25,000,000
Distilled liquor	$1\frac{1}{4}$ to $1\frac{3}{4}$	$30,000,000 to $42,000,000
Petroleum refining	$1\frac{3}{4}$	$193,000,000 ex transport facilities $225,000,000–$250,000,000 with transport facilities
Meat packing[b]	$\frac{1}{80}$ to $\frac{1}{5}$	Very small
	2 to $2\frac{1}{2}$	$10,000,000 to $20,000,000
Tires and tubes	3	$25,000,000 to $30,000,000
Category 2:		
Steel[c]	1 to $2\frac{1}{2}$	$265,000,000 to $665,000,000[d]
Metal containers[c]	$\frac{1}{2}$ to 3	$5,000,000 to $20,000,000
Rayon	4 to 6	$50,000,000 to $75,000,000[e] $90,000,000 to $135,000,000[f]
Soap	4 to 6	$13,000,000 to $20,000,000[g]
Farm machines ex tractors	4 to 6	No estimate
Cigarettes	5 to 6	$125,000,000 to $150,000,000
Category 3:		
Gypsum products[h]	$2\frac{1}{2}$ to 3	$5,000,000 to $6,000,000
Automobiles	5 to 10	$250,000,000 to $500,000,000
Fountain pens	5 to 10	Around $6,000,000
Copper	10	No estimate
Tractors	10 to 15	Around $125,000,000
Typewriters	10 to 30	No estimate

[a] These estimates generally exclude anticipated "shakedown losses" of new entrants, which in some cases may be large and prolonged.

[b] The two rows of estimates refer alternatively to fresh and diversified meat packing.

[c] Percentage of an efficient plant in the largest regional market may exceed 5 per cent.

[d] Excludes any investment in ore or coal.

[e] Acetate rayon.

[f] Viscose rayon.

[g] Excludes working capital.

[h] Percentage of an efficient plant in the largest regional market may exceed 10 per cent.

hensive, and are summarized in Table VII. Column 2 of this table shows the estimated percentage of national industry capacity provided by one efficient plant, and Column 3 the total investment required to establish such a plant (ordinarily including working capital) as of about 1951.

The industries are grouped according to the importance of scale economies from the previously emphasized percentage standpoint. The first category of industries are those in which a single efficient plant will supply no more than 5 per cent of the largest submarket or unsegmented national market; the second includes those where the corresponding percentage is 5 to 10 per cent; the third includes those where the percentage is above 10 per cent. We may thus observe the extent to which the "percentage effect" of scale economies is of the same order as their "absolute capital requirement effect."

The findings in Table VII speak fairly clearly for themselves, but a few comments may be in order. First, there is no evident correlation of the absolute capital requirements for an efficient plant with the percentage of market output supplied by it. The size of the market is an erratic variable forestalling such a correlation. Second, absolute capital requirements for an efficient plant in all the manufacturing industries examined are large enough to restrict seriously the ranks of potential entrants; even 500,000 dollars, the smallest amount listed, will not be forthcoming from savings out of salary or from the winnings in a poker game.

Third, the absolute capital requirements in some cases reinforce but in other cases weaken the "percentage effect" on entry of economies of scale of plant. For each of the eight industries in Category 1 in Table VII, for example, the percentage of market output supplied by a single plant seems small enough to provide no serious-deterrent to entry. In three of these cases—flour milling, shoes, and canned goods[20]— the absolute capital requirements are also so small that entry may not be seriously restrained thereby. But in four others, capital requirements ranging from 10 to 42 million dollars per plant provide a greater deterrent, and in one (petroleum refining) they impose a truly formidable barrier.

In the six industries of Category 2, where the "percentage effect" on entry of economies of scale of plant is moderate, it is strongly reinforced in four cases (possibly excepting metal containers, and farm machines, for which there is no estimate) by absolute capital requirements. The effect is very much increased in both the steel and cigarette industries. In the six industries of Category 3, where the "percentage effect" appears quite important, it is strongly reinforced in the cases of automobiles and tractors by absolute capital requirements, but in the fountain pen and gypsum industries capital requirements are relatively small. Thus a generally mixed picture regarding the dual effects of economies of large plant emerges.

[20] As well as in fresh meat packing.

The extent to which economies of multiplant firms as already noted increase the capital requirements for efficiency may be readily ascertained by comparing the findings of the Table VI with those of Table VII. Since the existence of such economies was denied in six industries, not estimated in eight others, and held to be slight in at least half the remaining six, detailed comment on this matter does not seem justified.

V. *Conclusions*

When the answer provided by empirical investigation to an initial inquiry concerning the values of certain economic data is that the values are highly irregular and variegated, and when the answer is therefore found only in a great array of numbers, any brief summarization of the findings may be difficult to make and misleading if attempted. Since this situation is encountered with respect to each of the major questions posed at the beginning of this paper, no comprehensive summary of findings will be attempted here. Certain salient conclusions may be restated briefly, however, in each case with the proviso that they may have general validity only so far as the sample of industries selected is generally representative of moderately to highly concentrated manufacturing industries in the United States.

Regarding the importance of economies of large plants, the percentage of a market supplied by one efficient plant in some cases is and in some cases is not sufficient to account for high firm concentration or to impede entry. Where it is, these economies might easily propagate high concentration and serious impediments to entry; the number of cases where it is sufficient increases as we refer to the smaller regional or product submarkets in various industries. A significant corollary of these findings is that the following popular horseback observations are apparently *not true:* that economies of scale of plant are never or almost never important in encouraging oligopoly or impeding entry, and that such economies always or almost always are important in these ways. The picture is not extreme in either direction and not simple.

The economies of large plants frequently erect formidable barriers to entry in the shape of absolute capital requirements. Moderately to very high barriers of this sort were found in all but four or five of the industries studied. The height of such barriers is not clearly correlated with percentage of the market supplied by a single plant, so that a relatively independent influence on entry is discovered.

The economies of large multiplant firms are left in doubt by this investigation. In half the cases in which definite estimates were received, such economies were felt to be negligible or absent, whereas in most of the remainder of cases they seemed slight or small. Perhaps the frequently expressed suspicion that such economies generally are unimportant after all is supported, and perhaps we are justified in saying that we have had difficulty in accumulating convincing support for the proposition that in many industries production or distribution economies of large firms seriously encourage concentration or discourage entry.

Our reference here has of course been strictly to the effect of the size of the plant or firm on the cost of production and distribution, and thereby on entry and on concentration. Needless to say, parallel studies of other factors bearing on entry, including the effects of scale on price and on sales promotion, are required for a full evaluation of the entry problem.

SCALE OF OPERATIONS—AN EMPIRICAL STUDY*

Edward H. Bowman

This study concerns the optimum size of an ice cream branch plant and territory. The company operated ten plants covering a seven state area. At the time of the study, management was uncertain as to even the approximate size of an optimum plant. The study revealed that about six larger plants would be a better system. The company now operates six plants and is considering cutting this number still further.

THIS PAPER reports one phase of a larger research project that involves the attempted application of several methods of analysis or models to one set of manufacturing problems. The problems are those posed by one company's system of ice cream branch plants.

THE PROBLEM

AT THE TIME of this study the company operated ten ice cream plants over an extended multistate area. The plants were essentially homogeneous and self-sufficient within their areas. The basic question being asked in this study was, *what is the optimum size for this company's ice cream plants?*

The relation between price asked and quantity sold is not part of this study. In addition it was felt that the customers will neither know nor care where their ice cream originates. Therefore, it is assumed for this study that both total sales and product mix were given. An answer to the question of optimum size plants then would also answer the question of an optimum number of plants. The study was not addressed to the proper location of the individual plants in the system.

The answer given to the question raised on the basis of this analysis is that nine out of ten of the plants are too small, most of them about half their optimum size, and that therefore the best number of plants would be five or six. The analysis leading to this conclusion follows.

* The research in connection with this paper has been partly supported by the Sloan Research Fund of MIT's School of Industrial Management and the U. S. Army Ordnance Corps. Thanks are due several individuals of the cooperating company for their assistance and to MR. T. A. MANGELSDORF and MR. A. G. GRASBERG, Graduate Assistants of M.I.T. A briefer version of this paper was presented at the Fifth Annual Meeting of the OPERATIONS RESEARCH SOCIETY OF AMERICA in Philadelphia on May 10, 1957.

Reprinted from *Operations Research*, 6 (1958), 320–328, by permission of the author and editor.

The basic nature of the method of analysis used here is to attempt to relate quantitatively the variations that do exist in actual costs per gallon between plants to variations in other important factors, some of which may be manipulated by management. If insight into these relations may be gained from present experience, then changes in these other variables may be made by management in order to reduce the cost per gallon.

A MEASURE OF EFFECTIVENESS

WITH THE restriction that total sales and product mix were given, it was determined that the objective was to attempt to minimize the cost per gallon of ice cream. This objective function, cost per gallon, itself, presented two problems, i.e., what was a cost and what was a gallon?

The cost used in this study was essentially a value added type or conversion cost. It included the costs of manufacturing and distribution without the raw material costs. Actually, each plant was well beyond economies of scale with respect to raw material procurement as all deliveries of milk and cream—the major components—were by tank car. In addition, the company itself, rather than the individual plants, contracts for these raw materials on a long-term basis. The company's own accounting system was relied upon to determine what costs occurred at the different plants in the given year under study. That is, the company kept books for each plant, including the usual labor accounts—direct, indirect, supervisory—supplies, local taxes, depreciation, transportation, etc. Obviously, accounting decisions with respect to allocating long-term expenses to a given time period had been made, e.g., the proportion of equipment depreciation to allot to this year. In addition to the accounting costs, opportunity costs for capital invested in plant, equipment, and inventory were also included. In order to do this, the replacement cost of each plant was determined, and this was multiplied by the company's opportunity cost of capital. Had the company not invested capital in a particular plant, the capital could have been used elsewhere in the firm and the value of its use elsewhere denied by this plant must be considered as part of the cost of operating the plant. Though in some cases such 'interest' costs might be important, here they were relatively small. That is, the decision sought would not be sensitive to the cost of capital used. As it was the total cost of the plant that was of interest for this analysis, there was no need nor desire to allocate these costs to the various products.

With respect to a measure of gallons, the company had developed for its own purposes a 'gallon-equivalent' system. With respect to pint, quart, gallon, and three-gallon packages, the conversion was the obvious one to gallon equivalents. For specialty products, it was necessary to determine the net weight including, for instance, a chocolate coating, and convert this weight into gallon equivalents of ice cream. Though, of course, the unit of measure lacks complete homogeneity, it is unlikely that this could seriously influence the analysis. This is due to the fact that the product mix each plant manufactures was explicitly considered as one of the variables that influence the cost per gallon. That is, allowance was made in the model predicting cost per gallon for the higher labor content in specialty products, e.g., ice cream cups, popsickles, etc.

It is interesting to note at this point that having determined the measure of effectiveness, cost per gallon equivalent, an initial check was made of the variation in this measure between plants. It turned out that the comparison of the highest to the lowest cost plant revealed a difference of more than two to one (as shown in Table I.)

TABLE I

	Predicted cost	Actual cost	Ratio, predicted/actual
Plant No. 1	98	98	1.00
Plant No. 2	87	87	1.00
Plant No. 3	117	105	1.11
Plant No. 4	82	63	1.30
Plant No. 5	98	134	0.73
Plant No. 6	118	118	1.00
Plant No. 7	92	87	1.06
Plant No. 8	109	90	1.21
Plant No. 9	115	141	0.82
Plant No. 10	170	167	1.02

THE MODEL

IT WAS FELT that the following variables were the major influences on differences in the cost per gallon between plants:

1. Volume of product manufactured by each plant.
2. Area size of the territory served by each plant.
3. Product mix manufactured at each plant.
4. Labor rates at the particular plant location.

The larger the volume handled by a plant, the lower the cost per unit was expected to be. For virtually any kind of an economic activity, there tend to be certain fixed costs such as, for instance, the plant manager's or night watchman's salary. The larger the number of units to which this cost is assigned or allocated, the lower the cost per unit.

The larger the area of the territory served by a plant, the higher the costs were expected to be. This was due mainly to the fact that the trucks would have to travel farther from the plant out into the territory and back again. As a gross approximation, this travel from the plant corresponds to spokes on a wheel or circle radii. Such a radius varies with the square root of the area, and therefore it was felt that the cost would increase approximately with the square root of the area.

The higher the amount of labor input required for a gallon of a plant's products, the higher costs were expected to be. Specialty items per gallon equivalent require substantially more labor than regular products. All plants do not make the same proportion of each product, i.e., mix of product differs. The company had developed for its own purposes a measure of the relative labor input into each product, and for each plant had computed a weighted average of this measure.

The higher the labor rates in the area, the higher the costs per gallon were expected to be. Actually, most of the cost involved in the conversion process was a labor cost—direct, indirect, and supervisory. Therefore, it was felt that all of the previously mentioned costs would increase somewhat as labor rates increased.

Two other factors were carried beyond the early stages of the analysis but were ultimately not used: (*a*) The number of retail outlets in a territory was found not to affect the cost per gallon significantly. (*b*) Technology differences between plants, though certainly of potential importance in some branch plant systems, were judged of no significance between these particular ice cream plants.

The model, as developed, was as follows*:

$$C = L\,(a + b/V + c\,\sqrt{A} + d\,M). \qquad (1)$$

Here *a*, *b*, *c*, *d* are constant parameters; the variables have the following meanings:

$C =$ Cost of manufacturing and distribution per 1000-gallon equivalents not including raw-material costs. This is the total cost for each plant secured from the company's books for the one-year period being used as the empirical base of the study divided by the plant's volume.

$L =$ Labor rates at the plant expressed as the average hourly wage payment.

$V =$ Volume manufactured and distributed by the plant during the year expressed in 1000-gallon equivalents.

$A =$ Area serviced by the plant expressed in square miles, and determined by placing a grid over the map of each of the territories.

$M =$ Mix of product expressed as a ratio of the average 'labor content' of the plant's products to the labor content of the company's least costly product, i.e., the variable allowing for high labor input into some products.

C, L, V, A, and *M* vary throughout the system of plants with their actual

* Though a model like $C = L^{\alpha}\,V^{\beta}\,A^{\gamma}\,M^{\delta}$ might have been employed using a regression on logarithms, it was felt that a direct sum of the cost components would more closely describe the actual circumstances. That is, it would give a better description of the physical and economic behavior, not necessarily a better statistical fit.

values determined for each of the plants. On the other hand, a, b, c, and d are treated as constant parameters of the system, and their values must be estimated. The same basic model (not including dM) was applied with some success to bulk plants (warehouses) of a major oil company, and to warehouses of another type of food processer.*

The underlying rationale of the analysis is that the 10 plants examined are a small sample from an infinite number of similar (possible) plants. The analysis infers from this sample that other plants in the same parent population with different configurations of the influencing variables will yield different (and in some cases lower) costs per gallon. Prediction of such costs is sought. The parameters of the system (a, b, c, and d) were estimated by standard least-squares multiple regression.

To summarize the procedure so far:

1. A measure of effectiveness, cost per gallon, was chosen.

2. Ten 'observations' were taken with actual cost per gallon as the dependent variable and labor rates, product volume, territory area, and plant product mix for that year as the independent variables. All observations covered a one-year period.

3. A model that related the dependent to the independent variables had been constructed from studying the problem (not the data).

4. Using the actual data 'observed,' the system parameters of the model were estimated by least-squares regression.

TESTING THE MODEL

SEVERAL TESTS of the model were made: (a) the significance of the estimates of the separate parameters was tested, and (b) the model was used to 'predict' the costs of the plants to compare against the actual costs. This comparison is shown first in Table I. The *actual cost* is the cost per gallon, C, the total cost for each plant for the particular year divided by the volume of that plant that year expressed in 1000-gallon equivalents. The *predicted cost* was calculated for each plant by inserting that plant's particular values of L, V, A, and M (labor rates, volume, area, and product mix) into the model that now has the regression estimates of the system parameters a, b, c, and d. The model then 'predicts' a cost for the plant. All costs (and only costs) are coded on a consistent basis, and may be considered analogous to cents per gallon.

The multiple-correlation coefficient for the comparison shown in Table I (with the error approximately normally distributed) is $R = 0.868$, which has a significance greater than 0.005. Adjusted for the relation between

---

* E. H. BOWMAN AND J. B. STEWART, "A Model for Scale of Operations," *J. Marketing*, January, 1956.

the number of unknowns (four) and the small sample size (ten) the adjusted multiple correlation coefficient is $R = 0.80$.*

Using the point estimates of the parameters, and the computed estimate of their standard deviations, the significance levels from a one tail 't' test (as economic reasoning ruled out the other tail), with the coefficients equal to zero as the null hypothesis, were as shown in Table II.

Admittedly, parameter c can hardly be called significant at this level. However, if the null hypothesis of $c = 0$ is accepted, then the decision rule that this analysis is seeking will call for one very large plant to serve the whole territory. In other words, *if* cost per gallon does *not* vary with territory area and it decreases with increasing volume, then the larger the plant the better. This point reappears later. For the moment at least, the analysis will accept all the point estimates (for a, b, c, and d).

TABLE II

Statistic	t	Significance level
b	3.459	>0.005
c	0.816	>0.22
d	1.413	>0.10
$R[f(b,c,d)]$	4.276	>0.005

DECISION RULE

HAVING determined the model that would in some sense predict the cost per gallon at a plant, given the plant's labor rates, volume, area, and product mix, the next step was to see how the variables in this model could be manipulated to minimize cost per gallon. On the assumption that the model represents the real world, if this minimum could be found in the model, then the branch plant system could be altered according to the model to yield the minimum cost per gallon of ice cream.

The decision rule sought was an expression for the optimum *size* plant. Neither the average labor rate nor the product mix would *necessarily* vary with an alteration by management in the volume of a plant. This is not true of area. With total sales for the company given or fixed, if the volume of a plant is to be increased (for instance), then the area of the territory served by the plant would have to be increased to pick up the additional customers to purchase this volume. It was necessary then to establish this relation between volume of production (and sales) and territory area. This relation was labelled sales density and noted by K, where $K = V/A$. This expression for sales density was in terms of sales volume (1000-gallon equivalents) per square mile, and was treated as a constant *within* each plant's territory.

* M. EZEKIEL, *Methods of Correlation Analysis*, Wiley, New York, 1941.

The substitution, $A = V/K$ can then be made in the model:

$$C = L\ (a + b/V + c\ \sqrt{A} + d\ M), \qquad (2)$$

$$C = L\ (a + b/V + c\ \sqrt{V/K} + d\ M); \qquad (3)$$

and the derivative taken with respect to V (the decision variable), and equated to zero to reveal the optimum volume:

$$dC/dV = Lb/V^2 + \tfrac{1}{2}\ Lc\ (V/K)^{-1/2} = 0,$$

$$V_{\mathrm{Opt}} = K^{1/3}\ (2\ b/c)^{2/3}. \qquad (4)$$

The optimum volume then is a function of b and c, cost parameters of the system, and K, defined as the sales density of the territory. This is the decision rule that has been sought by the analysis. It is an expression for

TABLE III

	Ratio of actual volume to optimum volume	Ratio of predicted cost at actual volume to predicted cost at optimum volume
Plant No. 1	1.50	1.01
Plant No. 2	0.72	1.02
Plant No. 3	0.60	1.03
Plant No. 4	0.53	1.06
Plant No. 5	0.54	1.05
Plant No. 6	0.54	1.05
Plant No. 7	0.53	1.04
Plant No. 8	0.49	1.05
Plant No. 9	0.38	1.11
Plant No. 10	0.15	1.63

the 'best' size of the company's ice cream plants based on the company's own technology, methods, and costs. The appropriate values of K (the sales density of the particular region), and b and c (the point estimates of the parameter values for the whole system) are inserted into the decision rule, equation (4), in order to determine the optimum volume for each plant. This information is presented in Table III. The ratio of costs in Table III was determined by inserting first the actual volume and then the optimum volume in the cost predicting model, equation (2).

It can be seen from Table III that according to this analysis, except for Plant No. 1, all the plants are operating at too small a volume. Half of them are operating at about half their optimum volume, while two are substantially below this figure. Taking total sales as given, then it appears that the company should operate five or six plants rather than ten. As an example, plants 1, 2, 3, 5, 7, and 9, all operating at their calculated *optimum* volumes, together would produce just about the total sales volume of all ten plants at their old volumes; that is, the total sales that are given.

An extension of the cost premium paid by the company for operating the smaller plants as suggested by the last column in Table III indicates that a total premium of approximately $230,000 per year has been incurred as a result of operating the small plants. That is, the total sales volume could have been supplied by fewer larger plants with this yearly dollar savings.

ADDENDA TO THE DECISION RULE

ACCORDING to the model, and depending on a territory's sales density, a plant that varies 50 per cent from optimum on the small side incurs a 5 to 8 per cent cost premium while a plant that varies 50 per cent from optimum on the large side incurs only a 1 or 2 per cent cost premium. Therefore, the analysis indicates not only that most plants should be larger, but if an error is to be made, it is better to make it on the large side.

Considering the fact that the parameter values used for b and c are point estimates, and that the estimating procedure presents distributions of these parameters, a case could be made for combining the economic cost functions $(b/V + c\sqrt{V/K})$ with the statistical distributions (of b and c) in order to carry out an explicit minimization of expected value rather than using the point estimates. While this was not done here, the following calculations served somewhat the same purpose.

The decision rule developed by the analysis centers around the ratio b/c, i.e., $V_{\mathrm{Opt}} = K^{1/3} (2 b/c)^{2/3}$. Both b and c have been estimated by least squares regression. The point can now be made again that the estimate of c had a relatively large standard deviation (significance level > 0.22).

A sensitivity check was made on the *limits* of the decision rule. Using the standard deviation estimates developed in the regression computation, one confidence interval of 80 per cent was placed around the point estimate of b, and another around the point estimate of c. As the distributions are assumed symmetrical, b and c would be outside their own limits 10 per cent of the time at either extreme. So far, this analysis reveals that virtually all of the plants are too small; however, if b were enough smaller and c were enough larger this would not be the case.

The value below which b could be expected in 10 per cent of the estimates, and the value above which c could be expected in 10 per cent of the estimates were determined. If independent, this would happen simultaneously in only 1 per cent of the estimates (0.1×0.1). With these new values, the plants that this present analysis reveals are about half their optimum size would be just about their optimum size, e.g., rather than 0.54 to 0.49, the ratio of actual to optimum size would be 1.09 to 0.97. This extreme (on the small side) answer for plant size, however, would be very unlikely. To give some balance to the picture, the large extreme (with $0.1 \times 0.1 = 0.01$ probability) was computed to be an infinite size plant, or to make it more meaningful that the company should make all their ice cream in only one plant. This is similar to accepting the null hypothesis that c (the coefficient of area) is not significant, i.e., cost per gallon does not increase with an area increase.

MANAGEMENT'S DECISION PROCESS

THIS ANALYSIS was carried on with the cooperation of several members of the ice cream company but independent of the decision-making group in the firm. While the optimum size of the company's plants would not be seriously recommended as *precise* answers following this analysis, considering the model explained only about two-thirds (0.8^2) of the cost variance, it was felt that the company's plants were too small, and that a system with fewer and larger plants would be a less costly one. Sometime after this study was completed (and to the best of our knowledge independent of it), the company started to make some changes. *They closed Plants Nos. 10, 4, 6, and 8.* In other words, they arrived at just about the system recommended by this analysis (i.e., size and number of plants, as no attention was given in this analysis as to which plants to close).

A check back with the company (our cooperating individuals) yielded the company's rationale. The management group suspected they had too many plants. Most of the plants had been acquired (with customers) rather than purposefully built. From the company's books and accounting cost models, they estimated, item by item, in the chart of accounts what costs would be saved by closing a particular plant (essentially manufacturing costs), and what costs would be increased at the adjacent plants (essentially manufacturing and transportation costs). According to the *company's* analysis, Plant No. 10 was studied and closed as it had a particularly poor layout. Plant No. 4 was studied and closed as its space was needed for storage for sales purposes. Plant No. 6 was studied and closed because it was built for another purpose originally and also the company desired to increase the operations of Plant No. 5, the adjoining plant. Plant No. 8 was studied and closed because it was becoming one of the most costly plants, as it is in a very difficult and high-cost labor market.

It is interesting to note that the company is now considering going still further with their consolidations, possibly even to a three-plant system.

Costs Associated with External Scale Economies

Production and Distribution in the Large Metropolis [1]

RAYMOND VERNON

Abstract: This is an examination of the present and future role of metropolitan areas in the fields of production and distribution and the problems that future growth will bring. Special attention is given to the implications of the outward movement of manufacturing activities from the central cities into the suburbs and open country beyond. The consequences of the relative growth of business services in metropolitan areas are also explored. These trends are related to the outward shift of populations in the metropolitan areas and some of the resulting problems are identified and discussed.

OUR purpose in this paper is to speculate on the problems and policies which are likely to confront the larger urban areas of this nation in the next quarter century as a result of developments in the fields of production and distribution. This calls first of all for economic projection. But to rely on economic projection, as Simon Kuznets has observed, is in some sense an act of faith. Projections are not true or false; they are simply more fully reasoned or

[1] This paper has been developed as a by-product of the New York Metropolitan Region Study. It incorporates some of the preliminary ideas of the author as well as his interpretation of some of the tentative conclusions of his colleagues in the Study. The Study, which is now winding up its first year, is planned for a three-year period. Undertaken by the Harvard Graduate School of Public Administration for the Regional Plan Association and financed jointly by the Ford Foundation and the Rockefeller Brothers Fund, its purpose is to analyze the economic life of the New York metropolitan region and to project the region's future growth. Nevertheless, the observations contained in the paper should not be regarded in any sense as conclusions of the New York Metropolitan Region Study. Two years hence, the Study's participants will probably be both wiser and more cautious in their observations about the future of metropolitan areas.

less so. And none knows more acutely than the economic analyst how often events may prove more subtle and more complex than the best reasoning and analysis could have anticipated.

When we speculate about the future role of the large metropolis in the fields of production and distribution, however, there is a certain seeming solidity in the factual background from which such speculations are launched. For the past fifty years or more, the growth patterns of the metropolitan areas of the United States have assumed a regularity calculated to gladden the heart of the forecaster. And as one inquires into the reasons for these patterns, he finds himself able to rationalize most of what he sees without wandering far into fields of pure fancy. To gain some sense of the future role of the metropolis, therefore, we shall begin by reviewing the main trends in their past growth; we shall then consider some of the significant shifts which have been occurring within the subareas of these large urban complexes; and we shall conclude by considering the problems and policies which these trends suggest.

Other essays in this volume will no doubt document the fact that our ur-

Reprinted from *The Annals of the American Academy of Political and Social Sciences,* 314 (1957), 15–29, by permission of the author and editor.

ban areas have accounted for a steadily growing share of the nation's population and the nation's jobs. In 1800, for instance, only 6 per cent of the nation's population lived in urban places. By 1850 the figure had reached 15 per cent; by 1900 it had climbed to 40 per cent; and by 1950 it was 59 per cent.[2] Part of this growth, of course, was simply due to the fact that many small towns and patches of open country during this period graduated into "urban places." But a considerable part of the increase was due to the fact that the large industrial areas—areas which were already urbanized by mid-nineteenth century—have persistently grown at a faster pace than the small towns and rural areas. For example, although the 33 largest industrial areas of the country accounted for only 23 per cent of the nation's population in 1870 they had come to account for 36 per cent in 1930; [3] and 52 "standard metropolitan areas" which represented 32 per cent of the nation's population in 1900 had come to represent 42 per cent by 1950.[4]

Meanwhile, the number of persons on farms and in small towns has grown more slowly than in the larger urban complexes. Indeed, lately there has been an absolute thinning out of the people in some agricultural areas of the country. Our next step is to consider the reasons for some of the basic shifts.

OUR CHANGING DEMANDS

The overriding characteristic of this nation's economy in the past century

[2] On the basis of a new definition of "urban places," the 1950 figure would be 64 per cent.
[3] G. E. McLaughlin, *Growth of American Manufacturing Areas* (Pittsburgh: University of Pittsburgh Press, 1938), p. 53. There is some evidence that medium sized industrial areas have been growing even faster than the largest areas but the differences are not marked.
[4] D. J. Bogue, *Population Growth in Standard Metropolitan Areas 1900–1950* (Washington: U. S. Housing and Home Finance Agency, 1953), p. 13.

has been the long-term growth in output per worker. This growth has been characteristic not only of manufacturing but of agriculture as well.[5] And it has, of course, been matched by an increase in the per capita consumption of goods and services by the American people.

But as incomes have grown, wants have tended to change. The principal change has been a decline in the relative importance of the consumption of food and fibers raised on the farm and an increase in the relative importance of that heterogeneous collection of demands which goes under the heading of "services." As a result, with farm productivity continually growing, many sons of farmers have had to look elsewhere for jobs. At the same time, employment in such fields as trade, amusement, education, and medical care has expanded dramatically, providing some of the jobs which agriculture could no longer offer.[6]

Meanwhile, the kinds of skill needed for making and distributing goods have also undergone shifts. The relative need for unskilled muscle in production and trade has gone down, while the demand for professional and technical men and for clerks and similar office-bound workers has risen.[7] As a matter of fact, one

[5] Cf. J. W. Kendrick, "National Productivity and Its Long-Term Projection," in the National Bureau of Economic Research's *Long-Range Economic Projection* (Princeton: Princeton University Press, 1954), p. 67 ff.
[6] From 1870 to 1950, workers in agriculture declined from 50 per cent to 12 per cent of the United States labor force (changes in definition of the labor force introduce slight elements of incomparability in the two figures). In the same period, jobs in government administration went up from 2.0 to 7.9 per cent; jobs in wholesale and retail trade rose from 6.1 to 18.0 per cent; and jobs in the professions increased from 1.6 to 6.3 per cent. See J. F. Dewhurst and Associates, *America's Needs and Resources* (New York: Twentieth Century Fund, 1955), p. 732.
[7] Cf. "Nonproduction Workers in Factories, 1919–56," *Monthly Labor Review*, Vol. 80, No. 4 (April 1957).

should not overlook the possibility that the shift has been even more marked than any data on the manufacturing industries might suggest. For some of the business functions which fifty years ago were performed under the heading of manufacturing—to the extent that they were being performed at all—are being carried on today by a different type of work force in the advertising services, management advisory services, research organizations, wholesalers, and specialized repair and maintenance organizations—in short, in some of the so-called service industries.[8]

In a later section—a section devoted to the changing function of the city's core—we shall argue that this curiously mixed bag of business services and some of the fast-growing consumer services have demanded large urban locations and have contributed to the disproportionate growth of such urban areas. For the present, let us take this conclusion for granted, subject to later proof. Once granted, the trend to urban growth feeds upon itself. For urban living has demanded more services still: some of these services have arisen from the "diseconomies" of urban living, leading to more building inspectors, laundries, and purveyors of fresh vegetables; other services such as ball games and hospital care have come closer to contributing to the real consumption of the urban dwellers.[9] The increased demand for services has

added to urban growth in still another way. In the past fifty years the real output per man of workers engaged in the service industries has not increased very rapidly—certainly not as rapidly as in agriculture and manufacturing. Accordingly, the share of the nation's labor force engaged in services has probably gone up even more than the share of the nation's output represented by services. And this has added further to the urban orientation of the nation's labor force.[10]

THE STRUCTURE OF MANUFACTURING

While jobs on the farms and in rural areas were declining in their relative importance and while service jobs were growing in urban areas at a very rapid rate, manufacturing jobs were being distributed between urban and rural areas in a pattern all their own. Historically, our large urban areas have harbored the majority of the country's manufacturing jobs. Yet despite this fact and despite the relatively rapid growth of the metropolitan labor force, the large urban areas' share of the nation's manufacturing jobs has undergone a gradual although moderate decline over the past thirty or forty years.[11] This means that manu-

---

[8] From 1910 to 1950, laborers declined from 16.8 to 6.9 per cent of the nonfarm United States work force; clerks and kindred workers went up from 7.9 to 13.9 per cent; and professional and technical workers rose from 6.7 to 9.9 per cent. G. L. Palmer, *Philadelphia Workers in a Changing Economy* (Philadelphia: University of Pennsylvania Press, 1956), App. Table 13, p. 161.

[9] Cf. Colin Clark, "The Economic Functions of a City in Relation to its Size," *Econometrica*, Vol. 13, No. 2 (April 1945), pp. 97–113. Clark appears to assume that the increased demand for services is entirely a reflection of changing household demands.

[10] This suggests that a rise must have occurred in the relative price of services which was not enough to stifle the increase in demand.

[11] Cf. Coleman Woodbury (Editor), *The Future of Cities and Urban Redevelopment* (Chicago: University of Chicago Press, 1953), p. 253. The 33 "industrial areas" comprising the nation's principal cities and their peripheries accounted for 58.3 per cent of the nation's manufacturing jobs in 1919, 56.2 per cent in 1929, 54.9 per cent in 1939, and 54.4 per cent in 1947. A group of 48 large standard metropolitan areas accounted for 59.8 per cent of the nation's manufacturing jobs in 1929, 58.2 per cent in 1939, 58.7 per cent in 1947, and 55.8 per cent in 1954. Compiled from E. M. Kitagawa and D. J. Bogue, *Suburbanization of Manufacturing Activity within Standard Metropolitan Areas* (Oxford, Ohio: Miami University Press, 1955), App. B, and

facturing jobs in the large urban areas have not kept pace with other jobs in these areas. Taken together these forces have reduced the comparative importance of manufacturing operations in large urban areas and have increased the importance of their office- and store-bound activities.

One is tempted to draw the conclusion from these facts that the pull of manufacturing establishments toward large urban areas may have decreased in the past fifty years. In a superficial sense, this is unquestionably the case. Half a century ago, when the railroad, the cart, and the boat were the principal means of moving people and goods, the importance of being close to transportation ganglia was critical for industry and commerce and for their labor force. Accordingly, large cities developed close to the ganglia and particularly at the nodes of the transportation system—at the juncture of the rivers and railroads—and industry and commerce competed for space close by these nodes.

The truck and the automobile loosened the bonds of manufacturing plants toward larger urban areas and allowed them to consider locations which were more distant from the center of urban complexes. In this sense, the tie of manufacturing plants to large urban areas can be said to have weakened. In another sense, however, we are inclined to suspect that the pull to large urban areas may have grown in importance relative to the pull of other factors in the locational equation such as the source of materials, the cost and availability of labor, and so on. Indeed, our working hypothesis at present is this: Over the course of time manufacturing establishments have been tending to group themselves about large urban areas, creating loose clusters of inter-related and interdependent plants. The

from preliminary *1954 Census of Manufactures* releases.

clusters, though oriented to large urban markets, have been so loose that they have spilled over into the countryside surrounding the metropolitan areas.[12] Moreover, with the passage of time, the clusters surrounding these areas have grown more like one another in their composition. In the aggregate they have tended to increase the self-sufficiency and independence of the large urban areas for industrial goods and to reduce the relative role of trade in goods between such areas.

These hypotheses have been built up from a number of initial impressions. One of these is the view that the balance between transportation savings and savings involved in large-scale production—a balance which, as we shall shortly see, is critical in locational decisions—has been undergoing a gradual shift over the past century; and that this shift has tended to locate manufacturing plants closer to the markets they are to serve.[13] Let us consider what this concept means.

LOCATION OF MARKETS

In the early period of American industrial history, manufacturing plants were typically located very close to their markets. Since the size of the market for any firm was circumscribed by high overland transport costs, our early factories and foundries had to make the best of local sources of supply and had to market their goods close to where

[12] Cf. D. J. Bogue, *The Structure of the Metropolitan Community* (Ann Arbor: University of Michigan, 1949), p. 41. The analysis indicates that as of 1940 persons engaged in manufacturing were less highly concentrated toward the center of metropolitan areas than persons engaged in services, retail trade, or wholesale trade. No analysis is available, however, with respect to the trend in such concentration over time.

[13] Cf. C. D. Harris, "The Market as a Factor in the Location of Industry in the United States," *The Appraisal Journal* (January 1956), pp. 58–61.

they were made.[14] But in the middle of the nineteenth century transport costs declined dramatically; at the same time, mass production methods gave a heavy edge in production costs to the larger firms over their smaller competitors. For a time, then, a new balance was struck. The new large-scale firms could afford to take advantage of superior materials, wherever they might be, and to ship their products for longer distances to their markets.

Then came the third stage: The relative fall of transportation costs which was so dramatic in the nineteenth century was arrested and finally reversed in the first half of the twentieth century. At the same time, many local markets grew sufficiently large to accommodate plants with most or all of the cost advantages associated with mass production.[15] As a result, the pattern of expansion of the large firms tended more and more toward the establishment of plants closer to their local markets.[16]

[14] The pattern described above is clearer for some industries than for others; it fits reasonably well, for example, with respect to boot and shoe manufacture, flour milling, iron and steel making, and non-ferrous metal refining. Cf. E. M. Hoover, Jr., *Location Theory and the Shoe and Leather Industries* (Cambridge: Harvard University Press, 1937), p. 115 *passim;* M. S. Gordon, *Employment Expansion and Population Growth* (Berkeley and Los Angeles: University of California Press, 1954), p. 36; Carter Goodrich and others, *Migration and Economic Opportunity* (Philadelphia: University of Pennsylvania Press, 1936), pp. 53–54, 305–9; H. F. Williamson (Editor), *The Growth of the American Economy* (New York: Prentice-Hall, 1951), pp. 154–88, 432–509, 699 *passim.*

[15] This implies that the optimum scale of plant had not been increasing during the period at a sufficient pace to offset the tendency toward market orientation created by other forces. For the present, this is in fact our working assumption.

[16] Notice that this analysis neglects altogether the role which may have been played by regional differences in costs other than materials such as labor costs, power costs, taxes,

During the same period of 50 to 100 years, another force was weakening the relative attraction of raw material sources for industrial location and was increasing the pull toward markets. This was the constantly increasing degree of fabrication characteristic of products offered to consumers. As time went on, the products of farm, forest, and mine were subjected to increasingly complex manufacturing processes and to increasingly intricate assembly. Indeed, in some cases, "raw" materials were entirely displaced by fabricated materials such as artificial fibers and plastic products produced in establishments whose locational choice was not nearly so restricted as the sources of the displaced raw materials.[17]

Of course, if manufacturing firms had chosen to elaborate their processes solely through the expansion of their existing plants or through the creation of multiple plant structures at their original sites, the developments suggested above might not have shifted the distribution of manufacturing plants and might not have increased the tendency toward industrial clusters. But the increasing complexity of the processes meant an increasing complexity of "inputs" both of raw materials and of intermediate products. This increasing complexity

rent, and so on. That such factors did play a role in the regional redistribution of some industries such as textiles and radio manufactures, goes without saying. Preliminary results of various studies now under way, however, leave one with the impression that the forces of raw material location, market size, and scale economies have been more important on the whole in redistributing industry than changing regional levels of factor costs.

[17] A crude reflection of these tendencies is found in the fact that between 1870 and 1950 the number of persons engaged in agriculture, forestry, fishing, and mining rose only 21 per cent while those engaged in manufacturing rose 589 per cent. Adapted from Harold Barger, *Distribution's Place in the American Economy* (Princeton: Princeton University Press, 1955), p. 4.

reduced the importance of the location of any one material in the locational calculus. Locations which might be unfavorable in the supply of one material were sometimes attractive in the supply of another. The question of materials location became less important and that of market location correspondingly more so, especially where the location of markets coincided with the location of industrial clusters capable of providing many of the needed intermediate "inputs."

What is more, there is an impression among some economists that the elaboration of manufacturing processes has led to the development and growth of new intermediate industries in the United States—industries devoted primarily to supplying other manufacturers with fabricated products for further construction or assembly.[18] This trend seems to have characterized the faster growing segments of our industrial structure such as the chemicals and metal-working industries. And the advantages of large-scale operation by these new producers of intermediate products have commonly led to the location of plants near the larger, diversified, industrial markets.[19]

[18] Cf. G. J. Stigler, "The Division of Labor is Limited by the Extent of the Market," *Journal of Political Economy*, Vol. 59, No. 3 (June 1951), pp. 187–91. Stigler's argument in support of the growth of specialization does not rely on the increasing complexity of the production process and is based rather on the effects of growth itself.

[19] The reader is warned, if warning were needed, that the assumption of disintegration implied by this description is no more than an impressionistic conclusion for which statistical verification is so far lacking. The warning is especially important because there have been striking illustrations flatly at variance with the specialization and disintegration trends suggested above, motivated by the desires of some producers to maintain control over their sources of material or their distribution channels. Besides, in some industries, economies have been developed which are dependent upon the extent of integration of an installation, such

Still another force may be operating to attract manufacturing firms toward their markets. In many lines of consumer goods, there has been a pronounced tendency over the years to depart from a few staple lines and to offer wider choices in colors, styles, packaging, and accessories. The classic case, perhaps, is that of house paints, where a proliferation of colors, textures, and packages has had a major impact on the industry. The effect of such an increase is twofold: It reduces the economies associated with large-scale operations; and it also increases the size of the inventories which have to be maintained at points of distribution, since the difficulty of forecasting the sales of many small lines is much greater than that involved in a few large lines.

Both results appear to have reduced the advantages of larger and more centrally located plants, that is, to the extent that such advantages may previously have existed. The opportunity for the larger firms to profit from large-scale operations and longer runs has declined. And the need for such firms to maintain decentralized regional shipping points has increased. As a result, the tendency has been for paint establishments to move toward the market. Other types of producers assailed by the same pressures may well have followed suit.

This chain of reasoning completes the picture for the present. If the sketch developed in the preceding pages is consistent with the facts, we are a nation

as economies through the recycling of scrap and the avoidance of the intermediate handling of bulky products; the development of the continuous strip mill in the steel industry is a case in point. A crude test of the validity of the concept that specialization and disintegration are growing might be made through comparing the structure of interindustry tables compiled for different years over an adequate period of time; but even this approach has its pitfalls and uncertainties.

ending toward regional self-sufficiency in the production of goods. The plants in each region are developing increasingly complex ties with one another. And although they are not showing any increasing tendency to settle within the borders of metropolitan areas, nevertheless one of the major determinants of their location is the size and location of these metropolitan clusters.

POPULATIONS AND JOBS

We have already observed that in the past half century urban areas of the United States have grown much faster than the nation as a whole. But during this time, the area of fastest population growth in the typical large metropolis appears to have lain in a ring surrounding the city center—a ring whose distance from the center has tended to increase as the city has grown.[20] The great mushrooming of suburbs after World War II carried on this long term trend at an accelerated tempo, perhaps as a reaction to the prior fifteen-year interruption occasioned by depression and war.

The shift in populations from city to suburb carried with it an inevitable shift in certain kinds of jobs. One may readily assume, for instance, that jobs in the retail trades and in household service lines followed the drift of households to the suburbs.[21] But solid figures

measuring the long-term shift in jobs between the periphery and the center of the large metropolitan areas are only available with respect to manufacturing employment. We shall begin, then, by exploring the movement of jobs for this sector of the nation's economy.

Manufacturing employment over the past half century has tended to grow at the periphery of the larger urban areas at a faster rate than at the center. The trend toward an outward redistribution of manufacturing jobs has been gradual but persistent, and it has characterized the overwhelming majority of the major metropolitan areas.[22] By 1955, manufacturing jobs in the centers of those areas were no longer a major element. In New York City, for instance, only 24 per cent of the total jobs were reported in manufacturing whereas the ring counties reported 39 per cent of their jobs in the manufacturing category.

To understand these shifts, we must first of all explore the differences in function between these two portions of the large urban area. A clue to some of

[20] The pattern is clearer for the larger metropolitan areas than for the smaller; see A. H. Hawley, *The Changing Shape of Metropolitan America: Deconcentration Since 1920* (Glencoe: Free Press, 1955), pp. 42–43. But this is probably due to the fact that the faster growing ring in the smaller metropolitan areas is usually contained within the political boundaries of the central city and is therefore not separately available from Census data.

[21] Manageable data on this point are not available prior to 1939. For 1939 to 1947, see R. P. Cuzzort, *Suburbanization of Service Industries within Standard Metropolitan Areas* (Oxford: Miami University Press, 1955), p. 17, Table II–4; although Cuzzort's measure-

ments unfortunately do not distinguish business from household services, they are reliable enough to indicate the shift. From 1947 to 1955, the experience of the New York metropolitan region illustrates the trend; counties outside the central city—New York City—recorded a rise in retail jobs of 41 per cent while retail jobs in New York City declined 6 per cent.

[22] Of the total production workers in 33 industrial areas in 1899, 68.3 per cent were in the "principal cities" of the areas whereas the comparable figure by 1947 was 59.2 per cent; conversely 31.7 per cent in 1899 were in the rings of these areas, whereas the 1947 figure was 40.8 per cent. Adapted from Coleman Woodbury (Editor), *op. cit.* (note 11 *supra*), p. 253. Of total production workers in 48 large standard metropolitan areas in 1929, 66.5 per cent were in the "central cities" of the areas whereas the comparable figure for 1954 was 58.6 per cent. Compiled from E. M. Kitagawa and D. J. Bogue, *op. cit.* (note 11 *supra*), App. B, and from preliminary 1954 *Census of Manufactures* releases.

these differences is offered by the fact that for large metropolitan areas, the manufacturing plants in the core of the area tend to be smaller than those located at the periphery. Part of this difference is due, of course, to the fact that the industries of the core differ in character from those of the ring. But part of the relationship is due also to the fact that even within any given industry the firms in the center are smaller than those at the periphery.

The situation in the New York metropolitan area in 1954 is typical. At that time, the average manufacturing firm in New York City had only 25 employees whereas the average for firms elsewhere in the region was 60 employees. This relationship held, industry by industry, for 19 of the 20 major industry groups into which manufacturing activity was divided; and spot-checks indicated that the relationship continued to hold for fairly fine subindustries as well.[23]

There are various reasons why small firms in a given industry should have a greater affinity for a core location than their larger competitors. As one pictures the situation of a small manufacturing firm in competition with larger establishments, one of its chief problems is to approximate the economies which are available to its larger competitors because of their size. The small firm may solve the problem, to the extent that it can be solved at all, by subcontracting portions of its manufacturing or maintenance operations to specialists whose scale of operations allows them to achieve the necessary economies. But where a variety of subcontracting operations is a vital and continuing portion of the operation, the manufacturer will wish to

be physically close to his suppliers. His suppliers, in turn—being specialists who rely on a variety of such customers— will wish to be close to the greatest cluster of such customers. The equilibrium point for such an interrelated mass is bound to be close to the center of the urban complex.

"EXTERNAL ECONOMIES"

The same concept, in fact, may be applied *in extenso* to the wide range of "external economies" of a metropolitan area. The small firm in a given industry usually needs the fractional use of transportation facilities; it is likely to use less-than-carload and less-than-truckload transport to a greater degree than its competitors. In securing fractional transport of this sort the small firm can often obtain better service and better terms in the center of the large metropolitan area than either at the periphery or in smaller metropolitan areas. For the volume of business in the large metropolitan area develops enough specialists in this kind of transportation to introduce scale economies and to push down rates and service toward levels more nearly competitive with the rates and service available for carload and truckload lots.[24]

The phenomenon of substituting "external economies" in the metropolitan

[23] For 48 large standard metropolitan areas in 1954, the average manufacturing firm in the central city had 38 employees while the average manufacturing firm in the ring had 62 employees. In 1947 the comparable figures were respectively 42 and 77.

[24] Freight forwarders accounted for 14 per cent of the outbound carload rail traffic of the New York metropolitan region in 1955, compared with less than $\frac{2}{10}$ of 1 per cent for the nation as a whole. Another reflection of these scale economies appears in the fact that the incidence of "commodity rates" as distinguished from "class rates" is greater in the larger metropolitan areas; "commodity rates," of course, are far lower than "class rates." A large shipper may have the bargaining power to compel carriers to initiate such rates for given commodities in locations outside metropolitan areas where they have not previously existed but the bargaining power of smaller shippers is proportionately weaker.

core for scale economies available elsewhere—more strictly, the phenomenon of securing the advantages of scale economies by buying from specialists in the product or service concerned—can be observed in a number of other production costs. Power, water, sewage, police, and fire protection can present similar problems for the small firm. Requirements which in a less populous area would involve a large indivisible expenditure, such as a power transformer or a plant policeman, may be satisfied in the city by a divisible service fee. And the service fee may reduce the small producer's handicap vis-à-vis his larger competitor.

The core of the metropolitan area offers opportunities not only to overcome the handicap of insufficient size but also to deal with the costs engendered by various uncertainties. The odds are that in any given industry small firms are more uncertain than large—more uncertain about their future sales, more uncertain about their future labor needs, and more uncertain about their future space needs. One way to meet such uncertainties is to control more inventory, more labor, and more space than is immediately needed; but it is a solution which does not recommend itself to the small typically capital-starved manufacturing firm. Another partial solution is to locate in rented quarters which are flexible in area and short-run as to commitment; to stay close by a large labor market from which temporary labor needs are readily mustered; and to be near sources capable of supplying added materials on short notice. These considerations have dominated the locational decisions of many small firms in the New York metropolitan region and have persuaded them to cling to a location near the region's center.

So far we have spoken of the large firm versus the small in some given industry. But the tendencies suggested above are stronger in some industries than in others. There are industries, for example, whose product is continually subject to significant change and whose outlook accordingly is constantly colored by uncertainty as to the quantity and nature of the "inputs." Such industries tend to deal in unstandardized materials and to produce unstandardized finished products. Firms in industries of this sort typically must make their locational decisions with due regard for their need to draw on a variety of collateral sources for materials and processes and their need to examine directly the color, texture, or degree of workmanship of these collateral products and processes. In such cases, too, firms must plan to display their unstandardized finished products at some point convenient to the prospective buyer in order to facilitate the comparative shopping which is characteristic of the sale of unstandardized products.

Industries which possess these characteristics are typically dominated by small sized firms. Where raw materials are unstandardized or constantly changing; where the processes involved are in continual flux; where the end product is not standardized; in such cases, there are few economies associated with large-scale operations and large firms cannot readily dominate the market. This interplay among size and standardization suggests why "unstandardized" industries organized on a small-firm basis such as high-style dresses and hats, buttons, furs, toys, jobprinting, and magazine publishing have an affinity to the city's center.

FACTORS IN FIRMS' SHIFT TO THE PERIPHERY

If these are the functions of the core and the ring of urban areas, what accounts for the pronounced shifts that have been taking place between the core and the ring within such areas? [25] One element in the outward shift has been the movement of small firms graduating to larger size in some given industry. Numerous analyses have been conducted on the subject of plant migration, covering a number of areas and varying circumstances.[26] All the surveys are vulnerable, of course, in the sense that they have sought to classify and categorize a decision-making process—a process culminating in a decision to move—which at best is complex, obscure, and highly subjective in character. What is more, since the firms involved were usually interviewed after they had made the decision, their reasons before the fact and their rationalizations after the fact are probably hopelessly intertwined.

Yet the studies are astonishingly consistent in one respect. They show that in a high percentage of cases the triggering factor which led manufacturing firms to move away from the center of metropolitan regions was that they were running out of existing space at their central location. Second in importance was a variety of other asserted problems: high labor costs, high taxes, traffic congestion, onerous city fire and health ordinances, local graft, and so on. But none of these problems appears to have had primacy over the space problem.

The decision to move, then, appears superficially to be associated with growth. And this is precisely what one would expect if the hypotheses outlined earlier have any validity. For the growth of firms, according to our reasoning, reduces their reliance on otherwise indivisible inputs of labor and capital, such as a few hours' work on electrical wiring or the part-time use of a metal-stamping machine. At some stage in the firm's growth, it is in a position to take on these indivisible elements at a unit cost which compares favorably with the subcontractors' price. What is more, the growth of a firm probably reduces the level of its uncertainty as well, allowing it to plan its space, inventory, and labor needs with a surer hand and with less concern for violent fluctuations in these needs. As a result, the special pull of the center of the urban complex is greatly weakened.

As the outward movement of growing firms has progressed, the small firms which have sprung up to fill the resulting vacuum have not been sufficient to allow the growth of manufacturing employment at the center of our large

[25] The explanation which follows places heavy emphasis on the cost side of the locational equation. But part of the explanation for the shift may perhaps be found on the demand side: Employment in the types of manufacturing which require a core location may be growing more slowly than other types of employment requiring this kind of location such as business services; see the succeeding section on the locational requirements of business services. Where central locations have been scarce, the latter group of demands may have bid space away from the former. This possibility needs more testing, however, before it can be seriously advanced.

[26] Cf. Business Executives' Research Council and Faculty Committee, *Chicago's Metropolitan Growth* (Evanston: Northwestern University, 1955), pp. 40–45; G. H. Ellis, "Why New Manufacturing Establishments Located in New England: August 1945 to June 1948," Federal Reserve Bank of Boston, *Monthly Review,* Vol. 31, No. 4 (April 1949), pp. 1–12; J. I. Griffin, *Industrial Location in the New York Area* (New York: City College Press, 1956); R. M. Haig, *Regional Survey of New York and Its Environs,* Vol. I (New York: Committee on Regional Planning of New York and its Environs, 1927); W. N. Leonard and C. D. Stonier, *Industry Looks at Long Island,* Part I (Hempstead: Hofstra College, 1956); G. E. McLaughlin and Stefan Robock, *Why Industry Moves South* (Washington, D. C.: National Planning Association, 1949); P. M. Reid, "Movement of Manufacturing Establishments 1937–1949 and Factors Influencing Location of Plants" (Detroit Metropolitan Area Regional Planning Commission, 1949, mimeographed); School of Business Administration of Seton Hall University, *Reasons for Relocation of New Jersey Manufacturing Firms, 1955* (South Orange: Seton Hall University, 1955).

metropolitan areas to keep pace with the growth of the ring; indeed, of late, there has even been an absolute decline in manufacturing jobs at the center of many large metropolitan areas.[27] This has been due in part, no doubt, to the fact that the truck has displaced the dray horse; interplant hauling, therefore, may now take place in a wider area. But there is a strong probability that it has been due also to the fact that the periphery of many of these urban areas, having developed their own industrial complexes, can now provide many of the "external economies" once available primarily at the center. In short, fractional transportation and service facilities and the easy availability of added space, materials, and labor, so indispensible in some industries for the small firm competing with larger rivals, now are available over wider geographical areas.[28]

The shift of the small manufacturing firm probably has not been the only factor contributing to the net outward movement of manufacturing jobs in metropolitan areas. The changing technical requirements of large firms also have added to the drift. Over the past half-century the tendency of large firms in many lines of manufacture has been to move from "batch" production to continuous production. Such a shift characteristically involves a basic change in the flow of materials inside the factory. In general, the shift consists of bringing the materials in a regular flow to fixed

[27] From 1947 to 1954, for instance, manufacturing jobs in the city of Chicago (not the "standard metropolitan area") fell by 8 per cent; in Boston by 6 per cent; in San Francisco by 8 per cent; in Cleveland by 3 per cent; and in St. Louis by 8 per cent.

[28] A striking illustration is afforded by the recent exodus of Alexander Smith & Co. from Yonkers, N. Y. The firm vacated 60 buildings on a 35-acre site with no obvious successor. But the space was taken up at once by a heterogenous collection of small manufacturing firms.

stations at which machines and labor are located; it reduces the movement of labor and the use of movable machines in the plant. Since it is ordinarily easier to engineer a continuous flow of materials in a single-level plant than in multi-story structures, this development has encouraged a preference for horizontal layouts in large plants. As a result, large establishments tend to avoid cramped sites more than they did in the past; the overwhelming preference is for open sites where horizontal expansion in any direction is relatively unimpeded.

SERVICES AT THE CENTER

The slack at the center of large metropolitan areas created by the shifting locus of manufacturing jobs has been taken up in part by jobs of other types. Data which might afford a long-term perspective of this process cannot be had readily, but recent figures for the New York metropolitan region illustrate the trend. From 1947 to 1955, for instance, while manufacturing jobs in New York City fell by 42,000, the number of jobs in finance, insurance, and real estate increased by 28,000.

Some of the reasons for the attraction of business services to the center are suggested by our discussion of the location of manufacturing establishments. It is a small step from the proposition that "unstandardized" manufacturing operations are attracted to the core of our urban areas to an understanding of the core's attraction for such business services as central offices, advertising agencies, law firms, commercial banks, and certain types of salesrooms. Some of these services, like the manufacturing establishments just discussed, have the need to gather up a heterogeneous and constantly changing mix of unstandardized "inputs." For the central office, these "inputs" consist of the counsel of lawyers and bankers, the gossip of the trade, the advice of advertising agencies and management firms, the major negotiated decisions of large suppliers or large customers; a varied, unstandardized mix requiring face-to-face confrontation with a wide variety of other entities. For the advertising agency or the publishing firm, one adds the materials obtained from free-lance writers and artists, the layouts of printers, and so on.

As we already intimated in our earlier discussion regarding manufacturing firms, it is the unstandardized nature not only of the inputs but also of the outputs which pulls the service industries toward the urban core. Purveyors of advertising space or high-style clothing, diamond merchants, and art dealers offer products which are unstandardized in character and which require face-to-face communication. The buyer of all these services or products will wish to see them and engage in comparative shopping before making a purchase. The seller whose service or product cannot be shopped at minimum cost to the buyer will be handicapped in the market, and his handicap will increase in proportion as the product is unstandardized.

FUTURE TRENDS AND FUTURE PROBLEMS

At this point, a certain amount of recapitulation may be in order. We have argued that the larger urban areas have grown in their relative importance because there has been a shift in demand from agriculture to services, because the relative importance of raw material locations has fallen, because the manufacturing role of individual establishments may have tended to become more specialized and interrelated, and because local markets may have grown sufficiently to support more local plants enjoying large-scale production economies.

It would be helpful if one could attach some rough quantitative measure to each of these forces, distinguishing the highly significant from the inconsequential. But our research has not yet reached this level of exactitude; perhaps it never will. Yet this limitation does not prevent us from concluding that if these are some of the major causes of comparative urban growth, we have not seen the end of it. Of course, the decline of agriculture's relative position cannot go much further; the agricultural work force is now down to under 10 per cent of the nation's total labor force. But the rise in business services will probably continue. New techniques for the planning and control of the production and distribution processes are spreading; data-processing devices are developing rapidly; research activities are constantly increasing; and all of these elements seem likely to add to the "nonproductive" functions associated with the making and transporting of goods.

Moreover, as new raw materials may affect the location of industry, they are likely to orient manufacturing plants toward larger urban locations.[29] While atomic power should be just beginning to have an effect on location in the next quarter century, it will free power generating stations and heavy power users from their affinity to coal and oil sources. As for other raw materials, the more spectacular locational shifts are likely to be movements from domestic interior sources to foreign sources; and this should add to the growth of urban areas surrounding the ports which are in a position to handle bulk materials.

This leaves for consideration one more tendency suggested above—the increasing specialization of the manufacturing

[29] One should note the distinction, however, between an urban "orientation" and an urban "location"; the former might well be in the countryside several trucking hours away from the urban center. Indeed, we have been struck by the frequency with which firms outlining their locational requirements have stated them in terms of the number of trucking hours from New York City.

process. Here the crystal ball is murkiest, just as the history is most obscure. But if events prove to be on the side of theory, this development also could contribute to future urban growth.

The odds are, then, that insofar as production and distribution trends have a hand in the process, they will encourage growth in the metropolitan areas at a rate faster than our total national growth. This growth, of course, will engender all sorts of problems even while it produces all sorts of benefits. The other essays of this volume are sure to deal in full with both. A recapitulation of them here would only be needlessly repetitive.

But there is one aspect of this shifting pattern which will offer a particular challenge to the economist. This is the changing distribution of economic activities between the ring and the core of the growing urban areas. Our research so far suggests that the core of these areas will be exposed to a confusing tangle of conflicting tendencies— tendencies whose relative quantitative importance may be somewhat clearer by the time such research has been completed. On the one hand, some of the demands for space in the core will grow; the space demands of the service industries, for instance, may increase radically. On the other hand, major productivity increases in some of these activities, such as the data-processing function of offices, may place a damper on such growth since comparatively fewer people and consequently less additional space may be needed to handle the larger output.

Besides, only certain elements of these activities demand a central urban location, namely, the elements which involve unstandardized inputs or outputs. Thus, while the executive suite is likely to stay fairly close to a downtown location, the data processors may be placed in less expensive and less congested space elsewhere. By the same token, though the showroom for high-style products may have to remain close to other showrooms for similar products, the manufacturing operations may well move to other quarters. Much depends on the extent to which industry and trade move in the direction of increased specialization, separating manufacturing from wholesaling.[30] Much depends on the rate of internal growth of the establishments involved and on their ability to make their overhead costs divisible: To separate the vice-president for finance, who demands a city location, from the cost accountant, who does not, and to separate the chief salesman of high-style dresses from the production supervisor.

"PROBLEMS" OF THE DECLINE OF THE CENTRAL CITY

The net effects of tendencies of this sort may differ from one urban area to the next. But some central cities are bound to lose on balance in population and in employment. Is this a "problem"? "Problems" are in the eye of the beholder. For some, any tendency which holds down the growth of the congested central city is not a problem but a solution; according to their lights, the psychic income from working and living outside the environment of the central city is so high as to offset other considerations. For others, street congestion or long journeys to work are minor inconveniences compared to the stimulation and rewards of the city environment.

However that may be, the decline of the central city where it occurs will be elevated to the status of a major prob-

[30] Note Stigler's view that there is a tendency for the wholesaling function to be more and more separated from the manufacturing function by specialization. G. F. Stigler, *Trends in Employment in the Service Industries* (Princeton: Princeton University Press, 1956), p. 144.

lem by city governments and city property owners and will command increasing attention from economists and political scientists. To arrest the trend, numerous proposals will be made to do something about the obvious irritations —to ease the suburbanites' journey to work and shop in the central city and to reduce the problems of downtown trucking traffic. Vigorous action on these fronts could slow the outward drift, no doubt; but if the hypotheses suggested above are valid, one wonders if relief on these fronts really gets at the heart of the problem.

If the "problem" as the larger city sees it is to arrest the outward job flow, its leverage might conceivably be greater if governmental action were directed to the provision of modern factory space at the core than if a similar effort were made in transportation, parking, and streets. From the viewpoint of the type of manufacturer who finds a city location most attractive, such space would be particularly desirable if it could be had on a flexible basis and a short-term lease; and it would be even more attractive if it could be organized in the type of clusters in which the unstandardized, disintegrated, smaller firm industries tend to arrange themselves. Such measures, of course, could exacerbate other "problems" for the city; they could load the streets with greater traffic and keep the use of commuting facilities close to their capacity. Yet they could well constitute the most effective approach to the "problem" of the city as the city conceived it.

The improvement of mass transit would probably have the effect of preserving some job opportunities in the central city. But the odds are that its greatest impact would be in slowing down the outward drift of the repetitive mass-production elements of the large-office operation. For the labor force involved in these operations—

young women marking time for marriage and older women returning to the labor force as the second breadwinner in the family—could well find the difficulties of an overburdened transit system too much to stand for the reward of a downtown working regime. If these were the jobs which the city were determined to retain, the leverage of mass transit improvement might be greater than any alternative.

But no two cities will put exactly the same priorities on their many "problems." And some may place a high premium on providing better job opportunities for the low-income groups—in the larger Eastern cities, for the Negroes and Puerto Ricans—crammed into the run-down private housing and the subsidized public housing bordering on the city's core. In these situations, the improvement of mass transit may be irrelevant, even inimical, to attaining the city's goal. For necessity is the mother of adaptation; and it could well be that employers who had no other choice would learn to staff their offices and their showrooms with the labor force at hand rather than to move their labor-using office operations to the suburbs. A great deal would depend on the training of these minorities, on the attitudes prevalent among employers in a given area, and on the speed of progress in office mechanization. But if the city saw its "problem" in these terms, the avoidance of mass transit improvement might prove, paradoxically, to be its most productive course.

FREIGHT MOVEMENT AND URBAN TRANSPORTATION WEB

Meanwhile, as manufacturing pushes its way into the suburbs, there is a considerable likelihood that new patterns of freight movement will develop. If regional self-sufficiency continues to grow and if the plants within each region continue to develop the extensive patterns of interrelationship which our analysis suggests, truck traffic from point to point within each large urban area may grow considerably faster than hauls between points situated in different areas. This would mean that urban areas would have to accommodate themselves to more diffused crosshauling from one suburb to the next, rather than to radial movements to and from the central city.

As one examines the transportation web of some of our major urban areas, he is struck by their inadequacy for dealing with these developments. The transportation system of the New York metropolitan region, for instance, consists of a series of rail lines converging in a radial pattern on the New York port. While lighterage facilities afford a link between these lines in a limited area of the region's core, there is no quick and easy means for rail connection between plants dispersed in different parts of the region. The highway pattern also is largely radial in nature, converging on the congested core of the region; and while fragments of circumferential routes do exist at some points, the easy linkage of plants situated at far-flung points on the region's circumference is still far from being developed.

Boston presents a somewhat similar picture, but illustrates at the same time the extent of the pent-up demand for circumferential routes; the recent development of one such route around portions of the Boston metropolis region produced a response of unanticipated dimensions in new plant locations and in added traffic. Chicago—to use another illustration—has overcome some of the limitations of a radial rail system through the development of various circumferential belt lines and rail interchange arrangements, but her highway system stresses the movement of goods in and out of the center of the region. Although radial traffic in goods in urban areas may not grow as fast as the circumferential flows, such traffic may create new problems because of an increasing shift to less-than-truckload lots. This should occur as wholesalers continue to move their warehousing operations to the periphery and as retailers grow increasingly insistent on smaller and more frequent deliveries to avoid the use of high-cost space for stocks. It might be prudent to plan for radial traffic, therefore, on the assumption that increasing proportions will be in small lots with frequent drops.

One last comment on a more general plane: The haul and pull between the city and its suburbs can be stated in terms of the rivalries of the sort which the paragraphs above have suggested. Or else they may be stated in terms of standards which look on the well-being of the metropolitan region as a whole as the planner's goal. It is not for the writer to make the choice; this will be made by the attitudes of the people in the region and by the political structure which they adopt. But for a long time economists have hammered home a point of homely wisdom which bears repeating in this connection. Different areas offer different opportunities for specialization which, when they are exploited, may add to the aggregate income and well-being of the region to which these areas belong. This creates a presumption that the land-using potentials of any metropolitan region are best exploited by a joint consideration of all the areas which go to make it up —not of the central city alone or of the fragmented suburbs. This is a presumption which may not stand up in the individual case; ineptness and corruption could be combined in a coalition of the central city and its suburbs, which would be more harmful than rivalry. But the presumption is still there, and it offers the safest starting point from which to view the economic problems of the larger metropolitan region.

CONTRASTS IN AGGLOMERATION: NEW YORK AND PITTSBURGH

Benjamin Chinitz

The natural inclination of a scientist when confronted with a new problem is to try to solve it with old tools. When he is finally convinced that the old tools will not do the job, he retreats to his shop to fashion some new tools. The burden of my argument in this paper is that we have reached the stage in regional economics when we must begin to fashion some new analytical tools.

When I say regional economics I have in mind specifically the analysis of the growth and structure of the economy of geographic subdivisions within a national economy. This type of analysis is now being carried on in at least a dozen metropolitan areas throughout the country and in numerous other types of subdivisions, large and small. I have been associated with two such studies: the New York Metropolitan Region Study, which just recently published its final report, and the Pittsburgh Economic Study, which is at its halfway mark, having been initiated in June, 1959, and being scheduled for completion in June, 1962. My observations, as the title of my paper suggests, are drawn from these two immersions in regional economics.

The basic-nonbasic approach to the analysis of a region has been under severe attack from many quarters in recent years. But I think it is fair to say that alternative approaches have differed in degree of refinement more than in kind. Fundamentally, we still go about our business in the same way. We try to identify the autonomous influences operating on the region and chart a network of interdependence between sectors within the region. I have no quarrel with this approach. I find it difficult to frame the problem otherwise. My quarrel is with the limitations of the maps of interdependence which are typically drawn.

I will surely be doing some of my colleagues an injustice with the following generalization but, begging their pardon, I state it anyway: our efforts so far have been almost exclusively devoted to the demand dimension of interdependence. The supply side has been virtually ignored. Let me elaborate.

The basic-nonbasic model is a way of coming to grips with the demand side of interdependence in one fell swoop. The links in the output-income-consumption chain, the links in the output-capital-

Reprinted from *American Economic Review, Papers & Proceedings* (May 1961), pp. 279–289, by permission of the author and editor.

formation chain, the links in the output-tax revenues-government spending chain, and the links in the output-materials purchased-output (i.e., input-output) chain, are all subsumed under one grand link between the exogenous and the endogenous elements of the system. Sometimes we can get away with this leap over a lot of treacherous ground just as in football a seventy-yard pass from the thirty-yard line occasionally results in a touchdown. To maintain the metaphor, most of us prefer to gain more yardage on the ground before passing into the end zone.

So we move in small steps. We try to chart the flows between our sectors in greater detail. A dollar of output of industry A, we observe, generates a demand for the output of industry C which is not equal to the demand generated for the output of industry C by a dollar of output of industry B. We observe, further, that a dollar of output of industry A generates more or less personal income than a dollar of output of industry B. If we are really keen observers, we might even discover that a dollar paid out to workers in industry A generates demands for consumer goods, housing construction, and government services which are different from the demands generated by a dollar paid out to workers in industry B.

My point is that in the main we improve upon the crude basic-nonbasic approach by a process of flow disaggregation—a process which hopefully will reduce our margin of error. I characterize this activity as the application of old tools to new problems for the obvious reason that input-output relationships, consumption functions, investment functions, and the like are old tools which were fashioned to solve the problems of a national economy. Furthermore, all those tools are used to come to grips with the demand side of the interdependence between sectors in a regional economy.

When I say that the supply side has been ignored, I mean simply that we have not come to grips with the following question: How does the level of activity in industry A in a given region influence the factor supply curves confronting industry B in the same region? Let me hasten to exclude one kind of effort from my indictment. We certainly have tried to incorporate the influence on industry B of the availability of the output of industry A as an input to industry B. Probably the best example of this kind of work is the Isard-Kuenne study of the impact of the Fairless Works. But this is only one of a number of supply relationships which need to be explored and, as far as I can tell, they have not received adequate attention from regional economists.

My former colleagues on the New York Metropolitan Region Study staff could certainly register a strong objection at this point. After all, another term for supply interdependence is external economies and diseconomies, and there is certainly a lot of discussion about them in a number of volumes of the New York study.

But this discussion is limited to two problems: one has to do with intraindustry external economies and diseconomies the other has to do with the influence of the aggregate size of the region on the costs of individual firms. The first problem is too narrowly defined and the second too broadly defined from my point of view.

Nevertheless, I believe, regional economics owes a great debt to the New York Metropolitan Region Study for highlighting these external relationships. It was only after we were confronted with the problem of understanding certain features of the Pittsburgh economy that we at the Pittsburgh Study felt compelled to probe more deeply into the nature of these interindustry effects.

Pittsburgh, as a metropolitan economy, stands in sharp contrast to New York with respect to these three summary variables: size, industrial structure, and rate of growth in recent decades. New York is between six and seven times the size of Pittsburgh. New York has a much more diversified industrial structure. And, while New York has grown at just a bit less than the national rate for the last thirty years, Pittsburgh has grown at less than half the national rate in the same period.

Superficially, all these contrasts fit a familiar pattern. Large areas are more diversified than small areas. Diversified areas exhibit more stability in their growth because their fortunes are not tied to the fortunes of a few industries. In these terms, Pittsburgh's story seems easy to tell.

Unfortunately the matter cannot rest there. Pittsburgh is much more specialized than any large SMA with the exception of Detroit, including many which are no larger than Pittsburgh and many which are considerably smaller. The question, why is it not diversified, therefore, remains largely unanswered. Of course, if we could accept the lack of diversification as inevitable, we might not have to try to understand it. For it is difficult to quarrel with the proposition that the future of such an area can be safely projected once we project the future for its one or two dominant industries. But here we may be caught on the horns of a dilemma. Suppose we project a sharp decline in the dominant industries along with a modest decline in the region's minor industries. True, the dominant industries will retard the growth of the region but in the process they will also decline in relative importance. The region will then become more diversified in its old age, so to speak. What then? Do we correct for the increased diversification? Does it open up new opportunities to the region?

The need to understand the whys and wherefores of diversification should therefore be quite apparent. This has led us to consider the question which I posed earlier: How does the growth of one industry in an area affect the area's suitability as a location for other industries? But we are not yet ready to assert that the latter question has to be answered. We might avoid it if we could show that different degrees of diversification in areas of comparable size are due simply to the fact that some areas have a variety of locational advantages which makes them attractive to a variety of industries while other areas offer advantages only to a small number of industries. Observe for example the figures in Table 1 for Cleveland and Pittsburgh.

TABLE 1

EMPLOYMENT IN SELECTED MANUFACTURING INDUSTRIES, 1957

	Cleveland	Pittsburgh
Food...................	14,532	20,459
Textiles and apparel........	14,130	3,550
Printing and publishing.....	14,618	10,042
Chemicals and products.....	17,959	6,823
Stone, clay and glass........	3,260	21,372
Primary metals............	46,894	154,215
Fabricated metals..........	38,378	31,298
Machinery, nonelectrical....	52,552	23,534
Electrical machinery........	20,746	27,652
Transportation equipment...	55,570	11,047
Total.................	311,471	358,239

SOURCE: Bureau of the Census, *Annual Survey of Manufactures*, 1957.

Pittsburgh is way ahead in glass and primary metals and leads also in food and electrical machinery. Cleveland, on the other hand, is ahead in textiles, printing, chemicals, fabricated metals, nonelectrical machinery, and transporation equipment. On the whole, Cleveland is a much more diversified manufacturing center. But maybe this is just the outcome of the process by which individual industries gravitate to those areas which are best for them. If Cleveland had attracted the 154,215 employees in primary metals, it might still look more like itself than like Pittsburgh in the rest of its manufacturing profile.

I cannot assert positively that this is an unsatisfactory way of approaching the matter, but I can suggest a number of reasons why I find it necessary to go beyond it. For one thing, this approach implies that location of industry is heavily determined by transportation factors or, as we say in our jargon, transport oriented. By this we mean that the location of markets and materials and the transport network determine the geographic distribution of industries. If a lot of industries end up in one place, presto, you have a diversified regional economy.

Nobody believes that the logic of location runs in these terms for the majority of manufacturing industries. My former colleague, Robert

Lichtenberg, of the New York Study, after a painstaking review of factors influencing industrial location classified 50 per cent of American manufacturing as nontransport oriented. P. Sargent Florence has repeatedly emphasized in his writings that transport orientation is a minor influence in location. There is also a fairly general consensus that the proportion of industry which is transport oriented is diminishing as time goes on.

Once we recognize that variations in production costs are important determinants of location, we cannot avoid the consideration of interindustry factor cost relationships. Production costs are not given by nature, except that nature may influence the cost of energy and the cost of plant. These are trivial determinants alongside the influence exerted by the way in which a region's natural advantages are exploited. If we ask why are wage rates higher in one area than another, it is only in rare cases that nature will provide the answer. In most cases the explanation will run in historical terms; that is, in terms of the heritage of each region as it bears on labor supply.

For many purposes it is sufficient to recognize the difference in wage rates, and there is no compulsion to explain why it exists. A firm which is seeking a maximum profit location for a new plant might very well take the wage-rate differential as given—a type of behavior which fits so well the textbook model of a competitive firm. Even so, a conscientious consultant might very well post a warning signal. After all, a plant represents a twenty-year commitment. What is the wage differential likely to be twenty years hence? Be that as it may, it is certainly inappropriate to take wage-rate differentials as given in a twenty-year projection for a region. A static atomistic approach will not do for a problem in aggregate dynamics.

I also find the multiple-locational-advantages theory of diversification unsatisfactory for another reason. It permits us to assess an area's potential for growth only with reference to industries with known locational requirements. But in a projection, it is difficult enough to anticipate the bill of goods, let alone to project the locational needs of the industries which will be producing them. This may suggest that we ought to give up the ghost. Those who have this alternative are blessed. The rest of us have to seek ways to mitigate the curse. One is to develop the concept of a region's capacity for attracting new industries with considerable freedom of location from a transport point of view. If we are to develop such a concept, we need to probe into the region itself more deeply than we do when we locate industries one by one.

I have said enough—perhaps too much—about my reasons for raising these questions. I will now proceed to the main business of this paper, which is to offer some hypotheses about interindustry influences on factor costs. To begin with, I think that the net has to be spread a lot wider than most people assume. I propose to consider all the traditional categories: entrepreneurship, capital, labor, and land, in that order.

Entrepreneurship. This is a production factor which, to my knowledge, no one has tried to price out at different locations. The implicit assumption, I suppose, is that the supply schedule of entrepreneurship is identical at all locations. Our colleagues studying international differences in growth reject this assumption explicitly. I am convinced that we need to reconsider its validity in regional economics.

When you tell a location analyst that a firm is where it is because its founders prefer to live there, he throws up his hands. Such cases, he claims, are outside his domain. Our own experience suggests that for many industries cost is almost invariant with location—or at least there is no "min min" location. Yet we are reluctant to treat such cases as random phenomena because we feel there are significant variations in the cost of entrepreneurship. Moreover, these differences may be large enough to offset other cost differences.

I came to this notion by reflecting on the differences between New York and Pittsburgh, but I hasten to say that area size is only one variable. For a given size of area, the entrepreneurial supply curve is also a function of certain traditions and elements of the social structure which are heavily influenced by the character of the area's historic specializations.

The proposition I offer is this: An industry which is competitively organized—in the neoclassical sense of the term "competition"—has more entrepreneurs per dollar of output than an industry which is organized along oligopolistic lines. The average establishment in the apparel industry, for example, has one-sixth as many employees as the average establishment in primary metals. Furthermore, multi-unit firms account for 82 per cent of the employment in primary metals, while they account for only 28 per cent of employment in apparel. Now you may have as much management per dollar of output in primary metals as you have in apparel, but you certainly do not have as many managers who are also risk-takers and this is my definition of an entrepreneur.

What is the consequence of this? My feeling is that you do not breed as many entrepreneurs per capita in families allied with steel as you do in families allied with apparel, using these two industries for illustrative purposes only. The son of a salaried executive is less likely to be sensitive to opportunities wholly unrelated to his father's field than the son of an independent entrepreneur. True, the entrepreneur's son is more likely to think of taking over his father's business. My guess is, however, that the tradition of risk-bearing is, on the whole, a more potent influence in broadening one's perspective.

I think I have formulated a proposition which can at least theoretically be tested, although I confess that I have not tested it yet. For all I know, this may already be a well-established proposition in entrepreneurial history.

But if an oligopolistic environment has a lower entrepreneurial birth rate, there remains the question of how receptive it is to the in-migration of entrepreneurs. Here, too, I would argue that the competitively organized area has an edge. Receptivity as measured by factor costs we shall discuss under separate headings later on. What I have in mind now is receptivity as it relates to the entrepreneur's "utility function." There is an aura of second-class citizenship attached to the small businessman in an environment dominated by big business. It manifests itself in many small ways, such as the kinds of social clubs he can belong to, the residential areas he will comfortably fit into, the business organizations he can join, and so forth. The ease of entry, to borrow a concept from industrial organization, is considerably greater in an environment dominated—not dominated, to be more exact—by small firm industries. I am not sure that we can satisfactorily test this notion, but I am hopeful.

Capital. Many of the same observations are relevant to regional differences in the availability of capital. Here, too, we are dealing with a factor whose cost is typically assumed to be invariant with respect to location. This is surely not so. It is true that capital is almost perfectly mobile, provided the probability distribution of returns is approximately known. G.M. and U. S. Steel can raise capital almost anywhere with equal ease. But a small firm embarking on a new enterprise will find a much more receptive ear over the home counter than it will over-the-counter in "foreign" places. The cost of transferring confidence may be high enough to give us a capital-supply function which has distance as an important independent variable.

Once we admit of such immobility, it becomes relevant to inquire into differences in local capital supply among areas. Again the industrial organization of the dominant industries strikes me as an important variable. A major source of capital to new firms in general is the undistributed profit and unexpended depreciation allowance of old firms. Now, the surplus capital which accumulates inside large multiplant companies, I would argue, is more mobile interregionally within the company than intraregionally outside the company. A large corporation is more likely to respond to investment opportunities in its traditional activity at other locations than to investment opportunities at home in unrelated industries. The small firm, by contrast, is more likely to make its surplus capital available to other local enterprise in another industry than to a distant enterprise in the same industry. (Actually, I have overstated the case to avoid a complex formulation. All I need to argue is that the marginal rate of substitution between local and foreign outlets is greater [smaller] for the large multiplant firm [small firm]. Given an equivalent array of investment opportunities at home, the surplus capital of the multiplant industry is more likely to "leak" out to other areas.)

The commercial banks, of course, also play a vital role in the initial financing of new business. Are banks in one area more receptive than banks in another area to the demands of new business and, if so, are these differences in attitude shaped by the industrial traditions of the area? I say yes, on both counts. My conviction on this point is based less on deductive than on inductive reasoning. I have been told that this is the case. Having been told, I can think of some fairly good reasons why this might be the case. When banks cater to a competitively organized industry, they are more likely to accept the insurance principle of making money, not on each customer, but on the average customer. If you have U. S. Steel and Westinghouse on your rolls, you do not have to learn to make money on the insurance principle.

In the present state of my knowledge, I am not too optimistic about being able to test these hypotheses empirically. However, I am not prepared to pronounce them as untestable. This is an altogether too easy way out. I believe if we think hard enough, we can spell out some corollaries which, if we dig hard enough, we can subject to empirical test.

Labor. Now we come to what most will assume and I am prepared to concede is the cost factor, which is most sensitive to interindustry influence. Yet, even here, I suspect I will be spreading my net farther than most people would.

First, the wage level. My colleague on the Pittsburgh Study, Mel Bers, is exploring this question in great detail. The presumption that the wage level in the dominant industry influences the wage level in other industries is one which no one can seriously question. I am confident that Bers's research will throw more light on the network of interdependence than anything that has been done so far. Bers is also immersed in the study of the influence of labor organization in the dominant industry on the structure of wages in the region. These two issues are inseparable in his framework.

But there are other influences relating to labor cost and supply which are not generally recognized. Bers found, for example, that the rate of participation of married women in the labor force in the

Pittsburgh region is far below the average for metropolitan areas. When standardized for industry mix, however, it turns out that the rate is as high as you would expect it to be. The question arises, therefore, do these women represent a potential supply or not? Why are not female-labor-using industries attracted by the surplus? Wages aside, there are at least two other factors relating to the character of the dominant industries which influence the outcome.

The first is the dispersion within the region of the plants of our dominant industries. The ratio of central city employment to SMA employment in manufacturing is much lower in Pittsburgh than in any of the large SMA's. Outside the Central City, the gradient in Pittsburgh is also flatter. The reasons are obvious. Our industries could not be piled up one on top of another as in the garment district even if our land were flat. The topography encourages still greater dispersion. But the importance of this for our purposes is that the early dispersion of manufacturing (plus the dispersion of mining) led to a dispersal of population which is also unmatched among our large SMA's. To the extent that pools of female labor are relevant to industrial location, Pittsburgh is at a disadvantage because a greater radius is required to form a pool of a given size. One must bear in mind that the areas in which the plants of the dominant industries operate are not exactly the most desirable as sites for other kinds of industry. (We shall return to this point later on.)

The second point has to do with the work schedule of the man in the family. Steel is a three-shift industry. The typical worker is not assigned to a particular shift for an indefinite period. Instead he works from 8:00 to 4:00 for some time, then 4:00 to 12:00 for some time, then 12:00 to 8:00 for some time. He also has to put in his share of weekends. It is reasonable to suppose that under these conditions the housewife is somewhat less willing to work than under ordinary conditions. Taken together, these factors tend to dissipate some of the labor force advantages we normally attribute to SMA's. And they are consequences of characteristics of the dominant industries.

Land. We normally assume that an SMA is large enough in area to nullify any considerations of site availability as a location factor except for industries with very special requirements like steel and chemicals. In general, I think this is a sensible approach. Nevertheless, I feel compelled to attach some importance to the impact of an industry's operations on the quality of the air and water in the surrounding area. Pittsburgh, as you all know, was notorious until recent years for its smoke and dust. There were three causes for this condition. The principal one was the use of soft coal as fuel in households and industry. A second was the steel industry. And a third was the railroads with their steam engines. All this has changed now and I do not mind using this forum as an opportunity to plug the radical improvement in the quality of Pittsburgh's air. A white shirt will now stay white in Pittsburgh for as long as it will in any city in the country. But it will take some time to work off our reputation. And furthermore, at a time when the reputation was founded in fact, it was bound to exercise a restraining influence on the growth of subsidiary industries in the region.

Intermediate Goods and Services. So much for the primary factors of production. I said earlier that location analysts have paid attention to a dominant industry's impact on the location of other industries which are oriented to the supply of the product of the dominant industry. But agglomeration is nourished more by the availability of a wide range of goods and services created in the first instance by the growth of the dominant industries. Transportation is the classic illustration of this phenomena. One industry attracts the service, and a second industry coming in finds that the service is available at costs which are lower than they would be in virgin territory. The second industry also finds already in existence a whole community of suppliers of business services such as legal, accounting, duplicating, etc.

The question I raise is whether the emergence of these services and their availability to other industries depends on the character of these industries which trigger development in the first instance. I think much depends on the internal organization of these industries. Large firms incorporate many of these services within their own operations because they can achieve scale economies within the firm. They are much more fully integrated and therefore depend less on outside suppliers. On the one hand, this means that, dollar for dollar, their business is less of a stimulus to the creation of a community of independent suppliers. On the other hand, the new entrant is not likely to find that the company is anxious to spread its fixed costs by making its services available to outsiders.

Again, consider the classic example of external economies: transport services. A firm which operates its own truck fleet on an exempt basis is specifically forbidden by the ICC to transport freight as a common carrier. Imagine then that you have two communities of equal size. In one of these, all the firms rely on common carriage. Hence service to and from a wide variety of places is available to all comers. In the other community, every firm has its private truck fleet. True, the roads are built and this helps a lot. But there is no service available to the new firm coming in unless it starts big.

We do know that Pittsburgh is not up to par in employment in ancillary services. This is indicated by a calculation of location quotients based on the 1950 Census of Population. The Duncans in their recent book, *Metropolis and Region,* also found that Pittsburgh had less than the national average per capita employment in service industries broadly defined. Only Detroit among the SMA's of 1,000,000 population or more shared this characteristic with Pittsburgh. It goes without saying, that much of my reasoning is applicable to Detroit as well.

Summary and Conclusions. It should be apparent by now that what I am reaching for is the specification of a function which relates external economies and diseconomies to industry structure, size being held constant. My feeling is that we have been too prone to associate external economies and diseconomies with size. We have been disturbed at not being able to derive a satisfactory correlation between the two. What I have tried to do is explore some of the residual variation around the size function. I recognize the difficulties of adequately formulating and testing these notions. But I do not think we can afford to ignore them because they are difficult if, as I maintain, they are relevant to an understanding of the dynamics of area development.

To come back to my first point: I think we are not using the optimal combination of tools in regional analysis. We know we can do a lot more to refine the methods we use to trap what I have called the demand side of interdependence. We need bigger and better regional input-output tables, regional capital coefficients, regional consumption functions. But we are not equating marginal returns in all directions if we do not, at the same time, push vigorously on the supply side of the problem.

I said we need new tools in regional analysis. I am prepared to modify that statement in favor of this one. We need to make better use of some old tools which we have not yet applied very extensively to regional analysis. We need to work out the regional implications of market organization.

Variations in Demand over Space

SIZE OF MARKETS VERSUS TRANSPORT COSTS IN INDUSTRIAL LOCATION SURVEYS AND THEORY

Melvin L. Greenhut[1]

I. INTRODUCTION

THE distinction between the 'size of market' factor on the one hand and the 'transport cost' factor on the other is a very fine one, and only recently has the former been taken into account in location theory.[2] At the beginning, it was given consideration only in the theory of spatial competition, and then as part of the broad subject of monopolistic competition. In turn, location theory proper followed the purely cost approach originated by von Thünen[3] and given rigorous formulation by Weber.[4] Significantly, however, there is reference to what is called market orientation in all the leading treatises on the subject, both old[5] and new,[6] a reference which traditionally made the one part of the other.

Empirical studies by planning and research groups did, it is true, request respondents to evaluate the market and transport cost factor as if they were fully separable. But the terms were never defined and the individual respondents ascribed their own meanings to them. Illustrative of the resulting confusion was the tradition of designating that location which took place 'near to the consumer' as a location which deferred to the market factor, and this was accepted regardless of whether the motivation was a sales advantage due to proximity, the desire to control a special market, or a saving of transport costs. Indeed, the last usage became so common in traditional descriptions that the most prevalent explanation for market-oriented location was that it resulted in transport savings and this usually was said to take place when the raw materials gained weight as a result of fabrication.

[1] An acknowledgment of thanks is hereby extended to Professors Frank H. Jackson and James E. Snover for their helpful comments, criticisms and suggestions and to the Florida State University Research Council for a grant which encouraged this investigation.
[2] A. Lösch, *Die räumliche Ordnung der Wirtschaft* (Jena, 1944) and translation by W. Woglom and W. Stopler for the Yale University Press, 1954, part 1.
[3] *Der Isolierte Staat in Beziehung auf Landwirtschaft und Nationalökonomie*, 3rd ed. (Berlin, 1875).
[4] C. J. Friedrich (trans.), *Alfred Weber's Theory of Location* (Chicago, 1928).
[5] E.g., see E. G. Holmes, *Plant Location*, 1st ed. (New York, 1930); T. Palander, *Beiträge zur Standortstheorie* (Uppsala, 1935); L. Dechesnes, *La localisation des Diverses Production* (Bruxelles, 1945); S. E. Dennison, *The Location of Industry and the Depressed Areas* (Oxford, 1935); E. M. Hoover, *Location Theory and the Shoe and Leather Industry* (Cambridge, 1937).
[6] E. M. Hoover, *Location of Economic Activity*, 1st ed. (New York, 1948); W. Isard, *Location and Space Economy* (New York, 1956); L. Yaseen, *Plant Location* (New York, 1956).

Reprinted from *Journal of Industrial Economics*, 8 (1959–1960), 172–184, by permission of the author and editor.

The market and transport cost factor should, however, be distinguished, for clearly it is of value to be able to differentiate between a market location which is due to a size of market advantage and one which is due to transport cost advantages. After we have established the general outlines of the model with which we intend to work, we will make this distinction clear by presenting a simple abstract case and generalizing from it.

II. THE GENERAL THEORY

We have elsewhere established a model which, while conforming to theory, can also be used in empirical studies.[7] Because the model does conform to theory, the empiricist who uses it is able to draw on the accumulated knowledge of others, benefiting from the consistency and functional value which are the results of years of thought and effort.

This model distinguishes essentially between three general types of plant location: (1) a first plant or a relocation by a firm; (2) a branch plant location due to the development of a distant market; and (3) a branch plant location selected after several alternative new markets have been considered, where at least one of the alternative markets has grown to significant size.

The first type is the one traditionally described in location theory. Disregarding non-economic locations both here and elsewhere in the paper, we hold that site-selection will proceed in accordance with cost or demand (locational interdependence) factors.[8] Assuming, for example, we are studying the reasons for new locations in a given state, one of the sub-factors of these two will bring the firm to a particular state. It may be that other factors will then induce a location within the state different than that which is indicated on the basis of the main one. Customarily, the factor behind the specific location is cost, such as a saving in labor cost or the discovery of a raw material source which results in savings in transport cost at a certain location.

The second case is readily described by illustration. Suppose the original plant of a firm was located in New Jersey, and that this plant was oriented to the Eastern industrial area. Suppose further that a modest amount of total output had for some years been sold in Florida but that latterly the development of the Florida market has caused a relatively expanding part of the output of the New

[7] Melvin L. Greenhut, 'Empiricism and Location Theory', *Review of Economics and Statistics*, vol. XLI, 1959, pp. 433-8.
[8] For an early analysis of the demand factor, see E. H. Chamberlin, *The Theory of Monopolistic Competition*, 3rd ed. (Cambridge, 1938), appendix C; also *infra*, references in note 11.

174   MELVIN L. GREENHUT

Jersey plant to be earmarked for sale in Florida. In time, either expansion of the original plant or an entirely new plant is indicated. But while the New Jersey plant may have been well oriented to the Pennsylvania, New York and adjacent markets, it may not be particularly well located with respect to Florida or let us say the deep South generally, in particular because of the high cost of transportation involved. Large savings could be realized in such a situation by location in or near to Florida.

Savings in transport cost might result in either of two ways. (1) It might be significantly cheaper to ship the raw materials over long distances and to minimize the length of movement of the finished product. Hence, a new branch plant rather than expansion of the original plant would be indicated by the developments noted above. (2) An alternative source of raw materials might be available which could be used by a new plant with resulting savings in transportation cost.

The reason for the location of a branch plant might clearly be something other than savings in transport costs, e.g. labor unrest or high insurance rates at the original plant site. Our interest here is simply to note that, in selecting the factors responsible for location, the plant locator tends naturally to compare his new branch plant with his old one in terms of the market to which the new plant sales are being directed. What attracts the firm to Florida may be cost (e.g. transport savings on raw materials) or demand (e.g. the desire to be proximate to Southern consumers), though on *a priori* grounds we would often expect significant transportation cost savings to prevail even where the demand factor is regarded as the most important.

It is probably the third type of plant location decision which is most common today. Many firms are finding rather suddenly that their original plants are both insufficient in size to meet growing demands and improperly located with respect to the new total market. A decision to locate a branch plant in one place entails often a preference for one area extremity over an alternative one, a preference either as to cost or demand or both. What is important about this is that the locator who seriously considered an alternative location in a different area tends to designate a different set of factors (or forces) as having governed his choice than the locator faced with a decision of the second type, i.e. where no alternative area was considered.

Compared to plant expansion, the establishment of a branch plant *may* offer advantages in transport or labor costs. On the other hand, compared to location of a branch plant in an alternative market area, the actual location *may* offer more favorable taxes, markets or insurance rates. The important point is that the advantages in the first case above may be entirely different from those in the second. And, going one step farther, the results of a spot check made by this writer among respondents during a survey suggest that locators of branch plants *where an alternative market area* was considered tend to regard as the main determinant of the particular new location the factor which appears most advantageous as compared to the alternative location. On the other hand, the factors making the branch plant economic compared to the original plant were customarily listed as secondary or tertiary forces.

To summarize, our model conforms with general location theory in distinguishing between cost, demand and, if desired, purely personal factors.[9] And it further differentiates between first plant locations (or relocations) and branch location as well as between branch locations where no alternative market areas exist and those where there are alternative market areas to consider.

It is precisely where alternative market areas do exist and where second, third, etc., branch plants are involved that the most serious problems arise in empirical research.[10] And it is in such situations that the fine distinction between the market and transport cost factors with which we are basically concerned may *have* to be drawn. All this having been noted, we can next propose the market and transport factor concepts which will distinguish the instances where one of these forces serves as the main factor behind branch plant locations.[11] In the process, we will realize that our distinction is truly a part of present-day location theory.

III. THE SPECIAL THEORY: DISTINGUISHING SIZE OF MARKETS AND TRANSPORT COSTS

Assume two different raw material centers, $M1$ and $M2$, and two point formed markets related to these centers, $C1$ and $C2$. In no case may a firm locate with reference to one buying center and sell also in the other, for the markets are distinctly and sharply separated in

---

[9] Example, see G. Katona and J. H. Morgan, 'The Quantitative Study of Factors Determining Business Decisions', *Quarterly Journal of Economics*, vol. LVI (1941-42), pp. 67-90. Also M. L. Greenhut, *Plant Location in Theory and in Practise* (Chapel Hill, 1956), especially chapter XII.

[10] Probably many would suspect that, at least in the earlier years of the industrial growth of the United States, the location of an original plant was conceived in terms of a total (more or less) nationwide market. The growth of rival market areas, the development of rival firms and rival products, the need for speedy delivery, personalized service, etc., in turn have caused conception of alternative market areas ... possibly even in the case of original plants today. And this particular conception is, of course, part and parcel of the theory of locational interdependence.

[11] We specify for the present in note that outside of the case where significant locational advantage stems from being situated near to consumers, the market factor will dominate the process of selecting a particular location only when alternative markets are under consideration.

space. Suppose that, as shown in Fig. 1, the distance between M_1 and C_1 is less than between M_2 and C_2. It follows that if the freight rates are proportional to distance and basically identical in each area, a transport cost advantage would appear to exist in the M_1C_1 market. If a *given* locator finds maximum profits at M_1C_1 and if the product is a weight-gainer in fabrication so that the plant is located near to C_1 (e.g. point P in Fig. 1A), theorists would tend to conclude that this is a market orientation formed along classic lines. Unfortunately, even in this simple model, the general theory related in section II might show that a different relation actually holds true.

The complexity of even this simple model is revealed by exploring the alternatives open to the theoretician. In doing this, reference to the output that maximizes profits at the best M_1C_1 location will help to serve as a focal point for analysis. Suppose, therefore, we assume the same output is produced in M_2C_2 as in M_1C_1. By definition profits are less in M_2C_2, but are they less because costs are higher at this output, such as transport costs, or are they less because demand is weaker and hence price is lower? Clearly, the net demand of buyers at the seller's plant is another way of allowing for transport costs, a principle which is well recognized in the literature of spatial competition and which signifies that the greater the costs of shipping the final product to buyers, that is, the more distant the buyer from the seller, the smaller is the magnitude of his net demand curve for the seller's product.[12] Clearly, a distinction exists between what is demand and what is cost (or between size of markets and transport costs). If we do not recognize this, then our theoretical and empirical studies must consider only the cost side of plant location, as was the practice of von Thünen, Weber and their followers.[13]

How may the magnitude of the demand in a market be distinguished from the cost of transporting the finished product in the market when the latter yields the net demand at the seller's plant? To answer, let us again return to the output that maximizes profits at M_1C_1, and let us consider the 'average' delivered price to buyers that would prevail if the same output is sold in the M_2C_2 area as in the M_1C_1 region. If the number of buyers in each buying place were the same and were possessed of equal effective demand, the 'average' delivered price for the given quantity would also have to be the

---

[12] See Lösch, op. cit., part 2; E. M. Hoover, 'Spatial Price Discrimination', *Review o Economic Studies*, vol. IV (1935-36), pp. 182-91; A. Smithies, 'Optimum Location in Spatial Competition', *Journal of Political Economy*, vol. XXXII, 1942, pp. 423-39.
[13] In this tradition see A. Linke, *Die Lederindustrie (Erzeugende und Verarbeitende)*, (Tübingen, 1913); D. C. Hague and P. K. Newman, *Costs in Alternative Locations: The Clothing Industry* (Cambridge, England, 1952).

same. It then would follow that the smaller profitability in the M_2C_2 region, *ceteris paribus*, would have to be due to higher transport cost. However, if to obtain the same sales total in M_2C_2, a lower 'average' delivered price must be charged, and if this price difference times the units sold exceeds any freight cost times units sold advantage that may hold in M_1C_1 (or, of course, any disadvantage that in other cases may exist), then it is the market which is the main factor that drew the firm to M_1C_1 in place of the alternative area M_2C_2. Significantly, it is only by a distinction such as this that we can speak in terms of a market factor distinct from a transport cost factor either in theory or in survey work.

This basic model can be extended in diverse ways. To illustrate: we may visualize that the buying market C_1 is point formed, such as in effect is New York City. In contrast, C_2 may be spread over an area (see Fig. 2). Imagine next that the best location in each region is at the material source. Assume further, as in Fig. 3, that a small town T is near to M_2. Sales can be effected to this place at very low transport cost compared to sales in the M_1C_1 market, but the conclusion that a transport cost advantage exists in M_2C_2 is, however, incomplete *if* we hypothesize greater profits for the firm in question in M_1C_1. To make our cases comparable, we must visualize sales in M_2C_2 beyond town T, such that they extend to towns T', T'', and T''' and a sales quantity equal to that obtained at the profit-making location in M_1C_1 is obtained. Then by noting the 'average' delivered price and all cost differentials, the chief disadvantage of location in M_2C_2 (and *ipso facto* the advantages of the other region) may be found.

It is manifestly part of our model that when the same 'average' delivered price (as formulated later in equation 3) yields the same total sales in M_2C_2, then the markets are equal and transport cost or other cost disadvantages must exist. If, on the contrary, the sales total at the M_1C_1 price is less than in the M_1C_1 area, or, equivalently, a lower average delivered price is necessary to attain the designated sales total, then the markets are different.

Whether the effective transport distance between the raw material supply and the market is less in one region than another, and hence whether transport cost or market advantages, *ceteris paribus*, dominate, cannot be decided except on the basis of a comparable footing. This, in turn, requires a comparison such as the one proposed herein based on the profit-maximizing position in the profit-maximizing region. Failure to establish such a basis for comparison might well lead an investigator to draw faulty conclusions as illustrated on p. 178.

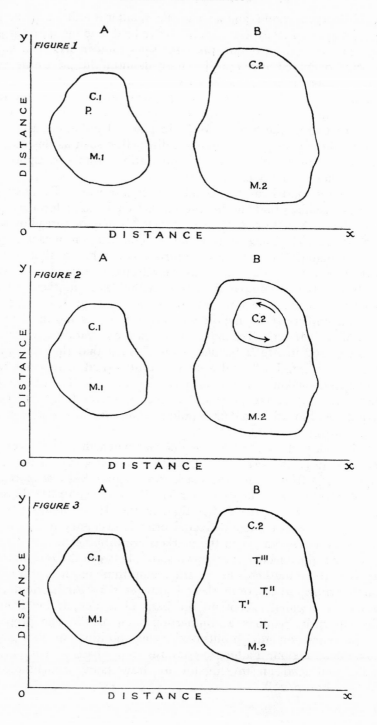

(A) Facts: M_1C_1 is more profitable than M_2C_2. In M_1C_1, all buyers are located at City C_1. In M_2C_2, some buyers are located at Town T. Town T is closer to supply source M_2 than is C_1 to M_1. The conclusion which would follow if no other facts were studied is that, while a transport cost advantage exists in area M_2C_2, because the most profitable location is in the M_1C_1 market and because it is there notwithstanding a transport cost disadvantage, the most profitable location must be attributable to the better market it controls, *ceteris paribus*. Of course, if the investigator included Towns T', T'' and T''', and no other buyers exist beyond T''', he might find that the number and demand of these buyers is great enough to yield an identical sales total in the area at the same 'average' delivered price as prevails in M_1C_1. The advantage of M_1C_1 over M_2C_2 would then be shown as one of transport cost saving rather than one of a better market, *ceteris paribus*.

(B) Facts: The same as above with respect to dispersion of buyers. Different data are that the investigator does include towns T', T'' and T''' in his calculations but obtains as further 'facts' the information that his buyers are generally more distant in M_2C_2 and his transport cost total accordingly higher. He concludes that M_1C_1 is more profitable because it has a transport cost advantage over M_2C_2. However, if the investigator had conjectured about sales possibilities, he might have found that a much lower 'average' delivered price would be necessary in M_2C_2 in order to yield the same sales total that is most profitable in M_1C_1. Indeed, the market discrepancy may actually have been greater than any economic difference in the transport distance.

(C) Facts: Assume finally that the given quantity cannot be sold in M_2C_2 because the f.o.b. price plus freight to distant buyers necessary to maintain the designated 'average' delivered price may be so high that another firm located elsewhere is able to undersell the subject firm at some certain distance and beyond. Reduction in net mill price and hence 'average' delivered price will have to be made in order to attain the sales total possible at the profit-maximizing site. Or a limit may exist which rules out even this possibility, such as in those situations where the sales area appears as if it suddenly breaks off. In either case, the market is clearly weaker than that available at the M_1C_1 location.[14]

[14] This case, by the way, shows that when the buyer concentration in one market is more favorable than in the other, the demand advantage actually appears in the form that the profit-maximizing sales total cannot be effected in the other market without an undue lowering of the 'average' delivered price, since competition from firms at distant places limits the sales radius of the firm and hence the magnitude of the demand which it faces. The upshot, of course, is that the total demand available in one market area location is greater than in the other.

The changing situations which may produce contradictory answers when one is not armed with an inclusive theoretical system are so complex as to suggest present advantage if we now provide a brief summary of two vital points. We maintain, first, that when transport distance is less in one area than another, profits will be greater there than elsewhere, *ceteris paribus*. And if location happens to take place near to the consumer, the orientation is, to be sure, to the market, but not because of the size of market (or demand) factor, rather because of a savings of cost. If, second, the distance is found to be less in one area than in another, it may nevertheless be that the greatest advantage in the former over the latter lies in other forces than transportation, and among these other forces may be the market. This market, we hold, is distinguishable from all other factors, including transport cost, and the distinction is made by comparing the 'average' delivered prices which are obtained from and are necessary to provide the profit-maximizing quantity of sales.

For those who find such desirable, our basic arguments may now be repeated below in mathematical form. Only a few simple equations are needed. But over and above preferences in the form an argument may take, this presentation has the independent advantage of permitting us to give simply a precise meaning to the term 'average' delivered price.

To review assumptions, remember that we are concerned with the situation of a branch plant location selected in the light of alternative market area possibilities for the branch plant. This kind of situation raises the possibility of the selection of one area rather than another because of either the market factor or transport cost factor, assuming, of course, that other readily identifiable differences, such as labor cost differences, do not exist.

In equation (1), Ei stands for the amount paid for the ith unit sold, P stands for the base mill price received by the seller, and is assumed to be the same for each unit sold, and fi is the freight cost on the ith unit.

(1) $Ei = P + fi$

If then $A1$ stands for the 'average' delivered price in market M_1C_1 and $A2$ for the 'average' delivered price in market M_2C_2, with M_1 representing the market M_1C_1 and M_2 the market M_2C_2, we find first for M_1 that:

$$(2) \ \frac{\overset{n}{\underset{\substack{M1 \\ i=1}}{\Sigma}} Ei}{n} = \frac{\overset{n}{\underset{\substack{M1 \\ i=1}}{\Sigma}} (P + fi)}{n} = \frac{nP + \overset{n}{\underset{\substack{M1 \\ i=1}}{\Sigma}} fi}{n} = P + \frac{\overset{n}{\underset{\substack{M1 \\ i=1}}{\Sigma}} fi}{n}$$

Then

$$(3) \ A_1 = P + \frac{\overset{n}{\underset{\substack{M1 \\ i=1}}{\Sigma}} fi}{n}$$

And similarly for market $M2$ where the 'average' delivered price is represented by

$$(4) \quad A2 = P + \frac{\overset{n}{\underset{\substack{M2 \\ i=1}}{\Sigma}} fi}{n}$$

With n the same in each market, it follows that $A1 \gtrless A2$, as the situation may be.

Under full market equality, that is where the same 'average' delivered price yields the same sales total, the profit advantage of one market area location over the other must be due to cost, and by assumption for our model, transport cost. In the present case, a transport cost advantage exists in the $M1C1$ region which, we note, is maximized customarily by minimizing freight cost on the finished product or on the raw material, as the situation may be. Thus a locator (and respondent) who selects $M1C1$ because of these gains has recognized transport cost as the factor which drew his plant to the area in question.

It may be, however, that to sell the given quantity in each market, the 'average' delivered price would have to be significantly lower in $M2C2$, a discrepancy which could amount to a price differential greater than the transport cost differential. In such a case, location in the $M1C1$ area would have been due first to the better market and second to the smaller distance between materials and market.

Extending this principle to the more complicated world, we assume that buyers are spread out over space in alternating waves with peaks and troughs of numbers at different towns and cities. This permits us to examine the true situation of sales over space, for realistically the centroid of a market area cannot be well designated, depending as it does on the quantity to be sold and on selling price. Notice now how the comparative method used in our simple model works out.

Imagine that of all conceivable locations in the M_1C_1 and M_2C_2 areas (where C_1 and C_2 cover a range of points or places in space) and of all conceivable outputs, a location can be found which offers greatest profits. These greatest profits exist at a certain production point. In turn, this certain output carries with it an 'average' delivered price to all buyers in the market area. Consider this output, i.e. the profit-maximizing output of M_1C_1, at the best practical location in the M_2C_2 area. What is the cost total at that location and what is the 'average' delivered price? Manifestly, we may find that in M_2C_2 the demand of buyers is relatively weak, and that to sell the output in question, the firm must charge a very low 'average' delivered price. Sales may or may not be made over a very extensive market area and accordingly transport costs may or may not be high. In any case, the location disadvantage, as indicated by equation (5) must be a market disadvantage, for we posit there that the freight cost per unit sold in M_1C_1 equals that in M_2C_2 and that the same number of units are sold.

$$(5) \quad \left[\frac{\underset{i=1}{\overset{n}{\Sigma}} f_i}{\frac{M_1}{n}} = \frac{\underset{i=1}{\overset{n}{\Sigma}} f_i}{\frac{M_2}{n}} \right]$$ and, of course, P in market $M_1 > P$ in market M_2.

As a consequence, the location advantage of M_1C_1 is a market advantage and similarly where equation (6) or (7) holds, provided, of course, we continue to assume that advantages in readily identifiable other costs (such as labor costs) do not explain M_1C_1's greater profitability. Incidentally, we let P_1 stand for P in market M_1C_1 and P_2 for P in market M_2C_2 in equations (6) and (7).

$$(6) \quad \left[\frac{\underset{i=1}{\overset{n}{\Sigma}} f_i}{\frac{M_1}{n}} \geq \frac{\underset{i=1}{\overset{n}{\Sigma}} f_i}{\frac{M_2}{n}} \right] \text{ and } \left[P_1 > P_2 \right]^{[15]}$$

[15] We record here in note, 'a' more general situation than the above, yet as a note rather than as body material because it is incidental to our main purpose of distinguishing between a market and transport cost advantage. We use equation (6a) below for this purpose, where, in equation (6a), C_1 stands for any one non-transport cost item in market M_1 and comparably for C_2 in M_2.

$$(6a) \quad \left[\frac{\underset{i=1}{\overset{n}{\Sigma}} f_i}{\frac{M_1}{n}} > \frac{\underset{i=1}{\overset{n}{\Sigma}} f_i}{\frac{M_2}{n}} \right] > \left[A_1 > A_2 \right] > \left| C_1 < C_2 \right|$$

Because M_1 is assumed to be more profitable than M_2, we therefore propose through equation (6a) that the market is the main location factor. Implicit to this is the idea that whenever the 'average' delivered price in the most profitable area is greater than in an

$$(7) \qquad \left| \begin{array}{cc} \sum\limits_{i=1}^{n} f_i & \sum\limits_{i=1}^{n} f_i \\ \dfrac{M_1}{n} & \leq \dfrac{M_2}{n} \end{array} \right| \text{ which difference is less than } \left[\begin{array}{c} P_1 > P_2 \end{array} \right]$$

Let us further note that demand may be uniform from region to region. However, though the same 'average' delivered price brings forth the same quantity of sales in M_2C_2 as in M_1C_1, it may be that in order to gain these sales in the less profitable region, buyers who are spread out over a greater spatial extent have to be attracted. In this event, transport costs would be high and a transport cost (not market) disadvantage would exist.

Suppose finally we observe how judgments of location shift with slight changes in data. For example, assume simply that there are two market areas with the same number of buyers dispersed differently in each, but with each buyer having an identical demand. Given the same 'average' delivered price, the given quantity may be sold. The difference in profit positions would be attributable to a difference of costs. But now imagine that the location of competitors in the one area limits the market (number of buyers) for our firm. To gain the given quantity of sales then requires reduction in 'average' delivered prices and the primary location factor may well become that of markets rather than savings in costs. Depending on the situation, either equation (6) or (7) will then prevail.

IV. EMPIRICAL SURVEYS AND THEORY: IN CONCLUSION

Plant location theory must stand ultimately behind any empirical survey which seeks to determine the reasons for industrial location. But how, it may be asked, are respondents to a questionnaire supposed to be able to provide meaningful answers, especially when the difference between such basic factors as a market advantage and a transport cost advantage rests on the fine distinctions that we described above? Admittedly, they cannot be instructed fully on a mail questionnaire, if indeed during a personal interview. And similarly, analysts cannot hope to be able to know whether it is the market or the transport distance (and hence transport cost between

alternative area by an amount which exceeds any other particular advantage (i.e. particular cost advantage) obtained in the same area, the market factor has dominated. Exception to this rule would, of course, lie in empirical work where the market advantage is expected to be short-lived and where, therefore, some other factors actually serve as the main force behind the location. In any case, where the first and second terms of equation (6a) hold true between two areas, we find that the demand is greater in the one than the other while, however, the transport relations between the raw material source and market is more than offsetting the gross demand advantage. For location then to proceed in that market area, some other cost advantages must prevail leaving, as net of all the advantages and disadvantages, a favorable residue.

the alternative and respective material centers and market points) which may happen to be the more favorable factor.

We suggest in answer that replies to plant location questionnaires will conform to theory whenever the questionnaire is carefully arranged.[16] This conclusion is advanced because a highly limited market (for example, one limited by competition within the same market by an unfavorable buyer concentration, by the competition of strategically located rivals, or by the existing small magnitude of individual and total demand), and the opposite, a potentially vast market potential, will be apparent and distinguishable from a pure case of different distance between material source and market. Alternatively stated, the intuitive reaction of the businessman is believed to conform generally to theory as he answers the question whether the market or transport cost factor controlled his location (assuming, of course, that it was either of the two). If this belief is not correct, then we must discard the difference between the demand or market factor and the transport cost factor in this kind of empirical work. Paradoxically, this will move us toward a cost approach in our empirical work, which kind of research has long attempted to speak in terms of distinctions between markets and transport costs while theory, on the other hand, now recognizes such distinctions but until lately spoke essentially just in terms of the latter.[17]

---

[16] To attempt detailed suggestion of how this can be done in the present paper would tend to increase the length of the paper a great deal. Suffice it to say that before the respondent reaches the typical part of the location questionnaire which contains a check list of factors, a brief description of the location process might be entered which leads him to think in terms of markets versus costs. For example, the questionnaire might contain the following:

Explanation of check list — The plant is located at a given place because this location is expected to yield greatest profits or satisfactions to the owner. Location in ————— may suggest that the market is so favorable that, even though (or if) cost is higher than at other places, the sales potential is sufficiently large to induce the location. Or, it may be that the market is about the same as at other locations, while certain cost savings indicate greater profits and thereby explain the location. Or, some combination of these forces may, in fact, prevail. Indeed, personal satisfactions alone may have dominated, with economic values being sacrificed. Below are listed by category some important factors of location. Please check those which were considered to be important in guiding your company to its new location in —————. Later on you will be asked to rank these factors according to their importance.

[17] See Lösch, op. cit., p. 19 original.

When is the Demand Factor Of Location Important? †

Melvin L. Greenhut

INTER-REGIONAL linear programming models, comparative cost, and industrial complex studies have assumed that the market is formed at a point and that the location objective is to find the site which minimizes the cost of producing and delivering the product. This tradition is traceable directly to the assumption of a point-formed market, which assumption, we have elsewhere observed,[1] makes cost alone, not cost and demand, an integral part of each of the models. This is not to say that demand has been completely ignored for, in effect, the subject models have included demand via the assumption of differential costs of delivering the product. Unfortunately, this technique is inadequate.[2] In compliance with tradition, we shall refer to the pure cost models, as well as those which treated demand essentially from the cost side (e.g., as additional transport inputs), as the cost theory of location. In turn, we shall reserve the expression "demand and cost" for models explicitly recognizing other sides of demand.

We believe that the cost theory of location requires analysis which deviates from that of general economic theory and, in particular, fails to explain fully the location patterns of industries in large nations, including a block of nations such as those in the common market. For certain research objectives, a demand-cost approach to industrial location is the much more informative. To support these beliefs, our paper will therefore (a) develop the full meaning of demand in location economics and (b) designate the conditions under which it is fundamentally important.

The Meaning of Demand in Location Economics

That an empirical study must reflect theory is probably well accepted. That plant location theory must give more

---

† Grants from the Florida State University Research Council and the Inter-University Committee for Research on Southern Economic Development led to empirical findings which have buttressed this writer's belief that the one-sided cost approach to plant location (which has more often than not been followed in theory and which has been followed basically in empirical studies) is insufficient in theory and should not be considered alone in empirical investigations. Appreciation is acknowledged to R. W. Pfouts, J. Airov, L. T. Wallace, and M. R. Colberg for their helpful comments and critiques.

[1] M. L. Greenhut, *Plant Location in Theory and in Practice* (Chapel Hill, North Carolina: University of North Carolina Press, 1956), Chapter III.

[2] When a market is considered *as if* at a point, the transport costs of a seller vary with his location but are constant with respect to offsetting changes in the quantities he sells to *particular buyers*. When, however, a more inclusive framework is used, e.g. buyers dispersed over space, transport costs vary not only with the seller's location but with his sales to particular buyers. Under such conditions, sales depend on transport distances, transport costs on the location of competitors, and the location of competitors on the price policy in the industry, among other things. Shall we say, the whole cost basis of location shifts when site demand elements are considered; more specifically, when the market is not conceived as point formed, what we call the site demand factor of location will be seen to be instrumental in determining locations.

Reprinted from *Land Economics*, 40 (1964), 175–184, by permission of the author and editor.

than lip service to demand is perhaps not so clear-cut, even though it may be readily apparent to many that the distribution of plants cannot be explained just by observing that fuel, labor, freight, taxes, or some other cost determinant accounts for the location. In the instances where buyers are dispersed the selection of a plant site involves more than just the minimization of costs of sales to some given buying point. Demand becomes, in fact, an important variable which *depends upon location* and which actually may be more variable than cost from place to place.

By its very nature, space involves monopolistic elements.[3] Hence, pure competition theory is sometimes irrelevant, depending ultimately, of course, on objectives.[4] A more realistic and informative market model for selected problems would be one based on the conception of an oligopoly market. This market type may be expected to dovetail more precisely with prevailing price practices and to predict location patterns more aptly than the simple competitive market type; at the same time it yields a theoretical picture of long-run profit differences among industries which relates to the varying uncertainties and practices intrinsic to business activity in a space economy. If, let us say, space does give empirical reality to an oligopoly market theory, and if it does therefore admit to theory the conception of long-run profits varying from industry to industry, the location model which hinges on cost alone must be invalid in the broader sense, just as was the pure cost analysis of the early classicists. Demand differentials over space, we should realize, influence location in some way. Moreover, they help account for economic value and hence for differences in the returns to the factors of produc-

tion.[5]

Generally speaking, demand influences the location of industry *in every instance*. However, unfortunately for simple reading, this claim amounts to such an elementary observation as to be theoretically insignificant in its present form. What then are we really saying when we argue that location theory and empirical research should consider demand? Surely, we must be regarding demand in a different light than the mere fact that the want for a good or service is the basis for all economic activity. What we must actually be saying is that demand is a prime location variable from place to place, that it causes, and at the same time reflects, varying uncertainties and profits, and that it influences and is influenced by the location of industry. It is, indeed, from this particular point of view that we propose two ways in which demand *is* a vital part of location theory.

Alternative Important Categories of Demand. We find in the first important category that significant freight costs on

[3] See Don Dewey, "Imperfect Competition No Bar to Efficient Production," *Journal of Political Economy*, February 1958, pp. 24-33. See also M. L. Greenhut, "Space and Economic Theory," *Papers and Proceedings of the Regional Science Association*, December 1958, pp. 267-280, where it is observed that only if all buyers are at a point will pure competition by a "logically true" market type. On the empirical side, M. R. Colberg mentions on p. 74, of our book, *Factors in Location of Florida Industry* (Tallahassee, Florida: Florida State University Studies, No. 36, 1962), the desire for a monopoly position by officials of a small furniture company who sought to dominate a comparatively small area. In similar vein, in a reading of the present paper, Colberg reminded me of the many retailers who locate at sites of high cost and high demand. Also see E. Smykay, D. Bowersox, and F. Mossman, *Physical Distribution Management* (New York, New York: The Macmillan Company, 1961), Chapters VI-VIII.
[4] M. Friedman, "The Methodology of Positive Economics," *Essays in Positive Economics* (Chicago, Illinois: University of Chicago Press, 1953) notes the importance of objectives in selecting a theory.
[5] M. L. Greenhut, *Microeconomics and the Space Economy* (Chicago, Illinois: Scott, Foresman, 1963).

the finished product may combine with a large geographic area of demand to leave more than one market area within which a given kind of plant could be located. Selection of the one area for location instead of some alternative area may be due to the greater "size" of market in the one. In effect, demand is an *area-determining* factor of location. In the second instance, we find that after some roughly designated market area is selected the particular site may be chosen on the basis of demand differentials throughout the area. Significantly, these differentials arise as firms "jockey for position." When the competition in the industry causes a certain location pattern (e.g., heavy localization with slight dispersion), future entrants visualize different sales potentials at the alternative locations open to them and we hold demand to be a site-determining factor of location.

Distinction between the area and site components of demand may be seen by examining the reasons for demand differentials over space. If geography is a prime factor accounting for differentials in demand over space, the area demand factor of location is defined to exist. That is to say, if natural barriers to trade exist, such as mountain ranges which are so nearly impassable that shipment of goods through these ranges is very costly, the trading area of a firm locating, say, between such mountain ranges is fixed in advance of any particular location. Similarly, if for example a series of price zones exist which mark off different sales potentials from area to area, geography will be said to be the basis for demand differentials over space. If, on the other hand, the trading area of a firm is based on market determined demand and cost elasticities, among other forces, and these elasticities account for continuous (not

wide area) differentials over space, the site-determining demand factor is defined to prevail. But let us embellish further upon the statement that geography might appear in some cases as a prime factor behind differentials in demand.

Whenever mountain ranges, waterways, converging transport lines, and other geographic characteristics (such as natural resources, population concentrations, and different city sizes) help form sharply defined polygonic market areas for given products, or when business practices (such as sales quotas, territorial allotments, and zone pricing) cause sharply defined market areas to emerge, or when national boundaries determine the trading area, geographical features, we will hold, are relevant to the location of industry. These features signify that noticeable differences in potential sales and net receipts would arise if location were shifted within the area to sites distant from the maximum profit location. Let us say that under this determinant there would be an insufficient number of would-be buyers located beyond the original market's peripheral points who would be attracted to a firm locating nearer to such peripheries; accordingly, sales to these buyers would be very inadequate compared to the increased costs that would be incurred if such location were adopted.

In order for the area demand factor to apply, those areas (or regions) that are marked off by natural, political, or institutional forces must be comparatively independent of the price and location policies followed by any group of firms in the given industry. That is to say, the market area must be readily identifiable apart from *particular* industrial locations and developments. It must have been set by, or be attributable to forces lying outside the influence of one, two, or a few plant locations. Though variations in market areas will, of course, generally take place from product to product as "a" firm shifts its site or changes its price, what is defined to be vital to the concept is whether or not we are able to visualize some more or less distinctive trading areas for the product. If we are, the area demand factor of location is applicable and will help determine the location of branch and original plants in the subject industry.[6] Besides this, the site-determining demand factor of location (or, as it more popularly is called, the locational interdependence factor), as next explained, may also be relevant.[7]

It is pointed out in the literature on locational interdependence that the degree of elasticity of demand (or let us say here the shape of the demand curve), the shape of the marginal cost curve, the height of the freight rate, the homogeneity of products within the industry, the type of competition between an industry and a rival industry, and related forces, influence the way firms view their spatial relations and select their plant sites. Unfortunately, because the site determining (or locational interdependence) factor of location has so many component parts, each requiring analytic discussion, only a generalized illustration of the effect of one of its elements on plant location can be included here. Pursuant to this limitation, consider the elasticity of demand that applies to the product of an industry and note that, given the existing demand elasticity, a certain price policy and related amount of freight absorption will tend to be followed. The derived price may prove to be comparatively high or low, depending next on transport costs. In turn, the ability of the firm to service all parts of a market area from any location is

thereby determined. Clearly, the ability —or inability—to service buyers at a substantial distance from a given location influences the way that would-be rival firms will resolve their problem of estimating the likely location of competitors. The demand curve type thus helps resolve the matter of locational interdependence and the location pattern in the industry.

Most of the interest in the present paper centers on situations where the effective demand *within* a given region is actually altered by the location of firms. We shall not really emphasize here the more elementary matter of how demand influences the selection of an area or region, i.e., the area demand factor of location. Studies of new industrial patterns in the southern part of the United States, or in the states of West Virginia and Oklahoma, are testimonials to the fact that it is not the area aspect of demand which American and other location empiricists have failed to include in their studies; rather, they have ignored the site-determining demand factor of location. By focusing attention on the monopolistic site-determining influences of demand, we shall be in a

[6] Articles by H. Nishioka, "A Reconsideration of the Economic Location Theory," *Aoyama Journal of Economics*, June 1962, pp. 25-42 and "Interregional Economic Differences in Japan," *op. cit.*, March 1962, pp. 37-57; and K. Doi, "The Industrial Structure of Japanese Prefectures," *Proceedings of IGU Regional Conference* in Japan 1957, pp. 310-316, and other writings in Japan albeit more or less cost oriented in approach (e.g., T. Aoki, "On the Cost Factors in the Location Theory of Industry," *The Annals of the Hitotsubashi Academy*, August 1959, pp. 91-107) are yet of profound interest and relevance here since one may observe there much of what we have called the area demand factor. Indeed, note 11 by Nishioka in his "A Reconsideration . . .", *op. cit.*, suggests that Kunimatsu and Kasuga are finding more than cost factors behind the locational patterns in Japan.

[7] For details on and references to locational interdependence theory, see this writer's *Plant Location*, *op. cit.*, Chapter VI.

position to show why location theory and location surveys must consider *all* main forces (all sides of demand as well as cost) in order to understand the place where economic activity may be found. We protest the heavy leaning to cost theories of location[8] and their related kind of empirical investigations.[9] We contend that the site demand factor of location is an independent force in much the same position as labor or transportation and, hence, must be included in the models used to explain industrial location. Therefore, we next attempt to show the conditions under which this factor of location is or is not particularly important.

Price Systems and the Demand Concept

There are three basic location-price policy practices which might be distinguished, one of which makes the site-determining demand factor of location vital to all firms. In the first of these, cost of production is of paramount importance; in the second, the area demand factor of location is instrumental in determining the location pattern along with the cost differences that may prevail at alternative places; in the third (possibly the most important case), the site-determining demand factor of location must also be considered as it influences the location pattern. This last situation, as already mentioned, is the one generally ignored in location economics.

Equalizing Delivered Price System. Imagine a finished good which is sold on an equalizing delivered price basis throughout the country. Frequently, commodities of this kind carry low freight cost, such as in the distribution of alarm clocks and razors. For the present, we assume this situation of negligible freight costs and also the condition that physical proximity to buyers is of no consequence in sales. Given then an equalizing delivered price system, we obtain a location effect similar to that which arises when all buyers are located next to (or near) each other in some industrial center. The industrial location pattern which develops among the sellers is based on the production-procurement differentials existing at all alternative locations. These differentials are the only impersonal variable forces

---

[8] In fact, as we have argued elsewhere in several places, most of present day location theory is still tied to the von Thünen-Weber tradition.

[9] For studies in this pattern, see E. Hedland, *The Transportation Economics of the Soybean Processing Industry* (Champaign, Illinois: University of Illinois Press, 1952); and S. E. Dennison, *The Location of Industry and the Depressed Area* (London, England: Oxford University Press, 1939). There are countless other studies which can be included. Among them, those which deal with the development areas in Great Britain fall within the cost framework, such as J. Jewkes, *The Control of the Location of Industry in Great Britain* (New York, New York: American Enterprise Association, 1952); D. C. Hague and P. K. Newman, *Costs in Alternative Locations: The Clothing Industry* (London, England: Cambridge University Press, 1952); and J. Sykes, "Some Results of Distribution of Industry Policy," *The Manchester School*, January 1955, pp. 1-21. Of course, each of these studies relates to a special legislative program and to some extent do not, accordingly, require a complete theoretical design. Indeed, the contiguous land surfaces over which the alternative locations are weighed are not so large that locational interdependence forces will be significant. Nonetheless, they fit readily as examples of studies under the cost framework. We should note also in connection with these studies that though costs alone are mentioned, e.g., see Sykes, p. 6, one may occasionally discern the area demand factor when references are made to the resource advantages of different areas. And see J. Dunning, "The Development Area: A Further Note," *The Manchester School*, January 1956, pp. 77-92, esp. 90-92 where the author speaks of branch plant location and changes in location factors (e.g., labor costs, proximity to research and technical developments), and further mentions alternative areas in a manner somewhat reflective of our meaning of the area demand factor of location. In American studies on industrial complexes and location, such as J. Airov's, *The Location of the Synthetic Fiber Industry: A Study in Regional Analysis* (New York, New York: John Wiley, 1959); and in our programming studies a similar leaning is in evidence.

which prevail in the market; they yield rent differentials among locations.

As in Weber's system,[10] each firm and company in this kind of industry seeks to minimize delivered (total) cost throughout the market area. So, if all other things are equal, the initial firm will locate in the center of this area. What happens, one may ask, when the second, third, and other producers enter the field? Is the total demand in the market invariable? Do the second, third, and later entrants select their sites on the basis of competitive location or do they ignore the location of rivals?

Because there is no sales advantage through close physical proximity to a buyer (i.e., advantage in close contact, regional bias, or its like), the overall effective demand in the market would be constant regardless of location. This conclusion stems naturally from our derived hypothesis of a finished product sold at a given price everywhere. Moreover, second, third, or later entrants who sell over the whole market (by definition of the model) are oblivious to the location of competitors. Hence, given the commodity and the adoption of a fixed price to all points in the market, there is no locational interdependence between firms; that is, no forces outside of fundamental cost differentials and production limitations would be considered and hence no forces outside of these would determine whether an ideal, or less than ideal dispersion of sellers takes place. The present case, therefore, does not contain either of the two theoretically significant sides of the demand factor.

Single exception to the last mentioned claim would occur if there are some small companies located, say, in the center of the market which do not sell to all market peripheries. Then, if a new company later enters which is willing to be, and remain, smaller in size than the large producers, it would reap a freight cost saving by location at some peripheral point of the market. This freight cost saving would of course reflect the site-demand differentials that arose in the market. If as is often the case and as we assumed, the equalizing delivered price system is tied up with negligible freight costs, the freight savings are, however, unimportant and the demand (sales) advantges at peripheral points are of small moment. If, however, freight costs, though not substantial, are still significant, then the site-demand factor of location (that is, the difference in profit returns traceable directly to the location of rivals) carries weight; some small firms, subject to this interdependence, will tend to locate away from the production center of the industry.

Basing Point Pricing. Imagine a commodity for which freight cost is significant and whose production involves substantive economies of size, such as the manufacture of steel or, say, soil pipe. Legal or otherwise, a basing point price pattern or some modification thereof may exist, whether by zones, somewhat unsystematic, or under good-faith claims, it matters not. What about location? Is it determined by cost alone, by the regional area demand factor, or possibly by the site-determining force of demand?

Let us follow our previous order of answer by observing first the total magnitude of demand in the market area. By definition, once the base point is selected and a basing point price system established, effective demand is datum

---

[10] See C. J. Friedrich's translation as Alfred Weber's *Theory of the Location of Industries* (Chicago, Illinois: University of Chicago Press, 1928).

hroughout the market. It matters not vhether the initial and (or later) producers locate at the base point, or elsevhere, in so far as effective demand is concerned for its value is fixed. In comparable manner, locational interdependence does not exist because it is of no import to any firm whether a competitor is situated nearby or at a distance unless we introduce some special considerations such as small size or advantages to be derived from physical proximity to selected buyers. The objective of the base point system is to enable centrally (or near centrally) located firms (i.e., those at or near the base point) to ship over the market area. They are, under our assumptions, oblivious to the location of competitors. And this is one reason why an agglomeration of locations tends to take place at the base point. Location under base point pricing involves an attempt to minimize both the cost of procuring and processing the raw material and of distributing the finished good over the whole market, a result usually best attained at the base point city. Indeed, this is a principal reason why the base point city was first developed.[11]

Commodities of the kind just described, unlike those in the previous case, do provide instances where some important aspects of the demand factor may find their way into theoretical explanations. For example, if we assume that freight costs on the final product are significantly large and overall demand is spread out over a vast area of space, a single basing point system often proves impractical and is replaced by the so-called multiple basing point system. Under this multiple base point price pattern, effective demand in the market appears as a variable since the aggregation of net demand curves at the

base point locations yields a different totality from system to system.[12]

We are able to visualize demand as a location determinant under base point pricing in still another way—that is, the site-determining demand factor of location. To see this, assume that a prospective firm aspires to only a smaller size than the one most prevalent among the base point leaders. Because sales are not intended to all parts of the market, a location toward the peripheral areas will offer phantom freight profits, hence making such location advantageous. In turn, other entrants with plants not designed to produce enough goods for sale over the whole market area will find varying demand magnitudes throughout as small firms cause competition to be uneven from place to place. The locations of such plants *depend* upon those of other plants and among small firms an interdependence develops which marks the site demand factor of location as a determinant, along with cost, of the particular place selected for a plant.

The paint industry in the United States can provide us with a helpful reference. This industry has been distinguished by its stepped-up zone price

[11] Fritz Machlup, *The Basing Point System* (Philadelphia, Pennsylvania: Blakiston, 1949), p. 192, writes that sellers compete for the same market under the basing point system by paying for unnecessary transportation. When the unnecessary transportation is very costly, a tendency to develop multiple base points arises.

[12] To understand the choice of wording, consider the demand curve of a buyer for the product of a seller; example, $p = f(x) = K - 2x$, where p stands for price, K is a constant and x is the quantity sold. Now assume a transport cost (t) so that the net demand of the buyer at the seller's location (i.e., the net receipts of the seller) appears as $p = g(x) = K - 2x - t$. Aggregate all the g functions of buyers to obtain the total demand curve of buyers at the seller's location. Then divide the total market into two parts thereby obtaining different values for (t). The magnitude of effective demand in the market, as a consequence, has change.

pattern.[18] For example, uniform delivered prices were found at one time within each zone in the marketing of linseed oil. For this product the North Central states, including Minnesota (the leading producer), were designated as zone 1. From this base, zone differentials were calculated to other zones, with the largest advances in prices being on the west coast. Similar patterns were uncovered in the sales of white lead and prepared paints though the actual price pattern followed depended in part on the type and size of the seller. Thus, the larger manufacturer who distributed paint on a national scale used a four-zone price system raising prices variously between 4 and 18 cents per gallon from zone to zone. Medium size producers operating regionally used f.o.b. destination prices with some equalization involved though they did allow freight to buyers who arranged their own transportation. In contrast, small size producers did little to equalize delivered cost.

There is no price information available today on the American paint industry through sources such as the Temporary National Economic Committee. The Federal Trade Commission, for one possibility, has not made a study of price practices in the industry; while a second possible source, the National Paint, Varnish and Lacquer Trade Association, disclaims the compilation of such figures. The only data on the industry available today are those provided by individual companies and unfortunately these are generally extended on a confidential basis, if at all. Selected interviews by this writer suggest that uniform pricing by zones applies to practically all of the raw materials used in the industry, while the outline of a multiple four-zone price system is, at least,

still roughly discernible on certain prepared paints.

By carrying low price lines, small independents enjoy a price advantage among trade consumers. Significantly for our purposes and interest, the stepped up zone pricing system is counterpart to the basing point system and the paint industry illustrates a case where large companies seek to minimize cost throughout the market often using the original plant for its main product and strategically located branches for special outputs. Corollary thereto, small independents disperse readily to higher priced zones and take advantage of the gains of phantom freight differentials. We find, in particular, that the area demand factor of location determines the branch plant decisions of large firms. Moreover, because practically all of the 1200 raw materials used in the industry are shipped on the kind of discriminatory price basis which has an equalizing effect, cost differences are slight. The tendency has therefore developed for production to be spread out and divided among an increasing number of plants and firms (there are over 1500 in the industry). The narrowing of cost differences over space, in turn, has tended to make the site-demand factor of location the chief variable for small firms as well as a force to be reckoned with by the large.

Non-Discriminatory Plenary or F.O.B. Mill Pricing. When a plenary or straight f.o.b. mill price system is adopted with no systematic freight absorption or discrimination involved we find the clearest picture of demand as a factor of plant location. As with our two previous

---

[18] *Economic Concentration and Corporate Power,* Temporary National Economic Committee (Washington, D. C.: 1940), pp. 314, 315.

odels we will demonstrate this claim y reference to the area magnitude of ffective demand in the market and 1en the matter of locational interdeendence.

Assume a homogeneous cost pattern ver space and commodities whose eight cost is significant but whose manfacture fails to offer large scale econo1ies. If natural (distinguishable) maret areas do not exist, the area demand 1ctor of location will have no identiiable role. Location will be attributable nly to cost differentials, and to locaional interdependence differences, with 1arket area boundaries and size limitaions set by forces which themselves are 1 a state of variation and flux. Maniestly, if the area demand factor of locaion does happen to be relevant in causng a firm to select a certain region, the ite-determining location factor may also pply. In such case, demand would apear in its two significant roles.

Visualize the initial firms in the inustry adopting a location central to the vhole market (or the individual market rea) or, if you want, at a quartile or extile point along a line in the market, r anywhere else; further assume condiions similar to those of previous models, uch as the irrelevance of physical proxmity as an industrial characteristic. For ur purposes, it does not matter where he original firm (or firms) selects its ite; what counts is only that, given a ocation, an aggregate net demand curve nay be identified for any firm and, in urn, given a later entry and independnt pricing, a new individual net aggreate demand curve will obtain for all ffected firms.[14] Significantly, the demand curve facing the individual firm s influenced by not only the number of lants but the places of plant location. iince the demand curve is partially a

variable *because of location,* it is, accordingly, a site-determining factor of location.

The entry of later firms, *regardless of size,* is clearly influenced by the location of earlier firms. Whether or not procurement and production costs vary from place to place, there will generally prevail a difference in transport costs on the finished product or a difference in size of markets from alternative locations, as the case be.[15] The location of any and all firms is influenced (if not determined) by the location of others. More generally, the elasticity of the demand function, the history of competition in location in the industry, the degree of competition from substitutable products at the various locations, the homogeneity or heterogeneity of the firms belonging to the industry, and many of the other demand factors of location which have been shown to influence the selection of plant sites—i.e., the determine the locational interdependence of firms—become relevant in such cases. They influence the firms in the industry to localize or disperse, as the case be.

Selection of the place to locate a plant cannot be determined simply by reference to costs at alternative locations. The type of commodity and the price pattern to be followed may combine to make the plant location subject to many other influences than just procurement, production, and distribution cost over some given distance. These other influences, as detailed in the literature of spatial competition, are, in sum, our site-determining demand factor of plant location. They are especially critical to the findings of an analyst whose interest centers on county economic development, or on location near regional borders or, in the case of common market countries, location within a given national border. They are part of and should be included in a general economic theory of plant location.

[14] The literature on space oligopoly abounds with discussions of this situation.

[15] See M. L. Greenhut, "Transport Costs vs Size of Markets," *Journal of Industrial Economics*, March 1960, pp. 172-184 for distinctions between market orientations due to transport cost advantages and those due to "demand" advantages.

THE MARKET POTENTIAL CONCEPT
AND THE ANALYSIS OF LOCATION

Edgar S. Dunn

THE IDEA OF USING CONTOUR MAPS in the analysis of location is an old one. Weber developed the idea of plotting contours of equal cost. He called them isotims or isodapanes.[1] More recently Hoover gave extensive treatment to the use of cost contours in location analysis.[2] Until recently, however, such techniques were conceptual tools and found very little empirical application. There are several reasons why this is so. (1) Before contours of cost could be developed to represent geographically the cost pattern for serving a market area, some means had to be derived for identifying the size and geographical character of the market area. No definite empirical technique was available for doing this. As a consequence, location analysis fell back on the more simple technique of approximating market contours as a point and applying the Weberian approach exemplified by the location triangle. (2) Another serious restraint upon the application of the contour technique has been the fact that it would necessitate large volumes of data and numerous computations. It was expensive and time consuming relative to the kind of results that could be expected.

Recent developments have removed to a considerable degree these restraints and it is my opinion that the contour technique will shortly find an important role in location analysis. First, computing machines and punch card equipment have made the cost and time considerations manageable. Second, Harris[3] following the leadership of Stewart[4] has provided the beginnings of a tool for dealing empirically with market areas.

REVIEW OF CONCEPTS

Review briefly, the techniques provided by these men. Stewart provided the spark by developing the concept of population potential. This concept

[1]Weber, Alfred, Theory of Location of Industries, edited by C.J. Friedrich, (Chicago, University of Chicago Press, 1920), pp. 102-104, 122, 144, 240-243.

[2]Hoover, E.M., Location Theory and the Shoe and Leather Industries, (Cambridge, Harvard University Press, 1937), pp. 41-49, 77-88.

[3]Harris, Chauncy D., "The Market as a Factor in the Localization of Industry in the United States," Annals of the Association of American Geographers, December 1954, pp. 315-348.

[4]Stewart, John Q., "Demographic Gravitation: Evidence and Applications," Sociometry, February-May 1948.

Reprinted from Papers, The Regional Science Association, 15 (1956), 183–194, by permission of the author and editor.

arose out of a dissatisfaction with the conventional concept of population center of gravity and a realization that the extent of control between peoples was diminished by the distance between them -- much as the force of gravitation between two bodies is diminished by distance. Adopting gravitation formulae from physics, Stewart measured the population potential for one county by summing the quotients of the population of all other counties divided by their respective distances from the base county $[\Sigma(P/d)]$. Once these potentials are computed for each county, lines of isopotential may be drawn on a map showing the characteristics of population distribution.

Harris recognized in this technique a tool for market analysis. Research by Isard, Ullman, Zipf, and many others had testified to the importance of distance of accessibility in determining the potential of a market. Harris replaced population with retail sales in the Stewart formula $[\Sigma(M/d)]$ and used transport costs as a refinement of distance. This resulted in the measure of market potential. The resulting maps for the United States describe its market structure with remarkable interest.

In addition to the measurement of market potential, Harris prepared a series of contour maps designed to measure the geographic distribution of costs in serving a market. The same retail sales and distance cost figures were used, arranged in the following formula: $T = \Sigma(Md)$. In this exercise the object is to locate minimum transport costs in serving the market rather than maximum market potential.[5]

Following Harris, I have computed the market potentials and the transport costs for 103 counties in Florida and Southern Georgia for 1948 (Figures 1 and 2).

SIGNIFICANCE FOR LOCATION ANALYSIS

It is obvious that contour maps are useful in picturing the general market structure and may be useful to picture shifts over time.[6] Such maps are undoubtedly useful pedagogical tools and useful instruments for regional policy making. To what extent, you might ask, are these techniques of use to the business firm seeking to identify its best production (or marketing) location.

The specific maps which have been shown would be of use only to firms producing simple manufactured goods and selling in a market area which coincided with those illustrated. A firm whose sales did not correlate highly with general retail sales, whose natural market area differed from those pictured, and whose transport rate structure differed from those

[5]Harris, op. cit.

[6]As a matter of interest the author developed the market potentials and transport costs for 1933 and 1954 as well as 1948. During all periods the Tampa Bay area formed the center of highest market potential. However, in 1933 the configurations were definitely oriented towards Jacksonville in the north and by 1948 they had shifted radically in response to the growth situation on the lower East Coast. Investigations of earlier population data suggest that the market center of highest potential in the early 20's was at Jacksonville. Thus, in the short span of 25 years the market center for serving the area pictured shifted from the East Coast in the North, to the Tampa Bay area. Further, the 1954 data show that the Tampa bay area holds its superiority by only a few percentage points and that the highest market potential may be on the verge of returning to the East Coast in the South.

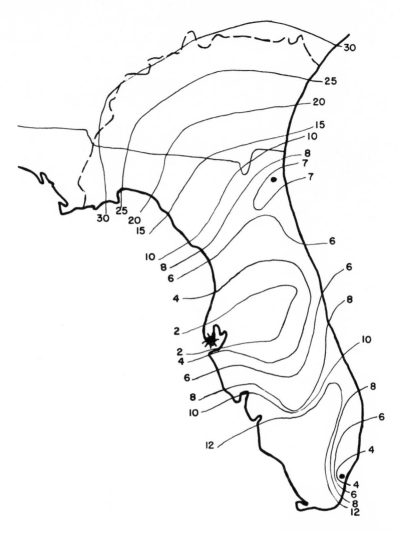

FIGURE 1. Market Potential, 1948. Percent below Pinellas County.

med in constructing the maps would find the contours pictured completely
levant to their location problem. The technique, however, is quite
ible. Different market areas and different measures of sales potential
distance costs appropriate to the special problem of each firm can be
to develop maps of use in analyzing the location problem of each firm.

as not been made clear in the literature that these techniques and
e contour maps as they stand can be used in analyzing the location of

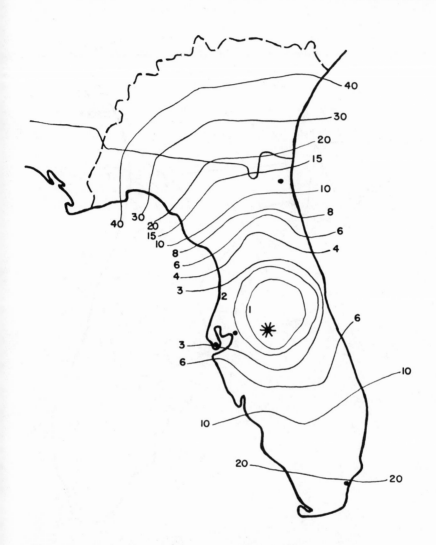

FIGURE 2. Transport Costs, 1948. Percent above Polk County.

only two very restricted types of firms. First, market potential by its
can provide a guide to location only for the firm that is not transp
oriented. By that it is meant that transport costs on inputs and prod
do not play a role in determining location. For such a firm market pot
tial could provide a guide in determining the location that will maxim
sales.[7] Second, the index of transport costs developed by Harris w

---

[7]One might respond by saying, "Doesn't the market potential concept of necessity imply transport orientation
transport costs are included in the denominator?" The answer is no. In this situation transport costs are simply

ply only to the firm that is transport oriented and market oriented
i.e., transport costs on inputs are unimportant). Even for such a firm
his index of transport costs will provide a guide to location only in
he event that its market potential is constant. This means that the
irm could locate anywhere within the specified geographic landscape
ithout suffering any loss in market. In such a case the location that
inimized transport costs in serving the market would be superior. Cost
ontours similar to Figure 2 would identify this location.

he two special location situations just discussed undoubtedly make up a
mall percentage of the location problems. Therefore, the geographical
easure of market potential and transport costs can be applied directly
o only a limited number of situations. A much more common location problem
ould involve a firm that is transport oriented and market oriented and
s faced with a variable market potential. In such a case maximum market
otential is no guide because it might be at a point with higher than
inimum transport costs. Similarly, minimum transport costs might be
ought at the expense of reducing sales volume.

he solution to this problem lies in combining the measure of market
otential and the measure of transport costs into what we might call an
ndex of location. This calls forth the use of the isodapane technique
n which the two contours are merged into a third which partakes of the
haracter of both. This can be accomplished statistically or graphically.
y the graphic technique the cost and market potential contours would be
verlayed and new contours generated by joining together appropriate
ntersection points.[8] However, it is easier and more accurate in this
ase to compute the index of location statistically.

irst, however, it must be pointed out that the cost contours such as
ontained in Figure 2 are not appropriate for computing the location index.
he reason is obvious. Consider this example. A firm locating in Polk
ounty (which has the lowest transport costs) instead of Pinellas County
which has the highest market potential) might lose .8 percent of its
arket potential. At the same time, according to the cost figures in
able IV, it would gain a 3.0 percent saving in transport cost. On this
asis one might assume a net advantage in locating in Polk County. The
efect in these cost data, however, is the fact that they are based upon
he assumption that the market potential is the same for every county.
n order to get a true basis for substituting transport costs for sales
olume (and vice versa), these transport cost figures need to be weighted
y market potential figures. Thus, in Polk County the transport costs
ould be more than 3.0 percent less than Pinellas because the size of
he market served is .8 percent smaller.

n Table I the transport cost figures by county are weighted by the market
otentials. These weighted transport costs are, in turn, converted into
ercentages of the county with the lowest transport cost. Since the market
otentials are expressed in percentages of the county with the highest

---

s an index of access to the market. In some cases distance in miles or even time required to travel might be better
ndexes of access.

[8]Op. cit., Hoover, p. 46.

TABLE I.   Computation of Index of Location, 1948. (Data for Selected C
ties Only.)

County	(1) Market Potential (Percent of Pinellas)	(2) Transport Costs (Percent of Polk)	(3) Weighted Transport Costs $[(1)\times(2)]$	(4) Shift Base to Pinellas $[(3)\div103]$	(5) Net Differ- ential $[(1)-(4)]$	(6 Index Locat (bas shift to Po
1. Monroe	66.8	155.4	103.8	100.8	-34.0	-36.
2. Dade	96.7	120.9	116.9	113.5	-16.8	-19.
3. Lee	89.3	111.0	99.0	96.1	- 6.8	- 9.
4. Hendry	92.2	108.6	100.1	97.2	- 5.0	- 7.
5. Charlotte	89.8	109.2	98.1	95.2	- 5.4	- 8.
6. Glades	93.5	107.0	100.0	97.1	- 3.6	- 6.
7. DeSoto	93.7	105.3	98.7	95.8	- 2.1	- 5.
8. Pinellas	100.0	103.0	103.0	100.0	0.0	- 2.
9. Hillsborough	99.3	102.5	101.7	98.7	+ .6	- 2.
10. Polk	99.2	100.0	99.2	96.3	+ 2.9	0.
11. Osceola	97.1	100.6	97.7	94.9	+ 2.2	- .
12. Pasco	98.1	101.1	99.2	96.3	+ 1.8	- 1.
13. Citrus	94.6	103.7	98.1	95.2	- .6	- 3.
14. Lake	97.4	101.0	98.4	95.5	+ 1.9	- 1.
15. Orange	97.9	100.5	98.4	95.5	+ 2.4	- .
16. Brevard	92.5	104.2	96.4	93.6	- 1.1	- 4.
17. Marion	95.4	103.3	98.5	95.6	- .2	- 3.
18. Dixie	86.8	113.4	98.4	95.5	- 8.7	-11.
19. Alachua	93.1	107.2	99.8	96.9	- 3.8	- 6.
20. Duval	93.4	111.4	104.0	101.0	- 7.6	-10.
21. Madison	82.4	123.3	101.6	98.6	-16.2	-19.
22. Leon	75.4	134.4	101.3	98.3	-22.9	-25.
23. Colquit	76.4	136.4	104.2	101.2	-24.8	-27.
24. Chatham, Ga.	73.1	143.6	105.0	101.9	-28.8	-31.

potential, the two series can be compared to generate the index of locati
When the data are graphed we develop the contours in Figure 3.

This computation would have to be made with extreme care in a speci
research problem. We developed the contours in Figure 3 on the sim
assumption that a 1 percent reduction in transport costs is a direct off
to a 1 percent loss in sales leaving no location preference. In order
this to give an accurate location index, transport costs as a percent
of sales would have to be the same as net revenue as a percentage of sal
In most cases such identity would not be found and the gain or loss
market potential and/or transport cost would have to be given a wei
appropriate to the experience of the individual firm. (For example,
might take a 3 percent reduction in transport cost to offset a 1 perc

188

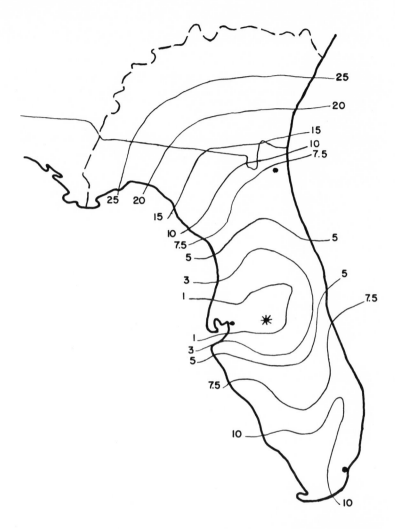

FIGURE 3. Index of Location, 1948. Percent below Polk
County. (An isodapane combining market potential
and weighted transport costs. Transport costs
diminished by 1/3.)

:tion in sales.) Because of the assumption made, the index of location
igure 3 is dominated by the pattern of transport cost in Figure 2.
:eater weight were given to sales the index of location would take
 configuration corresponding more closely to that of Figure 1. (See
:xample, Figure 4).

189

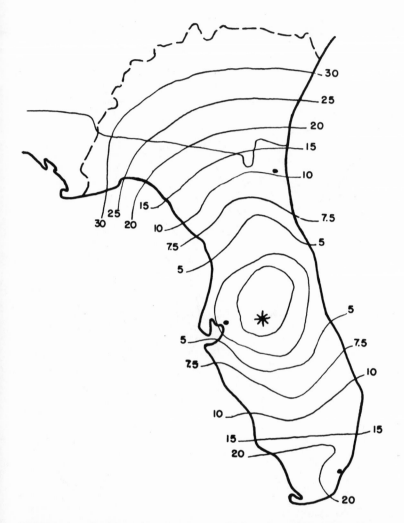

FIGURE 4.   Index of Location, 1948.   Percent below Polk
County.   (An isodapane combining market potential
and weighted transport costs.   Transport costs
and market potential weighted equally.)

The index of location just suggested above will probably work adequat
for firms selecting distribution or marketing locations and perhaps s
manufacturing concerns that are highly market oriented.   Some fir
however, are transport oriented and find that the transport costs on
material inputs are as important in reaching a location decision as tr
port costs in serving the market.   In the past these problems have usu

190

been approached with the classical Weberian location figure. Markets and raw material sources were considered as points. There was no technique for handling adequately the situation where markets or raw material sources are areally distributed. In such cases a meaningful index of location can be computed by extending the isodapane technique just described one step further. Two additional cases can be identified. **First, transport costs on inputs are important and market potential is constant.** In this case the isodapane composing the index of location would be composed of two elements: (a) transport costs on inputs, (b) transport costs in serving the market. **Second, transport costs on inputs are important and market potential is variable.** In this case the isodapane composing the index of location would be made of (a) transport costs on inputs, (b) the iso-dapane combining market potential and transport costs in serving the market.

APPLICATION TO LOCAL PROBLEMS

Most of the literature devoted to location analysis is devoted to the location of regional producing and distribution units. I feel a strong conviction that variations of these contour techniques can prove helpful in locating local economic units — particularly those engaged in distri-bution. Many indexes of sales potential (such as per capita income, bank deposits, population per family, retail sales, percent negro, etc.) can be generated on a square mile basis. My conviction is borne out by the fact that Eli Goldberg has been highly successful in locating retail outlets for Rayco by following a technique remarkably similar to the market potential concept. The end product was a set of contour maps for each metropolitan area which were used by the real estate men in negotiating for a site.

Similar techniques might prove very useful in the evaluation of retail areas served by suburban shopping centers.[9]

SOME SPECIAL ANALYTICAL CONSIDERATIONS

Up to this point, the mechanics of these techniques have been presented without devoting any special attention to their possible limitations. Two problems are worth consideration.

Those of you who are familiar with gravity models in the many applications that have been proposed for them[10] are aware that every researcher utilizing

[9]In this connection consult a very excellent paper by Dr. Reinhold P. Wolff of the University of Miami, "The Determination and Evaluation of Retail Areas Served by Suburban Shopping Centers," an unpublished paper presented at the Atlanta meeting of the Southern Economic Association, November 11, 1955.

[10]For example, Mr. Carroll read a paper before this group in Detroit last year in which the gravity model was applied to the measurement of spatial interaction and urban-metropolitan influence. J. Douglas Carroll, Jr., "Spatial Interaction and the Urban-Metropolitan Regional Description," Papers and Proceedings, (Publications of the Regional Science Association, 1955), Vol. I. Mr. Anderson, who sits on the panel with us this morning, has used the gravity model to study intermetro-politan migration. See, "Intermetropolitan Migration," American Sociological Review, June 1955, Vol. 20, No. 3. Isard and Freutel have explored the possibility for using this model in the statistical projection of gross regional product or in-come measures. In this connection they develop the concept of income potential. See, "Regional and National Product Projections and their Interrelations," Long-Range Economic Projection, (National Bureau of Economic Research, Studies in

191

these techniques has been plagued with doubts about the appropriateness of the variables included in both the numerator and denominator.

In connection with the numerator of the model, wide variations in content have been proposed. Some of these variations are naturally a consequence of the different uses which have been proposed for the gravity model. Thus, Stewart uses population in the numerator, while Isard uses income and Harris, retail sales. This is to be expected. However, researchers attempting to measure the same phenomena exhibit their uncertainty by disagreeing on the essential content of the numerator. Anderson,[11] for example, is concerned in his article with the fact that in measuring inter-metropolitan migration Zipf[12] uses population while Stouffer[13] claims superiority for data measuring "intervening opportunities." After reviewing carefully these alternative hypotheses, Anderson concludes that improving the accuracy of the gravity model for this purpose lies in the direction of including the influence of several factors in the numerator.

I think that this point has a great deal of relevance for using the contour technique in location analysis. It supports my statistical intuition which suggests that, in a practical problem, a preliminary multiple correlation study might indicate several highly important variables for which data can be generated on an area basis.[14] The final computations of market potentials might be based upon some weighted combinations of these elements.

It is in connection with the denominator of the gravity model that the greatest controversy arises. Should the attractive force represented by the numerator be diminished by the distance or the distance raised to some power? In keeping with this uncertainty the more recent writers usually present the model in the form, Attraction = P/d^a, where a is an unknown exponent. A good deal of concern has been expressed over the dimension of the exponent and a good deal of effort expended to measure it. The results are confusing. Zipf has argued that the exponent for distance is unity and has assembled data to demonstrate his hypothesis.[15] Reilly, in studying the pattern of retail trade attractions of Texas cities, concluded that the exponent is two.[16] Carroll, using data on telephone calls and intercity travel, concluded that the exponent was closer to three.[17] Anderson, in his recent article, has suggested that the exponent may be variable with the size of the exponent being a function of the size of the population base. Though the majority opinion is that the denominator is an exponential function, there is little agreement as to the size of the exponent.

Income and Wealth, 1954), Vol. 16, pp. 427-471. Again Isard has explored the use of the income potential concept in connection with the short-run analysis of international trade theory. See, "Location Theory and Trade Theory: Short-run Analysis," **Quarterly Journal of Economics**, May 1954, pp. 305-320.

[11]Op. cit.

[12]Zipf, George K., **Human Behavior and the Principle of Least Effort**, (Addison Wesley Press, Cambridge, 1948), chap. 9.

[13]Samuel A. Stouffer, "Intervening Opportunities: a Theory Relating Mobility and Distance," **American Sociological Review**, December 1940.

[14]In many cases it would be unnecessary to go beyond the scatter diagram.

[15]Zipf, op. cit.

[16]Reilly, William J., "Methods for the Study of Retail Relationships," University of Texas, Bulletin No. 2994, November 1929.

[17]Carroll, op. cit., p. D-10.

Such seeming inconsistency might lead one to the conclusion that techniques using the gravity models have not been sufficiently refined to be useful for predictive research. I do not feel that these results necessarily point to a serious restraint upon the practical application of contour analysis to location problems. To me there is one obvious interpretation of these varied results. Instead of there being a single exponential value to fit all cases, it is likely that the exponent is different for different types of social and economic intercourse. Mr. Carroll himself has indicated that the extent of urban dominance is different for different urban functions.[18] This fact might make it difficult to measure an exponent applicable to more vague and general measures of urban dominance or inter-metropolitan migration. However, it appears to me to hold the promise that, in the analysis of a specific location problem in which a single economic function is being subjected to examination, a realistic and operational exponent may not be too difficult to establish.

In this connection, Harris' use of economic distance based upon transport costs seems to be a reasonable first approximation to the rate at which the market potential of a given community for a given product is diminished. It is interesting to note that, since transport costs are a product of distance and the transport rate, and since the transport rate is itself a function of distance, the distance function in the denominator of the market potential concept is an exponential. This is in keeping with the majority opinion of previous researchers. It is also interesting to note that, implicit in this denominator is the fact that the exponent of distance is a variable exponent.[19] Thus, Harris has implicitly introduced a new element into the exponent discussion.

It should not prove too difficult, when faced with a specific location problem, to construct refinements of the denominator that would improve the accuracy of the predictive model.

There is a second problem associated with the mechanics of constructing market contours that deserves mention. It is obvious that the dimensions of the market potential contours depend upon the specific market area selected for study. The area represented on the maps presented was not taken to represent the market area for any specific commodity. It was simply taken arbitrarily to serve as the basis for exploring a technique. South Georgia was included and West Florida excluded purely on the basis of crude observation of the spatial extent of the dominance of Jacksonville as an urban metropolitan community.

For a specific research problem the extent of the market area to be used in developing the contour analysis would have to be established on the basis of techniques similar to those discussed by Reilly and Carroll. The basic joker in the procedure is the fact that the spatial extent of the market for a firm located in Duval County might be different from that for a firm located in Hillsborough County. This means that the number of counties

---

[18]Ibid., p. D-4.

[19]This is consistent with Anderson's comment on the possibility of a variable exponent. However, Anderson's exponent is a variable function of P. When distance costs are used the exponent becomes a variable function of d thus creating a transcendental function.

included in computing the market potential for a specific base county
might be different from those for another base county when the spatial
influence of economic rivalry is taken into account. This may, in some
cases, complicate the computation of the market contours. I think, however,
that I am not overly optimistic when I say that in many instances the
pressure of market rivalry will not be sufficiently strong to make this
refinement significant. In those cases where this modification is necessary
in order to derive useful predictive data, the mechanics of the adjustment
are not prohibitively complicated. Whether the economic costs would become
prohibitive in many cases I cannot say.

CONCLUSION

In conclusion it is my thought that the tools provided by contour analysis
of the type I have outlined here in combination with new techniques for
machine processing data may make feasible location analysis for many firms
of a degree of refinement heretofore not commonly possible. These techniques should be particularly important in breaking through the barriers
that have existed in analyzing market areas. Since the tool is completely
flexible, it can be used also as a research tool in analyzing supply areas.
For example, the problem of locating a woodpulp mill with reference to its
supply sources might be facilitated through the use of such a technique.

One further concluding comment. The presentation of these techniques by
means of the experimental research reported here overemphasizes the complexity of the practical research problem. For example, in locating a
firm within a relevant market area coinciding with the 78 counties in
this study, two-thirds or more of these counties could be eliminated from
serious consideration as base counties on the basis of preliminary studies.
In many cases it would be necessary to apply these techniques only to those
location possibilities that lie within the margin of uncertainty.

TENDENCIES IN AGRICULTURAL SPECIALIZATION AND REGIONAL CONCENTRATION OF INDUSTRY

Michael Chisholm

The purpose of this paper is to present a train of thought which I believe has not been stated before in the same terms and which I hope will provide a useful starting-point for discussion. Not one of the individual ideas incorporated here is new; if there is any originality, it lies in the association of ideas. May I also add that these thoughts are framed with reference to the more developed or more rapidly developing parts of the world and relate to large-scale regional trends.

Let me summarise my argument by making six bald statements, each of which I will then elaborate and qualify.

1) Very largely owing to the improvement of transport facilities, agricultural production is becoming regionally more specialized and increasingly production is in the areas which are better endowed for particular crops by reason of their climates and soils.

2) With industry, it is the market which is increasingly important for location, natural resources being of decreasing significance.

3) The territorial extent of what may be termed a 'market' is expanding for most commodities, often now embracing the whole world.

4) The 'market', which is a collection of consumers, is becoming more mobile.

5) People are increasingly attracted by regions possessing a good climate and/or terrain allowing outdoor leisure activities.

6) The areas to which the industrial population is moving are often precisely those best endowed for specialized and intensive agriculture.

Regarding agricultural specialization and the concentration of production into those areas which are best suited on account of climatic and soil conditions, there is not a great deal that needs to be said. The matter has been discussed at greater length than is here possible in my book *Rural Settlement and Land Use: An Essay in Location*[1]. The key point is that transport is a substantial item of cost for the distribution of agricultural products and that many products are very perishable. In the United States, the cost of transport from the farm to the first point of collection is in the order of 10 per cent of the gross value of output. Clearly, any reduction in the relative cost of transport substantially reduces the advantages of proximity to markets. The long-run tendency is for transport to become relatively cheaper, for a variety of

[1] London, Hutchinson, 1962.

Reprinted from *Papers, Regional Science Association*, European Congress, Zurich, 10 (1963), 157–162, by permission of the author and editor.

reasons that need not detain us. With perishable commodities, the speedin
up of transport (by the introduction of railways, road vehicles and even aer
planes) has greatly extended the radius over which fresh foodstuffs can b
marketed. Refrigeration has had a tremendous effect upon the world patter
of meat and dairy production in particular. Recent developments in parti
and complete dehydration and subsequent reconstitution of foods are likely t
have equally significant results in the future; the accelerated freeze-dry pr
cess is particularly promising. This not only preserves foodstuffs but make
them far easier to transport.

For these reasons, location of production near the consuming centres i
becoming less and less important. Conversely, other location factors assum
greater significance. Of these, it is the physical environment which has th
greatest effect upon regional costs. For this reason, production of particula
products tends to concentrate in those areas where the environmental advant
ages are the greatest relative to other products. One of the classic example
of this process is the revolution in Danish agriculture during the last century
whereby a general agricultural economy in which cash grains were importan
was transformed into a specialist livestock and dairy products system of agri
culture. Tropical products such as coffee, tea, cocoa and rubber also shov
marked specializations of production in different parts of the world.

Now it happens that many products have very similar requirements o
soil and climate and therefore they are likely to congregate into the sam
more favoured regions. The concentration of fruit and vegetable productio
in California is a particular case in point. This tendency is reinforced by th
increasing proportion of 'industrial' inputs—fertilisers, machinery, irrigatio
and the like. In order that full advantage can be taken of these developments
it is necessary that the physical environment should not be restrictive an
create conditions of diminishing returns. For example, the use of fertiliser
in arid plains is limited by the lack of water. Thus, those parts of the worl
with good soil, level land, plenty of sun and water for irrigation are likely t
find themselves at an increasing relative advantage.

This tendency is being reinforced by changes in diet. The growing con
sumption of fruits, vegetables, dairy produce and meat means that an increas
ing proportion of agricultural production is amenable to intensive methods o
farming. This can be done most economically in those areas where the solu
tion of one agronomic problem does not bring the farmer up against anothe
environmental problem which needs to be overcome before the first advanc
can be used.

The increasing importance of the market as a factor for the location o
industry has been remarked by many workers. To list the main reasons fo
this situation is to show that the trend is likely to continue.

1) Technical development is resulting in a greater economy in the use o
raw materials. For example, the iron and steel industry of the United Kingdom
used 4.2 tons of materials of produce one ton of pig iron in 1920–24 wherea
in 1955–59 the quantity had fallen to 3.4 tons.[2]

2) Materials are subjected to a much greater degree of processing than

---

[2] *Annual Statistics*, Iron and Steel Board, British Iron and Steel Federation.

362

ormerly so that the 'value added' is increasing in relation to the value of the materials.

3) Cheaper transport has a greater relative effect upon raw materials than upon the finished articles which are more valuable, thereby making it possible to carry the raw materials much further than formerly.

4) Natural raw materials are of diminishing importance relative to manufactured materials. G.A.T.T.[3] has culculated that for the industrial countries of Europe the use of natural raw materials and fuels increased by about one-third in the period 1938–1954. At the same time, the consumption of manufactured 'raw' materials and fuels increased six-fold. The significance of this fact is that the processing of these 'raw' materials—from coal, oil, wood pulp, etc.—often takes place in the industrial areas. Hence it follows that increasingly the 'market' is also the immediate source of materials for manufacture. The by-products of oil refineries is a notable case in question.

5) The changing structure of advanced economies means that manufacturing is becoming relatively less important. The provision of services of all kinds—whether those of a solicitor or of pre-packing foods—is taking a growing share of national incomes. It is impossible to give an adequate measure of this tendency because in censuses and national income calculations many services are classified under the manufacturing activity of which they are a part. Service industries are characterised by the need to be near the consumers.

But the meaning of the term 'market orientation' is changing. The local market of a few miles' radius is ceasing to be a relevant concept for a wide range of manufactures, except at the level of retail sales. It is regional, national and international territories over which goods are marketed. Hence, the desire of manufacturers to be located where they have good access to a large number of consumers and the all-too-familiar consequence of sprawling conurbations. This tendency is partly caused by the increasing scale of manufacturing units, dictated by the economies to be obtained from mass-production.

As a consequence of these factors, there is a strong tendency for economic activity to become progressively concentrated into heavily urbanised regions. This presents us with the familiar problems of severe congestion in the conurbations and their surrounding regions. The converse problem is that of getting vigorous development under way in the less developed regions, for there is often a cumulative divergence in living standards between the 'haves' and 'havenots'. The argument as presented so far suggests that there is an increasing 'polarisation' of economic activities: manufacturing and service industries being drawn to the existing market areas while agricultural production becomes orientated towards regions where the conditions of the natural environment are the most favourable for production.

This conclusion overlooks another set of considerations. The 'market' is made up of several elements, of which we may notice the distinction between manufacturers who buy in components and materials and final consumers who buy goods at retail. It is the latter aspect of the market with which I am concerned. One of the major social revolutions of our time is the provision of pension schemes, by employers or governments or both. In the absence of such provision, it is necessary for individuals to go on working until they are

[3] *Trends in International Trade*, G.A.T.T., 1958, p. 43.

physically incapable and to rely upon their offspring or close relatives fo support in their old age. Under these circumstances, elderly persons are ef fectively tied to the place in which they have lived and worked all their life as a class, they are immobile.

But this situation ceases to obtain when adequate pension schemes exist In most European countries, the United States, Canada, Australia and else where, those who retire at between 60 and 65 or 67 have their own means o support and still have a number of active years in front of them. Under thes circumstances, it is entirely natural that an increasing number of people choos to change their abode when they retire, selecting those parts of the countr which offer desirable conditions. Frequently, it is sun and a mild climat which attracts such people. In England, the south coast, particularly Bourne mouth, attracts large numbers of retired folk. In France, the Riviera tradi tionally plays the same part, while in the United States it is to Californi and, more recently, Florida that people flock.

In this way, entirely new market centres are being created which in par at least are orientated towards conditions of the natural environment. Th same thing is happening in a different but related way. A social developmen parallel to the one mentioned above is the increasing amount of leisure avail able to people. This takes the form of shorter working days and weeks an longer annual holidays. Much of this leisure is being taken up with outdoo activities such as boating, mountaineering, camping and gardening—taste vary. But there is a need common to most of these activities, especially wher undertaken in family groups, for good weather. For all that modern techni ques enable indoor climates to be controlled, the increase in outdoor leisure activities increases our dependence upon the natural environment.

The significance of this trend is that employers have increasingly to consider whether a particular location is likely to prove attractive for em ployees. If it is not, then it may prove difficult to obtain and then keep stuff of the right calibre. This fact has been recognized for many years, having been noted, for example, by the Barlow report on the *Distribution of the Industrial Population* in 1940.[4] It may not yet be a factor of major importance but from the nature of the case it is probable that it will assume increasing significance.

There is good reason to think that this consideration is influencing the distribution of employment and population in Great Britain. For several decades now, the greatest relative growth has been in the Midlands and south— the Birmingham-London region. This part of the country combines many advantages, of which two are particularly important: the relief is gentle, which facilitates the building of large works; the climate is relatively sunny and dry and there is lovely country side to hand.

Although it is dangerous to try refining ideas such as the above, the following propositions do seem worth making. In countries such as Britain and Germany, at the forefront of the Industrial Revolution, there grew up major concentrations of population on the coalfields. This was primarily because coal provided the only important source of power, transport was costly and

---

[4] Royal Commission, H.M.S.O., London, Cmd. 6153.

very large amount of coal were required because boilers and blast furnaces were very inefficient. With the advance of techiques and the introduction of alternative sources of power (electricity and oil), the attraction of coal as a locating factor has declined sharply. But the coalfields have remained as important centres of industry because here are large markets. Thus, the increasing importance of a market orientation has tended to maintain the *existing* major population centres in being. But now that leisure is becoming more generally available, the 'market' is itself becoming more mobile and the dominance of the coalfields is breaking down.

In those countries where industrial development has begun more recently, the coalfields have never assumed such importance. With these countries, the first step in the sequence outlined above is usually passed by. Industrial development is generally taking place in those regions which already have a substantial population because it is in such regions that markets may be found and facilities such as transport are more readily available than elsewhere. Japan provides a good illustration of this point, for most of the modern industrial development has occurred in the southern part of the main island, Honshu. Although Japan has some coal, this has not been the main factor in this pattern of growth. Southern Honshu has the largest tracts of flat land in Japan, the best possibilities for good communications and the best climate. This region has for centuries been the main centre of population in Japan and the base for her civilization. The point is reinforced by recent reports that, despite the rapid increase in total population for many decades, some of the remote mountain regions where conditions for agriculture are poor are actually *losing* population.

This brings me to my last substantial points. I have already argued that agricultural production is tending to be orientated towards conditions of the natural environment. It is also clear that the location of industrial production is also being increasingly affected by conditions of terrain and climate (though not sources of raw materials). The important thing to notice is that the kinds of environmental advantage desirable for both agriculture and industry are often very similar. The conclusion is inescapable: that in a world where resources are scarce, the increasing pressure on what we have is not evenly distributed. On a long-run view, the greatest demands are going to be made on relatively limited areas where the conflict between different possible uses for the same land is going to become increasingly severe.

In Britain, we already have this difficulty in quite an acute form. With the continued expansion of the urban area, there is a running battle between the desire of local authorities and private persons to build on flat and well-drained land on the one side and agriculturalists who want to preserve such terrain for farming since it is often first-class soil. My contention is twofold:

1) Even if there were no increase in total population and no improvement in the amount of dwelling space available per capita this conflict would build up for the reason which I have adduced.

2) What is now happening at a fairly local scale in Britain is likely to become a problem affecting progressively larger regions.

Finally, if one is interested in the stages of economic growth along the lines of Rostow's analysis, there is an interesting sub-division to be made of those economies which have passed the 'take-off' into sustained growth. The first class is one in which the location of the major markets is static, having been inherited from the past. The second is the phase in which the market itself takes on a degree of mobility. The two circumstances provide very different problems for planning and regional development.

In a sense, this last point is a tautology, for we are all of us workers and consumers. If workers flock to a coalfield, then consumers also are congregating there: if consumers choose to reside in Devon, then workers will follow to minister to their needs. Thus, the 'market' has always been mobile in the sense that workers are mobile. The new situation is that markets are mobile because consumers *as consumers* have a greater freedom of choice of where to live: this is reinforced by the fact that as workers we can also be more selective in where we work.

PART III
Alternative Views and Analyses of Decision-Making

INTRODUCTORY NOTE

As noted in the first part of this book, we envision the development of a more complete analysis for the location of manufacturing to be derived from the partial equilibrium and general equilibrium approaches. The preceding selections from the literature have elucidated what we consider to be the major contribution of the partial approach. Although these selections followed an abstract and theoretical tradition, they were also strongly rooted in reality. We wish to proceed to describe the role of the general equilibrium approach in guiding thought and research toward the more complete theory. However, before grappling with the complexity of general equilibrium solutions, it is important to become acquainted with other ways in which scholars attempt to explain locational decisions reached by firms.

One important premise of the partial model was the negligible influence of the firm upon the market price of its product. Hence, under conditions of pure competition, the firm was not concerned with the reactions of competitors. However, it was also noted earlier that the friction of distance (transportation costs) imparts to each producer a limited monopolistic position with regard to consumers closer to him than to other producers. This limited monopolistic position does allow the firm to influence prices; and accordingly, its setting of prices may provoke reactions and retaliatory measures by other firms. In seeking to maximize its profits by choosing the most desirable site, the firm of reality frequently must recognize the possible responses of other firms. It must choose its location, establish its prices, and determine its output after evaluating the direct and indirect repercussions of similar decisions by other firms.

The paper by Stevens illustrates how the influence of distance establishes a spatial monopoly by a producer over nearby customers. The subsequent pricing reactions by competing producers is then demonstrated by Stevens in the context of game theory wherein decision behavior is a critical ingredient in locational strategy. The following article, by Isard and Reiner, though not concerned with pricing as such, expands the framework within which an industrial entrepreneur must make a decision, and illustrates how the system administrator concerned with national goals and regional development can effectively exert leverage on an industrialist's locational strategy or choice.

Another assumption critical in the partial approach is the notion that the firm establishes a price for its product on the basis of costs or some other objectively determined consideration. Behavioral studies of the firm, however, indicate that certain variables internal to the firm influence price and output decisions. Cohen and Cyert present a behavioral approach to the theory of the firm which departs from the traditional view that market considerations and profit maximization dominate price and output decisions. By focusing upon a different set of questions specifically designed to uncover the way in which resources are allocated *within* the firm, they illustrate how the firm can affect the market by its behavior, and that the firm is not completely dominated by market considerations. Relative to behavioral characteristics of the firm, Cochran adds still another dimension by noting the influence of cultural and social forces upon the entrepreneur. Cochran stresses the importance of cultural conditioning to produce a definable modal personality; the entrepreneur assumes a role shaped by the social conditioning of his generation. The importance of goal-setting to the internal behavior of the firm is thus indicated as influenced by exogenous cultural variables.

The last section of this part of the book treats more empirical aspects of locational strategy. In contrast to the abstract, armchair approach toward explaining the existence of a specific manufacturing pattern, numerous studies have followed an interview procedure wherein entrepreneurs are asked why they chose a specific location for their establishments. While these surveys suffer from the unavoidable inadequacies of a "questionnaire," they do reveal a discrepancy between factors considered relevant by theorists and factors which industrialists state as critical. The survey by Mueller and Morgan of Michigan manufacturers illustrates one attempt to measure the importance of "nonpecuniary factors" — those factors which have no obvious effect on costs and revenues — such as personal preferences, good schools, etc. It also investigates those factors whose impacts are indirect and cannot be easily quantified, such as industrial climate, business contacts, etc. This survey and the Greenhut and Colberg survey of Florida manufacturers provide some measure of the relative importance of the usual cost factors in determining the location decision. Also, the latter study presents results by categories of manufacturing; thus, the different significance of certain cost and market factors are indicated for different industries. Both the Michigan and the Florida surveys make a special effort to weigh the relevance of the location decision with respect to new plants as against relocated plants, and with respect to the single-plant firm as against the branch-plant firm.

Market Competition and
Strategies in Locational Equilibrium

AN APPLICATION OF GAME THEORY
TO A PROBLEM IN LOCATION STRATEGY

Benjamin H. Stevens

This paper is an outgrowth of
a course paper written in the spring of 1955 at M.I.T. The autho
wishes to acknowledge the aid of Professor Harold Freeman wh
read the original manuscript of the first part of paper. Work o
the second part of the paper was done more recently and wa
supported, in part, by grants from the National Science Foundatio
and Resources for the Future, Inc. This support is gratefully acknowl
edged. The comments of Duane Marble and Walter Isard hav
been most helpful but neither they, nor anyone also mentioned here
are in any way responsible for the paper's shortcomings.

THIS PAPER EXPLORES the possibility of applying game theory to a simple problem of location strategy: the strategic problem of two competitive sellers locating along a line. The first part of the paper treats the Hotelling [4] and Chamberlin [2] formulation of this problem as a simple two-person zero-sum game, initially under the assumption of perfectly inelastic demand.[1] Then, following Lerner and Singer [7], this assumption is relaxed and results are compared. Some comparisons with Smithies' [10] conclusions are also made.

The second part of the paper deals with a somewhat more realistic problem in which two competitors bid for location franchises along a turnpike. Bidding procedures are developed for certain restricted cases. An appendix provides some more general bidding rules.

THE HOTELLING-CHAMBERLIN PROBLEM

General Assumptions

This problem can be stated simply (and somewhat inaccurately) as the problem of two sellers of a homogeneous product each attempting to locate along a line in such a way as to maximize his profits.[2] The line is assumed to be a main street, a highway, or a railroad. The distribution of buyers along the line is known and the assumption is made that every buyer will always purchase from

---

[1] Since the original work on this paper was done, both Dorfman [3] and Kemeny [6] have used a form of this problem as an example of the application of game theory to a "real" economic problem. The work here in part parallels what they have done but also extends their analyses.

[2] The divergencies from Hotelling's original formulation will be pointed out where they may have significant effects on the results of the analysis. For a brief but inclusive history of the work on this problem see Isard [5].

Reprinted from *Papers and Proceedings of the Regional Science Association*, **7** (1961), 143–157, by permission of the author and editor.

the seller who quotes the lowest delivered price: i.e., F.O.B. price plus transport cost.

Hotelling's formulation is based on the following assumptions: (1) a line of uniform market density, (2) equal and constant transport rates per unit distance in either direction anywhere along the line, and (3) complete inelasticity of demand.[3] Sellers are allowed to adjust both price and location. This latter assumption is difficult to incorporate in a simple game formulation. But since, at equilibrium, F.O.B. price and location are intimately connected, it is possible to analyze location while holding price constant. It is not possible to allow continuous adjustment of location in a game with finite numbers of strategies. The loss in generality here, however, is balanced by a gain in realism. It is more likely that there would be a limited number of desirable locations at towns, cross-roads, or other nodal points.[4] Finally, Hotelling assumes that the second seller locates after the first has already fixed his location. From the game theory viewpoint this is a less interesting problem than simultaneous location unless relocation is assumed to be costless. If it is indeed costless, then the problem reduces again to one of simultaneous location or dynamic adjustment. We will consider both of these possibilities in our game solutions[5].

Game Formulation of the Hotelling-Chamberlin Problem

Figure 1 describes a simple linear market, forty units long, with possible locations a, b, c, d, and e spaced equally along it. Assume that the F.O.B. price for both sellers I and II is $1 per unit and that they both operate without cost. Further assume a uniform transport rate of $.025 per unit commodity per unit distance and one buyer per unit length who will buy one unit no matter what the delivered price.

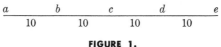

FIGURE 1.

We have already stated that each buyer will always purchase his unit from the seller who can offer the lowest delivered price. If both sellers choose the same location, we assume that they split the available market equally. Furthermore, in order to have a zero-sum game we make the entries in the payoff matrix equal to the advantage of one seller over the other. This advantage is equal to the difference in sales (and profits since seller's operations are assumed

---

[3] The transportation is assumed to be performed by the buyer who goes to the seller to make his purchase and returns home with it. The price paid is assumed to be equal to just the F.O.B. price at the seller plus the transportation to the point of consumption, however. The trip to the store is ignored.

[4] The existence of such nodal points seem to be inconsistent with the assumption of uniform market density. But to keep the game formulation from becoming unnecessarily complex, we will accept this inconsistency.

[5] The simultaneous-location problem is more realistic than it appears at first glance. The discussion in Part two of this paper of the problem of bidding for turnpike franchises is an example.

costless) between the two sellers at their respective locations.[6] For example, suppose one seller locates at a and the other at c. Under our assumptions they would split the market between a and c. The seller at a would sell to the ten consumers between a and b and have sales of $10. The seller at c would capture the whole market between b and e with sales of $30. The appropriate payoff to the seller at c would be $30 - $10 = $20.

The payoff matrix for this first case is given in Table I. We have employed the usual convention of positive signs on payoffs to seller I (whose strategies are listed in the left-hand column) and negative signs on payoffs to seller II (whose strategies are listed across the top of the table). As would be expected, the game is symmetrical and the two sellers completely interchangeable. A stable, unique, equilibrium solution exists when both players choose to locate at c and neithers gains an advantage.[7]

TABLE I. Payoff matrix for Fig. 1 with F.O.B. price $ 1, transport cost
$ 0.25/unit good/unit distance, each consumer buys 1 unit good.

Seller II

		a	b	c	d	e	Row Min.
	a	0	-30	-20	-10	0	-30
	b	30	0	-10	0	10	-10
Seller I	c	20	10	0	10	20	0
	d	10	0	-10	0	30	-10
	e	0	-10	-20	-30	0	-30
Col. Max.		30	10	0	10	30	

This solution is consistent with Hotelling's conclusions for his case where both sellers are free to move without cost. We can follow the dynamics of the adjustment process via the payoff matrix in Table 1. Suppose seller I enters the market first and locates at a. When seller II enters the market he will then locate at b and gain an advantage of $30. Seller I will then move to c with an advantage of $10. Finally, seller II will also move to c and all advantages will be eliminated. Neither can gain any advantage by moving from this point. The solution with both sellers at c is thus a stable solution under adjustment

---

[6] The use of advantages as payoffs is not particularly important in this first case because total sales are fixed at forty units. Thus the game is constant-sum and could be solved by zero-sum methods. It becomes important in later cases where the total value of sales by both sellers depends upon their *pattern* of location. Using advantages as payoffs allows us to make zero-sum games out of non-zero-sum situations. It could also be argued that advantage is the relevant criterion for a seller if his goal is long-run profit maximization achieved through ruining his opponent and driving him out of the market.

[7] Readers unfamiliar with game theory and the solution of simple matrix games are referred to Baumol [1], Luce and Raiffa [8], McKinsey [9], or the highly readable exposition by Williams [11]. For the moment, notice that the *expected* value of a symmetric game must be zero to both competitors. A seller can gain a *real* advantage only if his opponent uses a non-optimal strategy.

as well as the minimax solution under simultaneous location.[8] However, notice that this is not the optimum welfare solution. Total costs to consumers (and total transportation costs) would be minimized by having one seller at b and the other at d.

Game Formulation with Moderately Elastic Demand

Lerner and Singer [7] reanalyzed the problem of location along a line by putting heavier emphasis on the effects of transportation costs. They also considered cases where demand is moderately elastic so that the pattern of delivered prices becomes an important determinant of total sales. It is instructive to parallel their approach in a game formulation of the problem. Maintain, for the moment, all of the previous assumptions except that now each consumer will buy two units if the delivered price is between $1 and $1.25, one unit if it is between $1.25 and $1.50, and no units if it exceeds $1.50.

The appropriate payoff matrix is found in Table II. The minimax solution occurs again with both sellers located at c. However, our use of *advantages* as the payoffs here tends to obscure the fact that total sales at the minimax solution would be 60 units, while total sales with sellers located at b and d would be 80 units. Since we are assuming a strictly non-cooperative game, however, the "b-d" pattern would not normally arise. Were it possible to force such a pattern the outcome would be advantageous to both buyers and sellers.

TABLE II. **Payoff matrix for Fig. 1 with F.O.B. price $ 1, transport cost $ .025/unit good/unit distance. Each consumer buys 2 units of good if delivered price is between $ 1 and $ 1.25, 1 unit if price is between $ 1.25 and $ 1.50, and no units over $ 1.50.**

| | | Seller II | | | | | |
	a	b	c	d	e	Row Min.
a	0	-30	-30	-20	0	-30
b	30	0	-10	0	20	-10
c	30	10	0	10	30	0
d	20	0	-10	0	30	-10
e	0	-20	-30	-30	0	-30
Col. Max.	30	10	0	10	30	

Seller I labels rows.

It is interesting to consider Smithies' [10] conclusions on the problem of moderate elasticity of demand. He investigates the ratio of the cost of trans-

---

[8] Rather than assuming equal market division, Hotelling assumed that if both sellers locate at the same point, the one facing the larger market would gain an advantage. Thus, if seller I located first at a, seller II would also locate at a but to the right of seller I so as to capture the entire market to the right. Seller I would then move to b, seller II would follow him there but to his right and so on until both again settle permanently at c. However, it seems more realistic (and makes the game easier to formulate) to assume equal market division when both sellers locate at the same point. *Ceteris paribus*, there is no reason why either of two stores located side by side should be more attractive to consumers than the other (particularly if the only parking lot is located between them).

porting one unit of commodity the whole length of the market to the highest price that consumers are willing to pay. For the case described above this ratio is $40 \times \$0.025/\$1.50 = 2/3$. This is roughly equivalent to Smithies' "critical" value of 4/7 *below* which both competitors locate at the center and *above* which neither locates at the center.

We can give an approximate indication of this effect if we leave our demand assumptions unaltered but double our transport costs to $0.05 per unit commodity per unit distance.[9] The ratio is then $40 \times \$0.5/\$1.50 = 4/3$, substantially above the critical value of 4/7. The corresponding game matrix is presented in Table III. Notice that there are now three equally good strategies—*b*, *c*, and *d*—for each of the two competitors. If each chose his strategy randomly from this

TABLE III. Payoff matrix for Fig. 1 with F.O.B. price $ 1, transport cost $ .05/unit good/per unit distance. Each consumer buys 2 units of good if delivered price is between $ 1 and $ 1.25, 1 unit if price is between $ 1.25 and $ 1.50, and no units over $ 1.50.

		Seller II					
		a	b	c	d	e	Row Min.
Seller I	a	0	−30	−30	−30	0	−30
	b	30	0	0	0	30	0
	c	30	0	0	0	30	0
	d	30	0	0	0	30	0
	e	0	−30	−30	−30	0	−30
Col. Max.		30	0	0	0	30	

trio of possibilities, any one of nine minimax solutions could occur. But if it happened that both located at *b*, for example, and movement were costless it would pay for one of them to move to *d*. By so doing he would lose no advantage but would thereby share in a larger total of sales. Specifically, with both sellers at *b*, *c*, or *d* total sales would be 30 units; with one at *c* and the other at *b* or *d*, 45 units; and with one at *b* and the other at *d*, 60 units. Knowing this, and knowing that *b* and *d* strategies are not "punishable", rational sellers would choose only between *b* and *d*. A stable equilibrium solution would eventually come about with one seller at each of these two quartile points.[10]

Alternative Formulations

Further examples could be given with various combinations of transport

---

[9] Our first example, Table I, has already provided a case where the ratio is less than 4/7. In this case demand was perfectly inelastic so that the maximum price that consumers were willing to pay is theoretically infinite. Therefore, the ratio is $40 \times \$ .025/\$ \infty = 0$. As would be expected from this low a ratio, both sellers located at the center.

[10] In Smithies' more general analysis of continuous location, the actual equilibrium occurs with the two sellers located somewhat closer to the center than the quartile points. Our deviation from Smithies' solution is due to our assumptions of discrete locations and demand quantities.

costs and demand elasticities.[11] This would not, however, add appreciably to the demonstration of the use of game theory to solve the classical problem of location along a line nor would it substantially alter the conclusions of previous authors. Unfortunately the limitations of game theory seem to prevent the systematic treatment of more general location strategy problems with several sellers, continuous location choice, and so forth. Extension of the two-person theory to cases with discrete location choice over areas rather than lines and to cases with uneven spatial distribution of demand is possible but presents certain practical difficulties. These difficulties are ones of spatial aggregation rather than of the applicability of game theory. These problems are currently under study and the results of this work will be reported in a later paper.

THE BIDDING PROBLEM FOR TURNPIKE FRANCHISES

For the moment we turn to the somewhat more realistic problem of bidding for turnpike service franchises. This is clearly a strategic problem involving both the Hotelling-Chamberlin problem and more general bidding strategy problems. It has the distinct advantage that bids are, in fact, made simultaneously and, presumably, non-cooperatively by the competitors. Thus the problem realistically fulfills the criterion of "simultaneous" location choice.

For obvious reasons we again limit our analysis to cases involving two sellers. We also assume that the sellers have exactly equal funds available to bid.[12] Bids are sealed so that neither knows what the other is doing. Sites are awarded to the highest bidder with the flip of a coin used to decide ties: i.e. the expected value of a location to a seller is zero if both bid equal amounts on it. And again, each seller is attempting to maximize his advantage over his competitor.

Problem with Uniform Location Profitabilities

Suppose a turnpike has available for lease three service locations which are projected to have equal profitability. The payoff for winning a location is $1; the payoff for a losing bid is zero.[13] The equal funds allocated by the two

---

[11] One further example is of some interest. The present author attempted to duplicate the Lerner-Singer [7] three-seller case by the questionable expedient of allowing one of the two sellers to locate two stores while the other was limited to a single store. This avoided the problem of dealing with a three-person game and resulted in mixed strategies for both sellers. It was possible to trace through the matrix and demonstrate the three-plant instability found by Lerner and Singer [7] under the assumption of costless movement of stores.

[12] Obviously a seller with larger bidding resources can always gain some advantage over his competitor. But our assumption is not too restrictive if we consider that the two sellers are actually going to bid only a portion of their total capital available for such purposes for the locations on a particular turnpike. This portion is set with a view to the opportunity costs involved in overinvesting in a particular location or set of locations. If we can assume that both bidders are large corporations with similar cost and profit structures, the assumption of equal bidding power does not appear unreasonable. Alternatively, if the bids are to be in terms of percentages of gross sales at locations, we could assume that the market estimates of the two sellers would be approximately the same.

[13] Unexpended funds left over from losing bids are of no further use to the seller in bidding on this turnpike since it is assumed that franchise allocation is a one-shot process. Of course, such funds could be allocated to later bidding on another turnpike. Unfortunately, such a multi-stage process is beyond the scope of the present paper.

sellers to bidding for franchises on this turnpike are assumed to be entirely bid: i.e. if a seller wins all the locations he bids on, his bid funds will be exactly used up. Each then has the choice of bidding on any one, any two, or all three locations. In all cases we assume that the seller will divide his bid funds equally among the locations on which he bids.[14]

TABLE IV.   **Payoff matrix for bidding on three franchises, each with a profitability of $ 1 to the seller who wins it.**

		a	b	c	ab	bc	ac	abc	Row Min.
	a	0	0	0	0	−1	0	−1	−1
	b	0	0	0	0	0	−1	−1	−1
Seller I	c	0	0	0	−1	0	0	−1	−1
	ab	0	0	1	0	0	0	1	0
	bc	1	0	0	0	0	0	1	0
	ac	0	1	0	0	0	0	1	0
	abc	1	1	1	−1	−1	−1	0	−1
Col. Max.		1	1	1	0	0	0	1	

(Seller II across the top)

The appropriate payoff matrix is found in Table IV. The construction of the matrix is somewhat more complicated than in our previous cases. Take as an example the entry where seller I bids on a and b and seller II bids on b alone. Obviously seller I will win location a since seller II does not bid on it. However, seller II will win location b since he allocates all of his bid funds to it while seller I allocates only one-half of his. Since they have equal available funds, seller II's bid is larger. Each wins one location and all locations are equally profitable; therefore neither gains an advantage and the appropriate entry is zero.

There are three saddle-point solutions for this game. Each seller will always bid on two randomly-selected locations and gain no advantage over his rival. It is instructive that a bid on a single location is never worth-while and that a bid on all three locations is advantageous only if the other seller bids on only one location (which he will never do).

Problem with Different Location Profitabilities

Another simple example is provided by the case in which one location is definitely superior to the others. Suppose we retain our previous assumptions except that b is now twice as profitable as a or c: i.e. the payoff for winning b is $ 2 and for a or c is $ 1. The game matrix, Table V(a) gives a unique

---

[14] It is possible to show that if all locations are equally profitable, if both sellers have equal bid funds, and if both must bid all available funds it is irrational to bid differing amounts on different locations *if they are bid on at all*. Under these assumptions, any advantage gained at one location through unequal bids would be balanced by a loss at another location. The seller's expected advantage is just as high for equal bids as it would be for unequal bids. Thus each seller will bid all his funds on one location, one-half on each of two locations, or one-third on each of three locations.

addle-point solution with both sellers bidding all available funds on b. Notice
hat any other strategy by one seller can gain him nothing or lose him $1 as
ong as his rival sticks to a single bid on b. This case incorporates to some
xtent the problem of location, as well as bidding, strategy. It would, in fact,
e the relevant solution where demand was equally distributed along the turnpike,
here a and c were end-points and b the center-point, and where buyers could
nd would always go to the nearest service area.

TABLE V(a). Payoff matrix for bidding on three franchises Profitability of b is $2; profitability a or c, $1; Bids equally distributed among locations bid upon.

		Seller II							
		a	b	c	ab	bc	ac	abc	Row Min.
Seller I	a	0	−1	0	−1	−2	0	−2	−2
	b	1	0	1	1	1	0	0	0
	c	0	−1	0	−2	−1	0	−2	−2
	ab	1	−1	2	0	0	1	2	−1
	bc	2	−1	1	0	0	1	2	−1
	ac	0	0	0	−1	−1	0	0	−1
	abc	2	0	2	−2	−2	0	0	−2
Col. Max.		2	0	2	1	1	1	2	

A difficulty arises, however. If both competitors bid on b they are both
gambling all on the flip of a coin. If one knew that the other would always
bid on b, he could then win a and c by token bids. Under our assumptions he
ould not do this and also equal his rival's bid on b. Unfortunately, it is exactly
t this point that our assumption of equal bidding power seems most unrealistic.
Still, if both were willing to allocate extra funds to side bids on a and c, each
would be running the risk that his opponent would bid these extra funds all
n b or, better still, on a combination of b with a or c and gain a real advan-
age. As long as the sellers are actually equal in *total* bidding power, the
minimax solution dictates bidding all on b.

This result may be intuitively more obvious than the result for the case of
qual profitabilities. It is more difficult, however, to justify equal distribution
f bid funds among all locations bid upon where the locations differ in profitability. An alternative would be to assume that the sellers allocate their bid
unds in proportion to the values of the locations bid upon: e.g. in bidding on
a and b, 2/3 of the available funds would be bid on b and 1/3 on a. Table V(b)
gives the results of recalculating the payoffs for proportional bids.

Notice that the payoffs in Table V(b) differ from those in Table V(a) only
where an ac bid is matched against an ab or bc bid. These differences are
nough to produce another set of saddle-point solutions: each seller can now
play either b or ac or some mixture thereof without fear of any loss no matter
what his opponent does. One would still tend to favor strategy b, however, be-
ause of its effectiveness against non-optimal bidding by the opponent. Strategy
ac can never gain either seller an advantage; strategy b might. A later example
will demonstrate much more substantial differences between the solutions for

equal bids and for proportional bids.

TABLE V(b). Same as Table V(a) with bids by both sellers proportional to location profitabilities.

Seller II

		a	b	c	ab	bc	ac	abc	Row Min.
	a	0	−1	0	−1	−2	0	−2	−2
	b	1	0	1	1	1	0	0	0
Seller I	c	0	−1	0	−2	−1	0	−2	−2
	ab	1	−1	2	0	0	0	2	−1
	bc	2	−1	1	0	0	0	2	−1
	ac	0	0	0	0	0	0	0	0
	abc	2	0	2	−2	−2	0	0	−2
Col. Max.		2	0	2	1	1	0	2	

It is also interesting to consider what would happen if one seller used pro portional bidding while the other used equal bids. Table V(c) gives the payof matrix for our same simple problem with the difference that here seller I bids in proportion to location profitabilities while seller II distributes his bid funds equally among the locations he bids upon. Again the solution is only slightly altered. Seller I can use either strategy b or strategy abc with impunity; seller II can use strategy b or strategy ac; and the value of the game is still zero to both competitors so that neither gains an advantage.[15] For seller II, b is vastly better than ac against foolish bidding by seller I. Seller I might have a hard time deciding between b and abc as the best strategy against the contingency of non-optimal bidding by seller II.[16]

TABLE V(c). Same as Table V(a) but with bids of seller I proportional to profitabilities and equal bids by seller II.

Seller II

		a	b	c	ab	bc	ac	abc	Row Min.
	a	0	−1	0	−1	−2	0	−2	−2
	b	1	0	1	1	1	0	0	0
Seller I	c	0	−1	0	−2	−1	0	−2	−2
	a	1	−1	2	1	2	0	1	−1
	bc	2	−1	1	2	1	0	1	−1
	ac	0	0	0	−1	−1	0	0	−1
	abc	2	0	2	0	0	0	0	0
Col. Max.		2	0	2	2	2	0	1	

[15] Because of the simple nature of this problem and the numbers used, seller I does not gain any *real* advantage through the use of a seemingly preferable bidding procedure. The more complex problem discussed below will demonstrate that the advantage does, in fact lie with the proportional bidder.

[16] The non-optimality here refers to seller II's choice among his equal-bid strategies and not to his choice between equal bidding and proportional bidding. We have already made this latter choice for him in Table V(c).

380

Problem with Different Location Profitabilities and Mixed Strategies

A more interesting example is provided by a case where all three locations differ in profitability. Again assume a turnpike with an even distribution of demand but with the location arrangement of Figure 2.

| 1/9 | a | 4/9 | b | 4/9 | c |

FIGURE 2.

With this division of the total line-market, the relative sales (and profitabilities) are $a:b:c = 3:4:2$. Again we assume that two sellers, I and II, are each interested only in advantage over the rival seller, and that the expected value of a location to a seller is zero if both bid equal amounts on it.

TABLE VI(a). Payoff matrix for bidding on three franchises; Profitabilities: a-\$3, b-\$4, c-\$2; and bid funds equally distributed among locations bid.

		Seller II							
		a	b	c	ab	bc	ac	abc	Row Min.
Seller I	a	0	−1	1	−1	−3	1	−3	−3
	b	1	0	2	1	2	−1	−1	−1
	c	−1	−2	0	−5	−2	−1	−5	−5
	ab	1	−1	5	0	1	2	5	−1
	bc	3	−2	2	−1	0	−1	3	−2
	ac	−1	1	1	−2	−1	0	1	−2
	abc	3	1	5	−5	−3	−1	0	−5
Col. Max.		3	1	5	1	2	2	5	

The appropriate payoff matrix where both employ equal bid distribution is found in Table VI(a). Notice that there is no simple saddle-point solution. The solution is not difficult to determine, however, since strategies a, c, bc, and abc are all dominated. Both players should play a mixture of b, ab, and ac probabilities:[17]

$$X_b = 1/2$$
$$X_{ab} = 1/4$$
$$X_{ac} = 1/4$$

The expected advantage is, of course, zero for both sellers.

The solution where both players use proportional bids is not nearly so simple and, in this case, is quite different from the solution for equal bids. Table VI(b) is the payoff matrix for proportional bids. Strategy c is the only one which is strictly dominated although it turns out that strategy bc also is not used. The remaining strategies are employed with probabilities:

$$X_a = 7/23$$
$$X_b = 3/23$$
$$X_{ab} = 3/23$$

---

[17] The reader is again referred to any of the standard references on game theory for a discussion of dominance, mixed strategies, and the use of random devices in minimax problems.

$$X_{ac} = 9/23$$
$$X_{abc} = 1/23$$

TABLE VI(b). Same as Table VI(a) but with bids proportional to Location profitabilities by both sellers.

Seller II

		a	b	c	ab	bc	ac	abc	Row Min.
	a	0	−1	1	−1	−3	1	−3	−3
	b	1	0	2	1	2	−1	−1	−1
Seller I	c	−1	−2	0	−5	−2	−1	−5	−5
	ab	1	−1	5	0	−3	−1	5	−3
	bc	3	−2	2	3	0	−1	3	−2
	ac	−1	1	1	1	1	0	1	−1
	abc	3	1	5	−5	−3	−1	0	−5
Col. Max.		3	1	5	3	2	1	5	

It is particularly noteworthy that strategy a, which was dominated by strategy ab in the equal-bid case, should now be used with a probability of almost 1/3. This is partly explained by the changes in payoffs to strategy ab between the equal-bid and proportional-bid cases. Comparison of Tables VI(a) and VI(b) shows the substantial drop in the payoffs to ab when used against bc or ac. These reductions mean that ab no longer dominates a. The high probability on a is due to the fact that the reductions in payoffs to ab and bc when employed against ac makes a the best answering strategy against the latter: only a gives a positive payoff against ac. With the rises in payoffs to ac against ab and bc, ac gets a heavy play; therefore its counter-strategy, a, must also be heavily used in a minimax solution.

The question naturally arises as to what would happen if one seller used proportional bids while the other used equal bids. The relevant payoff matrix is given in Table VI(c). It is reasonable to assume for the moment that seller I uses proportional bids assuming that his opponent will do likewise. On the basis of this assumption he would play his strategies with the proportional-bid probabilities given above and expect a zero advantage. By the same token, we

TABLE VI(c). Same as Table VI(a) but with seller I using Proportional bids and seller II, equal bids.

Seller II

		a	b	c	ab	bc	ac	abc	Row Min.
	a	0	−1	1	−1	−3	1	−3	−3
	b	1	0	2	1	2	−1	−1	−1
Seller I	c	−1	−2	0	−5	−2	−1	−5	−5
	ab	1	−1	5	1	5	−1	5	−1
	bc	3	−2	2	3	2	−1	1	−2
	ac	−1	1	1	1	−3	1	1	−3
	abc	3	1	5	−5	−3	−1	2	−5
Col. Max.		3	1	5	3	5	1	5	

382

can assume that seller II uses equal bids because he thinks his opponent will do likewise. He therefore employs the equal-bid probabilities for strategies b, ab, and ac as previously given, and expects zero advantage.

Using the two different sets of probabilities for the two sellers and the payoff matrix of Table VI(c), it is then a simple matter to compute the actual advantages. If we look at the problem from the point of view of seller I, we can form Table VI(d). This shows that seller I would have an expected advantage of $\$3/23$ (and player II, an expected disadvantage of the same amount). This indicates that if it is not known whether the opponent will use equal or proportional bids, the use of proportional bids is the best strategy: it gives a player no worse than a zero advantage if his opponent uses proportional bids, and a positive advantage if he does not.[18]

TABLE VI(d). Expected advantage of seller I using optimal proportional-bid strategies over seller II using optimal equal-bid strategies.

Seller I's Strategies	Seller II's Strategies						Expected Payoff To Seller I	Seller I's Probabilities
	b		ab		ac			
	P'off	Prob.	P'off	Prob.	P'off	Prob.		
a	$-1 \times 1/2 +$		$-1 \times 1/4 +$		$1 \times 1/4 =$		$-1/2 \times$	$7/23$
b	$0 \times 1/2 +$		$1 \times 1/4 +$		$-1 \times 1/4 =$		$0 \times$	$3/23$
ab	$-1 \times 1/2 +$		$1 \times 1/4 +$		$-1 \times 1/4 =$		$-1/2 \times$	$3/23$
ac	$1 \times 1/2 +$		$1 \times 1/4 +$		$1 \times 1/4 =$		$1 \times$	$9/23$
abc	$1 \times 1/2 +$		$-5 \times 1/4 +$		$-1 \times 1/4 =$		$-1 \times$	$1/23$

Total expected advantage to I $= \$3/23$

Conclusions

The last example given was only the second in which the game was non-symmetrical and the first in which one seller could actually gain a real advantage over the other. One may wonder whether a game whose value is always zero (if both sellers bid optimally) is worth the bother of playing it. But the value is zero in both the Hotelling-Chamberlin problem, and in the turnpike probelm, only if both sellers are equally sophisticated. In any real situation it is unlikely that both sellers would be equally adroit at solving the location-strategy problem. And, as we have repeatedly pointed out, non-optimal play can be costly.

Furthermore, we must not forget that many of our basic assumptions were unrealistic. Preliminary work indicates, and we should expect, that bidding strategies would be very different where one seller has substantially greater total bidding power than the other. This will involve cases where the more

---

[18] Of course the probabilities assigned and the advantages expected by both sellers might be somewhat different if seller I knew that seller II would always use equal bids and seller II knew that seller I would always use proportional bids. It is possible, but not likely, that seller I could do better than an expected value of $\$3/23$ under these conditions. However, he could do no better with any combination of equal-bid and proportional-bid strategies. Any approach of this sort would give him an advantage equal to some weighted average of $\$0$ and $\$3/23$.

powerful seller is seeking maximize his positive advantage and the weaker is seeking to minimize his real disadvantage.

We have already mentioned the possibility of relaxing the assumptions of a line market and of even distribution of demand. But this work, together with the relaxation of the assumption of equal bidding power, is still not likely to allow us to draw very general conclusions or to develop bidding rules of universal applicability. It is in the nature of strategic games that the interesting cases, at least, do not permit easy generalization. We have found it possible to present in an appendix some bidding rules for n locations applicable under the restrictive assumptions of this paper. But we are not optimistic about the possibility that more complex cases will submit to even this minor sort of generalization. It is more likely that each case will have peculiar (and intriguing) features of its own.

Nevertheless, it is hoped that this brief paper is at least suggestive of the possibilities in the application of game theory to problems of location strategy. The writer shares the disappointment of many others that, after its hopeful beginnings, game theory has been stymied by the difficult mathematical and conceptual problems of non-zero sum and multi-person games. Still we should not overlook the potentialities of simple two-person, zero-sum theory. Even such limited theory can provide insights and suggest approaches to the solution of location problems as well as other problems in the realm of business competition.

APPENDIX ON BIDDING RULES FOR EQUAL BIDS

The rules given below are based on the writer's experience with location strategy games and, to some extent, on the symmetry of the simple games. The rules are intended to be suggestive and are presented without proof.

It is clear that neither seller can gain an advantage in a symmetric game. In the turnpike franchise problems, then, each seller's aim is to assure himself of at least one-half of the available profits. He is therefore most interested in those combinations of locations which will provide at least half the total sales. He is constrained, however, by the fact that if he bids on a great many or all locations, his rival can "punish" him by bidding on, for example, one fewer location. The rival thereby allocates a higher bid to each and wins all but one location. The bidder must therefore avoid combinations with large numbers of locations.

In cases where one location is more profitable than the others, the bidder will be interested in combinations involving this location. This will allow him to achieve the highest possible profits from the smallest number of locations thereby permitting high bids on each. The seller may also bid on the high-profit location alone in order to punish his opponent's use of strategies which contain both the high-profit location and one or a few other locations. The use of these strategies will depend heavily on the relative values of the high-profit and other locations. Finally, combinations which would give higher total profits than the high-profit location may be employed to punish the use of bids on the high-value location alone.

A. Consider a turnpike with n locations all of equal profitability; K:

$$v_1 = v_2 = \cdots = v_n = K$$

1. Then, if n is even, all strategies containing $n/2$ locations should be used with equal probability. Since there are $(n!/[(n/2)!(n/2)!]) = C_e$ such combinations, each should be used with probability $1/C_e$.

2. If n is odd, and $n > 3$, all strategies containing $(n - 1/2)$ or $(n + 1/2)$ locations should be used, again with equal probability. Since there are

$$2 \times \frac{n!}{\left(\dfrac{n+1}{2}\right)! \left(\dfrac{n-1}{2}\right)!} = C_0$$

such strategies, each should be used with probability $1/C_0$.

3. In each case, equal amounts should be bid on all locations in each bidding combination.

B. Consider a turnpike with n locations, one of which, the m-th, is more profitable than any of the others which are of equal profitability K:

$$v_1 = v_2 = \cdots = v_{m-1} = v_{m+1} = \cdots = v_n = K$$
$$v_m > K$$

1. If $v_m \geqq [(n - 1)K + v_m]/2)$, bid all funds on location m (use strategy m with probability of one).

2. If $v_m < [(n - 1)K + v_m]/2)$, use a mixture of strategies. This mixture *need not* contain strategies other than following:

   a). Strategy m

   b). Strategies containing m plus any g other locations such that:

$$[v_m + (g - 1)K] \leqq \frac{(n - 1)K + v_m}{2} \leqq [v_m + gK]$$

   c). Strategies excluding m and containing h locations such that:

$$(h - 1)K \leqq \frac{(n - 1)K + v_m}{2} \leqq hK$$

   d). Strategies excluding m and containing any f other locations such that: $fK \geqq v_m$

   e). Strategies containing m and any f other locations (definition of of f as above).

3. In each case, equal amounts should be bid on all locations in each bidding combination.

The foregoing may not appear to have eliminated many possible strategies. And even if it has, the ones left must still be placed in a payoff matrix and probabilities computed by suitable means. This may sometimes be an arduous task, but often there will be a simple saddle-point solution. In any case, substantial effort may be saved by concentrating attention on the strategies outlined above, especially in large-scale problems.

Unfortunately the writer has not been able, as yet, to develop a set of simple, workable rules for cases where several locations differ in profitability or where proportional bids are used. The examples given in the body of the paper ma indicate why this is so.

REFERENCES

[1] Baumol, W. J., *Economic Theory and Operations Analysis*, Prentice-Hall, Englewoc Cliffs, New Jersey, 1961, Chapter 18.
[2] Chamberlin, E., *The Theory of Monopolistic Competition*, Harvard University Pres Cambridge, Mass., 1937, Appendix C.
[3] Dorfman, R., P. A. Samuelson, and R. M. Solow, *Liniar Programming and Econom Analysis*, McGraw-Hill, New York, 1958, pp. 427-8.
[4] Hotelling, H., "Stability in Competition," in G. J. Stigler and K. E. Boulding (eds. *Readings in Price Theory*, Richard D. Irwin, Chicago, 1952, pp. 467-484.
[5] Isard, W., *Location and Space-Economy*, John Wiley & Sons, New York, 1956, p 158-165.
[6] Kemeny, J. G., J. L. Snell, and G. L. Thompson, *Introduction to Finite Mathematic* Prentice-Hall, Englewood Cliffs, New Jersey, 1956, p. 301, example 11.
[7] Lerner, A. P. and H. W. Singer, "Some Notes on Duopoly and Spatial Competition *The Journal of Political Economy*, Vol. XLV, 1937, pp. 145-186.
[8] Luce, R. D. and H. Raiffa, *Games and Decisions*, John Wiley and Sons, New York, 195
[9] McKinsey, J. C. C., *Introduction to the theory of Games*, McGraw-Hill, New Yor 1952.
[10] Smithies, A., "Optimum Location in Spatial Competition," *Journal of Political Econom* Vol. XLIX, 1941, pp. 423-9.
[11] Williams, J. D., *The Compleat Strategyst*, McGraw-Hill, New York, 1954.

ASPECTS OF DECISION-MAKING THEORY
AND REGIONAL SCIENCE

Walter Isard and Thomas A. Reiner

The authors are indebted to the National Science Foundation and to Resources for the Future, Inc., for grants in support of the research underlying this paper.

IN THIS PAPER we wish to explore the potential of certain new concepts and approaches pertaining to decision-making and related areas which have been developing in recent years. We wish to carry on this inquiry because we feel that traditional economic, sociological, political, psychological, and regional theories are highly inadequate for projecting behavior with respect to certain key problems of basic interest to regional scientists and planners.

The purpose of this paper is not, however, to present technical materials that have been developed elsewhere.[1] Our objective is to present a concrete illustration of how these new ideas and approaches in decision making can be used for the projection of behavior. The illustration will concern a basic location-investment decision.

Let there be the following:

(1) a hypothetical nation X, consisting of several regions, some of which are considerably underdeveloped;

(2) a major industrialist who has at his disposal a large sum of capital for investment purposes;

(3) concern on the part of one or more national planning units with national economic growth;

(4) concern of a regional planning unit in an underdeveloped region with attracting new industry and employment to the region, thereby to decreases unemployment and raise regional per capita income; and

(5) concern on the part of an urban planning unit with projecting and guiding the future land use pattern and transportation structure of a capital city.

To present the problem on a manageable scale, we construct Table 1. There it is assumed that the industrialist can only see four possible courses of action in terms of using and investing the capital at his disposal:[2]

[1] For detailed discussion of the points raised by this paper, and for supporting literature, see: W. Isard and M. Dacey, "On the Projection of Behavior in Regional Analysis," *Journal of Regional Science*, Vol. IV, 1962.

[2] In technical terms, his perceived action space consists of four alternatives.

Reprinted from *Papers and Proceedings of the Regional Science Association*, 9 (1962), 25–33, by permission of the authors and editor.

A) develop a textile complex in the underdeveloped region, taking advantag
   of the presence of an abundant supply of cheap labor;
B) purchase securities of foreign companies, depositing these securities out
   side the country;
C) construct an integrated steel works in the capital city; and
D) construct a metals fabricating complex in the capital city based upo
   the import of steel and metal ingots and shapes.

Also, let this individual believe that four (and only four) states of th
environment are possible in the relevant future. That is, the socio-politic
economic context may take any one of several forms; no one outcome on th
international, national, and regional scene can be forecast with certainty. W
have categorized these four states as follows:

I. nation X joins the Common Market; her present political regime stay
in office, and political stability obtains;

II. nation X does not join the Common Market; her present politic
regime stays in office and political stability obtains;

III. nation X does not join the Common Market; political revolution occurs
and the new regime socializes all industries without compensation; and

IV. nation X does not join the Common Market; her present politic
regime loses the election and the new government nationalizes all heavy in
dustries with partial compensation.

Then, if we assume that the actions of other individuals and groups ca
have no further influence whatsoever on the outcomes associated with eac
action of the industrialist, we may, for example, specify an outcome matri
for the industrialist as follows:

TABLE I. An Hypothetical Outcome Matrix.

		States of the Environment			
		I	II	III	IV
Industrialist's	A	225	196	0	100
	B	100	100	81	144
Alternatives	C	0	361	0	25
	D	100	324	0	25

As soon as we set down an outcome matrix of the type, a number of basi
questions arise. One refers to the manner in which the industrialist deter
mines that there are these four action alternatives and these four states of th
environment. Another concerns the way in which the numbers in the matri
cells are derived. The manner in which the industrialist assigns or associate
a probability (subjective) to the occurrence of each state of the environment i
yet another question.[3]

---

[3] Particularly enlightening discussion of these questions is in C. West Churchman
"Decision and Value Theorem," in Russell L. Ackoff, ed., *Progress in Operations Research*
Vol. 1, John Wiley, New York, 1961.

26

Such a matrix representation, furthermore, fails to take into account a number of vital considerations. First, the industrialist's action is a one-time decision: the outcome matrix in the simple form of Table 1 does not allow for any feedback effects between actions of the industrialist and the state of the environment. Neither does the information contained in the matrix offer any explicit knowledge as to the industrialist's motivations (money, power, prestige, etc.). Moreover, the matrix says nothing about how the industrialist internalizes the numbers in the matrix cells; that is, transforms the numbers (outcomes) into a set of payoffs (utilities) which have real meaning to him. Finally, such a matrix implies not only the assumption (already noted) that other individuals and groups can have no influence on these outcomes, but also that the industrialist has a complete set of relevant (if not accurate) information[4].

Before considering any of these basic matters, however, let us note the major step forward that this framework permits. Traditional economic and location theories and their operational counterparts (such as comparative cost and industrial complex analyses, and interregional linear programming) for the most part assume, implicitly at least, that there is no risk or uncertainty with respect to the states of the environment, or that the risks can be satisfactorily discounted. They assume that the industrialist has available complete knowledge about the (discounted) state of the environment that will exist. In effect, these assumptions which underlie such theories and techniques compress the matrix into one column. Then, of course, the problem of the maximizer (or optimizer) is to find the highest outcome in the single column—and the above mentioned theories and techniques become valuable as shortcut methods for identifying this highest outcome when many action-alternatives are possible.

In reality, however, there are many problems for which the concept of a multiple-column outcome matrix and statistical decision-making theory in general are much more relevant. As soon as we recognize this and allow the possibility that more than one state of the environment may occur, the problem of projecting behavior is no longer a simple one. The attitude of the industrialist immediately becomes a basic variable which must be identified before his behavior can be projected. For example, let us consider several possible attitudes:

a. The industrialist is a conservative-banker type. He does not want to take chances. For each action alternative (row), he finds the lowest possible (i.e., the worst possible) outcome. In Table 1. these are 0 for A, 81 for B, 0 for C, and 0 for D.

He then picks that action whose worst possible outcome is higher than any other — that is he adopts a "max-min" strategy. In Table 1, this approach calls for action B, which guarantees to the industrialist a minimum outcome of 81. If he pursues that action in which the max-min occurs, no matter what happens, he will get at least that much, namely 81. Note that this conservative person does not even consider the concept of prob-

---

[4] For further discussion of some of these points, see: M. Shubik, "Approaches to the Study of Decision-Making Relevant to the Firm," *The Journal of Business*, Vol. 34, April 1961, pp. 101–118.

27

ability. He choses action B even if the probability of the corresponding state of the environment (state III) is very small.

b. Closely associated with the conservative-banker type is the 100 per cent pessimist, who always imagines that nature is "out to get him." The pessimist, in essence, takes each row, orders the outcome elements in each row in terms of size, and tends to assign a probability factor of 1.0 (or close to 1.0) to the lowest element in each row. He therefore comes to focus his attention on the worst element in each row, and then selects the best of these. Like the conservative banker, he would select action B in Table 1, because 81, the minimum of row B, is higher than the minimum of any other row.

c. At the other extreme is the 100 per cent optimist. Like the conservative banker and the 100 percent pessimist, he doesn't evaluate the likelihoods of the several states of the environment. He considers each action-alternative (row) and picks out the highest element corresponding to it. In Table 1, these are 225 for A, 144 for B, 361 for C, aud 324 for D. Then pursuing a "max-max" strategy, he selects that action associated with the best of these maxima. In Table 1, the best of these maxima is 361, and the corresponding action is C.

d. Still another attitude is that of the cold, calculating strategist or businessman. He assigns probabilities to the occurrence of each state of the environment, and, *ceteris paribus*, chooses that action with the highest expected outcome. For example, in Table I, if the industrialist assigns a probability of .50 to state I, .20 to state II, .10 to state III, and .20 to state IV, the expected outcome for A will be:

$$.50(225)+.20(196)+.10(0)+.20(100)=171.$$

The outcome for B will, similarly, be 107, for C will be 77, and, for D, 120. The industrialist therefore selects action A.

e. The industrialist may have still another attitude. On one hand, he may not be as careful a calculator as is implied by his maximizing expected outcome. On the other hand, he may not be an extremist. He may mix both pessimism and optimism. For example, he may argue that the probability is 0.5 that the highest outcome associated with any action will be realized, and 0.5 that the least outcome will be realized. His strategy will then be to choose action C.[5]

f. Finally, let us mention one of many other possible attitudes, that of the person who is always regretting what he has not done. Such a person, after he has made his decision and after it becomes known which state of the environment has come about, compares his realized gains with what

---

[5] His computation will look as follows:
Expected Outcome of A = .5(225)+ .5(0) =112
Expected Outcome of B = .5(144)+ .5(81)=112
Expected Outcome of C = .5(361)+ .5(0) =180
Expected Outcome of D = .5(324)+ .5(0) =162
He will choose that action which is associated with the largest expected outcome, namely action C.

28

he could have received had he been able to anticipate the state of the environment which subsequently materialized. For example, if he had chosen action B, and the state of the environment which materializes is state 1, he would have received 100. But, had he known that state I would have materialized, he could have chosen action A (and not action B) and received 225. The difference between 225 and 100, namely 125, is a measure of his regret. Similar calculations give us the regret matrix of Table II.

TABLE II. An Hypothetical Regret Matrix.

		States of the Environment			
		I	II	III	IV
	A	0	165	81	44
Industrialist's	B	125	261	0	0
Alternatives	C	225	0	81	119
	D	125	37	81	119

Now, if this individual is dominated by regret, he may be motivated toward regret minimization. Again, there are several attitudes he may bring to this objective. Among others, he may be optimistic, pessimistic, or simply conservative. He may try to minimize expected regret based upon subjective probabilities assigned to the perceived environmental states, and so forth. For example, if he is a conservative individual, he may look at each row of the regret matrix, and focus on the maximum element in it (165 for action A, 261 for B, 225 for C, and 125 for D). He will then select that action-alternative, namely D, which is associated with the least of these worst possible regrets, namely, 125. In effect he adopts a "min-max" regret strategy.

Many other attitudes can be identified and considered. The point we wish to stress, however, is already obvious. The industrialist will choose different alternatives (A, B, C, or D) depending on his attitude, *ceteris paribus*.[6]

Let us next briefly touch upon a few additional basic variables. As already indicated, one of these is the manner in which the industrialist internalizes outcomes, or transforms them into a utility or satisfaction measure. There are many such ways. One simple procedure is for him to assign a value of either +1 (satisfactory) or 0 (unsatisfactory) to each outcome, depending on whether or not an outcome is not less than some predetermined value. A value of 0 can also be interpreted as an unrewarded or "lose" situation with corresponding interpretation given to +1[7].

---

[6] Interesting materials on these points are contained in Herman Chernoff and Lincoln E. Moses, *Elementary Decision Theory*, John Wiley, New York, 1959; John Milnor, "Games Against Nature," in R. M. Thrall, C.H. Coombs, and R.L. Davis, eds., *Decision Processes*, John Wiley, New York, 1954; and Robert Schlaifer, *Introduction to Statistics for Business Decisions*, McGraw-Hill, New York, 1961.

[7] See, for example Herbert Simon, *Models of Man*, John Wiley, New York, 1957, ch. 14.

29

Another method would be to adopt a three way classification: $+1$, 0, -1 (satisfactory, neutral and unsatisfactory—or win, draw and lose—or increased assets, unchanged assets and decreased assets). Still other transformations which have been frequently suggested view payoff as the square root, or as the log, or as some more complicated function of the outcome. The transformation which is relevant, however, in any given situation is not easily discerned. Despite recent developments in utility theory it must be admitted that there is very little knowledge about how a typical individual, let along an atypical one, internalizes outcomes. Yet this is an important variable which does affect decisions. For example, if we apply a simple utility formula, $U = \sqrt{O}$, a formula which is consistent with both a positive marginal utility as outcome (O) increases, then the alternative of Table 1 which yields highest expected utility (on the assumption that each state I—IV is equally probable) is B rather than A[8]. It would, of course, be A if the transformation were according to the formula $U = O$. Thus, it becomes clear that, without knowledge of the transformation, decisions are frequently not predictable. Unfortunately, such transformations are not usually available[9].

Our next questions concerns the way the figure in each cell in Table 1 is derived. For the moment, let us assume that figures refer to a single specified attribute of an outcome, such as money profit. At the one extreme these figures may be predetermined or given to an individual decision maker, and no computation is required of him. At the other extreme, the set of figures in each column may be derived by an extensive objective-like computation, as is possible using industrial complex analysis or interregional linear programming. But even here, the attitude of the industrialist enters in a very significant way. For example, in projecting a wage rate necessary for estimating his profits in an underdeveloped region, a conservative banker would select one of the higher possible wage rates, whereas an optimist would select a considerably lower wage rate; similarly with taxes, power costs, and so forth. Individuals with different attitudes come up with different figures in Table I, even though they may use the same techniques.

But the play of the attitude variable goes even deeper. It affects what one sees as relevant variables and what one considers as relevant techniques. It is clear that a conservative banker would shy away from input-output and prefer the simpler, possibly more reliable comparative cost analysis, while an

---

[8] The computation is:
$$EU_A = .25(15) + .25(14) + .25(0) + .25(10) = 9.75$$
$$EU_B = .25(10) + .25(10) + .25(9) + .25(12) = 10.25$$
$$EU_C = .25(0) + .25(19) + .25(0) + .25(5) = 6.00$$
$$EU_D = .25(10) + .25(18) + .25(0) + .25(5) = 8.25$$

[9] For example, see: Ernest W. Adams, "Survey of Bernoullian Utility Theory," in Herbert Solomon, ed., *Mathematical Thinking in the Measurement of Behavior*, Free Press, Glencoe, Ill., 1960; R. Duncan Luce and Howard Raiffa, *Games and Decisions*, John Wiley, New York, 1957; John von Neumann and Oskar Morgenstern, *Theory of Games and Economic Behavior*, Princeton University Press, Princeton, 1944; and S.S.Stevens, "Measurement, Psychophysics, and Utility," in C. West Churchman and Philburn Ratoosh, eds., *Measurement: Definition and Theories*, John Wiley, New York, 1959.

30

optimist, or a planner seeking to delve more deeply into an economy's inter-connections might prefer an input-output approach. Each would then tend to obtain different magnitudes[10].

To complicate matters still further, each figure in a given cell might represent a set of many outcomes, that is, an outcome vector rather than a simple outcome such as profit. One component of an outcome vector might measure profit, another prestige, a third life-expectancy, etc. In the usual situation, the industrialist would then be required in some manner to aggregate vector components prior to his making a decision. To project his behavior, it may then be necessary to estimate his aggregation procedure[11].

Other basic questions are involved. It is recognized that the industrialist's attitude also affects the action space which he perceives and the alternatives he is willing to consider as feasible and worthwhile to pursue—at least to the point of calculating outcomes. Further, even where the regional scientist knows what variables the industrialist considers relevant, his attitudes, and his perception of the environment in certain situations, the scientist must still identify, as best he can, the subjective probabilities which the industrialist assigns to the several states of the environment[12].

The upshot of all this, as well as the analysis of many other factors, leads to the conclusion that projecting behavior is no easy or simple task. The analyst might throw up his arms and revert to traditional procedures of economics and location theory. But now that we have dwelt briefly upon several basic variables in decision making, it is clear that the traditional economic and location theories make implicit, and in many cases, unwarranted assumption about the play of such variables. In situations where we can work with more realistic assumptions, even though they are based on scanty evidence, we should do so.

It is beyond the scope of this paper to deal in greater depth with the analysis of the above basic variables. In the few remaining paragraphs we wish to illustrate the importance of this type of approach for the urban, regional, and national planner in guiding his policies and actions. Suppose we have identified by interview that the industrialist does perceive the four states of the environment of Table I, does think in terms of the four possible actions of Table I, and has hired a research team of economists, regional scientists and others who derive the figures in the cells of Table I. Furthermore, suppose from past study of the industrialist's behavior, he can be characterized as a "conservative banker". Then one could project his choice of action B—investment of capital in foreign countries.

Now, to the national and regional planner, this choice may appear as highly undesirable. The national planner wants job opportunities from capital investments in his own country; the regional planner, in his own region. A

---

[10] See: Churchman and Ratoosh, *op. cit.*

[11] For possible relevant components, see: Harold D. Lasswell and Abraham Kaplan, *Power and Society*, Yale University Press, New Haven, 1950; and Shubik, *op. cit.*

[12] See: W. Edwards, "Behavioral Decision Theory," *Annual Review of Psychology*, Vol. 12, 1961, pp. 473-498.

31

study of Table I would reveal that 81 is the key figure (the best of the worst outcomes of the rows). It is clear that if the national or regional planner can guarantee to the industrialist a return of 81 in the event that state III of the environment materializes (their government may consider depositing such a sum in a foreign bank), the industrialist would tend to choose action A. In the eyes of the regional and national planners who make calculations on an expected payoff basis, this could well be the best course of action. Observe that 81 does not represent the expected cost to their government of this guarantee, since its payment to the industrialist is contingent on the occurrence of state III, and since the probability of this occurrence is presumably less that 1.0.

The above case thus illustrates how and where leverage is required to achieve certain policies, and how decision making required of a planner is related to the decision making which an industrialist undertakes[13].

If a matrix similar to Table I were to be prepared for a number of major industrialists and other investors, then it might be possible to identify directions capital investments are likely to take, and to institute preventive or ameliorative measures if such measures are seen desirable by the planners in pursuit of government goals. One measure might be an attack on prevalent views of subjective probability, by providing such information as may exist regarding likelihood of future states. Another measure might be associated with an expansion of the set of alternative actions perceived by the industrialists, through a systematic identification and study of means consistent with ends held. Still another may be through efforts to expand the horizons of enterpreneurs by publicizing possible new environmental states.

These activities on the part of planners require, of course, an explicit value position on their own part. Yet they have, to some extent at least, avoided a frontal attack on the more deeply held values of the industrialist: such as his Weberian protestant ethic or his utility transformation function. We close our brief introduction to this subject with the observation that this approach makes it possible to partition planning into directives which have

---

[13] Another case may help point out the leverage available to the planner. For example, suppose the industrialist were a "100 percent optimist". Scanning Table 1 he locates the largest figure, namely 361. This is the best of the best outcomes of the rows. The analyst then projects that the industrialist will adopt action C and construct an integrated steel mill in the capital city. This may however, not be best from the stand point of (1) the urban planner, who has judged that the capital city is already too large in terms of efficiency in operation; (2) the regional planner who would like to see new investment in his region and; (3) the national planner who considers the capital area overdeveloped compared to the rest of the country. Hence, course C ought to be discouraged. Likewise alternative D, which is to construct and operate a metals fabricating complex in the capital city ought to be discouraged. An appropriate policy might then be to levy a heavy tax or some other penalty (at least as great as 136) on locating in the capital city—a negative stimulus—or, in contrast, to provide a subsidy (at least as great as 136) on locating in the underdeveloped region (action A)—or, by means of public works, reduce the cost to the entrepreneur of action A so that an outcome of 361 can be attained.

32

values as their focus, and those which are primarily directed to enlarge or modify the subject's fund of information[14].

It summing up, we hope that in this brief paper some of the new concepts and approaches to decision making have been effectively brought to bear upon problems of regional scientist and the planner. These concepts and approaches permit not only an increased knowledge and understanding of society, but also a greater ability to project individual behavior within certain class of decision-making situations. In turn, this increased knowledge and analytical skill can lead to a more effective shaping of social and economic development.

---

[14] It is necessary to qualify this last statement, for values and facts cannot be easily split (see: C. West Churchman, *Prediction and Optimal Decision*, Prentice Hall, Englewood Cliffs, New Jersey, 1961). It is wiser to think of a fact—value continuum, with the planner, at least in a democratic society, concentrating his efforts on the factual end of this continuum.

33

The Decision Process of the Firm

New Considerations in the
Theory of the Firm[1]

Kalman J. Cohen and Richard M. Cyert

Up to this point we have assumed that the firm is attempting to maximize profits. We have implicitly taken the point of view that only market considerations determine the decisions of the firm. We have assumed that the internal organizational structure of the firm has no effect on the decisions that the firm makes. Now we shall look at the firm from a different viewpoint. In particular, we should like to rely on some of the results derived from a behavioral approach to the firm. The nature of the behavioral approach will become clear as we proceed.

[1] This chapter draws heavily from Richard M. Cyert and James G. March, *A Behavioral Theory of the Firm* (Englewood Cliffs, N.J.: Prentice-Hall, Inc., 1963), chaps. 3–5. Some of this material has been used directly without explicit indication of quotation; other material has been paraphrased.

Reprinted from Kalman J. Cohen and Richard M. Cyert, *Theory of the Firm: Resource Allocation in a Market Economy* (Englewood Cliffs, New Jersey: Prentice-Hall, Inc., 1965), pp. 329–351, by permission of the authors and publisher.

I. Motivation of the Behavioral Theory

Periodically in the history of the theory of the firm in economics, there have been attacks on the assumption of profit maximization. In particular, as one looks closely at the behavior of actual firms, the justification for the assumption of profit maximization seems to weaken. When one adds uncertainty to the firm's decision-making process, even defining the meaning of profit maximization becomes difficult to do in an empirically meaningful way. The behavioral theory of the firm takes the position that arguments over motivation are somewhat fruitless. The critical issue is not whether one assumes profit maximizing instead of satisficing behavior. Instead, it is fruitful to develop an understanding of the process of decision making within the firm.

The behavioral theory is viewed as supplementing the conventional theory of the firm. The traditional theory is essentially one in which certain broad questions are asked. Specifically, the conventional theory of the firm is designed to explain the way in which the price system functions as a mechanism for allocating resources among markets; relatively little is said about resource allocation within the firm. For the purposes of the classical theory, the profit maximization assumption may be perfectly adequate. It is clear, however, that as one asks a different set of questions, specifically questions designed to uncover the way in which resources are allocated within the firm, the profit maximization assumption is neither necessary nor sufficient for answering these questions. Therefore the behavioral theory of the firm should be viewed as focusing on a different set of questions, questions concerning the internal decision-making structure of the firm. Thus, with this theory we are interested in answering such questions as

1. How does the allocation of resources within the firm's budget relate to the organizational goals?
2. How do objectives change over time?
3. What happens to information as it flows through the organization?
4. Are there biases in the information?
5. How do these biases affect the decisions that are finally made?
6. What is the relationship between decisions made by management and the final form of the decision as it is implemented by the organization?

In general the behavioral theory is most applicable to those firms whose decisions are not completely determined by the market. These firms have some freedom to develop decision strategies or rules that become part of the decision-making system within the firm.

II. Key Concepts of the Behavioral Theory

A. ORGANIZATIONAL GOALS

The phrase, "organizational goals," is slightly misleading, since an organization as such cannot have goals. Only the individuals within the organization can have goals. When we speak of organizational goals, however, we mean essentially that there is agreement among some group responsible for the direction of the organization on the nature of the goals. In particular, this group (which we shall call a *coalition* within the organization) is an interacting group, and the goals will be modified by discussions and pressures within the group. Thus the decision on the final set of goals of the organization is in some sense a political decision. The coalition within the organization for a business firm may include managers, workers, stockholders, customers, and so on. In other words, all the individuals who have some stake in that particular organization may in one way or another affect the goals of the organization.

The concept of a coalition assumes a different type of firm than we have been dealing with in the preceding chapters of this book. Hitherto, the firm was implicitly regarded as controlled by an entrepreneur, and the goals of the entrepreneur were the goals of the organization. He purchased conformity to these goals by payments in the forms of wages to workers, interest to capital sources, and profits (when they existed) to himself.

To understand organizational goals it must be realized, first of all, that all resolutions of goals within the coalition are not made by money. Rather, many side-payments to members in an organization are made in the form of policy commitments. For example, in order to get the vice-president of marketing to stay within the organization, it may be necessary to commit resources to research on new products. It may well be that some of the policy demands are inconsistent with the side-payments that are made. Thus, every organization is continually undergoing the test of new demands, the test to see how these new demands conform to existing policy and, in general, pushing the policy toward new dimensions. In some sense, therefore, the goals of the organization are never completely consistent at any particular point in time.

The second point that must be understood about goals is that some objectives are stated in the form of a normative dictum. For example, we must have 46 per cent of the market, or we must expend 6 per cent of our gross revenue in advertising. Third, some objectives are stated in a nonoperational form. In other words, they are not necessarily in a form to have any effect on decisions. Thus, a nonoperational goal may be that the firm desires to be a leading innovator in the industry. In and of itself, this goal does not lead to a particular set of actions. A goal in nonoperational form may, however, be a guide in making certain sets of decisions on personnel or may more broadly affect the allocation of resources. In general, nonoperational demands are encouraged by the coalition, since these nonoperational objectives are consistent with virtually any other set of objectives.

Given a set of goals, an interesting question arises as to how these goals change over time. It is believed that an important phenomenon is the aspiration level mechanism. The aspiration level concept is taken from psychology. It assumes, first, that goals are stated in operational form, such as "our profit goal for this year is $5,400,000." The organization then periodically compares its performance with its aspiration level.

The following propositions describe the way in which we would expect goals in the form of aspiration levels to change:

1. In a steady state, i.e., one where the external environment in the form of the demand curve is constant, we would expect the aspiration level to be higher than actual performance by a small amount.

2. Where the performance is improving at an increasing rate, the aspiration level will generally lag in the short run behind achievement.

3. When performance is decreasing in quality, the aspiration level will tend to be above achievement.

These three propositions have not been empirically verified for a wide range of business firms. They are essentially based on a set of assumptions which postulate that current aspirations are an optimistic extrapolation of past achievements and past aspirations. The model does seem to be consistent with a wide range of human goal-setting behavior which has been observed in experiments reported in the psychological literature. We would expect the demands of the individual participants in the coalition to change over time, partly as a function of the achievement of the individual, and also as a function of the individual's achievement in relation to others that he deems comparable to him both in this and in other organizations. Thus, we would expect that aspirations with respect to salary would vary as a function of the payments actually received. Similarly, aspirations regarding advertising budget, volume of sales, capital investment, etc., will vary as a function of achievement. Unfortunately, until we know a great deal more about the nature of the relationship between achievement and aspiration, we can make only weak predictions. Even so, some of these predictions are still useful, as we shall see.

B. Organizational Slack

In terms of the present framework, a coalition is viable if the payments made to the various coalition members are adequate to keep them in the organization. If enough resources exist to meet all demands, the coalition is a feasible one. Since demands adjust to actual payments and alternatives external to the organization, there is a long-run tendency for payments and demands to be equal. In this sense, what we have called *coalition demands* are analogous to the factor prices of the more conventional view of the firm.

There is a critical difference, however. In the behavioral theory we focus on the short-run relation between payments and demands and on the imperfections in factor markets. The imperfections, in fact, dominate behavior, for three primary reasons:

1. As we have already noted, payments and demands are in a variety of forms: monetary payments, perquisites, policies, personal treatments, and private commitments. As a result, information on actual factor "prices" is hard to obtain, easily misinterpreted, and often unreliable.

2. Information about the "market" is not obtained automatically; it must be sought. Typically, the participants in the organization do not seek this information until stimulated to do so by some indication of failure.

3. Adaptations in demands are slow—even in the face of strong pressure.

Because of the frictions in the mutual adjustment of payments and demands, there is ordinarily a disparity between the resources available to the organization and the payments required to maintain the coalition. This difference between total resources and total necessary payments is called *organizational slack*. Slack consists in payments to members of the coalition in excess of what is required to maintain the organization. Many interesting phenomena within the firm occur because slack is typically not zero.

In conventional economic theory slack is zero (at least in equilibrium). In discussions of managerial economics, specific attention is generally paid to only one part of slack—payments to owners—and it is generally assumed that other slack is maintained at zero. Neither view is an accurate portrayal of an actual firm. Many forms of slack typically exist: stockholders are paid dividends in excess of those required to keep stockholders (or banks) within the organization; prices are set lower than necessary to maintain adequate income from customers; wages in excess of those required to maintain labor are paid; executives are provided with services and personal luxuries in excess of those required to keep them; subunits are permitted to grow without real concern for the relation between additional payments and additional revenues; public services are provided in excess of those required.

From time to time virtually every participant in any organization obtains slack payments. Some participants, however, ordinarily obtain a greater share of the slack then do other participants. In general, we would expect that those members of the coalition who are full-time, in a position to perceive potential slack early, or have some flexibility in the unilateral allocation of resources will tend to accumulate more slack than will other members.

In most cases we use the organizational slack concept not to explain differential payments but as a hypothetical construct for explaining overall organizational phenomena. In particular, it seems to be useful in dealing with the adjustment of firms to gross shifts in the external environment. For example, consider what happens when the rate of improvement in the environment is great enough so that it outruns the upward adjustment of aspirations. In a general way, this seems to be the situation that faces business firms during strong boom periods. When the environment outruns the aspiration-level adjustment, the organization secures, or at least has the potential of securing, resources in excess of its demands. Some of these resources are simply not obtained—although they are available. Others are used to meet the revised demands of those members of the coalition whose demands adjust more rapidly—usually those most deeply involved in the organization. The excess resources would not be subject to general bargaining because they do not involve allocation in the face of scarcity.

When the environment becomes less favorable, organizational slack represents a cushion. Resource scarcity brings on renewed bargaining and tends to cut heavily into the excess payments introduced during plush times. It does not necessarily mean that precisely those demands that grew abnormally during better days are pruned abnormally during poorer ones, but in general we would expect this to be approximately the case. More important, the cusion provided by organizational slack permits firms to survive in the face of adversity. Under the pressure of a failure (or impending failure) to meet some set of demands on the coalition, the organization discovers some previously unrecognized opportunities for increasing the total resources available. For example, it was reported that after losses of about $50 million for the first three quarters of 1946, the Ford Motor Company "announced that it had found methods of reducing operating costs (on a given volume of output) by about twenty million dollars per year."[2]

Organizational slack absorbs a substantial share of the potential variability in the firm's environment. As a result, it plays both a stabilizing and an adaptive role. We have already noted that the demands of participants adjust to achievement. Aspiration-level adjustment, however, tends to be a relatively slow process—especially downward adjustment. If the only adaptive devices available to the organization were adjustments in aspirations of the members of the coalition, the system would be quite unstable in the face of an environment with even moderate fluctuations. Slack op-

---

[2] M. W. Reder, "A Reconsideration of Marginal Productivity Theory," *Journal of Political Economy*, 55 (1947), 450–58.

erates to stabilize the system in two ways: (1) by absorbing excess resources, it retards upward adjustment of aspirations during relatively good times; (2) by providing a pool of emergency resources, it permits aspirations to be maintained (and achieved) during relatively bad times.

This is not to argue that slack is deliberately created for such a stabilizing purpose; in fact, it is not. Slack arises from the bargaining and decision process we have described, without conscious intent on the part of the coalition members to provide stability to the organization. In a sense, the process is reinforced because it "works" and it "works" partly because it generates slack, but we have seen no significant evidence for the conscious rationalization of slack in business firms. From the point of view of a behavioral theory of the firm, however, the critical question is whether predictions based on the concept can be verified. For example, we would predict that the costs of firms that are successful in the market place will, *ceteris paribus*, tend to rise. Such predictions are susceptible to direct test.[3] They also may be tested within the context of more complicated models of the behavior of firms.

III. Business Goals and Price and Output Decisions

Suppose we wish to use the foregoing general considerations to construct a model of organizational decision making by a business firm determining price, output, and general sales strategy. As we have already noted, we are not yet in a good position to develop a theory that focuses intensively on the formation of objectives through bargaining and coalition making (rather than on the revision of such objectives and selective attention to them). As a result, when we look at price and output determination in business firms, we do three things:

1. We assume a small set of operational goals. In making such an assumption we suggest that the demands of many parts of the coalition are not operative for this class of decisions most of the time or are substantially satisfied when the set of goals assumed is satisfied.

2. We assume that this set of goals is fixed in the sense that no other classes of goals will arise within the coalition. Such an assumption does not exclude changes in the levels of the goals nor in the attention directed at specific goals within the set.

3. We attempt to determine by empirical investigation what specific goals ordinarily enter into the price and output decisions. In general, we have observed that we can represent organizational goals reasonably well by using five different goals. In any organization, other considerations sometimes arise. For example, governmental demands occasionally become

---

[3] R. M. Cyert and J. G. March, "Organizational Factors in the Theory of Oligopoly," *Quarterly Journal of Economics*, 70 (1956), 44–46.

of prime importance. In a few organizations other considerations are as important as those we have identified. For example, in some organizations considerations of prestige or tradition are major goal factors. For most decisions concerning price, output, and general sales strategy in business firms, we think we can limit our primary attention to five goals.

We list the five goals here in an arbitrary order without attempting to establish any necessary order of importance; most of the time no order of importance is required. All goals must be satisfied. It should be clear in the model we shall present in Section V that there is an implicit order reflected in the way in which search activity takes place and in the speed and circumstances of goal-level change. These latent priorities appear to vary from organization to organization in a way that is not clear. It seems most probable that their variation should be explainable in terms of differences in either the current or historical bargaining position of the several participants in the coalition, but at present we treat the implicit priorities simply as organizational parameters.

A. Production Goal

We assume that an organization has a complex of goals surrounding the production operation. These can be summarized in terms of a production goal, with two major components. The first is a smoothing goal: we do not want production to vary more than a certain amount from one time period to another. The second is a level-of-production goal: we want to equal or exceed a certain production level. These two components can be summarized in terms of a production range: we want production to fall within a range of possible production.

The production goal represents in large part the demands of those coalition members connected with production. It reflects pressures toward such things as stable employment, ease of scheduling, development of acceptable cost performance, and growth. Thus, the goal is most frequently evoked in the production part of the organization and is most relevant to decisions (e.g., output) made in that part.

B. Inventory Goal

We assume certain aspirations with respect to finished-goods inventory levels. As in the case of the production goal, the inventory goal summarizes a number of pressures, most conspicuously the demands of some participants to avoid runouts in inventory and to provide a complete, convenient source of inventoried materials. We summarize these demands in terms of either an absolute-level-of-inventory goal or an inventory range (in which case we also attend to demands to avoid excessive inventory costs).

The inventory goal reflects the demands of those coalition members connected with inventory. Thus it is affected by pressures on the inventory department from salesmen and customers. Since inventory essentially serves as a buffer between production and sales, the inventory goal is most frequently invoked and is most relevant to decisions in the output and sales areas.

C. Sales Goal

We assume that most participants in business firms believe the firm must sell the goods or services it produces in order to survive. Thus, various members of the coalition demand that the organization meet some general criteria of sales effectiveness. The sales goal and the market-share goal (Section III.D) summarize these demands. In addition, the sales department itself (and the personnel in it) link subunit goals with sales. The sales goal is simply an aspiration with respect to the level of sales. It may be stated in terms of dollars, units, or both.

The sales goal represents primarily the demands of those members of the coalition closely connected with sales and secondarily those members of the coalition who view sales as necessary for the stability of the organization. The goal is most frequently evoked and is most relevant to decisions with respect to sales strategy.

D. Market-Share Goal

The market-share goal is an alternative to the sales goal insofar as the concern is for a measure of sales effectiveness. Either or both may be used, depending on the past experience of the firm and the traditions of the industry. In addition, the market-share goal is linked to the demands of those parts of the organization that are primarily interested in comparative success (e.g., top management, especially top sales management) and to the demands for growth.

Like the sales goal, the market-share goal is most frequently evoked and most relevant to sales strategy decisions.

E. Profit Goal

We assume that the business firm has a profit goal. This goal is linked to standard accounting procedures for determining profit and loss. It summarizes the demands for two things: (1) demands for accumulating resources in order to distribute them in the form of capital investments, dividends to stockholders, payments to creditors, or increased budgets to subunits; (2) demands on the part of top management for favorable performance measures. In general, we assume that the profit goal is in terms of an aspiration level with respect to the dollar amount of profit. In principle, of course, this goal might also take the form of profit share or return on investment.

The profit goal reflects the pressure of those parts of the coalition that share in the distribution of profits and in the distribution of credit for profitability. Thus, in general, this pressure comes from top-level managers throughout the firm, from stockholders, creditors, and from those parts of the organization seeking capital investment. The goal is usually most closely linked to pricing and resource allocation decisions.

Although our fivefold specification of goals deviates substantially from the conventional theory of the firm, it will not necessarily satisfy anyone who would like to reflect all the goals that might conceivably be of relevance to price, output, and sales strategy decisions. Without insisting on the necessary efficacy of five goals, we think a strong case can be made for expanding the set of goals beyond the single profit goal of the conventional theory, and even beyond the elaboration to include a sales goal which was suggested by Baumol.[4] We think, however, that expanding the list of assumed goals much beyond the present list of five rapidly meets a point of diminishing returns.

IV. Organizational Expectations

Just as the theory of the firm requires some understanding of goals and goal formation within the organization, it also requires an understanding of the generation and handling of information within the firm and the ways in which information about the environment enters into the decision process of the firm. As already indicated, we consider the organization to be a coalition, and that members of this coalition make decisions affecting the organization's resources. These decisions depend upon information and expectations formed within the organization.

On the basis of a number of empirical studies certain conclusions can be tentatively drawn. In particular, resource allocation within the firm reflects only gross comparisons of the marginal advantages of alternatives. Rules of thumb for evaluating alternatives provide some constraints on resource allocation, and there is no conscious comparison of specific alternative investments. Any alternative that satisfies the constraints and secures suitably powerful support within the organization is likely to be adopted. This means that decision making is likely to reflect heavily a response to local problems of pressing need.

Search activity is stimulated when a problem area is recognized. At the first stage, however, only rough expectational data are used to screen obviously inappropriate actions. In general the early search is stopped after a few suitable alternatives are generated. These alternatives are then considered in greater detail. In most cases studied, a rather firm commit-

---

[4] William J. Baumol, *Business Behavior, Value and Growth* (New York: The Macmillan Company, 1959).

ment to an action was taken before the search for information proceeded very far.

Computations by the organization of anticipated consequences seems to be quite simple. There appear to be two main reasons for the simplicity. First the major initial question about a proposed action was not how it compared with alternatives but whether it was feasible. There are two varieties of feasibility. The first is the budgetary constraint: Is money available for the project? The second is an improvement criterion: Is the project clearly better than existing procedures? The second reason relates to the difficulty of measuring all the relevant considerations on a single dimension. In the studies referred to, many factors, such as speed and accuracy of work, safety of personnel, and convenience of location, were not viewed by the firm as reducible, in a meaningful way, to dollars. As a result such variables were treated as independent constraints and as irrelevant to cost estimation.

Expectations in the firm seem to be related to the hopes and wishes of the decision maker. In each of the studies made there is some suggestion of unconscious or semiconscious adjustment of perceptions to hopes. Thus there is a tendency to bias estimates of costs, revenues, and other important variables in the direction desired. It would be a mistake to think of these biases as great or the result of dishonesty. They are no different from the biases a scientist has in reviewing the evidence for a favored hypothesis.

V. A Partial Model of Price and Output Determination

Much of what has been said here may be difficult for the reader to make operational in the form of a model; therefore, as a way of illustrating some of the points which have been made and as a way of demonstrating that models other than the classical models can be constructed we are going to describe a duopoly model which summarizes some of the implications of the concepts of goals and expectations that have been discussed. The model itself is solved by simulation. This is a methodology which economists are beginning to use for developing and analyzing complex formal models. The model is developed for a duopoly situation, the product is homogeneous and, therefore, only one price exists in the market. The major decision that each of the two firms makes is an output decision (this is similar to the duopoly models discussed in Chapter 12, Section I). In making this decision each firm must estimate the market price for varying outputs. When the output is sold, however, the actual selling price will be determined by the market. No discrepancy between output and sales is permitted, so there are no inventory problems in the model.

We assume the duopoly to be composed of an ex-monopolist and a firm developed by former members of the established firm. We shall call the latter the *splinter* and the former the *ex-monopolist*. Such a specific case is

TABLE 16–1

PROCESS MODEL FOR OUTPUT DECISION OF FIRM

1. *Forecast* Competitor's reactions	Compute conjectural variation term for period t as a function of actual reactions observed in the past.
2. *Forecast* Demand	Keep slope of perceived demand curve constant but pass it through the last realized point in the market.
3. *Estimate* Average unit costs	Cost curve for this period is the same as for last period. If profit goals have been achieved two successive times, average unit costs increase.
4. *Specify objectives* Profit goal	Specify profit goal as a function of the actual profits achieved over last periods.
5. *Evaluate* Examine alternatives	Evaluate alternatives within the estimate space. If an alternative which meets goal is available, go to (9). If not, go to (6).
6. *Reexamine* Cost estimate	Search yields a cost reduction. Go to (5). If decision can be made after evaluation there, go to (9). If not, go to (7).
7. *Reexamine* Demand estimate	Estimate of demand increased after search. Go to (5). If decision can be made after evaluation, go to (9). If not, go to (8).
8. *Reexamine* Profit goal	Reduce profit goal to a level consistent with best alternative in the estimate space as modified after (6) and (7).
9. *Decide* Set output	Selection of alternative in original estimate space to meet original goal, in modified estimate space to meet original goal, or in modified estimate space to meet lowered goal.

formulated so that some rough assumptions can be made about appropriate functions for the various processes in the model. The assumptions are gross but, hopefully, not wholly unreasonable. To demonstrate that the model as a whole has some reasonable empirical basis, we will compare certain outcomes of the model with data from the can industry in the United States, where approximately the same underlying conditions hold.

We can describe the specific model at several levels of detail. In Table 16–1 the over-all skeleton of the model is indicated.

The decision-making process postulated by the theory begins with a forecast phase (in which competitor's reactions, demand, and costs are estimated) and a goal specification phase (in which a profit goal is established). An evaluation phase follows, in which an effort is made to find the "best" alternative, given the forecasts. If this "best" alternative is inconsistent with the profit goal, a reexamination phase ensues, in which an effort is made to revise cost and demand estimates. If reexamination fails to yield a new best alternative consistent with the profit goal, the immediate profit goal is abandoned in favor of "doing the best possible under the circumstances."

The specific details of the model will now be presented, following the framework in Table 16–1.

A. FORECASTING COMPETITOR'S BEHAVIOR

Since we deal with a duopoly, an estimate of the rival firm's output is a significant factor in each firm's output decision. These estimates are essentially the same as the conjectural variation terms introduced in Chapter 12, Section I.[5] Our model assumes that these depend upon the actual reactions of the rival observed in previous periods.

To express this dependence, let $V_{m,t}$ denote the ratio of the actual change in the splinter's output between periods t and $t-1$ to the actual change in the ex-monopolist's output between periods t and $t-1$:[6]

$$V_{m,t} = \frac{Q_{s,t} - Q_{s,t-1}}{Q_{m,t} - Q_{m,t-1}} \qquad (16\text{-}1)$$

where $Q_{s,t}$ is the splinter's actual output during period t and $Q_{m,t}$ is the ex-monopolist's actual output during period t. Analogously, let $V_{s,t}$ denote the ratio of the actual change in the ex-monopolist's output between periods t and $t-1$ to the actual change in the splinter's output between these same periods:[7]

$$V_{s,t} = \frac{Q_{m,t} - Q_{m,t-1}}{Q_{s,t} - Q_{s,t-1}} \qquad (16\text{-}2)$$

We assume that the *ex-monopolist* estimates the ratio of the change in the splinter's output to his own change, that is, $V_{m,t}$, on the basis of the splinter's behavior during the past three time periods. Specifically, we assume that the ex-monopolist's estimate, $V'_{m,t}$, is a weighted average:

$$V'_{m,t} = V_{m,t-1} + [4(V_{m,t-1} - V_{m,t-2})$$
$$+ 2(V_{m,t-2} - V_{m,t-3}) + (V_{m,t-3} - V_{m,t-4})]/7 \qquad (16\text{-}3)$$

where $V'_{m,t}$ = the ex-monopolist's estimate of $V_{m,t}$.

---

[5] The only difference is that in Chapter 12, where a continuous time dynamic analysis was implicit, the conjectural variations were treated as partial derivatives. Here, where we explicitly use a discrete time dynamic analysis, the conjectural variations are formulated as the ratios of finite differences.

[6] In case $Q_{m,t} = Q_{m,t-1}$, we arbitrarily define $V_{m,t} = 1$.

[7] In case $Q_{s,t} = Q_{s,t-1}$, we arbitrarily define $V_{s,t} = 1$.

The ex-monopolist's estimate of the splinter's output, $Q'_{s,t}$, is

$$Q'_{s,t} = Q_{s,t-1} + V'_{m,t} (Q_{m,t} - Q_{m,t-1}). \tag{16-4}$$

We expect the *splinter* firm to be more responsive to recent shifts in its competitor's behavior and less attentive to ancient history than the ex-monopolist, both because it is more inclined to consider the ex-monopolist a key part of its environment and because it will generally have less computational capacity as an organization to process and update the information necessary to deal with more complicated rules. Our assumption is that the splinter will simply use the information from the last two periods in obtaining $V'_{s,t}$, its estimate of $V_{s,t}$. In particular,

$$V'_{s,t} = V_{s,t-1} + (V_{s,t-1} - V_{s,t-2}). \tag{16-5}$$

The splinter's estimate of the monopolist's output is

$$Q'_{m,t} = Q_{m,t-1} + V'_{s,t} (Q_{s,t} - Q_{s,t-1}). \tag{16-6}$$

B. FORECASTING DEMAND

We assume that the actual market demand curve is linear; i.e., the market price is a linear function of the total output offered by the two firms. We also assume that the firms forecast a linear market demand curve, which is not necessarily the same as the actual demand curve. There has been considerable discussion in the literature of economics concerning the alleged discrepancy between the "imagined" demand curve and the actual demand curve; and it is the former concept that is incorporated in the model. The values we assign to the parameters of the imagined demand curve are based on rough inferences about the nature of the two firms.

We assume that, because of its past history of dominance and monopoly, the *ex-monopolist* will be overly pessimistic with respect to the quantity that it can sell at lower prices; i.e., we assume its initially perceived demand curve will have a somewhat steeper slope than will the actual market demand curve. On the assumption that information about actual demand is used to improve its estimate, we assume that the ex-monopolist changes its demand estimate on the basis of experience in the market. The firm assumes that its estimate of the slope of the demand curve is correct and it re-positions its previous estimate to pass through the observed demand point.

We posit that the *splinter* firm will initially be more optimistic with respect to the quantity that it can sell at low prices than the exmonopolist. We further assume that initially the splinter firm perceives demand as increasing over time. Thus, until demand shows a downward turn, the splinter firm estimates its demand to be 5 per cent greater than that found by re-positioning its perceived demand through the last point observed in the market place.

C. ESTIMATING COSTS

We do not assume that the firm has achieved optimum costs. We assume, rather, that the firm has a simplified estimate of its average cost curve, i.e., the curve expressing cost per unit as a function of output. It is horizontal over most of the range of possible outputs; at high and low outputs (relative to capacity) average costs are perceived to be somewhat higher.

Further, we make the assumption that these cost estimates are "self-confirming"; i.e., the estimated costs will, in fact, become the actual per-unit cost. The concept of organizational slack as it affects costs is introduced at this point. Average unit cost for the present period is estimated to be the same as the last period, but if the profit goal of the firm has been achieved for two consecutive time periods, then costs are estimated to be 5 per cent higher than "last time." The specific values for costs are arbitrary.

The *ex-monopolist's* initial average unit cost is assumed to be $800 per unit in the range of outputs from 10 per cent to 90 per cent of capacity. Below 10 per cent and above 90 per cent the initial average unit cost is assumed to be $900.

It is assumed that the *splinter* will have somewhat lower initial costs because its plant and equipment will tend to be newer and its production methods more modern. Specifically, initial average costs are $760 in the range of outputs from 10 per cent to 90 per cent of capacity. Below 10 per cent and above 90 per cent costs are assumed to average $870 per unit produced.

D. SPECIFYING OBJECTIVES

The multiplicity of organizational objectives is a fact which will not be considered in this model. For simplicity, we limit ourselves to a single goal defined in terms of profit. In this model the function of the profit objective is to restrict or encourage search as well as to determine the actual decision made. If, given the estimates of rival's output, demand, and cost, there exists a production level that will provide a profit that is satisfactory, we assume the firm will produce at that level. If there is more than one satisfactory alternative, the firm will adopt that quantity level which maximizes profit.

We assume that the *ex-monopolist*, because of its size, substantial computational ability, and established procedures for dealing with a stable rather than a highly unstable environment, will tend to maintain a relatively stable profit objective. We assume that the objective will be a moving average of the realized profit over the last ten time periods. Initially the ex-monopolist seeks to achieve a profit level that is in the same proportion to the profit level achieved during its monopoly period as its current capacity is to total industry capacity.

The *splinter* firm will presumably be inclined to consider a somewhat shorter period of past experience, for reasons indicated earlier. We assume that the profit objective of the splinter will be the average of experienced profit over the past five time periods and that the initial profit objective will be linked to the experience of the former monopolist and the relative capacities of the two. Thus, we specify that the initial profit objective of the two firms will be proportional to their initial capacities.

E. Reexamination of Costs

We assume that when the original forecasts define a satisfactory plan, there will be no further examination of them. If, however, such a plan is not obtained, we assume an effort to achieve a satisfactory plan in the first instance by reviewing estimates and finally by revising objectives. We assume that cost estimates are reviewed before demand estimates and that the latter are reexamined only if a satisfactory plan cannot be developed by the revision of the former. The reevaluation of costs is a search for methods of accomplishing objectives at lower cost than appeared possible under less pressure. We believe this ability to revise estimates when forced to do so is characteristic of organizational decision making. It is, of course, closely related to the organizational slack concept previously introduced. In general, we have argued that an organization can ordinarily find possible cost reductions if forced to do so and that the amount of the reductions will be a function of the amount of slack in the organization.

It is assumed that the reexamination of costs under the pressure of trying to meet objectives enables each of the organizations to move in the direction of the "real" minimum cost point. For purposes of this model it is assumed that both firms reduce costs 10 per cent of the difference between their estimated average unit costs and the "real" minimum.

F. Reexamination of Demand

The reevaluation of demand serves the same function as the reevaluation of costs. In the present model it occurs only if the reevaluation of costs is not adequate to define an acceptable plan. It consists of revising upward the expectations of market demand. The reasoning is that some new alternative is selected that the firm believes will increase its demand. The new approach may be changed advertising procedure, a scheme to work salesmen harder, or some other alternative that leads the firm to an increase in optimism. In any event, it is felt that the more experienced firm will take a slightly less sanguine view of what is possible. As in the case of estimating demand, we assume that both firms persist in seeing a linear demand curve and that no changes are made in the perceived slope of that curve. In the case of the *ex-monopolist*, it is assumed that as a result of the reexamination of demand estimates, the firm revises its estimates of demand upward by 10 per cent. In the case of the *splinter*, the assumption is that the upward revision of demand is 15 per cent.

G. Reexamination of Objectives

Because our decision rule is one that maximizes among the available alternatives and our rule for specifying objectives depends only on outcomes, the reevaluation of objectives does not, in fact, enter into our present model in a way that influences behavior. The procedure can be interpreted as adjusting aspirations to the "best possible under the circumstances."

Table 16-2

Initial Conditions for Model

Initial market demand (unknown to firms)	$p = 2000 - q$
Ex-monopolist's initial perception of demand schedule	$p = 2200 - 3q$
Splinter's initial perception of demand schedule	$p = 1800 - q$
Ex-monopolist's average unit cost	
$\quad \begin{cases} 0.1q_{\max,m} < q_m < 0.9q_{\max,m} \\ q_m > 0.9q_{\max,m},\, q_m < 0.1q_{\max,m} \end{cases}$	$800 \\ 900$
Splinter's average unit cost	
$\quad \begin{cases} 0.1q_{\max,s} < q_s < 0.9q_{\max,s} \\ q_s > 0.9q_{\max,s},\, q_s < 0.1q_{\max,s} \end{cases}$	$760 \\ 870$
"Real" minimum average unit cost	$700
Ex-monopolist's capacity	400
Splinter's capacity	50
Market quantity	233
Market price	$1500
Ex-monopolist's profit goal	$163,100
Splinter's profit goal	$20,387
Conjectural variations ($V'_{m,t}$ and $V'_{s,t}$)	All 0 initially
Splinter's overoptimism of demand in forecast phase	5%
Splinter's raise of demand forecast upon reexamination	15%
Ex-monopolist's raise of demand forecast upon reexamination	10%
Cost reduction achieved in M's and S's search for lower costs (percentage of costs above "real" minimum average unit cost)	10%
Cost rise attributable to increase in "internal slack"	5%
Shift of actual demand schedule to right each time period	8%
Constraint on changing output from that of the last period	± 25%
Percentage of capacity at which firm must be producing before it may expand (subject to other conditions)	90%
Change in capacity, upon expansion	20%

TABLE 16-3

VALUES OF SELECTED VARIABLES AT TWO-PERIOD INTERVALS

	I	III	V	VII	IX	XI	XIII	XV	XVII	XIX	XXI	XXIII
Market												
Price	1420	1710	2196	2763	3283	3927	4430	4942	5425	3722	2785	2573
Output	290	311	262	205	209	195	303	466	713	914	855	534
Ex-monopolist												
Aspiration level	163,100	165,671	169,631	176,800	173,221	178,385	203,693	246,746	319,561	348,006	247,455	182,580
Conjectural variations	0	0	0.74	-22.4	1.09	0.74	0.26	0.35	0.28	0.30	-0.38	0.05
Costs (A.U.C.)	826	813	881	944	1041	1106	1219	1344	1482	1634	1801	1986
Output	240	251	206	153	161	150	233	363	566	703	658	369
No. reexam. steps	2	0	0	3	0	0	0	0	0	0	0	0
Splinter												
Aspiration level	20,387	27,107	31,448	39,763	46,218	39,684	54,245	79,090	113,595	121,973	86,083	60,742
Conjectural variations	0	0	9.2	-1.78	-6.58	8.72	3.39	3.96	4.76	3.91	6.3	-17.1
Costs	760	798	865	954	1023	1057	1166	1285	1417	1562	1623	1790
Output	50	60	56	52	48	45	70	103	147	211	197	165
No. reexam. steps	0	0	0	3	3	0	0	0	0	0	0	3
Profit ratio												
Splinter's profit ÷ ex-monopolist's profit	0.19	0.21	0.26	0.34	0.30	0.30	0.30	0.28	0.26	0.30	0.34	0.68
Share of market												
Ex-monopolist's output ÷ total output	0.83	0.81	0.79	0.75	0.77	0.77	0.77	0.78	0.79	0.77	0.77	0.69

TABLE 16-3 (continued)

	XXV	XXVII	XXIX	XXXI	XXXIII	XXXV	XXXVII	XXXIX	XLI	XLIII	XLV
Market											
Price	2229	1719	2286	2970	3355	3742	4099	4546	5463	6730	7294
Output	360	335	250	140	218	340	529	735	777	727	1126
Ex-monopolist											
Aspiration level	157,664	148,648	154,010	158,120	159,060	179,859	203,892	239,045	280,940	260,501	340,745
Conjectural variations	0.64	−1.07	28.4	−1.40	0.85	0.95	0.96	0.65	3.77	1.91	1.35
Costs (A.U.C.)	2085	1710	1609	1436	1363	1502	1656	1826	2013	2071	2283
Output	207	193	143	80	125	195	303	432	342	320	500
No. reexam. steps	1	3	0	3	0	0	0	0	0	0	0
Splinter											
Aspiration level	37,977	19,272	28,402	37,123	38,627	53,005	77,001	109,136	164,566	266,512	396,911
Conjectural variations	2.21	−0.32	2.43	50.7	1.32	1.31	1.32	2.3	−0.8	3.16	0.79
Costs	1853	1821	1608	1669	1840	2029	2237	2466	2719	2771	3055
Output	153	142	107	60	93	145	226	303	435	407	626
No. reexam. steps	0	1	0	0	0	0	0	0	0	0	0
Profit ratio											
Splinter's profit ÷ ex-monopolist's profit	0.98	0.74	0.75	0.64	0.49	0.49	0.49	0.47	0.90	0.97	0.95
Share of market											
Ex-monopolist's output ÷ total output	0.57	0.58	0.57	0.57	0.57	0.57	0.57	0.59	0.44	0.44	0.44

If our decision rule were different or if we made objectives at one time period a function of both outcomes and previous objectives, the reevaluation of objectives would become important to the decision process.

H. Decision

We have specified that the organization will follow traditional economic rules for maximization with respect to its perception of costs, demand, and competitor's behavior. The specific alternatives selected, of course, depend on the point at which this step is invoked (i.e., how many reevaluation steps are used before an acceptable plan is identified). The output decision is constrained in two ways:

1. A firm cannot produce, in any time period, beyond its present capacity. Both models allow for change in plant capacity over time. The process by which capacity changes is the same for both firms. If profit goals have been met for two successive periods and production is above 90 per cent of capacity, then capacity increases 20 per cent.

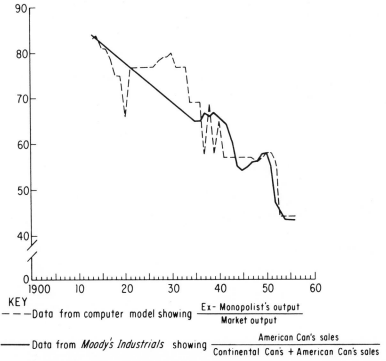

KEY

— — —Data from computer model showing $\dfrac{\text{Ex- Monopolist's output}}{\text{Market output}}$

————Data from *Moody's Industrials* showing $\dfrac{\text{American Can's sales}}{\text{Continental Can's + American Can's sales}}$

FIGURE 16–1. Comparisons of share-of-market data.

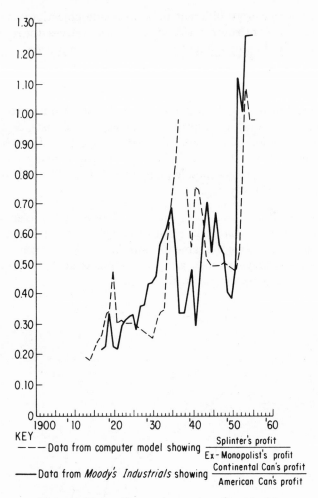

FIGURE 16–2. Comparisons of profit-ratio data.

2. A firm cannot change its output from one time period to the next more than ± 25 per cent. The rationale behind the latter assumption is that neither large cutbacks nor large advances in production are possible in the very short run, since there are large organization problems connected with either.

The various initial conditions specified previously are summarized in Table 16–2, along with the other initial conditions required to program the models.

We have now described a decision-making model with a large ex-monopolist and a splinter competitor. Table 16–3 shows some of the results of the model for selected periods.[8] By examining Table 16–3 we can determine the time paths of such variables as cost, conjectural variation, and output for each firm.

We also have compared the shares of market and profit ratio results with actual data generated from competition between an ex-monopolist, the American Can Company, and its splinter competitor, Continental Can Company, between 1913 and 1956. These results are shown in Figures 16–1 and 16–2. In general, we are encouraged by the surprisingly good fit of the behavioral model to real-world data, although we do not feel that this result *per se* constitutes a validation of our new approach to the theory of the firm.

VI. Summary

In this chapter we have considered a new, behavioral approach to the theory of the firm. This involves detailed consideration of the decision-making processes within a firm. Our major aim has been to show that the traditional theory is not the only way in which the economics of the firm can be analyzed. In order to acquire a complete understanding of the business firm as an institution it is necessary to analyze the effects of such variables as goal setting, goal adjustment, information flow, search patterns, and other internal organizational characteristics on the firm's decisions.

In general, the behavioral approach assumes that the firm is essentially an adaptively rational system. An adaptive system, as we use the term, has the following properties:

1. There exist a number of states of the system. At any point in time, the system in some sense "prefers" some of these states to others.

2. There exists an external source of disturbance or shock to the system. These shocks cannot be controlled.

3. There exist a number of decision variables internal to the system. These variables are manipulated according to some decision rules.

4. Each combination of external shocks and decision variables in the system changes the state of the system. Thus, given an existing state, an external shock, and a decision, the next state is determined.

5. Any decision rule that leads to a preferred state at one point is more likely to be used in the future than it was in the past; any decision rule that leads to a nonpreferred state at one point is less likely to be used in the future than it was in the past.

---

[8] Market demand was varied in the following way during this simulation: (1) The slope of the actual demand curve was held constant. (2) In each time period the intercept of the actual demand curve, I_t, was set equal to aI_{t-1}. The value of a was 1.08 for periods 1–16, 0.90 for periods 17–20, 1 for periods 21–26, and 1.08 from period 27 onward.

With this general assumption the behavioral approach then investigates effects of variables internal to the firm on price and output decisions. This approach is in sharp contrast to the traditional theory which ignores the internal structure of the firm. The latter approach assumes that market considerations dominate the internal structure of the firm in price and output decisions. This seems to be a valid position in the case of perfect competition. In the case of oligopoly, however, the firm can affect the market by its behavior and it is not completely dominated by market considerations. Thus a study of the internal factors affecting decisions can increase our understanding of firm behavior, especially in imperfect markets. Although the elaborations of the behavioral theory necessary for this have just begun, this seems a highly fruitful area for further research.

IE ENTREPRENEUR IN ECONOMIC CHANGE

Thomas C. Cochran

ᵗOR at least two centuries, during which
economists developed theories about
·ir own Western European culture, the lazy
.dity of man for pleasure and the laws of
·ration of reasonably free markets seemed
isfactory basic assumptions. Only when
itical needs for forced-draft economic
velopment in backward areas turned
· attention of economists to growth in
ange cultures were the social assumptions
t underlay classic theory clearly evident.
e more economists labored with the
·tic cultures of Asia, Africa, and Latin
ιerica, the more impressed they became
h both the force and intricacy of social
tors. Ten years after the end of World
ιr II some leading economists were ready
admit that "the really fundamental
·blems of economic development are
ιeconomic" (Buchanan & Ellis, 1955,
)).

MODELS OF ECONOMIC CHANGE

f for purposes of argument we may side
h these distinguished economists, their
tement implies the need for primarily
ial models of economic change. This in
n moves economic change from the
lusive realm of the economist or economic
torian into that of the general social
·ntist or historian.
But a model for social change either is
·ceived so broadly as to be a blunt tool

for analysis (for example: "Change occurs
when socially relevant new habits are
acquired via a learning process"), or in order
to provide detail introduces too many
variables. In spite of a wide recognition of
the importance of social and cultural factors
among economists, I know of no one who has
attempted a comprehensive general model.

A solution to this dilemma is to try to
narrow the scope of the problem by focusing
on a particular type of change where historical analogy can be of use. One way to do this
is by concentrating on how the variables
that seem most essential affect entrepreneurial decisions. If every economic
decision were made by a computer into
which social and economic factors were fed,
or by different individuals, each differently
conditioned and differently placed in the
social structure, it would be useless to focus
on the decision-maker. But fortunately this
is not the case. Decisions are normally made
in sequence by the same man, who is not a
random selection from the human species but
is, rather, a representative of a limited group
in his culture. Thus the noneconomic social
factors come in a definable set of influences
operating on the executive.

The role of the entrepreneur

As aggregates, managers or executives in a
given type of activity represent certain
ascertainable levels of education and social

Reprinted from *Behavioral Science,* 9 (1964), 111–119, by permission of the author
and editor.

status and types of cultural conditioning that produce a roughly definable modal personality. In making their decisions they play social roles anticipated by their associates and other groups in the culture. Therefore, in the modal entrepreneur (and in general the modes seem broad) there is a channel through which diverse, and in themselves intangible, social forces translate their effects into economic action; a point where social factors can be observed and estimated for relative intensities.

To begin with, the executives' inner character is largely conditioned by the type of child-rearing and schooling common to the culture. He receives the traditional admonitions, absorbs the family attitudes of his class, learns the ideologies and conceptual schemes of the society. Latin-American child-rearing, for example, even in the most advanced countries, tends to produce quite different characters from that of the United States (Landry, 1959, pp. 238 ff.). Similarly, American child-rearing and schooling before about 1920 produced differently conditioned individuals than did that of the 1920's and 1930's. Since this latter difference is of importance to the American business community, it will be well to use this as an illustration.

Middle-class parents of the turn of the century—and important executives have largely middle-class origins—were sure of the Christian moral values and the need for firm guidance and parental authority. A similar atmosphere permeated the school. By the 1920's the new psychology had undermined the old moral principles, up-to-date parents were Freudians or behaviorists, and good schools, public or private, were child- or community-centered (Cremin, 1961). Without going into all the complexities involved, it seems reasonable to suppose that a generation of executives was being trained with fewer fixed values, less secure principles, greater tendencies to be influenced by those around them: in a word, to be good organization men.

Whether this shift has been advantageous to the business community or not, it is probably too early to say, but it has fitted in with the needs of large-scale mass-production to give a particularly co-operative,

team-like aspect to American entrepreneu ship; one that is in quite striking contrast the individual- and family-centrism of l industrially advanced areas.

Returning to our model of the ent preneurial situation, the executive, therefo plays a social role partly shaped by t modal type of personality that comes fr the social conditioning of his generatic While unusual characters will always dep from the norms, in general invention a innovation will tend to be along lines cc genial to the type of conditioning. Anth pologists interested in change support t premise by saying that new items in t culture must be not only physically but a psychologically available. Subjective cc structions of the items must be made a these will depend on the value orientati of the culture (Vogt, 1960, p. 25). The r of change will be a function of the rate subjective construction. Thus executives one culture will conceptualize and use a n item, and in another culture, where the it is equally available, they may remain u aware of its existence.

Entrepreneurial roles are defined by t ideas of those important to the success of t actor. In the case of many new pursuits, su as manufacturing in an underdevelop country, the defining groups, those whom t executive seeks to satisfy, are often r connected with the industrial operation se. A role is established, therefore, that not necessarily instrumental to the ta involved. There is also much operatio trial and error. An Argentine manufactu of the 1920's, for example, wished primar to become an important family, busine and civic leader, achievements not necess ily functional to his role as an entreprene In operating a pioneer big business he had guide as to how he should divide his ti among production, finance, sales, and g ernment contacts. He could only learn experience how little working capital a what amount of time obligations would safe. But in a well-established corporatic defining groups such as the senior officers the board have well-formed expectatio and the entrepreneurial role may be said be closely defined.

It is obvious that the primarily cultu

factors operating on the personality of the executive and the defining of his role by those involved must accommodate to some degree to the necessities of the operations to be carried out. But the accommodation does not have to be an efficient one. For example, in West Texas in 1950, industrial risks in new lines such as furniture and other home fittings were relatively safe and offered high rates of return; but the banker role, as defined by both fellow officers and directors, was to loan only on cattle or land, and consequently the role was not efficiently adjusted to the actual needs or opportunities of the situation (Cochran, 1962, pp. 173–174).

This relatively simple framework of an entrepreneurial role defined by the personality of the actor, the expectations of groups with power to sanction deviations from expected behavior, and the operational needs of the function to be performed, subsumes all the social or cultural factors. But obviously, when so much is fitted into so little, each category must and does cover many complications (Jenks, 1949, pp. 108–152).

For example, observation of cultures making the change from agricultural-trading communities to industrial states shows that family obligations are one of the chief dysfunctional elements. But the force of the entrepreneur's feeling of obligation to the members of an extended family is hard to measure. It is easy enough to say that professional middle-management will only arise as this obligation grows weaker, but where are the critical points? How dysfunctional must this holdover from the static agrarian family become before a major alteration will occur in the entrepreneurial role?

It is because such questions, involving a variety of uncontrollable variables, cannot be directly answered by purely theoretical analysis that history becomes useful. The only plausible answers that can be offered have to be in terms of analogies taken from various historic situations. Once the factors are defined, as in the entrepreneurial-role model, it is possible to collect tolerably comparable data for such situations. Whether the facts are collected by economists or historians, whether the time span is two months or twenty years, it is still a

historical type of data; it is the record of what appears to have happened in a real situation where the variables could not be controlled to fit a research design. Thus Fayerweather's *The Executive Overseas* (1959), a study based chiefly on intimate observation of a small number of executives in Mexico over a 4-month period, is a history, even though the time-span is short and the data are unconventional.

ENTREPRENEURIAL INTERACTION WITH CHANGE

It is easier to demonstrate the dynamics of the entrepreneurial model by selecting instances from abroad where the pressures of advanced American technology have rapidly penetrated traditional agricultural cultures, but I believe it will be of more interest to American businessmen and economists to select some examples of entrepreneurial interaction with change from our own history, and to ignore events before the 19th century. In the last 150 years business executives have participated in three changes that cannot be neglected in any account of how we arrived at where we are: first, the rapid adoption of industrial machinery in the first half of the 19th century; second, the rise of professional management in the large corporation, starting in the second half of the century; and third, the spread of mass-production techniques in the 20th century. In each of these major changes the social factors in American culture operating through the entrepreneur appear to be well marked. The analysis may also be used to answer questions as to why corresponding changes did not occur in other cultures.

Rapid industrialization

In turning to the first type of change, it is striking that the usual problem of the present-day growth theorist is to account for overly-slow industrial expansion either in some less-advanced area or in the present United States, whereas in studying early 19th-century America the problem is to account for unusually rapid industrialization with novel characteristics. The major question is: Why did American entrepreneurs adopt machinery more rapidly than their counterparts in Western Europe? And the most convincing economic answer is because of shortage of labor. Habakkuk (1962) made an extensive analysis of this problem of labor shortage in relation to early American manufacturing methods, and came to the general conclusion that the development of the latter can be deduced from purely economic circumstances. In his arguments he sees certain entrepreneurial characteristics as products of the American economic environment. This is a chicken-egg problem, and my position is that if a modal personality trait exists at a given time it is more realistic to treat it as a cultural factor, regardless of what may have accounted for this trait historically.

While not contradicting any of Habakkuk's economic reasoning, the position taken by Sawyer (1954), that factors of culture and social structure were extremely important in early American manufacturing, seems to offer a more useful explanation, one applicable beyond manufacturing to other fields of entrepreneurial activity.

Using the work of both these scholars, let us see how their conclusions fit our model of entrepreneurial role. The American situation definitely emphasized certain operational needs. Since labor was scarce and valuable there was a greater inducement to plan for its efficient use. This in turn led to greater consciousness of costs and alertness to opportunities for substituting machinery; in other words, to rapid subjective construction of such new items. Habakkuk finds a contrast to England in these respects, and the contrast with Latin America or a nation like Greece would be even more striking.

But American entrepreneurial behavior also depended on different attitudes in such defining groups as fellow managers, customers, and bankers. Innovations within what anthropologists have called the "limits of sameness" met relatively little resistance. That is, if the innovation promised the same general type of product at less cost it was likely to be considered rationally on economic grounds, rather than resisted by both proprietors and labor from disinclination toward change. These matters, of course, are relative. Strassmann (1959) has emphasized early American resistance to risking addi-

tional capital. One can only say that comparatively Habakkuk finds British investors still more cautious, and in the nations destined to remain underdeveloped, the resistance was great enough to check almost all large-scale industrial investment.

American customers placed little value on fine craftsmanship–for that they would buy imports. In domestic goods they sought cheapness and utility. There was also a noticeable feeling that expenditure to produce exceptionally long life or permanence in an article was a waste. The migratory American purchaser would often sell his equipment before a move to another locality or replace it by something better.

As far as the general public was concerned the business executive was playing to an appreciative audience. Trade or manufacturing, even on a small scale, carried no social stigma. Financial success could immediately raise the executive to the top level of most American society. This pull of unrestricted opportunity was absent in the more rigid societies which characterized the rest of the civilized world.

These attitudes on the part of defining groups were necessarily reflected in the personality of the entrepreneur. Thus the executives of New England and the Middle States in the first half of the 19th century seem to have shared a feeling that work was a duty, and that a calling should be carefully selected and vigorously pursued. Child-rearing and education both placed emphasis on the busy, productive individual. Optimism about getting ahead was emphasized in the school texts, and presumably in family conversation (De Charms & Moeller, 1962).

Inadequate though it was, elementary education was probably more widespread in New England and the Middle States than in most Western nations. Governor DeWitt Clinton of New York illustrated a common cultural attitude when he said in 1826: "The first duty of government, and the surest evidence of good government, is the encouragement of education" (quoted in Cubberly, 1919, p. 112). Of executives born between 1790 and 1819 who came to be listed in the *Dictionary of American Bio-*

graphy, Mills (1945) found a total of 55 per cent with high school education or more, and only 23 per cent with only apprenticeship or a negligible formal education. Of manufacturing executives between 1789 and 1865 whose education is recorded in company histories, Brewer (1962, p. 49) also found 55 per cent with high school or college education and only 7 per cent with no formal education.

There are many characteristics of both the personality of entrepreneurs and the attitudes or expectations of defining groups that appear to be associated with the highly migratory character of the American population. Unfortunately there are few reliable statistics before 1850, but the case studies that exist suggest that the average American moved several times during his life, and that executives were probably more geographically mobile than the average. The elements associated with migration that would increase the efficiency of an entrepreneurial role were: emphasis on self-help as against aid from family status; willingness to cooperate with relative strangers, or impersonality; tolerance of, and adjustment to, strange conditions; and a tendency to innovate in making such adjustments (Lee, 1961). Recent studies have underlined the importance of moderate changes in environment in stimulating new ideas and practices (Barnett, 1953, pp. 87–88, 93).

One recognizes the above list as containing the elements that scholars have associated with successful industrialization. Co-operation and impersonality have been rated as specially important factors (Hirschman, 1958, p. 17). In the 1830's de Tocqueville was impressed with American co-operativeness. Very early, American executives engineered mergers, formed associations to control prices and production, and in general demonstrated a rational ability to put profits ahead of personal rivalries or animosities. This has not been so in other cultures, where pride in family companies has led to complete failure to meet changing market situations rationally (Cochran, 1959, pp. 91, 96). Impersonality, keeping personal friendships apart from business dealings, has led American executives to expect market considerations to govern patronage. There have been, of course, exceptions to this, but in general suppliers are changed for business reasons with a readiness not present in more traditional societies (Sawyer, 1954, pp. 365–366).

From the early 19th century on American executives showed what Hirschman has called the " 'growth perspective,' which comprises not only the desire for economic growth but also the perception of the essential nature of the road leading toward it." (1958, p. 10). On the basis of the rapid and creative subjective construction induced by American conditioning, whatever its original causes, the role of the entrepreneur becomes a major differentiating element in social and economic change. In spite of a level of technological knowledge below that of England, even in 1850, the American entrepreneur introduced a more highly mechanized industrialism and set in motion an upward spiral of labor-saving devices which continued to operate (Sawyer, 1954, pp. 365–366).

The rise of professional management

When we have a longer perspective, it may appear that the second type of entrepreneurially-guided change, the replacing of the owner entrepreneur by the professional executive as the chief managerial type, has been the most important socioeconomic development in American business. The need for readapting the attitudes of certain defining groups, chiefly officers and directors, and altering the role of the chief executives to meet the demands and opportunities of the large, widely-owned corporation inevitably brought about change. Whereas in our first example changes in operations appear to have been accelerated by the peculiar conditioning of American entrepreneurs, in this second example, a change in the methods of business operation gradually altered the role and the personality of the entrepreneur. It should be emphasized, however, that these American executives were peculiarly susceptible to role changes in the directions needed for the functioning of the large corporation.

Between 1850 and 1890, most of the new

obligations and opportunities associated with administering other people's money were worked out in the large railroads. In the 1850's, officers and directors saw nothing amiss in being on both sides of a bargain, of selling supplies to the railroad, buying land from the road for resale at a profit, or owning facilities such as bridges or stockyards that the road had to rent. Some of these arrangements had arisen because the early railroads were chronically short of capital, and as conditions became easier after 1865 ethics grew stricter. In the best-run companies, by the middle 1880's the executive role had been defined with a strictness that has not greatly altered since that time. In 1883 Charles E. Perkins, President of the Chicago, Burlington and Quincy Railroad, wrote to one of his top executives: "The smallest kind of an interest in a coal mine would be objectionable." Officers should not "make money out of side shows." (Cochran, 1953, p. 436).

As important as the improvement in ethics, essential to the continued attraction of capital, was the development of modern systems of big business management. Advancement on the basis of ability, security of tenure, delegation of authority, decentralization of operations, open but orderly channels of communication, and managerial co-operation for company welfare may all seem at first glance to be inevitable adjustments to the problem of size. But anyone who has studied the functioning of large organizations in other cultures knows this is not so. Until very recent years the biggest electrical machinery manufacturing firm in Latin America failed, in spite of the services of United States management consultants, to develop these characteristics (Cochran & Reina, 1962, pp. 184–191, 222–225). Delegation of authority, easy communication between levels of management, and co-operation among managers on the same level have all been difficult to achieve in Latin America, and in most other cultures. Even in England and Germany there is more difficulty in these respects than in the United States.

The decisive difference appears to be that American executives are reared in the equalitarian atmosphere of an outgoing, pragmatic, democratic society. They are taught from childhood on that co-operation for mutual benefit is good, and the type of individualism they develop does not stand in the way of easy relations with their peers.

This latter point is of particular importance. As the result of rather elaborate analyses of United States individualism in comparison to that of Latin America, some basically important differences appear. Fayerweather (1959, pp. 12–17, 194–195) calls Mexican executives "individualistic" in personality and Americans "group-oriented." To the former he attaches the characteristics of: distrust in the relations of managers with their superiors; hostility in relations with their peers; and a sense of separation in their relations with subordinates. To the group-oriented personality he attributes confidence and fellow-feeling in relations with superiors and peers, and a sense of union with subordinates. Research at the University of Pennsylvania has indicated that so-called American individualism is a matter of standing up for one's rights in the group or against government or other external encroachment, in contrast to the more subjective, inward-looking individualism of Latin Americans.[1]

The Latin type of personality, shared to some degree by entrepreneurs in most underdeveloped areas, has made it much more difficult to create efficient managerial structures for expanding business; or viewed another way, has tended to put a ceiling on corporate expansion at the level where one man or a small family group can give personal attention to the details of operation. In contrast to Latin distrust of fellow executives, the British missions sent between 1949 and 1952 to observe American manufacturing methods issued reports such as: "Among the executives we met, we encountered . . . a readiness to encourage and pass on knowledge to juniors" (Sawyer, 1954, p. 365). The United States attitudes have accelerated change through expansion, mergers, diversification of products, and decentralization (Chandler, 1962).

[1] For Latin American traits see Cochran (1959, pp. 122–125).

Mass-production techniques

Economists tend to see the third major change, the rapid spread of advanced mass-production techniques, as a function of both the state of technology and the size of the American domestic market. Since by 1900 the United States had more and wealthier customers than either England or Germany, it developed larger-scale processes and bigger companies. But social historians are impressed by additional factors.

To begin with, American culture as expressed in law and government demanded efforts to maintain the ideal of competition. The interpretation of restraint of trade by the courts and by both state and national antitrust laws deprived medium-sized businesses of the ability to protect their positions by legal agreements or cartels. This led to mergers into larger units which were judged legal as long as they did not try to, or threaten to, monopolize the trade. The bigger units resulting from this social pressure would perhaps have led in any case to a more intensive search for economies of scale than seems to have been pursued elsewhere. In addition to these exogenous forces that altered the operational demands of the entrepreneurial role, the personality characteristics noted in early American manufacturers persisted. The English missions of the mid-20th century reported that productivity "is part of the American way of life, an article of faith as much as a matter of economics . . . Americans believe it is their mission to lead the world in productive efficiency.

" 'Cost-consciousness' . . . does not simply mean cutting costs. . . . It also means not missing opportunities.

"American managements look continually towards the future. They base their decisions on an intelligent anticipation of trends rather than wait until the pressure of current events forces them to make the decisions." (Sawyer, 1954, p. 365).

Henry Ford, generally credited with being the most dramatic adapter of new mass-production techniques in the 20th century, shows interesting contrasts to the man who, more nearly than any other, was his counterpart in Argentina. Ford was literally obsessed by machinery (or, in more formal language, oriented toward change in mechanical items). His subjective constructions were in terms of new machines and processes (Nevins, 1954, pp. 49 ff.). Although each of his major innovations—the Model T, the power-driven continuous assembly line, and the 5-dollar minimum wage—can readily be attributed to the ideas of subordinates, Ford saw his entrepreneurial role in terms of these achievements. On the other hand, Torcuato Di Tella, who introduced household electric refrigeration and other electrical machinery to Argentina, saw his role in much broader terms, and delegated most of the purely technological work to trusted subordinates. In other words, Ford represented the classic American drives for mechanization and efficiency, Di Tella the Latin interests in the all-around social man who would be family leader, business leader, intellectual, and patron of the arts. Both were extremely "driven" individuals, but Ford had the singleness of purpose so usual to American entrepreneurial personality, Di Tella the more diffused ambitions of men of Latin and many other cultures.

SOCIAL STRUCTURE AND CHANGE

So far, little has been said about elements of social structure, as distinct from values, that may negate change. Most such elements are associated with rigidities. Their existence, however, is usually manifest in the conditioning of the modal entrepreneurial personality. An aristocratic social structure like 19th-century England, for example, made becoming an aristocrat a more attractive goal for the successful entrepreneur than continued expansion of his business. This structure tended to produce a cutoff point in expansion similar to that imposed by the limits of direct personal or family control.

Aside from caste or status lines per se, some cultures are more static and ceremonial than others. While these conditions might be traced back to geographical and economic circumstances, at any specific time they are given parts of the situation. Fear of change by the power elite, for example, may be based on low energy and resources, but it comes to exist as a separate factor.

CONCLUSIONS

My general position, as distinct from the specific application of role theory, is summed up in technical language by psychologists De Charms and Moeller. They say: "We propose that motivation, or cultural orientation be conceived as an intervening variable standing between antecedent environmental factors associated with economic and political changes and consequent behavior resulting in cultural changes such as technological growth . . . Thus two cultures undergoing similar economic or political change may react quite differently due to intervening variables of values, child rearing practices, and motives." (1962, p. 142).

The concepts of entrepreneurial role offer ways of defining and organizing these "intervening variables." But unfortunately, neither this nor other current systems can quantify the variables so that additions or subtractions can be made in the measurable terms of land, labor, capital, or market price. One cannot speak of units or doses of personality or values. For problems of change over time where the variables are numerous and nonquantifiable there seems no substitute for historical analogy applied to carefully defined situations. Location of social variables in terms of more or less, or below or above some norm, or as correlates of other variables is frequently possible. These operations do not lead to equations but rather to propositions stating probable relationships. The statement that limits are placed on motivation for achievement by "too large discrepancies between expectations and results," which "may develop an avoidance motive as far as achievement is concerned" (McClelland, Atkinson, Clark, & Lowell, 1953, p. 65), or Vogt's proposition that "the importance of value orientation in shaping the direction of change is proportional to the amount of economic and technological control a society has achieved" (1960, p. 26), are examples of useful but nonquantifiable relationships. They are, however, of the same degree of specificity as such economic maxims as "the larger the market the greater the division of labor."

Role theory allows for change by the deviant action of an individual, but the emphasis in my discussion has been change as the interaction of modal types personality with the culturally conditione expectations of defining groups and th operational needs of situations. Exogenou changes in population, resources, technolog consumer demand, or merely what Hur (1963, pp. 80–81) has called "cumulativ institutional drift," all seem most likely impinge first on the role structure by crea ing new operational needs; but the entr preneurial response to these needs may either successful innovation or dogge continuance of a dysfunctional way of doin things. The response will depend on variabl of personality and culture, which, as we hav seen, are predictable within certain limits.

There is no theoretical reason wh important innovation in role behavior cou not arise from inner-conditioning indepen ently of all immediate exogenous factors. is merely the bias of my historical observ tion that I think such instances rare. It ma be, for example, that the particular innov tions credited to Ford would only have bee prompted in the precise year by such uniquely conditioned character, but over 20-year span the exact timing seems re atively unimportant. The given innovation or superior ones usually seem to be in proces of introduction by several executives. general theory for relating economic an other social factors to change should de with normal responses of functional grou to at least partially repetitive situation From this standpoint a model of entrepre neurial role is a useful device.

REFERENCES

Barnett, H. G. *Innovation: the strategy of econom development.* New Haven: Yale Univ. Pres 1958.

Brewer, T. B. The formative period of 140 manu facturing companies, 1789–1929. Unpub lished doctoral dissertation, University Pennsylvania, 1962 (Microfilm).

Buchanan, N. S., & Ellis, H. S. *Approaches economic development.* New York: Twentiet Century Fund, 1955.

Chandler, A. D. *Structure and strategy.* Cambridge Mass: MIT Press, 1962.

Cochran, T. C. *Railroad leaders, 1845–1890.* Cam bridge, Mass.: Harvard Univ. Press, 1953

Cochran, T. C. *The Puerto Rican businessman* Philadelphia: Univ. of Pennsylvania Press 1959.

ochran, T. C. *The American business system.* New York: Torchbooks, 1962.

ochran, T. C., & Reina, R. E. *Entrepreneurship in Argentine culture.* Philadelphia: Univ. of Pennsylvania Press, 1962.

remin, L. A. *The transformation of the school.* New York: Knopf, 1961.

ubberly, E. P. *Public education in the United States.* Boston: Houghton Mifflin, 1919.

Charms, R., & Moeller, H. H. Values expressed in American children's readers, 1800–1950. *J. abnorm. soc. Psychol.*, 1962, 64, 136–142.

ayerweather, J. *The executive overseas.* Syracuse, N. Y.: Syracuse Univ. Press, 1959.

abakkuk, H. J. *American and British technology in the 19th century.* Cambridge, England: Cambridge Univ. Press, 1962.

irschman, A. E. *The strategy of economic development.* New Haven: Yale Univ. Press, 1958.

urst, W. *Law and the social process.* Ann Arbor: Univ. of Michigan Press, 1963.

Jenks, L. H. *Change and the entrepreneur.* Cambridge, Mass.: Harvard Univ. Press, 1949.

Landry, D. *Tropical childhood.* Chapel Hill: Univ. of North Carolina Press, 1959.

Lee, E. S. The Turner thesis re-examined. *Amer. Quart.*, 1961, 13, 77–83.

McClelland, D. C., Atkinson, J. W., Clark, R. A., & Lowell, E. L. *The achievement motive.* New York: Appleton-Century-Crofts, 1953.

Mills, C. W. The American business elite: a collective portrait. *J. econ. Hist.*, 1954, 5 (suppl).

Nevins, A. *Ford.* New York: Scribner's, 1954.

Sawyer, J. E. The social basis of the American system of manufacturing. *J. econ. Hist.*, 1954, 14, 361–379.

Strassman, W. P. *Risk and technological innovation.* Ithaca, N. Y.: Cornell Univ. Press, 1959.

Vogt, E. Z. On the concepts of structure and process in cultural anthropology. *Amer. Anthropol.*, 1960, 62, 18–33.

Empirical Evidence of the Subjective Bases of Location Decisions

LOCATION DECISIONS OF MANUFACTURERS

Eva Mueller *and* James N. Morgan

Better understanding of the process by which firms and workers move is crucial, not only to the theory of industrial location, but in developing public policies, for instance, to minimize the difficulties resulting from tariff reductions or to help depressed areas. The purpose of this paper is to analyze the factors which govern location decisions in the manufacturing sector of the economy, using data from a survey of *Location Decisions and Industrial Mobility in Michigan* [1] conducted by the Survey Research Center in spring 1961.

The study was based on personal interviews with top executives (presidents, vice-presidents, plant managers) of 239 Michigan manufacturing plants in spring 1961. The sample of plants was drawn by probability methods and was designed to be representative of all manufacturing plants in Michigan with only minor exclusions. The probability that a plant would fall into the sample was proportional to its employment, and responses were weighted by employment. Interviews were obtained with top executives of 91 per cent of the sampled plants, including the Big Three automobile companies. However, the data for these three companies were not included in the statistical tabulations, since they might have dominated the results. Each interviewer asked the identical sequence of questions, but respondents were encouraged to answer each question at length in their own words, describing fully their situation and attitudes.

We shall distinguish between three kinds of location decisions: (1) the location of new firms, (2) the decision of existing firms to stay at their present location or, alternatively, to relocate, and (3) location decisions which occur in connection with expansion of facilities. Although in practice this classification is not always clear cut, we shall demonstrate that these three kinds of decisions are arrived at in different ways and dominated by different considerations. It will be shown that the traditional cost and demand factors have indeed an important influence on location decisions, but that other economic as well as noneconomic factors may play a significant role under certain circumstances. Thus the assumption of profit maximization is too restrictive for an analysis of location decisions. The process of industrial location is clarified if we recognize other preferences in addition to the desire for maximum profits.

Reprinted from *American Economic Review, Papers & Proceedings*, 502 (1962), 204–217, by permission of the authors and editor.

429

Location has been studied in different ways. One can study the inputs and market locations of an industry and determine the locations which minimize the costs of manufacture and shipping (and possibly also costs in time). Insofar as transportation is a major cost, as markets and inputs are not themselves subject to movement and as necessary resources are available only in a limited number of locations, this type of analysis can lead to useful conclusions. This approach was used successfully, for instance, by Walter Isard in his analysis of the iron and steel industry [2] and in Edgar M. Hoover's classical study of the shoe and leather industry [3]. However, for many industries transport cost differentials are not a dominant location factor or major inputs are available in many places. Hence, although some locations are ruled out by cost and market considerations, there remain many alternative locations which are feasible. Under these circumstances there is a purpose to going beyond factors bearing directly on costs and market access and to examine also some "nonpecuniary factors." We mean by nonpecuniary factors those which have no obvious effect on dollar cost and revenue (personal preferences for a location, good schools) as well as those whose impact on costs and revenues is indirect and cannot be readily quantified (industrial climate, business contacts). We are not distinguishing between the theoretical and the empirical, nor between the deductive and the pragmatic—they should go hand in hand. But we are distinguishing between the limited use of a simple theory focused on a few economic factors as against a more comprehensive theory which attempts to select from among a larger number of possible influences those which really matter under given circumstances.[1]

Once we broaden the scope of our theory to include a larger range of preferences on the part of decision-makers, we must have more detailed information. It is appealing then to start with a representative sample of plants and interview their managers. Instead of checking out the presumptive influence of a few things which can be measured in dollars and cents, we find out by asking which of a large number of factors affect industrial location decisions.

The notion that firms may not maximize profits in the short run has been discussed primarily as regards decisions about the size of output and price. In relation to location decisions it would mean, among other things, that as costs and market advantages change over time, the firm may prefer stability of location to repeated moves in order to realize an optimum. Needless to say, when we speak of stability of location, we do not imply that adjustment to change will not take place under any circumstances. Rather, it is argued that change

[1] For an earlier discussion of this approach, see [4].

will take place when, but only when, the firm consciously recognizes a sizable deviation from the maximand.

With these ideas in mind, it was assumed that prevailing attitudes among industrialists—subjective feelings of satisfaction or dissatisfaction with the present location—are an important variable in any attempt to explain or predict location decisions. No doubt these attitudes are to a large extent an outgrowth of objective economic factors. Why then do we introduce attitudes into the analysis instead of the so-called "objective" conditions? There are two reasons. First, advantages and disadvantages of a location are difficult to measure in cost and revenue terms. For example, labor cost comparisons between states must take into account wage rates for equal work (which is not easy to define), costs of fringe benefits, as well as labor productivity, reliability, and versatility. Such factors as market potential or industrial climate are still more difficult to measure or compare. The measurement problem appears formidable if we consider that the attractiveness of a location may also be influenced by such factors as union attitudes, the legal climate, zoning regulations, schools, recreational facilities, and the like.

Second, even when it can be determined that certain cost differentials exist between locations—say that taxes differ by an amount equivalent to 3 per cent of the wage bill—it is not clear how important such a differential is to the manufacturer. Certainly, favorable and unfavorable locational factors are not additive in the simple sense that dollars and cents are. A combination of unfavorable factors may bring about serious discontent, even though each factor by itself may be of minor consequence. There may be a threshold below which unfavorable developments do not matter greatly, but above which they affect location decisions. The translation of objective developments into subjective-attitudinal rather than financial terms therefore not only facilitates the measurement problem but provides us with a meaningful variable for research on the decision-making process.

This is not the place to describe in detail how satisfactions and dissatisfactions were measured in the survey. It suffices to say that a large number of questions were asked to assess attitudes toward specific conditions and changes in Michigan. These were then combined to construct an attitude scale which achieves a rough rank-ordering of firms from the most to the least satisfied with their location in Michigan [1].

The Location of New Firms

The location of a new firm undoubtedly is a genuine decision in the sense that possible alternatives are carefully weighed and an optimum is sought. What are the considerations that enter into such decisions? Among other things, respondents were shown a list of twenty-one locational factors and asked to identify the five which would be most crucial in locating a plant such as theirs. According to Table 1, six factors each were rated as being of major importance by manufacturers accounting for 50 per cent or more of employment. They are, in order of frequency: labor costs, proximity to markets, availability of skilled labor, industrial climate, the tax bill, and proximity to materials. By and large, these are the cost and demand factors stressed by traditional location theory. The one nonpecuniary factor among the six top-ranking considerations is industrial climate, defined in the survey as "attitudes of the state and community toward industry."

The discussion was then shifted from general locational principles to a particular location decision. Executives of plants which were opened in Michigan since 1940 were asked why this specific plant was located in Michigan. In this context noneconomic reasons were mentioned much more often. Table 2 shows that executives of plants accounting for half of the employment in plants established in Michigan since 1940 reported that their plant was located in Michigan by historical accident—because the founder lived there, liked it there, or had valuable business connections there. Twenty per cent (in some cases the same executives) said that they happened to find a good plant site in Michigan or that they had an attractive opportunity to buy a business in Michigan.[2] The remaining responses related primarily to cost and demand factors, with proximity to customers receiving particularly frequent mention. Corresponding questions about selection of the specific plant site within Michigan again show that historical accident and personal preferences of the founder(s) play an important role.[3]

Many executives mentioned cost and market factors as well as personal and business ties. It may be inferred from the survey that often a number of alternative locations may be feasible for a new firm on the basis of cost and demand considerations. The owner's personal preferences and contacts may then be decisive in selecting among the feasible locations.

Both parts of Table 2 show sizable differences by size of firm. According to manufacturers' explanations, personal considerations and historical accident play a much greater role in the location of factories of smaller firms than in the location of factories which are part of large multiplant firms. In studying the interviews, one obtains the distinct impression that more careful cost and market calculations are made by

[2] All the analysis is in terms of the proportions of employment represented, but for ease in writing, phrases such as "proportion of executives" are used occasionally.
[3] Personal preferences also emerged as an important factor in [5] and [6].

TABLE 1
IMPORTANT LOCATIONAL FACTORS IN MICHIGAN BY INDUSTRY
(Percentage of Employment Represented)

Important Locational Factors Mentioned‡	All Michigan	INDUSTRY					
		Transportation Equipment	Machinery (including electrical)	Fabricated Metals	Rubber, Plastics, Petroleum, and Chemical Products	Manufactured Consumers Goods§	Primary Materials Industries**
Labor costs (wages, productivity)	65%	69%	59%	68%	76%	57%	73%
Proximity to markets (including transportation costs)	62	75	56	55	70	77	54
Availability of labor (skills, supply)	56	50	67	68	39	66	40
Industrial climate	53	19	55	50	61	54	67
Taxes	52	50	53	65	48	49	48
Proximity to materials (including transportation costs)	50	78	44	25	48	49	60
Water	41	44	35	25	70	29	54
Unionism	23	19	30	28	15	23	15
Community factors	14	23	12	11	9	12	14
Marketing facilities	11	*	8	10	3	20	23
Traffic access; parking	7	6	13	3	3	6	4
Zoning, other regulations	4	14	3	3	3	*	2
Local sources of financing	3	3	3	*	3	6	4
Total	†	†	†	†	†	†	†

* Less than ½ per cent.
† Totals differ from 100 per cent because respondents mentioned more than one factor.
‡ Factors either selected as important from list of twenty-one locational factors or mentioned in answer to the question: "Are there any minimum requirements which must be met for locating plants in this line of industry—for instance, a very large or very pure water supply, an unusually large or particularly skilled labor force?"
§ Includes such industries as food, textiles, and furniture.
** Includes such industries as lumber, paper, and primary metals.

TABLE 2

EXPLANATIONS GIVEN FOR LOCATION OF PLANT BY NUMBER OF PLANTS OPERATED BY FIRM

(Percentage of Employment Represented)

	All Michigan	NUMBER OF PLANTS OPERATED BY FIRM		
		One Plant	2–4 Plants	5 or More Plants
Main Reasons for Locating Plant in Michigan‡				
Personal reasons; chance................	50%	63%	52%	32%
Opportunity—found good site, etc.........	19	23	20	14
Proximity to customers; central location....	15	17	20	4
Proximity to auto industry..............	8	14	4	4
Labor advantages......................	7	*	12	14
Proximity to materials..................	6	3	8	9
Local concessions and inducements; encouragement by groups or persons...........	2	*	*	4
Better tax situation.....................	1	*	*	4
State already established as a center for the industry.............................	1	*	4	*
Total.......	†	†	†	†
Main Reasons for Locating Plant at Particular Site§				
Personal reasons; chance................	33%	55%	32%	20%
Opportunity—found good site, etc.........	18	27	16	14
Proximity to customers; central location....	15	16	15	14
Proximity to auto industry..............	13	7	14	12
Labor advantages......................	7	4	9	7
Proximity to materials..................	12	7	6	15
Local concessions and inducements; encouragement by groups or persons...........	4	2	4	7
Better tax situation.....................	3	4	6	2
Area already established as a center for the industry.............................	2	1	2	4
Total........	†	†	†	†

* Less than ½ per cent.

† Totals differ from 100 per cent because some respondents mentioned more than one reason, and for some others the reasons were not ascertained.

‡ Asked only at plants that started operating at present locations after 1940. The question was: "What were the main reasons for locating the plant in Michigan?"

§ The question was: "What were the main reasons that operations were set up here in [name of town]?"

larger than by smaller firms. It also seems that attempts to evaluate not only current costs and market factors but also future trends are more common among larger than among smaller firms. The following quotations may serve to illustrate the difference in approach.

A pattern maker company (current employment 20):

It's my home, I've never gone anywhere, I was trained here, my contacts are here, where else would I go? It takes me a while to catch on but once I take root I don't want to change. I like Michigan.

An electrical machinery and equipment company (current employment 1,100):

I come from Ohio. I came to Michigan with another company. When I thought I could see that the other company was going to fold, I started to develop this business, with the help and cooperation of a few fellow-workers. As we were still working with this company that had brought us to Michigan, the new business of course had to be in this state—and in this town.

One of Michigan's largest employers:

In locating plants that supply other plants, finding the minimum cost location amounts to finding an optimum location with respect to the already existing plants this new plant will feed, and the location of the inputs necessary for the new plant's operations. The dominant factors determining the location of a plant such as this, then, would be costs of transportation to the plants it will supply and the availability of resources, modified by considerations of labor supply, labor costs, and the availability of very large sites at alternate locations. Marginal rate changes and changes in regulations affecting transportation costs, or any other costs for that matter, will naturally alter the optimality of any given plant's location. All we can do is to sit down and try to find the minimum cost location in the light of conditions as they are today and in consideration of whatever changes we can foresee in the future.

Often new companies which start on a small scale with limited resources seem to have little real choice in the matter of location. Potential new entrepreneurs undoubtedly are most numerous in the older, heavily industrialized areas. Local business relationships and the attraction of familiar places and friends seem to have a tendency to keep them in these areas. Thus the impact of nonpecuniary factors may well be in the direction of slowing down shifts in the geographic distribution of manufacturing activity. This conclusion is less pertinent for firms which start with substantial resources or have a subsidiary relationship to a large established company.

It also appears that an area may improve its chances of attracting newly created firms by being a desirable place to live for new entrepreneurs and management. For the small entrepreneur in particular, a location decision is a consumer (or household) as well as a business decision; that is, the preference function which is relevant includes consumer as well as business preferences. This does not mean merely that the appeal of a community to business is enhanced by climate and scenery (as in the case of California). Fourteen per cent of Michigan manufacturers rated community factors (housing, size of town, schools, recreation facilities) among the five most important locational factors. When asked to evaluate the relative importance of proximity to markets and materials on the one hand and "such things as good community relations, favorable industrial climate, good schools, or adequate recreation facilities" on the other hand, 26 per cent of manufacturers argued that these latter matters are more important and another 12 per cent argued that they are equally important. It appears here that some importance attaches to location factors which are "manmade," in the sense that they can be altered by the actions of government, business, labor, and community groups.

The Decision to Relocate

As firms grow older and expand, many remain at or near their original locations, even though these locations may have become far from ideal. It is at this point that concepts like Simon's "satisficing" entrepreneur [7], Boulding's homeostasis (maintenance of the balance of the organism) [8], and Katona's habitual behavior [9] become relevant for location theory. Besides the obvious financial cost of relocation, stability in plant locations results from inertia, from uncertainty, from personal attachments of owners and managers to a place, or from reluctance to disrupt tested ways of operating or established business connections. Manufacturing firms have important ties to other business firms—retail and wholesale customers, their suppliers, subcontractors, service establishments which perform auxiliary functions, machine tool shops, banks, legal and accounting firms. Moreover, 40 per cent of manufacturing output in the U. S. is absorbed as inputs by manufacturing itself, a figure which illustrates the importance of interfirm connections [10]. Firms are groups of people, and business connections have an element of personal co-operation which is strengthened by proximity and long-standing relationships.

The power of inertia and the forces making for stability are evident in the Michigan data. Although there is widespread dissatisfaction with conditions in Michigan, manufacturers accounting for only 8 per cent of employment in sampled industries were thinking of relocating their plants in the next few years. Michigan manufacturers who had no relocation plans were asked: "If you could start from scratch again with this plant, do you think you would locate where you are now or somewhere else?" About 40 per cent of executives replied that they would prefer to be located in another state and named a specific state or region. In Ohio, where some interviews were also taken, the feeling that the present location is not optimal was expressed by a somewhat smaller, but still substantial, proportion of manufacturers.

Those few manufacturers who did indicate that there was a possibility of relocation were asked what advantages would be offered by the new location being considered. The first column of Table 3 shows that cost factors were mentioned far more frequently than market considerations. Lower labor costs, in particular, were often cited as a reason for preferring another location. Tax considerations ranked second in Michigan, and market factors were a close third.

The emphasis on cost factors in connection with relocation decisions is clarified when relocation plans are related to recent growth of the firm. The proportion of manufacturers with plans to relocate all or part

TABLE 3

REASONS GIVEN BY MICHIGAN MANUFACTURERS FOR POSSIBLE RELOCATION
OR EXPANSION AT NEW LOCATIONS

(Percentage of Employment Represented)

Cited as advantages of possible new locations‡	Among Michigan Firms Considering Relocation	Among Michigan Firms Considering Expansion
Labor costs, unionism............................	32%	23%
Taxes..	20	8
Lower costs—not specific..........................	4	3
Proximity to customers, marketing facilities.........	18	49
Availability of plant site, local concessions..........	10	10
Proximity to materials...........................	*	2
Industrial climate................................	3	1
Labor supply.....................................	2	*
Other..	3	14
Total..	†	†

* Less than ½ per cent.
† Total differs from 100 per cent because some respondents mentioned several advantages, while others (having no specific location in mind as yet) did not mention any.
‡ These questions were asked of 23 per cent of Michigan manufacturers who said that they definitely, probably, or possibly might relocate and of 29 per cent who said they would or might expand in other areas.

of their operations out of the state of Michigan is 14 per cent among those plants which experienced a decline in employment of at least 10 per cent over the past ten years; but it is only 5 per cent among plants with stationary employment and 4 per cent among plants with increases in employment of at least 10 per cent and/or increases in sales of at least 40 per cent.

The survey also shows a clear association between relocation plans and the attitude scale which measures degree of satisfaction or dissatisfaction with a Michigan location. Plans to relocate all or part of operations out of state are more frequent among those with the least favorable attitudes (11 per cent) than among those in the midrange category (8 per cent) or those with the most favorable attitudes (2 per cent). It should be stated here that unfavorable attitudes in Michigan relate primarily to cost factors: labor, taxes, and the state's legal climate.

Among the firms planning to relocate, there are of course a few with satisfactory sales trends and favorable attitudes toward a Michigan location; a change in product, market, or manufacturing process or costs may have prompted the plan to move in those cases. On the other hand, many managements which are highly critical of developments in Michigan have no thought of relocating their plant. Unfavorable attitudes seem to become decisive when established methods of operation no longer produce satisfactory results; for example, when the firm is experiencing falling profit margins, persistently declining sales, or increasing competition. Faced with the necessity of taking some action, an out-of-state move to a (supposedly) low-cost location becomes an alternative that might not have been considered in a more favorable climate of opinion.

Location Decisions in Connection with Expansion

New capital investment by established firms constitutes a major source of flexibility in location patterns. When growth in business leads to the need for expansion, a genuine choice of location is required, unless the contemplated addition to facilities is small or important indivisibilities exist. In contrast to relocation, which may not be consciously considered unless serious problems develop, when a location is selected for new facilities, the forces of inertia are relatively weak. The advantages of having the new facilities close-by will then be weighed carefully against the cost and marketing advantages of more distant locations. Where a new plant is to be opened or where capacity could be added at alternative branch plants located in different places, the firm planning expansion clearly has more latitude in its choice of location than small new plants or plants already in operation.

Sometimes expansion and relocation are jointly considered. Expansion elsewhere, if successful, may be the first step toward relocation. Or relocation may facilitate expansion. In these cases, expansion serves to bring the location problem to the fore and makes for greater latitude of choice.

The quantitative importance of location decisions in connection with expansion is illustrated by the 1961 data for Michigan. While manufacturers accounting for only 8 per cent of employment in sampled industries are considering relocation, 46 per cent are planning additions to plant or equipment during the next five years or so. This group consists of 18 per cent who have plans to expand in-state only and 28 per cent who have plans to expand wholly or partly out of state. (It might be worth mentioning here again that the Big Three are not included in these figures.)

The survey shows that factors which govern choice of location differ between relocation and expansion decisions. In contrast to plans to relocate, which are strongly influenced by changes affecting cost of production, plans to expand at new locations seem to be dominated by considerations of demand and efficient marketing. Obviously a great many factors are involved in both kinds of decisions, and this distinction is not always clear cut. The second column of Table 3 shows that by far the most frequently mentioned advantage of the contemplated location, cited by nearly half of those considering expansion in other areas, is proximity to markets and customers. Labor costs—the next most frequent consideration—were referred to with less than half the frequency of market factors.

The role of geographic decentralization in connection with expansion decisions is particularly clear in the case of the Michigan economy. Decentralization of the automobile industry has been progressing over several decades. More generally, Perloff and his colleagues have shown that the Manufacturing Belt, extending from the Middle and North Atlantic States to Illinois and Indiana, is experiencing a gradual decline in its share of the metal-fabricating industries. As the national market grows, and as areas in the Far West, Southwest, and South become increasingly industrialized, plants closer to these markets can realize the necessary internal economies of scale as well as external economies of agglomeration [10]. The importance of geographic decentralization is illustrated by the following figures for Michigan: 31 per cent of manufacturing employment outside the Big Three is accounted for by one-plant firms, 11 per cent by multiplant firms operating in Michigan only, and 58 per cent by firms operating one or more plants outside the state.

When the balance between in-state and out-of-state expansion plans is analyzed by characteristics of firms and plants, it appears that the ratio of out-of-state expansion plans is highest among firms serving regional or national markets, among the larger firms, and among firms which already have plants in more than one state. For the latter group, out-of-state expansion does not constitute a radical departure from current methods of operation.

Perloff has presented data which indicate that manufacturing activity has a much greater association with population (i.e., terminal markets) than with resource locations, even for the first stage resource users [10]. When market oriented firms consider expansion possibilities, their thinking seems to be dominated by the desire to realize the advantages of proximity to customers. Plans, as measured in this study, often relate to a period two to three years ahead and have an element of uncertainty. At this planning stage *no* visible relationship emerges between expressed attitudes of manufacturers and the pattern of planned in-state versus out-of-state expansion.

At the actual point of deciding where to expand, the situation seems to be different. Table 4 indicates that at this later stage attitudes do exert at least a marginal influence on the choice of location. Those manufacturers with the most critical attitudes reported less in-state expansion in the recent past and more out-of-state expansion than manufacturers with a more favorable opinion of a Michigan location. This finding establishes a link between attitudes and expansion decisions,

TABLE 4

RELATION OF EXPANSION DURING THE PAST TEN YEARS TO MANUFACTURERS' ATTITUDES TOWARD A MICHIGAN LOCATION

Percentage of Employment Represented by Michigan Manufacturers Who During the Past Ten Years:	All Michigan	INDEX OF CURRENT ATTITUDES TOWARD A MICHIGAN LOCATION		
		Least Favorable	Mid-range	Most Favorable
Expanded in-state only..................	36%	26%	39%	50%
Expanded both in-state and out-of-state.....	46	57	43	33
More in-state........................	13	19	11	12
About equally......................	11	7	12	14
More out-of-state.....................	22	31	20	7
Did not expand........................	14	16	12	17
Do not know; not ascertained whether expanded.............................	4	1	6	*
Total..............................	100%	100%	100%	100%

* Less than ½ per cent.

since we may assume that relative positions of manufacturers along the attitude scale have changed only slowly over time. In marginal cases, where two (or several) alternative locations may be almost equally satisfactory, attitudes seem to be influential, at the actual point of decision, in making one or the other location appear more attractive.

Conclusions

In conclusion, it is interesting to explore some of the policy implications of the findings presented, although further research is needed to corroborate the inferences drawn. The analysis points to a variety of stabilizing influences on location patterns: inertia, the importance of established business connections, the attraction of familiar places and people, the costs and uncertainties of relocation, and the multiplicity of important locational factors (so that a deterioration of one may be balanced by the favorable influence of another).

Shifts in location patterns seem to receive their chief impetus from expansion of facilities. Such changes may be reinforced by the location decisions of newly founded firms, but small new entrepreneurs often have to stay close to "home" and historical accident may play a large role in their location (the origin of the automobile industry in Michigan is a case in point). Relocations occur infrequently, and when they do occur, it is often in response to a decline in sales or profits. Relocations will benefit relatively low-cost locations, especially areas which are seen as having low labor costs.

Location decisions related to expansion are oriented to an important extent toward growing final and intermediate markets. Of course, the frequency and size of expansion projects depends on the rate of growth of the economy. Because of the interest of expanding firms in proximity to new customers and markets, a high rate of growth for the economy as a whole may entail very uneven growth rates for manufacturing activity in various regions and localities, accelerating incipient shifts. This implies that some of the older centers of industrial activity and the depressed areas cannot rely on the upward movement of the national economy as a whole to solve their unemployment problems.

Yet this conclusion does not mean that these older industrial areas are inevitably doomed to a decline in manufacturing activity. The survey clearly demonstrates that location decisions are governed only partly by the distribution of economic resources and population. To be sure, cost and demand factors exclude certain locations from the list of possible alternatives, but they seem to leave many firms with a considerable range of choice. Within that range, location decisions reflect in part historical accident, in part they are governed by locational factors which are "man-made" and can be altered. These include community factors such as housing, schools, and recreational facilities. They also include feelings of satisfaction and dissatisfaction on the part of business executives with labor conditions, taxes, legal climate, and their evaluations of the industrial climate. Dissatisfaction with these matters often stems from lack of co-operation between labor, government, and business. It hardly needs to be pointed out that the economic growth of a state depends to an important extent on the innovation-mindedness of its businessmen—the energy which they apply to the development of new products, new markets, and channels of distribution, and new production processes. Finally, the study indicates that a community can improve its chances of interesting new firms in locating there by having suitable plant sites (or even plants) available[4] and by being able to provide new firms with detailed information on local conditions and resources.[5]

[4] This factor also stood out in an early postwar interview study in New England [11].
[5] This last point is treated in more detail in [1] and [12].

REFERENCES

1. Eva Mueller, Arnold Wilken, and Margaret Wood, *Location Decisions and Industrial Mobility in Michigan, 1961* (Survey Research Center, Univ. of Michigan, Jan., 1962).
2. Walter Isard, "Some Locational Factors in the Iron and Steel Industry Since the Early Nineteenth Century," *J.P.E.*, 1948, pp. 203-17.
3. Edgar M. Hoover, Jr., *Location Theory and the Shoe and Leather Industries* (Harvard Univ. Press, 1937).
4. George Katona and James N. Morgan, "The Quantative Study of Factors Determining Business Decisions," *Q.J.E.*, Feb., 1952, pp. 67-90.
5. Melvin L. Greenhut, *Plant Location in Theory and Practice* (Univ. of North Carolina Press, 1956), Chap. X.
6. Helen Hunter, "Innovation, Competition, and Locational Change in the Pulp and Paper Industry, 1880-1950," *Land Econ.*, Nov., 1955, pp. 314-27.

7. Herbert A. Simon, "Theories of Decision-Making in Economics," *A.E.R.*, June, 1959, pp. 253-83.
8. Kenneth Boulding, *A Reconstruction of Economics* (New York, 1950), Chap. 2.
9. George Katona, *Psychological Analysis of Economic Behavior* (McGraw-Hill, 1951), pp. 49-52.
10. H. S. Perloff *et al.*, *Regions, Resources and Economic Growth* (Resources for the Future, Johns Hopkins Univ. Press, 1960), Chaps. 23-25.
11. George Ellis, "Why New Manufacturing Establishments Located in New England," *Monthly Rev.* (Fed. Res. Bank of Boston), Apr., 1949.
12. Glenn E. McLaughlin and Stefan Robock, *Why Industry Moves South* (Nat. Plan. Asso., 1949), pp. 110-11.

FACTORS IN THE LOCATION OF FLORIDA INDUSTRY: SUMMARY OF GENERAL FINDINGS OF FLORIDA SURVEY

Melvin L. Greenhut and Marshall R. Colberg

We may summarize the main points that were noted in previous paragraphs for the purpose of providing a concise review of vital data at this time as well as to form a reference point for the selected case illustrations which will follow:

(1) It was noted that the more northerly points tend to supply regional or national markets, while those to the south are geared to local markets.

(2) Fabricated metal products catering to the construction trade are tending to concentrate in South Florida.

(3) Electrical machinery, equipment, and supply companies are localizing in Central Florida.

(4) Lumber mills and wood products plants have been oriented to raw material supply points in the north and south.

Selected Case Examples of the Location of New Plants and Types of Industry

(1) That the more northerly plants supply regional or national markets reflects in part the transport cost saving that is possible by location in northern Florida. Thus the Chemstrand Company, which manufactures nylon filament yarns in its Northwest Florida plant, was located there in part to hold down the transportation cost in the chemical portion of its operation. At the same time, the company kept the transport cost on its finished yarn within reasonable bounds by locating there rather than in the states farther to the West.

The Florida plant of the Chemstrand Company is unique in the nylon industry because it produces the nylon filament yarns in one complete operation: from the basic chemical side to actual fiber making and packaging.

Chemstrand officials feel that their location in the Pensacola area holds down reasonably well the freight cost on the chemical portion of their business. The principal raw materials, cyclohexane and ammonia, are processed from sources in Texas and Louisiana. Freight costs on these materials are, therefore, reasonably low. Though freight cost on the yarn to the textile mills would be lower from locations in the Carolinas or Virginia, for example, the econo-

Reprinted from Melvin L. Greenhut and Marshall R. Colberg, *Factors in the Location of Florida Industry* (Tallahassee: The Florida State University, 1962), pp. 58–81, by permission of the authors and publisher.

mies gained on raw material deliveries, coupled with the gains made possible by a wholly unified operation in Florida, offset the rather high delivery cost of yarn. Transportation, while an important factor, is, of course, only one element in determining the optimum location for such a facility.

Somewhat similarly, the unique Foley branch plant of the Buckeye Cellulose Company was located to be near the company's raw material supply. This firm manufactures cellulose. Because the raw material it uses loses weight and bulk in fabrication, it is cheaper to transport the finished product over long distances than the raw material. Given this basic characteristic, it remained for the company to find a site at which adequate waste disposal facilities were possible and where a sufficient supply of water was available.

(2)   The tendency of the fabricated metal products industry to follow the construction industry is readily illustrated by the Adapto Steel Products Company of Miami. The president of this firm desired to isolate a small portion of the national market for steel shelving. Observation showed that Miami, because of its metropolitan nature and rapid growth, comprised a promising market. The spokesman pointed out that at the time of his location the Miami area was served chiefly by distant competitors. But customers prefer to buy from local producers because a local producer will install the final product and should be better able to supply the buyer readily on short notice. These considerations cause firms of this type to select the best available market area that can be found and then to locate at the center of gravity of this area.

(3)   The Minute Maid Company of Leesburg, Auburndale, and Plymouth and the Evans Properties of Dade City stress three vital gains from location in Central Florida. One, transport costs on raw materials are minimized. Two, the operation of company-owned groves is maintained at high standards as a result of the easy surveillance that is possible when the main plant is located nearby. Indeed, the ready availability of raw materials which follows from an integrated operation of this kind is a vital consideration and advantage. Three, the citrus codes of Florida and the Federal Marketing Acts require that higher grade fruits be shipped out of Florida to other states. Location, for example, in South Georgia would therefore involve higher priced fruits as well as high freight rates on these perishable raw materials.

Special Findings (Plant Types and the "Whys" of Location)

Branch Plants

It is interesting to note that a very significant number of the new plants established in Florida in 1956 and 1957 were plants of firms which also have facilities in other states. This is especially true of the larger plants.

Table 6 shows that 245 branch plants were established in the state. This compares with 367 plants of new firms. Among plants with less than 100 employees, the new firms dominated, but 26 branch plants with 100 or more employees were established compared with 18 plants of this size belonging to new companies.

The largest number of branch plants appeared in the non-electrical machinery and fabricated metal products fields. These fields also attracted large numbers of new firms.

TABLE 6.

Branch Plants Established in Florida, 1956-57

Industry	Number of Employees				
	0-24	25-99	100-499	500 & over	All Sizes
Metal mining	1	0	0	0	1
Mining and quarrying of non-metallic minerals, except fuels	2	1	0	0	3
Ordnance and accessories	0	0	0	1	1
Food and kindred products	13	1	1	1	16
Textile mill products	0	1	1	0	2
Apparel & similar products	15	0	1	0	16
Lumber and wood products except furniture	8	1	0	0	9
Furniture and fixtures	16	2	0	0	18
Paper and allied products	5	1	1	1	8
Chemicals and allied products	1	2	1	1	5
Petroleum refining and related industries	1	0	0	0	1
Stone, clay, and glass products	16	3	4	0	23
Fabricated metal products	27	0	1	0	28
Machinery, except electrical	37	6	0	0	43
Electrical machinery, equipment, and supplies	15	2	1	1	19
Transportation equipment	11	3	5	1	20
Professional controlling instruments, photographic and optical goods, watches, and clocks	10	1	1	0	12
Miscellaneous manufacturing industries	5	10	0	0	15
Miscellaneous services	1	1	3	0	5
Totals	184	35	20	6	245

The printing and publishing industry contrasts interestingly with the apparel industry in that 46 new independent establishments appeared in the former while no branch plants were set up. In the apparel industry 16 branch plants were set up, while no new firms were counted.

Relocations of Plants

An interesting phase of American economic history deals with the movement of textile mills from New England to the South. Most of Florida's new plants have been established without disturbing those in other states, but a number of relocations from out of state are occurring, especially of small plants. Often a *contributing* reason is that the owner wants to move to Florida.

In all industry groups there were 22 plants employing 25 or more persons which have moved to Florida from other states. Among these were eight plants with 100 or more employees in the "electrical machinery, equipment, and supplies" industry. In part this trend reflects the rapid development of Florida as a center for missile production and testing. Data on relocations from out of state are given in Table 7.

TABLE 7.
Relocation in Florida of Out-of-State Plants: 1956-57
(Number Relocated)

Industry	Number of Employees				
	0-24	25-99	100-499	500 & over	All Sizes
Construction	5	0	0	0	5
Ordnance and accessories	1	0	0	0	1
Food and kindred products	15	1	2	0	18
Textile mill products	5	0	1	0	6
Apparel and similar products	0	0	1	0	1
Lumber and wood products, except furniture	16	0	0	0	16
Printing, publishing, and related industries	5	0	0	0	5
Chemicals and allied products	2	2	1	0	5
Stone, clay, and glass products	1	0	0	0	1
Fabricated metal products	6	0	0	0	6
Machinery, except electrical	5	0	0	0	5
Electrical machinery, equipment and supplies	0	0	7	1	8
Transportation equipment	1	0	0	0	1
Motor freight transportation and warehousing	0	5	0	0	5
Wholesale trade	1	1	0	0	2
Totals	63	9	12	1	85

A total of 55 new plants were found to be relocations from one site in Florida to another. Although 45 of these were small plants, the rather large number points out a pitfall that exists when one counts the employee totals of these concerns as if they add to the net employment in the State. Figure 3 portrays the relative numerical importance of the new firms, branch plants, and in and out of state plant relocations.

The Factors of Location

A summary view of the frequency with which various factors were cited as the most influential in causing location in Florida is provided in Figure 4. Access to markets stands out as the primary factor for slightly over half of the firms surveyed. Expected growth of markets, a closely related factor, was mentioned next most frequently. On the cost side, low freight cost on shipping the final product and on obtaining raw materials stand out.

The relative frequency with which various factors were cited as of second greatest importance is portrayed graphically in Figure 5. Climate as it affects operations and as an attraction to top management shows up much more as a secondary factor than as a primary factor. Figure 6 indicates the relative number of times that factors were cited as of either first or second importance to the decision to locate in Florida.

Factors by Industry

Tables 8, 9, 10, and 11 show the frequency with which the various factors were cited as of first, second, or third greatest importance in the various industries.

(A) The printing and publishing industry, for example, is clearly one which should be near to the consumer because of contact advantages and need for speedy delivery. In practically every case, this factor served as the main cause for selecting the specific community in Florida. But whether the Florida market is superior to other markets in the country, or whether the cost level is lower or whether purely personal considerations caused the shop to be located in the State is another matter. Generally the respondents for this industry ventured the opinion that the Florida market was and is most enticing. It is clear that, theoretically, this is the correct response.

Fig. 3
Type of Plant

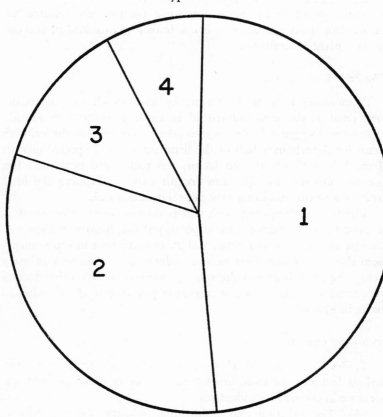

1. New Firm or Original Main Plant ___ 48.1%
2. New Branch Plant _____ 32.9
3. Relocation of Out-Of-State plant _____ 11.5
4. Relocation of In-State Plant _____ 7.5
                                          _____
                                          100.0%

Fig. 4

Percentage of Firms Citing Various Factors as the Most Influential
in Their Florida Location

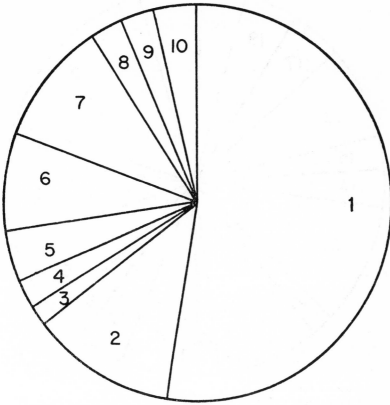

1.	Access to markets	51.9%
2.	Anticipation of growth of markets	12.8
3.	Amicable labor relations	1.7
4.	Lower wages	2.6
5.	Ease of attracting out-of-state personnel, incl. research	4.7
6.	Low freight cost on obtaining raw materials and components	7.7
7.	Low freight cost on shipping final product	10.7
8.	Climate, as it affects operations	1.8
9.	Community facilities (education, police, medical, fire)	2.9
10.	All other factors	3.2
		100.0%

Fig. 5
Percentage of Firms Citing Various Factors as Secondarily
Important in Their Florida Location

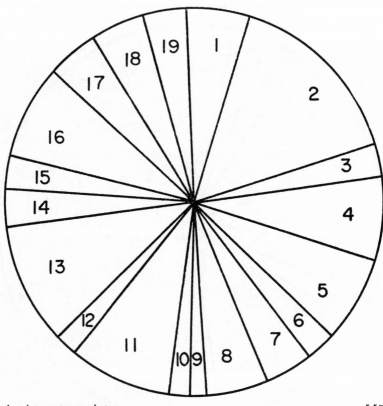

1.	Access to markets	5.5%
2.	Anticipation of growth of markets	15.8
3.	Amicable labor relations	2.3
4.	Lower wages	7.2
5.	Availability of labor already in Florida	7.1
6.	Ease of attracting out of state personnel, incl. research	2.5
7.	Low freight cost on obtaining raw materials and components	3.8
8.	Availability of raw materials	5.7
9.	Low cost of fuel	1.1
10.	Availability of capital	1.1
11.	Low freight cost on shipping final product	10.9
12.	Adequate waste disposal possibilities	1.2
13.	Climate (as it affects operations)	11.1
14.	Community facilities	2.9
15.	State and/or municipal tax structure	2.8
16.	Climate as an attraction to top management	7.5
17.	Personal, without economic advantage	4.2
18.	Personal, with economic advantage	4.6
19.	All other factors	2.7

100.0%

Fig. 6

Percentage of Firms Citing Various Factors, Either Primarily or Secondarily, As Most Influential in Their Florida Location

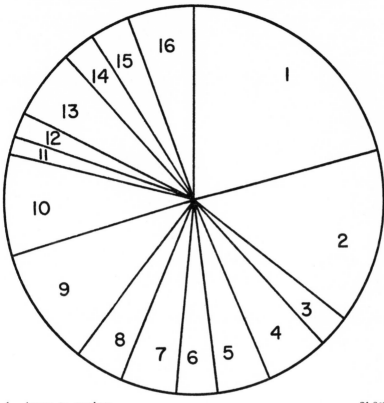

1.	Access to markets	21.8%
2.	Anticipation of growth of markets	14.7
3.	Amicable labor relations	2.1
4.	Lower wages	5.6
5.	Availability of labor already in Florida	4.9
6.	Ease of attracting out-of-state labor incl. research personnel	3.3
7.	Low freight cost on obtaining raw materials and components	5.2
8.	Availability of raw materials	3.9
9.	Low freight cost on shipping final product	10.8
10.	Climate, as it affects operations	7.8
11.	Community facilities (education, medical, police and fire)	1.9
12.	State and/or municipal tax structure	1.9
13.	Climate (as attraction to top management)	5.9
14.	Personal, with economic advantages, e.g., friendship with customers, suppliers, etc.	2.8
15.	Personal, without economic advantage	2.9
16.	All other factors	4.5

100.0%

TABLE 8.
First, Second, and Third Reasons for Location in Florida by Industry

Factor	Metal mining			Mining and quarrying of nonmetallic minerals			Construction— special trade contractors			Ordnance and accessories			Food and kindred products			Textile mill products		
	1	2	3	1	2	3	1	2	3	1	2	3	1	2	3	1	2	3
Access to markets				7				1		1			29	5	10	7		
Anticipation of growth of markets											1	1	10	15			1	5
Amicable labor relations																	5	
Lower wages														3	10	1	1	1
Higher productivity																		
Florida labor laws																		
Availability of labor already in Florida								5	5					11	8	1	1	1
Ease of attracting out-of-state skilled labor (including research personnel)										1	1							
Low seller's mill price on raw materials and components	1												2					
Low freight cost on obtaining raw materials and components					1	6												
Availability of raw materials		1			6	1							19	9	2			
Low cost fuel																		
Adequate supply and satisfactory type of water																		
Availability of capital																		
Low freight cost on shipping final product														10	22		6	
Adequate waste disposal possibilities																		
Climate (as it affects operations)															1			
Community facilities (educational, police and fire)												1			2			
Community attitudes and aid																		
State and/or municipal tax structure																		
Climate (as an attraction to top management)							5						5			5		
Personal (with economic adv. eg., friendship with customers, suppliers or bankers)							1							1	7			1
Personal (without economic adv.)														10				1
TOTALS	1	1	0	7	7	7	6	6	5	2	2	2	66	64	62	14	14	9

Industry

TABLE 9.

First, Second, and Third Reasons for Location in Florida of Industry

Industry

Factor	Apparel & other finished prod. made from fabrics & similar materials			Lumber & wood prod. except furniture			Furniture and fixtures			Paper & allied products			Printing, publishing and allied prods.			Chemicals and allied products		
	1	2	3	1	2	3	1	2	3	1	2	3	1	2	3	1	2	3
Access to markets		5		25	12		17	11	1	1	6		46	36		8	2	3
Anticipation of growth of markets	1		2	10	10		6	1	25	6	5	5		10		1	7	6
Amicable labor relations	1												11					
Lower wages		10				16		1					5				1	
Higher productivity											1							
Florida labor laws											1	1						
Availability of labor already in Florida	10				10	3	1	5	1									
Ease of attracting out-of-state skilled labor (including research personnel)																1		3
Low seller's mill price on raw materials and components							1											
Low freight cost on obtaining raw materials and components	5	2		22	5	1		1		1	1	1			5	6	2	1
Availability of raw materials	5			1	14	2		1	1	1		7				2	2	
Low cost fuel																		
Adequate supply and satisfactory type of water																		
Availability of capital																		
Low freight cost on shipping final product				14	8	18	11		1							7	7	2
Adequate waste disposal possibilities																	1	
Climate (as it affects operations)		6			6	5		15						5				
Community facilities (educational, police and fire)			10			5			1									2
Community attitudes and aid																		
State and/or municipal tax structure					5	10				5				11	5	1		
Climate (as an attraction to top management)			1			7			7						30			1
Personal (with economic adv. e.g., friendship with customers, suppliers or bankers)			10			5	1										2	
Personal (without economic adv.)						1									22			
TOTALS	22	23	23	72	70	66	37	35	37	14	14	14	62	62	62	25	25	18

TABLE 10.
First, Second, and Third Reasons for Location in Florida by Industry

Factor	Petroleum refining and related products			Rubber and misc. plastic products			Leather and leather products			Stone, clay and glass products			Primary metal ind.			Fab. met. prod. except ordnance mach. & trans. equipment		
	1	2	3	1	2	3	1	2	3	1	2	3	1	2	3	1	2	3
Access to markets	11									5	1	2	6	5		5	6	1
Anticipation of growth of markets	1		5							34	3	1	5			67	5	2
Amicable labor relations		1														3	26	1
Lower wages				1												1	6	1
Higher productivity														1		5	10	21
Florida labor laws																		
Availability of labor already in Florida																		
Ease of attracting out-of-state skilled labor (including research personnel)			1		1							1						1
Low seller's mill price on raw materials and components																		
Low freight cost on obtaining raw materials and components										2	6							
Availability of raw materials											18						5	
Low cost fuel																		
Adequate supply and satisfactory type of water																		
Availability of capital																		
Low freight cost on shipping final product		5					15			3	1	15			6	22	7	23
Adequate waste disposal possibilities																		10
Climate (as it affects operations)		6	1					15			3	20				5	28	5
Community facilities (educational, police and fire)																1		10
Community attitudes and aid																		
State and/or municipal tax structure			5							1		1					5	5
Climate (as an attraction to top management)									15		13	1			5	1		5
Personal (with economic adv. eg., friendship with customers, suppliers or bankers)																		5
Personal (without economic adv.)												2						2
TOTALS	12	12	12	1	1	0	15	15	15	45	45	43	11	6	11	110	98	92

TABLE 11.
First, Second, and Third Reasons for Location in Florida by Industry

Factor	Machinery, except electrical			Elec. mach. equipment and supplies			Transportation equipment			Instr. photo. goods, watches & clocks			Mis. mfg. industries			Motor freight trans. & warehsng.			Wholesale trade			Misc. services		
	1	2	3	1	2	3	1	2	3	1	2	3	1	2	3	1	2	3	1	2	3	1	2	3
Access to markets	54	6	5	24	9	16	42	30	1	12	1		22		1	5	5					2	3	3
Anticipation of growth of markets	10	10					1	1	2														1	
Amicable labor relations		1	1					1																
Lower wages	5	6	5	1	2		2	8	1	1										1				
Higher productivity				1	10																			
Florida labor laws									1															
Availability of labor already in Florida			5	3	2	1	9	8	18		11	1										4	1	
Ease of attracting out-of-state skilled labor (including research personnel)	7	5		2	4	6		2	1	7	1	11												
Low seller's mill price on raw materials and components																								
Low freight cost on obtaining raw materials and components									6						1									
Availability of raw materials		16											1									1		
Low cost fuel			15																					
Adequate supply and satisfactory type of water																								
Availability of capital					5		2	2	4															
Low freight cost on shipping final product	1	1		1	1	1	2	1	12						15			5						
Adequate waste disposal possibilities				1											5									
Climate (as it affects operations)	5	20		1	1	1		4				1			1				1					
Community facilities (educational, police and fire)		1				3																	1	
Community attitudes and aid		11				1																		
State and/or municipal tax structure			11						1		1													
Climate (as an attraction to top management)			6			3			8			1									1			
Personal (with economic adv. e.g., friendship with customers, suppliers or bankers)			6						2															
Personal (without economic adv.)						1					6			15										
TOTALS	82	77	54	34	34	34	58	57	57	20	20	14	23	15	23	5	5	5	1	1	1	7	6	3

"Amicable labor relations" was cited 11 times as the factor of first importance and 10 times as the second most significant matter in this industry. It appears that labor relations is a consideration of more concern in the printing and publishing industry than in most industries which were surveyed.

Climate as an advantage to top management was cited 30 times as the third most important factor by owners or managers of printing shops. Since a market exists for printing and publishing throughout the country, the Florida climate often appeared as the decisive factor in guiding plants to the State.

(B) Fabricated metal products plants place heavy stress on locating to gain access to markets and to secure low freight cost on shipping final products. The former determinant was cited 67 times as the primary factor and the latter 22 times. These plants are located mainly in the population centers, often producing items which enter into construction.

Significant advantage is gained by companies in this general field of activity which locate in or near the population centers. Both the Aetna Steel Company and the Florida Steel Corporation of Jacksonville stressed the advantage gained by being near selected customers. Proper servicing of a job is possible only under conditions of proximity; otherwise a local sales-engineering office would be in order if a substitute arrangement were desired. For small specialty companies that cannot afford to maintain extra offices, it becomes vital, if not imperative, to be located at places where close contact with a sufficient number of buyers is possible. Under the belief that the market in Florida offers greater demand than alternative and otherwise equivalent buying areas, a double market influence appears. We find that desire to have access to Florida markets brings the firm to Florida; in turn, the need for proximity then induces the firm to locate in a specific locality.

(C) The chemical industry shows heavy reliance on locating in such a way as to secure low freight cost on obtaining raw materials. Nevertheless, low freight cost on shipping the final product is also significant, and some branch plants which have located in Florida rather than in the Gulf states farther to the west have done so in order to be closer to the Eastern markets. Their location is an interesting compromise between getting low cost on material deliveries and low cost on shipping final products. "Access to markets" was mentioned as of first importance quite often, but scrutiny of individual returns shows that this factor is more important for chemical warehouses and packaging plants—which are located near local markets—than for the typical chemical manufacturer. (See Chapter III for detailed explanation of the difference between transport cost on the finished product and the market factor.)

(D) Furniture and fixtures manufacturing seeks access to markets and low freight cost on shipping the final product. Climate, at is affects operations, shows up as an important secondary factor. Lower manufacturing costs are possible in Florida because many items can be produced in relatively low cost factory buildings which normally require no heat. Outdoor work is also more feasible than in other states, and the sunshine is helpful in drying paint.

Successful operation in this industry requires either that the market be large or, if it is small, that rivals be few. This factor is especially vital in view of the relatively durable nature of the final product, the resulting irregular demand by any one set of buyers, the rather high freight cost involved in transporting the finished products and the resulting restricted radius over which a small manufacturer may sell. That both access to markets and low freight cost on shipping the final product appear as vital location factors in this industry is no surprise at all.

(E) Lumber and wood products other than furniture are often made near the raw material source. Access to markets was cited slightly more often as the primary factor, however, since the category covers a good number of products, such as roof trusses, which are used in construction.

Ease of Attracting Skilled Labor

Some interesting information can be obtained by examining Tables 8, 9, 10 and 11 horizontally rather than vertically. For example, "ease of attracting out-of-state skilled labor" is unimportant in many industries. It is a significant factor, however, in the production of transportation equipment (trailers, boats, etc.), instruments and machinery.

Notwithstanding the general findings noted above, there are selected industries which are greatly influenced by this factor. The Martin Company and the Sperry Electronic Tube Division of Sperry Rand, among others, were influenced greatly by considerations of this kind.

The Martin Company selected Orlando, Florida, as the home of its new division in 1956. The Division was organized to handle development and production of missiles and electronic systems under contract from the defense establishment. The Division now (1961) employs 10,000 persons and is the State's largest industrial firm.

The Orlando Division, incidentally, is the second of Martin's divisions to be set up away from Baltimore. The first, near Denver, Colorado, is engaged in the production and development of the Titan missile. The Colorado mountain area site was selected because the type of operations to be performed there—including static firings of missiles—requires a certain amount of seclusion.

The Orlando Division, on the other hand, has as its primary requisite a location which would attract an adequate supply of skilled personnel and provide space for plant expansion. The company conducted a nationwide survey to determine the regional location of this plant. The prime purpose of the survey was to determine where engineers and research personnel preferred to work. The results indicated that approximately 60 per cent of the persons surveyed preferred Florida. Accordingly, company officials were relatively sure that an adequate supply of the required type of personnel would be available in this State. The actual location in the city of Orlando was due to other special considerations, particularly community attitudes, and is a matter which takes us beyond our present interest and will be ignored.

The attraction of the Florida climate for skilled engineers and scientific personnel—an important element in the applied research function of the Sperry Electronic Tube Division of the Sperry Rand Corporation—is considered a decided asset by the Division's leadership. In 1961 the plant employed 600 persons with a staff of 1,100 planned for the future. Research and products of the Gainesville plant are taking many forms, including electronic food sterilization, microwave relay links, linear accelerators, radar apparatus, and airport landing and take-off equipment.

Plant management has found that the attitude of local employees has brought high productivity to the operation. A willingness to direct their efforts toward the opportunities for more technical training leading to more complex jobs has been manifest.

The mild climate is also credited with reducing operating costs in many cases through a variety of plant and personnel advantages, and is cited as a dominant factor behind Sperry's decision to locate in Florida.

Personal Factors with Economic Advantages

Personal factors with economic advantages due to friendship with customers, suppliers, bankers, and others do not rank high in most fields. They appear to be significant, however, in the manufacture of apparel, stone, clay, and glass products. Where relevant, these considerations serve to induce a businessman to stay near his hometown.

Wage Rates

Relatively low wage rates do not show up very often as a factor attracting plants. In part this seems to be due to a reluctance to cite this factor on a questionnaire since it is mentioned quite often in the course of personal interviews. Where labor is in abundant supply relative to demand, which is especially the situation in rural counties and in communities with many retired but still competent workers, the low wage rates in relation to productivity can be an important factor in making a business venture feasible. Lower wages as a factor among the first three in importance show up most often in the manufacture of food and kindred products, apparel, lumber and wood products, fabricated metal products, machinery, and transportation equipment. A substantial number of companies stressed the need for competitive wages, for an adequate supply of workers, for low labor turnover and, in general, their desire to have amicable labor relations. To many of these firms, amicable labor relations was synonymous with the non-existence of labor unions.[1]

Community Factors

Officials of new plants were asked not only to check and rank the factors which caused them to locate in Florida but also to state what factor or factors caused them to select a particular city. Answers to this question are often the same as for the State in general.

---

[1]The attraction of a relatively low wage area to new plants and the amount of employment afforded by existing plants can both be affected adversely by minimum wage legislation. See M. R. Colberg, "Minimum Wage Effects on Florida's Economic Development," *Journal of Law and Economics*, October, 1960, pp. 106-117.

TABLE 12.
First, Second, and Third Reasons for Location in Community by Industry

Factor	Metal mining			Mining and quarrying of nonmetallic minerals			Construction—special trade contractors			Ordnance and accessories			Food and kindred products			Textile mill products		
	1	2	3	1	2	3	1	2	3	1	2	3	1	2	3	1	2	3
Access to markets										1			17			5	2	3
Anticipation of growth of markets																		
Amicable labor relations																	1	
Lower wages								1			2			2	1			
Higher productivity																		
Florida labor laws																		
Availability of labor already in Florida	1												2	1		2		
Ease of attracting out-of-state skilled labor (including research personnel)										1						1		
Low seller's mill price on raw materials and components																		
Low freight cost on obtaining raw materials and components															1			
Availability of raw materials				7									5	2				
Low cost fuel																		
Low cost of elec. power																		
Adequate supply and satisfactory type of water														3	1			
Low cost of capital																		
Availability of capital													1					
Low freight cost on shipping final product													16	10	2			
Adequate waste disposal possibilities															2			
Climate (as it affects operations)																		
Community facilities (educational, police and fire)											1		7	6	2	6		
Community attitudes and aid														7	7			
State and/or municipal tax structure												1						
Climate (as an attraction to top management)																		
Personal (with economic adv. eg., friendship with customers, suppliers or bankers)							1						1	1				1
Personal (without economic adv.)							5											
TOTALS	1			7			6	1		2	3	2	51	33	16	14		1

TABLE 13.
First, Second, and Third Reasons for Location in Community by Industry

Industry

Factor	Apparel & other finished prod. made from fabrics & similar materials			Lumber & wood products furniture			Furniture and fixtures			Paper & allied products			Printing, publishing and allied prods.			Chemicals and allied products		
	1	2	3	1	2	3	1	2	3	1	2	3	1	2	3	1	2	3
Access to markets				8	6		17	11		7						7		
Anticipation of growth of markets	10						1						46	30				
Amicable labor relations																		
Lower wages																		
Higher productivity																		
Florida labor laws																		
Availability of labor already in Florida		1					5		10		1							
Ease of attracting out-of-state skilled labor (including research personnel)																		
Low seller's mill price on raw materials and components				2														
Low freight cost on obtaining raw materials and components		2		25	1					1	6			5		3	2	
Availability of raw materials						1				1						1		
Low cost fuel																1		
Low cost of elec. power																2		
Adequate supply and satisfactory type of water																		
Low cost of capital																		
Availability of capital																		
Low freight cost on shipping final product				12	2	1	10					1				1	5	1
Adequate waste disposal possibilities											1	1				1		
Climate (as it affects operations)																		
Community facilities (educational, police and fire)	10			10	4	1	1			5			1					
Community attitudes and aid	3				5	2							5			1	3	1
State and/or municipal tax structure				5			1									5		
Climate (as an attraction to top management)																		
Personal (with economic adv. eg., friendship with customers, suppliers or bankers)			1	10			1								5			
Personal (without economic adv.)													10	1		1		
TOTALS	23	3	1	72	18	5	36	11	10	14	8	2	62	36	5	23	13	2

TABLE 14.

First, Second, and Third Reasons for Location in Community by Industry

Factor	Petroleum refining and related products			Rubber and misc. plastic products			Leather and leather products			Stone, clay and glass products			Primary metal ind.			Fab. met. prod. except ordnance mach. & trans. equipment		
	1	2	3	1	2	3	1	2	3	1	2	3	1	2	3	1	2	3
Access to markets										9						71		
Anticipation of growth of markets	2	5	5							19	1		6			6	6	
Amicable labor relations				1														
Lower wages																		
Higher productivity																		
Florida labor laws																		
Availability of labor already in Florida					1											1		
Ease of attracting out-of-state skilled labor (including research personnel)																		
Low seller's mill price on raw materials and components																	20	
Low freight cost on obtaining raw materials and components	5						15				2	1				5		
Availability of raw materials																		
Low cost fuel																		
Low cost of elec. power																		
Adequate supply and satisfactory type of water																		
Low cost of capital																		
Availability of capital																		
Low freight cost on shipping final product										2	1					2	1	
Adequate waste disposal possibilities																		
Climate (as it affects operations)																		
Community facilities (educational, police and fire)										2	1					17	1	
Community attitudes and aid										1								
State and/or municipal tax structure						1										5		
Climate (as an attraction to top management)	5									12			5					1
Personal (with economic adv. eg., friendship with customers, suppliers or bankers)																1		1
Personal (without economic adv.)																1		20
TOTALS	12	5	5	1	1	1	15			45	5	1	11			109	28	22

TABLE 15.
First, Second, and Third Reasons for Location in Community by Industry

Factor	Machinery, except electrical			Elec. mach. equipment and supplies			Transportation equipment			Instr. photo. goods, watches & clocks			Mis. mfg. industries			Motor freight trans. & warehsng.			Wholesale trade			Misc. services		
	1	2	3	1	2	3	1	2	3	1	2	3	1	2	3	1	2	3	1	2	3	1	2	3
Access to markets	43	5		12			31	4		12			21			5						1	1	
Anticipation of growth of markets								10	1													1		
Amicable labor relations																								
Lower wages					10	10	6	1																
Higher productivity																								
Florida labor laws																								
Availability of labor already in Florida			10	3	1		1	15	7			10												
Ease of attracting out-of-state skilled labor (including research personnel)							7				1	1												
Low seller's mill price on raw materials and components													1									1		
Low freight cost on obtaining raw materials and components		5				1			1											1				
Availability of raw materials		16																						
Low cost fuel																								
Low cost of elec. power																								
Adequate supply and satisfactory type of water																								
Low cost of capital							3																	
Availability of capital	1	2		2	5		3	1																
Low freight cost on shipping final product								1			1												1	
Adequate waste disposal possibilities						1																		
Climate (as it affects operations)	5																							
Community facilities (educational, police and fire)	17	5	5	12	8	5	5	7	1	2	1								1			4		
Community attitudes and aid			5			1	1	1	1		11													
State and/or municipal tax structure	5	5		3	2	5																		
Climate (as an attraction to top management)								2																
Personal (with economic adv. e.g., friendship with customers, suppliers or bankers)	6	6	17	2	3																			
Personal (without economic adv.)		5	1						26	6														
TOTALS	77	49	38	34	29	23	57	42	37	20	14	11	22			5			1	1		7	2	

The question tends to bring out factors which vary a good deal from one community to another.

Personal factors with economic advantages are cited often as guiding a firm to a particular locality, as may be seen in Tables 12, 13, 14, and 15. Community facilities for education, medical care, police and fire protection are frequently named. Availability of labor in the community shows up often. Access to market appears regularly since the market is sometimes restricted to a single community and since cities can differ markedly as market centers. Quite vital in many cases was the attitude of civic leaders toward industrial development. The Tiffany Tile Corporation of Port Tampa was among those influenced favorably by community attitudes. The Martin Company selected its particular Florida location in part because it found the amount of land it needed readily available. The friendly attitude of bankers, civic leaders, and average citizens proved to be the extra inducement which caused the company to select Orlando.

Summary

Access to markets, ease of attracting skilled workers, relatively low wages, climate, and community facilities are but a few of the many factors that influenced the location of the diverse kinds of plants and industries which recently located in Florida. Reference to the tables and figures in this chapter will uncover data of special and even more restricted nature than most of those that were described above. Through such examination further insight and details can be obtained concerning the forces which have led new plants to selected localities in the State.

PART IV

Manufacturing Locations in
a General Equilibrium

AN INTRODUCTION TO SPATIAL GENERAL EQUILIBRIUM

David F. Bramhall

In the previous sections, manufacturing location has been examined one factor at a time, one industry at a time, often one establishment at a time. Solutions were based on certain assumptions regarding the constancy or invariance of a number of aspects of the problems: for example, production technology, transport rates and routes, and the location of markets and suppliers. In particular, it is the constancy of the last factor that a general equilibrium approach has traditionally sought to eliminate.[1]

If the location of the steel industry is partly dependent on the location of coal production, is it not equally true that the location of coal production is partly a function of the location of one of its major consumers — the steel industry? It is such locational interdependence that we analyze in a general equilibrium model.

History and Definition

The roots of the idea of general economic equilibrium go back at least to the scientific and economic transformations of the seventeenth century. Isaac Newton's model of heavenly bodies in perpetual motion controlled by their own masses, distances, and velocities is a conspicuous example of general equilibrium in the physical sciences. The shift from a hierarchal feudal economy to a relatively free market economy, at about the same time, led to Adam Smith's dramatic figure of the "invisible hand" which guides numerous independent decisions by economic producers and consumers into outcomes which display overall order. This idea is an affirmation of the existence of internal control mechanisms in the social order.

Leon Walras published the earliest fully specified general equilibrium

This section draws rather heavily on the extremely valuable book by Robert E. Kuenne, *The Theory of General Economic Equilibrium* (Princeton: Princeton University Press, 1963), and on the lectures and writings of Walter Isard, who pioneered in the introduction of the spatial dimension in general equilibrium systems.

[1] However, the most ambitious spatial general equilibrium systems seek also to make the other specified elements a part of the solution.

analysis in 1889,[2] which was followed shortly by the work of Vilfredo Pareto at the turn of the century.[3] In recent years extensions, elaboration, and improvements have been made by, among others, John Hicks and Paul Samuelson.[4] These writers provided mathematically complete models which could be solved conceptually, though not empirically, and which have led to a great many insights into the conditions under which a stable, unique, general economic equilibrium may exist.

Specifically, in the economic context a general equilibrium model is a set of statements about an entire economic system which specifies the motivating principles of economic actors, the physical-technological conditions of economic activity, and the nature of markets in which participants interact. One definition of general equilibrium is offered by Kuenne, paraphrasing Pareto. General equilibrium is "a specific solution to an economic model describing a state of rest and resulting from the opposition between identifiable desires of men and obstacles to their fulfillment, including among these latter the desires of actors other than any one of the specific firms or consumers under consideration."[5] An outline of a simple nonspatial general equilibrium model is presented in the next section.

The main differences among general equilibrium models are (1) the number and types of economic actors specified; (2) the set of relevant commodities; (3) the sectors of economic activity included; and (4) the nature of the motivating principles which drive the actors. In particular, a *spatial* general equilibrium system should include the dimensions of distance and direction, i.e., the locations of the actors; and it must include the transportation sector which describes flows of commodities from one location to another. Spatial general equilibrium theory has had an extremely short history dating perhaps from a tentative statement by August Lösch in 1939.[6] Elaborations of theoretical statements in the Walrasian tradition were first made by Walter Isard in a number of works.[7] We present basic elements of a spatial model in the second section to follow.

[2] *Elements d'Economie Politique Pure.* English edition, *Elements of Economics,* tr. Jaffe (London: Allen and Unwin, 1954).

[3] V. Pareto, *Cours d'Economie Politique* (Lausanne: Rouge, 1897); *Manuel d'Economie Politique* (Paris: Girard et Brière, 1909).

[4] J. R. Hicks, *Value and Capital* (Oxford: Oxford University Press, 1939); Paul Samuelson, *Foundations of Economic Analysis* (Cambridge: Harvard University Press, 1948).

[5] Kuenne, *Theory of General Economic Equilibrium,* p. 18.

[6] August Lösch, *The Economics of Location* (New Haven: Yale University Press, English translation 1954), Ch. 8.

[7] Walter Isard, *Location and Space-Economy,* (New York: M.I.T. Press and Wiley, 1956); "General Interregional Equilibrium," *Papers and Proceedings of the Regional Science Association,* 1957; with Ostroff, "General Interregional Equilibrium," *Journal of Regional Science,* Spring 1960, 67–74; with Peter Isard, "General Social, Political and Economic Equilibrium for a System of Regions, Part I and Part II," *Papers and Proceedings of the Regional Science Association, XIV and XV* (1965), 1–33, 7–25.

A somewhat different approach toward general equilibrium, derived from activity analysis, has been pursued by Isard, Stevens, Lefeber, Koopmans, and others.[8] The final section of this paper briefly treats this approach and mentions some of the associated operational models which have been applied to actual problems.

A Simple Nonspatial General Equilibrium Model

As Kuenne points out, there are a number of pedagogic functions which are served by the construction of general models even when they cannot be empirically applied. The scope of a field can be defined, showing specifically which elements must be taken as data and which should be determined by relationships of the model; the possibility of equilibrium can be proved for specified conditions so that unnecessary complications of theory can be avoided; in some cases qualitative statements can be made about the effect of variation of data upon variables in the model; and so on. In sum, these systems "provide maps of the whole economic terrain, within which models of lesser ambition obtain position and scale."[9]

It is not really possible to give an elementary example of an economic general equilibrium system; if there is enough interdependence to be of interest, complexity of exposition results. This section will briefly develop an illustrative system, although even for this we must use mathematical statements in which subscripted variables represent the large numbers of individual economic participants and commodities.[10] To make it easier for the nonmathematical reader to see the underlying basis of the model, the mathematical statements have been placed in footnotes.

We first specify the elements of our model. In this simple system, production is assumed to take place under conditions of fixed technological coefficients. For example, the same amount of an input such as labor is required per unit of output, no matter how much output is produced. There is unrestricted competition and any firm is free to enter or leave an industry. This eliminates surplus profits and makes revenues and costs equal. Hence no decision-making entrepreneurs are needed. The participants are therefore consuming individuals who may also sell stocks of commodities that they hold initially.[11] There are many commodities in

---

[8] Walter Isard, "Interregional Linear Programming," *Papers and Proceedings of the Regional Science Association* (1958); Benjamin Stevens, "An Interregional Linear Programming Model," *Journal of Regional Science I* (1958); Louis Lefeber, *Allocation in Space* (Amsterdam: North-Holland, 1958); and T. Koopmans (ed.), *Activity Analysis of Production and Allocation* (New York: Wiley, 1951).

[9] Kuenne, *Theory of General Equilibrium*, p. 11.

[10] This example is drawn from Walras in notation used by R. G. D. Allen in sections 10.1 and 10.2 of *Mathematical Economics* (London: Macmillan, 1963).

[11] Let there be n such individuals, designated by the subscript i $(i = 1, \ldots, n)$. An initial holding or commodity r by individual i is x_{ri}.

the system and they are classified either as factors of production or as consumer goods.[12]

We will consider this model solved when we have determined (1) the amount of each consumer good purchased by each individual; (2) the amount of each productive factor used up in production; (3) the amount of each consumer good produced; and (4) the price of each commodity.[13]

In choosing among commodities the consumer is motivated to maximize his utility. He is subject to a budget limitation (he cannot spend more than his income) and he can purchase and sell commodities only at prices ruling in the market. Each individual is assumed to have a utility function which indicates the utility he receives at the margin from a unit quantity of each commodity consumed (or retained, in the case of production factors).[14]

Each individual's income, i.e., the amount he may spend on purchasing commodities, is determined by his disposal of commodities he "owns" initially. (One of these may be thought of as labor if we are willing to let him value the unsold portion of it for himself at the market price.) His budget is therefore in balance when his expenditures on purchases exactly equal his receipts from "sales."[15]

Given the above, it follows that a first set of conditions for equilibrium consistent with each consumer maximizing his utility is that the rate at which he is willing to substitute between any two commodities is equal to the ratio of their respective prices.[16] Or in simpler terms, he can do

---

[12] Let the total number of commodities be m of which the first k are factors of production (such as labor and land) and the remaining $m - k$ are consumer goods. When any commodity is referred to in general, we use the subscript r ($r = 1, \ldots, m$). When we refer only to productive factors we use the subscript s ($s = 1, \ldots, k$). When we refer to consumer goods we use the subscript t ($t = k + 1, \ldots, m$).

[13] Actually, prices are stated only as ratios, the price p_m of some standard commodity being set at unity. Mathematically, the unknowns are (1) mn individual commodity purchases (designated x_{ri}); (2) k factor usages (designated Y_s) and $m - k$ commodity outputs (designated Y_t); and (3) $m - 1$ prices (designated p_r) since one price is given as numeraire. Altogether, therefore, there are $mn + 2m - 1$ unknowns.

[14] Mathematically:

$$(1) \qquad u_i = f_i(x_{1i}, x_{2i}, \ldots, x_{mi}) \qquad (\text{for } i = 1, 2, \ldots, n)$$

where u_i is the total utility for individual i. The partial derivatives are designated u_{ri}; they represent the amount at the margin by which an additional unit of commodity r increases the utility of individual i:

$$(2) \qquad u_{ri} = \frac{\partial u_i}{\partial x_{ri}} \qquad (\text{for } r = 1, 2, \ldots, m \text{ and } i = 1, 2, \ldots, n)$$

[15] That is, when the following equality holds:

$$(3) \qquad \sum_r p_r(x_{ri} - \bar{x}_{ri}) = 0 \qquad (\text{for } r = 1, 2, \ldots, m \text{ and } i = 1, 2, \ldots, n)$$

[16] This condition is presented in any modern price theory textbook. It is

$$(4) \qquad \frac{u_{ri}}{u_{mi}} = \frac{p_r}{p_m} \qquad (\text{for } r = 1, 2, \ldots, m \text{ and } i = 1, 2, \ldots, n)$$

no better only when the last dollar spent on each commodity yields him the same utility.

We turn now to the relations which determine commodity production and market prices. By assumption, only consumer goods can be produced, and only productive factors are used as inputs to production. In this simple system we assume, as already indicated, that there are no scale economies in production.[17] We also assume no joint production of commodities. A set of conditions for production equilibrium requires that the amount of each factor used in production be equal to the total amount of that factor sold by individuals.[18]

Still another set of conditions for equilibrium is that aggregate supply and demand of each commodity be equal.[19] By the assumption of a competitive economy with freedom of entry and exit, it follows that a final set of conditions of equilibrium is that costs of production equal receipts for each firm, or, equivalently, that unit cost equals price in the production of each consumer good.[20]

The above equilibrium conditions spell out as many mathematical equations as there are unknowns for the simple closed system. In this

---

But p_m has been stipulated as equal to one; therefore, by substitution and transposition of (4) we obtain

$$(5) \qquad \frac{u_{ri}}{p_r} = u_{mi} \qquad \text{(for } r = 1,2, \ldots, m - 1 \text{ and } i = 1,2, \ldots, n)$$

[17] That is, production coefficients are fixed. Let a_{st} equal the amount of production factor s required per unit output of consumer good t.

[18] This may be stated

$$(6) \qquad \sum_t a_{st} Y_t = -Y_s \qquad \text{(for } s = 1,2, \ldots, k)$$

where Y_s, as defined below, is a negative quantity such that $(-Y_s)$ is positive.

[19] Let

$$X_r = \sum_i x_{ri},$$

the aggregate final purchases of commodity r. Let

$$\bar{X}_r = \sum_i \bar{x}_{ri},$$

the total initial holdings of commodity r. For productive factors, $X_s < \bar{X}_s$, and the difference is the amount sold by individuals for use in production; for consumer goods, $X_t > \bar{X}_t$, and the difference, if any, is the required new production. The requirement that market supply and demand be equal is

$$(7) \qquad Y_r = X_r - \bar{X}_r \qquad \text{(for } r = 1,2, \ldots, m - 1)$$

There are only $m - 1$ independent conditions of this type, since in the final balance it can be shown that one equation is necessarily implied when others are added together.

[20] That is,

$$(8) \qquad \sum_s p_s a_{st} = p_t \qquad \text{(for } t = k + 1, k + 2, \ldots, m)$$

sense the statement is consistent with equilibrium.[21] With specific data and explicit forms of the utility functions, the system may turn out to have a unique solution, or no real solution, or multiple solutions.

The main feature of this model to be stressed here is that by the use of assumptions on economic behavior and production technology, it may be possible to solve at once for *all* prices, *all* commodity outputs, *all* factor uses, and *all* consumer demand quantities; and, under certain conditions, it is possible to obtain a single, unique magnitude for all these elements.

Extensions to a Spatial Model

Can we proceed on the foundations of the preceding section and solve also simultaneously for all productive locations and all commodity shipments? This section will illustrate a qualified "yes" answer to that question.

The broad outlines of changes necessary to bring the location dimension into the system are clear. We must identify the place where each industry produces its output and where each consumer makes his purchases. We must introduce the activity whereby at least some goods are transported from one location to another. Finally, we must require that markets be in balance (supply equal to demand) at all locations.

In this simple presentation we will not develop a full spatial general equilibrium system; rather, we will show separately how each of the necessary changes might be made in the previous model.

There are two ways in which the *locations* of economic actors might be specified. Locations may be indicated as belonging to one of a set of predefined regions, or they may be indicated as spatial coordinates which themselves are variables of the system. Since only the first of these alternatives has so far been successfully built into a complete system, let us concentrate upon a regional designation for each consumer and for the production of each commodity.[22] In adopting this approach we are treating space as a set of discrete points, each a region, at which all production and consumption occurs. Distances exist among these points, but not among the actors located at a single point.

What economic force causes shipments of commodities to take place

---

[21] The numbers of equations are

Equations		Number
(3)	—	n
(5)	—	$n(m-1)$
(6)	—	k
(7)	—	$m-1$
(8)	—	$m-k$
Total		$mn + 2m - 1$

[22] For example, we write $x_{ri}{}^L$, the quantity of commodity r demanded by i in region L; and $Y_t{}^L$, the production of good t in region L.

among regions? Basically, the consumer's desire to maximize utility, coupled with the fact that production costs (and therefore prices) of a good may vary from one region to another. Consumer utility maximization is already incorporated into the model. So too, are different regional production costs, since regional resource prices may differ, and since different regions may employ different production technologies.[23]

The condition (new) for interregional transportation of goods is that the delivered price of a good which moves from region A to region B be equal to or lower than the price of the good produced locally in region B.[24] Since the delivered price in region B is the production cost of the good in region A plus its transport cost from A to B, we must also add the latter cost as a new datum in the system.[25]

Now the unknowns of the spatial system must include the levels of shipments of goods among regions. For utmost simplicity, let us assume here that only consumer goods can move in interregional trade.[26]

Finally, market balancing of supply and demand must occur in each region. Furthermore, we must allow for the possibility of demand for consumer goods in any region being increased by exports to other regions, or of supply being increased by imports from other regions.[27]

When these (or alternative) spatial modifications have been introduced into an equilibrium model in ways which preserve the equality of unknowns and equations,[28] a solution can be obtained which includes the location — by region — of commodity production and consumption and the levels of commodity shipments among regions. It should be clear by now, however, that the ability to come to such a simultaneous solution, in

---

[23] This can be explicitly recognized by defining $a_{st}{}^L$ to be the productive factor input per unit output in region L, and by allowing $a_{st}{}^L$ to be different from the corresponding input $a_{st}{}^K$ in region K.

[24] In fact, at equilibrium, the two prices will be equal if commodities from different regions are perfect substitutes.

[25] Let $c_t{}^{AB}$ be the (given) cost of transporting a unit of good t from region A to region B. The condition for interregional transportation of goods is therefore $p_t{}^B \geq p_t{}^A + c_t{}^{AB}$. But if the inequality holds, there will be excess profits from export trade, which will be eliminated by competition. Hence at equilibrium the equality holds.

[26] If we define $S_t{}^{AB}$ as the quantity of good t shipped from region A to region B, the equilibrium condition that $p_t{}^B = p_a{}^t + c_t{}^{AB}$ for all goods that move between regions will assure that there will be no cross-hauling of a commodity, and that therefore $S_t{}^{AB} = -S_t{}^{BA}$. That is, if there are U regions there will be only $\dfrac{U(U-1)}{2}$ independent flows of any commodity. (Of course, many of these may equal zero).

[27] The demand equals supply equations become:

for productive factors, $\qquad\qquad Y_s{}^L = X_s{}^L - \bar{X}_s{}^L \qquad\qquad$ and

for consumer goods, $\qquad\qquad Y_t{}^L = X_t{}^L - \bar{X}_t{}^L + \sum_K S_t{}^{LK}$

[28] The most accessible fully specified spatial model of the broad type discussed here is in Isard and Ostroff, "General Interregional Equilibrium." It is considerably more elaborate, especially in its production relationships, than the simple model we have illustrated.

which each variable is determined by all others, is not without cost. When one looks back over the rich detail of some of the selections earlier in the book which deal with individual industries, or even individual cost elements, it is evident how much is sacrificed when a "clear" mathematically formulated general equilibrium model is constructed.

The location analyst, like all who seek to understand phenomena of the world we inhabit, must move between microscopic and cosmic views of his subject. At one stage he examines at close range, so that each object is seen in its own peculiarity and unique nature; but at other times he sees objects for their generic nature, abstracting from individual aberrations in order to see overall patterns and relationships. Thus general and partial equilibrium approaches are not competitors, but essential complements.

Operational Modifications and Theoretical Frontiers

Current developments of the general equilibrium approach are simultaneously proceeding in two very different directions. One of these is toward simplifications which allow application to empirical problems; the other is toward expanding the field of variables within the system to include more of the social and economic environment.

One way to simplify a system so that it can be applied is to reduce the number of actors and commodities by aggregating them. The Keynesian system of national economic sectors can be viewed as such a modification, although the maximizing conditions of the Walrasian system have been replaced by statistically derived behavioral equations. A regional counterpart might be the interregional models of Metzler and Chipman.[29]

Another method of achieving operationality retains large numbers of commodities and producer-participants, but simplifies the relationships which are used to solve the model. Particularly since the appearance of high-speed computers it is possible to regard very large models as operational if their relationships are measurable and relatively simple. Equations derived, for example, from utility maximization are ruled out; but production-shipment and market-balance relationships can be included, although data relevant to these relationships are often poor and incomplete.

The conspicuous examples of this type of operational general equilibrium are the input-output systems developed by Leontief, and the activity analysis-programming models stemming from the work of Kantorevich, Dantzig, Hitchcock, Koopmans, and others.[30] Spatial versions of these

---

[29] Lloyd Metzler, "A Multiple Region Theory of Income and Trade," *Econometrica* (October 1950); John Chipman, *The Theory of Intersectoral Money Flows and Income Formation* (Baltimore: Johns Hopkins Press, 1950).

[30] See the discussion in Kuenne, *Theory of General Economic Equilibrium;* also Dorfman, Samuelson, and Solow, *Linear Programming and Economic Analysis* (New

models, both conceptual and operational, have been elaborated in recent years, and many have actually been applied in ways ranging from corporate planning (e.g., physical distribution management) in the United States, to regional production planning in the Soviet Union and other planned economies.[31]

Still another approach to the construction of applied general systems eschews the notion of equilibrium central to the models which we have discussed so far. This approach, even more dependent upon the development of computers, seeks to simulate the operation of economic systems by solving successively a large number of relationships, each of which may be complex and often probabilistic in form.[32] Because no general or unique solution is sought, in principle these simulation systems may include nearly unlimited dimensions and complexities. However, many problems remain in the evaluation of the results of these models, and they do not have many of the pedagogic advantages cited previously for equilibrium models.

There is other research which does not place such high value upon the empirical applicability of general equilibrium models, but instead aims at improving their conceptual content. It is a goal of this research to change the status of elements of the socioeconomic system which have been given or assumed outside the model to unknowns to be derived within the model. Among the elements which have been tackled in this fashion with varying success are time, space, decision-making behavior, uncertainty, political goals, and psychological differences among individuals.[33] Of particular interest to our concern in this book are attempts to move from point-form space to continuous space, and to make the locational coordinates of actors and activities part of the solution of an equilibrium model.[34]

It should be evident that work on spatial general equilibrium models

York, McGraw-Hill, 1958) ; and Chenery and Clark, *Interindustry Economics* (New York, Wiley, 1959).

[31] See, for example, A. Charnes and W. W. Cooper, *Management Models and Industrial Applications of Linear Programming* (New York, Wiley, 1961) ; and J. Hardt, M. Hoffenberg, N. Kaplan, and H. Levine (eds.), *Mathematics and Computers in Soviet Economic Planning* (New Haven: Yale University Press, 1967).

[32] See the work of Guy Orcutt and associates, *Microanalysis of Socioeconomic Systems* (New York: Harper, 1961) ; and the more aggregative approach in Edward Holland, *Experiments on a Simulated Underdeveloped Economy* . . . (Cambridge: M.I.T. Press, 1963).

[33] See, for example, Kuenne, *Theory of General Economic Equilibrium,* Ch. 8; W. Isard and T. H. Tung, "Selected Non-Economic Commodities . . ." *Papers and Proceedings of the Regional Science Association, 13* (1964) ; W. Isard and M. Dacey, "On the Projection of Individual Behavior in Regional Analysis," *Journal of Regional Science, 4,* No. 1 (1962).

[34] See W. Isard, *Location and Space-Economy,* 1956, Chapter 10; Louis Lefeber, *Allocation in Space;* H. C. Bos, *Spatial Dispersion of Economic Activity* (Rotterdam: Rotterdam University Press, 1965) ; and Kuenne, *Theory of General Economic Equilibrium,* Ch. 7.

of all sorts is proceeding with considerable vigor. Whatever the advance in operational models (and it is reasonable to expect a good deal of such progress), the development of conceptual models will continue, in the words of Kuenne, to "throw brilliant light into dark corners."

In this part of the book only two other selections are presented. The first, by Isard and Kuenne, illustrates a practical application of an input-output system for business and planning purposes. A second article, by Walter Isard, Peter Isard, Barchas, and Epps, emphasizes the conceptual in an attempt to introduce important new unknowns into the system.

THE IMPACT OF STEEL UPON THE GREATER NEW YORK-PHILADELPHIA INDUSTRIAL REGION

Walter Isard and Robert E. Kuenne

For a long time the inadequacy of the traditional Weberian agglomeration analysis[1] has been fully recognized. Palander, in particular, has pointed up its shortcomings.[2] More recently, a fresh and more general approach has been made by P. Sargant Florence and others.[3] This approach, primarily an attempt to identify from processed census data meaningful geographical associations in industry, of necessity does not concern itself with the development of a theoretical framework.[4]

It is the purpose of this paper to attempt some development in the theory of agglomeration and of the broad spatial clustering of all economic activities by grafting on to the sounder elements of location theory a modified regional input-output schema. Viewed from a different standpoint, we attempt an impact study, wherein the direct and indirect reper-

Reprinted from *The Review of Economics and Statistics, 35* (1953), 289–301, by permission of the authors and editor.

This study was done partly under the auspices of the Social Science Research Center, the University of Puerto Rico, and of the Center of Urban and Regional Studies, the Massachusetts Institute of Technology. The basic projections were completed in February 1952 for investment use by the firm of Minot, De Blois and Maddison, who generously financed the work in the initial stage.

[1] C. J. Friedrich trans., *Alfred Weber's Theory of the Location of Industries* (Chicago, 1929), chs. 5–7.

[2] T. Palander, *Beiträge zur Standortstheorie* (Uppsala, 1935), ch. 8; see also E. M. Hoover, Jr., *Location Theory and the Shoe and Leather Industries* (Cambridge, Mass., 1937), pp. 89–99; and O. Engländer, "Kritisches und Positives zu einer allgemeinen reinen Lehre vom Standort," *Zeitschrift für Volkswirtschaft und Sozialpolitik,* Neue Folge, Vol. v (1926). For a defense of Weber's agglomeration theory, see E. Niederhauser, "Die Standortstheorie Alfred Webers," *Staatswissenschaftliche Studien,* Bd. xiv (1944), 181–187.

[3] National Resources Planning Board, *Industrial Location and National Resources* (Washington, 1943), ch. 5; and P. S. Florence, *Investment, Location, and Size of Plant* (Cambridge, England, 1948), esp. ch. iv.

[4] Florence's interpretations may be construed by some as implicit theorizing. In particular, objection may be made to a conversion of his coefficient of geographical association into a general indicator of economic spatial dependence between industries. It should be noted that such a conversion can be questioned in view of the statistical shortcomings of the coefficient. See Robert E. Kuenne, *The Use of Input-Output Techniques for the Estimation of Employment in the Delaware Valley* (Ph.D. dissertation, Harvard University, 1953), ch. 2.

cussions of the location of a basic industry in a region are evaluated.[5] In this sense, crucial elements of regional development theory are attacked. It is not our intent here to present a comprehensive analysis of the forces affecting the location of a basic industry. In other studies this has been attempted for the iron and steel industry.[6] Rather, we accept the conclusions of these studies as a starting point and attempt to appraise the direction and strength of the force generated by the basic industry upon all types of economic activity within the region. This may be defined as the "broad agglomeration effect."

This effect during the coming decade will be studied with reference to the Greater New York-Philadelphia urban-industrial region.[7] Some attention will be given to interregional repercussions, particularly upon the closely linked region of Puerto Rico. Throughout the study it is assumed that aggregate demand remains at a high level during the next decade, that no technological revolution in the production of steel takes place, and that no violent shocks such as a major destructive war impinge upon the economy.

[5] In many respects our impact study for a region resembles the pioneering, but neglected, study of Barfod's for a city. (Børge Barfod, *Local Economic Effects of a Large Scale Industrial Undertaking* (Copenhagen, 1938). Because of the larger quantities of data currently available, we have been able to adopt a more comprehensive approach.

Among other studies, somewhat related to ours, are: M. C. Daly, "An Approximation to a Geographical Multiplier," *Economic Journal*, L (June-September 1940), 248–258; Federal Reserve Bank of Kansas City, "The Employment Multiplier in Wichita," *Monthly Review*, 37 (September 1952); E. Ullman, "The Basic-Service Ratio and the Areal Support of Cities," forthcoming.

[6] W. Isard, "Some Locational Factors in the Iron and Steel Industry Since the Early Nineteenth Century," *Journal of Political Economy*, LVI (June 1948), 203–217; W. Isard and W. Capron, "The Future Locational Pattern of Iron and Steel Production in the United States," *Journal of Political Economy*, LVII (April 1949), 118–133; W. Isard and J. Cumberland, "New England as a possible Location for an Integrated Iron and Steel Works," *Economic Geography*, 26 (October 1950); John H. Cumberland, *The Locational Structure of the East Coast Steel Industry With Emphasis on an Integrated New England Steel Mill* (Ph.D. dissertation, Harvard University, 1951). For the analysis of locational factors in another basic industry, see John Krutilla, *The Structure of Costs and Regional Advantage in Primary Aluminum Production* (Ph.D. dissertation, Harvard University, 1952).

[7] This region includes the following counties: Fairfield and New Haven in Connecticut; Kings, Queens, Richmond, New York, Bronx, Westchester, Orange, Putnam, Rockland, Suffolk, and Nassau in New York; Bergen, Passaic, Morris, Essex, Hudson, Union, Middlesex, Monmouth, Ocean, Burlington, Atlantic, Salem, Gloucester, Camden, Mercer, Hunterdon, Somerset, Warren, and Sussex in New Jersey; and Chester, Delaware, Philadelphia, Montgomery, and Bucks in Pennsylvania.

Ideally, the area should be defined in such a way as to include all of those counties and parts of counties which together comprise a continuous spatial entity and which will undergo noticeable change as a result of the steel development. Practically, because of data inadequacies, only whole counties can be treated. From a consideration of the nature and direction of transportation facilities, industrial and residential land use, population distribution, and similar characteristics, the above listed counties seem to form the most appropriate spatial entity for our problem, although undoubtedly some contiguous areas will be directly affected, too.

The Scale of Basic Steel Operations

Past studies of the costs of assembling raw materials, production, and delivery of steel to market demonstrate that if there exists a market capable of absorbing the total output of a modern integrated steel-works, with its associated semifinishing mills, steel-producing capacity should be located in the vicinity of the market as closely as site conditions, transportation facilities, and socio-cultural factors permit. (There are of course exceptions when special conditions obtain, as when coal and ore sources coincide or are adjacent.) On the basis of these studies, it had been concluded that capacity on the eastern sea-board should be expanded. This conclusion has been borne out by the recent construction of the United States Steel Corporation's Fairless Works at Morrisville, Pennsylvania, the announcement of National Steel's intention to build at Paulsboro, New Jersey, and reports of the persistent interest of other steel companies in the Delaware Valley.

The cost rationale for the above conclusions and their subsequent fulfilment is presented succinctly in Table 1. Since the steel industry is a transport-oriented industry, transport costs alone need be presented.[8] The advantage of a Trenton location is clear-cut and marked.

From the standpoint of sound regional planning, the mere specification that an industry should be situated in an area on the basis of a cost advantage is insufficient; the scale of its operation must also be given. For such a market-oriented industry as steel, this entails the estimation of future demand for steel in the area. *Iron Age* estimated the consumption of steel by metal-working industry alone in the New York-Trenton-

Table 1. — Transportation Costs on Ore, Coal, and Finished Products for Selected Producing Locations Serving New York City*

(In dollars)

| Location | Transportation Costs on: | | | |
	Ore	Coal	Finished Products	Total
New London (hypothetical)	3.68	5.42	8.80	17.90
Pittsburgh	5.55	1.56	12.40	19.51
Cleveland	3.16	3.85	14.00	21.01
Sparrows Point	3.68	4.26	8.40	16.34
Buffalo	3.16	4.27	11.60	19.03
Bethlehem	5.56	5.06	5.80	16.42
Trenton	3.68	4.65	4.80	13.13

* The costs on iron ore and coal are calculated per net ton of steel. Source: Isard and Cumberland, *op. cit.*, p. 257.

[8] See Isard, *op. cit.*, pp. 203–204; and Isard and Capron, *op. cit.*, pp. 120–123.

Philadelphia industrial area in 1948 as 5.1 million tons.[9] (In 1948, for the nation as a whole, the metal-working industry received 46 million of the 66 million tons of steel shipped by steel mills.) The *Iron Age* estimation procedure, however, is subject to serious criticism.[10] The much more reliable Census data record consumption by metal-fabricating industries of 4.0 million tons for 1947 after appropriate adjustment of state data to correspond with our area.[11]

If the adjusted Census figure is blown up by 43 per cent to account crudely for consumption by nonmetal-working industry, if, in addition, allowance is made for a share of the coastwise trade and export markets of the United States,[12] and if the expected growth of effective demand by steel consumers in the area is considered, an optimist might predict steel consumption of at least 9 to 11 million tons annually by the early 1960's. On this basis he might contend that an almost equivalent amount of new capacity could be justified. Less sanguine observers, cognizant of the intense competition from Sparrows Point, Bethlehem, and Buffalo, might with good reason restrict their estimates of new capacity by 1962 to 5 or 6 million tons.[13]

For purposes of this article, a range of estimates would unduly complicate computations, as is easily seen later. The use of an average also is undesirable, since in terms of planning capital outlay and development of the greater metropolitan regions within the area it is more

[9] O. Johnson, *Steel Consumption in 1948: A Report by IRON AGE to the Metalworking Industry.* The New York-Trenton-Philadelphia industrial area, considerably smaller than our Greater New York-Philadelphia urban-industrial region, includes the following counties: Fairfield and New Haven in Connecticut; Bronx, Kings, Nassau, New York, Queens, Richmond, and Westchester in New York; Bergen, Burlington, Camden, Essex, Gloucester, Hudson, Mercer, Middlesex, Passaic, and Union in New Jersey; and Bucks, Chester, Delaware, Montgomery, and Philadelphia in Pennsylvania.

[10] For Connecticut the *Census of Manufactures,* 1947, Vol. I, pp. 244–245, reports consumption by metal-workers of 509,210 tons as against 1,194,694 tons in *Iron Age;* for New York, 2,109,010 tons as against 3,232,356 tons; for New Jersey, 1,130,845 tons as against 1,684,699 tons; and for Pennsylvania, 5,600,224 tons as against 5,498,654 tons.

[11] The adjustment procedure was as follows: for those sectors of our area in Connecticut, New York, and Pennsylvania, the consumption for each (as given in *Iron Age*) was taken as a percentage of the appropriate *Iron Age* state figure. These percentages were multiplied by the appropriate Census data for the state, and the products were added to the total consumption listed in the *Census* for New Jersey.

[12] Exports from the port districts of New York and Philadelphia of iron and steel mill products and semi-manufactures were 2.6 million tons and 451,800 tons respectively in 1947, and 1.6 million tons and 283,000 tons respectively in 1948. U.S. Army, Board of Engineers for Rivers and Harbors, *Commercial Statistics; Water-borne Commerce* (Washington, D.C.); and Annual Reports, pt. 2, 1947, pp. 231, 285–366, and pt. 2, 1948, pp. 255, 315–397.

[13] In view of such competition we postulate that only 50 per cent of the new steel demand arising as a result of this regional development will be supplied by producers in the area. For discussion of this point see page 489 and column 2, Table 5 below.

desirable to have firm estimates of minimum expansion effects than infirm estimates of most likely effects.[14] Hence, here, as throughout this paper, we attribute expansion to an industry in our area only when a sound basis exists for such a prospect. Our minimum estimate for new basic steel capacity for this area, exclusive of steel capacity induced by the new steel demand incident to the agglomeration effect in its broadest sense, is 3.0 million tons. This new steel capacity, in effect a displacement of extra-areal capacity, estimated as of autumn 1951, was based on the announced intention of the United States Steel Corporation to construct 1.8 million tons of capacity, and on our considered judgment — particularly in the light of National Steel's proposal to erect 1 million tons of capacity — that at least 1.2 million tons of additional new capacity was justified.[15]

From here on, the problem decomposes into two major parts: (1) to estimate the resulting direct expansion of existing and influx of new steel-fabricating activities within the area, and (2) to quantify the direct and indirect repercussions of the new steel production and associated new steel-fabricating operations upon all activities in the area.

Directly Induced Steel Fabrication

Several attempts have been made to identify the forces dictating the juxtaposition of industries representing consecutive stages in a production process or related in some other vertical or horizontal manner.[16] The approach of these attempts becomes more valid and useful when location theory and historical trend analysis supplement the location quotient and coefficient of geographical association upon which these studies heavily depend. In associating steel-fabricating activity with basic steel capacity, we have treated individually the steel-fabricating industries listed below in Table 4 by three-digit Census classification. For each such activity: (1) we compare, for each of 69 industrial areas

[14] It should also be noted that a secondary objective of this study was to isolate and pin-point those localities in our area which would experience highest rates of population growth and physical development and hence would be most attractive for nonspeculative real estate investment, ceteris paribus. For this objective, too, firm minimum estimates are more desirable insofar as they reduce the element of risk.

[15] It is interesting to note that the United States Steel Company in discussing the operation of the Fairless Works stated: "Initial operation of the plant starting in 1952 will require delivery of 3,300,000 gross tons of coal and foreign ore annually by water. . . . The rolling mills which will be installed at the Fairless Works in 1951–52 will have sufficient capacity to consume the output of probable future open hearths and blast furnaces requiring an additional annual tonnage of 3,700,000 gross tons of iron ore and coal." (*Statement by United States Steel Company at Public Hearing by U.S. Army Engineers March 14, 1951, Trenton, New Jersey*, mimeographed, pp. 2–3.) These statements, in addition to others, suggest a capacity well beyond the 1.8 million tons currently under construction.

[16] Florence, *op. cit.;* and National Resources Planning Board, *op. cit.*, ch. 5.

as defined by *Iron Age,* the number of production workers engaged in it and the capacity to produce the major basic steel items consumed by it;[17] (2) we observe the rates of growth of the given activity during the period 1939–47 in those areas where capacity for producing the major steel items consumed by the activity increased considerably more rapidly than for the nation as a whole, and we compare such rates with those of other areas;[18] and (3) we consider particular features and characteristics of the production process in the given activity, with special reference to transportation costs on raw materials and the finished product, economies of scale, industrial organization, and other location factors whose effect might easily and objectively be identified.

To illustrate the procedure, industry number 343, Heating Apparatus (Except Electric) and Plumbers' Supplies (S.I.C. code) is analyzed below. This industry produces the following major products: cast iron heating boilers; cast iron radiators; residential steel heating boilers; warm air furnaces; gas, coal, wood, and kerosene domestic heating stoves and cooking stoves, ranges, and appliances (except electric); steam and hot water unit heaters; floor furnaces; tanks for water heaters; oil burners, domestic and industrial; plumbing fixture fittings and trim; cast iron and steel kitchen sinks; cast iron and steel bathtubs. In Table 2 are recorded for 69 industrial areas and for the balance of each state not included in the industrial areas capacity for hot-rolled sheet and strip production in 1948 (column 1) and *Iron Age* estimates of production workers in 1948 (column 2). It should be noted that of the steel consumed by industry 343 in 1947, 86 per cent consisted of sheet and strip.[19]

Careful scrutiny of the table reveals two types of relationships. The fairly large concentrations of employment in the New York-Newark-Jersey City area (5,876), Bridgeport-New Haven (2,853), Hartford-New Britain (1,988), and other southern New England districts, indicate a strong market pull. This, too, is borne out when the disproportionately small capacity in the combined San Francisco-Oakland-Los Angeles area is contrasted with the large amount of employment in industry 343 (12,123).

Less clear-cut cases of strong market pulls are Philadelphia-Camden

---

[17] Though the quality of the *Iron Age* data is poor, they are used since there are no other data on three-digit steel-fabricating activities for such a fine breakdown of the United States.

Because of the aforementioned reasons and those cited in the source quoted in footnote 4, we have not computed the coefficient of geographical association. Rather we have carefully inspected these two sets of data.

[18] Moreover, because costs of relocation are significant, consideration was given to the rate at which each activity has been expanding nationally. It was felt that ceteris paribus, greater employment could be anticipated for our area in the faster growing than in the slower growing industries.

[19] *Census of Manufactures,* 1947, Vol. I, p. 238.

Table 2. — Production Employment in Industry 343 and
Hot-Rolled Sheet and Strip Capacity, 1948, by Selected Areas*

Industrial Area	Capacity (*in tons*)	Employment	Industrial Area	Capacity (*in tons*)	Employment
Chicago-Gary	3,879,700	12,959	Minneapolis-St. Paul	0	1,073
Youngstown	2,638,350	650	Seattle	0	943
Pittsburgh	2,614,520	3,437	Fall River-New Bedford	0	935
Detroit	2,451,000	3,875	Boston	0	885
Baltimore	1,195,000	2,031	Moline	0	717
Buffalo	1,155,380	2,540	Worcester	0	640
Cincinnati-Covington	950,000	3,960	Dallas-Ft. Worth	0	611
Balance of Ohio	793,000	791	Rochester	0	610
Birmingham	725,000	2,210	Utica	0	610
Cleveland	651,000	7,510	Ft. Wayne	0	565
Sharon-New Castle	600,000	1,101	Syracuse	0	565
Balance of Kentucky	374,000	300	San Diego	0	500
St. Louis	328,500	5,361	Akron	0	500
Canton	314,000	625	Benton Harbor	0	435
San Francisco-Oakland	238,926	2,918	Balance of Alabama	0	410
Mansfield-Marion	205,000	2,040	Balance of Texas	0	381
Los Angeles	113,284	9,205	Springfield-Holyoke	0	361
Bridgeport-New Haven	150,000	2,853	Trenton, N.J.	0	330
Philadelphia-Camden	105,100	3,909	Allentown-Bethlehem	0	275
Anderson-Muncie	95,000	855	Balance of Missouri	0	220
Columbus	61,500	2,715	Balance of Michigan	0	210
Indianapolis	55,000	1,477	Balance of Georgia	0	200
Atlanta	25,500	620	Toledo	0	186
New Castle, Ind.	25,000	0	Flint	0	175
Kansas City	23,500	426	Balance of Indiana	0	175
Houston	9,000	68	Balance of Washington	0	150
Balance of Minnesota	7,120	785	Evansville, Ind.	0	109
Louisville	0	6,820	Balance of Connecticut	0	80
New York-Newark-Jersey City	0	5,876	Dayton	0	65
Sheboygan	0	5,500	Albany	0	50
Milwaukee	0	3,768	Binghamton-Elmira	0	50
Balance of Wisconsin	0	3,734	Balance of California	0	40
Lansing	0	2,830	Balance of Maryland	0	25
Hartford-New Britain	0	1,988	Balance of New York	0	0
Peoria	0	1,875	Balance of Pennsylvania	0	0
Erie	0	1,760	Balance of New Jersey	0	0
South Bend	0	1,599	Hagerstown	0	0
Rockford	0	1,540	Danville, Ill.	0	0
Lancaster-York	0	1,450	Madison, Wis.	0	0
Springfield, Ill.	0	1,376	Balance of Kansas	0	0
Wichita	0	1,255			
Reading	0	1,206	Mobile	0	0
Balance of Illinois	0	1,167	New Orleans	0	0
Grand Rapids	0	1,097	Balance of Louisiana	0	0
Scranton-Wilkes-Barre	0	1,095	Beaumont	0	0

* Heating apparatus (except electric) and plumbers' supplies.

(3,909 employed), and the entire state of Wisconsin (13,002), including Milwaukee (3,768) and Sheboygan (5,500). However, each one of the areas already mentioned has some sheet and strip capacity or, aside from New England points, is no more than about 200 miles from a major sheet- and strip-producing point. This testifies to the pull of sheet- and strip-producing points which is even more forcibly illustrated by Chicago-Gary (12,959 employed); Cleveland (7,510); Louisville, somewhat over 100 miles from Cincinnati-Covington, (6,820); Cincinnati-Covington (3,960); Detroit (3,875); and Pittsburgh (3,437). In short, both market and sheet- and strip-producing points exert significant pulls upon the location of the industry. This suggests that with the addition of new sheet and strip capacity at the Fairless Works and elsewhere in the Delaware Valley, there should be a net positive attraction for industry 343, especially since, relative to the other major population focal points, such as Chicago-Gary and San Francisco-Oakland-Los Angeles, our area is deficient in its per capita representation of this industry.

A study of relevant historical materials is also illuminating. In Table 3 are presented Census data on the rates of growth of industry 343 for the United States and for Maryland and California, 1939–47. (Because

Table 3. — Production Employment in Industry 343

	1939	1947	Per cent Rate of Growth, 1939–47
United States	78,330	126,725	61.8
Maryland	1,128	2,499	121.5
California	4,652	9,373	101.5

of data shortcomings, a comparison over a longer historical period is not justified.) Maryland and California were during this period among the fastest growing states in terms of sheet and strip capacity,[20] and they embrace or are peripheral to major market areas. The growth rates for California and Maryland well exceed that for the nation. This suggests that in any given large market area growth of industry 343 is at least partially related to the existence and growth of sheet and strip capacity in that area. This adds further support to the thesis that installation of sheet and strip capacity in the Delaware Valley will induce additional employment in this industry, particularly since the existing Maryland capacity can be considered peripheral to our area.

[20] Hot-rolled sheet and strip capacity grew from 498,000 tons in 1938 to 1,195,000 in 1948 for Maryland; and for the same years from 85,100 tons to 352,210 tons for California. These represent respectively a more than doubling and tripling effect for these states. Data from American Iron and Steel Institute, *Annual Reports*.

Theoretical considerations reinforce the empirical suggestions. The products of industry 343 tend to be heavy and bulky and to bear high transport costs relative to their value if not produced at the market; similarly, transport costs on the raw material steel are high, although to a lesser degree, if production does not take place at a steel source. A situation which involves the coincidence of both market and raw material, as in our area, strongly argues for significant expansion of employment in this industry. Thus, since this industry is a relatively fast growing one, as indicated in Table 3, it seems logical that a decreasing proportion of the area's demand for the products of this industry will be met from plants in the Western Pennsylvania-Ohio area, and an increasing proportion from plants within the area.

Having established on three counts that the coexistence of market and capacity in our area warrants expansion in industry 343 during the coming decade, we confront the problem of estimating the specific magnitude of this expansion. No neat estimating formula exists. Judgment based on knowledge of the area and conversations with informed persons must be resorted to. In line with such knowledge and conversations and in view of the fact that in 1948 our area had 12,968 production workers whereas the Chicago-Gary area had 12,959 (exclusive of the very substantial employment in the 200-mile area about Chicago-Gary) we judge that 20 per cent represents a firm minimum rate of increase in production workers in industry 343 incident to our area's increased ability to compete as a result of new steel capacity. This 20 per cent increase represents an increment of 2,594 workers.

Similarly, for every other three-digit steel-fabricating activity, an estimate of numbers of new production workers was derived.[21] These estimates are listed in Table 4.[22] The total number of new production workers is 61,326 which, when divided by the 9,166 production workers to be associated with the 3.0 million tons of new steel capacity, yields a ratio of 6.7. Despite its serious shortcomings, a comparison of this ratio with the 8.9 national ratio of production workers in steel-fabricating activities to production workers in steel manufacture suggests the conservative nature of our estimates, especially since of all the areas in

---

[21] The lack of any clear-cut patterns in the three-digit industries of the two-digit categories, industry groups 36, 38, and 39, strongly argued for the use of the two-digit aggregates of these three-digit industries.

[22] It should be noted that expansion in metal furniture trades has been omitted. Difficulties of separating metal furniture from nonmetal furniture manufacture, both in the above steps and the steps to follow, argued for excluding this activity, although about 2,500 new production workers in metal furniture trades might be anticipated. This contributes to the minimal nature of our projections. It still further balances any overestimates that may have crept into the analysis, especially in the industry groups, 354–359, where a reexamination of procedure after computations were completed indicated that we had made less conservative estimates for these three-digit industries than for other three-digit industries.

Table 4. — Estimates of New Production Employees in the Area
by Steel-fabricating Activity

Industry No.	Title	Per cent Rate of Growth	New Production Employees
341	Tin cans and other tinware	10.0	923
342	Cutlery, hand tools, and general hardware	0.0	0
343	Heating apparatus (except electric) and plumbers' supplies	20.0	2,593
344	Fabricated structural metal products	4.6	1,132
346	Metal stamping, coating, and engraving	10.0	2,408
347	Lighting fixtures	2.5	1,911
348	Fabricated wire products	10.0	670
349	Miscellaneous fabricated metal products	17.5	2,695
351	Engines and turbines	8.0	723
352	Agricultural machinery and tractors	10.0	294
353	Construction and mining machinery and equipment	10.0	252
354	Metal-working machinery	13.5	2,137
355	Special-industry machinery (except metal-working machinery)	16.0	5,204
356	General industrial machinery and equipment	25.0	5,566
357	Office and store machines and devices	10.0	1,225
358	Service-industry and household machines	20.0	4,512
359	Miscellaneous machinery parts	25.0	5,666
36	Electrical machinery, equipment and supplies	5.0	8,025
371	Motor vehicles and motor-vehicle equipment	20.0	7,331
372	Aircraft and parts	3.0	871
373	Ship and boat building and repairing	5.0	1,989
374	Railroad equipment	3.0	364
375	Motorcycles, bicycles, and parts	0.0	0
379	Transportation equipment (n.e.c.)	7.0	32
38	Professional, scientific, and controlling instruments; photographic, etc.	0.0	0
39	Miscellaneous manufacturing industries	10.5	4,803
	Total		61,326

the United States our area represents the most concentrated market.[23]

In setting forth these estimates, we do not claim that each will be realized. It is well recognized that unpredictable events and inadequate

[23] For curiosity's sake alone, a multiple linear correlation between production workers and four explanatory variables was made for the 69 industrial areas of Table 2 (balances of states were excluded). The four variables were: (1) market proximity, as given by an index measuring distances of any given area from the eleven largest market centers in the United States; (2) distance of that area from a region of major steel capacity (arbitrarily defined as one capable of producing more than 1,250,000 tons annually); (3) population (1950) of that area; and (4) steel capacity of the given area.

A multiple correlation coefficient of .82 was obtained. However, only 11 of the estimates derived from the estimating equation were within plus or minus ten per knowledge of the interaction of basic underlying forces as they affect an individual industry may have led us astray in individual instances. However, as a whole, we feel that these estimates represent a set of firm minimum figures upon which subsequent analysis may rest.[24]

Repercussions of Initial Activities

To quantify the direct and indirect repercussions of the operation of the above new steel-frabricating industries as well as of the new steel capacity, a modified regional input-output schema is employed. The entire set of inputs absorbed directly by the steel and steel-fabricating activities constitutes, in a sense, the "bill of goods" that must be furnished to our area. This bill of goods is constructed: (1) by multiplying the cents' worth of every input required per dollar output of a given steel-fabricating activity by the dollar volume of that activity corresponding to the estimated new employment;[25] (2) by multiplying the cents' worth of every input per dollar output of steel by the dollar volume of new steel output corresponding to our estimate of new steel capacity; and (3) by summing horizontally for each of the 45 different industrial inputs the requirements by steel and each fabricating activity. The totals for each of the 45 inputs are recorded in column 1 of Table 5.[26]

---

cent of the actual employment data. Injection of new values for the variables to account for new steel capacity in the New York-Trenton-Philadelphia industrial area led to an estimate of 45,000 new production workers in metal-fabricating activities for this area. However, no significance should be attributed to this finding, since extreme items have seriously distorted the influence of steel capacity upon fabricating employment, and since, in any case, multiple correlation analysis has little meaning in this particular context. For a more detailed presentation of the correlation analysis, see Kuenne, *op. cit.*, ch. 2.

[24] To the extent that the input structures of these individual activities tend to resemble one another, errors of over- and under-estimation tend to cancel themselves when we proceed to quantify subsequent repercussions. In the limit, when input structures are identical, the industries may be aggregated into one industry without loss of accuracy.

[25] These cents' worth of inputs are simply the technical coefficients in the Leontief input-out model. The coefficients for a 50 x 50 matrix were developed for 1947 by the Bureau of Labor Statistics. See Table 5 in W. D. Evans and M. Hoffenberg, "The Interindustry Relations Study for 1947," this *Review*, xxxiv (May 1952).

The dollar volume corresponding to new employment in steel and each fabricating activity was crudely obtained by multiplying the dollar volume per production worker for steel and for each activity, as derived by the 1947 *Census of Manufactures* for the United States as a whole, by the anticipated new employment. This derivation of input requirements assumes linear homogeneous production functions. In addition it should be borne in mind that the production worker data of the *Census* and *Iron Age* diverge. Hence, unavoidable error is introduced, since new employment estimates of three-digit categories are stated in terms of *Iron Age* production workers while the dollar volume expansion of each activity is based on *Census* production worker data.

[26] An error of computation crept into the construction of this bill of goods. Production worker employment in industry 343 was overstated by 477. In view of the crudeness of the analysis and the smallness of the error, recomputation of the round effects did not seem to be warranted.

Table 5. — Direct and Indirect Repercussions of New Basic Steel Capacity

		Input requirements of initial steel and steel-fabricating activities (in $ thousand) (1)	Minimum percentage of input requirements to be produced in area (2)	First round expansions in area (in $ thousand) (3)	Second round expansions in area (in $ thousand) (4)	Third round expansions in area (in $ thousand) (5)	Sum of round expansions in area (in $ thousand) (6)	Total new employees corresponding to round expansions (7)	Total new employees in initial steel and steel-fabricating activities (8)	Over-all total of new employees (9)
1.	Agriculture & fisheries	50.0	0	0.0	0.	0.	0.	0		0
2.	Food & kindred products	294.6	60	176.8	17,660.	8,249.	42,492.	1,833		1,833
3.	Tobacco manufactures	0.0	0	0.0	0.	0.	0.	0		0
4.	Textile mill products	3,864.7	10	386.5	406.	39.	1,280.	142		142
5.	Apparel	1,285.6	75	964.2	10,124.	3,461.	21,155.	2,302		2,302
6.	Lumber & wood products	5,610.7	5	280.5	93.	36.	450.	64		64
7.	Furniture & fixtures	1,753.4	33	578.6	802.	198.	2,000.	234		234
8.	Paper & allied products	4,818.7	40	1,927.5	1,674.	1,297.	6,574.	426		426
9.	Printing & publishing	425.5	90	383.0	5,929.	3,014.	14,617.	1,667		1,667
10.	Chemicals	10,626.4	45	4,781.9	3,599.	1,630.	12,077.	601		601
11.	Products of petroleum & coal	10,936.6	25	2,734.2	2,547.	1,118.	7,634.	228		228
12.	Rubber products	8,381.5	15	1,257.2	355.	102.	1,879.	169		169
13.	Leather & leather products	647.7	20	129.5	679.	194.	1,371.	150		150
14.	Stone, clay, & glass products	9,031.7	15	1,354.8	441.	139.	2,083.	268		268
15.	Iron & steel	121,170.5	50	60,585.3	13,566.	2,965.	78,335.	6,093	11,666	17,759
16.	Nonferrous metals	33,997.4	20	6,799.5	1,667.	381.	9,063.	505		505
17.	Plumbing & heating supplies	3,192.4	25	798.1	248.	50.	1,189.	118	3,640	3,758
18.	Fabricated structural metal prod.	3,480.7	40	1,392.3	312.	33.	1,809.	151	1,420	1,571
19.	Other fabricated metal products	31,770.9	40	12,708.4	2,146.	561.	16,121.	1,537	10,060	11,597
20.	Agric'l, mining, & const. machinery	3,651.3	5	182.6	46.	11.	251.	22	707	729
21.	Metal-working machinery	7,389.1	25	1,847.3	270.	43.	2,210.	289	2,705	2,994
22.	Other machinery (except electric)	28,463.6	40	11,385.4	2,675.	551.	15,384.	1,486	28,607	30,093
23.	Motors & generators	11,265.9	20	2,253.2	226.	42.	2,560.	301	⎫	⎫
24.	Radios	4,562.2	30	1,368.7	428.	101.	2,026.	192	⎬ 10,392	⎬ 12,312
25.	Other electrical machinery	21,773.9	50	10,887.0	2,011.	432.	13,903.	1,427	⎭	⎭
26.	Motor vehicles	50,530.8	10	5,053.1	742.	260.	6,421.	389	8,770	9,159
27.	Other transportation equipment	2,605.5	20	521.1	276.	69.	938.	117	4,605	4,722
28.	Professional & scientific equip.	3,221.4	50	1,610.7	801.	287.	3,123.	416		416
29.	Miscellaneous manufacturing	5,116.8	60	3,070.1	2,888.	982.	8,418.	845	6,108	6,953
30.	Coal, gas, & electric power	7,767.0	50	3,883.5	1,843.	2,693.	11,079.	1,100		1,100
31.	Railroad transportation	13,575.8	75	10,181.9	6,010.	2,390.	21,532.	3,308		3,308
32.	Ocean transportation	457.3	75	343.0	331.	170.	1,021.	110		110
33.	Other transportation	4,179.4	95	3,970.4	343.	2,836.	19,694.	2,394		2,394
34.	Trade	13,969.8	95	13,271.3	8,422.	11,855.	83,642.	13,874		13,874
35.	Communications	1,790.7	90	1,611.6	36,585.	1,283.	7,305.	1,191		1,191
36.	Finance & insurance	3,086.2	90	2,777.6	2,409.	5,062.	25,252.	2,329		2,329
37.	Rental	3,018.8	95	2,867.9	9,472.	9,603.	55,680.	909		909
38.	Business services	5,338.5	95	5,071.6	26,222.	2,406.	13,384.	1,305		1,305
39.	Personal & repair services	396.9	95	377.1	2,385.	5,088.	24,212.	4,443		4,443
40.	Medical, educ., & nonprofit org's	000.0	90	0.0	14,399.	2,160.	17,271.	4,370		4,370
41.	Amusements	000.0	90	0.0	9,811.	1,066.	6,591.	1,100		1,100
42.	Scrap & miscellaneous industries	8,388.2	50	4,194.1	3,677.	727.	7,411.	771		771
43.	Undistributed	103,638.6	50	51,819.3	2,054.	6,019.	69,236.	7,208		7,208
44.	Eating and drinking places	000.0	95	0.0	16,916.	3,903.	29,551.	3,705		3,705
45.	Households	348,281.0	82	285,590.4	63,002.	80,894.	509,578.			
	Totals	903,807.7		521,377.2	282,024.	164,400.	1,177,822.	70,089	88,680	158,769

In designing our study we made an important modification of the traditional input-output matrix. Since in regional analysis it is important to catch the local multiplier effect resulting from the generation of new income, households have been introduced into the structural matrix as an industry. Hence, the labor and other household services required by the new activities are recorded.[27]

After the bill of goods had been constructed, it was necessary to determine the fraction of the total amount of each input minimally expected to originate in the area. (It is clear that of the bill of goods requirements some will be produced within the area, while others, such as coal, will come from outside the area.) This step was necessary since in this study the expansionary effect upon the economy of the area is maintained by only the outputs which are produced within the area. It is not to be denied that the area may expand as a result of new demands for its products by population elsewhere, for example as a result of new demands by the population in the Appalachian coalfields consequent to additional demand for coal within the area. However, the inability to apply an interregional model[28] which would quantify these feedbacks compels us to neglect this indirect expansionary effect. This is not inconsistent with our accumulated bias toward underestimation, and hence is fully in line with the objectives of this article.

The determination of the above fraction for each industrial activity was based on the small amount of location theory directly relevant, on the accumulated production and derived consumption data for our area, on data of flows of commodities into and out of the area, and, finally, upon judgments of informed persons within the area. These fractions are recorded in percentage terms in column 2 of Table 5. Again many subjective decisions had to be made, and in each case we attributed to the area the production of only that fraction of the inputs required of an activity for which we felt there was a firm basis. For example, because the new industry will draw upon existing agricultural labor in the area, because some of the best agricultural land will be diverted into industrial, commercial, and residential uses, and in view of the past relative decline of agriculture in the area, it was felt that there was no firm basis for projecting an expansion of agriculture incident to steel development. Hence, a percentage of zero is recorded for agriculture, even

---

[27] New construction was removed from the Bureau of Labor Statistics structural matrix because its inclusion is questionable. Given the data currently available, any separation of construction into that on current and that on capital account involves subjective judgments. As a consequence, results obtained on the requirements of construction when construction is included in the structural matrix tend not to be superior to those obtained by the crude rule-of-thumb method which will be employed later.

[28] See W. Isard, "Interregional and Regional Input-Output Analysis: A Model of a Space-Economy," this *Review,* xxxiii (November 1951). Experimentation with an interregional model is currently being undertaken.

though the likelihood exists that there will be some expansion. Similarly, in the case of chemicals, a 45 per cent figure represents an understatement in view of the rapid expansion of, and the natural advantages for, chemical production in the area. Observe, too, that the highest percentage figure associated with any activity is 95, even though it is likely that for certain service industries the percentage figure will be higher.[29]

Applying the percentages of column 2 to the corresponding items of column 1 yields column 3, which records (as firm minimums) the first round expansion of each industrial activity in the area which we anticipate will be required to maintain the new steel capacity and its associated fabricators in reasonably full operation. It should be noted that in column 3 of Table 5 the requirements of steel and of the diverse outputs of steel-fabricators are considered to represent demand which is over and above the demands for steel and fabricated steel products which initially justified the erection of new basic steel and steel-fabricating capacities; these industries must produce beyond their initial capacity. In effect, we have shaped the analysis so as to leave these activities within the structural matrix.

To produce the first round of expansions requires in turn a whole series of inputs. One can derive this series of inputs: (1) by multiplying the cents' worth of each input per dollar output of a given activity by the dollar volume of output of that activity recorded as the first round expansion; and (2) by summing horizontally over all activities the requirements so derived for inputs from each industrial category. However, not all of these second round input requirements will originate in the area. Multiplying these second round input requirements by the corresponding percentages in column 2 of Table 5 yields firm minimum estimates of the second round expansions for the area, which are recorded in column 4. In turn, third round input requirements and third round expansions (column 5) are derived, and so forth.[30] Since the rounds con-

---

[29] In the case of households a figure of 82 per cent was used in order to allow for some outflow to persons residing in other areas and to recognize leakages through savings and other channels.

A useful check on the percentages was furnished by data derived for 1939 in connection with regional input-output work of the Harvard Economic Research Project (see W. Isard, "Some Empirical Results and Problems of Regional Input-Output Analysis," ch. 5 in W. Leontief, *et al., Studies in the Structure of the American Economy,* New York, 1953). In this work, for each of a group of industries somewhat similar to ours, estimates were made of the consumption of outputs by states. Then, subtracting for any given activity the consumption estimate from the actual production for a given state yields a surplus or deficit which can be expressed as a percentage of total consumption of that activity in that state. This percentage gives some indication of the degree to which a state supplies its own needs for the outputs of any given industry. The percentages derived for 1939 for the states of Connecticut, New York, New Jersey, and Pennsylvania tend to have either smaller deficits than our percentages would yield or actual surpluses.

[30] Under certain circumstances, different sets of percentage reduction factors can and should be used from round to round to estimate expansions. See W. Isard and

verge rather rapidly, it was necessary for our problem to compute only the first six rounds of expansions with rough extrapolations to cover the infinite number of succeeding rounds. By industrial category, the sum of the first six rounds plus extrapolations are listed in column 6 of Table 5.[31]

For each industrial category (except the household sector), the value of output per worker in 1947 was used to obtain a crude estimate of new employment[32] corresponding to the sum of the round expansions of column 6. These estimates include nonproduction employment. They are listed in column 7 of Table 5, and total 70,089 workers. To them must be added the employees in the initial new capacity of steel,[33] and steel-fabricating activities (column 8, Table 5). This yields column 9 of Table 5, and a total of 158,769 workers.[34] Finally, new employees expected to be engaged in construction (8,574)[35] and government activity (12,884)[36] must be included. The over-all new employment thus amounts to 180,228 workers.

It should be emphasized that the above total is a gross figure and relates to change in employment only in activities which expand as a result of new steel capacity. Theoretically, one should subtract from this figure the decline in employment in activities which are forced to contract as a result of labor shortages, high wages, and the like. However, contractions are likely to be more severe in the shortrun than in the longrun when the new employment openings will have had an oppor-

---

M. J. Peck, "Location Theory and International and Interregional Trade Theory," *Quarterly Journal of Economics,* forthcoming.

[31] These, of course, represent the dollar value of each industry's product in 1947 prices.

[32] Data were obtained from the *Census of Manufactures,* 1947; *Census of Business,* 1948; *Minerals Yearbook,* 1947; *Survey of Current Business,* July 1949; various issues of the *Monthly Labor Review;* and from the Harvard Economic Research Project.

[33] The 11,666 estimate of number of total workers for the 3.0 million tons of initial new capacity is obtained from data available on the Fairless Steel Works. See Pennsylvania State Planning Commission, *Boom in Bucks County* (mimeographed), p. 1.

[34] Column 9 of Table 5, when converted into dollar figures, approximates the column vector X, where $X = (I-RA)^{-1}Y$. In the term on the right-hand side of the equation, Y represents the bill of goods column vector whose elements are the outputs of the initial steel and steel-fabricating activities. It is multiplied by the inversion of the matrix $(I-RA)$ where A is the coefficient (structural) matrix constructed to include households, and where R is the diagonal matrix whose elements are the set of percentages of column 2, Table 5.

[35] We estimated construction employees: (1) by dividing the total national labor force in 1947 less government and construction workers into the total of construction workers for the nation; and (2) by multiplying this ratio by the total of the estimates in column 9.

[36] We estimated government employees: (1) by dividing the total national labor force in 1947 less all government employees (state, local, and federal) into the total of state and local government employees in 1947 for the nation; and (2) by multiplying this ratio by the total of the estimates in column 9 plus new construction employees. This calculation, which excludes an allowance for federal employment, is in keeping with the probable less-than-proportional expansion of government employees, and also in line with our "firm minimum" objective.

tunity to exert a positive effect upon labor migration into the area. Since this study is concerned with conditions a decade hence, at which time we do not feel that such contractions will be of major proportions, and since we have already allowed for some contractions when we weighed expanding sectors against declining sectors for an industrial category in deriving the percentages of column 2 of Table 5, we retain the gross figure of 180,228 as an over-all firm minimum estimate of new employment. The reader may prefer to make a small downward adjustment.

In terms of the population engaged in the labor force (roughly 43 per cent) which characterized the area in 1950,[37] the total new population resulting, on the basis of the above gross employment figure, is 419,000. To the extent that the new wage jobs replace existing wage jobs and cause the decline of the industries associated with the latter, and to the extent that the above per cent increases in the future, the net increase in population supported by the new industrial stratum will be smaller.

Basic Qualifications

In appraising the above results, we need not discuss the qualifications springing from the use of constant production coefficients. They have been fully discussed elsewhere.[38] However, the inclusion of constant consumption coefficients in the structural matrix requires some discussion. To the extent that the new income generated does accrue as income to new job-holders (either from in-migration or natural population growth)[39] and does not increase wages of existing job-holders, and to the extent that the age and sex composition, ethnic and racial backgrounds, savings habits and other socio-cultural characteristics of the new job-holders and their families are similar to those of the population as a whole in 1947, the use of constant coefficients is not so tenuous a procedure as might appear at first sight. Also, it might be argued that in the light of the inadequacies of existing consumption studies, no better alternative exists.

In addition, we have abstracted from regional production coefficients and have assumed that production practices (as well as consumption habits) for the area are identical with those for the nation as a whole.

---

[37] According to the *Census of Population* 1950 (general characteristics reports by states), the percentages for New Jersey, for the New York-Northeastern New Jersey metropolitan area, and for the Philadelphia metropolitan area are 43.5, 44.0, and 42.2 respectively.

[38] Among others, see "Input-Output Analysis: Discussion," *Papers and Proceedings of the American Economic Association,* xxxix (May 1949), 226–240; and W. Leontief, *The Structure of American Economy, 1919–1929* (Cambridge, Mass. 1941), pp. 38–41.

[39] This is not at all unlikely since our problem concerns a long-term adjustment. In the longrun labor from other regions can be attracted to these industries in the area, and growth of the area's population can take place. As a consequence the new income is likely to be absorbed by new job-holders.

This assumption is necessary since only national coefficients exist. However, from our knowledge of the resource characteristics of our area and its industrial composition, it is considered unlikely that the use of national coefficients entails serious distortions.[40] Nor, because of obvious difficulties, have these coefficients been adjusted industry by industry for increases in labor productivity or for changes in technology on the horizon; hence, our results reflect the 1947 productivity-technological structure.[41]

Since our projection is made for a decade hence, by which time the construction and equipping of our new plants and facilities will have been completed, we exclude input requirements to build up this capital stock. Our analysis is aimed at the delineation of current intersectoral flows to be expected in the early 1960's.[42]

One major problem which is not readily apparent needs to be bared. To be of practical use all types of input-output analysis require some leakage factor or device which reflects social frictions and the retarding effects of a whole array of noneconomic factors, as well as resource limitations and other economic resistance to expansion. In the typical input-output study, this is implicitly obtained by excluding sufficiently important sectors from the structural matrix (households, government, foreign trade, inventory, and capital formation) and placing them in the bill of goods. In our analysis, the restoration of households to the structural matrix without compensating changes would yield a leakage factor insufficient to guarantee a realistic convergence by rounds. In other words, the sum of the rounds would yield an expansion effect which far exceeds the upper limit of a range of reasonable levels. The system would be insufficiently anchored.[43]

[40] These distortions are certainly not likely to be any greater than those arising in general input-output analysis from insufficient disaggregation of industrial categories into component activities, from insufficient attention to varying product-mix of firms encompassed by any one component industry, and from differential efficiencies among such firms. The latter, too, pervade our analysis.

[41] The reader may care to adjust our employment estimates by a net labor saving coefficient. See W. Leontief, *et al., op. cit.*, pp. 27–35, for some analysis of changes in coefficients in past periods.

[42] Included, however, is an allowance for "average" new construction activity. This activity plus replacement of depreciated facilities engages the labor of the new employees in construction.

[43] This point is neatly borne out by operations with the Leontief balanced regional model. (Leontief, *et al., op. cit.*, chs. 4 and 5.) In the Leontief model, households are removed from the bill of goods and put into the structural matrix without any compensating changes. Hence, the use of the resulting inverted matrix gives the following unrealistic results: an increase of one dollar in the bill of goods requirements for the output of agriculture and fishing necessitates an expansion of $7.59 in outputs for all industries in the nation; a similar increase in the bill of goods requirements for food-processing necessitates expansions amounting to $6.64 for all industries; and the same increase for iron and steel foundry products leads to a total expansion of $7.03 for all industries; and so forth. Clearly, these expansionary effects are extreme, and point up the inadequate leakage of the Leontief model. On the

The counterbalancing factor in our analysis is the leakage introduced through the omission of interregional feedback effects. In other words, no expansionary impulse comes from the increased income in other areas incident to their supply of inputs to our area. Though neglect of the interregional feedback effects is a shortcoming which calls for improved models,[44] nonetheless in our crude framework it provides anchorage and serves the desirable purpose of compensating, if not overcompensating, for the elimination of the customary household leakage. This point is strongly supported by the fact that if the bill of goods of the 1947 BLS national interindustry study were increased by amounts corresponding to the outputs of the new steel and steel-fabricating capacities (which form the bill of goods in the problem of this paper) the resulting expansions in all activities of the nation which would be required would yield a dollar total somewhat greater than that obtained in this paper for the subsequent expansions of activities in our area. Put otherwise, for every new employee in the initial steel and steel-fabricating plants, we estimate that on the average another 0.79 persons would be employed in the subsequent expansions of activities in our area. In comparison, where the same bill of goods increase is injected into the BLS national model a somewhat greater number of persons would be employed in the required expansions of all activities in the nation for every employee corresponding to this bill of goods increase.

Some Interregional Aspects

With all the required qualifications, it is firmly believed that the empirical results achieved have significance as firm minimum projections. The potential usefulness of the results and the associated technique,

---

other hand, when households are retained in the bill of goods, similar one dollar increases in the bill of goods requirements for the output of each of these three activities necessitate respective expansions of $1.73, $2.14 and $1.89 in the outputs for all industries.

These statements, however, do not constitute a criticism of the Leontief balanced regional model. The Leontief model was designed to obtain the percentage change of the output of each activity from its 1939 level when the bill of goods demand for any given activity is changed in order to make comparisons among these percentage changes. It was not designed to obtain absolute changes. The data resulting from various operations with this model are presented in percentage terms, and not in dollars.

[44] Ideally, as improved models are developed to encompass this interregional feedback effect, those elements of each industrial category which do not respond readily in approximately proportionate manner to general impulses and consequent changes in their outputs and the outputs of related industries should be removed from the structural matrix. For example, that set of inputs which households require but which are relatively unrelated to income and must be considered as functionally related to other variables should be taken out of the matrix and transferred to the bill of goods. Thus, the construction of better models necessitates the inclusion of more realistic response patterns in the matrix.

however, has not been fully developed. It has already been observed that the area will not furnish all of the inputs required to permit each round of expansion. This circumstance permits the isolation of the magnitude of those commodities which must be imported into the region. For regions well placed competitively for supplying these inputs, this leads to at least a partial analysis of the effects upon these regions and of their potentialities for development. An excellent example of such a region in terms of our area is Puerto Rico. In order to sketch the procedure in adding this partial interregional dimension to the analysis (the full development of this procedure must be left to a later paper) we now pose the question: to what extent can Puerto Rico benefit from the expansionary movement in the area?

To answer this question requires the identification of those activities for which Puerto Rico has a competitive advantage relative to the area. It is beyond the scope of this paper to present finely detailed cost studies. Suffice it to indicate that Puerto Rico with its abundant, cheap labor supply and niggardly endowment of mineral resources tends to excel in the cheap labor-oriented type of industry, such as certain types of textiles, assembly work, and the like. The gross industrial categories of the fifty-industry BLS classification precludes isolation of the specific textile and other activities which must be examined. Not so, however, with the 192-industry classification, which forms the basis of the BLS 192 x 192 matrix which is currently available for use.

A recent report containing suggestions for a planned industrial promotion program for Puerto Rico[45] has clearly indicated the feasibility of expansion and/or establishment of activities which fall in, among others, the following categories of the 192-industry classification: industry number 30, spinning, weaving, and dyeing; industry 31, special textile products; industry 69, footwear (excluding rubber); industry 139, radios and related products; and industry 140, tubes (electronic). Accordingly, we have asked what new demand for the products of these industries will ensue from the steel-induced expansion of the area. These new demands are easily approximated, since per dollar output of each of the 45 industrial categories employed in the previous sections we can obtain the cents' worth of inputs required from each of the five cited industries.[46] These new demands are recorded in Table 6. However, it should be remembered that portions of these new demands will not only be provided from the area and from Puerto Rico, but also from other regions which may be

---

[45] W. K. Joelson, "Suggestions for a Planned Industrial Promotion Program," Economic Development Administration, San Juan, P. R., October 1, 1952.

[46] To determine the cents' worth of any one of these five inputs per dollar output of a given industrial category of the fifty-industry breakdown requires the summation of the amounts of the specified input which went into each of the components of the given industrial category (as recorded in the 192 x 192 BLS Interindustry Flow Table) and the division of this sum by the gross output of this industrial category.

Table 6. — Requirements of the Products of Selected
Cheap Labor-Oriented Industries

Industry Number	Name	Induced Demand (*in $ thousand*)
30	Spinning, weaving, and dyeing	9,731
31	Special textile products	1,471
69	Footwear (excluding rubber)	4,560
139	Radio and related products	2,448
140	Tubes	163

in a position to compete in these lines. Therefore, the determination of the quantities of these new demands which will be supplied by Puerto Rico must be left to market area analysis and related research.

In conclusion, we have attempted to develop more adequate techniques to anticipate the impact of the location of a basic industry upon the various economic activities of a region. Our effort to achieve an improved agglomeration and regional development analysis has not involved pure theory alone. Rather it has involved a weaving together of diverse theoretical threads and existing empirical material in order to obtain a realistic fabric of an induced development. As they now exist, analytical tools for area study are far from adequate, and it is for this reason that we have been compelled to aim not at the most probable effects of new basic industry but rather at the firm minimum. In this guise, and only in this guise, are these tools currently useful. It is hoped that with continued research, still more valid techniques can be developed.

ON A GENERAL POLITICAL-SOCIAL-ECONOMIC EQUILIBRIUM THEORY ORIENTED TO COOPERATIVE SOLUTIONS AND CONFLICT RESOLUTION*

by Walter Isard, Peter Isard, Mark Barchas and Richard Epps

INTRODUCTION

This paper attempts to cast some new light on the possibility of cooperative solutions in interdependent decision-making situations in which conflicts among behaving units exist. The paper attacks this problem from a standpoint which is quite different from that employed in most conflict analysis. It views the problem against the background of a general political-social-economic equilibrium theory. Such a general theory has not been employed by those pursuing research on cooperative procedures and conflict resolution. There is, however, no reason why such a theory cannot be as effectively used here as it has in the fields of economics and regional science. We, therefore, proceed to sketch cooperative procedures that might be used by individuals belonging to organizations of various sorts, or by representatives in a legislature, and so forth. Since individuals and other behaving units engage in many activities in non-cooperative ways, our setting must embrace such behavior as well. In particular, since our general theory draws heavily upon the general theory in the fields of economics and regional science, (where such theory has been most fully developed), and since in these fields non-cooperative, self-interested behavior is typical, our statement of a general theory necessarily includes many elements involving non-cooperative behavior.

Additionally, the present paper attempts to go beyond the general equilibrium theory of economics by embracing the interplay of non-economic factors, such as political forces and cultural-social values and norms. It includes non-economic commodities in the utility functions of individuals and in the profit determinations of organizations. Further, the behavior of cooperative organizations is not tied to the normal economic price system. The behaving units considered are non-cooperative production organizations, cooperative production organizations, exporting units, government units, and the individual. Each individual behaves in a number of roles, both active and passive. The coordination of all activities is effected through the price-determining market process (at the economic market in each region), within each organization itself, and within the political (legislative) process.

* This paper is a summary of two chapters (verbal and mathematical) by the two senior authors in a forthcoming book on General Social, Economic, Political and Regional Theory. The authors gratefully acknowledge the financial support of their research by the National Science Foundation.

Reprinted from *Papers, Peace Research Society (International)*, VI (1967), 1–11, by permission of the authors and editor.

Due to limited space, much of the original detail, including all of the mathematical statement, and proof of the existence of an equilibrium, has been left out. However, most of the conceptual framework is included.

COMMODITIES

Four kinds of goods have been defined for consideration in the equilibrium system:

1. Economic goods—like wheat, money (the numeraire), labor and c-transfer (transport and communication) services. In the context of this paper, the prefix c-indicates that the term which follows refers to a precisely defined commodity.

2. Non-economic goods (except those in 3 and 4 below). These goods, like c-solidarity, c-power, and c-achievement, which play a central role in behavioral sciences, are included here to allow for a more complete treatment of motivation. In the equilibrium system, these goods can be produced and are traded on a market using money as the numeraire.

3. C-love tendered—a non-economic commodity involved in gift giving. The person who gives a gift while expecting no reciprocal act produces and immediately consumes a feeling of well-being. This feeling is defined to be c-love tendered. The amount produced, and thus consumed, will vary with the degree to which the giver expects the gift to influence the receiver's utility. The c-love tendered itself can be neither traded on any market nor given away.

4. C-sanctions—a non-economic good which society awards to an individual or organization as a result of the recipient's action or inaction. It is society's principal tool for the control of behavior patterns, and may be bestowed in either positive amounts, as a reward, or negative amounts, as a penalty. Units of this commodity cannot be produced; however, once received they may be traded on particular markets (the organizational market).

   The amount of c-sanctions awarded for an action will vary, depending upon the individual or organization taking the action, as well as the nature of the action. The amount awarded is always well defined and is thus weighed in decisions made by most actors in the system.

One additional non-economic commodity, c-power, requires comment. This commodity, like all others, has a money price equivalent and thus may be traded for any commodity except c-love tendered. It is received when a representative of an organization is in political office. Its amount is proportional to the welfare of the constituency of the office holder, and accrues to the organization in which the incumbent is a member.

Within each category of good described[1] there are a number of classes of goods, each class being a set of essentially identical goods. What falls within a class of economic goods is usually clear, for we can list the important aspects of economic goods. In contrast, non-economic goods are not so well defined.

---

[1] While each individual theoretically has a vote, and may influence government by its use, we do not treat the vote as a good in this system. The vote is a nonretractable act, and as such does not lend itself of continuous reevaluation. Thus, we must assume that our system only applies between elections.

It therefore is difficult to distinguish conceptually between different qualities or brands or other significant attributes of a broad range of non-economic goods. We speak of the commodity c-respect when we should speak of many different classes of non-economic commodities which might fall under the heading of "c-respect type" commodities. For example, a Nobel Prize award for outstanding research, or a Red Cross decoration for an act of bravery are two "c-respect type" commodities, each corresponding to a specific number of units of the general commodity c-respect, and only c-respect. Because of inadequate definitions and empirical investigations, we aggregate all "c-respect type" commodities into the one broadly defined commodity c-respect. However we must distinguish among the different "c-respect type" commodities in terms of their organizational origins, because the utility one receives from different units of this commodity partly varies according to the source. Thus we assume, for example, that a unit of c-respect from the University of Pennsylvania is different from a unit of c-respect from the United States Steel Corporation.

NON-GOVERNMENT PRODUCTION ORGANIZATIONS

Two types of non-government organizations producing goods and services are considered in our system—the non-cooperative and the cooperative. The non-cooperative, (alternately designated non-coop) corresponds to the firm of perfect competition, except that it deals in non-economic as well as economic commodities. It is a profit maximizing organization which takes market prices of economic goods as given. We conceive each non-coop to have a submarket (to be described later) where exchanges of non-economic commodities are allowed to take place between active participants of the non-coop, and where the non-coop itself makes exchanges with its active participants. The exchanges at this submarket are regulated through an internal pricing system based on supply and demand. Thus, the competitive nature of the non-coop is manifest both in its internal structure and in its dealings in economic commodities with the rest of the social system at the economic market.

One example of a non-coop might be an automobile manufacturing corporation with an international market. Its input and output structure would be geared to profit maximization. The directors would make their decisions with knowledge of government programs, tax rates, demand, and prices on all markets in all countries. The directors and other active participants would give their labor services in return for money and certain non-economic commodities, such as c-security. They would buy material inputs and sell their product on the economic market.

The cooperative production organization differs from the non-coop in that it is not guided by a profit maximizing goal. Rather, its production plans are determined in accordance with prescribed rules. It makes decisions in a prescribed manner after receiving proposals from its members. It has no internal pricing system and does not need one because issues are resolved through constitutional-type procedures.

Firms, churches, families, social groups, world regional authorities, are all production organizations. Some units may be considered cooperatives, some non-coops, and some both, depending upon the decision-making processes employed. One example of the cooperative might be an organization like the World

Health Organization. In such a body the goals are well defined, in terms of eradicating world diseases via educational and direct action programs. Problems arise on specific levels of programs and financial contributions. We may imagine that the members jointly determine the levels of each program, the distribution of services, and the responsibilities for budget support.

The United Nations is another example, albeit a somewhat more complex one. Accepted goals are more inclusive: the elimination of war, encouragement of equal rights for all peoples, promotion of social and economic progress, plus the increase of freedom. Within this framework a number of conflicts of interest may arise. For example, when goals are in conflict with each other or when resources are limited, member countries who place different priority rankings on the goals will find themselves in conflict with each other. Or, conflicts may arise over the regional distribution of the outputs of the United Nations. In either case, the analyst is faced with a situation quite different from our non-coop. Instead of unity of view on a single objective, the organization is confronted with diverse, incompatible objectives. Clearly, some means of solution more akin to a game than to simple maximization must be used.

Among some of the procedures available for conflict resolution might be the following: (1) The members may split the difference between each one's most desired proposals; (2) they may each take turns being leader over a restricted range of action; or (3) they may follow an inching-forward procedure where concomitantly each lets the other have his way a little in each of a sequence of moves. The exact procedure employed by a cooperative may be one of many; it is to be prespecified and to allow each participant to achieve at least as high a level of utility as would be possible were he not a member of the cooperative.

The equilibrium system specifies that the cooperative, unlike the profit maximizing non-coop, does not directly purchase economic goods from the economic market. Instead, individuals who are members of the cooperative supply these inputs by purchasing them from the regional economic market. Likewise, the cooperative does not sell its economic output directly, but rather distributes it among members who may then sell it on the economic market.

REGIONS, MARKETS, MARKET PROCESSES, AND EXPORTING UNITS

In each region there is one economic market.[2] Here economic commodities may be purchased and sold at money prices established for these commodities in accordance with the total supply and demand for them in that region. Within each non-cooperative production organization in each region, there is a non-cooperative market where all commodities, both economic and non-economic, except c-love tendered, may be exchanged.

The reason there is only one economic market in each region, while there are as many non-economic markets as there are non-coop production organizations, lies with the distinction made earlier between economic and non-economic commodities. Economic commodities have a value independent of where they are purchased. Non-economic commodities, on the other hand, differ greatly in value according to where they are purchased. For example, a unit

---

[2] Regions are considered here as points, to avoid dealing with internal transportation costs.

of c-respect purchased at the local barber shop would differ greatly in value from a unit of c-respect purchased from Harvard University. Both are called units of c-respect, but we can not say which has the greater value to any individual.

The prices of economic commodities at the non-coop market are identical to the prices for these commodities at the regional economic market. However, the non-tangible prices of non-economic commodities at each non-cooperative market are established by the supply and demand for these commodities at that particular non-cooperative market. (Although in this analysis non-economic commodities are assumed to have well-defined prices, in actuality these prices are not easily stated in terms of a currency. Thus they are here referred to as non-tangible prices.)

At both the economic and non-cooperative markets, market equilibrium with respect to any commodity is said to exist when the supply of and demand for that commodity are equated or when price is zero and there is an excess supply. The operation of the market might be viewed as if there were a fictitious participant in every market who controlled prices but had no direct control over demand. Now if each such participant had a payoff function equal to the price of a commodity times its excess demand (the total demand minus supply at a given price), and if the participant had no conception of the relationship between excess demand and price, then the participant would be motivated to increase price or nontangible price wherever excess demand was positive, and to continue to increase price until it rose sufficiently to decrease excess demand to zero. Likewise, the participant would be motivated to decrease price and thus reduce loss whenever excess demand was negative. Thus again, at equilibrium, either excess demand would be zero or price would be zero, but in either case the payoff to the fictitious participant would be zero.

As is true in the real world, we allow prices for economic commodities to vary between regions. However, since each region is treated conceptually as a point, only one price for a commodity may exist at any given time in any single region. With prices allowed to vary between regions on commodities, it becomes profitable for exporting to take place. We therefore introduce exporting units whose sole function is to ship economic goods whenever the price span between regions is great enough to make it profitable. We do not treat importing as such since one region's imports are another region's exports. We treat exporting of non-economic commodities as a function of the individual and not the function of exporting units. (This is described in the section on the individual.)

GOVERNMENT, THE LEGISLATIVE PROCESS, AND ADMINISTRATION

Our general theory covers only two types of government activities, namely (1) those administrative activities which are involved in carrying out production and collecting taxes, and (2) legislative functions related to determining levels of programs and tax rates. We do not cover the adjudicative process nor regulatory activities. We allow decision makers of government to be elected, but are not able to incorporate the election process in the general framework.

The legislative branch selects programs to be carried out, appropriates funds for the suggested programs, and sets tax rates. As a short cut, we combine tax rates and appropriations by assuming that the legislature sets a separate tax rate to finance each program. Thus, in our system the legislature selects programs by suggesting an operating level for each and a corresponding tax rate. We assume that all proposed programs are compatible with each other and that none have economies of scale.

One approximation to the political process of the legislative branch begins with a proposal by each representative of a level and a tax rate for every program. We assume that the proposal of each representative on each program maximizes some index of his constituents' welfare, subject to a constraint of reasonableness—the tax rate must have a reasonable relation to the suggested level of the program. (The reasonableness constraint may originate from a need to appear responsible either in the eyes of the constituency or in the eyes of other representatives.)

The proposals of all representatives are combined into a set of compromise proposals by some agreed-upon cooperative method. The compromise proposal for a program is accepted if the expected cost of that program matches the expected revenue from its tax rate. If the expected revenue and tax rate do not match, further proposals are offered, a new compromise determined, and so on until a compromise proposal is achieved for each program having expected costs and revenues in balance.

Having explained what happens during the legislative process, we shall now explain how this process arrives at a budget balance. Each legislator in trying to maximize his constituency's welfare has a natural tendency to overstate the amount of program that can be purchased with a given amount of tax money. We therefore must assume that the legislators have at their disposal a non-political expert who can evaluate every compromise program level and tax rate and determine whether the two are objectively in balance. If too much program is called for in the compromise proposal, in light of revenues, the expert adds an amount to program costs which when presented to the legislators will force them to either increase money allotments or reduce program levels. Likewise, if too little program is called for in the compromise proposal in light of revenues, the expert subtracts an amount from the program cost which when presented to the legislators will force them to either reduce money allotments or increase program levels. In the end no surplus or deficit is permitted.

A second approximation to the political process may be reached much more directly. The legislators may have previously agreed on a set of rules and procedures of the sort discussed below in connection with the cooperative organization. There would be no need for a bi-partisan expert. There might be proposals made in each of a sequence of moves, where each proposal is consistent with certain acceptable constraints; and these proposals would continue to be made until a compromise proposal on all programs and tax rates was reached.

The tax rate which is determined by the legislature becomes the budget constraint of the regional administrator. Within this limit the administrator tries to maximize the welfare of the constituency on each program. (Because he has a budget constraint for each program, and cannot move funds between programs or change the nature of programs, this maximization reduces to achieving the highest level for each program, i. e., the most efficient means of production and distribution.) Two alternative motives may lead to welfare maximization by the administrator. First, he is a member of the constituency and thus may maximize his own welfare when he maximizes that of his constituents. Second, he is a member of a political organization which receives c-power awards in proportion to the level of constituency welfare he achieves. Therefore, the organization may direct him. In either case, he is led to maximize constituency welfare.

His only control is the ability to choose the regional pattern of production and the final level of each program. (Program levels may differ from those determined by the legislature because the administrator is dealing with actual instead of expected prices.) Because we assume constituency welfare to be insatiable with respect to each program, the administrator always strives for the maximum program level. Production costs may vary between regions, but also cost is incurred in shipping the outputs of a program back to the region of distribution. The administrator considers these two dimensions of costs and finds that pattern of production which represents the least cost and thus provides the highest level of programs within the budget constraint.

THE FAMILY AND SUBSISTENCE

Traditionally the family has taken on importance in economics as the basic consumption unit. In this paper we add the notion of the family as the basic subsistence unit. This role is crucial, for one of the necessary conditions for an equilibrium in this system is that all individuals be able to subsist. There will always be a number of persons who, due to age or some mental or physical handicap, will not be able to subsist on their own. The introduction of the family unit eliminates most of this problem by assigning responsibility for their subsistence to other family members.

The family can produce all economic and non-economic goods, except c-sanctions. However, only economic goods are considered as necessary for subsistence. In particular, we assume that consumption of all economic goods except money must be non-negative, and that a strictly positive amount of labor must be left for each individual's own consumption for leisure.

THE INDIVIDUAL

Given our framework of production organizations, markets, regions, and commodities, we now examine the individual, his roles and options.

The individual is a utility maximizer. His utility-maximizing total action involves a consistent decision on how to participate in each of several active roles, consistent in the sense of satisfying certain constraints which interrelate the roles. Six active roles are defined. They are:

1. One-man producer in isolation from society.
2. One-man producer in society.
3. Gift giver to friends and family.
4. Active participant in non-cooperative organizations.
5. Purchaser of economic goods on economic market.
6. Seller of adjusted initial stocks at the economic market.

The individual also has passive roles in which he has no decision-making function. His passive roles include:

1. Recipient of a share of the money profits of non-coop production organi-

zations and exporting units in which he owns stock.

2. Tax payer and recipient of a share of government distributions of goods and services.

3. Recipient of gifts from other individuals.

Lastly, an individual may choose to belong to cooperative organizations. This role differs from the six active roles in that, once decided, membership in cooperatives is binding on the individual, and it differs from the passive roles because he has a decision function within the cooperative.

(1) One-man producer in isolation from society

In his option as a one-man producer outside society, the individual produces in isolation for his own and his family's consumption. He chooses this role based on utility considerations. Because he is outside society, he neither buys nor sells at the market nor has any relationship with non-coop organizations. Also, because he operates outside society, he is not subject to society's sanctions and is not a constituent of any government. In this role, the individual or jointly all individuals in one family are able to subsist through a division of labor and gift-giving within the family. However, in this role, the individual may be a member of cooperatives.

(2) One-man producer in society

Again depending on the individual's utility considerations and his circumstances, he may choose to be a one-man producer in society. This role is similar to the previous one, except here options attendant with societal membership are opened. Here the individual's production is more likely to be efficient than were he to produce in isolation from society because he is able to take advantage of a larger specialization of labor. For example, an individual might grow wheat in a single-man or family operation, sell the wheat on the economic market, and with the proceeds purchase other necessities for home consumption and gift-giving. Because the individual is active in society, he incurs society's sanctions on his production.

(3) Gift-giver

As stated earlier, our system makes a provision for dependent people through the introduction of gift-giving. However, we extend the individual's gift-giving action space to include the possibility of giving gifts to individuals other than family members. When an individual makes a unilateral gift to another individual, without expectation of anything in return, we conceive of two things happening. First, the giver's stock of goods is reduced by the amont of the gift and any transport inputs necessary in delivery. Second, the giver produces and consumes a certain non-negative amount of c-love tendered. The c-love tendered increases the giver's utility (inwardly experienced satisfaction), and this acts as the motivation in gift giving. The giver also receives c-sanctions on his gift.

The individual may act as gift-giver regardless of his economic position vis-à-vis society. However, when the individual is outside society he can only give gifts to other family members. Gifts of labor and c-love tendered are not allowed, and, as elsewhere, gifts of non-economic commodities have utility dependent upon their source of origin.

(4) Active member of non-cooperative organizations

The individual has a set of exchange plans with respect to each non-coop in which he is a member. Each plan specifies amounts of commodities to be supplied as contributions and demanded as receipts. An example of a non-coop exchange plan would be an individual's supplying labor services to a business and in return receiving money. However, the individual could also receive c-respect from the business, or c-sociality.

In our system, the individual receives c-sanctions on his exchange plans with non-coops. He is responsible for transporting his contributions and receipts to and from his residence if the non-coop he deals with is located in a foreign region. Finally, along with other non-economic commodities, sanctions may be traded by the individual at the submarket.

(5) Purchaser on economic market

The individual may spend his income by purchasing economic goods at the regional economic market of his region, economic goods from other regions being supplied by exporting units. We stipulate that no individual may purchase the labor (as opposed to services) of another. Also the individual receives c-sanctions on his purchases.

The individual is allowed to go into debt, but only in terms of money. Thus he may go to the economic market with no money, and return with a negative amount of money (a debt) while purchasing economic commodities he needs for home consumption and gift-giving. However, there is a debt limit above which no individual can borrow.

(6) Seller of stocks on economic market

At the point in time when our system starts, the individual has a stock of goods. We may consider these goods to be his initial stock, and when the gifts he receives are added to them, we have his adjusted initial stocks. The individual has the options of: consuming these stocks, giving them to family members as gifts, or using them as inputs to one-man production outside of society. Economic commodities remaining are taken to the economic market and sold, subject to sanctions, for money income.

THE INDIVIDUAL'S EQUILIBRIUM

The individual chooses plans for each of his roles with the objective of maximizing his utility. We make the usual assumptions of insatiability and continuity of the utility function. However, we have to make a slight departure from tradition to assure survival of all individuals. We have pointed out a division of responsibilities within each family for providing the subsistence requirements for all members of the family. To assure that these responsibilities are carried out, we assume that the individual prefers to fulfill completely his responsibilities to others before fulfilling all of his own subsistence requirements.

A number of constraints limit the choices of the individual. First, he cannot accumulate debts in anything but money, and his total debt must not exceed his pre-specified debt limit. Second, he cannot plan to use or sell all of his labor—he must have some left for leisure. Third, he must balance his budget, both on the economic market and on each non-cooperative organizational market with reference to both economic and non-economic commodities. This last requirement is consistent with the first requirement, as we treat a debt as an income of money. Finally, the money he does not save must be spent on the economic market.

The individual calculates his choices given the levels of government taxes and distributions, his responsibilities to cooperative organizations, his gifts from other individuals, and the current levels of prices. These givens represent the conditions which "society" imposes, having their effect on the individual's choice of action. The set of constraints assures the consistency of his total action. Thus subject to the constraints and the conditions imposed by other actors, the individual attempts to choose an action which maximizes his utility.

OTHER EQUILIBRIUM CONDITIONS

As already stated, our non-coop production organization generally corresponds in its actions to the firm of perfect competition. We assume the basic technology of production organizations to be such that: they have the option of operating at a zero level, they operate under diminishing or constant returns to scale, and their total production is bounded.

The traditional equilibrium condition of production organizations is that they maximize profits. We modify this to take account of the fact that in determining profits our non-coop production organizations also consider non-economic commodities. Further, they receive sanctions on their production and c-power if they have an incumbent in government office. Since the non-coop takes these factors into account in determining profit, we define effective profit to include profits from economic and non-economic commodities, plus value of c-sanctions and value of c-power. Thus our equilibrium condition is: the total action of each non-cooperative maximizes its *effective* profits over its set of possible action plans compatible with the combined actions of the rest of the system.

In the section on markets it was mentioned that special exporting units carry on interregional trade in economic commodities. We assume that no exporting unit can influence prices in any region, but must operate taking prices as given. We further assume that money moves freely between regions, but that the total money component of a shipment plan is bounded by a very large fixed positive real number. Last, exporting units are required to supply the transport inputs necessary to effectuate their exporting plans. Given these conditions, the exporting unit's equilibrium is to maximize its total money profits over its set of possible action plans.

Earlier it was stated that the motive of an administrator is to maximize a given preference or utility function which he takes to represent an index of his constituents' welfare. In aggregate then, the equilibrium total action of each government unit, covering all regional production over all programs, is to maximize constituency welfare over its set of possible plans compatible with the combined actions of the rest of the social system. Similarly, the legislature reaches an equilibrium when its compromise proposal with regard to each program maximizes the welfare of the constituency of each representative and has estimated cost equated to expected revenues.

There are other equilibrium conditions in our system which will be just touched upon here. We assume that in the economic market equilibrium exists when supply and demand for every economic commodity are equal at some finite price or when the price for commodity is zero. Likewise, at the non-coop market, equilibrium is a state where supply and demand for every non-economic commodity are balanced at some finite price or when price falls to zero.

THE COOPERATIVE SOLUTION

The cooperative production organization has no equilibrium condition, since its decision-making process differs from organization to organization, as prescribed by a set of rules. In general, the cooperative accepts proposals from each of its members and somehow arrives at a cooperative solution in the form of a combined optimal membership plan specifying the inputs and outcomes of each of its members such that:

1. all consistency requirements for the individual are satisfied, and
2. all members are receiving at least as great a level of utility as they could achieve were they not members of cooperatives.

Through an iterative process, a combined membership plan emerges for each cooperative, such that individually and in aggregate cooperatives satisfy the two conditions just stated. That is, cooperatives recognize that they do not operate in isolation, requiring that when they have members in common they coordinate their actions.

A combined action of all participants in the social system is said to be an interregional social equilibrium if it satisfies these conditions with some refinements. It then can be mathematically proven that such an equilibrium, involving certain types of cooperative solutions, does exist.

SUMMARY

We have sketched the main elements of a general theory of political-social-economic equilibrium oriented to cooperative solutions. It is recognized that all that has been done is on the statement of a general theory. Nonetheless, the implications of this general theory are major for the development of operational techniques. Just as the powerful techniques of multi-regional linear programming and input-output have been yielded by the Walrasian general equilibrium theory of economics, the hope is that a general theory such as that outlined in this paper, when further refined and elaborated, may yield equally powerful techniques, utilizing comprehensive and consistent cooperative procedures for the resolution of conflicts among nations of the world and among other interest groups. These procedures would presumably go beyond simple relationships; each studied in isolation would, rather, take into account interdependencies of the interests of various actors with each other and with outside parties. Further, the proof (mathematical) of the existence of an equilibrium suggests that the new operational techniques that may be developed will have internal consistency.

AUTHOR INDEX

Ackoff, R. L., 388n
Adams, E. W., 392n
Airov, J., 339n, 343n
Alexander, J. W., 15, 65, 68n, 79n
Allen, R. G. D., 469n
Alonso, W., 16, 18, 22n, 23n, 42, 60n, 61n, 62n, 221, 222n
Anderson, C. A., 357n, 358, 359n
Andrews, R. B., 251n
Aoki, T., 342n
Atkinson, J. W., 426, 427n

Bain, J. S., 18, 265, 266n, 270n
Barchas, M., 476, 497
Barford, B., 478n
Barger, H., 303n
Barloon, M. J., 16, 97
Barlow report, 364
Barlowe, R., 246n, 252n
Barnett, H. G., 423, 426n
Bartholomew, H., 246n
Barton, F. L., 68n
Bassett, E. M., 245n
Baumol, W. J., 374n, 405, 405n
Bentz, D. R., 254n
Bergson, A., 133
Bers, M., 321
Blair, J. M., 267
Bloom, C. C., 167
Bogue, D. J., 300n, 301n, 302n, 305n
Boley, R. E., 246n, 254n
Bos, H. C., 475n
Boulding, K. E., 144n
Bowersox, D., 340n
Bowman, E. H., 18, 290, 294n
Brackett, C. A., 5n
Brazer, H. E., 176
Brewer, T. B., 423, 426n
Bridges, B., 17, 178, 192, 193n
Brown, S. E., 15, 65
Buchanan, J. M., 207n
Buchanan, N. S., 419, 426n

Calef, W. C., 253n
Campbell, A. K., 169n, 170, 171
Campbell, L. H., 211n
Capron, W. M., 478n
Carroll, J. D., 357n, 358, 359

Carter, J., 68n
Cassel, 3
Chamberlin, E. H., 52n, 227, 228, 229, 327n, 372, 373, 377, 383
Chandler, A. D., 424, 426n
Chapin, F. S., 245n
Charnes, A., 475n
Chenery, 475n
Chernoff, H., 391n
Chinitz, B. C., 16, 19, 83, 87n, 94n, 314
Chipman, J., 474
Chisholm, M., 19, 361
Churchman, C. W., 388n, 392n, 393n, 395n
Clark, C., 301n
Clark, J. M., 258
Clark, R. A., 426, 427n
Clawson, M., 246n
Cochran, T. C., 218n, 219n, 370, 419, 421, 423, 426, 426n, 427n
Cohen, K. J., 370, 396
Colberg, M. R., 370, 339n, 340n, 443, 459n
Coombs, C. H., 391n
Cooper, O., 163
Cooper, W. W., 475n
Cremin, L. A., 420
Cubberly, E. P., 422
Cumberland, J. H., 478n
Cuzzort, R. P., 305n
Cyert, R. M., 370, 396, 402n

Dacey, M. F., 38n, 387n, 475n
Daggett, Stuart P., 68n
Dahlberg, R. E., 15, 65
Daly, M. C., 478n
Dantzig, 474
Daoust, C., 253n
Davis, R. L., 391n
deCharms, R., 422, 426
Dechesnes, L., 326n
Delafons, J., 254n
Dennison, S. E., 326n, 343
de Vyver, F. T., 16, 108, 112n, 113n
Dewey, D., 340n
Dewhurst, J. F., 300n
Doi, K., 342n
Dorfman, R., 372n, 474n
Due, J. F., 17, 167, 193n, 200n
Dunn, E. S., 19, 222n, 223n, 349

508

Dunning, J., 343n

Edwards, W., 393n
Ellis, G. H., 308n, 442n
Ellis, H. S., 419
Englander, O., 477n
Epps, R., 476, 497
Eutsler, R. B., 68n
Evans, W. D., 475n
Ezekiel, M., 295

Fayerweather, J., 421, 424
Feiss, C., 245n
Fellner, 267n
Fisher, E. M., 252n
Fisher, R. M., 252n
Florence, P. S., 267, 318, 477, 481n
Floyd, J. S., 169, 171, 172, 176, 185, 191n, 208n
Fogarty, M. P., 245n
Forbes, J. M., 104n
Freutel, G., 357n
Friedman, J., 22n
Friedman, M., 340n
Friedrich, C. J., 5n, 22n, 42, 326n, 344n, 349, 477n
Fuchs, V. R., 16, 125
Fulton, M., 172, 173

Garrabrant, R. B., 250n
Gilmore, D. R., 190n
Gitlow, A. L., 16, 130
Glover, J. G., 212n
Gobar, A. J., 206
Goffman, I. J., 208n
Gooding, E. C., 178, 181, 182, 186n, 188, 189, 191n, 206, 207n
Goodrich, C., 20n
Gordon, M. S., 303n
Grasberg, A. G., 290n
Gray, R., 208n
Greenhut, M. L., 19, 171, 247n, 326, 327n, 329n, 339, 340n, 348n, 370, 441n
Griffin, J. I., 308n

Haar, C. H., 249n
Habakkuk, H. J., 422
Haber, W., 170n
Hague, D. C., 330n, 343n
Haig, R. M., 58, 308n
Hall, M., 18, 255
Hardt, J., 475n
Harris, C. D., 66, 302n, 349, 350, 358, 359
Hawley, A. H., 305n
Hedlund, E., 343n
Held, R. B., 246n
Hicks, J. R., 468
Henderson, J. M., 49n

Hill, L. E., 202n
Hirschman, A. E., 423
Hitchcock, 474
Hodges, L. H., 208n
Hoffenberg, M., 475n
Holland, E., 475n
Hotelling, H., 372, 373, 374, 375n, 377, 383
Holmes, E. G., 326n
Hoover, E. M., 5, 18, 22n, 43, 69n, 223n, 303n, 326n, 330n, 349, 353n, 430, 441n, 477n
Hunter, H., 432n, 441n
Hurst, W., 426

Isard, P., 468n, 476, 497
Isard, W., 4, 5, 6, 7, 8n, 16, 18n, 23n, 38n, 41n, 47n, 152, 154, 166n, 222n, 223n, 225n, 226n, 227, 228, 229n, 315, 326n, 350, 357n, 358n, 369, 372, 387, 387n, 430, 441n, 468, 469, 473, 475n, 476, 477, 478n, 479n, 489n, 490n, 497

Jackson, F. H., 326n
Jenks, L. H., 421
Jewkes, J., 343n
Johnson, O., 480n
Joilson, W. K., 495n
Joubert, W. H., 68n

Kantorevich, 474
Kaplan, A., 393n
Kaplan, N., 475n
Karaska, G. J., 15, 22
Katona, G., 329n, 430, 436, 441n
Kemeny, J. G., 372n
Kendrick, J. W., 300n
Kitagawa, E. M., 301n, 305n
Koopmans, T., 469, 474
Knapp, J., 255n
Krutilla, John, 478n
Kuenne, R. E., 44, 45, 315, 467 ff, 477
Kuhn, H. W., 44, 45
Kuznets, S., 299

Lagai, R. L., 212n
Landry, D., 420
Lansing, J. B., 154n, 156n
Lasswell, H. D., 393n
Launhardt, W., 5
Lee, E. S., 423
Lefeber, L., 469, 475n
Lester, R., 108, 109, 111
Leonard, W. N., 308n
Leontief, W., 474, 490n, 492n, 493n, 494n
Lerner, A. P., 372, 375, 377n
Levine, H., 475n
Lichtenberg, R., 318
Lindberg, O., 68n, 69n

Linke, A., 330n
Locklin, D. P., 68n
Lösch, A., 5, 10, 22n, 229n, 326n, 330n, 338n, 468
Lowell, E. L., 426
Luce, R. D., 374n, 392n

MacGibbon, D. A., 68n
MacNeil, N., 211n, 216n
McClelland, D. C., 426
McComb, J. B., 104n
McCracken, P. W., 172n
McKinsey, J. C. C., 374n
McLaughlin, G. E., 108n, 111, 300n, 441n, 442n
McLean, M., 245n
Maclaurin, W. R., 142, 143, 144
Machlup, F., 219n, 345n
Mangelsdorf, T. A., 290n
March, J. G., 396, 402n
Mattila, J. M., 168
Mayer, H. B., 66n
Menke, J. R., 153
Metz, H. W., 211n, 216n
Metzbaum, J., 248n
Metzler, L., 474
Miller, N. G., 217n
Mills, E. S., 423
Milnar, J., 391n
Mitchell, G. W., 198n
Moes, J. E., 202n, 207, 208, 253n
Moiller, H. H., 422, 426
Moore, H. E., 65, 66n
Morgan, J. H., 329n
Morgan, J. N., 370, 429, 441n
Morgan, W. E., 186, 193n
Morgenstern, O., 392n
Moses, L. E., 47, 50n, 51n, 391n
Mossman, F., 340n
Mott, S. H., 251n
Mueller, E., 370, 429, 431, 441n
Myers, C. A., 142, 143, 144, 150

Nevins, A., 425
Newman, P. K., 330n, 343n
Niederhauser, E., 477n
Nishioka, H., 342n
Null, J. A., 254n

Ontko, M. J., 22n
Orcutt, G., 475n
Ostroff, 473n

Palander, T., 39n, 326n, 477
Palmer, G. L., 301n
Paveto, V., 3, 468
Pasma, T. K., 246n
Peck, M. J., 491n

Penrose, E. F., 66n
Perloff, H. S., 436, 439, 442n
Pick, G., 39n, 42, 43n
Pollard, W. L., 249n
Pfouts, R. W., 339n

Quandt, R. E., 49n

Raiffa, H., 374n, 392n
Ratcliff, R. V., 252n
Ratoosh, P., (ed.), 392n, 393n
Reder, M. W., 401n
Reid, P. M., 308n
Reilly, W. J., 358
Reina, R. E., 424
Reiner, T. A., 369, 387
Reynolds, L. G., 145, 146, 147, 148n, 149, 150, 151n
Rinehart, J. R., 202n
Robinson, R. I., 185
Robinson, E. A. G., 267
Roback, S., 108n, 111, 308n, 441n, 442n
Ross, W. D., 168n, 201, 204
Rostow, W. W., 366
Ruttan, V. W., 201
Rydell, C. P., 55n

Salkever, L. R., 132n
Salzenstein, M. A., 254n
Samuelson, P. A., 468, 474n
Sawyer, J. E., 422, 425
Schlaifer, R., 391n
Schurr, S. H., 153n, 163n, 165n
Shenkel, W. M., 18, 244
Shubik, M., 389, 393n
Shultz, G. P., 131, 144, 150
Simon, H. A., 391n, 436, 442n
Singer, H. W., 372, 375, 377n
Smith, A., 7
Smithies, A., 147, 147n, 330n, 372, 375
Smykay, E., 340n
Snover, J. E., 326n
Solberg, E. D., 248n
Soloman, H., 392n
Solow, R. M., 474n
Soule, D., 170
Steindel, 267
Stephenson, F. M., 109
Stevens, B. H., 5n, 55n, 369, 372, 469
Stevens, S. S., 392n
Stewart, J. B., 294n
Stewart, J. Q., 349, 350, 358
Stigler, G. F., 311
Stigler, G. J., 304n, 311n
Stoddard, C. H., 246n
Stolper, W. F., 5, 22n
Stonier, C. D., 308n
Stopler, W., 326n

Stouffer, S. A., 358
Strasma, J. D., 168n, 169, 170n, 173
Strassman, W. P., 422
Sufrin, S. C., 109, 114
Sussna, S., 249n
Swinyard, A. W., 109
Sykes, J., 343n

Taylor, G. R., 84
Thomas, C. A., 153ff
Thompson, J. H., 208n, 247n, 252n
Thrall, R. M., 391n
Tung, T. H., 475n
Turvey, R., 252n

Ullman, E. L., 66n, 350, 357n, 358, 478n

Vernon, R., 19, 299
Vogt, E. Z., 420
von Newmann, J., 392n
von Thunen, J. H., 5, 6, 18, 222n, 326, 330

Wallace, L. T., 201, 339n
Walras, L., 3, 467, 468n
Warntz, W., 44

Weber, A., 3, 5, 6, 22n, 28n, 30n, 39n, 43, 44, 45, 47, 326, 330, 349
Wehrly, M. S., 251n
Weintraub, S., 53n
Whitnall, G., 249n
Whitney, V., 16, 152, 166n
Whittlesey, D., 67, 68n, 69n
Wilhelm, P. A., 244n
Wilken, A., 429, 431, 441n
Will, R. A., 17, 210
Williams, J. D., 374n
Williams, N., 248n
Williamson, H. F., 303n
Winsten, C., 18, 255, 261
Woglom, W. H., 5, 22n, 326n
Wolff, R. P., 357n
Wonnacott, R. J., 194n, 195, 196
Wood, M., 429, 431, 441n
Woodbury, C., 301n, 305n

Yaseen, L., 326n
Yntema, D. B., 169

Zipf, G. K., 350, 358

SUBJECT INDEX

Aerospace industry
  influence of Federal government, 213
Agriculture
  land rent, specialization and markets,
    361–366
Aluminum industry
  influence of Federal government, 212
Apparel industry, Florida, 445 ff
Area Development Administration, 214
Atomic Energy Commission, 212, 217
Automobile industry, 269–289

Basing point system, 218
Bid price surface, 60 ff, 223n, 237–240
Bid rent function, 60 ff, 226
Branch plants, 328–329

Canned fruit and vegetable industry,
  269–289
Capital-supply function, 320
Cement industry
  atomic power, 161–162
  conditions of entry, concentration and
    scale, 269–289
Chemical industry, Florida, 445 ff
Cigarette industry, 269–289
Cleveland, employment, 317
Concentration (economies of scale), 265–
  289
Consumer surplus, Weberian problem,
  56–58
Copper industry, 269–289
Critical isodopane, 33
Cross-elasticity, pulls, 49–50

Decision-making. See Entrepreneurial decision-making
Decision theory, 387–395, 396–418, 419–
  427
  business goals, 402–405
  entrepreneur values, 419–427
  general equilibrium theory, 497–507
  organizational expectations, 405–406
  organizational goals, 398–399
  organizational slack, 399–402
Demand elasticity
  game theory, 375–376
  industrial land, 251
  Weberian problem, 52 ff

Diseconomies of scale, 301, 311–312

Economies of scale, external, 299–313,
  314–324
  capital influences, 320–321
  center-city services, 309–310
  core vs. periphery of cities, 305–313
  disintegration, 304n
  entrepreneurship, 319–320
  future trends, 310–313
  intermediate goods and services, 323–
    324
  labor factors, 321–322
  land, influence of, 322–323
  market considerations, 302–307
  New York Metropolitan Area, 299–
    313, 314–324
  Pittsburgh, 314–324
  size of firm, 307
  standardized vs. unstandardized in-
    dustries, 307
  supply interdependence, 315
  transportation rates, 306–307
Economies of scale, internal, 255–264,
  265–289, 290–298
  capital requirements, 285–289
  dimensions, 257–258
  Great Britain, 255–264
  markets, 279–289, 295–298, 303
  measurement, 259–260, 292–298
  multiplant firms, 279–289, 290–298
  optimal firm size, 279–285, 290–298
  optimal plant size, 270–279
  percentage effect, 287
  scale curves, 265–267, 268 ff
  selected industries, 269–289
  Weberian problem, 34–36, 50 ff
Efficiency analysis (economic), 255
Electrical machinery industry, Florida,
  445 ff
Entrepreneurial decision-making, 419–
  427
  empirical, Florida, 443–464
  empirical, Michigan, 429–442
  interaction with change, 421–425
  modal personality, 420
  nonpecuniary factors, 430–442
  social structure and change, 425–426
Entrepreneurship, 319–320

Entry, conditions of, 265–289
  defined, 266

Fabricated metal industry, Florida, 445 ff
Farm machinery industry, 269–289
Federal government, 210 ff
Firm, theory of, for decision-making, 396–418
Florida, empirical location decisions, 443–464
  food industry, 445 ff
  market potential, 349–360
Flour industry, 269–289
F.O.B. pricing, 346–348
  Weberian problem, 53–56
Food industry, Florida, 445 ff
Fountain pen industry, 269–289
Furniture and fixtures industry, Florida, 445 ff

Gaining factor, pulls, 50
Game theory, 372–386, 387–395
  bidding in turnpike franchises, 377 ff
  demand elasticity, 375–376
  Hotelling-Chamberlin problem, 372–386
General equilibrium
  commodities, 498–499
  decision criteria, 469
  economies of scale, 285 ff, 314
  elementary formulation, 467–472
  elementary spatial formulation, 472–476
  family, the, 503
  government, 501–503
  history and definition, 467–468
  individual, the, 503–506
  linear programming, 469, 474
  markets, 500–501
  nongovernment organizations, 499–500
  regional impact, steel and Delaware Valley, 477–496
  rent, 227–243
  theory, 467–472, 497–507
General social theory, 497–507
Georgia, southern
  market potential, 350–360
Glass industry
  atomic power, 162–163
  Florida, 445 ff
Government, 178–191, 192–209
  attitudes of state, Michigan, 432
  credit gap argument, 205–207
  development credit corporations, 186–191, 205
  direct loan programs, 182–183, 204–205
  general equilibrium theory, 501–503
  impacts on business costs, 194–200

loan guarantee programs, 179–182, 203–204
local bond financing, 183–185, 203–204, 220
questionnaire studies, 193–194
tax concessions, 185–186
wage-rate inflexibility, 207–208
Gravity model, 349–360
Great Britain, economies of scale, 225–264
Gypsum industry, 269–289

Heating apparatus and plumbing supply industry, 482–485
Hoover Commission Report, 211, 216
Hotelling location problem, 372–386

Ice cream industry, 290–298
Ideal weight, 28 ff, 43, 45
Industrial land
  elasticity of demand, 251
  zoning, 245–254
Inertia, 436
Input-output analysis
  economies of scale, external, 314–324
  interregional aspects, 489–490
  steel and Delaware Valley, 487–496
Instruments industry, Florida, 445 ff
Interdependence. *See* General equilibrium
  basic vs. nonbasic, 314
  market, 342
  supply vs. demand dimensions, 314–323
International Teamsters Union, 92
Interstate Commerce Commission, 67–68, 90–91, 218
Intervening opportunity model, 358
Iron and steel industry
  atomic power, 164–165
  basing point system, 218
  conditions of entry and scale, 269–289
  game theory, in, 388–395
  New York-Philadelphia Region, 477–496
  transport changes, 85
  transport service, 103–105
Isodapane, 30 ff, 43–44, 353, 355–357
Isophors, 69 ff
Isotim, 30, 69n
Isovecture, 69n

Labor, 108–124, 125–129, 130–151
  city-size differentials, 127–129
  color, age, and sex influence, 125–129
  costs, Weberian problem, 33
  economies of scale, external, 321–322
  economies of scale, internal, 260–263
  empirical study of Florida, 457–459

Labor (*continued*)
  empirical study of Michigan, 429–442
  geographic differences, 125–127, 131
  job attractiveness, 130–151
  job availability, 130–151
  legislative factors, 114–124, 219
  market boundaries, 147
  mobility, 133–144
  New England, 108 ff, 144–150
  opportunity costs, 132
  Pittsburgh, 321–322
  population size relations, 305–306
  South, the, 108 ff, 125–129
  steel and Delaware Valley, 491–493
  trade unionism, 111–114
  urban orientations, 301–302
Land. *See also* Rent
  economies of scale, external, 322–323
Liquor industry, 269–289
Location index, 353
Losing factor, pulls, 50
Lumber and wood industry, Florida, 445 ff

Machinery industry, Florida, 445 ff
Market area analysis, Weberian problem, 36 ff
Market orientation, 363
Markets
  agricultural specialization, 361–366
  area-determining factor, 341
  basing point pricing, 344–346
  demand, 339–348
  empirical study of Michigan, 429–442
  f.o.b. pricing, 346–348
  game theory, 373–386
  general equilibrium theory, 500–501
  geographic influences, 341
  market potential, 349–360
  price systems, 343–348
  transport costs vs. size of, 326–338
Material index, Weber's, 28–30
Meat industry, 269–289
Metal container industry, 269–289
Metal mining industry, Florida, 445 ff
Michigan, empirical location decisions, 429–442

New England, labor force, 108 ff, 144–150
New York, external economies of scale, 299–313, 314–324
New York-Philadelphia Industrial Region, 477–496

Ordnance industry, Florida, 445 ff
Organizational expectations, 405–406
Organizational goals, 398–399
Organizational slack, 399–402

Organized industrial districts, 248–249

Paint industry, 344–345
Paper industry, Florida, 445 ff
Petroleum industry, 269–289
  Florida, 445 ff
  transport service, 106
Pittsburgh, 314–324
  external economies of scale, 314–324
Poaching, in trade, 257
Population potential, 349
Potential competition, 266
Power
  atomic, cement industry, 161–162
  atomic, glass industry, 162–163
  atomic, iron and steel industry, 164–165
  costs, atomic, U.S., 152–153, 157–160
  costs, atomic, world, 153–157
  effects on industry relocation, atomic, 159–160
  regional differentials, steam, 158–159
  transport service, 106–107
Price
  basing point pricing, 344–346
  business goals, 402–405
  decision behavior, 399–400
  demand, 343–348
  f.o.b. pricing, 53–56, 346–348
  market considerations, 334–337
  rent, 221–222
Printing and publishing industry, Florida, 445 ff
Puerto Rico, 478, 494–496

Region, freight rates
  nodal, 68, 75 ff
  uniform, 66–67
Rent function, 223
Replacement deposit, Weberian problem, 33
Rubber industry
  conditions of entry, concentration, and scale, 269–289
  influence of Federal government, 212

San Francisco, demand for land, 246
Scale of output. *See* economies of scale
Shoe industry, 269–289
Soap industry, 269–289
South, labor force, 108 ff, 125–129
Steel fabricating industry, 481–484
Substitution, Weberian problem
  effect on costs, 49
  transport and agglomeration, 34–35
  transport and labor, 33–34
  transport and rent, 228, 228n
Sugar beet industry, 219

Taxes, 167–177, 178–191, 192–209
  business climate, 172–175
  concessions, 185–186
  empirical, Michigan, 429–442
  Gresham's Law, 175–176
  reform and business associations, 176–177
Tennessee Valley Authority, 215–216
Terminal or handling costs, 23 ff, 92
Textile industry
  Florida, 445 ff
  labor factors, 108–124, 144–150
  Puerto Rico, 494–496
  rayon, 269–289
Tool and die makers, labor mobility, 135–138
Total transportation costs, 25 ff
Transport costs
  class rates, 68
  commodity rates, 68n
  control point, 73, 344–346
  dock coal, 80
  fabrication-in-transit, 24, 28
  grouping principle, 73
  hold-downs, 80
  ice cream industry, 292–293
  influence of time, 98 ff, 302–303, 317–318
  Interstate Commerce Commission, 67–68, 90–91, 323
  land rent, 361

large vs. small shipments, 95 ff
line-haul costs, 92
long haul vs. short haul, 92 ff, 101–102
market costs, 326–338
market potential, 350–360
minimization, 47, 65 ff, 86 ff
negative anomaly, 80
piggy-back, 77, 98 ff
quoting of rates, "in-step," 75
rates vs. costs, Weberian problem, 23–27
scale economies, 306, 312–313
short line principle, 74–75
total transportation costs, 25 ff
Transportation equipment industry, Florida, 445 ff
Transportation service, 98 ff, 317–318
Typewriter industry, 269–289

Value added, 260–289
Varignon frame, 30, 42–43, 45

Weberian model, 23 ff
  market considerations, 329–330
Weight triangle, Weberian problem, 39
Wisconsin, freight rates, 69 ff

Zoning, 244–254
  effect on industry location, 245 ff
  progressively inclusive districts, 251
  prohibited industries, 250